WEISSENBERGER'S INDIANA EVIDENCE
2013–2014 Courtroom Manual

A.J. STEPHANI
Adjunct Professor
University of Cincinnati College of Law

GLEN WEISSENBERGER
Professor of Law Emeritus
University of Cincinnati and
Former Dean
DePaul University College of Law

LexisNexis

QUESTIONS ABOUT THIS PUBLICATION?

For questions about the **Editorial Content** appearing in these volumes or reprint permission, please call:

Mary Anne Lenihan at 908-673-3364

Email: .... maryanne.lenihan@lexisnexis.com

For assistance with replacement pages, shipments, billing or other customer service matters, please call:

Customer Services Department at . . . . (800) 833-9844
Outside the United States and Canada, please call . . . . (518) 487-3000
Fax Number . . . . (518) 487-3584
For information on other Matthew Bender publications, please call

Your account manager or . . . . (800) 223-1940
Outside the United States and Canada, please call . . . . (518) 487-3000

ISBN: 978-0-7698-8789-0 (print)
ISBN: 978-0-7698-8790-6 (eBook)

Cite as:

Stephani and Weissenberger, Weissenberger's Indiana Evidence Courtroom Manual, Chapter XXX (LexisNexis Matthew Bender)

This publication is designed to provide authoritative information in regard to the subject matter covered. It is sold with the understanding that the publisher is not engaged in rendering legal, accounting, or other professional services. If legal advice or other expert assistance is required, the services of a competent professional should be sought.

Editorial Offices
121 Chanlon Rd., New Providence, NJ 07974 (908) 464-6800
201 Mission St., San Francisco, CA 94105-1831 (415) 908-3200
www.lexisnexis.com

MATTHEW⬥BENDER

Acknowledgments

Professor Weissenberger would like to acknowledge the assistance of his research editor, Daniella A. Roelker.

Table of Contents
VOLUME CONTENTS

INDIANA RULES OF EVIDENCE

Table of Contents

Table of Contents

Using This Book

As its title suggests, this publication has been designed specifically for courtroom use. Its purpose is to provide fast, concise, and authoritative answers to most of the evidentiary questions that arise in the course of trials and hearings, as well as in trial preparation. It accomplishes this through a unique combination of trial-tested features, which are discussed below.

Locating a Topic

Index—This book's Index is located inside the front cover. It refers the user directly to the Evidence Rule covering each topic. When you are uncertain which rule covers an issue, this is the place to begin.

Rules—The Indiana Rules of Evidence are reprinted in their entirety in a separate section in the front of the book. They are preceded by a complete Table of Contents.

Section Locator—If you know the rule or article in which your topic is covered and need to review the author's Analysis, cases, incorporated statutes, or any of the book's other features, the Section Locator on the back cover directs you to the section of the book where this information is found.

Finding an Answer

Rules—If your question can be answered simply by reading the applicable rule, you can find the language of the rule either in the Rules of Evidence in the front of the book where all the rules are collected or at the beginning of the chapter in which the individual rule is discussed. The Section Locator on the back cover will guide you to either location.

Committee Commentary—The Committee Commentary is contained in an appendix at the end of the manual. In adopting the Rules of Evidence, the Supreme Court stated: "The Court has elected to adopt only the text of the Indiana Rules of Evidence. Practitioners may find the published committee proposal and its commentary helpful as history but should exercise care in its use, inasmuch as the Court has made changes from the committee proposal based on comments received from members of the bench and bar."

Analysis—Perhaps the most important part of this book, the author's Analysis, provides a quick overview of the rule under discussion, authoritative guidance in interpreting the rule, and pointers for applying the rule in actual practice. In many chapters, the Analysis contains special features such as Illustrations, Constitutional Considerations, and Current Trends and New Developments.

Incorporated Statutes—Some rules require reference to sections of the Indiana Code. When this is the case, the incorporated statutes appear in the appropriate chapter.

Authority—Additional authorities are cited following each chapter's Analysis. These give the user a starting point for additional research.

Comparison to Federal Rule—A brief comparison of the Indiana and Federal Rules in each chapter provides additional insight.

Cases—Significant cases are summarized at the end of each chapter. These provide support for argument and decisions required during the course of proceedings.

Indiana Evidence Courtroom Manual is published annually. This edition contains the Indiana Rules of Evidence with amendments current through May 1, 2013. The comments and suggestions of users are welcome.

INDIANA RULES OF EVIDENCE

[Author's Note: Practitioners should be aware that the Federal Rules of Evidence underwent a comprehensive re-styling project in 2011. Because the Indiana Rules of Evidence were patterned on the Federal Rules of Evidence, practitioners have come to expect a similarity in wording and structure between the two sets of Rules. Currently, however, there are numerous discrepancies in wording between the two sets of Rules because of the Federal re-styling amendments, though most of these differences are not attributable to a substantive conflict between the Rules.

In March 2013, the Indiana Supreme Court proposed a comprehensive set of amendments that would, once again, conform the rules stylistically to the recently re-styled Federal Rules. Passage is expected, and the re-styled Indiana Rules of Evidence may very well be in effect by the time of publication. Complete coverage of the re-styled Indiana Rules, including several small substantive changes, will be included in a future edition. Nonetheless, it should be noted that the Indiana Rules depart from the Federal Rules on a number of substantive issues because of the desire to preserve Indiana common law or the vagaries of state court practice.]

Current through May 1, 2013

I. GENERAL PROVISIONS

Rule 101 Scope

These rules govern proceedings in the courts of this State to the extent and with the exceptions stated in this rule.

(a) General Applicability. These rules apply in all proceedings in the courts of the State of Indiana except as otherwise required by the Constitution of the United States or Indiana, by the provisions of this rule, or by other rules promulgated by the Indiana Supreme Court. If these rules do not cover a specific evidence issue, common or statutory law shall apply. The word "judge" in these rules includes referees, commissioners and magistrates.

(b) Rules of Privilege. The rules and laws with respect to privileges apply at all stages of all actions, cases, and proceedings.

(c) Rules Inapplicable. The rules, other than those with respect to privileges, do not apply in the following situations:

(1) *Preliminary questions of fact.* The determination of questions of fact preliminary to admissibility of evidence when the issue is to be determined by the court under Rule 104(a).

(2) *Miscellaneous proceedings.* Proceedings relating to extradition, sentencing, probation, or parole; issuance of criminal summonses, or of warrants for arrest or search, preliminary juvenile matters, direct contempt, bail hearings, small claims, and grand jury proceedings.

Rule 102 Purpose and Construction

These rules shall be construed to secure fairness in administration, elimination of unjustifiable expense and delay, and promotion of growth and development of the law of evidence to the end that the truth may be ascertained and proceedings justly determined.

Rule 103 Rulings on Evidence

(a) Effect of Erroneous Ruling. Error may not be predicated upon a ruling which admits or excludes evidence unless a substantial right of the party is affected, and

(1) *Objection.* In case the ruling is one admitting evidence, a timely objection or motion to strike appears of record, stating the specific ground of objection, if the specific ground was not apparent from the context; or

(2) *Offer of proof.* In case the ruling is one excluding evidence, the substance of the evidence was made known to the court by a proper offer of proof, or was apparent from the context within which questions were asked.

(b) Record of Offer and Ruling. The court may add any other or further statement which shows the character of the evidence, the form in which it was offered, the objection made, and the ruling thereon. It may direct the making of an offer in question and answer form.

(c) Hearing of Jury. In jury cases, proceedings shall be conducted, to the extent practicable, so as to prevent inadmissible evidence from being suggested to the jury by any means, such as making statements or offers of proof or asking questions in the hearing of the jury.

(d) Fundamental Error. Nothing in this rule precludes taking notice of fundamental errors affecting substantial rights although they were not brought to the attention of the court.

Rule 104 Preliminary Questions

(a) Questions of Admissibility Generally. Preliminary questions concerning the qualification of a person to be a witness, the existence of a privilege, or the admissibility of evidence shall be determined by the Court, subject to the provisions of subdivision (b). In making its determination, the Court is not bound by the Rules of Evidence, except those with respect to privileges. Where a determination of admissibility under this paragraph requires resolution of a question of fact, the question shall be resolved by the preponderance of the evidence.

(b) Relevancy Conditioned on Fact. When the relevancy of evidence depends upon the fulfillment of a condition of fact, the Court shall admit it upon, or subject to, the introduction of evidence sufficient to support a finding of the fulfillment of the condition.

(c) Hearing of Jury. Hearings on the admissibility of confessions shall in all cases be conducted out of the presence and hearing of the jury. Hearings on other preliminary matters shall be so conducted when the interests of justice require, or when an accused is a witness and so requests.

(d) Testimony by Accused. The accused does not, by testifying upon a preliminary matter, become subject to cross-examination as to other issues in the case.

(e) Weight and Credibility. This rule does not limit the right of a party to introduce before the jury evidence relevant to weight or credibility.

Amended eff. 1/1/09.

Rule 105 Limited Admissibility

When evidence which is admissible as to one party or for one purpose but not admissible as to another party or for another purpose is admitted, the court, upon request, shall restrict the evidence to its proper scope and admonish the jury accordingly.

Rule 106 Remainder of or Related Writings or Recorded Statements

When a writing or recorded statement or part thereof is introduced by a party, an adverse party may require at that time the introduction of any other part or any other writing or recorded statement which in fairness ought to be considered contemporaneously with it.

II. JUDICIAL NOTICE

Rule 201 Judicial Notice

(a) Kinds of Facts. A court may take judicial notice of a fact. A judicially-noticed fact must be one not subject to reasonable dispute in that it is either (1) generally known within the territorial jurisdiction of the trial court, or (2) capable of accurate and ready determination by resort to sources whose accuracy cannot reasonably be questioned.

(b) Kinds of Laws. A court may take judicial notice of law. Law includes (1) the decisional, constitutional, and public statutory law, (2) rules of court, (3) published regulations of governmental agencies, (4) codified ordinances of municipalities, (5) records of a court of this state, and (6) laws of other governmental subdivisions of the United States or of any state, territory or other jurisdiction of the United States.

(c) When Discretionary. A court may take judicial notice, whether requested or not.

(d) When Mandatory. A court shall take judicial notice if requested by a party and supplied with the necessary information.

(e) Opportunity to be Heard. A party is entitled, upon timely request, to an opportunity to be heard as to the propriety of taking judicial notice and the tenor of the matter noticed. In the absence of prior notification, the request may be made after judicial notice has been taken.

(f) Time of Taking Notice. Judicial notice may be taken at any stage of the proceeding.

(g) Instructing the Jury. In a civil action or proceeding, the court shall instruct the jury to accept as conclusive any fact judicially noticed. In a criminal case, the court shall instruct the jury that it may, but is not required to, accept as conclusive any fact judicially noticed.

Amended eff. 1/1/10.

III. PRESUMPTIONS IN CIVIL ACTIONS AND PROCEEDINGS

Rule 301 Presumptions in Civil Actions and Proceedings

In all civil actions and proceedings not otherwise provided for by constitution, statute, judicial decision or by these rules, a presumption imposes on the party against whom it is directed the burden of going forward with evidence to rebut or meet the presumption, but does not shift to such party the burden of proof in the sense of the risk of nonpersuasion, which remains throughout the trial upon the party on whom it was originally cast. A presumption shall have continuing effect even though contrary evidence is received.

IV. RELEVANCY AND ITS LIMITS

Rule 401 Definition of "Relevant Evidence"

"Relevant evidence" means evidence having any tendency to make the existence of any fact that is of consequence to the determination of the action more probable or less probable than it would be without the evidence.

Rule 402 Relevant Evidence Generally Admissible; Irrelevant Evidence Inadmissible

All relevant evidence is admissible, except as otherwise provided by the U.S. or Indiana constitutions, by statute not in conflict with these rules, by these rules or by other rules applicable in the courts of this State. Evidence which is not relevant is not admissible.

Rule 403 Exclusion of Relevant Evidence on Grounds of Prejudice, Confusion, or Undue Delay

Although relevant, evidence may be excluded if its probative value is substantially outweighed by the danger of unfair prejudice, confusion of the issues, or misleading the jury, or by considerations of undue delay, or needless presentation of cumulative evidence.

Rule 404 Character Evidence Not Admissible to Prove Conduct; Exceptions; Other Crimes

(a) Character Evidence Generally. Evidence of a person's character or a trait of character is not admissible for the purpose of proving action in conformity therewith on a particular occasion, except:

(1) *Character of accused.* Evidence of a pertinent trait of character offered by an accused, or by the prosecution to rebut the same;

(2) *Character of victim.* Evidence of a pertinent trait of character of the victim of the crime offered by an accused, or by the prosecution to rebut the same, or evidence of a character trait of peacefulness of the victim offered by the prosecution in a homicide case to rebut evidence that the victim was the first aggressor;

(3) *Character of witness.* Evidence of the character of a witness, as provided in Rules 607, 608 and 609.

(b) Other Crimes, Wrongs or Acts. Evidence of other crimes, wrongs, or acts is not admissible to prove the character of a person in order to show action in conformity therewith. It may, however, be admissible for other purposes, such as proof of motive, intent, preparation, plan, knowledge, identity, or absence of mistake or accident, provided that upon request by the accused, the prosecution in a criminal case shall provide reasonable notice in advance of trial, or during trial if the course excuses pre-trial notice on good cause shown, of the general nature of any such evidence it intends to introduce at trial.

Rule 405 Methods of Proving Character

(a) Reputation or Opinion. In all cases in which evidence of character or a trait of character of a person is admissible, proof may be made by testimony as to reputation or by testimony in the form of an opinion. On cross-examination, inquiry is allowable into relevant specific instances of conduct. Upon reasonable pre-trial notice by the accused of the intention to offer character evidence, the prosecution in a criminal case shall provide the accused with any relevant specific instances of conduct to be used in cross-examination.

(b) Specific Instances of Conduct. In cases in which character or a trait of character of a person is an essential element of a charge, claim, or defense, proof may also be made of specific instances of that person's conduct.

Rule 406 Habit; Routine Practice

Evidence of the habit of a person or of the routine

practice of an organization, whether corroborated or not and regardless of the presence of eyewitnesses, is relevant to prove that the conduct of the person or organization on a particular occasion was in conformity with the habit or routine practice.

Rule 407 Subsequent Remedial Measures

When after an event, measures are taken which, if taken previously, would have made the event less likely to occur, evidence of the subsequent measures is not admissible to prove negligence or culpable conduct in connection with the event. This rule does not require the exclusion of evidence of subsequent measures when offered for another purpose, such as proving ownership, control, or feasibility of precautionary measures, if controverted, or impeachment.

Rule 408 Compromise and Offers to Compromise

Evidence of (1) furnishing or offering or promising to furnish, or (2) accepting or offering or promising to accept a valuable consideration in compromising or attempting to compromise a claim, which was disputed as to either validity or amount, is not admissible to prove liability for or invalidity of the claim or its amount. Evidence of conduct or statements made in compromise negotiations is likewise not admissible. This rule does not require exclusion when the evidence is offered for another purpose, such as proving bias or prejudice of a witness, negating a contention of undue delay, or proving an effort to obstruct a criminal investigation or prosecution. Compromise negotiations encompass alternative dispute resolution.

Rule 409 Payment of Medical and Similar Expenses

Evidence of paying or furnishing, or offering or promising to pay medical, hospital, or similar expenses occasioned by an injury, or damage to property is not admissible to prove liability for such injury or damages.

Rule 410 Withdrawn Pleas and Offers

Evidence of a plea of guilty or admission of the charge which was later withdrawn, or a plea of nolo contendere, or of an offer so to plead to the crime charged or any other crime, or of statements made in connection with any of the foregoing withdrawn pleas or offers, is not admissible in any civil or criminal action, case or proceeding against the person who made the plea or offer.

However, such a statement is admissible (i) in any proceeding wherein another statement made in the course of the same plea or plea discussion has been introduced and the statement ought in fairness to be considered contemporaneously with it, or (ii) in a criminal proceeding for perjury or false statement if the statement was made by the defendant under oath, on the record and in the presence of counsel.

Amended eff. 1/1/94.

Rule 411 Liability Insurance

Evidence that a person was or was not insured against liability is not admissible upon the issue whether the person acted negligently or otherwise wrongfully. This rule does not require the exclusion of evidence of insurance against liability when offered for another purpose, such as proof of agency, ownership, or control, or bias or prejudice of a witness.

Rule 412 Evidence of Past Sexual Conduct

(a)   In a prosecution for a sex crime, evidence of the past sexual conduct of a victim or witness may not be admitted, except:

   (1)   evidence of the victim's or of a witness's past sexual conduct with the defendant;

   (2)   evidence which shows that some person other than the defendant committed the act upon which the prosecution is founded;

   (3)   evidence that the victim's pregnancy at the time of trial was not caused by the defendant; or

   (4)   evidence of conviction for a crime to impeach under Rule 609.

(b)   If a party proposes to offer evidence under this rule, the following procedure must be followed:

   (1)   A written motion must be filed at least ten days before trial describing the evidence. For good cause, a party may file such motion less than ten days before trial.

   (2)   The court shall conduct a hearing and issue an order stating what evidence may be introduced and the nature of the questions to be permitted.

(c)   If the state acknowledges that the victim's pregnancy is not due to the conduct of the defendant, the court may instruct the jury accordingly, in which case other evidence concerning the pregnancy may not be admitted.

Rule 413 Medical Expenses

Statements of charges for medical, hospital or other

health care expenses for diagnosis or treatment occasioned by an injury are admissible into evidence. Such statements shall constitute prima facie evidence that the charges are reasonable.

V. PRIVILEGES

Rule 501   Privileges

(a) General Rule. Except as provided by constitution or statute as enacted or interpreted by the courts of this State or by these or other rules promulgated by the Indiana Supreme Court or by principles of common law in light of reason and experience, no person has a privilege to:

(1) refuse to be a witness;

(2) refuse to disclose any matter;

(3) refuse to produce any object or writing; or

(4) prevent another from being a witness or disclosing any matter or producing any object or writing.

(b) Waiver of Privilege by Voluntary Disclosure. Subject to the provisions of Rule 502, a person with a privilege against disclosure waives the privilege if the person or person's predecessor while holder of the privilege voluntarily and intentionally discloses or consents to disclosure of any significant part of the privileged matter. This rule does not apply if the disclosure itself is privileged.

(c) Privileged Matter Disclosed Under Compulsion or Without Opportunity to Claim Privilege. A claim of privilege is not defeated by a disclosure which was (1) compelled erroneously or (2) made without opportunity to claim the privilege.

(d) Comment Upon or Inference from Claim of Privilege; Instruction. Except with respect to a claim of the privilege against self-incrimination in a civil case:

(1) *Comment or inference not permitted.* The claim of a privilege, whether in the present proceeding, or upon a prior occasion, is not a proper subject of comment by judge or counsel. No inference may be drawn therefrom.

(2) *Claiming privilege without knowledge of jury.* In jury cases, proceedings shall be conducted, to the extent practicable, so as to facilitate the making of claims of privilege without the knowledge of the jury.

(3) *Jury instruction.* Upon request, any party against whom the jury might draw an adverse inference from a claim of privilege is entitled to an instruction that no inference may be drawn therefrom.

Amended eff. 1/1/12.

Rule 502   Attorney-Client Privilege and Work Product; Limitations on Waiver

The following provisions apply, in the circumstances set out, to disclosure of a communication or information covered by the attorney-client privilege or work-product protection.

(a) Intentional Disclosure; Scope of a Waiver. When a disclosure is made in a court proceeding and waives the attorney-client privilege or work-product protection, the waiver extends to an undisclosed communication or information only if:

(1) the waiver is intentional;

(2) the disclosed and undisclosed communications or information concern the same subject matter; and

(3) they ought in fairness to be considered together.

(b) Inadvertent Disclosure. When made in a court proceeding, a disclosure does not operate as a waiver if:

(1) the disclosure is inadvertent;

(2) the holder of the privilege or protection took reasonable steps to prevent disclosure; and

(3) the holder promptly took reasonable steps to rectify the error, including (if applicable) following Indiana Rule of Trial Procedure 26(B)(5)(b).

(c) Controlling Effect of a Party Agreement. An agreement on the effect of disclosure in a proceeding is binding only on the parties to the agreement, unless it is incorporated into a court order.

(d) Controlling Effect of a Court Order. If a court incorporates into a court order an agreement between or among parties on the effect of disclosure in a proceeding, a disclosure that, pursuant to the order, does not constitute a waiver in connection with the proceeding in which the order is entered is also not a waiver in any other court proceeding.

Eff. 1/1/12.

VI. WITNESSES

Rule 601   General Rule of Competency

Every person is competent to be a witness except as otherwise provided in these rules or by act of the Indiana General Assembly.

Rule 602   Lack of Personal Knowledge

A witness may not testify to a matter unless evidence is introduced sufficient to support a finding that the witness has personal knowledge of the matter. A witness does not have personal knowledge as to a matter recalled or remembered, if the recall or remembrance occurs only during or after hypnosis. Evidence to prove personal knowledge may, but need not, consist of the testimony of the witness. This rule is subject to the provisions of Rule 703, relating to opinion testimony by expert witnesses.

Rule 603   Oath or Affirmation

Before testifying, every witness shall swear or affirm to testify to the truth, the whole truth, and nothing but the truth. The mode of administering an oath or affirmation shall be such as is most consistent with, and binding upon the conscience of the person to whom the oath is administered.

Rule 604   Interpreters

An interpreter is subject to the provisions of these rules relating to qualification as an expert and the administration of an oath or affirmation to make a true translation.

Rule 605   Competency of Judge as Witness

The judge presiding at the trial may not testify in that trial as a witness. No objection need be made to preserve the point.

Rule 606   Competency of Juror as Witness

(a) At the Trial. A member of the jury may not testify as a witness before that jury in the trial of the case in which the juror is sitting. If the juror is called so to testify, the opposing party shall be afforded an opportunity to object out of the presence of the jury.

(b) Inquiry into Validity of Verdict or Indictment. Upon an inquiry into the validity of a verdict or indictment, a juror may not testify as to any matter or statement occurring during the course of the jury's deliberations or to the effect of anything upon that or any other juror's mind or emotions as influencing the juror to assent to or dissent from the verdict or indictment or concerning the juror's mental processes in connection therewith, except that a juror may testify (1) to drug or alcohol use by any juror, (2) on the question of whether extraneous prejudicial information was improperly brought to the jury's attention or (3) whether any outside influence was improperly brought to bear upon any juror. A juror's affidavit or evidence of any statement by the juror concerning a matter about which the juror would be precluded from testifying may not be received for these purposes.

Rule 607   Who May Impeach

The credibility of a witness may be attacked by any party, including the party calling the witness.

Rule 608   Evidence of Character and Conduct of Witness

(a) Opinion and Reputation Evidence of Character. The credibility of a witness may be attacked or supported by evidence in the form of opinion or reputation, but subject to these limitations: (1) the evidence may refer only to character for truthfulness, and (2) evidence of truthful character is admissible only after the character of the witness for truthfulness has been attacked by opinion or reputation evidence or otherwise.

(b) Specific Instances of the Conduct of a Witness. For the purpose of attacking or supporting the witness's credibility, other than conviction of a crime as provided in Rule 609, specific instances may not be inquired into or proven by extrinsic evidence. They may, however, in the discretion of the court, if probative of truthfulness or untruthfulness, be inquired into on cross-examination of the witness concerning the character for truthfulness or untruthfulness of another witness as to which character the witness being cross-examined has testified.

Rule 609   Impeachment by Evidence of Conviction of Crime

(a) General Rule. For the purpose of attacking the credibility of a witness, evidence that the witness has been convicted of a crime or an attempt of a crime shall be admitted but only if the crime committed or attempted is (1) murder, treason, rape, robbery, kidnapping, burglary, arson, criminal confinement or perjury; or (2) a crime involving dishonesty or false statement.

(b) Time Limit. Evidence of a conviction under this rule is not admissible if a period of more than ten years has elapsed since the date of the conviction or, if the conviction resulted in confinement of the witness then the date of the release of the witness from the confinement unless the court determines, in the interests of justice, that the probative value of the conviction supported by specific facts and circumstances substantially outweighs its prejudicial effect. However, evidence of a conviction more than ten years old as calculated herein, is not admissible unless the proponent gives to the adverse party sufficient advance written notice of intent to use such evidence to provide the adverse party with a fair opportunity to contest the use of such evidence.

(c) Effect of Pardon, Annulment, or Certificate of Rehabilitation. Evidence of a conviction is not admissible under this rule if (1) the conviction has been the subject of a pardon, annulment, certificate of rehabilitation, or other equivalent procedure based on a finding of the rehabilitation of the person convicted, and that person has not been convicted of a subsequent crime which was punishable by death or imprisonment in excess of one year, or (2) the conviction has been the subject of a pardon, annulment, or other equivalent procedure based on a finding of innocence.

(d) Juvenile Adjudications. Evidence of juvenile adjudications is generally not admissible under this rule. The court may, however, in a criminal case allow evidence of a juvenile adjudication of a witness other than the accused if conviction of the offense would be admissible to attack the credibility of an adult and the court is satisfied that admission in evidence is necessary for a fair determination of the issue of guilt or innocence.

(e) Pendency of Appeal. The pendency of an appeal therefrom does not render evidence of a conviction inadmissible. Evidence of the pendency of an appeal is admissible.

Rule 610   Religious Beliefs or Opinions

Evidence of the beliefs or opinions of a witness on matters of religion is not admissible for the purpose of showing that, by reason of their nature, the witness's credibility is impaired or enhanced.

Rule 611   Mode and Order of Interrogations and Presentations

(a) Control by Court. The court shall exercise reasonable control over the mode and order of interrogating witnesses and presenting evidence so as to (1) make the interrogation and presentation effective for the ascertainment of the truth, (2) avoid needless consumption of time, and (3) protect witnesses from harassment or undue embarrassment.

(b) Scope of Cross-Examination. Cross-examination should be limited to the subject matter of the direct examination and matters affecting the credibility of the witness. The court may, in the exercise of discretion, permit inquiry into additional matters as if on direct examination.

(c) Leading Questions. Leading questions should not be used on the direct examination of a witness except as may be necessary to develop the witness's testimony. Ordinarily, leading questions should be permitted on cross-examination. Whenever a party calls a hostile witness, an adverse party, or a witness identified with an adverse party, interrogation may be by leading questions.

Rule 612   Writing or Object Used to Refresh Memory

(a) While Testifying. If, while testifying, a witness uses a writing or object to refresh the witness's memory, an adverse party is entitled to have the writing or object produced at the trial, hearing, or deposition in which the witness is testifying.

(b) Before Testifying. If, before testifying, a witness uses a writing or object to refresh the witness's memory for the purpose of testifying and the court in its discretion determines that the interests of justice so require, an adverse party is entitled to have the writing or object produced, if practicable, at the trial, hearing, or deposition in which the witness is testifying.

(c) Terms and Conditions of Production and Use. A party entitled to have a writing or object produced under this rule is entitled to inspect it, to cross-examine the witness thereon, and to introduce in evidence those portions which relate to the testimony of the witness. If production of the writing or object at the trial, hearing, or deposition is impracticable, the court may order it made available for inspection. If it is claimed that the writing or object contains matters not related to the subject matter of the testimony, the court shall examine the writing or object in camera, excise any portions not so related, and order delivery of the remainder to the party entitled thereto. Any portion withheld over objections shall be preserved and made available to the appellate court in the event of an appeal. If a writing or object is not produced, made available for inspection, or delivered pursuant to order under this rule, the court shall make any order justice requires, but in criminal cases if the prosecution elects not to comply, the order shall be one striking the testimony or, if the court in its discretion determines that the interests of justice so require, declaring a mistrial.

Rule 613   Prior Statements of Witnesses

(a) Examining Witness Concerning Prior Statement. In examining a witness concerning a prior statement made by the witness, whether written or not, the statement need not be shown nor its contents disclosed to the witness at that time, but on request the same shall be shown or disclosed to opposing counsel.

(b) Extrinsic Evidence of Prior Inconsistent Statement of Witness. Extrinsic evidence of a prior inconsistent statement by a witness is not admissible unless the witness is afforded an opportunity to explain or deny the same and the opposite party is afforded an opportunity to interrogate the witness thereon, or the interests of justice otherwise require. This provision does not apply to statements of a party-opponent as defined in Rule 801(d)(2).

Rule 614   Calling and Interrogation of Witnesses by Court and Jury

(a) Calling by Court. The court may not call witnesses except in extraordinary circumstances or except as provided for court-appointed experts, and all parties are entitled to cross-examine witnesses thus called.

(b) Interrogation by Court. The court may interrogate witnesses, in an impartial manner, whether called by itself or by a party.

(c) Objections. Objections to the calling of witnesses by the court or to interrogation by it may be made at the time or at the next available opportunity when the jury is not present.

(d) Interrogation by Juror. A juror may be permitted to propound questions to a witness by submitting them in writing to the judge, who will decide whether to submit the questions to the witness for answer, subject to the objections of the parties, which may be made at the time or at the next available opportunity when the jury is not present. Once the court has ruled upon the appropriateness of the written questions, it must then rule upon the objections, if any, of the parties prior to submission of the questions to the witness.

Rule 615   Separation of Witnesses

At the request of a party, the court shall order witnesses excluded so that they cannot hear the testimony of or discuss testimony with other witnesses, and it may make the order on its own motion. This rule does not authorize the exclusion of (1) a party who is a natural person, or (2) an officer or employee of a party that is not a natural person designated as its representative by its attorney, or (3) a person whose presence is shown by a party to be essential to the presentation of the party's cause.

Rule 616   Bias of Witness

For the purpose of attacking the credibility of a witness, evidence of bias, prejudice, or interest of the witness for or against any party to the case is admissible.

Rule 617   Unrecorded Statements During Custodial Interrogation

(a) In a felony criminal prosecution, evidence of a statement made by a person during a Custodial Interrogation in a Place of Detention shall not be admitted against the person unless an Electronic Recording of the statement was made, preserved, and is available at trial, except upon clear and convincing proof of any one of the following:

(1) The statement was part of a routine processing or "booking" of the person; or

(2) Before or during a Custodial Interrogation, the person agreed to respond to questions only if his or her Statements were not Electronically Recorded, provided that such agreement and its surrounding colloquy is Electronically Recorded or documented in writing; or

(3) The law enforcement officers conducting the Custodial Interrogation in good faith failed to make an Electronic Recording because the officers inadvertently failed to operate the recording equipment properly, or without the knowledge of any of said officers the recording equipment malfunctioned or stopped operating; or

(4) The statement was made during a custodial interrogation that both occurred in, and was conducted by officers of, a jurisdiction outside Indiana; or

(5) The law enforcement officers conducting or observing the Custodial Interrogation reasonably believed that the crime for which the person was being investigated was not a felony under Indiana law; or

(6) The statement was spontaneous and not made in response to a question; or

(7) Substantial exigent circumstances existed which prevented the making of, or rendered it not feasible to make, an Electronic Recording of the Custodial Interrogation, or prevent its preservation and availability at trial.

(b) For purposes of this rule, "Electronic Recording" means an audio-video recording that includes at least not only the visible images of the person being interviewed but also the voices of said person and the interrogating officers; "Custodial Interrogation" means an interview conducted by law enforcement during which a reasonable person would consider himself or herself to be in custody; "Place of Detention" means a jail, law enforcement agency station house, or any other stationary or mobile building owned or operated by a law enforcement agency at which persons are detained in connection with criminal investigations.

(c) The Electronic Recording must be a complete, authentic, accurate, unaltered, and continuous record of a Custodial Interrogation.

(d) This Rule is in addition to, and does not diminish, any other requirement of law regarding the admissibility of a person's statements.

Adopted eff. 1/1/11.

VII. OPINIONS AND EXPERT TESTIMONY

Rule 701   Opinion Testimony by Lay Witnesses

If the witness is not testifying as an expert, the witness's testimony in the form of opinions or inferences is limited to those opinions or inferences which are (a) rationally based on the perception of the witness and (b) helpful to a clear understanding of the witness's testimony or the determination of a fact in issue.

Rule 702 Testimony by Experts

(a) If scientific, technical, or other specialized knowledge will assist the trier of fact to understand the evidence or to determine a fact in issue, a witness qualified as an expert by knowledge, skill, experience, training, or education, may testify thereto in the form of an opinion or otherwise.

(b) Expert scientific testimony is admissible only if the court is satisfied that the scientific principles upon which the expert testimony rests are reliable.

Rule 703 Bases of Opinion Testimony by Experts

The facts or data in the particular case upon which an expert bases an opinion or inference may be those perceived by or made known to the expert at or before the hearing. Experts may testify to opinions based on inadmissible evidence, provided that it is of the type reasonably relied upon by experts in the field.

Rule 704 Opinion on Ultimate Issue

(a) Testimony in the form of an opinion or inference otherwise admissible is not objectionable merely because it embraces an ultimate issue to be decided by the trier of fact.

(b) Witnesses may not testify to opinions concerning intent, guilt, or innocence in a criminal case; the truth or falsity of allegations; whether a witness has testified truthfully; or legal conclusions.

Rule 705 Disclosure of Facts or Data Underlying Expert Opinion

The expert may testify in terms of opinion or inference and give reasons therefor without first testifying to the underlying facts or data, unless the court requires otherwise. The expert may in any event be required to disclose the underlying facts or data on cross-examination.

VIII. HEARSAY

Rule 801 Definitions

The following definitions apply under this Article:

(a) **Statement.** A "statement" is (1) an oral or written assertion or (2) nonverbal conduct of a person, if it is intended by the person as an assertion.

(b) **Declarant.** A "declarant" is a person who makes a statement.

(c) **Hearsay.** "Hearsay" is a statement, other than one made by the declarant while testifying at the trial or hearing, offered in evidence to prove the truth of the matter asserted.

(d) **Statements Which are Not Hearsay.** A statement is not hearsay if:

(1) *Prior statement by witness.* The declarant testi-

fies at the trial or hearing and is subject to cross-examination concerning the statement, and the statement is (A) inconsistent with the declarant's testimony and was given under oath subject to the penalty of perjury at a trial, hearing, or other proceeding, or in a deposition; or (B) consistent with the declarant's testimony, offered to rebut an express or implied charge against the declarant of recent fabrication or improper influence or motive and made before the motive to fabricate arose; or (C) one of identification of a person made shortly after perceiving the person;

(2) *Statement by party-opponent.* The statement is offered against a party and is (A) the party's own statement, in either an individual or a representative capacity; or (B) a statement of which the party has manifested an adoption or belief in its truth; or (C) a statement by a person authorized by the party to make a statement concerning the subject; or (D) a statement by the party's agent or servant concerning a matter within the scope of the agency or employment, made during the existence of the relationship; or (E) a statement by a coconspirator of a party during the course and in furtherance of the conspiracy.

Amended eff. 1/1/94.

Rule 802 Hearsay Rule

Hearsay is not admissible except as provided by law or by these rules.

Rule 803 Hearsay Exceptions; Availability of Declarant Immaterial

The following are not excluded by the hearsay rule, even though the declarant is available as a witness.

(1) *Present Sense Impression.* A statement describing or explaining a material event, condition or transaction, made while the declarant was perceiving the event, condition or transaction, or immediately thereafter.

(2) *Excited Utterance.* A statement relating to a startling event or condition made while the declarant was under the stress of excitement caused by the event or condition.

(3) *Then Existing Mental, Emotional, or Physical Condition.* A statement of the declarant's then existing state of mind, emotion, sensation, or physical condition (such as intent, plan, motive, design, mental feeling, pain and bodily health), but not including a statement of memory or belief to prove the fact remembered or believed unless it related to the execution, revocation, identification, or terms of declarant's will.

(4) *Statements for Purposes of Medical Diagnosis or Treatment.* Statements made by persons who are

seeking medical diagnosis or treatment and describing medical history, or past or present symptoms, pain, or sensations, or the inception or general character or the cause or external source thereof insofar as reasonably pertinent to diagnosis or treatment.

(5) *Recorded Recollection.* A memorandum or record concerning a matter about which a witness once had knowledge but now has insufficient recollection to enable the witness to testify fully and accurately, shown to have been made or adopted by the witness when the matter was fresh in the witness's memory and to reflect that knowledge correctly. If admitted, the memorandum or record may be read into evidence but may not itself be received as an exhibit unless offered by an adverse party.

(6) *Records of Regularly Conducted Business Activity.* A memorandum, report, record, or data compilation, in any form, of acts, events, conditions, opinions, or diagnoses, made at or near the time by, or from information transmitted by, a person with knowledge, if kept in the course of a regularly conducted business activity, and if it was the regular practice of that business activity to make the memorandum, report, record, or data compilation, all as shown by the testimony or affidavit of the custodian or other qualified witness, unless the source of information or the method or circumstances of preparation indicate a lack of trustworthiness. The term "business" as used in this rule includes business, institution, association, profession, occupation, and calling of every kind, whether or not conducted for profit.

(7) *Absence of Entry in Records Kept in Accordance with the Provisions of Paragraph (6).* Evidence that a matter is not included in the memoranda, reports, records, or data compilations, in any form, kept in accordance with the provisions of paragraph (6), to prove the nonoccurrence or nonexistence of the matter, if the matter was of a kind of which a memorandum, report, record, or data compilation was regularly made and preserved, unless the sources of information or other circumstances indicate lack of trustworthiness.

(8) *Public Records and Reports.* Unless the sources of information or other circumstances indicate lack of trustworthiness, records, reports, statements, or data compilations in any form, of a public office or agency, setting forth its regularly conducted and regularly recorded activities, or matters observed pursuant to duty imposed by law and as to which there was a duty to report, or factual findings resulting from an investigation made pursuant to authority granted by law. The following are not within this exception to the hearsay rule: (a) investigative reports by police and other law enforcement personnel, except when offered by an accused in a criminal case; (b) investigative reports prepared by or for a government, a public office, or an agency when offered by it in a case in which it is a party; (c) factual findings offered by the government in criminal cases; and (d) factual findings resulting from special investigation of a particular complaint, case, or incident, except when offered by an accused in a criminal case.

(9) *Records of Vital Statistics.* Records or data compilations in any form, of births, fetal deaths, deaths, or marriages, if the report thereof was made to a public office pursuant to requirements of law.

(10) *Absence of Public Record or Entry.* To prove the absence of a record, report, statement, or data compilation in any form, or the nonoccurrence or nonexistence of a matter of which a record, report, statement, or data compilation in any form was regularly made and preserved by a public office or agency, evidence in the form of a certification in accordance with Rule 902, or testimony, that a diligent search failed to disclose the record, report, statement, or data compilation, or entry.

(11) *Records of Religious Organizations.* Statements of births, marriages, divorces, deaths, legitimacy, ancestry, relationship by blood or marriage, or other similar facts of personal or family history, contained in a regularly kept record of a religious organization.

(12) *Marriage, Baptismal, and Similar Certificates.* Statements of fact contained in a certificate that the maker performed a marriage or other ceremony or administered a sacrament, made by a clergyman, public official, or other person authorized by the rules of practices of a religious organization or by law to perform the act certified, and purporting to have been issued at the time of the act or within a reasonable time thereafter.

(13) *Family Records.* Statements of fact concerning personal or family history contained in family Bibles, genealogies, charts, engravings on rings, inscriptions on family portraits, engravings on urns, crypts, or tombstones, or the like.

(14) *Records of Documents Affecting an Interest in Property.* The record of a document purporting to establish or affect an interest in property, as proof of the content of the original recorded document and its execution and delivery by each person by whom it purports to have been executed, if the record is a record of a public office and an applicable statute authorized the recording of documents of that kind in that office.

(15) *Statements in Documents Affecting an Interest in Property.* A statement contained in a document purporting to establish or affect an interest in property if the matter stated was relevant to the purposes of the document, unless dealings with the property since the document was made have been inconsistent with the truth of the statement or the purport of the document.

(16) *Statements in Ancient Documents.* Statements in a document in existence thirty years or more, the authenticity of which is established.

(17) *Market Reports, Commercial Publications.* Market quotations, tabulations, lists, directories, or other published compilations, generally used and relied upon by the public or by persons in particular occupations.

(18) *Learned Treatises.* To the extent called to the attention of an expert witness upon cross-examination or relied upon by the expert witness in direct examination, statements contained in published treatises, periodicals, or pamphlets that contradict the expert's testimony on a subject of history, medicine, or other science or art, established as a reliable authority by the testimony or admission of the witness or by other expert testimony or by judicial notice. If admitted, the statements may be read into evidence but may not be received as exhibits.

(19) *Reputation Concerning Personal or Family History.* Reputation among members of a person's family by blood, adoption, or marriage, or among a person's associates, or in the community, concerning a person's birth, adoption, marriage, divorce, death, legitimacy, relationship by blood, adoption, or marriage, ancestry, or other similar fact of a person's personal or family history.

(20) *Reputation Concerning Boundaries or General History.* Reputation in a community, arising before the controversy, as to boundaries of or customs affecting lands in the community, and reputation as to events of general history important to the community or state or nation in which located.

(21) *Reputation as to Character.* Reputation of a person's character among associates or in the community.

(22) *Judgment of Previous Conviction.* Evidence of a final judgment entered after a trial or upon a plea of guilty (but not upon a plea of nolo contendere) adjudging a person guilty of a crime punishable by death or imprisonment in excess of one year, to prove any fact essential to sustain the judgment, but not including, when offered by the government in a criminal prosecution for purposes other than impeachment, judgments

against persons other than the accused. The pendency of an appeal may be shown but does not affect admissibility.

(23) *Judgment as to Personal, Family, or General History, or Boundaries.* Judgments as proof of matters of personal, family or general history, or boundaries, essential to the judgment, if the same would be provable by evidence of reputation.

Amended eff. 1/1/12.

Rule 804 Hearsay Exceptions; Declarant Unavailable

(a) Definition of Unavailability. "Unavailability as a witness" includes situations in which the declarant

(1) is exempted by ruling of the court on the ground of privilege from testifying concerning the subject matter of the declarant's statement; or

(2) persists in refusing to testify concerning the subject matter of the declarant's statement despite an order of the court to do so; or

(3) testifies to a lack of memory of the subject matter of the declarant's statement; or

(4) is unable to be present or to testify at the hearing because of death or then existing physical or mental illness or infirmity; or

(5) is absent from the hearing and the proponent of a statement has been unable to procure the declarant's attendance by process or other reasonable means.

A declarant is not unavailable as a witness if exemption, refusal, claim of lack of memory, inability, or absence is due to the procurement or wrongdoing of the proponent of a statement for the purpose of preventing the witness from attending or testifying.

(b) Hearsay Exceptions. The following are not excluded by the hearsay rule if the declarant is unavailable as a witness.

(1) *Former Testimony.* Testimony given as a witness at another hearing of the same or a different proceeding, or in a deposition taken in compliance with law in the course of the same or another proceeding, if the party against whom the testimony is now offered, or, in a civil action or proceeding, a predecessor in interest, had an opportunity and similar motive to develop the testimony by direct, cross, or redirect examination.

(2) *Statement Under Belief of Impending Death.* A statement made by a declarant while believing that the declarant's death was imminent, concerning the cause or circumstances of what the declarant believed to be impending death.

(3) *Statement Against Interest.* A statement which was at the time of its making so far contrary to the

declarant's pecuniary or proprietary interest, or so far tended to subject the declarant to civil or criminal liability, or to render invalid a claim by the declarant against another, that a reasonable person in the declarant's position would not have made the statement unless believing it to be true. A statement or confession offered against the accused in a criminal case, made by a codefendant or other person implicating both the declarant and the accused, is not within this exception.

(4) *Statement of Personal or Family History.* (A) A statement concerning the declarant's own birth, adoption, marriage, divorce, legitimacy, relationship by blood, adoption, or marriage, ancestry, or other similar fact of personal or family history, even though declarant had no means of acquiring personal knowledge of the matter stated; or (B) a statement concerning the foregoing matters, and death also, of another person, if the declarant was related to the other by blood, adoption, or marriage or was so intimately associated with the other's family as to be likely to have accurate information concerning the matter declared.

(5) *Forfeiture by Wrongdoing.* A statement offered against a party that has engaged in or encouraged wrongdoing that was intended to, and did, procure the unavailability of the declarant as a witness for the purpose of preventing the declarant from attending or testifying.

Amended eff. 1/1/09.

Rule 805   Hearsay Within Hearsay

Hearsay included within hearsay is not excluded under the hearsay rule if each part of the combined statements conforms with an exception to the hearsay rule provided in these rules.

Rule 806   Attacking and Supporting Credibility of Declarant

When a hearsay statement, or a statement defined in Rule 801(d)(2)(C), (D), or (E), has been admitted in evidence, the credibility of the declarant may be attacked, and if attacked may be supported, by any evidence which would be admissible for those purposes if declarant had testified as a witness. Evidence of a statement or conduct by the declarant at any time, inconsistent with the declarant's hearsay statement, is not subject to any requirement that the declarant may have been afforded an opportunity to deny or explain. If the party against whom a hearsay statement has been admitted calls the declarant as a witness, the party is entitled to examine the declarant on the statement as if under cross-examination.

IX. AUTHENTICATION AND IDENTIFICATION

Rule 901   Requirement of Authentication or Identification

(a) **General Provision.** The requirement of authentication or identification as a condition precedent to admissibility is satisfied by evidence sufficient to support a finding that the matter in question is what its proponent claims.

(b) **Illustrations.** By way of illustration only, and not by way of limitation, the following are examples of authentication or identification conforming with the requirements of this rule:

(1) *Testimony of Witness with Knowledge.* Testimony of a witness with knowledge that a matter is what it is claimed to be.

(2) *Nonexpert Opinion on Handwriting.* Nonexpert opinion as to the genuineness of handwriting, based upon familiarity not acquired for purposes of the litigation.

(3) *Comparison by Trier or Expert Witness.* Comparison by the trier of fact or by expert witnesses with specimens which have been authenticated.

(4) *Distinctive Characteristics and the Like.* Appearance, contents, substance, internal patterns, or other distinctive characteristics, taken in conjunction with circumstances.

(5) *Voice Identification.* Identification of a voice, whether heard firsthand or through mechanical or electronic transmission or recording, by opinion based upon hearing the voice at any time under circumstances connecting it with the alleged speaker.

(6) *Telephone Conversations.* Telephone conversations, by evidence that a call was made to the number assigned at the time by the telephone company to a particular person or business, if (i) in the case of a person, circumstances, including self-identification, show the person answering to be the one called, or (ii) in the case of a business, the call was made to a place of business and the conversation related to business reasonably transacted over the telephone.

(7) *Public Records or Reports.* Evidence that a writing authorized by law to be recorded or filed and in fact recorded or filed in a public office, or a purported public record, report, statement, or data compilation, in any form, is from the public office where items of this nature are kept.

(8) *Ancient Documents or Data Compilation.* Evi-

dence that a document or data compilation, in any form, (i) is in such condition as to create no suspicion concerning its authenticity, (ii) was in a place where it, if authentic, would likely be, and (iii) has been in existence 30 years or more at the time it is offered.

(9) *Process or System.* Evidence describing a process or system used to produce a result and showing that the process or system produces an accurate result.

(10) *Methods Provided by Statute or Rule.* Any method or authentication or identification provided by the Supreme Court of this State or by a statute or as provided by the Constitution of this State.

Rule 902   Self-Authentication

Extrinsic evidence of authenticity as a condition precedent to admissibility is not required with respect to the following:

(1) *Domestic Public Documents.* The original or a duplicate of a domestic official record proved in the following manner: An official record kept within the United States, or any state, district, commonwealth, territory, or insular possession thereof, or within the Panama Canal Zone, the Trust Territory of the Pacific Islands, or the Ryukyu Islands, or an entry therein, when admissible for any purpose, may be evidenced by an official publication thereof or by a copy attested by the officer having the legal custody of the record, or by his deputy. Such publication or copy need not be accompanied by proof that such officer has the custody. Proof that such officer does or does not have custody of the record may be made by the certificate of a judge of a court of record of the district or political subdivision in which the record is kept, authenticated by the seal of the court, or may be made by any public officer having a seal of office and having official duties in the district or political subdivision in which the record is kept, authenticated by the seal of his office.

(2) *Foreign Public Documents.* The original or a duplicate of a foreign official record proved in the following manner: A foreign official record, or an entry therein, when admissible for any purpose, may be evidenced by an official publication thereof; or a copy thereof, attested by a person authorized to make the attestation, and accompanied by a final certification as to the genuineness of the signature and official position:

(a) of the attesting person; or

(b) of any foreign official whose certificate of genuineness of signature and official position relates to the attestation or is in a chain of certificates of genuineness of signature and official position relating to the attestation.

A final certification may be made by a secretary of embassy or legation, consul general, consul, vice consul, or consular agent of the United States, or a diplomatic or consular official of the foreign country assigned or accredited to the United States. If reasonable opportunity has been given to all parties to investigate the authenticity and accuracy of the documents, the court may, for good cause shown:

(i) admit an attested copy without final certification; or

(ii) permit the foreign official record to be evidenced by an attested summary with or without a final certification.

(3) *Official Publications.*   Books, pamphlets, or other publications issued by public authority.

(4) *Newspapers and Periodicals.* Printed materials purporting to be newspapers or periodicals.

(5) *Trade Inscriptions and the Like.* Inscriptions, signs, tags, or labels purporting to have been affixed in the course of business and indicating ownership, control, or origin.

(6) *Acknowledged Documents.* Original documents accompanied by a certificate of acknowledgment executed in the manner provided by law by a notary public or other officer authorized by law to take acknowledgments.

(7) *Commercial Paper and Related Documents.* Commercial paper, signatures thereon, and documents relating thereto to the extent provided by general commercial law.

(8) *Presumptions Created by Law.* Any signature, document, or other matter declared by any law of the United States or of this state, to be presumptively or prima facie genuine or authentic.

(9) *Certified Domestic Records of Regularly Conducted Activity.* Unless the source of information or the circumstances of preparation indicate a lack of trustworthiness, the original or a duplicate of a domestic record of regularly conducted activity within the scope of Rule 803(6), which the custodian thereof or another qualified person certifies under oath (i) was made at or near the time of the occurrence of the matters set forth, by or from information transmitted by, a person with knowledge of those matters; (ii) is kept in the course of the regularly conducted activity, and (iii) was made by the regularly conducted activity as a regular practice. A record so certified is not self-authenticating under this subsection unless the proponent makes an intention to offer it known to the adverse party and makes it available for inspection

sufficiently in advance of its offer in evidence to provide the adverse party with a fair opportunity to challenge it.

(10) *Certified Foreign Records of Regularly Conducted Activity.* Unless the source of information or the circumstances of preparation indicate lack of trustworthiness, the original or a duplicate of a foreign record of regularly conducted activity within the scope of Rule 803(6), which is accompanied by a written declaration by the custodian thereof or another qualified person that the record (i) was made at or near the time of the occurrence of the matters set forth, by or from information transmitted by, a person with knowledge of those matters; (ii) is kept in the course of the regularly conducted activity; and (iii) was made by the regularly conducted activity as a regular practice. The record must be signed in a foreign country in a manner which, if falsely made, would subject the maker to criminal penalty under the laws of that country, and the signature certified by a government official in the manner provided in subsection (2) above. The record is not self-authenticating under this subsection unless the proponent makes his or her intention to offer it known to the adverse party and makes it available for inspection sufficiently in advance of its offer in evidence to provide the adverse party with a fair opportunity to challenge it.

Amended eff. 1/1/04; 1/1/05.

Rule 903   Subscribing Witness' Testimony Unnecessary

The testimony of a subscribing witness is not necessary to authenticate a writing unless required by the laws of the jurisdiction whose laws govern the validity of the writing.

X. CONTENTS OF WRITINGS, RECORDINGS, AND PHOTOGRAPHS

Rule 1001   Definitions

For purposes of this Article the following definitions are applicable:

(1) *Writings and Recordings.* "Writings" and "recordings" consist of letters, words, sounds, or numbers, or their equivalent, set down by handwriting, typewriting, printing, photostating, photographing, magnetic impulse, mechanical or electronic recording, or other forms of data compilation.

(2) *Photographs.* "Photographs" include still photographs, x-ray films, videotapes, and motion pictures.

(3) *Original.* An "original" of a writing or recording is the writing or recording itself or any counterpart intended to have the same effect by a person executing or issuing it. An "original" of a photograph includes the negative or any print therefrom. If data are stored in a computer or similar device, any printout or other output readable by sight, shown to reflect the data accurately, is an "original."

(4) *Duplicate.* A "duplicate" is a counterpart produced by the same impression as the original, or from the same matrix, or by means of photography, including enlargements and miniatures, or by mechanical or electronic rerecording, or by chemical reproduction, or by facsimile transmission, or video tape, or by other equivalent techniques which accurately reproduces the original.

Rule 1002   Requirement of Original

To prove the content of a writing, recording, or photograph, the original writing, recording, or photograph is required, except as otherwise provided in these rules or by statute. An electronic record of the Indiana Bureau of Motor Vehicles obtained from the Bureau that bears an electronic or digital signature, as defined by statute, is admissible in a court proceeding as if the signature were an original.

Rule 1003   Admissibility of Duplicates

A duplicate is admissible to the same extent as an original unless (1) a genuine question is raised as to the authenticity of the original or (2) in the circumstances it would be unfair to admit the duplicate in lieu of the original.

Rule 1004   Admissibility of Other Evidence of Contents

The original is not required, and other evidence of the contents of a writing, recording, or photograph is admissible if:

(1) *Originals Lost or Destroyed.* All originals are lost or have been destroyed, unless the proponent lost or destroyed them in bad faith;

(2) *Original Not Obtainable.* No original can be obtained by any available judicial process or procedure;

(3) *Original in Possession of Opponent.* At a time when an original was under the control of the party against whom offered, such party was put on notice, by the pleadings or otherwise, that the contents would be a subject of proof at the hearing, and such party does not produce the original at the hearing; or

(4) *Collateral Matters.* The writing, recording, or photograph is not closely related to a controlling issue.

Rule 1005   Public Records

The contents of an official record, or of a document

authorized to be recorded or filed and actually recorded or filed, including data compilations in any form, if otherwise admissible, may be proved by copy, certified as correct in accordance with Rule 902 or testified to be correct by a witness who has compared it with the original. If a copy complying with the foregoing cannot be obtained by the exercise of reasonable diligence, other evidence of the contents may be admitted.

Rule 1006   Summaries

The contents of voluminous writings, recordings, or photographs which cannot conveniently be examined in court may be presented in the form of a chart, summary, or calculation. The originals, or duplicates, shall be made available for examination or copying, or both, by other parties at a reasonable time and place. The court may order that they be produced in court.

Rule 1007   Testimony or Written Admissions of Party

Contents of writings, recordings, or photographs may be proved by the testimony or deposition of the party against whom offered or by a written admission, without accounting for the nonproduction of the original.

Rule 1008   Functions of Court and Jury

Whenever the admissibility of other evidence of contents of writings, recordings, or photographs under these rules depends upon the fulfillment of a condition of fact, the question whether the condition has been fulfilled is ordinarily for the court to determine in accordance with the provisions of Rule 104. However, when an issue is raised whether (1) the asserted writing ever existed, or (2) another writing, recording, or photograph produced at the trial is the original, or (3) other evidence of contents correctly reflects the contents, the issue is for the trier of fact to determine as in the case of other issues of fact.

XI. MISCELLANEOUS RULES

Rule 1101   Evidence Rules Review Committee

A. The Supreme Court Committee on Rules of Practice and Procedure, as constituted under Ind. Trial Rule 80, shall serve as the Evidence Rules Review Committee.

B. The Evidence Rules Review Committee shall conduct a continuous study of the Indiana Rules of Evidence and shall submit to the Supreme Court from time to time recommendations and proposed amendment to such rules. The Committee shall follow the procedure set forth in Ind. Trial Rule 80(D) in the amendment of the Rules of Evidence. Amendments or additions may be suggested by the Supreme Court of Indiana in current case law or the Indiana General Assembly through enactment of legislation. Proposed amendments or comment on published amendments offered by the Bench, Bar, and Public, shall be delivered in writing to the Committee's Executive Secretary, 30 South Meridian Street, Suite 500, Indianapolis, Indiana 46204.

Amended eff. 2/1/96; 1/1/04; 1/1/08.

I
GENERAL PROVISIONS

Chapter 101

Rule 101. Scope

Rule 101 reads as follows:

These rules govern proceedings in the courts of this State to the extent and with the exceptions stated in this rule.

(a) General Applicability. These rules apply in all proceedings in the courts of the State of Indiana except as otherwise required by the Constitution of the United States or Indiana, by the provisions of this rule, or by other rules promulgated by the Indiana Supreme Court. If these rules do not cover a specific evidence issue, common or statutory law shall apply. The word "judge" in these rules includes referees, commissioners and magistrates.

(b) Rules of Privilege. The rules and laws with respect to privileges apply at all stages of all actions, cases, and proceedings.

(c) Rules Inapplicable. The rules, other than those with respect to privileges, do not apply in the following situations:

(1) *Preliminary questions of fact.* The determination of questions of fact preliminary to admissibility of evidence when the issue is to be determined by the court under Rule 104(a).

(2) *Miscellaneous proceedings.* Proceedings relating to extradition, sentencing, probation, or parole; issuance of criminal summonses, or of warrants for arrest or search, preliminary juvenile matters, direct contempt, bail hearings, small claims, and grand jury proceedings.

---

*   *   *   *   *

ANALYSIS

Applicability Generally. Rule 101 identifies the proceedings in which the Evidence Rules apply. Functionally, the rule directs that the rules are applicable to all proceedings, subject to the exceptions set forth in subdivision (c).

Proceedings Generally. The rules provide for a unitary system of evidence. Accordingly, the rules apply to all proceedings, civil and criminal, regardless of whether the matter is tried to the court or to a jury. In certain instances, however, the rules draw distinctions between certain types of cases. For example, under Rule 404 certain applications of character

3

evidence are available only in criminal cases. Other examples may be found in Rules 104(c), 803(8), and 804(b)(3).

Exceptions. Subsection (c) identifies proceedings in which the Rules of Evidence are inapplicable. The following proceedings are not subject to the Rules of Evidence:

- Grand juries
- Proceedings in extraction
- Sentencing
- Probation
- Parole
- Bail
- Direct contempt
- Preliminary juvenile matters
- Small claims

Recent Developments

   In *Dumas v. State*, 803 N.E.2d 1113 (Ind. 2004), the Indiana Supreme Court reviewed the applicability of the Indiana Rules of Evidence at the penalty phase of a capital trial. The Court held that, although Rule 101 clearly renders the rules inapplicable to proceedings in which evidence is presented to a trial judge alone without the intervention of a jury, the penalty phase of a capital trial requires the introduction of evidence with the burden on the State to prove its case beyond a reasonable doubt. Accordingly, the penalty phase is "in the nature of a trial" to which the rules of evidence apply. In *Malenchik v. State*, 928 N.E.2d 564 (Ind. 2010), the Supreme Court expanded on this reasoning, holding that the due process clause of the United States and Indiana Constitutions guarantee that persons may not be convicted with "unreliable" information.

Stages of Proceedings; Privileges. Rule 101(b) specifically provides that privilege rules apply to all stages of all proceedings conducted under the rules. Also, consistent with Rule 104, admissibility determinations are not subject to the rules, except those with respect to privileges.

ADDITIONAL AUTHORITY

WEISSENBERGER'S FEDERAL EVIDENCE § 1

1 WEINSTEIN 2d §§ 101.01–101.03

1 MUELLER & KIRKPATRICK § 1

Cooper, *Recent Developments in Indiana Evidence Law*, 32 IND. L. REV. 811 (1999)

Bodensteiner, *Indiana Rules of Evidence*, 27 IND. L. REV. 1063 (1993)

COMPARISON TO FEDERAL RULE

Indiana Rule 101 is modeled after Uniform Rules of Evidence 101 and 1101. Exceptions

to the applicability of the Federal Rules are set forth in Federal Rule 1101.

SIGNIFICANT CASES

Malenchik v. State, 928 N.E.2d 564 (Ind. 2010) (although the Indiana Rules of Evidence, except with respect to privileges, do not apply in trial court sentencing proceedings, the accused still has rights under the due process clause not to be sentenced with unreliable evidence).

Dumas v. State, 803 N.E.2d 1113 (Ind. 2004) (although Rule 101 makes clear that the rules of evidence do not apply in proceedings in which evidence is presented to a trial judge alone without the intervention of a jury, the penalty phase of a capital trial requires the introduction of evidence with the burden on the State to prove its case beyond a reasonable doubt, and is thus "in the nature of a trial" to which the rules of evidence apply; however, the error was invited, as the court permitted the introduction of the hearsay statement based on the party's own contention that the penalty phase of trial was essentially a sentencing hearing to which the rules of evidence do not apply).

Carter v. State, 711 N.E.2d 835 (Ind. 1999) (the evidence rules, other than those with respect to privilege, do not apply to sentencing hearings; thus, uncharged crimes may properly be considered at a sentencing hearing).

Thacker v. State, 709 N.E.2d 3 (Ind. 1999) (trial court conducting sentencing hearing is not limited to admissible evidence in evaluating aggravating and mitigating circumstances).

McEwen v. State, 695 N.E.2d 79 (Ind. 1998) (rules of evidence apply over conflicting statutory provisions).

Yamobi v. State, 672 N.E.2d 1344 (Ind. 1996) (in the absence of a unique Indiana policy, constitutional or statutory consideration, courts in Indiana should normally construe Indiana Rules of Evidence consistent with the prevailing body of decisions from other jurisdictions interpreting the same rules).

Hawkins v. Auto-Owners Ins. Co., 608 N.E.2d 1358 (Ind. 1993), *overruled in part*, *State ex rel. Crawford v. Delaware Circuit Court*, 655 N.E.2d 499 (Ind. 1995) (where Indiana statute conflicted with a rule of procedure adopted by the Indiana Supreme Court, the Court held that the statute was the correct statement of the law).

Dillon v. State, 492 N.E.2d 661 (Ind. 1986) (rules of evidence are not applied strictly at sentencing).

Lindsey v. State, 485 N.E.2d 102 (Ind. 1985), *reh'g denied with opinion*, 491 N.E.2d 191 (Ind. 1986) (rules regarding cross-examination are more relaxed at a suppression hearing).

L.H. v. State, 878 N.E.2d 425 (Ind. Ct. App. 2007) (the purpose of the child hearsay hearing is to determine the admissibility of certain hearsay statements, considering specific factors that demonstrate the reliability of the statements; accordingly, it is a preliminary juvenile matter to which the rules of evidence do not apply).

In re Z. H., 850 N.E.2d 933 (Ind. Ct. App. 2006), *transfer denied*, 860 N.E.2d 594 (Ind. 2006) (the Indiana Rules of Evidence apply to the full evidentiary hearing afforded a juvenile facing a state petition to place the juvenile on the sex offender registry).

Whatley v. State, 847 N.E.2d 1007 (Ind. Ct. App. 2006) (although the rules of evidence are inapplicable in probation revocation hearings, evidence must still bear substantial indicia of reliability; in this instance, a probable cause affidavit was admissible).

Harris v. State, 836 N.E.2d 267 (Ind. Ct. App. 2005), *transfer denied*, 841 N.E.2d 192 (Ind. 2005) (in a parole revocation hearing, the Indiana Rules of Evidence are inapplicable, and the Indiana Parole Board may consider any relevant evidence that bears some substantial indicia of reliability).

Marsh v. State, 818 N.E.2d 143 (Ind. Ct. App. 2004) (the hearsay rules under the Indiana Rules of Evidence are inapplicable to probation revocation; accordingly, the trial court, in revoking defendant's probation, is permitted to consider any relevant evidence bearing some "substantial indicia of reliability").

Citizens Action Coalition of Ind., Inc. v. N. Ind. Pub. Serv. Co., 796 N.E.2d 1264 (Ind. Ct. App. 2003) (administrative hearings, unlike judicial proceedings, are to be conducted in an informal manner, without the strictures of the Indiana Rules of Evidence; nevertheless, an administrative agency's findings must be based upon the kind of evidence that is substantial and reliable).

Black v. State, 794 N.E.2d 561 (Ind. Ct. App. 2003) (a probation revocation hearing is not to be equated with an adversarial criminal proceeding, and the Rules of Evidence do not apply; in such hearings, judges may consider any relevant evidence bearing some substantial indicia of reliability, including expert testimony and scientific evidence, but are not required to admit all evidence; rulings on the admissibility of evidence in probation revocation proceedings are subject to appellate review).

M.J.H. v. State, 783 N.E.2d 376 (Ind. Ct. App. 2003) (the Indiana Rules of Evidence do not apply in probation proceedings).

White v. State, 756 N.E.2d 1057 (Ind. Ct. App. 2001) (the rules of evidence, other than those concerning matters of privilege, do not apply at the sentencing phase of a criminal trial).

Pitman v. State, 749 N.E.2d 557 (Ind. Ct. App. 2001) (Indiana Rules of Evidence do not apply in probation proceedings; thus, courts may consider any relevant evidence bearing some substantial indicia of reliability, including reliable hearsay).

Carter v. State, 685 N.E.2d 1112 (Ind. Ct. App. 1997), *superseded*, 706 N.E.2d 552 (Ind. 1999) (in a proceeding, such as a probation revocation hearing, where the Indiana Rules of Evidence do not apply, case law provides the applicable law and hence the *Frye* common law rule is still valid to govern the admissibility of expert testimony).

Brim v. State, 624 N.E.2d 27 (Ind. Ct. App. 1993) (court held that state statute admitting evidence of a previous battery to show motive or intent was null because the Indiana Supreme Court had adopted the language of Fed. R. Evid. 404(b)).

Ray v. State, 496 N.E.2d 93 (Ind. Ct. App. 1986) (formal requirements for introducing evidence at full trial do not apply at postconviction relief hearings).

P. v. State, 446 N.E.2d 17 (Ind. Ct. App. 1983) (prior statement could not be admitted at trial against juvenile where juvenile refused to testify).

Chapter 102

Rule 102. Purpose and Construction

Rule 102 reads as follows:

> These rules shall be construed to secure fairness in administration, elimination of unjustifiable expense and delay, and promotion of growth and development of the law of evidence to the end that the truth may be ascertained and proceedings justly determined.

* * * * *

ANALYSIS

Construction Generally. The purpose of Rule 102 is to establish the spirit within which the rules should be applied and construed. While the rule imparts discretion to the trial judge, it is not intended to be applied in a manner which subverts the express requirements or limitations of other specific Rules of Evidence.

The reference to the "growth and development of the law of evidence" in the Rule provides a continuing role for Indiana common law in creating interstitial evidence law. For example, the Indiana Supreme Court has pointed to the spirit of Rule 102 in allowing an English language translation of a transcripted recording between a criminal defendant and a police informant. *See Romo v. State*, 941 N.E.2d 504 (Ind. 2011). Although the principles of the best evidence rule in Rule 1002 and the exceptions thereto in Rule 1004 were explored by the *Romo* Court, they were found to be inapplicable. Nonetheless, the Court allowed the translation, reasoning that the transcripts, not the original recording, constituted the source of the relevant information.

ADDITIONAL AUTHORITY

WEISSENBERGER'S FEDERAL EVIDENCE § 102.1

1 WEINSTEIN 2d §§ 102.01–102.06

1 MUELLER & KIRKPATRICK §§ 2–3

Weissenberger, *Evidence Myopia: The Failure to See the Federal Rules of Evidence as a Codification of the Common Law*, 40 WM. & MARY L. REV. 1613 (1999)

Weissenberger, *The Elusive Identity of the Federal Rules of Evidence*, 40 WM. & MARY L. REV. 1613 (1999)

COMPARISON TO FEDERAL RULE

Indiana Rule 102 is identical to Federal Rule 102.

SIGNIFICANT CASES

United States v. Bibbs, 564 F.2d 1165, 1170 (5th Cir. 1977) (court is free to fashion an evidentiary procedure with regard to subsequent inconsistent statements which will accord with objectives of Federal Rule 102).

United States v. Thorne, 547 F.2d 56, 59 (8th Cir. 1976) (Federal Rules permit exercise of discretion by trial judge to implement Rule 102).

Chapter 103

Rule 103. Rulings on Evidence

Rule 103 reads as follows:

(a) Effect of Erroneous Ruling. Error may not be predicated upon a ruling which admits or excludes evidence unless a substantial right of the party is affected, and:

(1) *Objection.* In case the ruling is one admitting evidence, a timely objection or motion to strike appears of record, stating the specific ground of objection, if the specific ground was not apparent from the context; or

(2) *Offer of proof.* In case the ruling is one excluding evidence, the substance of the evidence was made known to the court by a proper offer of proof, or was apparent from the context within which questions were asked.

(b) Record of Offer and Ruling. The court may add any other or further statement which shows the character of the evidence, the form in which it was offered, the objection made, and the ruling thereon. It may direct the making of an offer in question and answer form.

(c) Hearing of Jury. In jury cases, proceedings shall be conducted, to the extent practicable, so as to prevent inadmissible evidence from being suggested to the jury by any means, such as making statements or offers of proof or asking questions in the hearing of the jury.

(d) Fundamental Error. Nothing in this rule precludes taking notice of fundamental errors affecting substantial rights although they were not brought to the attention of the court.

---

* * * * *

ANALYSIS

Scope of Rule. Rule 103 establishes the trial procedures necessary to preserve errors for appellate review. The rule does not purport to provide substantive standards under which a reversal is required.

There are two circumstances in which the record must clearly reflect the alleged error:

(1) Error predicated on improper admission of evidence (objection overruled improperly).

(2) Error predicated on improper exclusion of evidence (objection sustained improperly).

Basis of Objection or Motion.   In the first instance, error is easily preserved by stating the basis of the objection or the motion to strike. If the basis of the objection is not stated, error is waived unless the reason for the objection is apparent from the context of the testimony. Even if the court rules before hearing the basis of the objection, counsel should state the reason for the record. The reason may be abbreviated. If there is any doubt regarding the adequacy of an objection and whether it has been stated with sufficient specificity, parties should always err on the side of too much detail. Indiana courts of appeals are reluctant to overturn the evidentiary rulings of trial courts, and insufficiently specific objections are frequently the basis upon which courts of appeal hang their deferential hat. For example, an objection than an expert witness is not "qualified" as an expert will not support a claim of error on appeal relating to the reliability of the expert witness's testimony, as the objections are derived from distinct evidentiary requirements that are nonetheless contained within the same Evidence Rule (Rule 702).

Proffer.   If the objection to admissibility of the evidence is sustained, the proponent should make a proffer of the evidence that he or she expects to elicit from the witness. A proffer, or an offer to prove, is an "offer" from counsel concerning what a witness would say if permitted to testify. An offer to prove must convey to the trial court the substance of the evidence.

Recent Developments

In *State v. Wilson*, 836 N.E.2d 407 (Ind. 2005), the Indiana Supreme Court reconsidered its earlier guidance concerning the adequacy of offers of proof in *Hilton v. State*, 648 N.E.2d 361 (Ind. 1995). In *Hilton*, the Court noted that the offer of proof in that case was insufficient because it lacked specificity and failed to establish such material facts as, when the conversation took place, where the conversation took place, and who was present at the time. The *Hilton* Court also questioned the offer on the ground that Hilton phrased his offer of proof "I believe," and he failed to adequately assure the Court that the offer truly represented the substances of the testimony. As reformulated in *Wilson*, however, these guidelines overstate the requirements for an adequate offer of proof. Accordingly, a proffer need only show: (1) the facts sought to be proved; (2) the relevance of that evidence, and; (3) the answer to any objection to exclusion of the evidence. The *Wilson* Court noted that details that are immaterial to the ultimate facts are not necessary, and also disapproved language from *Hilton* suggesting that "an offer of proof must vouch for the anticipated testimony."

Additionally, the offer to prove should identify the grounds for admission of the testimony as well as the relevance of the testimony. The proffer permits the reviewing court to determine whether the ruling was prejudicial error. A proffer is simply a statement on the record, outside the hearing of the jury, summarizing the import of the offered evidence.

Illustration

Counsel: And then what did defendant tell you?

Objection: Hearsay.

Court: Sustained.

Counsel: Your Honor, I wish to make a proffer.

Court: Proceed.

Counsel: *(Out of hearing of the jury)* This witness would have testified that the defendant said to her, "I should have seen that traffic signal."

Rule 103(c) provides that, whenever practical, discussions concerning rulings on evidence should be conducted outside the hearing of the jury. Obviously, the purpose of the procedure set forth in Rule 103(a) and (b) would be wholly defeated if the jury were permitted to hear a proffer of excluded evidence or to hear a lengthy explanation on the highly prejudicial nature of evidence sought to be admitted over objection.

Substantial Right Affected; Fundamental Error.   It should be noted that in order for evidentiary error to operate as the basis for appeal, a substantial right must be affected. Moreover, it should be noted that under Rule 103(d), error may be reviewed on appeal even if it has not been preserved where it falls within the category of "fundamental error."

Bench Trial.   As noted, error in the admission of evidence does not warrant a reversal unless a substantial right of the party is affected. Any harm from evidentiary error is lessened, if not completely obviated, when the trial is by the court sitting without a jury. Accordingly, in reviewing a judgment from a bench trial, an appellate court presumes that the lower court disregarded inadmissible evidence and rendered its decision solely on the basis of relevant and probative evidence. Moreover, in a bench trial, any error in the admission of evidence which is merely cumulative of evidence properly admitted is harmless.

ADDITIONAL AUTHORITY

WEISSENBERGER'S FEDERAL EVIDENCE §§ 103.1–103.5

MCCORMICK §§ 51–52, 54–55

1 WEINSTEIN 2d §§ 103.01–103.02

1 MUELLER & KIRKPATRICK §§ 4–23

1 WIGMORE §§ 17, 18

COMPARISION TO FEDERAL RULE

Indiana Rule 103 substitutes "proper offer of proof" in Indiana Rule 103(a)(2) for "offer" in Federal Rule 103(a)(2) and Indiana Rule 103(d) refers to "fundamental" error rather than "plain" error.

Federal Rule 103 was amended in December 2000. It now states:

(a) Effect of erroneous ruling. Error may not be predicated upon a ruling which admits or excludes evidence unless a substantial right of the party is affected, and

(1) *Objection.* In case the ruling is one admitting evidence, a timely objection or motion to strike appears of record, stating the specific ground of objection, if the specific ground was not apparent from the context; or

(2) *Offer of proof.* In case the ruling is one excluding evidence, the substance of the evidence was made known to the court by a proper offer of proof, or was apparent from the context within which questions were asked.

Once the court makes a definitive ruling on the record admitting or excluding evidence, either at or before trial, a party need not renew an objection or offer of proof to preserve a claim of error for appeal.

(b) Record of offer and ruling. The court may add any other or further statement which shows the character of the evidence, the form in which it was offered, the objection made, and the ruling thereon. It may direct the making of an offer in question and answer form.

(c) Hearing of the jury. In jury cases, proceedings shall be conducted, to the extent practicable, so as to prevent inadmissible evidence from being suggested to the jury by any means, such as making statements or offers of proof or asking questions in the hearing of the jury.

(d) Plain error. Nothing in this rule precludes taking notice of plain errors affecting substantial rights although they were not brought to the attention of the court.

The amendment applies to all rulings on evidence whether they occur at or before trial. The amendment also applies to "in limine" rulings.

A claim of error with respect to a definitive ruling is now preserved for review when the party has otherwise satisfied the objection or offer of proof requirements of Rule 103(a). A party may still renew its objection or offer of proof at the time the evidence is to be offered, but it is more a formalism than a necessity.

If there is doubt as to whether an *in limine* or evidentiary ruling is definitive, the amendment imposes upon counsel the obligation to clarify the court's ruling.

Even if a court's ruling is definitive, the court may revisit its decision when the evidence is to be offered. If the court changes its initial ruling, or if the opposing party violates the terms of the initial ruling, objection must be made when the evidence is offered to preserve the claim of error for appeal. The error, if any, in such a situation occurs only when the evidence is offered and admitted.

On appeal, a definitive ruling is reviewed in light of the facts and circumstances before the trial court at the time of the ruling. If the relevant facts and circumstances change materially after the advance ruling has been made, those facts and circumstances cannot be relied upon on appeal unless they have been brought to the attention of the trial court by way of a renewed, and timely, objection, offer of proof, or motion to strike.

Nothing in the amendment affects the provisions of Fed. R. Civ. P. 72(a), 28 U.S.C. § 636(b)(1), or the rule set forth in *Luce v. United States*, 469 U.S. 38, 105 S. Ct. 460, 83 L. Ed. 2d 443 (1984). Nor does the amendment purport to answer whether a party waives the right to appeal the trial court's ruling when it objects to evidence that the court finds admissible in a definitive ruling and then offers the evidence to "remove the sting" of its anticipated prejudicial effect.

SIGNIFICANT CASES

Baxendale v. Raich, 878 N.E.2d 1252 (Ind. 2008) (a simple explanation of the relevance of a question to which an objection has been sustained does not constitute an offer of proof sufficient to sustain the objection for appeal, as there was no demonstration of what the testimony would have revealed).

State v. Wilson, 836 N.E.2d 407 (Ind. 2005) (the only requirement for an offer of proof is that it indicate the relevance of the offered testimony and that it not violate some rule of evidence; an offer of proof may begin with the words, "We expect the witness to testify that" or "I believe," as the attorney making the offer must have a good faith and reasonable belief that the witness will testify as the attorney states, but the attorney is not a warrantor of the witness's reliability and should not vouch for the witness).

Azania v. State, 730 N.E.2d 646 (Ind. 2000), *superseded*, 875 N.E.2d 701 (Ind. 2007) (absent either a ruling admitting evidence accompanied by a timely objection or a ruling excluding evidence accompanied by a proper offer of proof, there is no basis for a claim of error on appeal).

Hauk v. State, 729 N.E.2d 994 (Ind. 2000) (error in the exclusion of evidence is not a basis for reversal on appeal, or otherwise modifying a judgment, unless refusal to take such action is inconsistent with substantial justice).

Fayson v. State, 726 N.E.2d 292 (Ind. 2000) (evidence outside the scope of cross-examination testimony does not affect defendant's substantial rights and provides no basis for reversal).

Marcum v. State, 725 N.E.2d 852 (Ind. 2000) (testimony did not affect defendant's substantial rights; therefore, any error in its admission was harmless).

Noble v. State, 725 N.E.2d 842 (Ind. 2000) (in attempted murder and child molestation case, defendant waived issue of identity because although he attempted to introduce evidence that another person committed the crime, he failed to make an offer to prove what witness would have said when trial court sustained objection without explanation; Rule 103(a) requires that the substance of the evidence be made known to the trial court and that the offer to prove identify the grounds for admission and the relevance of the testimony).

Roach v. State, 695 N.E.2d 934 (Ind. 1998) (an offer to prove must make known to the trial court the substance of the evidence, the grounds for admission of the testimony, and the relevance of the testimony).

Rule 103(a)

Raess v. Doescher, 883 N.E.2d 790 (Ind. 2009) (a trial court objection to the qualification of an expert witness was not sufficient to preserve a claim of error relating to the lack of reliability of the underlying expert testimony; no reference to an objection under Rule 702 or scientific reliability was made).

McCarthy v. State, 749 N.E.2d 528 (Ind. 2001) (a claim of error in the exclusion or admission of evidence will not prevail on appeal, unless the error affects the substantial rights of the moving party).

Murray v. State, 742 N.E.2d 932 (Ind. 2001) (in an attempted murder prosecution, the alleged error in permitting the state to cross-examine defendant about his illegal carrying of a handgun, at the time of the charged shooting, was preserved at trial because the defense counsel objected to the cross-examination during a colloquy between the counsel and the Court that concluded with the trial judge advising counsel and the Court reporter to note the objection).

Small v. State, 736 N.E.2d 742 (Ind. 2000) (when a trial court fails to give the requisite admonishment to the jury, a timely objection must be made to preserve the error for appeal; defendant failed to interpose an objection at the time the transcripts of a videotaped statement were distributed to the jury and, thus, he waived his error on appeal).

Cason v. State, 672 N.E.2d 74 (Ind. 1996) (evidentiary rulings are presumptively correct; any error in admitting holster found by police at defendant's aunt's home did not affect substantial rights of defendant and did not justify reversal of murder conviction).

Brown v. State, 671 N.E.2d 401 (Ind. 1996) (erroneous admission of evidence does not constitute reversible error if, in light of all the evidence in the case, the probable impact of the error on the jury is minor enough so as not to affect the substantial rights of the parties).

Moore v. State, 669 N.E.2d 733 (Ind. 1996) ("[w]here a defendant fails to object to the introduction of evidence, makes only a general objection, or objects only on other grounds, the defendant waives the suppression claim").

Isaacs v. State, 659 N.E.2d 1036 (Ind. 1995) (where defendant failed to object to judge's response to the defendant's original objection or to the clarifying statement later made by the judge, defendant failed to preserve his claim that trial judge invaded jury's province by summarizing witness's testimony while ruling on objection during the closing argument).

Fleener v. State, 656 N.E.2d 1140 (Ind. 1995) (in general, objection to question asked at trial must be made before answer is given, but where answer of witness was long narrative and objection was made after only a small part of that answer was given, objection was sufficient to preserve claim of error as to witness's subsequent testimony; once objection had been made, argued, and overruled, defense counsel could not be defaulted for failing to repeat objection to psychotherapist's testimony in prosecution for child molesting).

Mullins v. State, 646 N.E.2d 40 (Ind. 1995) (to preserve claim of error in admission or exclusion of evidence, objection must be stated with specificity at the time evidence is first offered; once prosecution has responded to timely objection in admission of results of alcohol breath test, defense may not rely on its first objection if it believes prosecution has still not established proper foundation, but must object again, stating what part of the required foundation the prosecution has failed to establish).

Willis v. State, 510 N.E.2d 1354 (Ind. 1987), *rev'd*, *Willis v. Cohn*, 956 F.2d 1165 (7th Cir. 1992) (in order to preserve an issue for review, an objection at trial must be specific).

Leggs v. State, 501 N.E.2d 431 (Ind. 1986) (failure to object waived claim of error in admission of evidence of unrelated crime).

Scott v. State, 260 Ind. 67, 292 N.E.2d 252 (1973) (failure to timely object constitutes a waiver of any error in the admission of evidence).

Kinsman v. State, 77 Ind. 132 (1881) (if the grounds for an objection are apparent or obvious from the context, specific grounds need not be stated at trial).

Witte v. M.M., 800 N.E.2d 185 (Ind. Ct. App. 2003), *superseded*, 820 N.E.2d 128 (Ind. 2005) (an offer of proof must (1) make the substance of the excluded evidence or testimony clear to the court, (2) identify the grounds for admission of the testimony, and (3) identify the relevance of the testimony).

King v. State, 799 N.E.2d 42 (Ind. Ct. App. 2003) (a party who does not make an offer of proof, before or after the trial court sustained the opposing party's objection and the substance of the evidence sought to be elicited was not apparent from the context of the questions, fails to create a record of the substance and nature of the precluded testimony and thus waives the issue on appeal).

Wohlwend v. Edwards, 796 N.E.2d 781 (Ind. Ct. App. 2003) (in determining whether an evidentiary error requires reversal, the appellate court should assess the probable impact of the evidence on the trier of fact).

East v. Estate of East, 785 N.E.2d 597 (Ind. Ct. App. 2003) (the requirement that a party make an offer of proof is not dispensed with simply because the witness whose testimony is at issue has been called by the party seeking admission of the evidence; such an offer is required for the trial and appellate courts to properly rule of the evidentiary issue).

Oldham v. State, 779 N.E.2d 1162 (Ind. Ct. App. 2002) (in determining whether an error in the admission or exclusion of evidence affects a party's substantial rights, the reviewing court must assess the probable impact of the evidence on the jury).

Roser v. Silvers, 698 N.E.2d 860 (Ind. Ct. App. 1998) (because the danger from evidentiary harm is almost nonexistent in a bench trial, an appellate court presumes that a lower court sitting without a jury disregarded inadmissible evidence and rendered its decision solely on the basis of relevant and probative evidence).

Rule 103(b)

Isaacs v. State, 659 N.E.2d 1036 (Ind. 1995) (where defendant failed to object to judge's response to the defendant's original objection or to the clarifying statement later made by the judge, defendant failed to preserve his claim that trial judge invaded jury's province by summarizing witness's testimony while ruling on objection during the closing argument).

Rule 103(c)

Baker v. State, 750 N.E.2d 781 (Ind. 2001) (after a court has made a ruling *in limine* on the admissibility of evidence, the proponent of that evidence must make a proffer of that evidence to preserve the claim for appellate review, unless its substance was apparent from the context in which the questions were asked).

Bryant v. State, 270 Ind. 268, 385 N.E.2d 415 (1979) (discussions on evidentiary issues should be conducted outside the presence of the jury to avoid the jury hearing inadmissible evidence).

Rule 103(d)

Bowman v. State, 577 N.E.2d 569 (Ind. 1991) (in order for an error in the admission of evidence to be harmless, there must be "no substantial likelihood that the evidence contributed to the verdict").

Gosnell v. State, 483 N.E.2d 445 (Ind. 1985) ("[f]undamental error is a clearly blatant violation of basic and elementary principles. The harm or potential must be substantial and appear clearly and prospectively from the record").

Malo v. State, 266 Ind. 157, 361 N.E.2d 1201 (1977) (in a criminal case, fundamental error is error which would deprive defendant of due process).

Williams v. State, 634 N.E.2d 849 (Ind. Ct. App. 1994) (fundamental error did not result where evidence of defendant's prior criminal activity was erroneously admitted at trial).

Carter v. State, 634 N.E.2d 830 (Ind. Ct. App. 1994) (objection made prior to trial, after motion *in limine*, is denied is insufficient to preserve error; party must object at trial also).

United Farm Bureau Family Life Ins. Co. v. Fultz, 176 Ind. App. 217, 375 N.E.2d 601 (1978) (fundamental error results where the erroneous admission of evidence was prejudicial to a party, went to the heart of the party's case, and was beyond the party's power to prevent or correct it).

Chapter 104

Rule 104. Preliminary Questions

Rule 104 reads as follows:

(a) Questions of Admissibility Generally. Preliminary questions concerning the qualification of a person to be a witness, the existence of a privilege, or the admissibility of evidence shall be determined by the Court, subject to the provisions of subdivision (b). In making its determination, the Court is not bound by the Rules of Evidence, except those with respect to privileges. Where a determination of admissibility under this paragraph requires resolution of a question of fact, the question shall be resolved by the preponderance of the evidence.

(b) Relevancy Conditioned on Fact. When the relevancy of evidence depends upon the fulfillment of a condition of fact, the Court shall admit it upon, or subject to, the introduction of evidence sufficient to support a finding of the fulfillment of the condition.

(c) Hearing of Jury. Hearings on the admissibility of confessions shall in all cases be conducted out of the presence and hearing of the jury. Hearings on other preliminary matters shall be so conducted when the interests of justice require, or when an accused is a witness and so requests.

(d) Testimony by Accused. The accused does not, by testifying upon a preliminary matter, become subject to cross-examination as to other issues in the case.

(e) Weight and Credibility. This rule does not limit the right of a party to introduce before the jury evidence relevant to weight or credibility.

---

* * * * *

ANALYSIS

Purpose of Rule; Foundation Generally. Rule 104 governs the allocation responsibility between judge and jury for determining questions of admissibility. The primary focus of the rule is on situations where a prerequisite showing must be made in order for certain evidence to be properly admitted. This procedure is commonly referred to as "laying a foundation" for the admission of evidence. The necessity of a foundation may be indicated by the Rules of Evidence or by substantive case law or statutes.

Court Determines Admissibility. Rule 104(a) provides that preliminary questions regarding the admissibility of evidence shall be determined by the trial judge. Where the trial judge considers the foundation to be sufficient, the primary evidence will be admitted to the jury or trier of fact. Subdivision (a) was amended in 2009 to clarify that the standard used by the Court in determining preliminary questions is a preponderance of evidence. This standard applies even in criminal cases with respect to preliminary questions. However, there may be cases in which there is substantial overlap between the resolution of the preliminary question and proof of an element of the crime charged. In these cases, the higher "beyond a reasonable doubt" standard is appropriate.

Examples. As the rule specifies, preliminary questions may involve the qualifications of a person to be a witness (e.g., whether a person is qualified to testify as an expert, or whether a lay witness is competent or incompetent by virtue of the exclusionary provisions of Rule 601); the existence of a privilege (i.e., whether the criteria exist for invocation of a privilege); and questions of admissibility of the evidence itself. This latter category includes a broad range of questions for example, whether the prerequisites for applicability of an exception to the hearsay exclusionary rule have been met?

Foundational Evidence May Be Inadmissible. Rule 104(a) contains a significant principle relating to foundational evidence. Foundational evidence which is directed exclusively to the trial judge need not be "admissible" evidence under the rules. For example, foundational evidence directed exclusively to the trial judge may consist of inadmissible hearsay or unauthenticated documents. The only limitation is that privileged information may not be utilized.

Illustration

Q: Did he say anything to you regarding his condition?

A: Yes—he said, "I know I haven't long to live. The doctor told me I have about five minutes left."

(*Note:* Objections based on hearsay or even multiple hearsay as to what the doctor told the victim would not be appropriate because the Rules of Evidence do not apply in admissibility determinations.)

Q: Did the victim say anything to you after that?

A.   Yes, he told me who shot him.

Opposing Counsel: Objection—hearsay.

Court: Overruled—I find the elements of a foundation for a dying declaration to have been met.

Conditional Relevance. Rule 104(a) is qualified in certain situations by Rule 104(b) which pertains to conditional relevance. Where conditional relevance applies, both the foundation and the primary evidence is considered by the jury in reaching its verdict. The standard of Rule 104(b) applies whenever the existence of one fact is necessary for the relevance of some connected fact. Whenever this is the case, the first fact must be proven in satisfaction of the standard of Rule 104(b) in order to enable the trier of fact to use the second fact as evidence. Authentication under Article IX, where authenticating testimony is conditional to the admission of a document or objects, represents a clear example of conditional relevance.

Illustration

Q: I am handing you now what has been marked as Plaintiff's Exhibit Number 5. Please look at the last line of the document.

A: Yes.

Q: Please describe what you see.

A: I see the signature of the defendant, Ralph Jackson.

Q: Please state the basis for your testimony that this is Mr. Jackson's signature.

A: I was present when he wrote his name on this document, and I recognize both the document and Mr. Jackson's signature.

Counsel: *(After showing document to opposing counsel)* I would now like to offer Plaintiff's Exhibit Number 5 into evidence.

In the foregoing illustration, the evidence is subject to Rule 104(b) because the trier of fact would be required to believe the foundational testimony in order to attach relevance to the document.

Another example of conditional relevance is the determination of factual competency of a witness.

Under Rule 104(b), a trial court may admit the evidence only after it makes a preliminary determination that there is sufficient evidence to support a finding that the conditional fact exists. The trial court must determine only that a reasonable jury could make the requisite factual determination based on the evidence before it. The trial court, however, is not required to weigh the credibility of the evidence or to make a finding. An appellate court reviews the lower court's decision regarding the sufficiency of the evidence under 104(b) for an abuse of discretion.

Hearing of Jury; Criminal Defendant; Weight or Credibility. Rule 104(c) identifies situations in which testimony on preliminary matters should be conducted outside the hearing of the jury. Rule 104(d) contains a provision applicable only in criminal cases in providing that the accused does not, by testifying on preliminary matters, subject himself to cross-examination on other issues in the case. Finally, Rule 104(e) clarifies the effect of the rule in not limiting the right of a party to introduce evidence to affect the weight or credibility of any evidence.

ADDITIONAL AUTHORITY

WEISSENBERGER'S FEDERAL EVIDENCE §§ 104.1–104.14

McCormick § 53 at 124

1 Weinstein 2d §§ 104.01–104.60

1 Mueller & Kirkpatrick §§ 24–37

9 Wigmore § 2550

COMPARISON TO FEDERAL RULE

Federal Rule 104 and Indiana Rule 104 are identical except that Indiana has added "out of the presence" of the jury in Rule 104(c).

SIGNIFICANT CASES

United States v. Zolin, 491 U.S. 554, 109 S. Ct. 2619, 105 L. Ed. 2d 469 (1989), *vacated,* **Church of Scientology v. United States**, 506 U.S. 9, 113 S. Ct. 447, 121 L. Ed. 2d 313 (1992) (Federal Rule 104 does not prohibit in camera review of attorney-client communications to determine the applicability of the crime-fraud exception to the attorney-client privilege).

Huddleston v. United States, 485 U.S. 681, 108 S. Ct. 1496, 99 L. Ed. 2d 771 (1988) (in theft case involving stolen videotapes, evidence of defendant's prior television sales was admissible in accordance with Federal Rule 104(b), where jury could have reasonably concluded that televisions were stolen from the low price, large quantity offered for sale, and defendant's inability to produce bill of sale).

Bourjaily v. United States, 483 U.S. 171, 107 S. Ct. 2775, 97 L. Ed. 2d 144 (1987), *superseded by statute,* **United States v. Kemp**, 2005 U.S. Dist. LEXIS 2072 (E.D. Pa. Feb. 10, 2005) (court was permitted to listen to tape recording in determining the recording's admissibility where statements on tape were corroborated by independent evidence).

Jackson v. Denno, 378 U.S. 368, 84 S. Ct. 1774, 12 L. Ed. 2d 908, 28 Ohio Op. 2d 177 (1964) (the Court held as unconstitutional New York's procedure of allowing the jury to determine the voluntariness of a confession).

United States v. Franco, 874 F.2d 1136 (7th Cir. 1989) (in determining the admissibility of evidence, court used a preponderance of the evidence standard and used hearsay evidence in making the determination).

Cox v. State, 696 N.E.2d 853 (Ind. 1998) (pursuant to Rule 104(b), a trial court may admit evidence only after it makes a preliminary determination that there is sufficient evidence to support a finding that the conditional fact exists such that a reasonable jury could make the requisite factual determination based on the evidence before it).

Lindsey v. State, 485 N.E.2d 102 (Ind. 1985) (evidence rules are not applied strictly at pretrial suppression hearing).

Lewis v. State, 904 N.E.2d 290 (Ind. Ct. App. 2009) (where the existence of a warrant was not an element of the State's case, but instead was relevant to the question of the admissibility of evidence obtained under the warrant, a court may consider hearsay when ruling on the admissibility of evidence).

Cardin v. State, 540 N.E.2d 51 (Ind. Ct. App. 1989) (document not admissible without the testimony of custodian).

Chapter 105

Rule 105. Limited Admissibility

Rule 105 reads as follows:

> When evidence which is admissible as to one party or for one purpose but not admissible as to another party or for another purpose is admitted, the court, upon request, shall restrict the evidence to its proper scope and admonish the jury accordingly.

* * * * *

ANALYSIS

When Appropriate.　Rule 105 provides for the "limiting instruction" or "admonition." A party is entitled to a limiting instruction by the trial judge directed to the jury whenever evidence might be misapplied by the jury in reaching its final determination.

Examples Under the Rules.　The following rules illustrate that evidence may be admissible for one purpose while at the same time remaining inadmissible for another purpose:

- Rule 407, Subsequent Remedial Measures
- Rule 408, Compromise and Offers to Compromise
- Rule 411, Liability Insurance
- Rule 609, Impeachment by Evidence of Conviction of Crime

Evidence admitted under any of these rules is subject to limiting instruction upon the request of opposing counsel.

Time of Request.　Trial counsel may request a limiting instruction when appropriate during the course of trial. Where anticipated prior to trial, a pretrial request for a limiting instruction is also appropriate. Where trial counsel wishes to suggest the tenor of the limiting instruction to the trial judge during the course of trial, counsel should ask to approach the bench for a sidebar conference.

Illustration

Counsel:　And isn't it true that the testimony that you have just provided is

21

> inconsistent with the statement you made to the plaintiff shortly after the automobile accident that "It was the blue car that ran the red light."
>
> **Witness:** Well, yes, I believe I said something like that.
>
> **Counsel:** And that statement you made to the plaintiff is inconsistent with your trial testimony here today that "It was the black car that ran the red light." Isn't that correct?
>
> **Witness:** Well, I don't remember the exact words I said, but I said something like that.
>
> **Opposing Counsel:** Your Honor, may I approach the sidebar? *(At the sidebar)* Your Honor, the prior inconsistent statement of this witness may not be received as substantive evidence. Consequently, a limiting instruction is necessary in order to ensure that the jury consider it only for its impeachment value.
>
> **Judge:** Yes, I will instruct the jury accordingly. *(To the jury)* Ladies and gentlemen of the jury, the statement that this witness may have made prior to trial which is inconsistent with his trial testimony may be considered by you only for the purposes of affecting the credibility of this witness. Ladies and gentlemen of the jury, I admonish you, you may not consider that prior statement as substantive evidence in this case. You may not base your verdict upon it. You may only consider it for the purposes of deciding the weight to be given to this witness's testimony while providing testimony on the witness stand here today.

Relationship to Rule 403. A limiting instruction is often used as a second line of defense after an attorney has unsuccessfully attempted to exclude evidence under Rule 403, the rule which balances probative value against such adverse influences as unfair prejudice. For example, if a party seeks to impeach a witness with a prior conviction under Rule 609, the party's opponent may seek to preclude use of the conviction entirely under Rule 403. If he or she fails to convince the judge that the conviction should not be used, the opponent may, as a second line of defense, ask the judge for an instruction which limits the jury's use of the prior conviction to the evaluation of the witness's credibility.

When Mandatory; Sua Sponte. Where appropriate, a limiting instruction is mandatory on request. The court, of course, retains the discretion to determine whether a limiting instruction is appropriate in the first instances, but the ruling by the court on the underlying objection will make this determination clear in most cases. The Rule also indicates that the court may provide a limiting instruction in the absence of a request. Such action may be prudent simply as a matter of jury education or instruction, and it may also help to sustain on appeal the trial court's ruling on the underlying objection.

ADDITIONAL AUTHORITY

WEISSENBERGER'S FEDERAL EVIDENCE §§ 105.1–105.3

MCCORMICK §§ 56, 59

1 WEINSTEIN 2d §§ 105.01–105.07

1 MUELLER & KIRKPATRICK §§ 38–41

1 WIGMORE §§ 13.215, 216.5

COMPARISON TO FEDERAL RULE

Indiana Rule 105 is identical to Federal Rule 105 except that Indiana refers to limiting instructions as admonitions.

SIGNIFICANT CASES

Richardson v. Marsh, 481 U.S. 200, 107 S. Ct. 1702, 95 L. Ed. 2d 176 (1987) (the Confrontation Clause is not violated when the nontestifying codefendant's confession is redacted to eliminate not only the defendant's name, but any reference to her existence, and proper limiting instructions are provided).

Cruz v. New York, 481 U.S. 186, 107 S. Ct. 1714, 95 L. Ed. 2d 162 (1987) (where a nontestifying codefendant's confession not directly admissible against the defendant was admitted at a joint trial, and the jury was instructed not to consider the confession against the defendant, the defendant's rights under the Confrontation Clause were nonetheless violated).

Marley v. State, 747 N.E.2d 1123 (Ind. 2001) (where defendant claims that battered women's syndrome has affected her ability to appreciate the wrongfulness of her conduct, she must proceed under the insanity defense; barring battered women's syndrome evidence as to a defendant's state of mind where defendant has not complied with the insanity statute does not affect its admissibility for other purposes).

Martin v. State, 736 N.E.2d 1213 (Ind. 2000) (defendant's claim, that evidence of a witness's prior inconsistent statement was improperly admitted for impeachment purposes because the jury might have considered the statement as substantive evidence, was rejected because defendant's proper remedy was to request that the jury be admonished to the effect that the statement was only to be used to judge the witness's credibility, which defendant did not do).

Small v. State, 736 N.E.2d 742 (Ind. 2000) (trial court properly admonished the jury as to the limited admissibility of recorded recollection evidence; a trial court has no affirmative duty to *sua sponte* admonish a jury as to evidence admitted for impeachment purposes).

Humphrey v. State, 680 N.E.2d 836 (Ind. 1997) (Rule 105 imposes no *sua sponte* duty on the Court to admonish the jury regarding the limited admissibility of certain evidence; a party's failure to request such an admonition operates as a waiver of any error based on the absence of such an admonition).

Grund v. State, 671 N.E.2d 411 (Ind. 1996) (defendant was not prejudiced by failure to request limiting instruction regarding testimony of defendant's sister, even though defendant would have been entitled to such limiting instruction since there was other evidence sufficient to show that defendant had opportunity to steal gun).

Jones v. State, 536 N.E.2d 267 (Ind. 1989) (jury presumed to have followed admonition to disregard police officer in photograph reenacting defendant's conduct).

Wilhelmus v. State, 824 N.E.2d 405 (Ind. Ct. App. 2005) (because Rule 105 requires the court to provide a limiting instruction in certain cases upon the request of the party opposing the evidence, trial courts should immediately provide a limiting instruction to the jury in addition to addressing the weight to be given to the evidence in its final instruction).

King v. State, 799 N.E.2d 42 (Ind. Ct. App. 2003) (the trial court correctly informed the jury when it stated that the jury was the exclusive judge of the credibility of witnesses and that with careful consideration it could disregard the testimony of any witness if it had reason to do so).

Brim v. State, 624 N.E.2d 27 (Ind. Ct. App. 1993) (where evidence of prior acts was admitted at defendant's criminal trial, court of appeals held that limiting instructions were available in other act cases upon request of defendant; court encouraged the use of such instructions).

Chapter 106

Rule 106. Remainder of or Related Writings or Recorded Statements

Rule 106 reads as follows:

> When a writing or recorded statement or part thereof is introduced by a party, an adverse party may require at that time the introduction of any other part or any other writing or recorded statement which in fairness ought to be considered contemporaneously with it.

*   *   *   *   *

ANALYSIS

Function of Rule. Rule 106 codifies the common law "completeness doctrine" in Indiana. Under the doctrine, when a party introduces a writing or recording in whole or in part into evidence at trial, the adverse party may require him to introduce any other recording or writing, or the remainder of the evidence introduced, which in fairness should be considered contemporaneously with the admitted evidence.

Scope of Rule. The rule is procedural in nature, requiring only that the complementary evidence be introduced at a time when it is needed to place the primary writing or recording into proper context or perspective. In other words, the proper remedy for a violation of the rule is admission of the remainder of the document, rather than a reversal of the underlying verdict or criminal conviction. The rule is limited to writings and recordings and does not expressly include conversations or other evidence.

Purpose of Rule; Judicial Discretion. In practice, Rule 106 operates to avoid the need for an adverse party to wait until cross-examination or rebuttal to introduce the writing or recording. Accordingly, it is intended to prevent consideration of matters out of context. Obviously, the rule contemplates a very high degree of discretion to be exercised by the trial judge.

Testimony; Depositions. As to testimonial matters, Rule 611 should be consulted regarding testimonial completeness. Also, it should be noted that Trial Rule 32(A)(4) provides: "If only part of a deposition is offered in evidence by a party, an adverse party may require him to introduce all of it which is relevant to the part introduced, and any party may introduce any other parts."

ADDITIONAL AUTHORITY

WEISSENBERGER'S FEDERAL EVIDENCE § 106.1

McCORMICK § 56

1 WEINSTEIN 2d §§ 106.01–106.08

1 MUELLER & KIRKPATRICK §§ 42–46

7 WIGMORE §§ 2094–2125

COMPARISON TO FEDERAL RULE

Indiana Rule 106 is identical to Federal Rule 106.

SIGNIFICANT CASES

Donaldson v. State, 904 N.E.2d 294 (Ind. Ct. App. 2009) (under the doctrine of completeness, the proper remedy is not a reversal of a criminal conviction, but simply the introduction into the record of the remainder of the statement which, in fairness, ought to be considered with the admitted portion).

Sanders v. State, 840 N.E.2d 319 (Ind. 2006) (the "completeness doctrine" does not require the inclusion of redacted material in a letter where the material would not have changed the context of the letter from one of confession to arguably one of sympathy; the redacted material did not cause the jury to be misled in any material way).

Brown v. State, 728 N.E.2d 876 (Ind. 2000) (although doctrine of completeness allows party to place remainder of a statement or document before the jury after the opposing party has introduced a portion of the statement or document into evidence, the remainder of the statement or document is subject to the general rules of admissibility, and portions that are immaterial, irrelevant, or prejudicial must be redacted).

Evans v. State, 643 N.E.2d 877 (Ind. 1994), *reh'g denied* (under "doctrine of completeness," party may place before jury remainder of statement or document after opposing party has introduced a portion of it into evidence, but the entire statement or document is subject to general rules of admissibility, and portions found immaterial, irrelevant, or prejudicial must be redacted; though admissibility of witness's prior consistent statement to rebut charges of improper motive overlaps with doctrine of completeness, these are distinct evidentiary categories).

Johnston v. State, 517 N.E.2d 397 (Ind. 1988) (if the remaining portions of the document are irrelevant, they may be omitted).

Saperito v. State, 490 N.E.2d 274 (Ind. 1986) (when a conversation or transaction is put into evidence, the other party may call for the entire conversation or transaction to be admitted).

Walker v. Cuppett, 808 N.E.2d 85 (Ind. Ct. App. 2004) (although Rule 106 embodies what was known as the "completeness doctrine," which was designed to avoid misleading impressions caused by taking a statement out of its proper context or otherwise conveying a distorted picture by the introduction of only selective parts of the statement, the redacted portions of a document are still subject to normal rules of admissibility before they may be admitted; because the party offering medical records did not prove the expert qualifications of the doctors who rendered opinions or made statements in the redacted portions of the records, the trial court properly allowed the redactions to stand).

Norton v. State, 772 N.E.2d 1028 (Ind. Ct. App. 2002) ("doctrine of completeness" does not change common law with regard to admissibility of omitted portions which party wishes to include; omitted portions are still subject to normal rules of admissibility, and portions found to be immaterial, irrelevant, or prejudicial must be redacted).

Atwell v. State, 738 N.E.2d 332 (Ind. Ct. App. 2000) (the doctrine of completeness under Rule 106 may be invoked to admit portions of a statement in order to (1) explain the admitted portion, (2) place the admitted portion in context, (3) avoid misleading the trier of fact, or (4) insure a fair and impartial understanding of the admitted portion; however, a court need not admit the remainder of the statement, or portions thereof, that are neither explanatory of nor relevant to the portions already introduced).

Vinson v. State, 735 N.E.2d 828 (Ind. Ct. App. 2000), *overruled in part, Long v. State*, 743 N.E.2d 253 (Ind. 2001) (eyewitness's entire written statement was admissible on redirect under the doctrine of completeness after defendant introduced a portion of the written statement while cross-examining an investigating officer about the eyewitness's description of a robber).

Lieberenz v. State, 717 N.E.2d 1242 (Ind. Ct. App. 1999) (rule of completeness may be invoked to admit omitted portions of a statement in order to explain the portion of the statement that was admitted, to place the admitted portion in context, to avoid misleading the trier of fact, or to insure a fair and impartial understanding of the admitted portion; however, a court need not admit the remainder of the statement, or portions thereof, that are neither explanatory of nor relevant to the portions already introduced; Rule 106 is designed to avoid misleading impressions caused by taking a statement of out its proper context or otherwise conveying a distorted picture by the introduction of only selective parts).

Stanage v. State, 674 N.E.2d 214 (Ind. Ct. App. 1996) (prejudicial parts of defendant's videotaped interview containing statements about defendant's prior bad acts were excludable by trial court when defendant sought to have whole interview admitted, under doctrine of completeness, into evidence after state moved to use specific statements from interview for purposes of impeachment).

II
JUDICIAL NOTICE

NOTICE

Chapter 201

Rule 201. Judicial Notice

Rule 201 reads as follows:

(a) Kinds of Facts. A court may take judicial notice of a fact. A judicially-noticed fact must be one not subject to reasonable dispute, in that it is either (1) generally known within the territorial jurisdiction of the trial court or (2) capable of accurate and ready determination by resort to sources whose accuracy cannot reasonably be questioned.

(b) Kinds of Laws. A court may take judicial notice of law. Law includes (1) the decisional, constitutional, and public statutory law, (2) rules of court, (3) published regulations of governmental agencies, (4) codified ordinances of municipalities, (5) records of a court of this state, and (6) laws of other governmental subdivisions of the United States or of any state, territory or other jurisdiction of the United States.

(c) When Discretionary. A court may take judicial notice, whether requested or not.

(d) When Mandatory. A court shall take judicial notice if requested by a party and supplied with the necessary information.

(e) Opportunity to be Heard. A party is entitled, upon timely request, to an opportunity to be heard as to the propriety of taking judicial notice and the tenor of the matter noticed. In the absence of prior notification, the request may be made after judicial notice has been taken.

(f) Time of Taking Notice. Judicial notice may be taken at any stage of the proceeding.

(g) Instructing the Jury. In a civil action or proceeding, the court shall instruct the jury to accept as conclusive any fact judicially noticed. In a criminal case, the court shall instruct the jury that it may, but is not required to, accept as conclusive any fact judicially noticed.

* * * * *

ANALYSIS

Definition. Judicial notice is the process by which a court takes recognition of a fact in the absence of any formal proof. Judicial notice is a substitute for formal proof where the facts sought to be proved are reasonably beyond dispute.

The principles of judicial notice are employed by the trial judge at numerous points during the course of the trial, often without the awareness of the participants in the courtroom. Judicial notice is taken of the English language and of the many human qualities that permit a conclusion that testimony is relevant and material. It is virtually impossible to identify all the occasions on which judicial notice is appropriate.

Rule 201 changes pre-Rule Indiana law in several respects. First, in addition to judicial notice of adjudicative facts, Rule 201 also provides certain judicial notice of law provisions in subdivision (b). Most public documents that can be said to contain "law" may be judicially noticed, including administrative regulations, court rules, court records, and, in a departure from Indiana common law, codified municipal ordinances. Second, Rule 201(g) provides that, in civil cases, a court should instruct the jury to accept judicially noticed facts as conclusive. Finally, pursuant to Rule 201(d), judicial notice is mandatory when requested by a party who provides the court with the necessary information.

Adjudicative Facts; Legislative Facts.   Rule 201 provides for the judicial notice of facts and laws. Where a fact is judicially noticed, it must be reasonably indisputable according to the standards set forth in Rule 201(a). Laws subject to judicial notice are identified in Rule 201(b). It should be noted that Rule 201(a) applies to so-called adjudicative facts and not "legislative facts." Simply stated, adjudicative facts are those facts that concern the immediate parties and that are determinative of the outcome of the case. Adjudicative facts are customarily established through formal proof and only through judicial notice pursuant to the conditions identified in Rule 201. By comparison, legislative facts are those facts that are used by the court in the decisional process of a case, in the expansion of the law, or in the interpretation or construction of legislative enactments. Accordingly, when a court makes new law, it "legislates." Inevitably, this lawmaking function relies upon factual assumptions as to the way in which the world operates.

Courts occasionally refer to the propriety of taking judicial notice of the pleadings and filings in the case before it. However, this kind of proof is not judicial notice, strictly speaking, as the introduction into evidence of the pleadings or papers merely raises a rebuttable presumption that arises with respect to the truth of the facts contained within the pleadings. The opposing party may come forward with evidence to dispute the presumption—an opportunity not available for facts formally noticed by the judge.

Conditions Precedent; Authoritative Sources.   In accordance with subdivision (a) of Rule 201, the conditions precedent to a court taking judicial notice are that the subject must be well known within the jurisdiction or, in the alternative, subject to verification by resort to a reasonably reliable source. The judge determines what a reasonably well informed person within the jurisdiction would know to be true beyond reasonable dispute. Otherwise, resort to an authoritative source is necessary. Representative authoritative sources for verification include such reference materials as historical works, science and art books, language and medical journals and dictionaries, calendars, encyclopedias, commercial lists and directories, maps and charts, statutes, and legislative reports.

Illustration

Counsel: Your Honor, may I approach the sidebar? *(At the sidebar)* Your Honor, I would like the court to take judicial notice of the fact that January 19, 1989, occurred on a Thursday.

Judge: Are you suggesting that the day of the week on which January 19 occurred is a matter of common knowledge?

Counsel: No, Your Honor, I am providing you with an almanac as well as a calendar which will conclusively demonstrate that January 19 fell on a Thursday in 1989.

Judge: Does opposing counsel have any objection?

Opposing Counsel: Your Honor, it would appear that this should be a matter of testimony from a witness sworn under oath. Consequently, I object to your taking judicial notice of this fact.

Judge: I will overrule the objection. These sources are essentially beyond dispute as to the day of the week on which January 19 occurred in 1989. Regardless of what a witness's memory may indicate, these sources are sufficient bases for judicial notice, and I will so instruct the jury. No formal evidence will be necessary.

When Appropriate. Judicial notice is appropriate if requested by a party where the party supplies necessary information or, in the alternative, the court may take judicial notice on its own initiative. In any event, a party is entitled to an opportunity to be heard in opposition to the taking of judicial notice or in support of the taking of judicial notice. Moreover, judicial notice may be taken at any time at any stage of the proceeding. Accordingly, judicial notice may be taken by the trial court or even on appeal. However, judicial notice should never be used by an appeals court to fill in missing evidentiary gaps in the trial record.

Contradictory Evidence. Rule 201(g) provides once a fact has been judicially noticed in a civil action, it is conclusively established and the adverse party may not introduce evidence to contradict the noticed fact. In a criminal case, however, the Rule respects the principle that a conviction may only rest upon a finding that each element of the charged offense has been proved beyond a reasonable doubt. In accordance with this doctrine, the Rule provides that where judicially noticed facts represent an element of the charged crime, the jury may be instructed that the taking of the judicial notice raises a rebuttable presumption as to the truth of the fact. Effectively, the jury may, but is not required to, accept as conclusive any fact judicially noticed in a criminal case.

ADDITIONAL AUTHORITY

WEISSENBERGER'S FEDERAL EVIDENCE §§ 201.1–201.9

MCCORMICK §§ 328–335

1 WEINSTEIN 2d §§ 201.01–201.03, 201.10–201.13, 201.30–201.35, 201.50–201.52

1 MUELLER & KIRKPATRICK §§ 47–60

9 WIGMORE §§ 2565–2583

COMPARISON TO FEDERAL RULE

Indiana Rule 201 is a modification of Uniform Rule of Evidence 201. Federal Rule 201 differs from Indiana Rule 201, in that Federal Rule 201 is limited to adjudicative facts.

SIGNIFICANT CASES

Lutz v. Erie Ins. Exch., 848 N.E.2d 675 (Ind. 2006) (although the color of a traffic light is not an appropriate subject for judicial notice, the fact that a party admitted in her pleading that the light was red may be judicially noticed, as a statement contained in a pleading is inadmissible as a matter of law).

French v. State, 778 N.E.2d 816 (Ind. 2002) (the failure to instruct a new jury, that it was not required to accept as conclusive any judicially noticed fact, is not a fundamental constitutional error where there was no claim the judicially noticed facts were incorrect).

Sanquenetti v. State, 727 N.E.2d 437 (Ind. 2000) (request granted to take judicial notice of facts related to accomplice's prosecution, conviction, and sentence from information in certified copies of accomplice's case summary, charging information, and verdict form signed by the jury).

Dye v. State, 717 N.E.2d 5 (Ind. 1999), *cert. denied*, 531 U.S. 957, 121 S. Ct. 379, 148 L. Ed. 2d 292 (2000) (uncompleted study in a pending capital case, examining the possible systematic exclusion of African Americans from jury venires, was not a proper subject of judicial notice; the subject matter was neither generally known within the jurisdiction nor did the conclusions of such a study seem to be capable of accurate and ready determination by resort to sources that could not be reasonably questioned).

Baran v. State, 639 N.E.2d 642 (Ind. 1994) (where defendant was charged with driving under the influence of alcohol, trial court effectively took judicial notice of three facts without notifying the parties; because this was a bench trial and the court was commanded by statute to take judicial notice of the facts, the absence of notice was not reversible error; procedures required for jury trials in Rule 201(g) did not apply).

O'Laughlin v. Barton, 582 N.E.2d 817 (Ind. 1991), *reh'g denied* (trial court erred by judicially noticing affidavits of two former legislators as to their intent in passing a statute because the intent of the sponsors could not be attributed to the entire Legislature).

Miller v. State, 563 N.E.2d 578 (Ind. 1990), *reh'g denied*, 577 N.E.2d 587 (Ind. 1991) (court judicially noticed defendant's testimony at bail hearing).

Coates v. State, 518 N.E.2d 1086 (Ind. 1988) (Supreme Court properly judicially noticed that a particular county was in Indiana).

Smith v. State, 443 N.E.2d 1187 (Ind. 1983) (court could not take judicial notice of evidence in a different case even though the same trial court was involved).

Roeschlein v. Thomas, 258 Ind. 16, 280 N.E.2d 581 (1972) (it was proper to take judicial notice of a statute's legislative history).

Banks v. Banks, 980 N.E.2d 423 (Ind. Ct. App. 2012) (though Rule 201(f) provides that judicial notice may be taken at any stage of a proceeding, including appeals, it may not be used to fill evidentiary gaps in a trial record).

Filter Specialists, Inc. v. Brooks, 879 N.E.2d 558 (Ind. Ct. App. 2007) (Rule 201 changed the prior common law rule that a court could not take judicial notice of ordinances of municipalities; furthermore, an appeals court may take judicial notice of an ordinance for the first time even though no party has requested that the court do so).

Gray v. State, 871 N.E.2d 408 (Ind. Ct. App. 2007) (although Rule 201(a)(2) has been interpreted to permit judicial notice of court records, which presumably would include a chronological case summary, the notice is limited to the fact of the record's existence, rather than to any facts found or alleged within the record of another case except for situations involving claim preclusion).

Rosendaul v. State, 864 N.E.2d 1110 (Ind. Ct. App.) (a court may take judicial notice of the pleadings and filings in the very case that is being tried; once this occurs, a rebuttable presumption arises with respect to the truth of the facts contained within the pleadings, and the opposing party is required to come forward with evidence to dispute the presumption), *transfer denied*, 878 N.E.2d 204 (Ind. 2007).

Lutz v. Erie Ins. Exch., 838 N.E.2d 1181 (Ind. Ct. App. 2005), *superseded in part*, 848 N.E.2d 675 (Ind. 2006) (although a trial judge may take judicial notice of the pleadings and filings in a case, the facts recited within the pleadings and filings, that are not capable of ready and accurate determination, are not suitable for judicial notice).

Reemer v. State, 817 N.E.2d 626 (Ind. Ct. App. 2004), *superseded*, 835 N.E.2d 1005 (Ind. 2005) (judicial notice may not be used on appeal to fill evidentiary gaps; judicial notice may not be taken concerning the chemistry of drugs).

Sanders v. State, 782 N.E.2d 1036 (Ind. Ct. App. 2003) (a trial judge may take judicial notice of the contents of the pleadings and filings in a case; subdivision (d) requires the court to take judicial notice when the requirements of subdivision (a) have been met and a request has been made by one of the parties).

Haley v. State, 736 N.E.2d 1250 (Ind. Ct. App. 2000) (court properly took judicial notice of the fact that a military institution was a private school because the jury was not required to accept the fact as conclusive and the trial court afforded defendant a hearing on the matter).

Berry v. State, 720 N.E.2d 1206 (Ind. Ct. App. 1999) (trial court erred in not taking judicial notice of Administrative Code sections regarding the effect of a breath test in a DUI case and failing to instruct the jury that it may, but is not required to, accept as conclusive any fact judicially noticed in a criminal case).

Sales v. State, 715 N.E.2d 1009 (Ind. Ct. App. 1999), *vacated by* 735 N.E.2d 219 (Ind. 2000) (trial court cannot take judicial notice pursuant to Evidence Rule 201(b) of a breath test machine report that a person has 0.14 grams of alcohol in 210 liters of his breath or that the person has 0.14 grams of alcohol in 100 milliliters of his blood because there is no statute or regulation which explains the correlation between the amount of alcohol in grams in 210 liters of breath and the amount of alcohol in grams in 100 milliliters of blood; appellate court takes no opinion whether there exists a conversion formula of which the court may take judicial notice under Evidence Rule 201(a)).

Grimes v. State, 693 N.E.2d 1361 (Ind. Ct. App. 1998) (trial court's refusal to take judicial notice of Indiana case law when requested by the defendant was error, but harmless error in light of the fact that the defendant could not have suffered any prejudice from the court's failure to take judicial notice).

McGrew v. State, 673 N.E.2d 787 (Ind. Ct. App. 1996), *aff'd in part, vacated in part by*, 682 N.E.2d 1289 (Ind. 1997) (court may take judicial notice of reliability of scientific principles underlying expert testimony if it is not subject to reasonable dispute).

Griffin v. Acker, 659 N.E.2d 659 (Ind. Ct. App. 1995), *reh'g denied* (in personal injury action, trial court erred in refusing to take judicial notice of interest-rate tables where jury could have used tables to calculate present value of damage award; error was harmless, however, where court allowed defendant to argue that any damage award should reflect present value of total award and defendant did not establish that jury did not reduce total award to its present value).

Patterson v. State, 659 N.E.2d 220 (Ind. Ct. App. 1995) (trial court in probation revocation proceeding not required to take judicial notice of criminal case underlying revocation to

NOTICE

establish mental illness; letter written by probationer's treating physician was inadmissible hearsay, and included conclusions about probationer's mental condition that would constitute facts subject to reasonable dispute; court may not take judicial notice of different case, even if before same court and on related subject between related parties).

Woods v. State, 654 N.E.2d 1153 (Ind. Ct. App. 1995) (trial judge may take judicial notice of fact if it is either generally known within court's territorial jurisdiction or is capable of accurate determination by reference to service whose accuracy cannot reasonably be disputed; trial court may not take judicial notice of its own records in another case previously before court, even on related subject and related parties such as previous recognition of Head Start school as "school" for purposes of statute).

Sturgis v. State, 654 N.E.2d 1150 (Ind. Ct. App. 1995) (failure to instruct jury that it could, but was not required to, accept as conclusive judicially noticed sections of administrative code governing breath-test equipment was error but harmless where there was other evidence regarding the equipment).

Pigman v. Ameritech Publishing, 650 N.E.2d 67 (Ind. Ct. App. 1995) (in taking judicial notice of facts subject to proof, court of appeals should exercise extensive caution; circumstances that merely provide context for legal issue are not "adjudicative facts" requiring hearing).

Godar v. State, 643 N.E.2d 12 (Ind. Ct. App. 1994) (where trial court did not take express judicial notice of regulations requiring breath-test equipment to measure blood alcohol content as percentage of weight by volume and did not instruct jury accordingly, and where no evidence in record showed equipment measured blood alcohol content by weight, evidence was insufficient to support conviction for operating vehicle while intoxicated with at least 0.10 percent by weight of alcohol in blood).

Ritz v. Indiana & O. R.R., 632 N.E.2d 769 (Ind. Ct. App. 1994), *reh'g denied* (exact boundaries and geographical features of property is not a proper subject for judicial notice; a court may take judicial notice of the well known nature of property).

Lake County Div. of Family & Children Servs. v. Charlton, 631 N.E.2d 526 (Ind. Ct. App. 1994) (court may not take judicial notice of evidence that was presented in a related court case).

Sharp v. State, 569 N.E.2d 962 (Ind. Ct. App. 1991) (appellate court could take judicial notice of information against defendant in prior proceeding to determine if subsequent drug conspiracy convictions from which defendant was appealing violated double jeopardy, in spite of defendant's failure to provide record from which appellate court could review as allegations regarding his former appeal).

Hammond v. Doody, 553 N.E.2d 196, 198 (Ind. Ct. App. 1990) ("facts that are judicially noted must be generally known or capable of accurate determination by resort to sources whose accuracy cannot reasonably be questioned").

III

PRESUMPTIONS IN CIVIL ACTIONS AND PROCEEDINGS

PRESUMPTIONS

Chapter 301

Rule 301. Presumptions in Civil Actions and Proceedings

Rule 301 reads as follows:

> In all civil actions and proceedings not otherwise provided for by constitution, statute, judicial decision or by these rules, a presumption imposes on the party against whom it is directed the burden of going forward with evidence to rebut or meet the presumption, but does not shift to such party the burden of proof in the sense of the risk of nonpersuasion, which remains throughout the trial upon the party on whom it was originally cast. A presumption shall have continuing effect even though contrary evidence is received.

* * * * *

ANALYSIS

Scope of Rule; Presumption Defined. Rule 301 governs the effect of presumptions on the allocation of the burden of proof in civil actions and other civil proceedings. Its scope is thus somewhat limited, leaving to case law the resolution of corollary issues that are raised by the invocation of a presumption. Under the Rule, a presumption is a procedural device that operates to shift the evidentiary burden of producing evidence, that is, the burden of going forward, to the party against whom the presumption is directed.

Burden of Producing Evidence; Burden of Proof. The burden of producing evidence operates generally to expose a party to an adverse result where evidence on the issue has not been advanced. The burden of proof, that is, the risk of nonpersuasion, is not affected under the Rule and it remains on the party on whom it was originally cast by the law and the pleadings. The Rule provides that the burden of proof, that is, the risk of nonpersuasion, may not be shifted from one party to another during the course of an action. It should be noted that in the Committee Commentary, the committee proposed a rule that followed Federal Rule 301, providing that once contrary evidence is produced, the presumption disappears and is not mentioned to the jury. The Supreme Court of Indiana instead adopted a rule modeled after Uniform Rule of Evidence 301, which provides that the presumption continues to have an effect after the production of contrary evidence. This represents a change in Indiana law because previously the presumption vanished once contrary evidence was introduced. The Rule, of course, creates no presumption. It merely governs the operation and effect of presumptions.

Terms.   At the outset, a clarification of terms is helpful in identifying the appropriate occasion for the use of any evidentiary presumption.

"Inference."   An inference is a conclusion that may be drawn from facts admitted in evidence as to a matter material to the case. An inference exists as a matter of common experience and logic, and while it may be recognized or even specifically authorized as a matter of law, its function is limited to permitting the trier of fact to find the facts sought to be established. An inference is the basic ingredient of all circumstantial evidence. Sometimes statutes use the term "inference" when either prima facie evidence or presumptive evidence is intended.

Recent Developments

In *Schultz v. Ford Motor Co.*, 857 N.E.2d 977 (Ind. 2006), the Indiana Supreme Court provided its most extensive discussion on the meaning of presumptions and inferences, the approach to presumptions taken by Rule 301, the effect of the Rule on jury instructions, and the relationship of the Rule to statutory "presumptions." In *Schultz*, the court instructed the jury that it may "presume" that Ford was not negligent in its design of the automobile in question if it found that Ford complied with applicable federal safety standards—an instruction seemingly indicated by Ind. Code §§ 34-20-1-1 to 34-20-9-1. However, the court also instructed the jury that the plaintiffs may "rebut" the presumption if they introduced evidence tending to show that the automobile was, in fact, defective.

After laying out the competing theories of presumptions endorsed by Professors Thayer and Morgan, the *Schultz* Court noted that the Court, in adding the final sentence of the Rule to the original draft, intended to strike a balance between the two approaches. Accordingly, Rule 301 adopts Professor Thayer's "bursting bubble" theory of presumptions but nonetheless continues to give presumptions some weight after the presumptive "bubble" has been "burst." In other words, the effect of Rule 301 on statutory presumptions such as the one set forth in Ind. Code §§ 34-20-1-1 to 34-20-9-1 is to create both a true presumption as well as an inference; the statute imposes a burden of production that disappears once the burden is satisfied, but it also has a "continuing effect" as accurately reflected in the jury instruction as originally given.

Accordingly, the *Schultz* Court held that a presumption is properly given "continuing effect" under the last sentence of Rule 301 when the trial court instructs the jury that when a basic fact is proven, the jury may infer the existence of a presumed fact. Rule 301 thus authorizes a court to instruct the jury on permissible inferences that may be drawn from the basic facts that give rise to presumptions, notwithstanding the traditional prohibition on instructing juries about presumptions.

"Conclusive Presumption."   A conclusive presumption is in reality a rule of substantive law, not a rule of evidence. It is, by definition, not rebuttable. Once the facts giving rise to the conclusive presumption are established, there is no further evidentiary function involved. It is, in effect, a policy determination that removes an issue from factual contest. For

example, a conclusive presumption that a child under a specified age is incapable of committing a felony precludes any attempt to prove that such a child committed a felony once the child's age has been established.

"Rebuttable Presumption." A rebuttable presumption exists only as a matter of law established either by common law, rule of court, or statute. If underlying facts giving rise to a presumption are offered into evidence, the presumption, as a matter of law, imposes on the party against whom it is directed the burden of going forward with evidence to rebut the presumption. It does not shift to that party the burden of proof in the sense that the party now bears the risk of nonpersuasion.

"Presumptions in Criminal Cases." Presumptions in criminal cases raise difficult constitutional issues. On the one hand, the burden of production may not be placed upon the defendant such as to impose the risk of a directed or instructed verdict on an element of the case, and the burden of persuasion may not be shifted to the defendant on an element necessary for conviction.

Limitation of the use of presumptions in criminal cases is established by case law construing constitutional and statutory provisions relating to the burden of proof in criminal cases. These cases require the prosecution to prove each and every element of the case beyond a reasonable doubt, including those elements subject to a presumption. The role of the presumption is limited to imposing the obligation upon the defendant to introduce evidence on a subject (a type of production requirement), which then establishes a burden upon the prosecution to meet the matter raised by the defendant by evidence justifying a jury finding that the claim by defendant has been negated.

ADDITIONAL AUTHORITY

WEISSENBERGER'S FEDERAL EVIDENCE §§ 301.1–301.4

MCCORMICK §§ 336–348

1 WEINSTEIN 2d §§ 301.01–301.05

1 MUELLER & KIRKPATRICK §§ 61–72

9 WIGMORE §§ 2483–2493

COMPARISON TO FEDERAL RULE

Indiana Rule 301 is modeled after Uniform Rule of Evidence 301, which provides that the presumption has a continuing effect even after contrary evidence is produced. Federal Rule 301 provides that once contrary evidence is produced, the presumption disappears.

SIGNIFICANT CASES

Civil Presumptions

Clay City Consol. Sch. Corp. v. Timberman, 918 N.E.2d 292 (Ind. 2009) (Indiana law recognizes a rebuttable presumption that children between the ages of seven and 14 are incapable of contributory negligence).

Schultz v. Ford Motor Co., 857 N.E.2d 977 (Ind. 2006) (Rule 301 authorizes a court to instruct the jury on permissible inferences that may be drawn from the basic facts that give rise to presumptions, notwithstanding the traditional prohibition on instructing juries about presumptions; the Rule adopts the Thayer "bursting bubble" approach to presumptions in which only the burden of production, not burden of persuasion, is affected, but modifies the approach with the addition of the second sentence of the rule, which instructs that a presumption shall have continuing effect even though contrary evidence is received).

Rosendaul v. State, 864 N.E.2d 1110 (Ind. Ct. App.) (a court may take judicial notice of the pleadings and filings in the very case that is being tried; once this occurs, a rebuttable presumption arises with respect to the truth of the facts contained within the pleadings, and the opposing party is required to come forward with evidence to dispute the presumption), *transfer denied*, 878 N.E.2d 204 (Ind. 2007).

Kelley v. Tanoos, 840 N.E.2d 342 (Ind. Ct. App. 2005), *superseded*, 865 N.E.2d 593 (Ind. 2007) (under Rule 301, a presumption met by rebutting evidence may effectively become an inference, which remains in the case despite the presentation of contrary proof and may be weighed with all the evidence), *reaffirmed, on rehearing*, 840 N.E.2d 342 (Ind. Ct. App. 2006).

Witham v. Norfolk & W. R. Co., 561 N.E.2d 484 (Ind. 1990) (proof that plaintiff violated a safety regulation created a rebuttable presumption of negligence by plaintiff).

Young v. State, 258 Ind. 246, 280 N.E.2d 595 (1972) (evidence of violation of a safety regulation creates a rebuttable presumption of negligence).

Criminal Presumptions

Sandstrom v. Montana, 442 U.S. 510, 99 S. Ct. 2450, 61 L. Ed. 2d 39 (1979), *overruled in part*, *Manson v. Haponik*, 2007 U.S. Dist. LEXIS 51934 (E.D.N.Y. July 13, 2007) (holding improper an instruction that the law presumes that a person intends the ordinary consequences of his voluntary acts; this was found to be a conclusive presumption that conflicted with the presumption of innocence and would invade the factfinding function that belonged solely to the jury).

Reid v. State, 529 N.E.2d 1309 (Ind. 1988) (harmless error where trial court gave a jury instruction worded similarly to the instruction condemned in *Sandstrom*, summarized above).

Eads v. Hill, 563 N.E.2d 625 (Ind. Ct. App. 1990) (pre-rule case which held that a presumption disappeared once contrary evidence was introduced to rebut the presumption).

Hall v. State, 560 N.E.2d 561 (Ind. Ct. App. 1990) (blood alcohol test results do not create a conclusive presumption of intoxication against the accused).

Chilcutt v. State, 544 N.E.2d 856 (Ind. Ct. App. 1989) (in a criminal case, a presumption may properly shift the burden of going forward with evidence).

IV
RELEVANCY AND ITS LIMITS

RELEVANCY

Chapter 401

Rule 401. Definition of "Relevant Evidence"

Rule 401 reads as follows:

> "Relevant evidence" means evidence having any tendency to make the existence of any fact that is of consequence to the determination of the action more probable or less probable than it would be without the evidence.

* * * * *

ANALYSIS

Function of Rule; Relevant Evidence Presumptively Admissible.   Considered in conjunction with Rule 402, Rule 401 constitutes the cornerstone of Indiana's evidentiary system. In essence, Rule 401 provides that in order for evidence to qualify for admissibility, the evidence must meet the threshold of relevance. Once relevance is established, however, evidence may be excludable for affirmative reasons identified in Rule 402. Accordingly, relevant evidence is presumptively admissible. The proponent of evidence must establish its relevance, and the opponent of the evidence must seek to establish its inadmissibility predicated on one of the bases cited in Rule 402.

Direct Evidence.   Evidence may be relevant because it is direct evidence of the event sought to be proved, for example, the eyewitness account of the murder or the exhibit establishing an element of the case, such as the executed contract or the letter constituting libel.

Circumstantial Evidence.   Alternatively, evidence may be relevant because it is of a quality that leads to an inference that a provable event did or did not occur. This is called circumstantial evidence. Rebuttal evidence may be thought of as a kind of circumstantial evidence, as it affects the likelihood that direct evidence may or may not exist. Accordingly, certain kinds of evidence, though irrelevant and inadmissible on direct examination, may become relevant and admissible on rebuttal.

Broadly Defined.   Determining whether evidence is relevant is ordinarily not a question of law, but one of common experience and logic. Under Rule 401 the definition of relevance requires only that the evidence have any tendency to make the fact to be proved more or less likely than if the evidence were not introduced. The term "any" indicates that the merest tendency will suffice. This broad definition is tempered, however, by Rule 403, which excludes relevant evidence which is remote, misleading, or unfairly prejudicial.

RELEVANCY

Practical Considerations

The doctrine of *"res gestae"* is a longstanding doctrine of the common law of evidence used to describe the facts that are part of the story of a particular crime. The doctrine has been used to admit evidence of acts which are part of an uninterrupted transaction, including acts of prior bad acts occurring before the charged crime. In *Swanson v. State*, 666 N.E.2d 397 (Ind. 1996), the Indiana Supreme Court clarified that the doctrine of res gestae no longer exists, as it did not survive the adoption of the Indiana Rules of Evidence. Admissibility of such evidence is now governed solely by Rule 401, Rule 404, and other rules of evidence that may touch upon its admissibility.

No listing of all relevant evidence or irrelevant evidence would be complete, possible, or helpful. Cases on the subject of relevance are generally legal limitations on the definition or the verbalized logic of the court deciding the case. The reasoning of the court in the latter instance is often of little authoritative value since it is so intimately related to the facts peculiar to the case.

Conditional Relevance. By its terms, Rule 401 does not purport to deal with the concept of "conditional relevance." Where evidence is conditionally relevant, its probative value depends upon not only satisfying the basic requirement of relevance, but also upon establishing the existence of some other fact. Under conditional relevance, one item of evidence is relevant only if another item of evidence is established. The discussion of conditional relevance appears in connection with Rule 104, which specifically addresses the concept.

Current Trends and New Developments

The U.S. Supreme Court has recently held that a videotape of a defendant's response when asked if he knew the date of his sixth birthday, filmed after police had arrested the defendant for drunk driving but before police informed him of his *Miranda* rights, was not admissible evidence. *Pennsylvania v. Muniz*, 496 U.S. 582, 110 S. Ct. 2638, 110 L. Ed. 2d 528 (1990). The Court determined the defendant's response to be testimonial in nature. Therefore, by not informing the defendant of his *Miranda* rights, police violated his Fifth Amendment privilege against self-incrimination. Evidence on the videotape of the defendant's slurred speech and lack of muscular coordination, however, was not testimonial, but physical evidence.

Practical Considerations

In reviewing the sufficiency of evidence in a criminal case, the Indiana Supreme Court will not weigh evidence nor judge the credibility of witnesses. The Court considers only the evidence favorable to the judgment, together with all reasonable inferences flowing therefrom to determine if there was substantial evidence to support the judgment. For a discussion of this standard, *see Lloyd v. State*, 669 N.E.2d 980 (Ind. 1996).

ADDITIONAL AUTHORITY

WEISSENBERGER'S FEDERAL EVIDENCE §§ 401.1–401.9

McCORMICK § 185 at 541–548

2 WEINSTEIN 2d §§ 401.01–401.08

1 MUELLER & KIRKPATRICK §§ 82–89

1 WIGMORE §§ 24–43

COMPARISON TO FEDERAL RULE

Federal Rule 401 and Indiana Rule 401 are identical.

SIGNIFICANT CASES

Pennsylvania v. Muniz, 496 U.S. 582, 110 S. Ct. 2638, 110 L. Ed. 2d 528 (1990) (videotaped evidence of the defendant's slurred speech and lack of muscular coordination obtained without *Miranda* warnings is not testimonial and is admissible; defendant's videotaped response when asked if he knew the date of his sixth birthday also obtained without *Miranda* warnings is testimonial and is not admissible).

Conley v. State, 972 N.E.2d 864, 872 (Ind. 2012) (a psychiatrist's rebuttal testimony limited to explaining and contradicting evidence offered by the defendant relating to his mental health was relevant and admissible under Rule 401).

Houser v. State, 823 N.E.2d 693 (Ind. 2005) (although it is doubtful whether a correlation exists between an individual's enjoyment of a particular piece of music and the individual's behavior, the threshold test of "relevance" under Rule 401 requires only that the evidence have "any tendency" to make the existence of any fact of consequence more probable or less probable than it would be without the evidence, and there are certainly circumstances where the evidence would be relevant; the more important evidentiary questions are whether the evidence is offered to prove the character of the defendant in violation of Rule 404(b), or whether the probative value of the evidence is substantially outweighed by the dangers articulated in Rule 403).

Stroud v. State, 809 N.E.2d 274 (Ind. 2004) (because shoes were a key piece of evidence linking the defendant to the crime scene, DNA evidence introduced through questioning of police performed on the inner soles of the shoes was relevant, as it was introduced to demonstrate that the testing showed the defendant was excluded; given the importance of the shoes, the possibility of misleading the jury would not substantially outweigh the probative value of the DNA test on the shoes).

Williams v. State, 749 N.E.2d 1139 (Ind. 2001) (evidence of witness's prior drug use was irrelevant and inadmissible; defendant was permitted to cross-examine the witness concerning her drug use on the day of the killing and at the time of trial).

Majors v. State, 748 N.E.2d 365 (Ind. 2001) (officer's testimony in a murder case was relevant because the victim's threat against defendant established a motive for future conduct; the officer's testimony related to the same event and took up, in more detail, where the victim had called the police. This evidence makes it more probable that defendant robbed and killed the victim in retaliation for her aggression two days before the murder).

Murray v. State, 742 N.E.2d 932 (Ind. 2001) (the fact that defendant openly displayed a handgun, knowing that there were penal consequences to being caught by the police with the gun, tended

RELEVANCY

to show that defendant had a serious, affirmative purpose in taking the handgun from the waistband of his pants and was relevant to his intent and tended to negate his defense that the shooting was accidental).

Ortiz v. State, 741 N.E.2d 1203 (Ind. 2001) (police officer's testimony in a murder prosecution, that defendant's girlfriend told the officer that she had argued with defendant before the murder and that he had left with a knife, was not hearsay because it was not offered for the truth of the statements made but rather to prove that the girlfriend said the things to which the officer was an eyeball witness; however, the evidence was inadmissible because it was not relevant and its minimal probative value was outweighed by the prejudice to defendant from having the jury hear about his other crimes).

Pope v. State, 737 N.E.2d 374 (Ind. 2000) (the fact that a person has in his possession the same instrumentality as that used in a crime has only the slightest tendency to support an inference that the person committed the crime, especially where possession of the instrumentality is remote in time from the date the crime occurred; thus, trial court properly excluded evidence that the accomplice may have possessed bullets which could have been consistent with those used in the murders because the bullets were not the same, there was no evidence in the record that any witness had compared the bullets, and there was no evidence that defendant's mother had any familiarity with firearms in general or bullets in particular).

Roop v. State, 730 N.E.2d 1267 (Ind. 2000) (evidence which tends to show that someone else committed the crime is admissible because it logically makes it less probable that the defendant committed the crime).

Wright v. State, 730 N.E.2d 713 (Ind. 2000) (defendant failed to object to hearsay during cross-examination; reversal may not be predicated upon the erroneous admission of evidence when evidence having the same probative effect is admitted without objection or without contradiction).

Jenkins v. State, 729 N.E.2d 147 (Ind. 2000) (trial court did not err in limiting defendant's cross-examination regarding rape victim's prior drug conviction because such evidence was not relevant to the fact of whether or not she was raped; if relevant at all to the highly collateral issue of whether she purchased drugs from defendant, it is outweighed by the danger of unfair prejudice).

Lowrimore v. State, 728 N.E.2d 860 (Ind. 2000) (in murder case where identity of murderer was issue, it was improper to admit a bag of marijuana and two pipes into evidence because whether defendant had smoked marijuana near the time of the offense was not relevant; error was harmless in light of other evidence of defendant's guilt).

Cline v. State, 726 N.E.2d 1249 (Ind. 2000) (crisis counselor's statements to a police officer, regarding defendant's statement that she would not hurt her baby, were irrelevant because they did not make more or less probable any issue before the jury; error was harmless).

Wallace v. State, 725 N.E.2d 837 (Ind. 2000) (autopsy photographs of victim were relevant and properly admitted because photographs illustrated the witness's testimony regarding "stippling").

Jester v. State, 724 N.E.2d 235 (Ind. 2000) (hearsay testimony regarding prior statements by defendant's wife that she believed defendant was having an affair, and that she had considered leaving defendant, were not relevant in prosecution of defendant for murder of wife, where defendant did not put his relationship with wife in issue during trial).

Smith v. State, 721 N.E.2d 213 (Ind. 1999) (although victim's state of mind is relevant evidence where defendant puts it in issue, only relevant evidence is admissible; thus, trial court erred in admitting evidence of victim's state of mind because it only turned on the truth of the matters reported and did not tend to make a fact in consequence more probable or less probable).

Phillips v. State, 719 N.E.2d 809 (Ind. 1999) (evidence of prior altercation between defendant and victim was relevant because it had some tendency to make it more probable than not that the killing was intentional).

Shane v. State, 716 N.E.2d 391 (Ind. 1999) (evidence of defendant's conversation with a friend regarding how to commit "a perfect murder" was improperly admitted because the discussion did not evidence a plan to murder the victim, did not involve the murder victim, and the murder was not carried out as described in the conversation; it was not more probable with the evidence of the discussion that defendant committed the murder than it was without it).

Lloyd v. State, 669 N.E.2d 980 (Ind. 1996) (evidence is admissible if it tends to prove or disprove material fact and is not otherwise excluded by evidentiary rule; in reviewing, the Indiana Supreme Court does not weigh evidence or judge its credibility but looks at the evidence in support of the decision to determine if the court has abused its discretion).

Swanson v. State, 666 N.E.2d 397 (Ind. 1996) (because res gestae has not survived adoption of Rules of Evidence, admissibility of evidence previously claimed admissible as part of res gestae should be determined by asking if evidence is relevant in that it makes more or less probable the existence of a pertinent fact).

Tynes v. State, 650 N.E.2d 685 (Ind. 1995) (to determine if evidence is relevant and admissible, the Indiana Supreme Court asks whether it proves or disputes material fact or sheds light on accused's guilt or innocence).

Butler v. State, 647 N.E.2d 631 (Ind. 1995) (photographs of victims' bodies and videotape of crime scene were admissible as relevant to establish the identity of the alleged victim and assailant, injury to the alleged victim and its source, death of the alleged victim and its cause, and physical surroundings in which injury and death occurred, even though defense counsel offered to stipulate that defendant had killed victims with a knife and said in opening statement that the victims died as the result of defendant's use of a knife on them).

Evans v. State, 643 N.E.2d 877 (Ind. 1994) (witness's statement in which the witness named a person he thought might have given money to defendant, charged with cocaine possession with intent to distribute, and in which the witness explained he heard their names mentioned together in the past, was too vague to be a reference to extrinsic offense and, thus, was not subject to redaction).

Craig v. State, 630 N.E.2d 207 (Ind. 1994) (where defendant was charged with molesting his son, trial court erred by admitting a hearsay statement made by the victim's mother to a police officer; the statement had no relevance except to prove the facts asserted in the statement; error held to be harmless in light of other evidence; court discussed the interplay of Rules 401 and 403 when a hearsay objection was made at trial).

Elliott v. State, 630 N.E.2d 202 (Ind. 1994) (where defendant was charged with murdering his ex-wife's boyfriend, trial court did not err in admitting testimony from the victim's mother concerning her son's background, including his relationship with the defendant's ex-wife; such evidence was relevant background information).

Pigg v. State, 603 N.E.2d 154 (Ind. 1992) (trial court limited defendant's cross-examination of an informant regarding the informant's address on the grounds of relevance; court held that in cases where the trial court limits cross-examination of a witness, prejudice is presumed when an informant is the sole witness to a controlled buy with defendant and there has been no in-camera hearing at which defendant had an opportunity to show prejudice).

Valinet v. Eskew, 574 N.E.2d 283 (Ind. 1991) (evidence of landowner's experience as a real estate developer and land holder was relevant to impeach his testimony that he had not noticed condition of dead tree).

Martin v. State, 528 N.E.2d 461 (Ind. 1988) (admission of evidence that has only a slight tendency to connect defendant to the crime is within the discretion of the trial court).

RELEVANCY

Williams v. State, 491 N.E.2d 540 (Ind. 1986) (evidence that defendant possessed sunglasses used in robberies was relevant).

State v. Hall, 432 N.E.2d 679, 682 (Ind. 1982) ("[r]elevancy is the logical tendency of evidence to prove a material fact").

Southtown Props. v. City of Fort Wayne, 840 N.E.2d 393 (Ind. Ct. App. 2006) (the rule announced in *State v. Sovich*, 253 Ind. 224, 252 N.E.2d 582 (1969), is essentially a rule of the relevance of evidence; *Sovich* stands for the proposition that evidence of changes in the value of property brought about by the project for which the property is being taken is irrelevant to the determination of the value of the property on the date of condemnation, that is, the date the condemnation action is filed).

Carlson v. Warren, 878 N.E.2d 844 (Ind. Ct. App. 2007) (an attorney's habit of engaging in dialogue with and observing the demeanor of individuals prior to executing deeds for those individuals is highly relevant habit evidence of whether the individual in question was incompetent or an involuntary participant in the transaction).

Willingham v. State, 794 N.E.2d 1110 (Ind. Ct. App. 2003) (a consideration of the admissibility of evidence under Rule 404(b) necessarily includes the relevance test of Rule 401 and the balancing test of Rule 403).

Custis v. State, 793 N.E.2d 1220 (Ind. Ct. App. 2003) (to admit a photograph into evidence, a trial court must first determine the photograph is relevant; the relevance of photographs depicting the body of a victim is determined by whether a witness would be permitted to describe the scene photographed; if so, the photograph will be admissible unless the probative value is substantially outweighed by the danger of unfair prejudice).

Lush v. State, 783 N.E.2d 1191 (Ind. Ct. App. 2003) (evidence that tends to show that someone else committed a crime logically makes it less probable that the defendant committed the crime, and thus meets the definition of relevance under Rule 401).

Martin v. State, 784 N.E.2d 997 (Ind. Ct. App. 2003), *overruled in part*, *Stewart v. State*, 866 N.E.2d 858 (Ind. Ct. App. 2007) (photographs that depict a victim's injuries generally meet the definition of "relevant" evidence and are thus admissible).

Carnahan v. State, 681 N.E.2d 1164 (Ind. Ct. App. 1997) (evidence of battered women's syndrome was admissible as being relevant to the credibility of defendant's wife who previously had admitted that the defendant hit her and threatened to kill her but recanted her story and denied any abuse at trial).

Angleton v. Estate of Angleton, 671 N.E.2d 921 (Ind. Ct. App. 1996) (evidence that life-insurance policy beneficiary was responsible for insured's death was irrelevant in proceeding to declare beneficiary constructive trustee of policy proceeds where certified copies of grand jury's indictment of beneficiary and abstract of judgment in criminal matter served as conclusive proof of beneficiary's conviction for murdering insured).

Lycan v. State, 671 N.E.2d 447 (Ind. Ct. App. 1996) (evidence, to be relevant, need only tend, however slightly, to make existence of fact more or less probable, or to shed light on accused's guilt or innocence).

Lacey v. State, 670 N.E.2d 1299 (Ind. Ct. App. 1996) (photographs are relevant, and thus generally admissible, if they depict scenes that witness is allowed to describe in his or her testimony).

Hopkins v. State, 668 N.E.2d 686 (Ind. Ct. App. 1996) (relevant evidence may be admissible even if prejudicial).

McKinstry v. State, 660 N.E.2d 1052 (Ind. Ct. App. 1996) (adoption of Rules of Evidence did not abolish common-law rule that defendant's false alibi statements are admissible to show consciousness of guilt; trial court has discretion to determine if consciousness of guilt may be inferred from false alibi statements and if danger of unfair prejudice outweighs evidence's probative value).

Sturgis v. State, 654 N.E.2d 1150 (Ind. Ct. App. 1995) (evidence is relevant if it tends to make existence of any fact important to determination of action more or less probable than it would be without evidence).

Hyundai Motor Co. v. Stamper, 651 N.E.2d 803 (Ind. Ct. App. 1995) (relevance at trial and relevance for discovery purposes are not the same, relevance for discovery includes possibility that information sought may be relevant to subject matter of action).

Sevits v. State, 651 N.E.2d 278 (Ind. Ct. App. 1995) (evidence is relevant if it is offered to prove matter in issue and if it tends to make existence of any material fact more or less probable than it would be without such evidence).

Schnitz v. State, 650 N.E.2d 717 (Ind. Ct. App. 1995), *aff'd*, 666 N.E.2d 919 (Ind. 1996) (crime-scene photographs are relevant if they help trier of fact become oriented to circumstances surrounding crime).

Christian-Hornaday v. State, 649 N.E.2d 669 (Ind. Ct. App. 1995) (evidence is relevant and admissible if it tends, however slightly, to prove or disprove material fact).

Swain v. State, 647 N.E.2d 23 (Ind. Ct. App. 1995) (evidence of defendant's prior cocaine-dealing convictions was irrelevant and its prejudicial effect substantially outweighed its probative value, making the evidence inadmissible despite argument that evidence was offered in response to defendant's theory that actions were motivated by racial prejudice).

Kiner v. State, 643 N.E.2d 950 (Ind. Ct. App. 1994) (evidence is relevant if it tends, however slightly, to shed light on accused's guilt or innocence).

Fisher v. State, 641 N.E.2d 105 (Ind. Ct. App. 1994) (to be relevant, evidence must tend to prove or disprove a material issue of fact; remoteness of evidence is consideration in determining relevance and admissibility).

McLean v. State, 638 N.E.2d 1344 (Ind. Ct. App. 1994) (photographs are relevant if they depict scenes that witness is allowed to describe in his or her testimony).

Robinson v. State, 634 N.E.2d 1367 (Ind. Ct. App. 1994) (trial court properly limited defense cross-examination of a prosecution witness upon the witness's invocation of his right against self-incrimination; defendant wanted to cross-examine witness regarding witness's involvement in unrelated drug transactions and witness's knowledge of drugs; court held that witness's knowledge of drugs was irrelevant).

RELEVANCY

Chapter 402

Rule 402. Relevant Evidence Generally Admissible; Irrelevant Evidence Inadmissible

Rule 402 reads as follows:

> All relevant evidence is admissible, except as otherwise provided by the U.S. or Indiana constitutions, by statute not in conflict with these rules, by these rules or by other rules applicable in the courts of this State. Evidence which is not relevant is not admissible.

*   *   *   *   *

ANALYSIS

Policy Reasons. Rule 402 is central to understanding the operation of the Indiana Rules of Evidence and, indeed, the structure of all evidence law. Evidence which is regarded as "relevant" is admissible unless there are express reasons invoked justifying exclusion. Policy reasons of exclusion are sometimes paramount to the accurate determination of facts in a lawsuit. Obvious examples of values of greater import are those associated with privileges, conclusive presumptions, subsequent repairs, and compromise negotiations.

Trustworthiness; Constitutional Inadmissibility. Other limitations on relevance arise from concerns over trustworthiness such as those found in the hearsay rule and best evidence rule. Rule 402 implicitly indicates that no attempt is made within the Indiana Rules of Evidence to codify constitutional principles of exclusion. Evidence which is relevant may appear to be admissible because no specific rule within the Indiana Rules of Evidence would require its exclusion. Nevertheless, the evidence may be subject to exclusion in order to protect the constitutional rights of a litigant. Consequently, constitutional inadmissibility may be a distinct basis for precluding the admission of evidence. Like other bases, the opponent of the evidence generally must assert the constitutional doctrine in an effort to exclude the evidence in question. While there is no embodiment within the rules of constitutional doctrines such as unlawful search, seizure or incriminating statements, or the right of confrontation, such doctrines of constitutional inadmissibility may be the basis for excluding evidence.

ADDITIONAL AUTHORITY

WEISSENBERGER'S FEDERAL EVIDENCE §§ 402.1–402.5

2 WEINSTEIN 2d §§ 402.01–402.06

1 MUELLER & KIRKPATRICK §§ 90–91

COMPARISON TO FEDERAL RULE

Indiana Rule 402 provides that all relevant evidence is admissible unless otherwise provided by the Indiana or U.S. Constitution or by a statute not in conflict with the Indiana Rules of Evidence. Accordingly, Indiana Rule 402 is modeled after Federal Rule 402, but conformed to Indiana practice.

SIGNIFICANT CASES

Wright v. State, 730 N.E.2d 713 (Ind. 2000) (defendant failed to object to hearsay during cross-examination; reversal may not be predicated upon the erroneous admission of evidence when evidence having the same probative effect is admitted without objection or without contradiction).

Smith v. State, 721 N.E.2d 213 (Ind. 1999) (although victim's state of mind is relevant evidence where defendant puts it in issue, only relevant evidence is admissible; thus, trial court erred in admitting evidence of victim's state of mind because it only turned on the truth of the matters reported and did not tend to make a fact in consequence more probable or less probable).

Smoote v. State, 708 N.E.2d 1 (Ind. 1999) (a ballistics expert's demonstration on the loading and preparation of a shotgun for firing did not constitute an abuse of discretion in prosecution for murder in which victim was killed by shotgun blast, even though demonstration was of marginal relevance and probative value where state made it clear that shotgun used in demonstration was not the one used in murder).

Edgecomb v. State, 673 N.E.2d 1185 (Ind. 1996) (in prosecution for aiding in felony murder, photographs showing victim's injuries tended to corroborate testimony about severity of injuries and therefore were relevant even though they were evidence of coconspirator's acts offered before introduction of evidence of conspiracy, as 911 call recording of defendant describing victim's injuries had been played and police witnesses had also testified about injuries; photographs taken just before autopsy of victim provided more clinical picture of injuries than first photographs taken at hospital and supported pathologist's description of cause of death).

Yamobi v. State, 672 N.E.2d 1344 (Ind. 1996) (the court did not abuse its discretion in allowing prosecution to demonstrate, with defendant's help, the physical sequence of events in which murder victim was shot in front seat of his car; demonstration permitted defendant to show jury precisely how victim allegedly aimed gun at him and what he did to push it away before it discharged, simulation of exchange was not complex, and trial court made sure of its accuracy by repositioning prosecution and defendant to recreate seating arrangement in victim's car).

Thompson v. State, 671 N.E.2d 1165 (Ind. 1996) (it is within sound discretion of trial court to determine admissibility of evidence or testimony even if only marginally relevant; evidence that defendant and accomplice possessed and disposed of murder victim's guns was relevant).

Tompkins v. State, 669 N.E.2d 394 (Ind. 1996) (evidence of defendant's racial bias was relevant as creating an inference of motive).

Cliver v. State, 666 N.E.2d 59 (Ind. 1996) (given witness's testimony that defendant intended to pay portion of his child-support debt with proceeds from victim's life-insurance policy, evidence of defendant's child-support debt was relevant to establish motive for murder and was thus admissible).

Isaacs v. State, 659 N.E.2d 1036 (Ind. 1995) (trial court's decision to admit testimony about battered woman syndrome at murder trial was within court's discretion; testimony was offered to refute defense claim that he and victim were on friendly terms prior to her death).

Tynes v. State, 650 N.E.2d 685 (Ind. 1995) (evidence that assault rifle and pistol were found in truck which defendant had been driving at time of his arrest was irrelevant in prosecution for murder where victim was fatally shot with shotgun; weapons found in truck were not used in crime charged and did not help "complete the picture" of the crime).

Butler v. State, 647 N.E.2d 631 (Ind. 1995) (with court's approval, parties' stipulations may limit facts in issue and therefore admissibility of evidence relevant to establishing those facts).

Harrison v. State, 644 N.E.2d 1243 (Ind. 1995), *superseded by statute*, **Kroegher v. State**, 774 N.E.2d 1029 (Ind. Ct. App. 2002) (once it is established that photograph accurately depicts what it is intended to depict, its admissibility depends upon its relevance in capital murder prosecution; autopsy photographs of victim's stab wounds were relevant to illustrate pathologist's testimony and were not excessively prejudicial).

Lambert v. State, 643 N.E.2d 349 (Ind. 1994) (in exercising its discretion regarding courtroom demonstrations, court should consider whether accurate record of demonstration could be made for purposes of appeal, whether demonstration accurately portrays the real intent, as well as the duration and complexity of the demonstration, availability of other means to prove same facts, and risks to fairness of trial; trial court did not abuse its discretion by admitting videotaped demonstration of handcuffed person's capacity to fire gun from back seat of police car because only two people were in car, so little variation was possible from the actual incident).

Brennan v. State, 639 N.E.2d 649 (Ind. 1994) (photograph of burned face which illustrated witness testimony was admissible, where there was bullet wound on top of victim's head and part of skull and scalp was missing and where this was apparent in photograph; but accomplice's violent act in jail after arrest for murder was inadmissible in defendant's murder trial where acts were not related to attack on victim at time of his murder or on any other prior occasion).

Booker, Inc. v. Morrill, 639 N.E.2d 358 (Ind. Ct. App. 1994) (in case against alcohol provider, evidence of driver's blood alcohol content was relevant where such evidence tended to prove that driver was visibly intoxicated when he was served alcoholic beverages and that bartenders knew he was intoxicated).

Kimberlin v. DeLong, 637 N.E.2d 121 (Ind. 1994) (criminal felony judgment was relevant and admissible at related civil action).

Pilarski v. State, 635 N.E.2d 166 (Ind. 1994) (court was within its discretion in admitting photograph of murder victim attached to life support prior to her death which showed multiple bruises on her face; photograph showed nature and extent of victim's injuries and was properly admitted during testimony of physician who examined victim, and photograph was neither prejudicial nor inflammatory).

Martin v. State, 490 N.E.2d 309 (Ind. 1986) (evidence that has a slight tendency to prove a material fact is relevant and, therefore, admissible).

Downs v. State, 482 N.E.2d 716 (Ind. 1985) (evidence must be relevant to be admissible).

Lake County Council v. Arredondo, 266 Ind. 318, 363 N.E.2d 218 (1977) (trial court's determination is to rest on relevant evidence and irrelevant evidence should be excluded).

Hancock Truck Lines, Inc. v. Butcher, 229 Ind. 36, 94 N.E.2d 537 (1950) (trial court shall make relevance determinations on a case-by-case basis).

Custis v. State, 793 N.E.2d 1220 (Ind. Ct. App. 2003) (to admit a photograph into evidence, a trial court must first determine the photograph is relevant; the relevance of photographs depicting the body of a victim is determined by whether a witness would be permitted to describe the scene photographed; if so, the photograph will be admissible unless the probative value is substantially outweighed by the danger of unfair prejudice).

Lycan v. State, 671 N.E.2d 447 (Ind. Ct. App. 1996) (evidence is relevant which tends to make existence of material fact more or less probable; trial courts have latitude regarding evidence's

RELEVANCY

admissibility and decisions will only be disturbed for abuse of discretion that have the effect of denying the accused a fair trial).

Lacey v. State, 670 N.E.2d 1299 (Ind. Ct. App. 1996) (photographs are relevant and therefore generally admissible if they show scenes that a witness is allowed to describe in testimony).

Gouge v. Northern Ind. Commuter Transp. Dist., 670 N.E.2d 363 (Ind. Ct. App. 1996) (admissibility of evidence on grounds of relevance is within discretion of trial court; reviewing court reverses for abuse of discretion only).

Williams v. State, 669 N.E.2d 178 (Ind. Ct. App. 1996), *vacated by* 683 N.E.2d 594 (Ind. 1997) (all relevant evidence is admissible except as otherwise provided by law).

Ross v. State, 665 N.E.2d 599 (Ind. Ct. App. 1996) (videotape of lab performing DNA analysis was admissible in rape case, even though defendant argued that procedures depicted were different from those of lab performing DNA analysis in this case; expert witness on DNA analysis had testified that videotape would be instructive and would help jury understand DNA and general way in which DNA analysis is performed).

Boyd v. State, 650 N.E.2d 745 (Ind. Ct. App. 1995) (although victim had been stabbed repeatedly with folding lock-blade knife, hunting knife owned by defendant was relevant to contradict statement by defendant that he had never owned knife).

Caley v. State, 650 N.E.2d 54 (Ind. Ct. App. 1995) (by introducing an issue at trial, defendant may let in otherwise inadmissible evidence; photographs are admissible if reliant to any material issue and if they tend to prove or disprove material fact or shed light on accused's guilt or innocence).

Link v. State, 648 N.E.2d 709 (Ind. Ct. App. 1995) (Court of Appeals will disturb superior court's decision on evidence's admissibility and relevance only for abuse of discretion).

Kiner v. State, 643 N.E.2d 950 (Ind. Ct. App. 1994) (where identification testimony is suspect, evidence that witness mistakenly identified a different person as the defendant is relevant).

Fisher v. State, 641 N.E.2d 105 (Ind. Ct. App. 1994) (evidence which tends to prove material fact, even if tendency is slight, is admissible; remoteness of evidence is considered in determination of relevance and, thus, admissibility).

Meisberger v. State, 640 N.E.2d 716 (Ind. Ct. App. 1994) (autopsy photographs are relevant if witness would be allowed to describe in words what photographs depict; photograph should not be admitted if relevant portion is obscured by irrelevance).

Turnbow v. State, 637 N.E.2d 1329 (Ind. Ct. App. 1994) (in ruling on an objection to relevance of questions about witness's address, trial court should conduct cross-examination in camera hearing and listen to proposed questions and answers of witness; ruling is reviewed for abuse of discretion, with burden on defendant).

Davis v. State, 635 N.E.2d 1117 (Ind. Ct. App. 1994) (attempts by defendant to conceal his participation in crime held to be relevant as evidence of defendant's consciousness of guilt).

Biberstine v. State, 632 N.E.2d 377 (Ind. Ct. App. 1994) (without a link between sexually explicit magazine and crimes charged, the magazine and related testimony were not relevant in child molestation trial; state failed to prove defendant showed magazine to victim prior to molestations, and victim was not requested to identify magazine).

Rust v. Watson, 141 Ind. App. 59, 215 N.E.2d 42 (1966) (only evidence which is pertinent to the issues presented by the case is admissible).

Chapter 403

Rule 403. Exclusion of Relevant Evidence on Grounds of Prejudice, Confusion, or Undue Delay

Rule 403 reads as follows:

> Although relevant, evidence may be excluded if its probative value is substantially outweighed by the danger of unfair prejudice, confusion of the issues, or misleading the jury, or by considerations of undue delay, or needless presentation of cumulative evidence.

*   *   *   *   *

ANALYSIS

Rule 403 provides that relevant evidence may be excluded where the probative value is substantially outweighed by the danger of unfair prejudice, confusion of the issues, misleading the jury, undue delay, or needless presentation of cumulative evidence.

Rule 403 codifies that longstanding authority of the trial judge to exclude relevant evidence where the probity of the offered evidence is outweighed by one or more of certain identified countervailing considerations. The underlying premise of the rule is that certain relevant evidence should not be admitted to the trier of fact where the admission would result in an adverse effect upon the effectiveness or integrity of the factfinding process. This same policy generally underpins the succeeding Rules contained in Article IV, and Rules 404 through 411 represent applications of the balancing of relevance and countervailing adverse effects which have recurred with sufficient frequency to have resulted in a specific rule.

When the court is requested to exclude evidence for one of the reasons specified under Rule 403, the trial judge must determine whether the adverse effect *substantially* outweighs the probative value of the evidence. The word "substantial" is undoubtedly a word of some elasticity, and ultimately in applying that standard, the trial judge has broad discretion. Consequently, it is generally held that a trial judge's determination based on Rule 403 will be overturned only upon a showing of abuse of his discretion. No precise definition of the term "substantial" appears in the rules, yet it is clear that, at least symbolically, Rule 403 favors a presumption of admissibility by mandating that the negative attribute of the evidence must substantially outweigh its probative value before exclusion is justified. At minimum, intelligent advocacy under the rule suggests that a litigant seeking exclusion based on Rule 403 should never argue that the balance is a "close question." At other times, Indiana courts have expressed the principle contained in Rule 403 through the word "merely," as in the admonition that "[e]vidence that is merely cumulative is not grounds for reversal." *See Tobar v. State*, 740 N.E.2d 106, 108 (Ind. 2000).

Alternative Methods of Proof; Limiting Instructions.   In applying Rule 403, the trial judge should consider alternative means by which the facts sought to be proven can be established. Obviously, if the same facts can be proven by evidence unattended by the risk of prejudice, confusion, or inefficiency, the trial judge should exercise his or her inherent power under Rule 403 to compel the use of the alternative method of proof. A trial judge should also consider whether a limiting instruction pursuant to Rule 105 will sufficiently diminish the danger of prejudice, confusion, or inefficiency.

Excessive Prejudice.   Rule 403 provides that the trial judge may exclude evidence that is excessively prejudicial. Accordingly, if the evidence arouses the jury's emotional sympathies, evokes a sense of horror, or appeals to an instinct to punish, the evidence may be unfairly prejudicial under Rule 403. Usually, although not always, unfairly prejudicial evidence appeals to the jury's emotions rather than intellect.

Current Trends and New Developments

In *Old Chief v. United States*, 519 U.S. 172, 117 S. Ct. 644, 136 L. Ed. 2d 574 (1997), the U.S. Supreme Court ruled under Federal Rule 403 that the trial court had abused its discretion in permitting the prosecution to refuse the defendant's offer of stipulation to a prior offense and instead admitting evidence concerning the nature of the offense. The nature of the prior offense was assault causing serious bodily injury, which raised the danger of prejudice to the defense. The Court found that, in this case, the sole purpose for admission of evidence regarding the nature of the prior offense was to prove the element of prior conviction and the trial court erred in admitting this evidence where defendant's admission was available.

In *Sams v. State*, 688 N.E.2d 1323 (Ind. Ct. App. 1997), the Second District Court of Appeals accepted and applied the reasoning of *Old Chief* in a prosecution for operating a motor vehicle after driving privileges were forfeited. Although it recognized that the U.S. Supreme Court had limited its holding to cases involving proof of felon status, the court held that the trial court abused its discretion in admitting the defendant's entire motor vehicle driving record rather than allowing the defendant to admit that his license was suspended for life. However, the court held that this error did not mandate reversal of defendant's conviction due to the strong evidence of defendant's guilt and the fact that the defendant failed to request a limiting instruction regarding his driving record.

Confusing and Misleading Evidence.   Confusion of the issues and misleading the jury may be bases for exclusion of evidence in instances where evidence is partially inadmissible or where evidence is admissible for one purpose and not for another. Exclusion based upon confusion is usually justified where the offered evidence would require the trier of fact to engage in intricate, extraordinary, or impossible mental gymnastics in order to comprehend the import of the evidence or to evaluate its weight. Likewise, if the jury is likely to ascribe excessive, unwarranted importance or weight to the evidence, the offered evidence is susceptible to exclusion under Rule 403.

Practical Considerations

Rule 403 does not designate unfair surprise as a ground for exclusion. While surprise may undoubtedly result in injustice in certain situations, the granting of a continuance is considered to be the more appropriate method of achieving fairness in this context.

ADDITIONAL AUTHORITY

WEISSENBERGER'S FEDERAL EVIDENCE §§ 403.1–403.7

MCCORMICK § 180

2 WEINSTEIN 2d §§ 403.01–403.07

2 MUELLER & KIRKPATRICK §§ 92–98

2 WIGMORE §§ 443–444

6 WIGMORE §§ 1904–1907

COMPARISON TO FEDERAL RULE

Federal Rule 403 is similar to Indiana Rule 403 except that the Federal Rule recognizes waste of time as a factor that may result in evidence being excluded.

SIGNIFICANT CASES

Old Chief v. United States, 519 U.S. 172, 117 S. Ct. 644, 136 L. Ed. 2d 574 (1997) (the U.S. Supreme Court ruled under Federal Rule 403 that the trial court had abused its discretion in permitting the prosecution to refuse the defendant's offer of stipulation to a prior offense and instead admitting evidence concerning the nature of the offense; in this case, the sole purpose for admission of evidence regarding the nature of the prior offense was to prove the element of prior conviction and the trial court erred in admitting this evidence where defendant's admission was available).

Baer v. State, 866 N.E.2d 752 (Ind. 2007), *cert. denied*, 128 S. Ct. 1869, 170 L. Ed. 2d 750 (2008) (excerpts of recorded telephone calls in which a criminal defendant admitted to feigning a claim of mental illness were certainly prejudicial to the defendant, but because the defendant raised the defense of guilty but mentally ill, the highly probative nature of the statements was not outweighed by any unfair prejudice).

Hardister v. State, 849 N.E.2d 563 (Ind. 2006) (when a defendant stipulates to his status as a felon to prove an element of the crime charged, admitting the full record of the prior felony conviction into evidence is an abuse of discretion).

Witte v. Mundy, 820 N.E.2d 128 (Ind. 2005) (an admission by an eight-year-old child on cross-examination that someone did not do "anything wrong" in an accident occurring three years earlier requires further support, and it is not cumulative to admit police testimony on the same issue).

Helsley v. State, 809 N.E.2d 292 (Ind. 2004) (although autopsy photographs frequently pose unique problems where the pathologist has manipulated the corpse during the autopsy, and are generally inadmissible where the body is in an altered condition, there are situations where some alteration of the body is necessary to demonstrate the testimony being given).

Stroud v. State, 809 N.E.2d 274 (Ind. 2004) (because shoes were a key piece of evidence linking the defendant to the crime scene, DNA evidence introduced through questioning of police performed on the inner soles of the shoes was relevant, as it was introduced to demonstrate that the testing showed the defendant was excluded; given the importance of the shoes, the possibility of misleading the jury would not substantially outweigh the probative value of the DNA test on the shoes).

Bostick v. State, 773 N.E.2d 266 (Ind. 2002) (probative value of transcript of defendant's interrogation by police after she failed polygraph test outweighed prejudicial value).

Wilson v. State, 765 N.E.2d 1265 (Ind. 2002) (photographs, even those gruesome in nature, are admissible if they act as interpretative aids for the jury and have strong probative value).

Wheeler v. State, 749 N.E.2d 1111 (Ind. 2001) (trial court did not abuse its discretion in admitting "mug shot" photographs of defendant that were taken when he was arrested for the current crime because the photographs had probative value; the photographs showed the head wound defendant sustained while he was attacked by the victim and corroborated testimony describing the murder, nor were the photographs unfairly prejudicial because they were taken at the time of the arrest on the current charges, from which a jury could not have inferred a prior criminal history).

Wheeler v. State, 749 N.E.2d 1111 (Ind. 2001) (trial court did not abuse its discretion in admitting autopsy photographs of the victim's body after being beaten and hit by a train because it assisted the jurors in understanding the pathologist's description of the victim's injuries and the probable cause of death. Admitting photographs of a dismembered corpse is not an abuse of discretion where the pathologist is uncertain exactly what caused the victim's death. Although there are cases in which a distorted and disturbing photograph may be too prejudicial to be admitted, this case was not one of them).

McCarthy v. State, 749 N.E.2d 528 (Ind. 2001) (the probative value of "other bad acts" testimony outweighed any prejudicial impact because if, as defendant maintained, he had never heard of the "strip perdiddle" game and had certainly never played it, then it would appear that the victim's testimony was made of whole cloth).

Swigeart v. State, 749 N.E.2d 540 (Ind. 2001) (trial court did not abuse its discretion in excluding two magnified photographs offered by defendant to demonstrate angle at which police officer allegedly observed defendant walking near crime scene because there was no reason for the magnified photographs, the photographs could have misled the jury, and the photographs were cumulative of other photographs in the record).

Majors v. State, 748 N.E.2d 365 (Ind. 2001) (officer's testimony as to an incident between the murder victim and defendant, during which the victim waved a gun at defendant and claimed she wanted defendant to move out because defendant had not paid rent, was not unfairly prejudicial on the ground that jury was allowed to consider defendant to be a shiftless, irresponsible sort of person because she had not paid rent to victim, who had been her landlord, as officer's testimony focused primarily, if not exclusively, on victim's prior misconduct).

Marley v. State, 747 N.E.2d 1123 (Ind. 2001) (the trial court did not abuse its discretion in excluding a videotape that contained over 100 minutes of defendant and her victim engaged in a variety of sexual activities because the defense could not lay a foundation for it and could not authenticate it, the date the tape was made was unknown, the circumstances of the sexual encounter were unknown, it would be distracting to a jury, and it could cause an undue consumption of time).

Brown v. State, 746 N.E.2d 63 (Ind. 2001) (motive evidence was highly probative of defendant's interest in permanently silencing the victim; the trial court acted within its discretion in allowing evidence that defendant knew that his victim was a key state's witness to a murder committed by defendant's sister).

Murray v. State, 742 N.E.2d 932 (Ind. 2001) (trial court did not err in admitting evidence that defendant unlawfully possessed a handgun because the purported prejudice did not substantially outweigh its probative value).

Sears Roebuck & Co. v. Manuilov, 742 N.E.2d 453 (Ind. 2001) (in the customer's personal injury action against the department store, the trial court did not abuse its discretion by excluding the testimony of the customer and his girlfriend, concerning the customer's prior domestic violence against his girlfriend, to prove that the customer was the type of lying unsavory character that would establish him as a malingerer because the probative value of the testimony was substantially outweighed by the danger of unfair prejudice).

Williams v. State, 741 N.E.2d 1209 (Ind. 2001) (testimony of victim's sister identifying defendant was undoubtedly prejudicial to defendant, but in light of the fact that identity was a key issue at trial, its probative value was not substantially outweighed by the danger of unfair prejudice).

Ortiz v. State, 741 N.E.2d 1203 (Ind. 2001) (police officer's testimony in a murder prosecution, that defendant's girlfriend told the officer that she had argued with defendant before the murder and that he had left with a knife, was not hearsay because it was not offered for the truth of the statements made but rather to prove that the girlfriend said the things to which the officer was an eyeball witness; however, the evidence was inadmissible because it was not relevant and its minimal probative value was outweighed by the prejudice to defendant from having the jury hear about his other crimes).

Tobar v. State, 740 N.E.2d 106 (Ind. 2000) (defendant was prosecuted for three murders, and the trial court erroneously admitted transcripts of defendant's videotaped statements to the police; however, the error was harmless because the transcripts were merely meant to aid the jury and defendant's statements alone were so damaging that the admission of the transcripts could not have been decisive; the cumulative impact of the transcripts with the videotaped statements was harmless in light of the evidence).

Swingley v. State, 739 N.E.2d 132 (Ind. 2000) (admission of autopsy photographs depicting the victim's gaping neck wound that had been cleaned by the pathologist was proper because their probative value outweighed their prejudicial effect; however, an autopsy photograph that depicted the victim's windpipe removed from the body and lying on the sheet was an altered photograph that should have been excluded because its potential for prejudice outweighed its probative value, but the error was harmless).

Crain v. State, 736 N.E.2d 1223 (Ind. 2000) (the state's use of the murder victim's actual skull to demonstrate healing stages of various injuries, colorations of bone, and staining in skull was admissible because its probative value outweighed any prejudicial effect because the skull was not particularly gruesome or ominous, was in three separate pieces, and was relevant given defendant's claim of accidental death and the state's corresponding need to show those injuries occurred at the time of death).

Wright v. State, 730 N.E.2d 713 (Ind. 2000) (17 photographs of stabbing victim with 65 wounds were not unduly prejudicial, not particularly gruesome, and not introduced solely for the purpose of inflaming the jurors' emotions; to exclude photographs from evidence on relevance grounds, the improper influence on the jury must outweigh their probative value to the extent of being unduly prejudicial; to exclude photographs because they are cumulative, the probative value must be substantially outweighed by the needless presentation of cumulative evidence).

Maxey v. State, 730 N.E.2d 158 (Ind. 2000) (if an investigating officer's "course of police work" testimony is comprised solely of inadmissible evidence, the danger of unfair prejudice might very well exceed any probative value, regardless of a trial judge's repeated and strong admonishments to the jury).

Mitchell v. State, 726 N.E.2d 1228 (Ind. 2000) (trial court did not err in admitting six autopsy photographs of victim who had been locked in outdoor closet for one month after death; the photographs depicted various parts of victim's body from different angles, were relevant, had

RELEVANCY

strong probative value, and served as interpretive aids for the jury in understanding the number and location of injuries inflicted upon the victim's body).

Wallace v. State, 725 N.E.2d 837 (Ind. 2000) (trial court did not err in allowing autopsy photographs of victim who was shot in the eye; photographs showing the deceased victim, before the pathologist makes incisions, can be admitted even when they are gruesome and gory because they allow the jury to see the wounds or trauma inflicted upon the victim and are often accompanied by testimony regarding the cause of death; therefore, the probative value of the photographs was not substantially outweighed by their prejudicial effect).

Cutter v. State, 725 N.E.2d 401 (Ind. 2000) (autopsy photographs of pathologist holding open victim's vagina were properly admitted; although autopsy photographs in which a pathologist distorts a victim's body parts are ordinarily objectionable, the distortion was necessary to show the jury the victim's largely internal injuries).

Allen v. State, 720 N.E.2d 707 (Ind. 1999) (identity of victim's attacker was a crucial issue at trial, so evidence of prior bad acts used to prove identity was probative of the issue and not substantially outweighed by danger of unfair prejudice; although court may have decided case differently, it reverses only when convinced that the trial judge's call was an abuse of discretion).

Coy v. State, 720 N.E.2d 370 (Ind. 1999) (six autopsy photographs taken at various stages of the police investigation were properly admitted into evidence although the probative value and prejudicial effect were in equipoise; evidence should only be excluded when its prejudicial effect substantially outweighs its probative value).

Ewing v. State, 719 N.E.2d 1221 (Ind. 1999) (photographs and videotape of crime scene showing large amounts of blood on the floor, but not the victim, were properly admitted into evidence because the probative value was not substantially outweighed by the danger of unfair prejudice).

Wise v. State, 719 N.E.2d 1192 (Ind. 1999) (the probative value of demonstrative evidence—videotape of fire in baby's nursery—was not substantially outweighed by the danger of unfair prejudice even when the videotape spent a considerable amount of time focusing on the warmth, comfort, and baby decorations in the room; trial courts are given wide latitude in balancing these concerns, and the standard of review is abuse of discretion).

Phillips v. State, 719 N.E.2d 809 (Ind. 1999) (evidence of altercation between defendant and victim one week before murder, although slightly prejudicial, was properly admitted because it was highly probative of defendant's animosity toward victim, his motive, and his intent to kill).

Anderson v. State, 718 N.E.2d 1101 (Ind. 1999) (the nonhearsay purpose of statements must be relevant and their probative value cannot be substantially outweighed by the danger of unfair prejudice; statements were relevant and properly admitted).

Ortiz v. State, 716 N.E.2d 345 (Ind. 1999) (trial court did not abuse its discretion in finding that the probative value of motive was not substantially outweighed by any potential prejudice that might arise from defendant's generally unfavorable portrait).

Ingram v. State, 715 N.E.2d 405 (Ind. 1999) (trial court did not abuse its discretion in admitting partial transcript of bond hearing, during which murder defendant made statements conveying anger at his brother's testimony, to attack credibility because the probative value was not substantially outweighed by danger of unfair prejudice).

Berry v. State, 704 N.E.2d 462 (Ind. 1998) (trial court did not abuse its discretion in admitting a specific threat of violence that was both equivocal and temporally remote (six months) from the crime for which the defendant was charged, because the testimony indicated the extent to which the defendant's relationship with his family had become strained).

Charlton v. State, 702 N.E.2d 1045 (Ind. 1998) (evidence that murder victim sought a protective order against defendant prior to the murder was relevant to establish the hostile relationship between the victim and defendant and defendant's motive for murder, and any prejudicial impact did not substantially outweigh probative value of such evidence).

Smith v. State, 702 N.E.2d 668 (Ind. 1998) (trial court did not abuse its discretion in admitting DNA evidence that linked defendant to a crime even though the DNA was allegedly mishandled, some control tests were not performed, and confidence intervals were not used).

Sauerheber v. State, 698 N.E.2d 796 (Ind. 1998) (evidence in a murder trial of defendant's incarceration for a single, undefined offense, though not a fundamental error, is perhaps inadmissible under Rule 403 and Rule 404(b); however, appellate review is inappropriate because defense counsel failed to object to the question at trial thus waiving appellate review unless the admission constituted a fundamental error).

Amburgey v. State, 696 N.E.2d 44 (Ind. 1998) (gory and revolting photographs may be admissible as long as they are relevant to some material issue or show scenes that a witness could describe orally, although they should be excluded if their prejudicial effect outweighs their probative value).

Barker v. State, 695 N.E.2d 925 (Ind. 1998) (evidence that defendant previously assaulted one murder victim should have been excluded where defendant's identity was not at issue at trial; the assaults occurred 28 and 19 months before the murder, and assaults were irrelevant to defendant's motive for the kidnapping which led to murder).

Thompson v. State, 690 N.E.2d 224 (Ind. 1997) (prior crimes evidence is presumptively prejudicial and therefore requires a strong showing of probative value; even if a prior criminal act is relevant to a material fact, the potential for unfair prejudice dictates that the evidence of the prior misconduct be limited to that necessary to prove the disputed fact).

Cason v. State, 672 N.E.2d 74 (Ind. 1996) (photographs from which defendant was identified by witnesses as perpetrator were admissible in murder prosecution because photos did not include potentially prejudicial features of mug shots, like information about previous criminal record or nameplates on suspects' necks, and identity of perpetrator was at issue; while "mug shots" may prejudice jury against defendant by implicating him in previous crimes, such photos are admissible if they are not unduly prejudicial and have substantial independent probative value).

Mayberry v. State, 670 N.E.2d 1262 (Ind. 1996) (excluding manuscript chronicling defendant's relationship with victim because its probative value was substantially outweighed by risk of unfair prejudice was not abuse of discretion, even though defendant raised insanity defense and manuscript demonstrated defendant's state of mind before the murder; manuscript contributed no information about defendant's state of mind just before the murder that was not disclosed during her testimony, and contained hearsay statements attributable to victim and others).

Tompkins v. State, 669 N.E.2d 394 (Ind. 1996) (two passing references by state's witness to possibility that defendant would be charged as habitual offender did not clearly signify to jury that defendant had previously been convicted of crime and did not warrant mistrial; trial court could have found that state did not intend to elicit comment or create evidentiary harpoon and trial court could have found that defendant failed to show that he was put in position of grave peril).

Isaacs v. State, 659 N.E.2d 1036 (Ind. 1995) (photograph or videotape may not be excluded merely because it depicts gruesome details of crime, videotape depicting coroner turning over body of murder victim and examining head, neck, and arm injuries was admissible at defendant's murder trial; where defendant claimed accident and self-defense, videotape helped jury determine nature and extent of victim's injuries and whether they were deliberate or accidental, and videotape was relevant to illustrate pathologist's and coroner's testimony).

Johnson v. State, 653 N.E.2d 478 (Ind. 1995) (independent evidence supporting *corpus delicti* required for admissibility of extrajudicial confession of defendant need not rule out all possible explanations of circumstances).

Steward v. State, 652 N.E.2d 490 (Ind. 1995) (if defense discusses or presents evidence of child's

RELEVANCY

behavior indicating child sexual abuse syndrome, or if, during trial testimony, child recants previous allegation of abuse, trial court may consider allowing expert testimony on child sexual abuse syndrome about frequency of specific unexpected behavior within general class of reputed child abuse victims to be admissible; such scientific evidence must help finder of fact to comprehend child's reactions to abuse, must fulfill requirements for reliability, and its probative value must outweigh risk of unfair prejudice).

Butler v. State, 647 N.E.2d 631 (Ind. 1995) (probative value of photographs of victims' bodies and videotape of crime scene was not outweighed by their prejudicial impact, where photos did not depict any alteration to bodies by physician who did autopsy, and defendant did not claim that crime-scene videotape was inaccurate).

Mullins v. State, 646 N.E.2d 40 (Ind. 1995) (opponent of evidence has duty to demonstrate why evidence is not admissible).

Harrison v. State, 644 N.E.2d 1243 (Ind. 1995), *opinion after remand*, 659 N.E.2d 480 (Ind. 1995) (in capital murder prosecution, autopsy photographs of stab wounds on murder victim were relevant to illustrate pathologist's testimony and were not unduly prejudicial; pretrial *Frye* hearing was necessary to decide admissibility of DNA test results).

Harris v. State, 644 N.E.2d 552 (Ind. 1994) (witness's testimony in murder prosecution that she had heard defendant joke that "he wanted to see how it felt to kill somebody" was relevant and admissible, especially given accomplice's testimony that defendant made very similar comment immediately after robbery or murder).

Mitchell v. State, 644 N.E.2d 102 (Ind. 1994) (even though photographs of injuries to victim's companion had no direct relation to issues in prosecution for attempted murder, they were not prejudicial where attack on victim's companion by defendant's companion was part of the total picture of the altercation and both testified to it, and photos merely depicted severe laceration to eye of victim's companion).

Evans v. State, 643 N.E.2d 877 (Ind. 1994) (in prosecution for cocaine possession with intent to deliver, jail officer's testimony that he found a baggie with white powder residue in defendant's shirt pocket during search was admissible, even though state had lost or discarded the baggie and failed to test the residue, and even though jury might have overestimated the testimony's value; its value was not substantially outweighed by risk of unfair prejudice).

Burris v. State, 642 N.E.2d 961 (Ind. 1994) (in capital murder prosecution, photographs of victim lying nude in alley where he had been shot, lying face down in frozen pool of blood, and pictures of victim's upper torso after police officer had turned him over showing that victim had been frozen to ground, were admissible and were not unduly prejudicial; photographs illustrated police officer's testimony, were not tampered with or mutilated and were only as gruesome as would be expected given the circumstances of the crime).

Splunge v. State, 641 N.E.2d 628 (Ind. 1994), *cert. denied*, *Splunge v. Anderson*, 528 U.S. 833, 120 S. Ct. 91, 145 L. Ed. 2d 77 (1999) (harmless error where prosecution introduced mug shot of defendant where identity was not at issue; although a mug shot is not *per se* inadmissible, a typical mug shot is likely to imply a prior arrest record and Rule 403 should exclude it unless there is particular probative value that substantially outweighs the prejudicial effect), *superseded by statute as stated in Wheeler v. State*, 749 N.E.2d 1111 (Ind. 2001).

Lowery v. State, 640 N.E.2d 1031 (Ind. 1994) (harmless error where trial judge referred to a photograph of defendant as a mug shot; jury was informed that the photograph was taken incident to defendant's arrest for the charged crime not for a prior crime).

Donahoo v. State, 640 N.E.2d 702 (Ind. 1994) (defendant in rape trial was not prejudiced by introduction of prior rape conviction to establish defendant's status as habitual offender, even though same exhibit also demonstrated that defendant had been charged with deviate sexual conduct, where the exhibit was introduced during bifurcated part of trial after trial on the instant charge was finished).

Koo v. State, 640 N.E.2d 95 (Ind. Ct. App. 1994), *disapproved*, ***Floyd v. State***, 650 N.E.2d 28 (Ind. 1994) (in trial of physician charged with rape of patient during examination, testimony from two witnesses about alleged prior uncharged acts of sexual conduct by physician was admissible to rebut specific factual claim that victim hallucinated sexual misconduct).

Barnes v. State, 634 N.E.2d 46 (Ind. 1994) (photographs of murder victim were admissible despite defendant's objection that the photos were gruesome and cumulative; police officer testified as to what he found when he arrived at the scene and identified the photographs; while defendant claimed he believed he was on government mission to kill victim, prosecutor argued that single shot to victim's head killed her and that other gunshots to pelvic area showed personal animosity toward victim, and additional photographs illustrated testimony of the doctor who did autopsy).

Craig v. State, 630 N.E.2d 207 (Ind. 1994) (where defendant was charged with molesting his son, trial court erred by admitting a hearsay statement made by the victim's mother to a police officer; the statement had no relevance except to prove the facts asserted in the statement; error held to be harmless in light of other evidence; court discussed the interplay of Rules 401 and 403 when a hearsay objection is made at trial).

Elliott v. State, 630 N.E.2d 202 (Ind. 1994) (no reversible error where trial court admitted an autopsy photograph that showed the victim's heart removed from his body; photograph was admitted to demonstrate the path of the bullet and to refute defendant's claim that the shooting was accidental; court held that photographs, even if gruesome, are generally admissible if they assist the jury in understanding a witness's testimony).

Barnes v. Barnes, 603 N.E.2d 1337 (Ind. 1992), *superseded by statute*, ***Sears Roebuck & Co. v. Manuilov***, 742 N.E.2d 453 (Ind. 2001) (only where evidence is marginally relevant does a trial court have the discretion to exclude evidence by balancing the probative value against its prejudicial impact).

Bellmore v. State, 602 N.E.2d 111 (Ind. 1992) (trial court may properly admit into evidence photographs that graphically depict a victim's injuries; such photographs are inadmissible where their prejudicial effect outweighs their probative value such that they are unduly prejudicial).

McWherter v. State, 569 N.E.2d 958 (Ind. 1991) (trial court did not err in admitting a videotape of the crime scene and photographs of the decedent's body, showing points of entry of the bullets).

Minnick v. State, 544 N.E.2d 471 (Ind. 1989), *cert. denied*, 528 U.S. 1006, 120 S. Ct. 501, 145 L. Ed. 2d 387 (1999) (trial court did not abuse its discretion in admitting photographs of decedent where the photographs were used by witnesses to identify the decedent).

Thompson v. State, 492 N.E.2d 264 (Ind. 1986) (photographs of the crime scene were admissible in a homicide case where their prejudicial value did not outweigh their relevance).

Wagner v. State, 474 N.E.2d 476 (Ind. 1985) (although gruesome in nature, photographs of deceased victim were properly admitted because any prejudice was clearly outweighed by probative value).

Raess v. Doescher, 858 N.E.2d 119 (Ind. Ct. App. 2006), *corrected, on reh'g*, 861 N.E.2d 1216 (Ind. Ct. App. 2007), *superseded*, 883 N.E.2d 790 (Ind. 2008) (it was an abuse of discretion for the trial court to admit witness testimony that a party was a bad person, a "workplace bully" who commits assault; the probative value of the testimony was minimal, as the testimony was relevant only to the extent that it bore on the opposing party's perception, and the opposing party testified that he had no prior fear of the party; consequently, the testimony was unduly prejudicial and confused the jury).

Samaniego-Hernandez v. State, 839 N.E.2d 798 (Ind. Ct. App. 2005) (all relevant evidence is inherently prejudicial in a criminal prosecution, so Rule 403 emphasizes the balance of the

RELEVANCY

probative value of the evidence against the "unfair" prejudicial impact of the evidence).

Sandifur v. State, 815 N.E.2d 1042 (Ind. Ct. App. 2004) (although evidence that a person related to defendant had died from a drug overdose was prejudicial to the defendant, the trial court did not abuse its discretion in admitting the evidence because it was not substantially outweighed by the danger of unfair prejudice).

Kiefer v. State, 239 Ind. 103, 153 N.E.2d 899 (1958) (autopsy photographs are not admissible if they show the body in an altered state as a result of the autopsy, and if they do not tend to prove or disprove a material fact).

Willingham v. State, 794 N.E.2d 1110 (Ind. Ct. App. 2003) (a consideration of the admissibility of evidence under Rule 404(b) necessarily includes the relevance test of Rule 401 and the balancing test of Rule 403).

Custis v. State, 793 N.E.2d 1220 (Ind. Ct. App. 2003) (to admit a photograph into evidence, a trial court must first determine the photograph is relevant; the relevance of photographs depicting the body of a victim is determined by whether a witness would be permitted to describe the scene photographed; if so, the photograph will be admissible unless the probative value is substantially outweighed by the danger of unfair prejudice).

Wales v. State, 768 N.E.2d 513 (Ind. Ct. App. 2002) (unlike Rule 403, which favors the admissibility of evidence, Rule 609 presumes the exclusion of convictions more than 10 years old).

Spry v. State, 720 N.E.2d 1167 (Ind. Ct. App. 1999) (trial court did not err in admitting photographs of victim's injuries that were relevant to show the placement and severity of injuries, were clinical in nature, were not cumulative, and would not have been unduly prejudicial to defendant nor inflammatory for the jury).

Giles v. State, 699 N.E.2d 294 (Ind. Ct. App. 1998) (evidence that a defendant, charged with theft for cashing two payroll checks to himself on an account lacking sufficient funds, also cashed 14 other checks was highly probative as evidenced by the numerous similarities between the incidents for which he was charged and the prior 14 incidents).

Benton v. State, 691 N.E.2d 459 (Ind. Ct. App. 1998) (defendant's bald assertion that the probative value of a witness's testimony was outweighed by its prejudicial effect was insufficient to convince the court of appeals that the trial court abused its discretion in admitting the testimony).

Sams v. State, 688 N.E.2d 1323 (Ind. Ct. App. 1997) (holding, in light of the U.S. Supreme Court's ruling in *Old Chief*, that the trial court abused its discretion in admitting the defendant's entire motor vehicle driving record rather than allowing the defendant to admit that his license was suspended for life).

McGrew v. State, 673 N.E.2d 787 (Ind. Ct. App. 1996), *aff'd in part, vacated in part by* 682 N.E.2d 1289 (Ind. 1997) (evidence of dildo found at home of defendant charged with criminal deviate conduct was admissible despite claim that probative value was substantially outweighed by danger of unfair prejudice; even though dildo was not used during incident, it had probative value because it corroborated victim's account of incident and no specific prejudice was claimed at trial beyond defendant's assertion that if dildo were admitted, "that's all we're going to hear during final argument").

Spires v. State, 670 N.E.2d 1313 (Ind. Ct. App. 1996) (otherwise admissible evidence is inadmissible if risk of unfair prejudice substantially outweighs probative value of evidence).

Lacey v. State, 670 N.E.2d 1299 (Ind. Ct. App. 1996) (photograph showing gunshot wound to chest of murder victim was admissible; photo was relevant because location of wound tended to prove victim was turning away from defendant, photo's scope was limited, and its relevance was not clearly outweighed by any tendency to inflame jury's passions).

Buzzard v. State, 669 N.E.2d 996 (Ind. Ct. App. 1996) (testimony of psychologist was irrelevant and unduly prejudicial in child molestation trial where psychologist did not examine defendants or victims; psychologist defined "pedophile" so broadly as to include those who do not act on their sexual desires for children, and psychologist stated that one pedophile fitting this definition could molest 5 to 800 children during his lifetime; admission of psychologist's testimony about pedophiles, together with prosecutor's references to it, was not harmless error).

Lawson v. State, 664 N.E.2d 773 (Ind. Ct. App. 1996) (to determine if prejudicial effect of evidence substantially outweighs its probative value, that court must use a balancing test).

Carson v. State, 659 N.E.2d 216 (Ind. Ct. App. 1995) (determination of admissibility of evidence of other crimes involves balancing test which weighs probative value against prejudicial impact of evidence; balancing test is necessary since evidence with some probative value might still unfairly affect trial's outcome, violating defendant's due process right to a fair trial).

Vega v. State, 656 N.E.2d 497 (Ind. Ct. App. 1995) (in criminal prosecution, offer or refusal to take polygraph examination, or results of exam, are not admissible without waiver or stipulation by parties).

Sloan v. State, 654 N.E.2d 797 (Ind. Ct. App. 1995) (in order for evidence of accused's prior bad acts to be admissible, evidence must (1) be directed toward proving matter in issue other than defendant's propensity to commit crime, (2) show prior act as similar enough and close enough in time to be relevant, (3) be such that reasonable jury could find that act occurred and that defendant committed the act, and (4) be such that evidence's probative value is not substantially outweighed by danger of unfair prejudice).

Sevits v. State, 651 N.E.2d 278 (Ind. Ct. App. 1995) (the potentially prejudicial effect of evidence on jury did not render evidence inadmissible).

Boyd v. State, 650 N.E.2d 745 (Ind. Ct. App. 1995) (in prosecution for attempted murder, prejudicial effect on jury of defendant's possession of hunting knife did not outweigh its probative value, even though victim had been stabbed repeatedly with folding lock-blade knife, because jury was clearly told that hunting knife was not used to attack victim and that it was relevant only to refute defendant's statement that he had never owned knife).

Link v. State, 648 N.E.2d 709 (Ind. Ct. App. 1995) (relevant evidence is not inadmissible simply because it is prejudicial).

Kiner v. State, 643 N.E.2d 950 (Ind. Ct. App. 1994) (evidence of out-of-court identification is inadmissible if the identification procedure, given all the circumstances, was impermissibly and unnecessarily suggestive, thus causing a very substantial likelihood of misidentification; just as prosecution may not introduce identification evidence resulting from impermissibly suggestive procedure, defendant may not misrepresent facts to a witness to obtain misidentification).

Meisberger v. State, 640 N.E.2d 716 (Ind. Ct. App. 1994) (where defendant was charged with murder, admission of a videotape of the autopsy of the victim was not error because the probative value of the videotape outweighed its prejudicial effect; the part of the videotape that depicted the coroner attempting to remove fluid from the victim's brain had no tendency to prove any material issues in the case, and should have been excised; however, because most of the tape was either unobjectionable or extremely relevant, the trial court did not abuse its discretion in admitting it into evidence).

Houchen v. State, 632 N.E.2d 791 (Ind. Ct. App. 1994) (detective's testimony that he asked defendant if he wished to take polygraph test was so prejudicial to defendant that even if defense counsel had objected and jury been admonished, defendant's case was irreparably harmed; defendant could not have been convicted without detective's testimony and detective's introduction of polygraph issue was indelibly etched in jurors' minds).

Greathouse v. Armstrong, 601 N.E.2d 419 (Ind. Ct. App. 1992) (remoteness and confusion of the issue are grounds for excluding evidence of prior occurrences).

RELEVANCY

Indiana Ins. Co. v. Plummer Power Mower & Tool Rental, Inc., 590 N.E.2d 1085 (Ind. Ct. App. 1992) (trial court has wide discretion to exclude evidence on grounds of remoteness).

Stone v. State, 536 N.E.2d 534 (Ind. Ct. App. 1989) (trial court has the discretion to exclude relevant evidence that is cumulative where the potential prejudice outweighs the probative value).

Chapter 404

Rule 404. Character Evidence Not Admissible to Prove Conduct; Exceptions; Other Crimes

Rule 404 reads as follows:

(a) Character Evidence Generally. Evidence of a person's character or a trait of character is not admissible for the purpose of proving action in conformity therewith on a particular occasion, except:

(1) *Character of accused.* Evidence of a pertinent trait of character offered by an accused, or by the prosecution to rebut the same;

(2) *Character of victim.* Evidence of a pertinent trait of character of the victim of the crime offered by an accused, or by the prosecution to rebut the same, or evidence of a character trait of peacefulness of the victim offered by the prosecution in a homicide case to rebut evidence that the victim was the first aggressor;

(3) *Character of witness.* Evidence of the character of a witness, as provided in Rules 607, 608 and 609.

(b) Other Crimes, Wrongs or Acts. Evidence of other crimes, wrongs, or acts is not admissible to prove the character of a person in order to show action in conformity therewith. It may, however, be admissible for other purposes, such as proof of motive, intent, preparation, plan, knowledge, identity, or absence of mistake or accident, provided that upon request by the accused, the prosecution in a criminal case shall provide reasonable notice in advance of trial, or during trial if the course excuses pre-trial notice on good cause shown, of the general nature of any such evidence it intends to introduce at trial.

*　*　*　*　*

ANALYSIS

Risks of Character Evidence. Evidence of a person's character or character traits tends to distract the trier of fact from the primary issues of the case. Such evidence creates a substantial risk that a finding will be predicated on the trier's attitude toward a person's character, rather than upon an objective determination of the facts. Consequently, specialized rules have developed to limit the use of character evidence in order to protect the integrity of the factfinding process.

"Propensity Rule."   Rule 404(a) codifies the basic rule that evidence of a person's character or character traits is not admissible for the purpose of proving that such a person acted in conformity with his character on a particular occasion. This basic prohibition is often called the "propensity rule." Essentially, the fundamental exclusionary rule creates a forbidden inferential pattern. Under the rule, a person's character or propensity to act in a certain way may not be offered as a basis for the inference that on a specific occasion he acted in conformity with the propensity or the character trait. The basic exclusionary rule applies both in civil and criminal cases, but it most frequently will be applied to exclude evidence in a criminal case. For example, a negative character trait of an accused may not be established by the prosecution as evidence of the propensity of the accused to commit the crime in question.

Illustration

In a prosecution for murder, the state cannot seek to show the violent character or the violent propensity of the accused in order to establish that, in connection with the operative facts of the case, the accused acted in conformity with his propensity and murdered the victim in question. Such evidence of the accused's character trait or propensity would be relevant under Rule 401. It would tend to alter the probabilities that the accused committed the murder in question, that is, as a matter of common experience, murders are more frequently committed by those with violent propensities than by those who lack such propensities. Nevertheless, such evidence is rejected under Rule 404(a) because evidence of a person's character may unduly excite the emotions and prejudices of the trier of fact; the trier might seek to penalize the accused for his violent propensities rather than making a dispassionate and objective evaluation of the facts of the case.

"Inference Forbidden."   It should be noted that the basic exclusionary principle of Rule 404(a) prohibits the use of a specific type of inference. It does not forbid the use of character evidence generally. Consequently, when character evidence is used to establish something other than conforming conduct, such character evidence is not within the forbidden inferential pattern prohibited by Rule 404(a).

"Character in Issue."   Such situations where character evidence is used in a manner other than to prove conforming conduct will generally fall into the application of character evidence known as "character in issue." Where character is "in issue," character evidence itself forms an essential element of a charge, claim, or a defense. Character is "in issue" where it is not used as a basis for a further inference, but it is a terminal point of proof.

Illustration

In a libel or slander case involving certain alleged character traits, the character traits may constitute an element of a defense. Accordingly, if the substantive law dictates that character or a character trait is an element of a defense, character then is "in issue," and it is outside the basic prohibition of Rule 404(a). Consequently, if *P* charged *D* with slander claiming that *D* said, "*P* is dishonest," and *D* pleads truth as a defense, *D* must prove *P*'s dishonesty to prevail. *P*'s character trait of dishonesty is a terminal point of proof. It is not used as the basis for a further inference. Consequently, *P*'s trait is "in issue," and such use of character evidence is not prohibited by Rule 404(a).

Exceptions: Criminal Defendant's Good Character.   Rule 404(a) sets forth three exceptions where the exclusionary rule will not apply to character used to prove conforming conduct. First, the accused in a criminal case may seek to introduce pertinent evidence of his good character in order to raise the inference that on a particular occasion involving the crime for which he is charged, he acted in conformity with his good character and did not commit the operative facts of the crime. It should be noted that this exception applies only to an accused in a criminal proceeding.

Illustration

Where an accused is charged with murder, he may introduce evidence of his character trait for peacefulness in the hope that the jury will make the inference that he acted in conformity with his peaceful character on the particular occasion and did not commit the murder. Such application of character evidence is particularly useful where the prosecution's case is based on circumstantial evidence. Character evidence is often used by the accused in this situation to establish reasonable doubt as to whether or not he committed the crime. Once defendant has attempted to establish himself as a hardworking, decent, and peaceful individual in defense to a murder charge, the state is entitled to elicit character evidence of defendant's reputation for violence when he became drunk. *See Schwestak v. State*, 674 N.E.2d 962 (Ind. 1996).

RELEVANCY

Crime Victim's Character.   The second exception to the exclusionary rule provides that an accused may introduce pertinent evidence of the character of a victim of the charged crime. Again, the term "accused" indicates that, like the first exception to Rule 404, Rule 404(a)(2) is applicable only in a criminal case. Rule 404(a)(2) is triggered by the accused offering a character witness in accordance with the procedures of Rule 405 who testifies to a "pertinent trait" of the victim of the charged crime. Additionally, a special application in homicide cases is provided in Rule 404(a)(2). In homicide prosecutions, a plea of self-defense, coupled with evidence that the deceased was the first aggressor, is sufficient to trigger the prosecutor's right to offer rebuttal evidence that the victim was a person of peaceful character. This provision is based upon the peculiar need for this kind of evidence in situations where the victim, by the nature of the crime, is unavailable. Evidence that the victim was the first aggressor may be of any competent type to avail the prosecution of the opportunity to offer evidence of the victim's peaceful character. Any evidence so offered by the prosecution must, of course, conform to the directives of Rule 405.

> *Practical Considerations*
>
> It is important to note that Rule 404(a)(1) and Rule 404(a)(2) are mutually exclusive. When an accused injects the issue of the victim's character into the case, either by offering character evidence in accordance with Rule 405 or by coupling self-defense with evidence of first-aggression of the victim in a homicide case, the accused does not, by virtue of these elections, open the issue of the accused's own character. The issue of the accused's character is only introduced in accordance with the provisions of Rule 404(a)(1), that is, when the accused offers positive character evidence as prescribed by the procedures delineated in Rule 405.

Veracity of Witness. A third exception to Rule 404(a) provides that the character of a witness may be explored as to the witness's traits of veracity or truth-telling. This exception to the basic exclusionary rule is more specifically codified in Rules 607, 608, and 609. *See* Analysis to Rules 607, 608, and 609, *below*. It is important to note that the exception relating to the character of witnesses will apply to the accused if he takes the stand on his own behalf. Consequently, if the accused elects to be a witness in his own case, certain aspects of his character may be explored by the prosecution pursuant to Rules 608 and 609.

Other Crimes, Wrongs, or Acts. Rule 404(b) codifies an extension of the exclusionary principle of Rule 404(a), and it is a restatement of implicit limitations on the proof of character evidence set forth in Rule 405. Rule 404(b) provides that evidence of other crimes, wrongs, or acts is not admissible to prove the character of a person in order to show that the person acted in conformity with the character on a particular occasion. As in the application of Rule 404(a), Rule 404(b) embraces the customary construction of the term "character," that is, a general form of propensity. Accordingly, the term "character" essentially pertains to a person's distinct traits or propensities to act in a particular way, and it applies to such traits of character as dishonesty, violence, peacefulness, and veracity. It is important to note that the rule applies in both civil and criminal cases, and its scope encompasses any extrinsic act, not merely acts resulting in criminal conviction or subject to criminal prosecution. As used in Rule 404(b), an "other act" or an "extrinsic act" is simply any act which is not part of the operative facts or episode of the case; that is, it is "extrinsic" usually because of a separation in time, space, or both.

Like Rule 404(a), Rule 404(b) creates a prohibited inferential pattern, but the pattern forbidden in Rule 404(b) extends one step further than the forbidden inferential pattern of Rule 404(a). Rule 404(b) creates a forbidden two-step inference pursuant to which an extrinsic specific act inferentially indicates a character trait or general propensity, which in turn inferentially indicates commission of the act which is part of the operative facts of the case. Actually, Rule 404(b) is largely redundant, because the final inferential step of Rule 404(b) is identical to the forbidden inferential pattern of Rule 404(a). The rule, in essence, prohibits the argument which would suggest that because a person acted in a particular way on a distinct, specific occasion, that person likely acted in the same way with regard to the operative facts of the instant litigation. The force of such an argument relies upon the intermediate operative inference of character.

Rule 404(b) contains two distinct functions. The first sentence sets forth the basic rule of exclusion. A clarifying provision is then added to emphasize the limited scope of the basic exclusionary rule contained in the first sentence. After stating the basic rule of exclusion, Rule 404(b) indicates that evidence of other crimes, wrongs, or acts may be admissible where offered to prove consequential facts other than conforming conduct. It should be appreciated that although a specific inference involving extrinsic acts is prohibited in the first sentence of Rule 404(b), the rule does not, by its terms, absolutely prohibit the admissibility of extrinsic crimes, wrongs, or acts. A person's extrinsic acts, including criminal acts, may be relevant for a purpose other than demonstrating a general propensity to commit a similar act. Some of these purposes are suggested in Rule 404(b). Evidence of such acts used for these purposes would not be subject to the exclusionary principle expressed in the first sentence of Rule 404(b). Although cases under Rule 404 typically involve prior acts of a party, the Rule applies equally to acts occurring after the charged conduct.

Current Trends and New Developments

In *Hicks v. State*, 690 N.E.2d 215 (Ind. 1997), the Indiana Supreme Court was urged to accept the four-pronged test used by the Seventh Circuit to determine the admissibility of prior acts evidence pursuant to Rule 404(b). Under that test, prior act evidence is admissible in a criminal case only if (1) the evidence is directed toward establishing a matter other than the defendant's propensity to commit the charged act; (2) the prior act is similar enough and close enough in time to be relevant to the matter at issue; (3) the evidence is sufficient to support a jury finding that the defendant committed the prior act; and (4) the probative value of the evidence must not be outweighed by its prejudicial effect. The Indiana Supreme Court declined to adopt the Seventh Circuit's test, electing instead to apply the two-prong test it has consistently used to evaluate prior bad acts evidence. Under this test, in order for a trial court to admit prior acts evidence, (1) the court must determine that the prior acts evidence is relevant to a matter at issue other than the defendant's propensity to commit the charged act, and (2) the court must balance the probative value of the evidence against its prejudicial effect pursuant to Rule 403.

Although *Hicks* purportedly refused to adopt the four-pronged Seventh Circuit approach, it has ruled in a manner consistent with that approach. For example, Rule 404 does not specify the requisite degree of proof necessary to establish the existence of the prior act or crime. However, Indiana has adopted the approach taken in *Huddleston v. United States*, 485 U.S. 681, 690, 108 S.Ct. 1496, 1501, 99 L.E.2d 771 (1988) that requires "sufficient proof from which a reasonable jury could find the uncharged conduct proven by a preponderance of the evidence." *See Camm v. State*, 908 N.E.2d 215 (Ind. 2009); *Clemens v. State*, 610 N.E.2d 236, 242 (Ind. 1993). It should be noted that the standard for finding preliminary matters in Rule 104(b) is the identical "sufficient to support a finding" standard considered in *Huddleston*. The Indiana Supreme Court has applied this standard in other contexts as well, rejecting the argument that the corpus delicti rule applies to evidence of other crimes admitted under Rule 404(b). Relying in part on the observation that the proof under Rule 404(b) is considerably less than that required for conviction, the court in *Wilkes v. State*, 917 N.E.2d 675 (Ind. 2009) noted that "admission under Rule 404(b) does not require proof sufficient for conviction."

Practical Considerations

The list of bases for properly offering an extrinsic act set forth in the second sentence of Rule 404(b) is not exhaustive, and the fundamental issue is whether the act is offered only to prove character and conforming conduct. If so, the evidence is rendered inadmissible by the first sentence of Rule 404(b). Moreover, the list of possible bases for offering an extrinsic act should not be seen as a list of exceptions to the rule, but rather as a suggestive, nonexhaustive catalogue of bases which do not violate the exclusionary principle of the first sentence of Rule 404(b).

Illustration 1

A prior act may be utilized to show the motive of the accused rather than to show the accused's propensity to commit antisocial acts. For example, if the defendant is charged with stealing an expensive diamond cutting device, the prosecution may seek to offer evidence that the month prior to the alleged theft of the diamond cutting device, the defendant stole a bag of uncut diamonds. Proof of the prior act would give rise to the inference that the defendant had a motive for stealing the diamond cutting machine.

Illustration 2

Often, prior acts of an accused are offered by the prosecution to establish the identity of the perpetrator of the crime which is charged. Where the defendant is charged with a crime and denies that he is the perpetrator, the prosecution may seek to establish his identity through the accused's unique *modus operandi* of committing crimes. When evidence is admitted under this theory of relevance, courts have required a heightened degree of similarity of the prior act to the charged crime. The "identity exception" thus exists only for crimes "so nearly identical that the modus operandi is virtually a 'signature.'" *Ortiz v. State*, 716 N.E.2d 345, 350 (Ind. 1999) (citing *Thompson v. State*, 690 N.E.2d 224, 234 (Ind. 1997)). Indiana courts have held consistently that the crimes must be so strikingly similar that it can be said with "reasonable certainty" that the same person committed them. *See Nicholson v. State*, 963 N.E.2d 1096 (Ind. 2012); *Penley v. State*, 506 N.E.2d 806 (Ind. 1987).

For example, if the defendant is charged with armed robbery, committed by a man wearing a Halloween mask who claimed to have dynamite wired to his body, and the accused has committed robberies on three prior occasions using the same method of operation, evidence of the accused's prior acts would tend to identify him as the perpetrator of the crime. The prosecution would argue that the prior acts of the defendant are outside the exclusionary rule because they are not offered to establish character or criminal propensity.

Illustration 3

Prior acts may be admissible to counter the allegation that a defendant acted with a particular intent. Such evidence is particularly appropriate when a defendant goes beyond merely denying the charged crime and affirmatively presents a claim of a contrary intent. For example, in *Bryant v. State*, 984 N.E.2d 240 (Ind. Ct. App. 2013), the prosecution alleged that the defendant committed aggravated battery. However, the defendant claimed that he acted in self-defense, and was permitted to introduce evidence of his own prior jail fights as evidence of his intent. When this occurs, of course, the State may respond by offering evidence of prior crimes, wrongs, or acts to the extent genuinely relevant to prove the defendant's intent at the time of the charged offense.

Notice in Criminal Cases. According to pre-Rule Indiana law, Rule 404(b) evidence should be evaluated as to whether it is unfairly prejudicial and subject to exclusion under Rule 403. *See Brewer v. State*, 562 N.E.2d 22 (Ind. 1990). Also, in a criminal case where requested by the accused, before the prosecution introduces evidence of the accused's acts or crimes, the prosecution must notify the accused of the general nature of any Rule 404(b) evidence it intends to introduce.

RELEVANCY

Current Trends and New Developments

In *Wickizer v. State*, 626 N.E.2d 795 (Ind. 1993), the Indiana Supreme Court analyzed newly enacted Indiana Rule 404(b) extensively and determined that "Indiana is best served by a narrow construction of the intent exception in Evid. R. 404(b)." The court found that Rule 404(b) permits the prosecution to offer evidence of prior crimes to prove a criminal defendant's intent only where the issue of intent is genuinely contested. The court rejected a broader interpretation that would permit the admission of evidence of prior crimes when a defendant entered a plea of "not guilty," and held that admissibility under Rule 404(b) "will be available when a defendant goes beyond merely denying the charged culpability and affirmatively presents a claim of particular contrary intent."

In *Swanson v. State*, 666 N.E.2d 397 (Ind. 1996), the Indiana Supreme Court held that relevant "bad acts" occurring on the same day as the charged crime are *not* inadmissible as evidence of prior bad acts under Rule 404(b). Inadmissible prior bad acts are antisocial acts committed on another day, in another place whose only apparent purpose is to prove that defendant is person who committed the charged crimes.

Limiting Instruction. In any case in which the court accepts the proponent's theory of the admissibility of evidence of a prior act and proceeds to admit the prior act, the judge should be asked to provide the jury with a limiting instruction. Such an instruction would advise the jury that the evidence of the prior act may not be considered as a basis for an inference that the individual in question acted in conformity with his prior conduct or with his indicated propensity. *See* Analysis to Rule 105, *below.*

INCORPORATED STATUTES

Ind. Code § 35-37-4-2. [Credibility of witnesses—Evidence of general moral character]

In all questions affecting the credibility of a witness, his general moral character may be given in evidence.

Ind. Code § 35-37-4-14. [Admissibility of evidence of previous battery]

(a) This section applies even if no criminal charges were filed concerning the act that is the basis of the evidence of a previous battery.

(b) As used in this section, "evidence of a previous battery" means evidence that a person charged with a crime described in subsection (c)(1) through (c)(3) committed a prior unrelated act of battery or attempted battery on the victim of a crime described in subsection (c)(1) through (c)(3) within five (5) years before the person allegedly committed the crime described in subsection (c)(1) through (c)(3).

(c) In a prosecution for:

    (1)   Battery;

    (2)   Aggravated battery;

    (3)   Murder; or

    (4)   Voluntary manslaughter;

evidence of a previous battery is admissible into evidence in the state's case-in-chief for purposes of proving motive, intent, identity, or common scheme and design.

(d) If the state proposes to offer evidence described in subsection (b), the following procedure must be followed:

    (1)   The state shall file a written motion not less than ten (10) days before trial stating that the state has an offer of proof concerning evidence described in subsection (b) and the relevancy of the evidence to the case. The motion must be accompanied by an affidavit in which the offer of proof is stated.

    (2)   If the court finds that the offer of proof is sufficient, the court shall order a hearing out of the presence of the jury. At the hearing, the court shall allow the questioning of the victim or witness regarding the offer of proof made by the state.

At the conclusion of the hearing, if the court finds that evidence proposed to be offered by the state is admissible, the court shall make an order stating what evidence may be introduced by the state and the nature of the questions to be permitted. The state may then offer evidence under the order of the court.

(e) This section shall not be construed to limit the admissibility of evidence of a previous battery in any civil or criminal proceeding.

Ind. Code § 35-37-4-15. [Child molestation; evidence of prior acts]

(a) In a prosecution for child molesting under IC 35-42-4-3, a prosecution for incest under IC 35-46-1-3, or a prosecution for an attempt or a conspiracy to commit child molesting or incest, evidence that the defendant has committed another crime or act of child molesting or incest or attempted or conspired to commit another crime or act of child molesting or incest:

    (1)   against the same victim; or

    (2)   that involves a similar crime or act of child molesting or incest against a different victim;

is admissible.

(b) If the state proposes to offer evidence described under subsection (a), the state must disclose the evidence to the defendant, including statements made by witnesses or a summary of the substance of any testimony that is expected to be offered at the defendant's trial:

    (1)   at least fifteen (15) days before the date the defendant's trial is scheduled to begin; or

    (2)   at a later date as determined by the court for good cause.

(c) The court shall hold a hearing out of the presence of the jury regarding the admissibility of the evidence described under subsection (a). Even if the court determines that the evidence is relevant, the evidence may be excluded if the probative value of the evidence is substantially outweighed by:

    (1)   the danger of:

        (A)   unfair prejudice;

        (B)   confusion of the issues; or

        (C)   misleading the jury; or

    (2)   considerations of:

        (A)   undue delay;

        (B)   waste of time; or

        (C)   needless presentation of cumulative evidence.

However, if the court finds that all or some of the evidence is admissible, the court shall enter an order stating what evidence may be introduced.

(d) This section may not be construed to limit the right to introduce evidence at a trial that would otherwise be admissible to prove any of the following:

    (1)   Motive.

(2)   Opportunity.

(3)   Intent.

(4)   Plan.

(5)   Knowledge.

(6)   Identity.

(7)   Absence of mistake or accident.

Ind. Code § 34-45-4-1. [Impeachment by evidence of bad character]

(a) Except as provided in subsections (b) and (c), the party producing a witness shall not be allowed to impeach the credibility of the witness by evidence of bad character.

(b) The party producing a witness may impeach the credibility of the witness by evidence of bad character if:

(1)   it was indispensable that the party produce the witness; or

(2)   it is a case of manifest surprise.

(c) In all cases, the party producing the witness may contradict the witness:

(1)   by other evidence; and

(2)   by showing that the witness has made statements different from the present testimony of the witness.

ADDITIONAL AUTHORITY

McCORMICK §§ 186–193 at 539–574

2 WEINSTEIN 2d §§ 404.01–404.02, 404.10–404.12, 404.20–404.23

2 MUELLER & KIRKPATRICK §§ 99–118

1 WIGMORE §§ 52–81

COMPARISON TO FEDERAL RULE

Federal Rule 404 was amended on December 1, 2000. It now provides:

Rule 404.   Character Evidence Not Admissible to Prove Conduct; Exceptions; Other Crimes

(a) **Character evidence generally.** Evidence of a person's character or a trait of character is not admissible for the purpose of proving action in conformity therewith on a particular occasion, except:

(1) *Character of accused.* Evidence of a pertinent trait of character offered by an accused, or by the prosecution to rebut the same, or if evidence of a trait of character of the alleged victim of the crime is offered by an accused and admitted under Rule 404(a)(2), evidence of the same trait of character of the accused offered by the prosecution;

(2) *Character of alleged victim.* Evidence of a pertinent trait of character of the alleged victim of the crime offered by an accused, or by the prosecution to rebut the same, or evidence of a character trait of peacefulness of the alleged victim offered by the prosecution in a homicide case to rebut evidence that the

alleged victim was the first aggressor;

(3) *Character of witness.* Evidence of the character of a witness, as provided in Rules 607, 608 and 609.

(b) Other crimes, wrongs, or acts. Evidence of other crimes, wrongs, or acts is not admissible to prove the character of a person in order to show action in conformity therewith. It may, however, be admissible for other purposes, such as proof of motive, opportunity, intent, preparation, plan, knowledge, identity, or absence of mistake or accident, provided that upon request by the accused, the prosecution in a criminal case shall provide reasonable notice in advance of trial, or during trial if the court excuses pretrial notice on good cause shown, of the general nature of any such evidence it intends to introduce at trial.

Federal Rule 404(a)(1) now provides that when the accused attacks the character of an alleged victim under Federal Rule 404(a)(2), the door is opened to attack the same character trait of the accused. The accused is no longer shielded from the disclosure of equally relevant evidence regarding the same character trait when attacking the alleged victim's character. Federal Rule 404(b) now provides that, upon request by the accused, the prosecution must provide reasonable notice in advance of trial (or at trial if the court excuses pretrial notice on good cause shown) of the general nature of any other evidence for proof of motive, opportunity, intent, preparation, plan, knowledge, identity, or absence of mistake or accident.

SIGNIFICANT CASES

Rule 404(a)

Michigan v. Lucas, 500 U.S. 145, 111 S. Ct. 1743, 114 L. Ed. 2d 205 (1991) (court of appeals erred in adopting a *per se* rule that notice and hearing requirements violate the Sixth Amendment in all cases where used to preclude evidence of past sexual conduct between a rape victim and a defendant).

Albrecht v. State, 737 N.E.2d 719 (Ind. 2000) (trial court's decision to exclude a deposition was correct because the record supported the conclusion that defendant was attempting to use evidence of character solely for the forbidden purpose of showing action in conformity therewith).

Williams v. State, 724 N.E.2d 1070 (Ind. 2000), *cert. denied*, 531 U.S. 1128, 121 S. Ct. 886, 148 L. Ed. 2d 793 (2001) (although an accused is permitted to introduce evidence of a victim's character trait pertinent to the crime, evidence of victim's sexual proclivities were inadmissible because they were not relevant to the crimes of murder and stealing electronic equipment).

Spar v. Cha, 881 N.E.2d 70 (Ind. Ct. App. 2008), *superseded, cause remanded,* 907 N.E.2d 974 (Ind. 2009) (in a tort case alleging the failure of a doctor to obtain informed consent, evidence of a patient's consent to previous surgeries to prove the patient had a propensity for risk-taking was improperly admitted under Rule 404 because it constituted prohibited character evidence).

Camm v. State, 812 N.E.2d 1127 (Ind. Ct. App. 2004) (evidence of defendant's extramarital affair was introduced to prove that he was a person of poor character who was more likely to commit murder because of that character; accordingly, the evidence was improperly admitted, as this is precisely what Rule 404 prohibits).

Ware v. State, 816 N.E.2d 1167 (Ind. Ct. App. 2004) (evidence of extra-jurisdictional sexual acts are relevant only to demonstrate the defendant's propensity to commit the crimes and is thus prohibited by Rule 404(b)).

Blevins v. Clark, 740 N.E.2d 1235 (Ind. Ct. App. 2000) (exception under Rule 404(a)(1) did not

RELEVANCY

apply in medical malpractice action because it was a civil case and Rule 404(a)(1) applies to criminal cases or, perhaps, civil cases that are criminal in nature).

Rule 404(a)(1)

Clark v. State, 668 N.E.2d 1206 (Ind. 1996), *reh'g denied* (evidence of a person's character is generally not admissible to show that person acted in manner consistent with that character; testimony will be admissible, where such testimony was not used to demonstrate defendant's propensity to attack others but was used to show that he was in possession of a knife; because there was sufficient testimony that defendant had been drinking all evening, any error in admitting testimony of defendant's character trait for drinking was harmless).

Cliver v. State, 666 N.E.2d 59 (Ind. 1996) (evidence of defendant's prior acts, even those reflecting badly on defendant's character, may be admissible for purposes other than character, such as motive).

Johnson v. State, 655 N.E.2d 502 (Ind. 1995) (evidence of defendant's four previous uncharged fights to show character trait of aggression was not admissible in trial of defendant charged with voluntary manslaughter for shooting a man who came to his door; evidence that defendant, two months prior to homicide, threatened to shoot apartment managers, was also inadmissible "prior act" evidence where prosecution did not offer it as proof of motive or intent).

Eguia v. State, 468 N.E.2d 559 (Ind. Ct. App. 1984) (where defendant presented witnesses who testified to defendant's good character, prosecution was entitled to rebut this evidence by asking the witnesses whether they were aware of defendant's prior convictions).

Rule 404(a)(2)

Brooks v. State, 683 N.E.2d 574 (Ind. 1997) (in a prosecution for murder, the trial court did not err in excluding evidence of the victim's prior violent acts; although evidence of a victim's violent character is relevant and may be admitted pursuant to Rule 404(a)(2), it may only be proven through evidence of reputation, not by specific prior acts).

Phillips v. State, 550 N.E.2d 1290 (Ind. 1990) (where a defendant claims self-defense and the prosecution wants to present evidence of the victim's character for peacefulness, defendant must first introduce evidence of aggression by the victim and establish that defendant was aware of this aggression).

Williams v. State, 669 N.E.2d 178 (Ind. Ct. App. 1996), *vacated by* 683 N.E.2d 594 (Ind. 1997) (evidence of a character trait is not admissible to prove action conforming with that trait on particular occasion, except that accused may offer evidence of relevant character trait of crime victim; this rule is not limited to battery or homicide defendants claiming self-defense).

Eldridge v. State, 627 N.E.2d 844 (Ind. Ct. App. 1994) (exception to inadmissibility of character evidence rule allows prosecutor to introduce evidence about victim's reputation for peacefulness if self-defense claim alleges victim was first aggressor).

Rule 404(b)

Dowling v. United States, 493 U.S. 342, 110 S. Ct. 668, 107 L. Ed. 2d 708 (1990) (testimony regarding a robbery of which defendant had been acquitted was admissible under Federal Rule 404(b) in a trial for a second, unrelated robbery because the jury could "reasonably conclude" that the defendant committed the crime even if the jury did not believe so beyond a reasonable doubt; consequently, there was no violation of the double jeopardy clause).

Huddleston v. United States, 485 U.S. 681, 108 S. Ct. 1496, 99 L. Ed. 2d 771 (1988) (under Federal Rule 404(b), the court need not make a preliminary finding that the Government has proved defendant's "other acts" consistent with Rule 104(b) before submitting the evidence to the jury).

United States v. Levine, 5 F.3d 1100 (7th Cir. 1993), *vacated,* 1997 U.S. App. LEXIS 34124 (7th Cir. Dec. 3, 1997), (evidence of defendant's flight after discovering that he would be indicted for murder of his brother and sister-in-law was admissible as proof of consciousness of guilt).

Nicholson v. State, 963 N.E.2d 1096, 1100 (Ind. 2012) (prior crimes admitted under the identity exception to Rule 404 must be so strikingly similar that we can say with reasonable certainty that the same person committed them).

Turner v. State, 953 N.E.2d 1039, 1049–1053 (Ind. 2011) (evidence that a defendant expressed an interest in robbing the family at a particular address was admissible to prove motive, which is always relevant in the proof of a crime).

Kubsch v. State, 934 N.E.2d 1138 (Ind. 2010) (criminal defendant's attorney may be found to constitute ineffective assistance of counsel for failing to object to the state's notice of intent to use evidence of prior crimes under Rule 404(b)).

Wilkes v. State, 917 N.E.2d 675 (Ind. 2009) (the corpus delicti rule does not apply to evidence of other crimes permitted by Rule 404 (b)).

Clark v. State, 915 N.E.2d 126 (Ind. 2009) (an entry on the defendant's MySpace page constituted statements to be analyzed under the hearsay rules rather than acts to be analyzed as prior acts under Rule 404(b)).

Lafayette v. State, 917 N.E.2d 660 (Ind. 2009) (a defendant does not put intent at issue at any stage of the proceedings simply by questioning the alleged victim's credibility).

Garland v. State, 788 N.E.2d 425 (Ind. 2003) (Rule 404(b) acts as an appropriate restraint on the admissibility of evidence about events or acts that are by definition largely extraneous to those for which a defendant is on trial; accordingly, the admissibility of evidence about prior bad acts by persons other than defendants is subject to Rule 404(b)).

Bassett v. State, 795 N.E.2d 1050 (Ind. 2003) (evidence of conduct of a party 12 and 16 years prior to the event in question and not involving the present victim did not bear sufficient similarity to constitute "signature" crimes, and was thus inadmissible).

Wrinkles v. State, 749 N.E.2d 1179 (Ind. 2001) (defendant did not object to the introduction of defendant's aggressive behavior toward his wife through two witnesses. On appeal, defendant claimed that he was prejudiced because the testimony made him appear violent and dangerous. The testimony was admissible to show motive. Moreover, he was not prejudiced in light of the facts that he donned himself in camouflage, cut the phone lines, and shot his wife, brother-in-law, and sister-in-law in the presence of children).

McCarthy v. State, 749 N.E.2d 528 (Ind. 2001) (testimony regarding the "strip perdiddle" incident and the Michigan trip was admissible at defendant's trial even though he claimed that the evidence portrayed him as a sexual predator; it was neither clear that the "strip perdiddle" activity represented "other crimes, wrongs, or acts" within the meaning of Rule 404(b), nor was the evidence introduced for the forbidden inference. Rather, the evidence was introduced to show that defendant had knowledge of the existence of "perdiddle" or "strip perdiddle," something he consistently denied, and the evidence was relevant because it was after engaging in this activity that the victim testified that defendant molested her. Evidence that defendant apparently played this "game" with students on an earlier occasion certainly went to the heart of his defense, but it was not rendered inadmissible by Rule 404(b)).

Fry v. State, 748 N.E.2d 369 (Ind. 2001) (trial court did not abuse its discretion in admitting evidence of a plan to steal a television set because it showed defendant's motive for killing two people; although defendant contended that the evidence was admitted to show his bad character and his propensity to act in conformity with the prior bad acts, the trial court specifically found that the testimony went to motive, which satisfied Rule 404(b)).

Murray v. State, 742 N.E.2d 932 (Ind. 2001) (the trial court did not err in admitting evidence that defendant unlawfully carried a handgun because such evidence was admissible for another purpose, namely to show intent, and not for the forbidden inference).

Stephenson v. State, 742 N.E.2d 463 (Ind. 2001) (testimony of a state's witness that he had to cancel telephone services and charges billed to a car repair shop rented by him and defendant was not evidence of uncharged prior bad acts).

Ortiz v. State, 741 N.E.2d 1203 (Ind. 2001) (evidence that defendant's prior attack on someone other than the murder victim was not admissible to show defendant's intent to commit the murder in question because the incidents involved two different victims, and the attack of the first victim did not make it more or less likely that the defendant knowingly or intentionally killed the second victim; however, error in admitting the evidence was harmless in light of the other evidence of defendant's guilt).

Johnson v. State, 740 N.E.2d 118 (Ind. 2001) (the court held that the trial court abused its discretion by allowing the prosecutor to dismiss and refile as a tactic to circumvent a proper evidentiary ruling under Rule 404(b), after the prosecutor missed the deadline for notifying defendant of its intent to use Rule 404(b) evidence in a molestation case).

Martin v. State, 736 N.E.2d 1213 (Ind. 2000); *Small v. State*, 736 N.E.2d 742 (Ind. 2000) (officer testified that three months before the victim's death, defendant told him where he lived; this prior conduct (a response to a question asked during a routine traffic stop) was not a prior bad act from which the jury could have drawn a forbidden inference about defendant's character of guilt).

Hatcher v. State, 735 N.E.2d 1155 (Ind. 2000) (state's six-day notice to defendant of its intent to offer evidence of other crimes, wrongs, or acts at his murder trial was reasonable because (1) defendant was not surprised by the offered evidence because it had been disclosed to him during discovery, and (2) the notice was sufficient to promote early resolution of the questions of admissibility).

Roop v. State, 730 N.E.2d 1267 (Ind. 2000) (trial court did not abuse its discretion in rejecting defendant's argument that father-in-law may have molested his granddaughter because of allegations that he molested his own daughter; the evidence was not offered for a proper purpose—to prove intent, plan, or absence of mistake; admissibility of such argument was further undermined by remoteness in time and lack of any evidence that the molestation was in any way similar to the alleged prior act).

Hauk v. State, 729 N.E.2d 994 (Ind. 2000) (trial court properly admitted evidence of cohort's bad acts from crime; additional bad act evidence was presented merely to persuade the jury that it was cohort who murdered and robbed victim and that defendant did not resist aiding him out of fear—this goes to nothing but propensity and was properly excluded).

Thompson v. State, 728 N.E.2d 155 (Ind. 2000) (trial court did not err in admitting evidence that defendant attempted to sell gun to another before the murder; such evidence was admissible under Rule 404(b) because it showed defendant had access to the murder weapon and the probative value of the evidence was not substantially outweighed by unfair prejudice).

Jackson v. State, 728 N.E.2d 147 (Ind. 2000) (although originally excluded, trial court properly admitted evidence of prior battery in case where defendant murdered his wife because defendant opened the door by claiming that he loved his wife every day of his 20-year marriage, and the evidence rebutted the suggestions or false impression that defendant would not knowingly or intentionally harm someone he loved).

Boone v. State, 728 N.E.2d 135 (Ind. 2000) (trial court properly admitted evidence of defendant's prior car chase of victim in a case where defendant claimed the killing was due to the heat of the moment; the prior bad act evidence was admitted to prove intent—the intent exception is available when a defendant goes beyond merely denying the charged culpability and affirmatively presents a claim of particular contrary intent).

Evans v. State, 727 N.E.2d 1072 (Ind. 2000) (defendant's prior act of choking ex-girlfriend was properly admitted to prove intent and rebut defendant's claim of self-defense where he alleged that victim was the aggressor).

Cline v. State, 726 N.E.2d 1249 (Ind. 2000) (evidence that defendant's boyfriend was involved in a gang and committed prior acts of violence was properly excluded by the trial court because it was only offered to show his propensity and that he likely acted in conformity with the acts and harmed victim).

Monegan v. State, 721 N.E.2d 243 (Ind. 1999) (testimony that defendant bragged that he had killed a young girl in a gang-related drive-by shooting was not relevant to defendant's claim that murder for which he was charged was accidental and, thus, was not admissible under the intent exception to the evidence rule excluding prior bad act evidence).

Smith v. State, 721 N.E.2d 213 (Ind. 1999) (trial court erred in admitting defendant's general statements regarding his past criminal history; state's claim of relevance relied on motive but the statements did not bear on the motive).

Allen v. State, 720 N.E.2d 707 (Ind. 1999) (trial court made a close call in admitting evidence of prior rape with use of duct tape to bind victims as evidence of identity but court was "hard-pressed to say the trial judge erred" on the point; prior bad acts are admissible to prove identity, the rationale being that the crimes, or means used to commit them, were so similar and unique that it was highly probable that the same person committed all of them).

McIntyre v. State, 717 N.E.2d 114 (Ind. 1999) (trial court erred in permitting statement defendant voluntarily gave to police regarding his prior bad acts; while defendant may waive the protections of Rule 404(b) by offering evidence of his own character at trial, he does not waive the protections of Rule 404(b) by volunteering his previous bad acts at some point before trial).

Ortiz v. State, 716 N.E.2d 345 (Ind. 1999) (evidence that defendant fought with his mother, stole money from her, stole checks from her and forged her signatures, had run up her phone bill, and used her car without permission, was properly admitted to prove motive to kill and not as prior bad acts; evidence of motive is always relevant in the proof of a crime, and a defendant's prior actions with respect to the victim are also usually admissible to show the relationship between the two).

Berry v. State, 715 N.E.2d 864 (Ind. 1999) (evidence that defendant committed prior crime—shooting stranger with shotgun while wearing a blue coat—was improperly admitted in case where he shot acquaintance with shotgun while wearing blue coat; state did not present evidence that the same shotgun was used and a blue coat was too commonly found, and thus, the evidence of the prior crime was not relevant to any matter besides defendant's propensity to commit crime).

Byers v. State, 709 N.E.2d 1024 (Ind. 1999) (in order for a trial court to admit prior acts evidence, the court must (1) determine that the evidence is relevant to a matter at issue other than the defendant's propensity to commit the charged act, and (2) balance the probative value of the evidence against its prejudicial effect pursuant to Rule 403).

Sanders v. State, 704 N.E.2d 119 (Ind. 1999) (evidence that defendant committed a battery was not offered to prove propensity to act in conformity with a character trait for violence, but rather was offered and properly admitted for the "other purpose" of proving defendant's intent by negating his claim of self-defense).

Berry v. State, 704 N.E.2d 462 (Ind. 1998) (trial court did not abuse its discretion in admitting a specific threat of violence that was both equivocal and temporally remote (six months) from the crime for which the defendant was charged, because the testimony indicated the extent to which the defendant's relationship with his family had become strained).

Charlton v. State, 702 N.E.2d 1045 (Ind. 1998) (evidence that murder victim sought a protective order against defendant prior to the murder was relevant to establish the hostile relationship between the victim and defendant and defendant's motive for murder, and any prejudicial impact

RELEVANCY

did not substantially outweigh probative value of such evidence).

Barker v. State, 695 N.E.2d 925 (Ind. 1998) (evidence that defendant had previously assaulted one murder victim should have been excluded where defendant's identity was not at issue at trial, the assaults occurred 28 and 19 months before the murder, and assaults were irrelevant to defendant's motive for the kidnapping which led to murder).

McEwen v. State, 695 N.E.2d 79 (Ind. 1998) (in prosecution for murder, trial court did not err in admitting evidence of a previous battery committed by the defendant against the victim as the previous battery evidenced a pattern of hostility between defendant and victim and was also relevant to the defendant's claim that the victim was stabbed accidentally).

Stevens v. State, 691 N.E.2d 412 (Ind. 1997), *vacated in part, **Stevens v. McBride***, 489 F.3d 883 (7th Cir. 2007) (holding that the prohibition against admission contained in Rule 404(b) applies only to "uncharged misconduct" or "prior bad acts" and does not operate to exclude evidence of prior mundane acts by the defendant where such acts do not reflect adversely on his character).

Thompson v. State, 690 N.E.2d 224 (Ind. 1997) (although evidence concerning events surrounding a prior murder committed by the defendant was relevant and admissible to show how the defendant obtained the weapon with which he committed the charged murder, the quantity and nature of the evidence admitted by the trial court, which fully detailed the prior murder, went beyond the scope of evidence admissible pursuant to the exception contained in Rule 404(b)).

Lee v. State, 689 N.E.2d 435 (Ind. 1997) (holding that Rule 404 does not bar the admission of other acts evidence where those other acts are intrinsic to the charged offense).

Grund v. State, 671 N.E.2d 411 (Ind. 1996) (evidence of previous burglary at defendant's home did not violate other crimes rule, since prosecutor did not link defendant with previous burglary; instead, evidence that the two burglaries were "mirror images" raised inference that defendant charged with murder of her husband had copied previous burglary to make it appear that burglar killed her husband).

Tompkins v. State, 669 N.E.2d 394 (Ind. 1996) (testimony that Caucasian defendant named road leading to his property "no nigger lane" and liked "to mess with black people" was relevant to show motive for murder of African American victim; evidence of motive is relevant to proof of crime, and thus decision to admit such evidence is within discretion of trial court; defendant's reference to murder victim as "nigger" was not relevant to motive since the statement did not make it more probable that defendant had motive to kill victim).

Buell v. State, 668 N.E.2d 251 (Ind. 1996) (in murder prosecution, even if trial court erred in admitting evidence that defendant was using drugs while discussing what to do with victim, no reversal was necessary given strong evidence against defendant).

Swanson v. State, 666 N.E.2d 397 (Ind. 1996) (evidence that defendant slapped his girlfriend and fired a handgun at the ceiling was not inadmissible as evidence of prior bad acts; paradigm of such inadmissible evidence is a crime committed on another day in another place, evidence whose only apparent purpose is to prove the defendant commits crime).

Cliver v. State, 666 N.E.2d 59 (Ind. 1996) (evidence of defendant's prior acts, even those reflecting badly on defendant's character, may be admissible for purposes other than character, such as motive).

Lay v. State, 659 N.E.2d 1005 (Ind. 1995) (where alleged basis for mistrial is jury hearing evidence of previous bad acts, severity of harm is to be judged by probable persuasive impact of evidence on jury; trial court admonished jury to disregard testimony, and independent evidence of guilt made error in admission of testimony harmless).

Taylor v. State, 659 N.E.2d 535 (Ind. 1995) (prejudicial impact of evidence that murder defendant had previously been accused of sexually abusing victim was outweighed by its probative value; evidence was relevant to show motive because there was testimony that defendant accused victim of lying about sexual charges prior to shooting her).

Greenlee v. State, 655 N.E.2d 488 (Ind. 1995) (trial court did not abuse its discretion in denying motion for mistrial by defendant charged with attempted murder after police officer testified to having arrested defendant in past, even though such testimony was improper to demonstrate guilt, where court admonished jury to disregard remark, where strong eyewitness testimony against defendant existed, and where record revealed no evidence of deliberate effort to inject the testimony into the trial; to decide if testimony of prior uncharged misconduct necessitates a new trial, it must be determined whether evidence was intentionally or inadvertently introduced and to what extent jury speculated improperly about defendant).

Evans v. State, 643 N.E.2d 877 (Ind. 1994) (evidence of extrinsic offense is usually inadmissible because juries might otherwise convict defendants on basis of prior bad acts and bad character).

Arndt v. State, 642 N.E.2d 224 (Ind. 1994) (appeal of child molestation case in which trial was held several months prior to Supreme Court's *Lannan* decision and defendant filed his *praecipe* before *Lannan* decision was subject to *Lannan* holding; defendant objected to remoteness of evidence of his past sexual misconduct but not to admission of that evidence to prove intent or sexual propensities and therefore failed to preserve his entitlement to remedy provided by *Lannan*'s abandonment of depraved sexual instinct rationale for admission of prior crimes evidence).

Brennan v. State, 639 N.E.2d 649 (Ind. 1994) (trial court did not err in preventing defendant from introducing evidence that his accomplice had been involved in a number of fights while in jail to rebut evidence that the violent acts in the charged crime were committed by defendant alone; a person's reputation for peace can only be shown by general reputation evidence, not specific acts).

Douglas v. State, 634 N.E.2d 811 (Ind. Ct. App. 1994), *opinion corrected on reh'g*, 640 N.E.2d 73 (Ind. Ct. App. 1994) (evidence that defendant had been in Indiana Boys School was not properly admitted as part of res gestae of crime of attempted robbery on ground that defendant and codefendant had planned crime there; even though it was significant that the two discussed and planned the crime in advance, such evidence did not assist jury).

Tingle v. State, 632 N.E.2d 345 (Ind. 1994) (in prosecution for robbery, aggravated battery, confinement, and theft, evidence that defendant and his companions stole car and license plate and that they drove toward area where defendant had been incarcerated was admissible as part of res gestae of crime, in spite of few hours' time lapse; stolen car, plate and trip to area were instrumental in getting defendant and companion to scene of charged crime and were part of same transaction).

Elliott v. State, 630 N.E.2d 202 (Ind. 1994) (where defendant was charged with murdering his ex-wife's boyfriend, evidence of past threats and statements made by defendant toward his ex-wife and the victim, including a taped telephone call, were properly admitted to show the relationship between the parties, and to show defendant's motive, plan, and absence of mistake or accident).

Wickizer v. State, 626 N.E.2d 795 (Ind. 1993) (Indiana Supreme Court held that Rule 404(b) permits the prosecution to offer evidence of prior crimes to prove criminal defendant's intent only where issue of intent is genuinely contested; court found that where defendant was charged with child molestation, evidence that he had previously touched other children's penises was reversible error).

Hatton v. State, 626 N.E.2d 442 (Ind. 1993) (where defendant was charged with murdering store manager, prosecution was permitted to prove that defendant had been fired by the manager for theft and had been convicted of theft; such evidence was admissible to show motive).

Hardin v. State, 611 N.E.2d 123 (Ind. 1993) (evidence of other uncharged criminal activity by defendant is admissible where the other acts were committed with an identical modus operandi

such that the methods employed were so strikingly similar as to comprise a signature of defendant).

Pirnat v. State, 607 N.E.2d 973 (Ind. 1993) (holding in ***Lannan v. State***, adopting new rule regarding admissibility of prior bad acts evidence in sex offense cases, applied to cases pending on direct appeal when *Lannan* was decided).

Lannan v. State, 600 N.E.2d 1334 (Ind. 1992) (Indiana Supreme Court adopted the language of Federal Rule 404(b)).

Brewer v. State, 562 N.E.2d 22 (Ind. 1990) (trial court may consider whether the prejudicial impact of uncharged crimes outweighs its probative value).

Kindred v. State, 254 Ind. 127, 258 N.E.2d 411 (1970) (to be admissible, evidence of other crimes must be substantial and amount to a prima facie case).

Bryant v. State, 984 N.E.2d 240 (Ind. Ct. App. 2013) (when a defendant alleges in trial a particular contrary intent, whether in opening statement, by cross-examination of witnesses, or by presentation of his own case-in-chief, the State may respond by offering evidence of prior crimes, wrongs, or acts to the extent genuinely relevant to prove the defendant's intent at the time of the charged offense).

Harris v. State, 878 N.E.2d 504 (Ind. Ct. App. 2007) (because the question of whether the defendant was, in fact, driving the truck on the day in question was not in dispute, there was no reason for the State to introduce into evidence the defendant's many prior criminal convictions for the same type offense).

Southern v. State, 878 N.E.2d 315 (Ind. Ct. App. 2007), *transfer denied*, 891 N.E.2d 41 (2008) (although cases under Rule 404 typically involve prior acts of a party, the language of the Rule does not exclude its application to subsequent acts; similarly, acts occurring after the charged conduct are admissible under the Fed. R. Evid. 404(b) if it satisfies the same test for prior acts).

Hines v. State, 856 N.E.2d 1275 (Ind. Ct. App. 2006) (because the rules of evidence do not apply in sentencing hearings, the court's consideration of the defendant's admission that he molested his daughter was not similar to a violation of Rule 404(b)).

Gillespie v. State, 832 N.E.2d 1112 (Ind. Ct. App. 2005) (testimony concerning the criminal defendant's actions prior to the alleged crime had no effect but to lead the jury to make the prohibited inference that the defendant had a propensity to commit criminal acts and thus engaged in the charged conduct, and is therefore inadmissible).

Samaniego-Hernandez v. State, 839 N.E.2d 798 (Ind. Ct. App. 2005) (the "intent" exception of Rule 404(b) is available where a defendant goes beyond merely denying the charged culpability and affirmatively presents a claim of particular contrary intent).

Guillen v. State, 829 N.E.2d 142 (Ind. Ct. App. 2005), *transfer denied*, 841 N.E.2d 182 (Ind. 2005) (a defendant who asserts self-defense does not make the victim's character an essential element of his defense, and the trial court therefore did not abuse its discretion by excluding the evidence of specific instances of reckless conduct by the victim to prove a relevant trait of character).

Holden v. State, 815 N.E.2d 1049 (Ind. Ct. App. 2004), *overruled in part*, *Waldon v. State*, 829 N.E.2d 168 (Ind. Ct. App. 2005) (Rule 404 does not bar the admission of evidence of uncharged acts that are "intrinsic" to the charged offense, or acts occurring at the same time and under the same circumstances as the charged crimes).

Manuel v. State, 793 N.E.2d 1215 (Ind. Ct. App. 2003) (a child victim's testimony concerning prior molestations were extremely vague and thus inadmissible to prove identity under Rule 404(b); accordingly, the only purpose of the testimony was to establish that defendant had a propensity to commit child molesting and was thus inadmissible).

Krumm v. State, 793 N.E.2d 1170 (Ind. Ct. App. 2003) (evidence of prior instances of alleged child molestation that were not relevant to prove motive, intent, preparation, plan, knowledge, identity, or absence of mistake or accident, and outweighed by the potential prejudice of such evidence, were properly excluded).

Swann v. State, 789 N.E.2d 1020 (Ind. Ct. App. 2003) (a party's attempt to introduce evidence of his prior false confession improperly sought to use proof of that prior extrinsic act to bolster his statement that he lied when giving his confession in the instant case, and was thus properly excluded).

Cowan v. State, 783 N.E.2d 1270 (Ind. Ct. App. 2003) (Rule 404 does not prohibit evidence of uncharged criminal acts that are "intrinsic—occurring at the same time and under the same circumstances as the crimes charged—to the charged offense").

Reynolds v. State, 797 N.E.2d 864 (Ind. Ct. App. 2003) (prior acts evidence is inadmissible when a party offers the evidence only to produce the "forbidden inference" that the defendant has engaged in other misconduct and the charged conduct was in conformity with the misconduct).

Law v. State, 797 N.E.2d 1157 (Ind. Ct. App. 2003) (a defendant's prior bad acts generally are admissible to show the relationship between the defendant and the victim).

Johnson v. State, 785 N.E.2d 1134 (Ind. Ct. App. 2003) (when evaluating the admissibility of evidence under Rule 404(b), a trial court must first (1) decide if the evidence of other crimes, wrongs, or acts is relevant to a matter at issue other than the defendant's propensity to commit the charged act; and (2) balance the probative value of the evidence against its prejudicial effect pursuant to Rule 403).

Willingham v. State, 794 N.E.2d 1110 (Ind. Ct. App. 2003) (a consideration of the admissibility of evidence under Rule 404(b) necessarily includes the relevance test of Rule 401 and the balancing test of Rule 403).

Jones v. State, 708 N.E.2d 37 (Ind. Ct. App. 1999) (defendant does not waive a Rule 404(b) argument on appeal where the party fails to make a specific Rule 404(b) objection at trial; rather, where the defense objects to evidence of prior convictions on the basis of relevance, a trial court should be alerted to Rule 404(b) concerns).

Roche v. State, 699 N.E.2d 752 (Ind. Ct. App. 1998) (the state may offer evidence of a defendant's prior acts only if the defendant goes beyond denying the charged culpability and affirmatively presents a claim of a particular contrary intent in opening statement, by cross-examination of the state's witnesses or through his case-in-chief).

Utley v. State, 699 N.E.2d 723 (Ind. Ct. App. 1998) (evidence of a person's sexual preference or propensities is generally considered character evidence).

Giles v. State, 699 N.E.2d 294 (Ind. Ct. App. 1998) (pursuant to the common plan or scheme exception to the rule excluding evidence of uncharged conduct, court properly admitted evidence that a defendant charged with theft for cashing two payroll checks to himself on an account lacking sufficient funds also cashed 14 other checks in much the same way during the same month).

Robinson v. State, 682 N.E.2d 806 (Ind. Ct. App. 1997) (the court stated that, assuming that gang membership qualifies as misconduct, evidence of the defendant's and a witness's membership in the same gang was admissible to show the witness's bias toward the defendant).

Abdul-Musawwir v. State, 674 N.E.2d 972 (Ind. Ct. App. 1996) (notice is required for evidence of other wrongful acts to be admissible, and failure to comply with notice requirement renders evidence inadmissible).

Spires v. State, 670 N.E.2d 1313 (Ind. Ct. App. 1996) (where crime is committed on a different day in a different place, and where introduction of evidence of such crime is solely to prove defendant is person who commits crimes, such evidence is inadmissible under other-crimes rule).

Hopkins v. State, 668 N.E.2d 686 (Ind. Ct. App. 1996) (defendant's previous dealing with police

RELEVANCY

informant was not inadmissible prior bad acts evidence; where issue of their previous involvement in transport of marijuana was offered in response to defense counsel's implication that informant was established drug dealer who acted as police informant not only to retaliate against defendant but also to help himself, and where even after state stipulated that informant was drug dealer, defense counsel questioned informant about his prior drug trafficking, his supplier, and his drug connections).

Poindexter v. State, 664 N.E.2d 398 (Ind. Ct. App. 1996) (if state tries to offer evidence of defendant's uncharged misconduct, trial court must decide if purpose of evidence is proving defendant's bad character or propensity to commit charged crime, and if evidence's sole purpose is to create forbidden influence that defendant had committed uncharged misconduct with which charged crime was in conformity then evidence is inadmissible).

DeBerry v. State, 659 N.E.2d 665 (Ind. Ct. App. 1995) (simply because police officers were discussing defendant did not mean he was implicated in any collateral crimes; trooper's testimony constituted invited error at most and did not necessitate new trial; trooper's statement that numerous charges were filed against defendant in other counties was merely answer to defense attorney's question regarding how attorney and defendant could have contacted police before charges in present case were filed).

Carson v. State, 659 N.E.2d 216 (Ind. Ct. App. 1995) (if state tries to offer evidence of defendant's uncharged misconduct, trial court must determine if evidence is offered solely to prove defendant's bad character or propensity to commit charged crime; error in admission of evidence of collateral criminal conduct may be harmless where jury's verdict is supported by independent evidence of guilt and reviewing court finds no substantial likelihood that improperly admitted evidence was factor in defendant's conviction).

Kimble v. State, 659 N.E.2d 182 (Ind. Ct. App. 1995) (evidence of previous conduct is admissible only where it is offered to prove something other than defendant's character or propensity to commit charged crime, the so-called forbidden influence; even if evidence is admissible under rule of evidence concerning uncharged conduct, it may still be excluded if its prejudicial effect substantially outweighs its probative value).

Forrest v. State, 655 N.E.2d 584 (Ind. Ct. App. 1995) (uncharged misconduct evidence is admissible if it demonstrates motive of defendant to commit crime).

Sloan v. State, 654 N.E.2d 797 (Ind. Ct. App. 1995) (the introduction of extraneous bad acts evidence requires that a rational, legitimate connection be shown between evidence and some matter at issue; to be admissible, evidence of accused's extraneous bad acts must (1) be directed to proving matter in issue other than propensity of defendant to commit crime, (2) show previous act was similar enough and close enough in time to be relevant, (3) be such that reasonable jurors could find that act occurred and that defendant committed the act, and (4) be such that evidence's probative value is not substantially outweighed by risk of unfair prejudice).

Moore v. State, 653 N.E.2d 1010 (Ind. Ct. App. 1995) (similarity by itself does not suffice to make evidence admissible under common scheme or plan exception; evidence of woman's rape which happened 11 months after charged offense of attempted criminal deviate conduct was not admissible under either the identity or preconceived plan branches of the "common scheme or plan" exception or under the identity exception to general rule that evidence of other crimes is not admissible; the uninterrupted transaction exception requires that crimes be committed in conjunction with each other; here, the incidents were 11 months apart and occurred in separate counties and there was no issue regarding defendant's identity).

Gardner v. State, 641 N.E.2d 641 (Ind. Ct. App. 1994) (where defendant was charged with burglary, trial court did not err in admitting evidence of two other burglaries for which defendant was not charged as evidence of defendant's common plan or identity; the two other burglaries were nearly identical to the charged crime: All were committed on the same morning in rural areas of adjacent counties, similar items were taken from each house, and doors were broken to gain entrance into each house; trial court properly found the similarities sufficient to establish a signature or *modus operandi*).

Williams v. State, 634 N.E.2d 849 (Ind. Ct. App. 1994) (fundamental error did not result where evidence of defendant's prior criminal activity was erroneously admitted at trial).

Bolin v. State, 634 N.E.2d 546 (Ind. Ct. App. 1994) (under *modus operandi* exception to general rule against admission of other crimes evidence, state may prove identity by demonstrating that similarities between previous offense and crime charged are so strong and the method so clearly unique that it is highly probable that perpetrator of both is same person; extrinsic offenses are admissible to demonstrate state of mind, although lesser degree of similarity between the acts is necessary).

Levi v. State, 627 N.E.2d 1345 (Ind. Ct. App. 1994) (evidence of defendant's previous conviction for burglary was not admissible to prove intent in trial on subsequent burglary charges, where defendant generally denied his culpability by pleading not guilty, but did not claim any specific contrary intent in either opening statement or cross-examination of state's witness; intent exception applies only where defendant goes further than simple denial of charge and affirmatively claims particular contrary intent either in opening statement, cross-examination of state's witness, or presentation of defendant's case-in-chief; then, state may respond by introducing evidence of previous criminal conduct to show defendant's intent at time of charged offense).

Brim v. State, 624 N.E.2d 27 (Ind. Ct. App. 1993) (where defendant was charged with beating the victim, evidence of other beatings by defendant was properly admitted where identity was a disputed issue at trial; the other beatings were sufficiently similar to the charged crime to constitute a signature, and the probative value of the evidence was not substantially outweighed by the potential unfair prejudice).

Schumpert v. State, 603 N.E.2d 1359 (Ind. Ct. App. 1992) (applying Rule 404(b) to identity exception).

Johnson v. State, 544 N.E.2d 164 (Ind. Ct. App. 1989) (evidence of defendant's involvement in other criminal acts must be weighed against unfair prejudice to defendant).

Chapter 405

Rule 405. Methods of Proving Character

Rule 405 reads as follows:

(a) Reputation or Opinion. In all cases in which evidence of character or a trait of character of a person is admissible, proof may be made by testimony as to reputation or by testimony in the form of an opinion. On cross-examination, inquiry is allowable into relevant specific instances of conduct. Upon reasonable pre-trial notice by the accused of the intention to offer character evidence, the prosecution in a criminal case shall provide the accused with any relevant specific instances of conduct to be used in cross-examination.

(b) Specific Instances of Conduct. In cases in which character or a trait of character of a person is an essential element of a charge, claim, or defense, proof may also be made of specific instances of that person's conduct.

---

* * * * *

ANALYSIS

Scope of Rule. Rule 405 provides the methodology for proving character where it is determined that character evidence is admissible under Rule 404. Rule 405 recognizes three devices for proving a person's character or character trait. First, reputation within a pertinent community may be used to establish circumstantially the character of an individual. Second, a person familiar with the character of an individual may provide opinion testimony as to the character in question. Third, specific instances of conduct may be offered to establish the character of an individual. Under pre-Rule Indiana law, opinion testimony was not available as a method for proving character.

Methods Available. The use of a particular methodology depends upon the way in which character is used in conjunction with the issues of a case. Where character is "in issue," all methodologies of proving character are available. Where character is used circumstantially to establish conforming conduct, only reputation and opinion evidence are available. Where, however, character evidence is utilized to impeach the credibility of a witness, methodology of proof is governed by Rules 608 and 609.

Character Witnesses. Character or character traits are established through a character witness. A person qualifies as a character witness where he is a member of some pertinent community in which the person characterized is known, and where the character witness has been a member of that community for a reasonably extensive period of time. Both of these elements must be established through a foundation in the course of the preliminary examination of the character witness. The character witness must also know the reputation of the person characterized and be prepared to testify to such reputation within the pertinent community. Reputation is the collective opinion of persons within the pertinent community. Rule 405 also provides that the character witness may respond to questions as to the character witness's personal opinion of the individual who is characterized. Consistent with Rule 701, the character witness is permitted to testify to his personal opinion of the existence of the pertinent trait.

Illustration

Embezzlement trial.

Q: Are you acquainted with the defendant, Mr. Bowman?

A: Yes.

Q: Please state the basis for your acquaintance?

A: I have worked with him at the downtown branch of the Mega Bank Corp. for twelve years.

Q: And during that time, have you had an opportunity to become familiar with Mr. Bowman's reputation for trustworthiness in the downtown banking community?

A: I have.

Q: What is his reputation?

A: He is known to be an honest and trustworthy person.

Q: During the twelve years you have known Mr. Bowman, have you had an opportunity to observe him in situations in which you would be able to determine his trustworthiness?

A: I have.

Q: And as consequence, have you developed a personal opinion as to Mr. Bowman's trustworthiness?

A: Yes.

Q: What is that opinion?

A: It is my opinion that Mr. Bowman is honest and trustworthy.

Character in Issue.   It should be noted that in the rare situation where character is "in issue," specific instances of conduct of the person characterized may be proven in order to establish the person's character or character traits. Character is in issue when it constitutes an element of a claim, charge, or defense. Specific instances of conduct may be proven through a character witness or through the testimony of any person who has first-hand knowledge of the relevant specific acts of the person characterized.

Cross-examination of Character Witnesses. Rule 405(a) also governs the cross-examination of the character witness. On cross-examination of a character witness, the witness may be asked about specific instances of conduct of the person characterized which are pertinent to the trait being considered. The question on cross-examination may be asked in the traditional form which provides that the cross-examiner may ask, "[h]ave you heard that Mr. X was terminated from his job in May of 1989 because of embezzlement?" Alternatively, the cross-examiner may use the more contemporary form: "Do you know that Mr. X was terminated from his job in May of 1989 because of embezzlement?"

Notice in Criminal Cases. Rule 405(a) expressly provides that upon reasonable pretrial notice in a criminal case, the prosecution must provide the accused with a description of the specific instances of conduct to be used in cross-examination.

ADDITIONAL AUTHORITY

WEISSENBERGER'S FEDERAL EVIDENCE §§ 405.1–405.6

MCCORMICK § 191 at 566

2 WEINSTEIN 2d §§ 405.01–405.05

2 MUELLER & KIRKPATRICK §§ 119–122

7 WIGMORE §§ 1981–1986

COMPARISON TO FEDERAL RULE

Indiana Rule 405 is identical to Federal Rule 405 except for the addition of the notice requirement in Indiana Rule 405(a).

SIGNIFICANT CASES

Michelson v. United States, 335 U.S. 469, 69 S. Ct. 213, 93 L. Ed. 168 (1948), *superseded by statute*, *People v. Vichroy*, 76 Cal. App. 4th 92, 90 Cal. Rptr. 2d 105 (1999), *superseded by statute as stated in McKinstry v. Ayers*, 2007 U.S. Dist. LEXIS 31709 (government permitted to cross-examine defendant's character witness about defendant's conviction from 27 years earlier).

United States v. Alvarez, 860 F.2d 801 (7th Cir. 1988) (government could cross-examine witnesses about their awareness of defendant's alleged violations of immigration laws 10 years before witnesses knew defendant).

Price v. State, 765 N.E.2d 1245 (Ind. 2002) (criminal defendant is not entitled to introduce evidence of a specific instance of victim's prior conduct to show that victim had violent propensities; evidence of specific incidents is permissible only on cross-examination of a character witness).

Brennan v. State, 639 N.E.2d 649 (Ind. 1994) (trial court did not err in preventing defendant from introducing evidence that his accomplice had been involved in a number of fights while in jail to rebut evidence that the violent acts in the charged crime were committed by defendant alone; a person's reputation for peace can only be shown by general reputation evidence, not specific acts).

Phillips v. State, 550 N.E.2d 1290 (Ind. 1990) (witness was permitted to testify that the victim had a reputation for being violent, but the court prevented the witness from testifying that the victim carried a firearm).

Lineback v. State, 260 Ind. 503, 296 N.E.2d 788 (1973) (cross-examination of defendant's character witness as to whether witness was familiar with defendant's prior arrest and conviction was proper).

Guillen v. State, 829 N.E.2d 142 (Ind. Ct. App. 2005), *transfer denied*, 841 N.E.2d 182 (Ind. 2005) (a defendant who asserts self-defense does not make the victim's character an essential element of his defense, and the trial court therefore did not abuse its discretion by excluding the evidence of specific instances of reckless conduct by the victim to prove a relevant trait of character).

Bell v. State, 820 N.E.2d 1279 (Ind. Ct. App. 2005), *transfer denied*, 831 N.E.2d 744 (Ind. 2005) (defendant's elicitation of testimony of specific instances of the victim's conduct to illustrate her behavior in situations when she was upset is erroneous; Rule 405 allows evidence only in the form of opinion or reputation in such situations).

In re Matter of Termination of Parent-Child Relationship of D.G., 702 N.E.2d 777 (Ind. Ct. App. 1998) (given the nature of a termination proceeding, a parent's character is also an integral factor in assessing a parent's fitness and in determining the child's best interest; accordingly, specific instances of a parent's character, including evidence regarding a previous termination of parental rights, are admissible character evidence in a subsequent termination proceeding).

Johnson v. State, 671 N.E.2d 1203 (Ind. Ct. App. 1996) (in murder prosecution, where evidence was not proof of motive, identity, plan, intent, or any other exception to rule forbidding prior bad act character evidence, evidence of defendant's four previous uncharged fights, to demonstrate defendant's character trait of aggression, was not admissible; nor could such evidence be admitted to rebut defense's evidence concerning murder victim's previous aggression conduct, as defendant's claim of self-defense and offer of evidence of victim's aggressive conduct did not put defendant's character into issue).

Williams v. State, 669 N.E.2d 178 (Ind. Ct. App. 1996), *vacated by* 683 N.E.2d 594 (Ind. 1997) (in all cases in which evidence of character or trait of character of person is admissible, proof may be made by testimony as to reputation or by testimony in form of opinion; in cases in which character or trait of character is essential element of defense, proof may also be made of specific instances of that person's conduct).

In re J.L.V., 667 N.E.2d 186 (Ind. Ct. App. 1996) (evidence of mother's previous involvement with county social services agency concerning four of her other children, was admissible character evidence in child in need of services (CHINS) proceeding because in CHINS proceeding, parents' character is at issue and therefore specific instances of parents' character are admissible).

Forrest v. State, 655 N.E.2d 584 (Ind. Ct. App. 1995) (previous arrest of defendant for disorderly conduct when defendant wrestled with police and his previous arrest for resisting law enforcement when he tried to prevent his sister's lawful arrest were relevant to rebut defense witness's claim that defendant had a peaceful nature; therefore, state's cross-examination of defendant's character witnesses about witness's awareness of defendant's arrests was proper).

Smith v. State, 655 N.E.2d 532 (Ind. Ct. App. 1995) (evidence that defendant allowed her daughter and daughter's boyfriend to have sex in defendant's home and permitted 15-year-old girl and girl's boyfriend to live together in defendant's home was relevant to explain defendant's relationship with daughter's boyfriend and girl's boyfriend who testified defendant solicited them to kill victim).

Dynes v. Dynes, 637 N.E.2d 1321 (Ind. Ct. App. 1994) (court of appeals, interpreting the rules of evidence, held that evidence of reputation at the workplace was admissible; such evidence must be general, must be held by an identifiable group with a basis to form an opinion, and the testifying witness must have sufficient contact with the community or group).

Chapter 406

Rule 406. Habit; Routine Practice

Rule 406 reads as follows:

> Evidence of the habit of a person or of the routine practice of an organization, whether corroborated or not and regardless of the presence of eyewitnesses, is relevant to prove that the conduct of the person or organization on a particular occasion was in conformity with the habit or routine practice.

* * * * *

ANALYSIS

Scope of Rule. Rule 406 governs the admissibility of the habit of a natural person and the routine practice of a business or organization. Habits of persons and the routine practices of businesses are equivalent in concept for the operation of Rule 406.

Practical Considerations

Habit is a person's regular practice of meeting a particular kind of situation with a specific type of responsive conduct. In behavioral terms, habit refers to the tendency of a person to exhibit a regular response to a specific stimulus. Habit is unquestionably a form of propensity, and consequently, it is, in many cases, difficult to distinguish habit from what evidentiary law would designate as character. The distinction, nevertheless, is important, because the admissibility of character evidence is highly restricted by Rule 404, whereas the admissibility of habit evidence is authorized under Rule 406. Where the form of propensity is general and represents a behavioral inclination, it constitutes character governed by Rule 404; where the form of propensity is specific and connected with an identifiable prompting circumstance, it constitutes habit governed by Rule 406. While gradations of gray undoubtedly exist between these polar concepts, the law requires designation of the propensity as either character or habit to determine whether Rule 404 or Rule 406 applies.

Relevance of Habit; Corroboration Unnecessary. Rule 406 essentially serves two functions. First, the rule confirms the relevance of habit or routine practice when used to establish conduct which conforms with the habit or routine practice. In this regard, Rule 406 is dissimilar from most other evidentiary rules in Article IV. It is essentially a rule of admissibility rather than inadmissibility. Its function is declaratory in light of any confusion that might have been engendered by pre-Rule case law. The second function of Rule 406 is to confirm that the admissibility of habit or routine practice is not affected by the absence of eyewitnesses or corroboration. Again, the rule is declaratory.

Method of Proof. Habit evidence is normally used in the stimulus-response format. The proponent of habit evidence usually seeks to establish that a habitual response occurred on a particular occasion. In order to establish such a conclusion, the proponent must first establish that the habit, in fact, exists.

Use of Testimony. Proof of the existence of a habit is normally effected through the testimony of a person who has first-hand knowledge of the individual or business whose habit is sought to be proven. The witness must testify that he is familiar with the person or business, and that practice of meeting a particular kind of situation with a response that approaches invariability. Alternately and additionally, the witness may testify that he has observed the person or business conform to the habit on several occasions.

Illustration

A party might seek to establish that an individual punched a time clock on a particular day. The proponent of such a consequential fact could offer testimony from the individual or other witnesses that the individual punched the time clock on the day in question. Such testimony would be based upon the first-hand knowledge of these witnesses. In addition, however, the proponent may wish to offer habit evidence to reinforce the testimony of the witnesses. In order to establish the conclusion indicated by the habit evidence, the proponent would first have to establish the existence of the habit of the individual to invariably punch the time clock when he or she arrived at work. Then the proponent of the evidence would establish that the individual in fact arrived at work on the particular day in question. The evidence having established that the individual arrived on the day in question, the operation of the habit rule would permit the inference that the individual punched the time clock on the particular day in question. The use of habit evidence creates a permissible, but not a mandatory, inference that the habitual conduct occurred. In other words, the trier of fact may find that the habitual response occurred, but it is not required to make such a finding.

After establishing the existence of the habit, the proponent of the evidence then submits evidence that would prove that the stimulus for the response occurred on a particular occasion. Such stimulus can be established through any witness possessing firsthand knowledge as required by Rule 602. Having established the habit and the stimulus, the response will be inferentially indicated by the habit rule.

ADDITIONAL AUTHORITY

WEISSENBERGER'S FEDERAL EVIDENCE §§ 406.1–406.4

McCORMICK § 195

2 Weinstein 2d §§ 406.01–406.06

2 Mueller & Kirkpatrick §§ 123–126

1 Wigmore §§ 92–97

Cooper, *Recent Developments in Indiana Evidence Law*, 32 Ind. L. Rev. 811 (1999)

COMPARISON TO FEDERAL RULE

Indiana Rule 406 and Federal 406 are identical.

SIGNIFICANT CASES

Carlson v. Warren, 878 N.E.2d 844 (Ind. Ct. App. 2007) (an attorney's habit of engaging in dialogue with and observing the demeanor of individuals prior to executing deeds for those individuals is highly relevant habit evidence of whether the individual in question was incompetent or an involuntary participant in the transaction).

Morphew v. State, 672 N.E.2d 461 (Ind. Ct. App. 1996) (evidence supported finding that Bureau of Motor Vehicles (BMV) mailed notice of suspension to defendant's last known address, as required to support conviction for driving while suspended as habitual traffic offender; witness testified as to BMV's routine practice of mailing notices, and jury could infer that notice had been sent to then-current address, based on testimony by defendant's girlfriend about length of time defendant had lived at current address).

Bottoms v. B & M Coal Corp., 405 N.E.2d 82 (Ind. Ct. App. 1980) (admission of evidence of similar acts transactions rests within discretion of trial court).

In re Adoption of Dove, 174 Ind. App. 464, 368 N.E.2d 6 (1977) (where party attempts to introduce evidence of similar act to prove that certain act occurred, trial court has the discretion to admit such evidence).

RELEVANCY

Chapter 407

Rule 407. Subsequent Remedial Measures

Rule 407 reads as follows:

> When after an event, measures are taken which, if taken previously, would have made the event less likely to occur, evidence of the subsequent measures is not admissible to prove negligence or culpable conduct in connection with the event. This rule does not require the exclusion of evidence of subsequent measures when offered for another purpose, such as proving ownership, control, or feasibility of precautionary measures, if controverted, or impeachment.

* * * * *

ANALYSIS

Scope of Rule. Rule 407 excludes evidence of subsequent remedial actions where such actions would be offered to prove negligence or any type of culpable conduct in connection with the event which caused the injury. Virtually any kind of subsequent corrective action is within the scope of Rule 407. The rule is not directed only to the repair of a mechanical device after that device causes personal injury. The rule is sufficiently broad to apply to the discharge of an employee subsequent to an accident or to a change in product design. As a basic principle, the rule will apply to any measure, which if taken prior to the accident, would have made the injury less likely to occur.

When Admissible. As the second sentence of Rule 407 indicates, exclusion of evidence of subsequent remedial measures is only required where the evidence is offered to prove negligence or culpable conduct. Evidence of subsequent remedial action may be offered to establish other relevant issues within a case, such as ownership, control, or feasibility of precautionary measures. In order for such corrective actions to be admissible, the issue must be generally controverted in the case and the remedial action must be probative of the controverted consequential fact.

Judicial Discretion; Limiting Instruction. Where the subsequent remedial action is only minimally probative of an issue other than negligence or culpability, the trial judge possesses discretion to exclude the evidence of the corrective action on the basis of prejudice, confusion of the issues, or misleading the jury. *See* Rule 403, *above.* The trial judge should provide a limiting instruction pursuant to Rule 105 where evidence of remedial action is admitted on a theory of relevance outside the forbidden inferential pattern prohibited by the first sentence of Rule 407.

Illustration

Subsequent to an accident at a construction site, one of the subcontractors erects a barrier around the instrumentality of the injury. Where there is a dispute as to which subcontractor was responsible for the instrumentality of the injury, such action by a particular subcontractor would be probative of ownership or control. Under these facts, the subsequent remedial measure may be admissible on a theory other than to show negligence or culpability.

ADDITIONAL AUTHORITY

WEISSENBERGER'S FEDERAL EVIDENCE §§ 407.1–407.5

McCORMICK § 275 at 815–818

2 WEINSTEIN 2d §§ 407.01–407.10

2 MUELLER & KIRKPATRICK §§ 127–133

2 WIGMORE § 283

COMPARISON TO FEDERAL RULE

Although Indiana Rule 407 and Federal Rule 407 are similar, Federal Rule 407 was amended in 1997 to (1) extend the exclusionary principle to product liability and design defect cases, and (2) clarify that the rule applies only to remedial measures made after the event giving rise to the action. Indiana did not adopt the language of the 1997 amendments to the Federal Rules of Evidence that specifically extended Federal Rule 407 to product liability and design defect cases.

As amended, Federal Rule 407 makes it clear that its exclusionary principle applies only to remedial measures which are taken after the event that gave rise to the injury or harm. Thus, the Rule cannot be used to exclude evidence of changes which are made subsequent to the manufacture or design of a product, but prior to the occurrence that causes injury. However, as explained by the Advisory Committee, such evidence may still be excluded under Federal Rule 403 if it offers so great a danger of prejudice or confusion so as to outweigh the probative value of the evidence.

The 1997 amendments to the Federal Rules of Evidence also serve to end the tension among the circuits regarding the applicability of Federal Rule 407 to products liability actions by adopting the view of a majority of the circuits interpreting the rule. As noted, however, Indiana has not adopted the extension of the exclusionary principle to product liability or design defect cases. Under amended Federal Rule 407, evidence of subsequent remedial measures may not be used to prove either the existence of a defect in a product or in its design or the necessity for a warning or instruction to accompany the product. The amendment thus reflects the concerns of those who opposed the admissibility of evidence of subsequent remedial measures in products liability actions, and appears to recognize that such evidence is at best irrelevant and at worst highly prejudicial. In adopting this position,

Federal Rule 407 also ensures that the plaintiff retains the burden of persuasion in a products liability action.

The scope of the Federal Rule 407 exclusion should not be forgotten, however, particularly in products liability actions. Federal Rule 407 only excludes evidence of subsequent remedial measures when such evidence is offered to prove a defect in a product, a defect in a product's design, or a need for a warning or instruction. If the evidence is offered for other reasons, including proving the feasibility of precautionary measures or other reasons identified in the second sentence of Federal Rule 407, then its admission is not barred by the rule. The evidence may still be deemed inadmissible, though, if its potential for prejudice or confusion substantially outweighs the probative value of the evidence, as discussed under Federal Rule 403.

SIGNIFICANT CASES

Rimkus v. Northwest Colorado Ski Corp., 706 F.2d 1060 (10th Cir. 1983) (if defendant alleges contributory negligence on the part of plaintiff, evidence of subsequent remedial measures may be admissible on the issue of contributory negligence).

Utley v. Healy, 663 N.E.2d 229 (Ind. Ct. App. 1996) (testimony about terms of city work order relating to allegedly obstructed stop sign was admissible for purpose other than proving negligence, even if testimony was evidence of subsequent remedial measure; testimony was admissible to prove city was notified of dangerous condition and therefore city rather than defendant was responsible for accident).

Blackburn v. City of Rochester, 640 N.E.2d 1068 (Ind. Ct. App. 1994) (evidence of subsequent remedial measures is not generally admissible to prove even negligence because its probative value is so slight).

Dukett v. Mausness, 546 N.E.2d 1292 (Ind. Ct. App. 1989) (firing of an employee at fault held to be a subsequent remedial measure).

Welch v. Railroad Crossing, Inc., 488 N.E.2d 383 (Ind. Ct. App. 1986) (trial court has the discretion to admit evidence of subsequent remedial measures if the need for the evidence outweighs the danger of admitting the evidence).

Ragsdale v. K-Mart Corp., 468 N.E.2d 524 (Ind. Ct. App. 1984), *superseded by statute, Koske v. Townsend Engineering Co.*, 551 N.E.2d 437 (Ind. 1990), *superseded by statute as stated in In re Inlow Accident Litig.*, 2002 U.S. Dist. LEXIS 8318, CCH Prod. Liab. Rep. P16346 (in products liability action, trial court did not err in excluding evidence of a design change in the product).

Ortho Pharmaceutical Corp. v. Chapman, 180 Ind. App. 33, 388 N.E.2d 541 (1979) (in products liability case, the trial court erred in admitting a magazine advertisement for defendant's product dated after plaintiff's injury that contained a patient warning; advertisement was inadmissible because it constituted a post-occurrence remedial measure).

RELEVANCY

Chapter 408

Rule 408. Compromise and Offers to Compromise

Rule 408 reads as follows:

> Evidence of (1) furnishing or offering or promising to furnish, or (2) accepting or offering or promising to accept a valuable consideration in compromising or attempting to compromise a claim, which was disputed as to either validity or amount, is not admissible to prove liability for or invalidity of the claim or its amount. Evidence of conduct or statements made in compromise negotiations is likewise not admissible. This rule does not require exclusion when the evidence is offered for another purpose, such as proving bias or prejudice of a witness, negating a contention of undue delay, or proving an effort to obstruct a criminal investigation or prosecution. Compromise negotiations encompass alternative dispute resolution.

* * * * *

ANALYSIS

Scope of Rule. Rule 408 operates to exclude statements or other evidence relating to an offer of compromise or to a completed compromise. The policy of the Rule is to facilitate settlement by promoting candor in settlement discussions. Rule 408 also excludes evidence of conduct or statements made during the course of compromise negotiations, including statements accepting fault or liability made during a period in which negotiation and settlement is actively being sought by all parties—so-called "interim negotiating concessions." It should be noted that the exclusionary principle of Rule 408 does not apply where a dispute does not exist as to liability or the amount of the claim. The rule cannot be invoked where settlement discussions relate to an amount that is admittedly due. The amount of the claim must be in dispute, or alternatively, liability for the claim must be contested in order for the exclusionary principle to apply.

Rule 408 is incorporated into Ind. Alternative Dispute Resolution Rule 2.11, which provides:

> Mediation sessions shall be closed to all persons other than the parties of record, their legal representatives, and other invited persons.

> Mediators shall not be subject to process requiring the disclosure of any matter discussed during the mediation, but rather, such matter shall be considered

103

confidential and privileged in nature. The confidentiality requirement may not be waived by the parties, and an objection to the obtaining of testimony or physical evidence from mediation may be made by any party or by the mediators.

Accordingly, Rule 408 has been read in light of the ADR Rules and the purposes for which those conflict resolution mechanisms exist. Indiana Supreme Court, in *Horner v. Carter*, 981 N.E.2d 1210 (Ind. 2013), rejected an exception to Rule 408 akin to that under the parol evidence rule, noting that the strong policy favoring open disclosure and frankness during mediation mandates a robust confidentiality provision. The *Horner* Court rejected a suggestion by a lower appeals court that oral statements made in a prior mediation proceeding could be admitted as extrinsic evidence to aid in the construction of an ambiguous agreement.

Principle of Exclusion.   Rule 408 excludes evidence of compromise negotiations only where such evidence is offered to establish liability for, or invalidity of a claim or its amount. The principle of exclusion does not operate when compromise-related evidence is used to establish some other fact of consequence in the litigation. For example, evidence of statements during the course of settlement discussions are not made inadmissible by Rule 408 where the statements are offered to establish bias or prejudice of a witness, or where offered to show an effort to obstruct a criminal investigation or prosecution.

ADDITIONAL AUTHORITY

WEISSENBERGER'S FEDERAL EVIDENCE §§ 408.1–408.6

McCORMICK § 274

2 WEINSTEIN 2d §§ 408.01–408.10

2 MUELLER & KIRKPATRICK §§ 134–138

4 WIGMORE § 1061

Cooper, *Recent Developments in Indiana Evidence Law*, 32 IND. L. REV. 811 (1999)

COMPARISON TO FEDERAL RULE

Indiana Rule 408 is similar to Federal Rule 408 except that Indiana Rule 408 specifically states that alternative dispute resolution is included within compromise negotiations. Additionally, Federal Rule 408 provides that evidence otherwise discoverable is not to be excluded merely because it was presented in the course of settlement negotiations.

SIGNIFICANT CASES

Kritikos v. Palmer Johnson, Inc., 821 F.2d 418 (7th Cir. 1987) (trial court erred in admitting letters by one party proposing a compromise solution).

Bules v. Marshall County, 920 N.E.2d 247 (Rule 408 is designed to facilitate settlement by promoting candor in settlement discussions and therefore excludes interim negotiating concessions).

Horner v. Carter, 981 N.E.2d 1210 (Ind. 2013) (ADR Rule 2.11 incorporates Rule 408, and absolutely prohibits statements made during mediation, even to clarify an ambiguous provision in the settlement agreement).

Dep't of Local Gov't Fin. v. Commonwealth Edison Co. of Ind., Inc., 820 N.E.2d 1222 (Ind. 2005) (Rule 408 encourages parties to engage in settlement negotiations by prohibiting the use of settlement terms or settlement negotiations to prove liability for or invalidity of a claim or its amount; such a policy is persuasive in not providing settlements with precedential effect in property tax cases).

Worman Enters. v. Boone County Solid Waste Mgmt. Dist., 805 N.E.2d 369 (Ind. 2004) (interim negotiating concessions are included within the scope of Rule 408; accordingly, letters written in an attempt to reach a compromise regarding a permit reached under a settlement agreement of a prior lawsuit were inadmissible in the subsequent lawsuit).

Vernon v. Acton, 732 N.E.2d 805 (Ind. 2000) (until reduced to writing and signed by the parties, mediation settlement agreements must be considered as compromise settlement negotiations under Rule 408).

Bell v. State, 622 N.E.2d 450 (Ind. 1993) (criminal defendant's confession made during the course of plea discussions with the prosecutor held not admissible when case went to trial).

Manns v. State Dep't of Highways, 541 N.E.2d 929 (Ind. 1989), *superseded by statute*, ***R. R. Donnelley & Sons Co. v. N. Tex. Steel Co.***, 752 N.E.2d 112 (Ind. Ct. App. 2001) (in civil cases, the fact of a settlement involving a third party is admissible to the jury, but not the details of the settlement).

Gast v. Hall, 858 N.E.2d 154 (Ind. Ct. App. 2006) (observations made during mediation are not rendered inadmissible under ADR Rule 2.11, which is based on Rule 408, because the observations are not being used to prove liability or invalidity of a claim, but rather were admitted to prove someone's testamentary capacity).

Bridges v. Metromedia Steakhouse Co., L.P., 807 N.E.2d 162 (Ind. Ct. App. 2004) (nonverbal conduct is not included within the scope of Rule 408; accordingly, a witness's testimony concerning a party's appearance during settlement proceedings could not be characterized as evidence of an offer of valuable consideration in settlement of a disputed claim, and was thus admissible).

Shanabarger v. State, 798 N.E.2d 210 (Ind. Ct. App. 2003) (Rule 408 does not apply in criminal proceedings).

Boehning v. State Bd. of Tax Comm'rs, 763 N.E.2d 502 (Ind. Tax 2001) (the general purpose of Rule 408, which precludes admission of compromises and settlements, is to encourage parties to engage in settlement negotiations without a judgment or admission of liability or wrongdoing).

R. R. Donnelley & Sons Co. v. N. Tex. Steel Co., 752 N.E.2d 112 (Ind. Ct. App. 2001) (Rule 408 does not require the exclusion of any evidence otherwise discoverable merely because it is presented in the course of compromise negotiations).

Indiana Dep't of Envtl. Mgmt. v. Adapto, Inc., 717 N.E.2d 646 (Ind. Ct. App. 1999) (stipulations in settlement proceeding that failed as parties prepared to litigate the substantial compliance issue were not made for the purpose of compromise within the meaning of the rule).

Kerkhof v. Kerkhof, 703 N.E.2d 1108 (Ind. Ct. App. 1998) (trial court acted within its discretion in determining that husband's statement, that he would have to pay his wife an amount of money due to a pending divorce, was made during settlement negotiations and was therefore not competent evidence).

Simon v. Clark, 660 N.E.2d 634 (Ind. Ct. App. 1996) (in personal injury action, trial court rightly excluded plaintiff's proffered testimony of insurance adjuster to rebut testimony that plaintiff's injuries and medical expenses were due to subsequent accident; trial court could have found that proffered testimony as whole suggested to jury that defendant was liable for any damages resulting from accident in question).

Reed v. Dillon, 566 N.E.2d 585 (Ind. Ct. App. 1991) (where parties could not successfully agree to a settlement, the proposed settlement agreement was admissible to prove the terms of the agreement).

Burrington v. Howard, 521 N.E.2d 371 (Ind. Ct. App. 1988) (draft of a custody agreement held to be

RELEVANCY

inadmissible).

Chapter 409

Rule 409. Payment of Medical and Similar Expenses

Rule 409 reads as follows:

Evidence of paying or furnishing, or offering or promising to pay medical, hospital, or similar expenses occasioned by an injury, or damage to property is not admissible to prove liability for such injury or damages.

* * * * *

ANALYSIS

Scope of Rule. Rule 409 functions to exclude evidence of the furnishing, or the offering, or the promising to pay medical, hospital or similar expenses occasioned by an injury or damage to property where the evidence is offered to establish liability for the injury or harm. Rule 409 does not, however, render inadmissible conduct or statements which are part of the act of furnishing, or offering, or promising to pay expenses.

Express Admissions of Liability. Whenever an express admission of liability arises in conjunction with an offer to pay medical expenses, the trial judge should make an effort to sever any aspect of the statement which relates to the payment of medical expenses. The express admission of liability is admissible, whereas any offers to pay medical expenses would be insulated from admissibility by Rule 409.

Nonliability Issues. Unlike Rule 408 relating to compromises, Rule 409 does not expressly address the question of whether evidence relating to the payment of medical expenses is admissible to establish issues other than liability. Nevertheless, it is clear that Rule 409 only limits admissibility where the evidence of the payment or offer of payment is directed to liability. Other consequential facts may be established by such evidence.

ADDITIONAL AUTHORITY

WEISSENBERGER'S FEDERAL EVIDENCE §§ 409.1–409.4

MCCORMICK § 275 at 815–819

2 WEINSTEIN 2d §§ 409.01–409.03

2 MUELLER & KIRKPATRICK §§ 139–141

2 WIGMORE § 283(a) at 159–160

COMPARISON TO FEDERAL RULE

Indiana Rule 409 is similar to Federal Rule 409 but specifically includes damage to property. Federal Rule 409 is limited to an injury.

Chapter 410

Rule 410. Withdrawn Pleas and Offers

Rule 410 reads as follows:

> Evidence of a plea of guilty or admission of the charge which was later withdrawn, or a plea of *nolo contendere*, or of an offer so to plead to the crime charged or any other crime, or of statements made in connection with any of the foregoing withdrawn pleas or offers, is not admissible in any civil or criminal action, case or proceeding against the person who made the plea or offer.
>
> However, such a statement is admissible (i) in any proceeding wherein another statement made in the course of the same plea or plea discussion has been introduced and the statement ought in fairness to be considered contemporaneously with it, or (ii) in a criminal proceeding for perjury or false statement if the statement was made by the defendant under oath, on the record and in the presence of counsel.

* * * * *

ANALYSIS

Inadmissible Evidence. Rule 410 insulates from admissibility certain pleas and certain statements made in conjunction with the plea bargaining process. Rule 410 renders inadmissible any evidence of the following in any criminal or civil proceedings when offered against the person who made the plea or offer: (1) a plea of guilty that was later withdrawn; (2) an admission of the charge that was later withdrawn; (3) a plea of *nolo contendere*; (4) an offer to make such a plea to the crime charged or any other crime; (5) any statements made in the course of the foregoing pleas or offers.

Exceptions. Rule 410 further provides that statements otherwise rendered inadmissible under the rule are nevertheless admissible in the following situations: (1) when offered in a proceeding in which another statement made in the course of the same plea or plea discussions has been introduced and the statement should, in fairness, be considered contemporaneously with it; (2) when offered in a criminal proceeding for perjury or false statement if the statement was made by the defendant under oath, on the record, and in the presence of counsel.

Current Trends and New Developments

In *United States v. Mezzanatto*, 513 U.S. 196, 115 S. Ct. 797, 130 L. Ed. 2d 697 (1995), the U.S. Supreme Court held that an agreement to waive the exclusionary provisions of Federal Rule 410 and Federal Rule of Criminal Procedure 11(c)(6) is valid and enforceable absent some affirmative indication that the defendant entered the agreement unknowingly or involuntarily.

Practical Considerations

The preexisting common law rule governing exclusion of statements made during plea negotiations remains even after the adoption of the Indiana Rules of Evidence. In order for the statement to qualify for a plea negotiation privilege, (1) defendant must have been charged with a crime *at the time statement was made*, (2) statement must have been made to an official with *authority* to enter a binding plea agreement, and (3) whether parties were undertaking plea negotiations at time statement is made is a question for the trial court. For discussion of this rule, *see Gilliam v. State*, 650 N.E.2d 45 (Ind. Ct. App. 1995).

Apologies. Rule 410 has been read broadly by the Indiana Supreme Court in an effort to encourage apologies or expressions of regret or sorrow made by criminal defendants. In *Gonzalez v. State*, 929 N.E.2d 699 (Ind. 2010), the Court ruled that a statement made to a victim or to the court in an effort to gain acceptance of a plea agreement by the court are statements "in connection with a plea agreement" and thus covered by Rule 410. Accordingly, such statements will be inadmissible, but only if they are made during the course of plea discussions or within the plea bargaining process.

ADDITIONAL AUTHORITY

Weissenberger's Federal Evidence §§ 410.1–410.5

McCormick § 265

2 Weinstein 2d §§ 410.01–410.11

2 Mueller & Kirkpatrick §§ 142–151

4 Wigmore §§ 1066–1067

COMPARISON TO FEDERAL RULE

Rule 410 is modeled after Uniform Rule of Evidence 410 with the second paragraph taken from Federal Rule 410.

SIGNIFICANT CASES

United States v. Mezzanatto, 513 U.S. 196, 115 S. Ct. 797, 130 L. Ed. 2d 697 (1995) (U.S. Supreme Court held that an agreement to waive the exclusionary provisions of Federal Rule 410 and Fed. R. Crim. P. 11(c)(6) is valid and enforceable absent some affirmative indication that the defendant entered the agreement unknowingly or involuntarily).

Gonzalez v. State, 929 N.E.2d 699 (Ind. 2010) (a defendant's statements made to a victim or to the court in an effort to gain acceptance of a plea agreement by the court are statements in connection with a plea agreement and therefore are not admissible in evidence pursuant to Rule 410).

Reed v. State, 748 N.E.2d 381 (Ind. 2001) (even if the state's taped interview with a key prosecution witness contained statements made in connection with a contemplated plea agreement, which could not be used against that witness if the agreement were not finalized, no privilege insulated the witness's dialogue with the state from discovery or use in defendant's case because the use of plea negotiations is prohibited only as to the negotiating accused person).

Bell v. State, 622 N.E.2d 450 (Ind. 1993) (defendant's confession made during plea discussions held to be inadmissible pursuant to state statute; court noted that statute was consistent with Rule 410).

Martin v. State, 537 N.E.2d 491 (Ind. 1989) (where defendant made statements to a police officer before defendant was charged with a crime and the officer had no authority to enter into a binding plea agreement, the statements were admissible).

Chase v. State, 528 N.E.2d 784 (Ind. 1988) (a statement made during a plea bargain attempt will be excluded only where the statement was made to a party that has the authority to make a binding agreement).

Shanabarger v. State, 798 N.E.2d 210 (Ind. Ct. App. 2003) (a conversation in anticipation of the course of action to follow should the state file a death penalty request amounted to a discussion of future plea negotiations and was thus subject to exclusion under Rule 410).

Gilliam v. State, 650 N.E.2d 45 (Ind. Ct. App. 1995) (defendant's statements made to police officer who lacked authority to enter binding plea agreement are not privileged plea negotiations and are admissible; for statement to qualify for plea negotiation privilege, defendant must have been charged with crime at time of statement and statement must have been made to person with authority to enter binding plea agreement; whether parties were undertaking plea negotiations when defendant made incriminating statements is question of fact for trial court).

Mundt v. State, 612 N.E.2d 566 (Ind. Ct. App. 1993) (statement given after plea agreement was already reached was not barred by state statute regarding plea negotiations).

Hensley v. State, 573 N.E.2d 913 (Ind. Ct. App. 1991) (trial court erred in permitting police officer to testify at sentencing regarding an uncharged crime to which defendant confessed during failed plea negotiations).

State v. Wolff, 545 N.E.2d 39 (Ind. Ct. App. 1989) (statements made by defendant under oath at his guilty plea hearing which allegedly misrepresented his prior record could serve as a basis for a subsequent perjury charge).

Tyree v. State, 518 N.E.2d 814 (Ind. Ct. App. 1988) (where defendant withdrew guilty plea, statements made by defendant forming factual basis for the plea are not admissible).

Chapter 411

Rule 411. Liability Insurance

Rule 411 reads as follows:

> Evidence that a person was or was not insured against liability is not admissible upon the issue whether the person acted negligently or otherwise wrongfully. This rule does not require the exclusion of evidence of insurance against liability when offered for another purpose, such as proof of agency, ownership, or control, or bias or prejudice of a witness.

*   *   *   *   *

ANALYSIS

Policy and Rationale.   Rule 411 provides that the fact that a person was or was not insured against liability is not admissible in order to establish negligent or wrongful conduct by the individual. The rule is designed to minimize unfair prejudice relating to the consideration of liability insurance. On one hand, the probative value of liability insurance is exceedingly low regarding issues of liability. On the other hand, the risks of prejudice are extremely high.

Scope of Rule.   The exclusionary principle of Rule 411 applies by its express terms to the fault of a defendant and to the possible contributory negligence or other fault of a plaintiff. Also, it should be noted that Rule 411 specifically excludes evidence of not only the existence, but also the nonexistence of insurance where such evidence is offered to establish negligence or wrongful conduct.

Purpose of Evidence Offered.   The exclusionary operation of Rule 411 applies only where liability insurance is offered to establish negligence or culpability. Where liability insurance is offered to establish some other consequential fact, the exclusionary principle will not prevent the admissibility of the evidence.

As the second sentence to Rule 411 confirms, evidence of liability insurance is admissible where offered to prove some other fact such as agency, ownership or control, or to establish the bias or prejudice of a witness.

RELEVANCY

113

Illustration

Where a defendant claims that he is not the owner of a vehicle that was involved in an automobile accident, evidence that the defendant had purchased insurance for that vehicle may be admissible as tending to establish the fact that he owned the vehicle or had sufficient control over it to be liable for its use. If such evidence were admitted, it would be subject to a limiting instruction under Rule 105.

ADDITIONAL AUTHORITY

WEISSENBERGER'S FEDERAL EVIDENCE §§ 411.1–411.4

McCORMICK § 201

2 WEINSTEIN 2d §§ 411.01–411.06

2 MUELLER & KIRKPATRICK §§ 151–154

2 WIGMORE § 282

COMPARISON TO FEDERAL RULE

Indiana Rule 411 and Federal Rule 411 are identical.

SIGNIFICANT CASES

Pickett v. Kolb, 250 Ind. 449, 237 N.E.2d 105 (1968) (evidence that a defendant carries liability insurance is irrelevant and potentially prejudicial).

Mullins v. Parkview Hosp., Inc., 830 N.E.2d 45 (Ind. Ct. App. 2005), *aff'd in part and superseded in part*, 865 N.E.2d 608 (Ind. 2007), (Rule 411 prohibits a finding that contractual agreements between one of the parties and a third person establishes the liability of the party; the fact that a facility was contractually obligated to carry malpractice insurance on its student learners who spent time at a party hospital, and thus contemplated being liable for the negligence of its students, cannot be admitted for the purpose of estopping the facility from claiming it was not liable).

Stone v. Stakes, 755 N.E.2d 220 (Ind. Ct. App. 2001) (requiring law firms to indicate their association with an insurance company as part of their name to prospective jurors does not impinge upon Rule 411's proscription against admissibility of the existence of insurance).

Osborne v. Wenger, 572 N.E.2d 1343 (Ind. Ct. App. 1991) (plaintiff may not introduce evidence of insurance coverage for a compensatory damage claim after defendant testified concerning his small net worth on a punitive damage claim).

Spratt v. Alsup, 468 N.E.2d 1059 (Ind. Ct. App. 1984) (reversible error where evidence that a party has or does not have insurance is admitted).

Antcliff v. Datzman, 436 N.E.2d 114 (Ind. Ct. App. 1982) (if issue of insurance is admitted, the trial court may declare a mistrial or admonish the jury to disregard the insurance evidence and allow the case to continue).

Rust v. Watson, 141 Ind. App. 59, 215 N.E.2d 42 (1966) (evidence of insurance coverage may prejudice case because jury may award higher damages if aware that defendant will not bear the loss).

Chapter 412

Rule 412. Evidence of Past Sexual Conduct

Rule 412 reads as follows:

(a) In a prosecution for a sex crime, evidence of the past sexual conduct of a victim or witness may not be admitted, except:

(1) evidence of the victim's or of a witness's past sexual conduct with the defendant;

(2) evidence which shows that some person other than the defendant committed the act upon which the prosecution is founded;

(3) evidence that the victim's pregnancy at the time of trial was not caused by the defendant; or

(4) evidence of conviction for a crime to impeach under Rule 609.

(b) If a party proposes to offer evidence under this rule, the following procedure must be followed:

(1) A written motion must be filed at least ten days before trial describing the evidence. For good cause, a party may file such motion less than ten days before trial.

(2) The court shall conduct a hearing and issue an order stating what evidence may be introduced and the nature of the questions to be permitted.

(c) If the state acknowledges that the victim's pregnancy is not due to the conduct of the defendant, the court may instruct the jury accordingly, in which case other evidence concerning the pregnancy may not be admitted.

---

* * * * *

ANALYSIS

Function of Rule. Rule 412(a) precludes the admission of evidence of either the victim's or a witness's past sexual conduct in a criminal case unless the evidence falls within the rule's exceptions. First, evidence of the victim's or a witness's past sexual conduct is admissible if it involved defendant. The rule also permits the admission of such evidence if it shows that some person other than the defendant committed the criminal act. Third, evidence that the victim's pregnancy at the time of trial was not caused by defendant is not excluded by Rule 412. Finally, Rule 412 provides that evidence of past sexual conduct is admissible if it amounts to evidence of conviction for a crime to impeach the victim or witness pursuant to Rule 609. Rule 412 is based on and replaces Indiana's rape shield statute, Ind. Code § 35-37-4-4.

Notice and Hearing. Rule 412(b) provides a notice procedure that must be followed if a party intends to offer evidence under Rule 412. Pursuant to 412(b)(1), the party must file a written motion at least 10 days prior to trial describing the evidence. The trial court should hold a hearing to determine if the proffered evidence falls within one of Rule 412(a)'s exceptions.

Pregnancy. Finally, Rule 412(c) provides that if the state acknowledges that the defendant is not responsible for the victim's pregnancy, the trial court may instruct the jury of that fact. In that situation, no further evidence concerning the pregnancy shall be received.

INCORPORATED STATUTES

Ind. Code § 35-37-4-4. [Sex crimes; admissibility of evidence of past sexual conduct; procedure]

(a) In a prosecution for a sex crime as defined in IC 35-42-4:

    (1)   evidence of the victim's past sexual conduct;

    (2)   evidence of the past sexual conduct of a witness other than the accused;

    (3)   opinion evidence of the victim's past sexual conduct;

    (4)   opinion evidence of the past sexual conduct of a witness other than the accused;

    (5)   reputation evidence of the victim's past sexual conduct; and

    (6)   reputation evidence of the past sexual conduct of a witness other than the accused;
        may not be admitted, nor may reference be made to this evidence in the presence of the jury, except as provided in this chapter.

(b) Notwithstanding subsection (a), evidence:

    (1)   of the victim's or a witness's past sexual conduct with the defendant;

    (2)   which in a specific instance of sexual activity shows that some person other than the defendant committed the act upon which the prosecution is founded; or

    (3)   that the victim's pregnancy at the time of trial was not caused by the defendant;

may be introduced if the judge finds, under the procedure provided in subsection (c) of this section, that it is material to a fact at issue in the case and that its inflammatory or prejudicial nature does not outweigh its probative value.

(c) If the defendant or the state proposes to offer evidence described in subsection (b) of this section, the following procedure must be followed:

    (1)   The defendant or the state shall file a written motion not less than ten (10) days before trial stating that it has an offer of proof concerning evidence described in subsection (b) and its relevancy to the case. This motion shall be accompanied by an affidavit in which the offer of proof is stated.

    (2)   If the court finds that the offer of proof is sufficient, the court shall order a hearing

out of the presence of the jury, and at the hearing allow the questioning of the victim or witness regarding the offer of proof made by the defendant or the state. At the conclusion of the hearing, if the court finds that evidence proposed to be offered by the defendant or the state regarding the sexual conduct of the victim or witness is admissible under subsection (b) of this section, the court shall make an order stating what evidence may be introduced by the defendant or the state and the nature of the questions to be permitted. The defendant or the state may then offer evidence under the order of the court.

(d) If new information is discovered within ten (10) days before trial or during the course of the trial that might make evidence described in subsection (b) of this chapter admissible, the judge shall order a hearing out of the presence of the jury to determine whether the proposed evidence is admissible under this chapter.

(e) This section does not limit the right of either the state or the accused to impeach credibility by a showing of prior felony convictions.

(f) If:

(1)   a defendant files a motion under subsection (c)(1) concerning evidence described in subsection (b)(3); and

(2)   the state acknowledges that the victim's pregnancy is not due to the conduct of the defendant;

the court shall instruct the jury that the victim's pregnancy is not due to the conduct of the defendant. However, other evidence concerning the pregnancy may not be admitted, and further reference to the pregnancy may not be made in the presence of the jury.

ADDITIONAL AUTHORITY

Weissenberger's Federal Evidence §§ 412.1–412.7

2 Weinstein 2d §§ 412.01–412.05

COMPARISON TO FEDERAL RULE

A proposed amendment to Federal Rule 412 took effect December 1, 1994. Federal Rule 412 differs from Indiana Rule 412 in several respects. First, Federal Rule 412 applies in both criminal and civil proceedings, and in any case involving sexual misconduct, whether or not the alleged victim or the accused person is a party in the case. Second, Federal Rule 412 specifically bars evidence relating to the alleged victim's sexual predisposition, as well as the alleged victim's sexual behavior. Both Federal Rule 412 and Indiana Rule 412 provide exceptions for situations in which evidence of incidents of sexual behavior shall be admitted. However, Federal Rule 412 permits the admission of such evidence in cases where barring such evidence would result in a violation of the constitutional rights of a defendant. Additionally, Federal Rule 412 provides a balancing test for a trial court to follow in admitting evidence of an alleged victim's sexual predisposition or sexual behavior in a civil case. Both Federal Rule 412 and Indiana Rule 412 provide for a notice and hearing procedure when a party proposes to offer evidence under the rule, although the specific procedures are different.

SIGNIFICANT CASES

Olden v. Kentucky, 488 U.S. 227, 109 S. Ct. 480, 102 L. Ed. 2d 513 (1988) (where consent was the issue in a rape case, court erred in not admitting a black defendant's evidence that the white victim was living with a black man, and that the rape claim may have been an attempt to protect that relationship).

Stephens v. Miller, 13 F.3d 998 (7th Cir. 1994) (rape shield statute did not unconstitutionally deprive defendant of his right to testify on his own behalf; court applied statute to prohibit defendant from testifying regarding certain statements he allegedly made to the victim during what he claimed was consensual sexual intercourse; the statements were barred because they implicated the victim's past sexual conduct).

Baker v. State, 750 N.E.2d 781 (Ind. 2001) (prohibiting defendant on rape charge from offering evidence of his alleged recent and regular sexual relationship with victim was reversible error, as the defense on the charge was consent and only the defendant and victim were present).

Miller v. State, 716 N.E.2d 367 (Ind. 1999) (evidence of victim's past sexual relationship with defendant was improperly excluded but defendant failed to preserve error for appeal because the evidence was not offered at trial—motion *in limine* was insufficient to preserve error; requirement of offering evidence of victim's past sexual relationship at trial is explicitly applicable to exclusions under the rape shield doctrines, even though Rule 412 and the rape shield laws include specific provisions for ruling on the admissibility of the proposed evidence after pretrial notice and hearing).

State v. Walton, 715 N.E.2d 824 (Ind. 1999) (as matter of first impression, (1) evidence of prior false accusations of rape made by complaining witness does not constitute evidence of "prior sexual conduct" for purposes of common law exception to rape shield statute; (2) general exclusionary rule applicable to proof of specific instances of untruthfulness does not bar such evidence; and (3) evidence was sufficient to permit conclusion that complaining witness had in fact made such accusations).

Jenkins v. State, 627 N.E.2d 789 (Ind. 1993) (rape shield statute held to apply even after rape victim's death).

Barnes v. Barnes, 603 N.E.2d 1337 (Ind. 1992), *superseded by statute*, ***Sears Roebuck & Co. v. Manuilov***, 742 N.E.2d 453 (Ind. 2001) (rape shield law is not applicable in civil cases).

Thomas v. State, 471 N.E.2d 677 (Ind. 1984) (trial court ruled that defendant was prohibited from showing that the victim had intercourse with her boyfriend prior to the alleged crime and that the boyfriend could have been the source of the semen found in the victim's vagina; court held that this ruling was within the trial court's discretion).

Blair v. State, 877 N.E.2d 1225 (Ind. Ct. App. 2007), *transfer denied*, 891 N.E.2d 40 (2008) (Rule 412 is designed to exclude evidence of a complaining witness's prior sexual conduct only, and evidence of prior false accusations of rape made by a complaining witness does not constitute prior sexual conduct for rape shield purposes; evidence of prior false accusations may be admitted only if (1) the complaining witness admits that she had made a prior false accusation of rape; or (2) the accusation is demonstrably false).

Redding v. State, 844 N.E.2d 1067 (Ind. Ct. App. 2006) ("partial corroboration" occurs when the state introduces evidence of the victim's physical or psychological condition to prove that sexual contact occurred and, by implication, that the defendant was the perpetrator; when this occurs, the defendant should be permitted to introduce evidence that someone else was responsible for the condition admitted).

Candler v. State, 837 N.E.2d 1100 (Ind. Ct. App. 2005) (under Rule 412, the admission of evidence relating to a victim's past sexual conduct is inadmissible, subject to the exceptions listed in the Rule and the common law exceptions that survived the Rule; these common law exceptions are:

(1) when the victim has admitted that his or her prior accusation of rape is false; or (2) when the victim's prior accusation is demonstrably false, that is, when the charges have been disproved).

Fugett v. State, 812 N.E.2d 846 (Ind. Ct. App. 2004) (Rule 412 embodies the basic principles of Indiana's Rape Shield Statute, but was not adopted verbatim; accordingly, to the extent that any differences in the two provisions exist, Rule 412 controls).

Sallee v. State, 785 N.E.2d 645 (Ind. Ct. App. 2003) (evidence of a victim's past sexual conduct may not be admitted, with the exceptions noted in Rule 412; in addition, a common law exception also exists, which provides that evidence of a prior accusation of rape is admissible if (1) the victim has admitted that her prior accusation of rape is false, or (2) the victim's prior accusation is demonstrably false; the rule requires a defendant to give written notice any time the defendant proposes to offer evidence under both the general rule prohibiting the admission of past sexual conduct and the exceptions listed thereafter).

Law v. State, 797 N.E.2d 1157 (Ind. Ct. App. 2003) (evidence of a victim's past sexual conduct with a defendant is admissible in a prosecution for a sex crime).

Williams v. State, 779 N.E.2d 610 (Ind. Ct. App. 2002) (the common law exception to the rule excluding evidence of a victim's prior sexual history, thus permitting the admission of the victim's prior false accusations of rape, also applies to prior false accusations of other sex crimes).

Sallee v. State, 777 N.E.2d 1204 (Ind. Ct. App. 2002) (evidence concerning the victim's prior sexual history is not admissible during a prosecution for rape and other sex crimes; none of the proffered evidence fit within one of the exceptions for the admission of past sexual conduct of a victim, and the evidence sought to be introduced did not make the victim's testimony any more or less likely).

Turner v. State, 720 N.E.2d 440 (Ind. Ct. App. 1999) (in child molestation case, trial court did not abuse discretion in excluding evidence that child was seen partially clothed with a neighborhood boy and also seen masturbating because such evidence were not specific instances of sexual activity that showed some other person other than defendant committed the acts).

Little v. State, 650 N.E.2d 343 (Ind. Ct. App. 1995) (rape shield statute prevented defendant from asking victim about her alleged statement to him concerning her past sexual experience, by which defendant hoped to support his alleged good faith belief that defendant was over age of consent; policy of rape shield law is to shield sex crime victims from general inquiry into their past sexual conduct and to keep victims from feeling that they are on trial).

Knisley v. State, 474 N.E.2d 513 (Ind. Ct. App. 1985), *disapproved*, *Stout v. State*, 612 N.E.2d 1076 (Ind. Ct. App. 1993) (rape shield law protects witnesses from having to be cross-examined concerning their sexual history).

Killian v. State, 467 N.E.2d 1265 (Ind. Ct. App. 1984), *vacated on other grounds by* 512 N.E.2d 411 (Ind. 1987) (rape shield act prevented the admission of evidence that the male victim of a homosexual rape was himself charged with child molesting in an unrelated incident).

RELEVANCY

Chapter 413

Rule 413. Medical Expenses

Rule 413 reads as follows:

Statements of charges for medical, hospital or other health care expenses for diagnosis or treatment occasioned by an injury are admissible into evidence. Such statements shall constitute prima facie evidence that the charges are reasonable.

---

* * * * *

ANALYSIS

In most tort cases, expert testimony is usually required to prove the reasonableness and necessity of medical expenses as part of a damage calculation. Rule 413 provides a simpler method when there is no substantial issue of reasonableness and the damages were caused by the actionable conduct. Accordingly, Rule 413 provides that written statements of charges for medical expenses for diagnosis or treatment of an injury are admissible and are prima facie evidence that the charges are reasonable. The opposing party may, of course, come forward with contrary evidence or reasonableness, which may or may not take the form of expert testimony. It should be noted that, under many agreements between insurance companies and medical providers, the amount charged and the amount paid for medical expenses may be different. The jury may decide that the reasonable value of medical care is the amount originally billed, the amount the medical provider accepted as payment, or some amount in between. Any difference between the original amount of a medical bill and the amount accepted as the bill's full payment is not a "benefit" under the collateral source rule because it is not a payment, but both the original bill and the discounted amount are evidence relevant to the reasonable value of medical expenses.

The Federal Rules of Evidence do not contain a counterpart to Indiana Rule 413.

ADDITIONAL AUTHORITY

WEISSENBERGER'S FEDERAL EVIDENCE §§ 803.28–803.36

MCCORMICK §§ 304–314

2 WEINSTEIN 2d §§ 413.01–413.05

2 MUELLER & KIRKPATRICK §§ 139–141

3 WIGMORE §§ 735–755

5 Wigmore §§ 1517–1561

COMPARISON TO FEDERAL RULE

The Federal Rules do not contain a comparable provision.

SIGNIFICANT CASES

Stanley v. Walker, 906 N.E.2d 852 (Ind. 2009) (if "discounted" medical expenses under an agreement between an insurance company and a medical provider may be introduced without referencing the existence of insurance, they may be used to determine the reasonable value of medical services).

Butler v. Ind. Dep't of Ins., 904 N.E.2d 198 (Ind. 2009) (under Indiana's wrongful death statute, Ind. Code § 34-23-1-2(c)(3)(A), the common law standard as set forth in Rule 413 to recover the reasonable value of medical care and treatment is not applicable; instead, the only those damages that are necessitated by the wrongful conduct, that is, actually paid, are permitted).

Cook v. Whitsell-Sherman, 796 N.E.2d 271 (Ind. 2003) (under Rule 413, bills for actual charges for past medical treatment are admissible, but not written statements purporting to estimate future medical costs).

Smith v. Syd's, Inc., 598 N.E.2d 1065 (Ind. 1992) (where party seeks to recover medical expenses, party must prove that the expenses were necessary and reasonable; party can prove reasonableness by submitting the bill paid, because it is assumed the party would not have paid an unreasonable bill; expert testimony is generally offered to prove necessity).

Wolfe v. Estate of Custer, 867 N.E.2d 589 (Ind. Ct. App. 2007), *transfer denied*, 878 N.E.2d 212 (Ind. 2007) (although expert testimony is usually required to prove the reasonableness and necessity of medical expenses as part of a damage calculation, Rule 413 provides a simpler method when there is no substantial issue of reasonableness and were caused by the tort; the opposing party may offer contrary evidence, including expert testimony).

Wilkinson v. Swafford, 811 N.E.2d 374 (Ind. Ct. App. 2004) (unless the opposing party presents evidence to dispute that medical treatment and the resulting expenses are necessary, medical bills are admissible to show not only the reasonableness of the charge, but also that the medical services performed were necessary).

Burge v. Teter, 808 N.E.2d 124 (Ind. Ct. App. 2004) (Rule 413 provides a simpler method of proving the amount of medical expenses when there is no substantial issue that they are reasonable and were caused by the tort).

Washington County Mem. Hosp. v. Hattabaugh, 717 N.E.2d 929 (Ind. Ct. App. 1999) (statement of charges for medical or health care expenses constitutes prima facie evidence that charges are reasonable; although amount of statement is not conclusive, it is prima facie proof of the amount owed on the account).

Chemco Transport, Inc. v. Conn, 506 N.E.2d 1111 (Ind. Ct. App. 1987) (paid medical bills were relevant to show damages incurred; bills tended to prove the reasonableness of the expenses).

V
PRIVILEGES

PRIVILEGES

123

Chapter 501

Rule 501. Privileges

Rule 501 reads as follows:

(a) General Rule. Except as provided by constitution or statute as enacted or interpreted by the courts of this State or by these or other rules promulgated by the Indiana Supreme Court or by principles of common law in light of reason and experience, no person has a privilege to:

    (1) refuse to be a witness;

    (2) refuse to disclose any matter;

    (3) refuse to produce any object or writing; or

    (4) prevent another from being a witness or disclosing any matter or producing any object or writing.

(b) Waiver of Privilege by Voluntary Disclosure. Subject to the provisions of Rule 502, a person with a privilege against disclosure waives the privilege if the person or person's predecessor while holder of the privilege voluntarily and intentionally discloses or consents to disclosure of any significant part of the privileged matter. This rule does not apply if the disclosure itself is privileged.

(c) Privileged Matter Disclosed Under Compulsion or Without Opportunity to Claim Privilege. A claim of privilege is not defeated by a disclosure which was (1) compelled erroneously or (2) made without opportunity to claim the privilege.

(d) Comment Upon or Inference from Claim of Privilege; Instruction. Except with respect to a claim of the privilege against self-incrimination in a civil case:

    (1) *Comment or inference not permitted.* The claim of a privilege, whether in the present proceeding, or upon a prior occasion, is not a proper subject of comment by judge or counsel. No inference may be drawn therefrom.

    (2) *Claiming privilege without knowledge of jury.* In jury cases, proceedings shall be conducted, to the extent practicable, so as to facilitate the making of claims of privilege without the knowledge of the jury.

(3) *Jury instruction.* Upon request, any party against whom the jury might draw an adverse inference from a claim of privilege is entitled to an instruction that no inference may be drawn therefrom.

*   *   *   *   *

ANALYSIS

Overview. Rule 501 recognizes privileges provided by constitution, statute, and common law and simultaneously provides for specific procedural matters governing privileges. The Rule should be read in conjunction with Rule 502, which was enacted in 2012 to provide some measure of protection for inadvertent disclosures of privileged matter during litigation. In addition to these Rules, other Evidence Rules are pertinent to privileges. Rules 101 and 104 relate to procedural aspects of the application of privilege laws. Rule 101 sets forth the broad applicability of privilege law by providing in subdivision (b) that "[t]he rule with respect to privileges applies at all stages of all actions, cases and proceedings conducted under these rules." Rule 104 provides that the question as to whether a privilege exists in a given situation is a preliminary question to be determined by the trial court. In making its determination, as well as making the determination as to all preliminary questions of admissibility, the court remains bound by the rules and statutes with respect to privilege even though it is not bound at this stage by other evidentiary rules.

Policy Basis of Privileges. In understanding privilege law, it should be appreciated that a privilege is essentially a personal right to preserve the confidentiality of certain private communications. Inadmissibility is an incidental and derivative ramification of this right. Consequently, privilege law is anchored in considerations of policy that exist independently of the usual evidentiary concerns with accuracy and reliability of evidence.

Effect of a Privilege. A privilege may involve a refusal to testify, a refusal to disclose a matter during the discovery stage of litigation, a refusal to produce real proof, or the right to prevent other persons from doing any of these things. A privilege permits a person to resist any judicial or governmental process aimed at eliciting protected information. As such, it is the only right that relieves an individual from the duty of revealing facts in response to governmental or judicial process and from the corollary risk of contempt for failure to respond.

Covered Communications. Privileges generally only apply to privileged communications. In this regard, the protected status applies to oral or written communications. It may additionally extend in certain instances to nonverbal actions and to knowledge gained by means of observation. As a further qualification, privileges generally attach only to communications made in confidence. Consequently, a privilege will not apply where confidentiality is compromised by a showing that the communication was made in the presence of a third person who was not essential to the transaction or communication. Nevertheless, third persons who are essential to the communication will not destroy confidentiality.

Statutory Privileges. Indiana has followed the lead of most states by codifying most of its privilege law in statutory form. Although privileges historically were primarily the product of common law, most of Indiana's privileges are now governed by the Indiana legislature. A sampling of these statutory provisions are set out at the conclusion of this Chapter. Although a conclusive discussion of these privileges is beyond the scope of this manual, a brief description of some of the noteworthy ones is set out below.

The testimonial privileges are covered primarily in Ind. Code § 34-46-3-1. The statute protects certain communications made within four types of confidential relationships. The relationships covered by the statute are those between: An attorney and his client, a physician and his patient, a clergyman and his parishioner, and a husband and a wife.

Another Indiana Statute pertinent to the concept of privileges is found in Ind. Code § 34-46-4-1. This statute allows a reporter or other employee of a news organization to withhold the source of any information "procured or obtained in the course of his employment" in any legal proceeding. Additionally, pursuant to Ind. Code § 34-30-15-1, all communications to and records of a medical peer review committee are privileged. This statute provides broad protection to committee activities by providing that proceedings and records of review committees are immune from discovery or introduction in evidence "in any judicial or administrative proceeding." Another "privilege," in a sense, is codified at Ind. Code. § 34-29-2-1, which provides that the Governor of the State of Indiana has an absolute privilege to be free from arrest on civil process, and from obeying any subpoena to testify. A distinctive feature of the "Governor's privilege" is that it is absolute: the statute does not contain any limits on the privilege or exceptions.

Indiana's "victim advocate privilege" at Ind. Code § 35-37-6-9 protects victims, victim advocates, and victim service providers from being compelled to give testimony, or produce records or other information concerning confidential communications in a judicial or administrative hearing. In *State v. Fromme (In re Crisis Connection, Inc.)*, 949 N.E.2d 789 (Ind. 2011), the Indiana Supreme Court held that this provision creates a strong shield for victims and victim advocates, and testimony or information that falls within this provision is not subject to additional analysis or balancing to determining its admissibility. If the evidence satisfies the provisions of the statute, it is absolutely privileged.

Competency Distinguished; Work Product Doctrine Distinguished. Rules of privilege should be distinguished from two other doctrines. The first of these is Rule 601 governing competency. While both privilege and competency involve limitations on who may testify and the subject matter of testimony, these distinct concepts approach the subject from entirely different policies. Competency, on one hand, generally concerns the reliability of witnesses. Privilege, on the other hand, precludes the introduction of possibly reliable testimony due to extrinsic policy considerations directed toward protecting certain confidential relationships. Privilege should also be distinguished from the work product doctrine set forth in Trial Rule 26(b)(3). This doctrine may operate to shield from discovery the attorney's work product generated in anticipation of litigation. As such, its design is to preserve the adversary nature of our judicial system, and this policy is distinguishable from that supporting the protection of confidential relationships.

PRIVILEGES

Current Trends and New Developments

In *Swidler & Berlin v. United States*, 524 U.S. 399, 118 S. Ct. 2081, 141 L. Ed. 2d 379

(1998), a controversy arising out of grand jury investigation into the firing of White House travel office employees in which notes from a conversation between a deceased White House official and his private attorney were subpoenaed, the U.S. Supreme Court confirmed that the attorney-client privilege survives the client's death. The district court had held that the notes were protected by the privilege, but the appellate court reversed, holding that the attorney-client privilege was not absolute and that there is a posthumous exception to the privilege for communications whose relative importance to particular criminal litigation is substantial. The Supreme Court reversed, holding that the notes were protected by the attorney-client privilege.

The Supreme Court began its analysis by stating that its "inquiry must be guided by 'the principles of common law . . . as interpreted by the courts . . . in light of reason and experience.'" The Court then reemphasized the importance of keeping attorney-client communications confidential as such confidentiality encourages clients to communicate fully and frankly with counsel, and noted that posthumous disclosure may be as feared as disclosure during a client's lifetime. Further, the Court noted, no case law supports the conclusion that the attorney-client privilege operates differently in criminal cases than in civil cases. Finally, the Court stated that such an exception to the privilege would result in uncertainty as a client may not know, at the time he discloses information to an attorney, whether it will later be relevant to a civil or criminal matter, let alone whether it will be of substantial importance to a criminal investigation.

INCORPORATED STATUTES

Ind. Code § 20-1-1.9-6. [Disclosure of information]

A school psychologist who is endorsed under this chapter may not disclose any information acquired from persons with whom the school psychologist has dealt in a professional capacity, except under the following circumstances:

(1) Trials for homicide when the disclosure related directly to the fact or immediate circumstances of the homicide.

(2) Proceedings:

(A) to determine mental competency; or

(B) in which a defense of mental incompetency is raised.

(3) Civil or criminal actions against a school psychologist for malpractice.

(4) Upon an issue as to the validity of a document.

(5) If the school psychologist has the expressed consent of the client or, in the case of a client's death or disability, the express consent of the client's legal representative.

(6) Circumstances under which privileged communication is lawfully invalidated.

Ind. Code § 20-6.1-6-15. [Immunity of counselors]

Except as provided in IC 31-32-11-1, a school counselor is immune from disclosing privileged or confidential communication made to the counselor as a counselor by a student. Except as provided in IC 31-32-11-1, the matters communicated are privileged and protected against disclosure.

Ind. Code § 25-2.1-14-1. [Confidentiality preserved]

A certified public accountant, a public accountant, an accounting practitioner, or any employee is not required to divulge information relative to and in connection with any professional service as a certified public accountant, a public accountant, or an accounting practitioner.

Ind. Code § 25-2.1-14-2. [Disclosures required by standards of profession]

The information derived from or as the result of professional services is confidential and privileged. However, this section does not prohibit a certified public accountant, a public accountant, or an accounting practitioner from disclosing any data required to be disclosed by the standards of the profession:

    (1)   In rendering an opinion on the presentation of financial statements;

    (2)   In ethical investigations conducted by private professional organizations;

    (3)   In the course of quality reviews; or

    (4)   In making disclosure where the financial statements or the professional services of an accountant are contested.

Ind. Code § 25-2.1-14-3. [Property rights in client records and reports of licensee]

All statements, records, schedules, working papers, and memoranda made by a licensee or a partner, a member, a shareholder, an officer, a director, or an employee of a licensee, including information prepared by the client for the work and services rendered to a client in the practice of accountancy, except the reports submitted by the licensee to the client and records that are part of the client's records, must remain the property of the licensee except in an express agreement between the licensee and the client to the contrary.

Ind. Code § 25-2.1-14-4. [Transfer of records without consent of client; prohibition]

A statement, record, schedule, working paper, or memorandum may not be sold, transferred, or bequeathed without the consent of the client or the client's personal representative or assignee, to anyone except for surviving partners, members, stockholders, new partners, or new stockholders of the licensee, or any combined or merged firm or successor in interest to the licensee.

Ind. Code § 25-2.1-14-5. [Quality review use of papers; duration of record keeping required of licensee]

(a) This chapter does not prohibit a temporary transfer of work papers or other material necessary to carry out quality reviews or to comply with the disclosure of information under this chapter.

(b) A licensee is not required to keep any work paper beyond the period prescribed in any applicable statute.

Ind. Code § 25-23.6-6-1. [Matters related in official capacity; exceptions to privilege]

Matters communicated to a counselor in the counselor's official capacity by a client are privileged information and may not be disclosed by the counselor to any person, except under the following circumstances:

(1) In a criminal proceeding involving a homicide if the disclosure relates directly to the fact or immediate circumstances of the homicide.

(2) If the communication reveals the contemplation or commission of a crime or a serious harmful act.

(3) If:

    (A) the client is an unemancipated minor or an adult adjudicated to be incompetent; and

    (B) the information communicated to the counselor indicates the client was the victim of abuse or a crime.

(4) In a proceeding to determine mental competency, or a proceeding in which a defense of mental incompetency is raised.

(5) In a civil or criminal malpractice action against the counselor.

(6) If the counselor has the express consent of:

    (A) the client; or

    (B) in the case of a client's death or disability, the express consent of the client's legal representative.

(7) To a physician if the physician is licensed under IC 25-22.5 and has established a physician-patient relationship with the client.

(8) Circumstances under which privileged communication is abrogated under Indiana law.

Ind. Code § 25-26-13-15. [Confidentiality of prescriptions, patient information, etc.; disclosure; immunity]

(a) A pharmacist shall hold in strictest confidence all prescriptions, drug orders, records, and patient information. He may divulge such information only when it is in the best interest of the patient or when requested by the board or its representatives or by a law enforcement officer charged with the enforcement of laws pertaining to drugs or devices or the practice of pharmacy.

(b) A person who has knowledge by virtue of his office of any prescriptions, drug order, record, or patient information may not divulge information except in connection with a criminal prosecution or proceeding or a proceeding before the board, to which the person to whom the information relates is a party.

(c) A pharmacist or pharmacy is immune from civil liability for any action based on its good faith release of information under this section.

Ind. Code § 35-37-4-1. [Competency of witnesses]

A person who is competent to testify in civil actions is also competent to testify in criminal proceedings.

Ind. Code § 34-45-2-2. [Insane persons deemed incompetent witnesses]

Except as otherwise provided by statute, persons who are insane at the time they are offered as witnesses are not competent witnesses, whether or not they have been adjudged insane.

Ind. Code § 34-46-3-1. [Persons not required to testify]

Except as otherwise provided by statute, the following persons shall not be required to testify regarding the following communications:

(1) Attorneys, as to confidential communications made to them in the course of their professional business, and as to advice given in such cases.

(2) Physicians, as to matters communicated to them by patients, in the course of their professional business, or advice given in such cases.

(3) Clergymen, as to the following confessions, admissions, or confidential communications:

    (A) Confessions or admissions made to a clergyman in the course of discipline enjoined by the clergyman's church.

    (B) A confidential communication made to a clergyman in the clergyman's professional character as a spiritual adviser or counselor.

(4) Husband and wife, as to communications made to each other.

Ind. Code § 34-46-3-2. [Husband or wife]

When the husband or wife is a party, and not required to testify in his or her own behalf, the person's spouse shall also be excluded.

Ind. Code § 34-45-2-9. [Husband or wife]

When the husband or wife is a party, and not a competent witness in his or her own behalf, the other shall also be excluded.

Journalist's privilege against disclosure of information source

Ind. Code § 34-46-4-1. [Applicability of chapter]

This chapter applies to the following persons:

(1) any person connected with, or any person who has been connected with or employed by:

    (A) a newspaper or other periodical issued at regular intervals and having a general circulation; or

    (B) a recognized press association or wire service;

    as a bona fide owner, editorial or reportorial employee, who receives or has received income from legitimate gathering, writing, editing and interpretation of news; and

(2) any person connected with a licensed radio or television station as owner, official, or as an editorial or reportorial employee who receives or has received income from legitimate gathering, writing, editing, interpreting, announcing or broadcasting of news.

Ind. Code § 34-46-4-2. [Privilege against disclosure of source of information]

A person described in section 1 [IC 34-46-4-1] of this chapter shall not be compelled

to disclose in any legal proceedings or elsewhere the source of any information procured or obtained in the course of the person's employment or representation of a newspaper, periodical, press association, radio station, television station, or wire service, whether:

    (1)   published or not published:

        (A)   in the newspaper or periodical; or

        (B)   by the press association or wire service; or

    (2)   broadcast or not broadcast by the radio station or television station

by which the person is employed.

Ind. Code § 34-30-15-1. [Confidentiality; peer review committee proceedings]

(a) All proceedings of a peer review committee are confidential.

(b) All communications to a peer review committee shall be privileged communications.

(c) Neither the personnel of a peer review committee nor any participant in a committee proceeding shall reveal any content of:

    (1)   communications to;

    (2)   the records of; or

    (3)   the determination of;

a peer review committee outside of the peer review committee.

(d) However, the governing board of:

    (1)   a hospital;

    (2)   a professional health care organization;

    (3)   a preferred provider organization (including a preferred provider arrangement or reimbursement agreement under IC 27-8-11); or

    (4)   a health maintenance organization (as defined in IC 27-13-1-19) or a limited service health maintenance organization (as defined in IC 27-13-34-4);

may disclose the final action taken with regard to a professional health care provider without violating the provisions of this section.

Ind. Code § 34-30-15-2. [Confidentiality; peer review committee proceedings; persons attending]

Except as otherwise provided in this chapter, a person who attends a peer review committee proceeding shall not be permitted or required to disclose:

    (1)   any information acquired in connection with or in the course of a proceeding;

    (2)   any opinion, recommendation, or evaluation of the committee; or

    (3)   any opinion, recommendation, or evaluation of any committee member.

Ind. Code § 34-30-15-3. [Confidentiality; otherwise discoverable information]

(a) Information that is otherwise discoverable or admissible from original sources is not immune from discovery or use in any proceeding merely because it was presented during proceedings before a peer review committee.

(b) A member, an employee, an agent of a committee or other person appearing before the committee may not be prevented from testifying:

(1) as to matters within the person's knowledge; and

(2) in accordance with the other provisions of this chapter.

(3) However, the witness cannot be questioned about this testimony or other proceedings before the committee or about opinions formed by the witness as a result of committee hearings.

Ind. Code § 34-30-15-8. [Confidentiality; persons information may be disclosed to]

(a) Communications to, the records of, and determinations of a peer review committee may only be disclosed to:

(1) the peer review committee of:

(A) a hospital;

(B) a nonprofit health care organization (described in IC 34-6-2-117(23));

(C) a preferred provider organization (including a preferred provider arrangement or reimbursement agreement under IC 27-8-11);

(D) a health maintenance organization (as defined in IC 27-13-1-19) or a limited service health maintenance organization (as defined in IC 27-13-34-4); or

(E) another health facility;

(2) the disciplinary authority of the professional organization of which the professional health care provider under question is a member; or

(3) the appropriate state board of registration and licensure that the committee considers necessary for recommended disciplinary action;

and shall otherwise be kept confidential for use only within the scope of the committee's work, unless the professional health care provider has filed a prior written waiver of confidentiality with the peer review committee.

(b) However, if a conflict exists between this section and IC 27-13-31, the provisions of IC 27-13-31 control.

Ind. Code § 34-30-15-9. [Waiver of privilege]

Except in cases of required disclosure to the professional health care provider under investigation, no records or determinations of or communications to a peer review committee shall be:

(1) subject to subpoena or discovery; or

(2) admissible in evidence;

in any judicial or administrative proceeding, including a proceeding under IC

34-18-11 (or IC 27-12-11 before its repeal), without a prior waiver executed by the committee.

Ind. Code § 34-30-15-10. [Invoking privilege]

Except in cases as authorized in this chapter, the evidentiary privileges created by this chapter shall be invoked by all witnesses and organizations in all judicial and administrative proceedings unless the witness or organization first has a waiver of the privilege executed in writing, on behalf of the peer review committee holding the privilege, by its chairman, vice chairman, or secretary.

Ind. Code § 34-30-15-11. [Limited waiver of privilege for attorney general investigation]

If a waiver of the privilege is executed on behalf of the peer review committee in favor of the attorney general for the purpose of conducting an investigation under IC 25-1-7, the records of, determinations of, or communications to a peer review committee are confidential and privileged under this section, except for the attorney general's use in an investigation to identify information otherwise discoverable or admissible from original sources under section 3 [IC 34-30-15-3] of this chapter.

Ind. Code § 34-30-15-12. [Subpoena powers of attorney general]

This chapter does not prevent the attorney general from obtaining by subpoena as part of an investigation under IC 25-1-7 for a violation under IC 25-1-9:

(1) the application for privileges or employment completed by the professional staff member under investigation regardless of whether the member is the subject of peer review committee proceedings;

(2) except for reports prepared as part of a peer review investigation, incident reports prepared contemporaneously to document the circumstances of an accident or unusual occurrence involving a professional staff member regardless of whether the member is the subject of peer review committee proceedings; or

(3) information otherwise discoverable from original sources, that is not the communications to, records of, or determinations of a peer review committee;

from a professional health care provider.

Ind. Code § 34-30-15-13. [Subpoena powers of attorney general; requirements]

A subpoena issued by the attorney general to obtain the records necessary to an investigation shall identify with reasonable particularity the documents sought and the specific professional health care provider under investigation.

Ind. Code § 35-37-6-9. [Privileged communication and victim counseling: Confidential communications; compelling testimony; records; temporary emergency shelters]

(a) The following persons may not be compelled to give testimony or to produce records concerning confidential communications in any judicial, legislative, or administrative proceeding:

(1) A victim.

(2) A victim counselor, unless the victim consents to the disclosure.

(3) An unemancipated child less than eighteen (18) years of age or an incapacitated victim, unless a custodial parent, custodian, guardian, or guardian *ad litem* who is not accused of a covered act consents to the disclosure.

(b) A victim counselor or a victim may not be compelled to provide testimony in any judicial, legislative, or administrative proceeding that would identify the name, address, location, or telephone number of any facility that provided temporary emergency shelter to the victim of the offense or transaction that is the subject of the proceeding unless the facility is a party to the proceeding.

For other applicable statutes, *see* Ind. Code § 31-39-8-7 (certain juvenile proceedings); Ind. Code § 33-2.1-6-6 (communications concerning the Judicial Qualifications Commission); Ind. Code §§ 16-41-7-1 to 16-41-7-4 (medical patient's HIV, AIDS, or hepatitis B diagnosis); Ind. Code §§ 16-39-6-3, 34-43-1-1 to 34-43-1-12 (hospital and mental health records); Ind. Code § 9-26-3-4 (accident reports); Ind. Code § 8-21-3-6 (aircraft accident reports); Ind. Code § 16-41-14-15 (communicable disease information for semen donors); Ind. Code § 9-14-3-7(e) (records of traffic violations); Ind. Code § 8-3-1-21 (railroad accident reports); Ind. Code § 35-47-7-3 (reports to a fire marshal); Ind. Code § 5-1-15-5 (bond issues); Ind. Code § 4-6-9-4(b) (consumer protection complaints); Ind. Code § 5-2-5-1 (criminal histories); Ind. Code § 27-8-8-10 (life insurance company records); Ind. Code § 6-1.1-35-12 (property taxes).

ADDITIONAL AUTHORITY

WEISSENBERGER'S FEDERAL EVIDENCE §§ 501.1–501.8

McCORMICK §§ 72–76.1 at 171–182

3 WEINSTEIN 2d §§ 501.01–501.05

2 MUELLER & KIRKPATRICK §§ 169–231

8 WIGMORE §§ 2201–2396

COMPARISON TO FEDERAL RULE

Indiana Rule 501 is modeled after Uniform Rules of Evidence 501, 510, and 511. Federal Rule 501 provides that privileges are governed by common law principles as interpreted by the federal courts, or, in civil actions in which state law supplies the rule of decision as to an element of a claim or defense, by principles of state law.

SIGNIFICANT CASES

University of Pa. v. EEOC, 493 U.S. 182, 110 S. Ct. 577, 107 L. Ed. 2d 571 (1990) (the Supreme Court declined to recognize a privilege against disclosure of peer review information).

Attorney-Client Privilege

Swidler & Berlin v. United States, 524 U.S. 399, 118 S. Ct. 2081, 141 L. Ed. 2d 379 (1998) (the Supreme Court reaffirmed the concept that the attorney-client privilege survives the client's death, and denied the existence of an exception to the privilege where the subject matter of the communication is of substantial importance to a criminal investigation).

United States v. Zolin, 491 U.S. 554, 109 S. Ct. 2619, 105 L. Ed. 2d 469 (1989), *vacated*, ***Church of Scientology v. United States***, 506 U.S. 9, 113 S. Ct. 447, 121 L. Ed. 2d 313 (1992) (addressing in camera review of allegedly privileged communications to determine applicability of the crime-fraud exception to the attorney-client privilege).

PRIVILEGES

Simon Prop. Group L.P. v. mySimon, Inc., 194 F.R.D. 644 (S.D. Ind. 2000) (an intentional disclosure of work-product to a testifying expert witness effectively waives the work-product privilege; an attorney should not be permitted to give a testifying expert witness a detailed "road map" for the desired testimony without also giving the opposing party an opportunity to discover that "map" and to cross-examine the expert about its effect on the expert's opinions in the case).

Brown v. State, 746 N.E.2d 63 (Ind. 2001) (defendant's sister had not been sentenced when her attorney took the stand in defendant's case and properly invoked the privilege; The trial court did not err when it ordered defense counsel not to ask questions likely to produce a legitimate claim of privilege in the jury's presence).

Rubalcada v. State, 731 N.E.2d 1015 (Ind. 2000) (husband's threat to do violence to his wife if she reveals his criminal actions is not privileged because such communications do not enhance the mutual trust and confidence of the marital relationship that the privilege is intended to cover).

Mayberry v. State, 670 N.E.2d 1262 (Ind. 1996) (information subject to attorney-client privilege retains its privileged character until client has consented to disclosure; victim's communication with friend who worked as paralegal was privileged as victim requested friend consult attorney about his legal concerns).

Hayworth v. Schilli Leasing, 669 N.E.2d 165 (Ind. 1996) (fact that defendant previously called its former employee as expert witness in unrelated litigation did not effect complete waiver of claim that attorney-client privilege precluded former employee from testifying in the instant action).

Taylor v. Taylor, 643 N.E.2d 893 (Ind. 1994) (wife waived any attorney-client privilege that may have applied to communications with decedent's son by submitting deposition for evidentiary use).

Lindsey v. State, 485 N.E.2d 102 (Ind. 1985), *reh'g denied*, 491 N.E.2d 191 (Ind. 1986) (voluntary testimony by client concerning his recollection of the confidential communications he made to his attorney constituted a waiver of client's privilege).

State v. Pelley, 800 N.E.2d 630 (Ind. Ct. App. 2003), *superseded*, 828 N.E.2d 915 (Ind. 2005), (the specific language of the social worker-client privilege relates to the time of the disclosure, not the time of the communication; furthermore, the statute granting the privilege is remedial in nature and may be applied retroactively; the trial court did not abuse its discretion in reviewing the documents in camera and finding that the documents did not fall within the exceptions to the privilege).

JWP Zack, Inc. v. Hoosier Energy Rural Elec. Coop., 709 N.E.2d 336 (Ind. Ct. App. 1999) (when information privileged as attorney-client communications is accidentally disclosed, a court deciding whether the privilege may be later invoked should consider all relevant circumstances including the reasonableness of the precautions to prevent inadvertent disclosure, the time taken to rectify the error, the scope of discovery, the extent of disclosure, and an overreaching issue of fairness and the protection of an appropriate privilege that must be judged against the care or negligence with which the privilege is guarded with care and diligence or negligence and indifference).

Owens v. Best Beers, 648 N.E.2d 699 (Ind. Ct. App. 1995) (attorney-client privilege did not protect evidence concerning existence or nonexistence of compensation agreement between employer and former employee, or other information regarding agreement derived from discussions between employer and its attorney in which employee participated from discovery request where employee is suing employer).

Corll v. Edward D. Jones & Co., 646 N.E.2d 721 (Ind. Ct. App. 1995) (communications during group meetings between counsel and investors to discuss potential lawsuit are privileged and, thus, not discoverable; however, not every communication between attorney and client is a confidential communication and a client's identity is not usually considered to be protected by the attorney-client privilege).

Brown v. Edwards, 640 N.E.2d 401 (Ind. Ct. App. 1994) (husband and wife waived attorney-client privilege in regards to will by requesting attorney and his assistant to witness wills, thus implicitly requesting attorney to defend wills against attack).

Accountant-Client Privilege

First Community Bank & Trust v. Kelley, Hardesty, Smith & Co., 663 N.E.2d 218 (Ind. Ct. App. 1996) (the common law did not recognize accountant-client relationship, but Indiana has recognized through statute).

Landau v. Bailey, 629 N.E.2d 264 (Ind. Ct. App. 1994) (affidavit by accountant submitted in favor of attorney in legal malpractice action violated accountant-client privilege).

Governor's Privilege

State v. IBM, 964 N.E.2d 206 (Ind. 2012) (the "Governor's privilege" set out at Ind. Code Ann. § 34-29-2-1(6), which provides that the Governor has an absolute privilege to be free from arrest on civil process, and from obeying any subpoena to testify, also clearly precludes a deposition of a sitting Governor).

Husband-Wife Privilege

State v. Wilson, 836 N.E.2d 407 (Ind. 2005) (although Ind. Code Ann. § 34-1-14-5 refers to husbands and wives as being incompetent witnesses as to "communications made to each other," it has been long held that this provision creates a privilege, not a disqualification of the witness, except in cases of will disputes, cases involving the dead man's statute, and actions by a husband for the seduction of his wife; in all other cases, it protects only confidential communications between spouses, and does not prevent a spouse from testifying as to any other matter).

Barajas v. State, 627 N.E.2d 437 (Ind. 1994) (defendant was not entitled to spousal privilege to prevent the woman he married from disclosing communications between them where, at the time of the marriage, he was still married to another woman so the marriage was not valid).

Leonard v. State, 537 N.E.2d 480 (Ind. 1989) (communications to spouse concerning defendant's escape plan was within the spousal privilege).

House v. State, 535 N.E.2d 103 (Ind. 1989) (marital privilege is limited to confidential communications and private information gained because of the marital relationship).

Pinkerton v. State, 258 Ind. 610, 283 N.E.2d 376 (1972) (held to be improper to comment on the exercise of an evidentiary privilege).

Hunt v. State, 235 Ind. 276, 133 N.E.2d 48 (1956) (discussion of spousal privilege).

Glover v. State, 816 N.E.2d 1197 (Ind. Ct. App. 2004), *vacated*, 831 N.E.2d 737 (Ind. 2005) (declining to follow federal law and create a "fraudulent" marriage exception to the spousal privilege, leaving instead the issue to the legislature).

State v. Farber, 677 N.E.2d 1111 (Ind. Ct. App. 1997) (statutory privilege encompasses only confidential communications and information gained by reason of marital relationship; only those communications passing from one married partner to the other are privileged; where wife consented to allow police to monitor conversation "fruit of the poisonous tree" doctrine did not apply to evidence discovered after that conversation).

Van Donk v. State, 676 N.E.2d 349 (Ind. Ct. App. 1997) (victim could be required to testify against her husband in battery prosecution; information sought was not gained in reliance upon marital relationship).

State v. Roach, 669 N.E.2d 1009 (Ind. Ct. App. 1996) (because privileges interfere with the search for truth and were mostly unknown at common law, they are disfavored and strictly construed;

wife could not avoid testifying against her husband in battery prosecution by claiming spousal testimonial privilege which is not recognized under Indiana law; only confidential marital communications are subject to spousal privilege in Indiana).

Journalist Privilege

Branzburg v. Hayes, 408 U.S. 665, 92 S. Ct. 2646, 33 L. Ed. 2d 626 (1972) (First Amendment does not create journalist privilege).

Patient-Psychotherapist Privilege

Jaffee v. Redmond, 518 U.S. 1, 116 S. Ct. 1923, 135 L. Ed. 2d 337 (1996) (the Supreme Court recognized a privilege against disclosure of confidential communications between patient and psychotherapist, including licensed social workers in the course of psychotherapy).

Ross v. Delaware County Dep't of Pub. Welfare, 661 N.E.2d 1269 (Ind. Ct. App. 1996) (psychologist-patient privilege does not apply in proceeding to terminate parental rights).

Peer Review Privilege

Mulder v. Vankersen, 637 N.E.2d 1335 (Ind. Ct. App. 1994) (allegedly defamatory statements made during hospital executive committee about registered nurse were protected from discovery by peer review privilege).

Physician-Patient Privilege

Elliott v. State, 630 N.E.2d 202 (Ind. 1994) (where defendant was charged with murdering his ex-wife's boyfriend, a therapist, who counseled defendant at a mental hospital defendant checked himself into, testified at trial; the therapist was not covered by the physician-patient privilege because, although she worked with the psychiatrist at the hospital regarding the prescription of drugs, she also worked independently in interviewing and counseling patients; consequently, her testimony was not barred by the physician-patient privilege).

In re C.P., 563 N.E.2d 1275 (Ind. 1990) (physician-patient privilege should be strictly construed).

Darnell v. State, 674 N.E.2d 19 (Ind. Ct. App. 1996) (physician-patient privilege does not always extend to communications made to nurses, and determination depends on patient's expectation it is a confidential communication to be relayed to his physician; here, statement to emergency room nurse was not privileged; test is whether nurse works under close supervision of doctor).

Rocca v. Southern Hills Counselling Ctr., Inc., 671 N.E.2d 913 (Ind. Ct. App. 1996) (public policy supports exception to physician-patient privilege where communications are made for unlawful purposes, and the objective is commission of crime).

Hayes v. State, 667 N.E.2d 222 (Ind. Ct. App. 1996) (physician-patient relationship is abrogated in cases where child is a victim of abuse or neglect).

Devore v. State, 658 N.E.2d 657 (Ind. Ct. App. 1995), *overruled in part*, *Biddinger v. State*, 868 N.E.2d 407 (Ind. 2007) (physician-patient privilege is abrogated "in any judicial proceeding resulting from a report of a child who may be a victim of child abuse"; therefore, medical records from hospital where defendant admitted himself to learn how to control child molesting were admissible for sentencing).

Thomas v. State, 656 N.E.2d 819 (Ind. Ct. App. 1995) (victim impliedly waived physician-patient privilege in regards to the details of attack she related to police officer).

Watters v. Dinn, 633 N.E.2d 280 (Ind. Ct. App. 1994) (physician-patient privilege is to be strictly construed).

In re Estate of Beck, 143 Ind. App. 291, 240 N.E.2d 88 (1968) (discussion of the physician-patient's privilege).

Therapist-Patient Privilege

Kavanaugh v. State, 695 N.E.2d 629 (Ind. Ct. App. 1998) (communications to a family therapist in the therapist's official capacity are normally privileged and may not be disclosed by the therapist, except under certain enumerated circumstances; however, where a patient discloses information in the presence of a therapist in response to a question posed by another person, and where the communication was conducted for nontherapeutic reasons, the communication is not protected by the therapist-client privilege).

Victim Advocate Privilege

State v. Fromme (In re Crisis Connection, Inc.), 949 N.E.2d 789 (Ind. 2011) (the three-step test for the discoverability of information outlined in *State v. Cline (In re WTHR-TV)*, 693 N.E.2d 1, 6 (Ind. 1998), is not reached when information is protected by an unqualified privilege unless a criminal defendant's constitutional rights would be violated by enforcing the privilege).

PRIVILEGES

Chapter 502

Rule 502. Attorney-Client Privilege and Work Product; Limitations on Waiver

Rule 502 reads as follows:

The following provisions apply, in the circumstances set out, to disclosure of a communication or information covered by the attorney-client privilege or work-product protection.

(a) Intentional Disclosure; Scope of a Waiver. When a disclosure is made in a court proceeding and waives the attorney-client privilege or work-product protection, the waiver extends to an undisclosed communication or information only if:

(1) the waiver is intentional;

(2) the disclosed and undisclosed communications or information concern the same subject matter; and

(3) they ought in fairness to be considered together.

(b) Inadvertent Disclosure. When made in a court proceeding, a disclosure does not operate as a waiver if:

(1) the disclosure is inadvertent;

(2) the holder of the privilege or protection took reasonable steps to prevent disclosure; and

(3) the holder promptly took reasonable steps to rectify the error, including (if applicable) following Indiana Rule of Trial Procedure 26(B)(5)(b).

(c) Controlling Effect of a Party Agreement. An agreement on the effect of disclosure in a proceeding is binding only on the parties to the agreement, unless it is incorporated into a court order.

(d) Controlling Effect of a Court Order. If a court incorporates into a court order an agreement between or among parties on the effect of disclosure in a proceeding, a disclosure that, pursuant to the order, does not constitute a waiver in connection with the proceeding in which the order is entered is also not a waiver in any other court proceeding.

*   *   *   *   *

ANALYSIS

Rule 502 was adopted in 2012. It was modeled after Federal Rule of Evidence 502, which itself was adopted in 2008 to address growing concerns about the inadvertent disclosure of privileged materials during discovery. Accordingly, Rule 502 governs several narrow parameters of the attorney-client privilege and work product doctrine during discovery in the course of litigation.

The scope of Rule 502 is very narrow, as it was created to address the rising costs of civil litigation due to the risk of forfeiting the attorney-client privilege or work product protection through inadvertent disclosure of privileged documents during discovery. Because of ambiguity in the caselaw governing the waiver of the privilege and work product protection, attorneys frequently took an overprotective approach to document requests, engaging in rigorous scrutiny of documents that ultimately had little to no importance in the case. Under the Rule, the inadvertent disclosure of privileged or protected information would not result in a waiver of the privilege if reasonable steps were taken to prevent the disclosure, and if retrieval of the information is promptly demanded. Also, the disclosure of privileged or protected information would not result in a waiver of the privilege or protection accorded other information concerning the same subject matter, unless fairness so requires.

The rule applies only to waiver of the attorney-client privilege and work product, and then only to those circumstances in which inadvertent disclosure of privileged or protected information does not result in a waiver. It does not address: (1) the circumstances under which attorney-client privilege or work product doctrine arises in the first instance; (2) waiver of the privilege and protection through means other than disclosure during discovery; or (3) waiver of other privileges, such as doctor-patient or spousal privilege. These areas continue to be addressed by statute or by common law.

Fundamentally, Rule 502 resolves a conflict as to when the inadvertent disclosure of protected material during litigation or agency proceedings may operate as a waiver of privilege or work product protection. Under the standard set out in the Rule, an "inadvertent disclosure" of protected material does not constitute a waiver if the holder of the protection "took reasonable steps" to prevent disclosure and rectify the error. Under this standard, a waiver will be found only if the disclosing party acted carelessly in disclosing the protected material, or failed to request its return in a timely manner.

Prior to the adoption of Rule 502, courts occasionally held that the disclosure of protected material during discovery would result in what was called "subject matter waiver," thus rendering all documents and materials in the possession of the disclosing party and concerning the same subject matter similarly waived and discoverable. This possibility led to a structural incentive for parties to engage in disproportionately expensive pre-production document review out of the fear that the accidental production of a single document might result in the waiver of protection for a vast collection of related materials. To combat this development, Rule 502 states, first, that waiver will never extend to undisclosed communications or information unless the waiver was "intentional." The effect of this provision is that inadvertent or accidental disclosure of protected materials will never operate as a "subject matter waiver." Furthermore, even if the disclosure was intentional, "subject matter waiver" will result only when "the disclosed and undisclosed communications or information concern the same subject matter," and "they ought in fairness to be considered together." According to the Committee Note accompanying Federal Rule of Evidence 502 (after which the Indiana Rule was modeled), the purpose of this restriction is to clarify that "subject matter waiver (of either privilege or work product) is reserved for those unusual situations in which fairness requires a further disclosure of related, protected information, in order to prevent a selective and misleading presentation of evidence to the disadvantage of the adversary." *See* Committee Note to Rule 502(a).

ADDITIONAL AUTHORITY

WEISSENBERGER'S FEDERAL EVIDENCE §§ 502.1–502.4

COMPARISON TO FEDERAL RULE

Indiana Rule 502 is modeled after Federal Rule of Evidence 502, which was enacted in 2008. The Federal version of the Rule contains provisions distinct to federal court practice and also sets out specific definitions for "attorney-client privilege" and "work-product protection." Otherwise, the Rules are effectively identical.

VI
WITNESSES

WITNESSES

Chapter 601

Rule 601. General Rule of Competency

Rule 601 reads as follows:

> Every person is competent to be a witness except as otherwise provided in these rules or by act of the Indiana General Assembly.

* * * * *

ANALYSIS

Purpose and Construction. In essence, the object of Rule 601 is to declare all persons competent to testify in all cases, criminal or civil, except where other Rules explicitly render a party incompetent or where an applicable state law disqualifies a witness. The reference to "an act of the Indiana General Assembly" preserves the statutory classifications of persons presently not competent as witnesses under Indiana law. *See* Ind. Code §§ 34-1-14-4 to 34-1-14-11. The purpose of Rule 601 is to create an assumption of competency except in expressly specified situations.

Notwithstanding the broad presumption of competency in Rule 601, there are still some situations in which a witness will be found incompetent to testify. A witness must be able to testify in an understandable manner, either directly or through an interpreter, and must be able to understand the duty to tell the truth. The situations affecting a witness's ability to testify in an understandable fashion are discussed in this chapter, whereas a witness's understanding of his or her duty to tell the truth is incorporated into Rule 603 and discussed briefly in Ch. 603, *Oath or Affirmation.*

Although many of the common law grounds for incompetency have been abolished in Illinois, the Dead Man's Statute remains as an incorporated statute. In addition, of course, every witness must have a sufficient foundation for testifying—that is, the requirement of first hand knowledge, as discussed in Ch. 602, *Lack of Personal Knowledge.*

In general, every person, regardless of age, is qualified to be a witness unless the person is incapable of expressing himself or herself in an understandable manner or incapable of understanding the duty to tell the truth. Accordingly, children are no longer disqualified because of an age limitation. In addition, a witness will not be automatically rendered incompetent as a witness because of the presence of a mental disability, current residence in a psychiatric facility or institution, adjudication of mental incompetence, or present mental condition. Under Ind. Code § 34-45-2-2, "insane" persons are deemed incompetent, but

147

Indiana follows the modern trend in not rejecting institutionalized persons categorically, instead relying on a case-by-case evaluation of the purported witness's ability to express himself clearly and understand what it means to tell the truth.

In every instance, the question is always whether the witness meets the general criteria for competency, i.e., whether the witness is capable of expressing himself or herself in an understandable manner. Despite the fact that a witness's mental condition will not render the witness incompetent per se, evidence of the mental condition, or any other fact bearing on the witness's capacity to express himself or herself in an understandable fashion, should generally be admissible to the extent that it relates to the credibility of the witness. The fact or mental condition must be relevant to the witness's capacity to express himself or herself in an understandable fashion.

Witnesses' inability to speak do not render them incompetent to testify or violate the defendant's right to cross-examine witnesses so long as they are able to communicate the facts by other methods and otherwise meet the tests of legal competency.

INCORPORATED STATUTES

Ind. Code § 35-37-4-1. [Competency of witnesses]

A person who is competent to testify in civil actions is also competent to testify in criminal proceedings.

Ind. Code § 34-45-2-2. [Insane persons deemed incompetent witnesses]

Except as otherwise provided by statute, persons who are insane at the time they are offered as witnesses are not competent witnesses, whether or not they have been adjudged insane.

Ind. Code § 34-46-3-1. [Persons not required to testify]

Except as otherwise provided by statute, the following persons shall not be required to testify regarding the following communications:

    (1)   Attorneys, as to confidential communications made to them in the course of their professional business, and as to advice given in such cases.

    (2)   Physicians, as to matters communicated to them by patients, in the course of their professional business, or advice given in such cases.

    (3)   Clergymen, as to the following confessions, admissions, or confidential communications:

        (A)   Confessions or admissions made to a clergyman in the course of discipline enjoined by the clergyman's church.

        (B)   A confidential communication made to a clergyman in the clergyman's professional character as a spiritual adviser or counselor.

    (4)   Husband and wife, as to communications made to each other.

Ind. Code § 34-46-3-2. [Husband or wife]

When the husband or wife is a party, and not required to testify in his or her own behalf, the person's spouse shall also be excluded.

Ind. Code § 34-45-2-9. [Husband or wife]

When the husband or wife is a party, and not a competent witness in his or her own behalf, the other shall also be excluded.

Ind. Code § 34-45-2-3. [Mentally incompetent persons and guardians]

(a) This section applies in all suits by or against any person adjudged to be a mentally incompetent person or against the mentally incompetent person's guardian:

    (1)   founded upon any contract with, or demand against the protected person;

    (2)   to obtain possession of the real or personal property of the protected person; or

    (3)   to affect the protected person's property in any manner.

(b) Except as provided in subsection (c), neither party to the transaction is a competent witness to any matter that occurred before the appointment of the incompetent person's guardian.

(c) If the party to the transaction who is under guardianship is adjudged by the court to be competent to testify, the other party to the suit shall not be excluded.

(d) This section does not apply to a contract made or transaction had before February 27, 1903.

(e) Either party to a suit under this section has the right to call and examine an adverse party as a witness. The court may require a party to a suit or other person to testify. An abuse of discretion under this subsection is reviewable on appeal.

Ind. Code § 34-45-2-4. [Executors or administrators; depositions; evidence given by decedent]

(a) This section applies to suits or proceedings:

    (1)   in which an executor or administrator is a party;

    (2)   involving matters that occurred during the lifetime of the decedent; and

    (3)   where a judgment or allowance may be made or rendered for or against the estate represented by the executor or administrator.

(b) Except as provided in subsection (c), a person:

    (1)   who is a necessary party to the issue or record; and

    (2)   whose interest is adverse to the estate;

is not a competent witness as to matters against the estate.

(c) In cases where:

    (1)   a deposition of the decedent was taken; or

    (2)   the decedent has previously testified as to the matter;

and the decedent's testimony or deposition can be used as evidence for the executor or administrator, the adverse party is a competent witness as to any matters embraced in the deposition or testimony.

WITNESSES

Ind. Code § 34-45-2-5. [Heirs or devisees; title or possession of property]

(a) This section applies to suits by or against heirs or devisees founded on a contract with or demand against an ancestor:

    (1)   to obtain title to or possession of property, real or personal, of, or in right of, the ancestor; or

    (2)   to affect property described in subdivision (1) in any manner.

(b) Neither party to a suit described in subsection (a) is a competent witness as to any matter that occurred before the death of the ancestor.

Ind. Code § 34-45-2-6. [Agent of decedent; transactions]

(a) This section applies:

    (1)   when an agent of a decedent testifies on behalf of an executor, administrator, or heirs concerning any transaction the agent had:

        (A)   with a party to the suit, or the party's assignor or grantor; and

        (B)   in the absence of the decedent; or

    (2)   if any witness testifies on behalf of the executor, administrator, or heirs, to any conversation or admission of a party to the suit, or the party's assignor or grantor, made in the absence of the deceased.

(b) The party against whom the evidence is adduced, or the party's assignor or grantor, is competent to testify concerning the matters described in subsection (a).

Ind. Code § 34-45-2-7. [Agent of decedent; contracts]

(a) Except as provided in subsection (b), a person who acted as an agent in the making or continuing of a contract with any person who has died, is not a competent witness, in any suit upon or involving the contract, as to matters occurring before the death of the decedent, on behalf of the principal to the contract, against the legal representatives or heirs of the decedent.

(b) If the person is called by the decedent's heirs or legal representatives, the person is a competent witness, as to matters about which the person is interrogated by the heirs or representatives.

Ind. Code § 34-45-2-8. [Unlawfully taking or damaging personal property]

If the defendant in a case:

    (1)   is charged with unlawfully taking or detaining personal property or having done damage to personal property; and

    (2)   defends the charge in the defendant's pleading by asserting that the defendant is the executor, administrator, guardian, or heir, and, as such, has taken or detained the property or has done the acts charged;

a person is not competent to testify who would not be competent if the defendant were the complainant. However, when the person complaining cannot testify, the defendant shall also be excluded.

Ind. Code § 34-45-2-10. [Assignor or grantor; adverse party]

(a) In all cases in which:

    (1)   executors, administrators, heirs, or devisees are parties; and

    (2)   one (1) of the parties to the suit is incompetent under this chapter to testify against the parties described in subdivision (1);

the assignor or grantor of a party making the assignment or grant voluntarily shall be considered a party adverse to the executor or administrator, heir, or devisee.

(b) However, in all cases referred to in sections 4 through 9 [IC 34-45-2-4 through IC 34-45-2-9] of this chapter, any party to the suit has the right to call and examine any adverse party as a witness.

(c) The court may require any party to a suit or other person to testify. Any abuse of the court's discretion under this subsection is reviewable on appeal.

Ind. Code § 34-45-2-11. [Executors or administrators; contracts assigned]

In all actions by an executor or administrator, on contracts assigned to the decedent, when the assignor is alive and a competent witness in the cause:

    (1)   the executor or administrator; and

    (2)   the defendant or defendants;

are competent witnesses as to all matters that occurred between the assignors and the defendant or defendants before notice of the assignment.

Ind. Code § 34-45-2-12. [Effect of lack of religious belief; moral character]

Lack of belief in a supreme being or in the Christian religion does not render a witness incompetent. However, lack of religious belief may be shown upon the trial. In all questions affecting the credibility of a witness, the general moral character of the witness may be given in evidence.

Ind. Code § 34-45-2-13. [Facts shown to affect credibility of witness]

Any fact that might have been shown to render a witness incompetent may be shown to affect the credibility of the witness.

ADDITIONAL AUTHORITY

Weissenberger's Federal Evidence §§ 601.1–601.6

McCormick §§ 61–67 at 155–164

3 Weinstein 2d §§ 601.01–601.05

3 Mueller & Kirkpatrick §§ 232–235

Wigmore §§ 483–721

COMPARISON TO FEDERAL RULE

    Indiana Rule 601 and Federal Rule 601 both provide that all witnesses are competent to testify unless otherwise provided by the rules. Indiana Rule 601 preserves statutory law pertaining to competency. Federal Rule 601 further provides that in civil actions as to which state law supplies the rule of decision, the competency of the witness is determined in accordance with state law.

SIGNIFICANT CASES

Pennsylvania v. Muniz, 496 U.S. 582, 110 S. Ct. 2638, 110 L. Ed. 2d 528 (1990) (videotaped

evidence of the defendant's slurred speech and lack of muscular coordination obtained without *Miranda* warnings is not testimonial and is admissible; defendant's videotaped response when asked if he knew the date of his sixth birthday, also procured without *Miranda* warnings, is testimonial and is not admissible).

Rock v. Arkansas, 483 U.S. 44, 107 S. Ct. 2704, 97 L. Ed. 2d 37 (1987) (criminal defendant's right to testify on her own behalf was violated by the Arkansas per se rule excluding all hypnotically refreshed testimony).

Kentucky v. Stincer, 482 U.S. 730, 107 S. Ct. 2658, 96 L. Ed. 2d 631 (1987) (in a sodomy case, defendant's rights under the Confrontation Clause of the Sixth Amendment and defendant's rights under the due process clause were not violated by his exclusion from a competency hearing of two child witnesses).

Bonham v. State, 644 N.E.2d 1223 (Ind. 1994) (pastor was competent to testify about defendant's statement describing crime where church had no course of discipline that required formal confession of sins).

Russell v. State, 540 N.E.2d 1222 (Ind. 1989) (child witness's answers to the court's questions demonstrated her understanding of the necessity to tell the truth).

Strong v. State, 538 N.E.2d 924 (Ind. 1989) (child knew the importance of testifying to the truth in court and was therefore, a competent witness).

Shields v. State, 490 N.E.2d 292 (Ind. 1986) (witness was not incompetent because he had visited a psychiatrist and attempted suicide).

Carlson v. Warren, 878 N.E.2d 844 (Ind. Ct. App. 2007) (statements that bore on the relationship between affected persons were clearly related to the circumstances surrounding a deed transaction and which could have been refuted by the deceased, if he had been living; accordingly; the trial court did not abuse its discretion in determining that the plaintiffs waived the application of the Dead Man's Statute by relying upon this evidence).

Richard v. State, 820 N.E.2d 749 (Ind. Ct. App. 2005) (although a determination of a child's competency to testify as a witness under Rule 601 would be helpful in reviewing probable cause cases involving child informants, the police is not required to make an inquiry into the child's competency for the purposes of establishing probable cause to issue a search warrant), *transfer denied*, 831 N.E.2d 741, *cert. denied*, 546 U.S. 1091, 126 S. Ct. 1034, 163 L. Ed. 2d 856 (2006).

Howard v. State, 816 N.E.2d 948 (Ind. Ct. App. 2004), *superseded*, 853 N.E.2d 461 (Ind. 2006) (the court should establish a child's competency to testify before allowing the witness to testify; however, where the witness's testimony or subsequent inclusion of deposition testimony makes it clear that the witness understood the difference between the truth and a lie and the importance of telling the truth at trial, the error was harmless).

Harrington v. State, 755 N.E.2d 1176 (Ind. Ct. App. 2001) (Rule 601 does not prohibit a special inquiry into the competency of children to testify, even though Rule 601 does not presumptively exclude children from serving as witnesses).

Buchanan v. State, 742 N.E.2d 1018 (Ind. Ct. App. 2001), *superseded*, 767 N.E.2d 967 (Ind. 2002) (six-year-old victim of child molestation was competent to testify at trial because she was able to distinguish between telling the truth and telling a lie, she identified examples of true statements and lies, and she acknowledged the importance of telling the truth).

Burrell v. State, 701 N.E.2d 582 (Ind. Ct. App. 1998) (five-year-old child was competent to testify where the child evinced an understanding of the distinction between truth and falsehood by articulating an unpleasant consequence for telling a lie and a pleasant consequence for telling the truth).

Newsome v. State, 686 N.E.2d 868 (Ind. Ct. App. 1997) (holding that the adoption of Rule 601 did not affect prior Indiana case law regarding the competency of children to testify. Hence, before allowing a child to testify, the trial court must first conduct an inquiry to determine whether the child understands the difference between telling the truth and telling a lie, knows she has a duty to tell the truth, and knows what a true statement actually is; it is not sufficient for a child witness to simply indicate that she understands that you get punished for telling a lie unless the child also demonstrates that she understands the difference between the truth and a lie).

Van Donk v. State, 676 N.E.2d 349 (Ind. Ct. App. 1997) (victim could be required to testify against her husband in battery prosecution).

Darnell v. State, 674 N.E.2d 19 (Ind. Ct. App. 1996) (physician-patient privilege does not always extend to communications made to nurses, and determination depends on patient's expectation, it is a confidential communication to be relayed to his physician; here, statement to emergency room nurse was not privileged; test is whether nurse works under close supervision of doctor).

Woodworth v. Estate of Yunker, 673 N.E.2d 825 (Ind. Ct. App. 1996) (testimony of witnesses who had cared for testator in claimant's absence were incompetent to testify under Indiana's dead man's statute because of the agency relationship between claimant and witnesses and therefore even if statements would otherwise have been admissible under an exception to dead man's statute, the court appropriately excluded).

Rocca v. Southern Hills Counselling Ctr., 671 N.E.2d 913 (Ind. Ct. App. 1996) (public policy supports exception to physician-patient privilege where communications are made for unlawful purposes and physician is competent to testify about such information).

Hayes v. State, 667 N.E.2d 222 (Ind. Ct. App. 1996) (therapist is not required to advise client of the child abuse reporting statute prior to counseling).

Ross v. Delaware County Dep't of Pub. Welfare, 661 N.E.2d 1269 (Ind. Ct. App. 1996) (psychologist who examined parents is competent to testify in proceeding to terminate parental rights as psychologist-patient privilege does not apply).

Stone v. Daviess County Div. of Children & Family Servs., 656 N.E.2d 824 (Ind. Ct. App. 1995) (social worker-patient privilege is abrogated in proceedings to terminate parental rights just as physician-patient privilege does not apply in these proceedings).

White v. White, 655 N.E.2d 523 (Ind. Ct. App. 1995) (court did not abuse its discretion in determining child's testimony regarding custody preference was improper subject to rebut testimony of husband's witness that mother kicked her son).

Thornton v. State, 653 N.E.2d 493 (Ind. Ct. App. 1995) (witness is presumed competent and defendant has burden of demonstrating that witness testifying in criminal case is not competent; evaluation of witness's competency is within discretion of trial court whose decision is reviewable only for manifest abuse of discretion).

Gardner v. State, 641 N.E.2d 641 (Ind. Ct. App. 1994) (defendant's right to confront witnesses against him was not violated by the failure of the state to procure his presence at a competency hearing for the prosecution's key witness because defendant had a sufficient opportunity to cross-examine the witness face-to-face at trial, as well as the option of requesting another competency hearing; good general discussion of a defendant's confrontation rights under the U.S. and Indiana Constitutions).

Brown v. Edwards, 640 N.E.2d 401 (Ind. Ct. App. 1994) (attorney was competent to testify in regards to wills where he witnessed wills and, in allowing this, husband and wife waived attorney-client privilege, implicitly requesting attorney to defend wills against attack).

Hall v. State, 634 N.E.2d 837 (Ind. Ct. App. 1994) (discussion of factors trial court should consider in determining the competency of a nine-year-old witness).

Paullus v. Yarnelle, 633 N.E.2d 304 (Ind. Ct. App. 1994) (dead man's statute does not exclude evidence, but it prevents classes of witnesses from testifying to protect decedent's estate from spurious claims).

Taylor v. Taylor, 632 N.E.2d 808 (Ind. Ct. App. 1994), *superseded*, 643 N.E.2d 893 (Ind. 1994) (where decedent's estate made a specific request to admit a transaction with the decedent, the estate waives the incompetency for that transaction).

Summit Bank v. Quake, 631 N.E.2d 13 (Ind. Ct. App. 1994), *disapproved by Mitchell v. Mitchell*, 695 N.E.2d 920 (Ind. 1998) (dead man's statute did not apply to testimony of decedent's daughter regarding matters occurring after decedent's death and about transactions occurring outside the presence of decedent).

Boyko v. State, 566 N.E.2d 1060 (Ind. Ct. App. 1991), *rev'd*, *Boyko v. Parke*, 259 F.3d 781 (7th Cir. 2001) (witness's intoxication at the time he was called to testify does not make him incompetent to testify; trial court did not abuse its discretion in permitting the witness to testify where he testified in a lucid manner).

Chapter 602

Rule 602. Lack of Personal Knowledge

Rule 602 reads as follows:

A witness may not testify to a matter unless evidence is introduced sufficient to support a finding that the witness has personal knowledge of the matter. A witness does not have personal knowledge as to a matter recalled or remembered, if the recall or remembrance occurs only during or after hypnosis. Evidence to prove personal knowledge may, but need not, consist of the testimony of the witness. This rule is subject to the provisions of Rule 703, relating to opinion testimony by expert witnesses.

*   *   *   *   *

ANALYSIS

Requirement Generally. The preliminary interrogation of every witness must establish that the witness has first-hand knowledge or personal knowledge of the facts as to which he or she will testify.

Pre-Rule Practice Changed. Rule 602 changes pre-Rule Indiana practice which presumed a witness to possess personal knowledge when called to testify. The party opposing the witness was required to raise the lack of competency. First-hand knowledge is knowledge acquired through one or more of the senses. Foundational testimony, as provided by Rule 602, may be developed from the witness whose competency is being established, and no extrinsic foundational evidence is required. Consequently, in a preliminary examination of a witness, it is only necessary to establish that he or she was in a physical position to see, hear, or otherwise perceive the matters as to which he or she is to provide testimony.

Practical Considerations. Frequently, it will be established during cross-examination that the witness lacks first-hand knowledge to testify to certain facts presented in the direct examination testimony. Where this occurs, the cross-examining attorney should move to strike the direct examination testimony because of its failure to satisfy Rule 602.

Rule 602 preserves preexisting Indiana law by providing that a witness lacks the requisite first-hand knowledge to be competent where the knowledge of the factual matter in question is recalled or remembered only during or after hypnosis.

Practical Considerations

According to the express terms of Rule 602, experts qualified under Rule 702 are not subject to the personal knowledge requirement. *See* Rule 703. A lay witness testifying in the form of opinion must base his or her opinion on first-hand knowledge. *See* Rule 701.

ADDITIONAL AUTHORITY

WEISSENBERGER'S FEDERAL EVIDENCE §§ 602.1–602.4

MCCORMICK § 69 at 167

3 WEINSTEIN 2d §§ 602.01–602.04

3 MUELLER & KIRKPATRICK §§ 236–237

2 WIGMORE §§ 650–670

COMPARISON TO FEDERAL RULE

Indiana Rule 602 is identical to Federal Rule 602 except that Indiana Rule 602 adds the provision concerning hypnosis.

SIGNIFICANT CASES

Rock v. Arkansas, 483 U.S. 44, 107 S. Ct. 2704, 97 L. Ed. 2d 37 (1987) (criminal defendant's right to testify on her own behalf was violated by the Arkansas per se rule excluding all hypnotically refreshed testimony).

Stephens v. State, 506 N.E.2d 12 (Ind. 1987) (court permitted a witness who had undergone hypnosis to testify where the witness's recollection was not significantly altered by the hypnosis and it was established that the witness's testimony had a factual basis independent of the hypnosis).

Wagner v. State, 474 N.E.2d 476 (Ind. 1985) (error to permit witnesses to speculate about the state of mind or attitude of another person).

Buck v. State, 453 N.E.2d 993 (Ind. 1983) (witnesses are permitted to testify concerning only those matters about which they have first-hand knowledge).

Pritchard v. State, 810 N.E.2d 758 (Ind. Ct. App. 2004) (under the "silent witness" theory, video recordings and photographic evidence may be admitted as substantive evidence, rather than merely as demonstrative evidence; however, the doctrine is inapplicable in this case, where the witnesses testified concerning matters within their personal knowledge, such as what the video recording showed).

Baran v. State, 639 N.E.2d 642 (Ind. 1994) (arresting officer's failure to recall every detail of facts leading up to motorist's arrest goes toward weight, not admissibility of officer's testimony at suppression hearing).

Chapter 603

Rule 603. Oath or Affirmation

Rule 603 reads as follows:

> Before testifying, every witness shall swear or affirm to testify to the truth, the whole truth, and nothing but the truth. The mode of administering an oath or affirmation shall be such as is most consistent with, and binding upon the conscience of the person to whom the oath is administered.

*　*　*　*　*

ANALYSIS

Requirement Generally. Rule 603 is consistent with pre-Rule Indiana practice in requiring that every witness must be sworn to testify to "the truth, the whole truth, and nothing but the truth." *See* Ind. Code § 35-45-1-2. Consistent with the Indiana Constitution, the oath must be "such as may be most consistent with, and binding upon, the conscience of the [witness]." Ind. Const. art. I, § 8.

Waiver. The requirement of an oath may be waived either expressly or by implication, such as when an adverse party goes forward in the matter without inquiry or objection.

INCORPORATED STATUTES

Ind. Code § 34-45-1-2. [Oath]

Before testifying, every witness shall be sworn to testify the truth, the whole truth, and nothing but the truth. The mode of administering an oath must be the most consistent with and binding upon the conscience of the person to whom the oath may be administered.

ADDITIONAL AUTHORITY

Weissenberger's Federal Evidence §§ 603.1–603.3

McCormick § 63

3 Weinstein 2d §§ 603.01–603.05

3 Mueller & Kirkpatrick §§ 238–239

6 Wigmore §§ 1818–1829

COMPARISON TO FEDERAL RULE

Federal Rule 603 is similar to Indiana Rule 603, in that it requires a witness to declare his

WITNESSES

intention to testify truthfully and permits a form of an oath that the witness believes will be binding on his conscience.

SIGNIFICANT CASES

United States v. Fowler, 605 F.2d 181 (5th Cir. 1979) (court refused to permit defendant to testify where he refused to either swear or affirm that he would tell the truth or submit to cross-examination).

Sweet v. State, 498 N.E.2d 924 (Ind. 1986) (failure to object to the trial court's failure to administer an oath or affirmation to a witness constitutes a waiver).

Tomlin v. State, 247 Ind. 277, 215 N.E.2d 190 (1966) (failure of court to administer an oath to a witness is prejudicial error).

Pooley v. State, 116 Ind. App. 199, 62 N.E.2d 484 (1945) (oath requirement is waived upon failure to object).

Chapter 604

Rule 604. Interpreters

Rule 604 reads as follows:

An interpreter is subject to the provisions of these rules relating to qualification as an expert and the administration of an oath or affirmation to make a true translation.

---

* * * * *

ANALYSIS

Requirement Generally. Rule 604 subjects an interpreter to the qualification requirements of other expert witnesses pursuant to Rule 702. Consistent with Rule 702, the determination of an interpreter's qualifications is an issue within the discretion of the trial court. Close relatives or friends of the witness are not precluded from serving as interpreters where such individuals qualify as experts.

Attacking Translation. Interpreters, like all experts, are subject to an attack on credibility. Nevertheless, where the trial judge finds that the interpreter satisfies the requirements of Rule 702 and allows the interpreter to testify, the accuracy of the translation becomes an issue for the trier of fact. In such cases, the credibility of the interpreter and his or her competence to translate, become issues for the jury.

Recent Development

In *Romo v. State*, 941 N.E.2d 504 (Ind. 2011), the Indiana Supreme Court had to determine whether to allow an English language translation of a transcripted recording of a conversation between the defendant and a police informant. Although the Court did not discuss Rule 604, it pointed to the safeguards in place to assure that the translation was accurate: the original translation was made by a bilingual specialist with the Indiana police department; the transcripts were also repeatedly reviewed and compared with the original audio by a number of others, including a Certified Indiana Court Interpreter. Presumably, each of the individuals reviewing the transcript filed an affidavit attesting to the accuracy of the translation, which would satisfy the Rule 604 requirement.

WITNESSES

INCORPORATED STATUTES

Ind. Code § 34-45-1-3. [Interpreters; entitlement]

Every person who cannot speak or understand the English language or who because of hearing, speaking, or other impairment has difficulty in communicating with other persons, and who is a party to or a witness in a civil proceeding is entitled to an interpreter to assist the person throughout the proceeding.

Ind. Code § 34-45-1-4. [Interpreters; appointment and qualifications]

(a) An interpreter assisting a person under section 3 [IC 34-45-1-3] of this chapter may be:

    (1)   retained by the party or witness; or

    (2)   appointed by the court before which the action is pending.

(b) If an interpreter is appointed by the court, the fee for the services of the interpreter shall be:

    (1)   set by the court; and

    (2)   paid in a manner as the court may determine.

Ind. Code § 34-45-1-5. [Interpreters—oath]

Every interpreter for another person who is either a party or a witness in a court proceeding described in this chapter shall take the following oath:

Do you solemnly swear (or affirm) that you will justly, truly, and impartially interpret to _____ the oath about to be administered to him (her), and the questions which may be asked [sic] him (her), and the answers that he (she) shall give to such questions, relative to the cause now under consideration before this court so help you God (or under the pains and penalties of perjury)?

ADDITIONAL AUTHORITY

WEISSENBERGER'S FEDERAL EVIDENCE §§ 604.1–604.3

3 WEINSTEIN 2d §§ 604.01–604.04

3 MUELLER & KIRKPATRICK §§ 240–241

6 WIGMORE § 1824

COMPARISON TO FEDERAL RULE

Indiana Rule 604 and Federal Rule 604 are identical.

SIGNIFICANT CASES

United States ex rel. Negron v. New York, 434 F.2d 386 (2d Cir. 1970) (failure to provide a criminal defendant with an interpreter held to violate Due Process Clause).

Valle v. State, 550 N.E.2d 746 (Ind. 1990) (trial court did not err in failing to provide a non-English-speaking defendant with a simultaneous translation where defendant indicated that it was not necessary and instead accepted a translated summary of the evidence).

Martinez Chavez v. State, 534 N.E.2d 731 (Ind. 1989) (indigent defendant who could not speak or understand English had a right to have the proceedings translated).

Bielich v. State, 189 Ind. 127, 126 N.E. 220 (1920) (court-appointed interpreter shall not appear to favor either party).

Skaggs v. State, 108 Ind. 53, 8 N.E. 695 (1886) (trial court may appoint the number of interpreters necessary to present evidence).

Angeles v. State, 751 N.E.2d 790 (Ind. Ct. App. 2001) (translator was qualified to act as interpreter even though translator stated that she was not bilingual; translator stated that she was fluent in Spanish, translator taught Spanish at high school and college levels for 34 years, and translator had traveled to Spanish-speaking countries).

Chapter 605

Rule 605. Competency of Judge as Witness

Rule 605 reads as follows:

> The judge presiding at the trial may not testify in that trial as a witness. No objection need be made to preserve the point.

* * * * *

ANALYSIS

Rule 605 provides that the trial judge presiding at the trial may not testify in that trial as a witness, and further, that no objection need be interposed at trial to preserve error for appeal. The Rule, however, does not prevent a judge from testifying at a later trial about matters occurring in the original trial, such as where a trial judge is called as a witness in a hearing on a petition for postconviction relief from a previous judgement.

ADDITIONAL AUTHORITY

Weissenberger's Federal Evidence §§ 605.1–605.4

McCormick § 68

3 Weinstein 2d §§ 605.01–605.07

3 Mueller & Kirkpatrick §§ 242–244

6 Wigmore § 1909

COMPARISON TO FEDERAL RULE

Indiana Rule 605 and Federal Rule 605 are identical.

SIGNIFICANT CASES

Lillie v. United States, 953 F.2d 1188 (10th Cir. 1992) (error for trial judge to view the scene of the accident outside the record).

State v. Hindman, 159 Ind. 586, 65 N.E. 911 (1903) (judge from a previous trial permitted to testify in a collateral proceeding).

Cornett v. Johnson, 571 N.E.2d 572 (Ind. Ct. App. 1991) (judge was not permitted to testify in a subsequent malpractice case under the Code of Judicial Conduct).

WITNESSES

Chapter 606

Rule 606. Competency of Juror as Witness

Rule 606 reads as follows:

> **(a) At the Trial.** A member of the jury may not testify as a witness before that jury in the trial of the case in which the juror is sitting. If the juror is called so to testify, the opposing party shall be afforded an opportunity to object out of the presence of the jury.
>
> **(b) Inquiry into Validity of Verdict or Indictment.** Upon an inquiry into the validity of a verdict or indictment, a juror may not testify as to any matter or statement occurring during the course of the jury's deliberations or to the effect of anything upon that or any other juror's mind or emotions as influencing the juror to assent to or dissent from the verdict or indictment or concerning the juror's mental processes in connection therewith, except that a juror may testify (1) to drug or alcohol use by any juror, (2) on the question of whether extraneous prejudicial information was improperly brought to the jury's attention or (3) whether any outside influence was improperly brought to bear upon any juror. A juror's affidavit or evidence of any statement by the juror concerning a matter about which the juror would be precluded from testifying may not be received for these purposes.

* * * * *

ANALYSIS

At Trial. Rule 606(a) declares incompetent any witness who is a member of the jury impaneled to hear the case in question.

Subsequent Proceeding. Rule 606(b) governs the competency of a juror to testify at a subsequent proceeding concerning the original verdict or indictment. The first half of the first sentence of Rule 606(b) represents the embodiment of the common law tradition of protecting and preserving the integrity of jury deliberations by declaring jurors generally incompetent to testify as to any matter directly pertinent to, and purely internal to, the emotional or mental processes of the jury's deliberations. The Rule is designed to protect the finality of verdicts and to ensure that jurors are insulated from being unceasingly harassed by defeated parties.

When Impeachment Allowed. The remainder of the first sentence of Rule 606(b) recognizes situations in which a juror is competent to impeach a verdict or indictment after

165

it has been returned. A juror may testify to drug or alcohol use by any member of the jury. A juror may also offer testimony concerning whether extraneous prejudicial information was improperly brought to the attention of the jury during deliberations. Finally, a juror may testify whether an outside influence was improperly brought to bear upon any member of the jury.

Current Trends and New Developments

Juror use of mind-altering substances was held not to be admissible under *Tanner v. United States*, 483 U.S. 107, 107 S. Ct. 2739, 97 L. Ed. 2d 90 (1987).

An alternate juror is considered an "outside influence" for purposes of Rule 606(b), at least to the extent that the alternate juror is involved in a discussion of the merits of the case. *See Griffin v. State*, 754 N.E.2d 899, 903 (Ind. 2001). However, mere "antics" of an alternate juror that do not expressly involve deliberation on the verdict will not rise to the level of "gross misconduct" that prejudices a party in a degree sufficient to warrant impeachment. *See Henri v. Curto*, 908 N.E.2d 196 (Ind. 2009).

ADDITIONAL AUTHORITY

WEISSENBERGER'S FEDERAL EVIDENCE §§ 606.1–606.5

McCORMICK § 605

3 WEINSTEIN 2d §§ 606.01–606.07

3 MUELLER & KIRKPATRICK §§ 245–255

6 WIGMORE § 1910

COMPARISON TO FEDERAL RULE

Indiana Rule 606(a) and Federal Rule 606(a) are identical. Indiana Rule 606(b) is similar to Federal Rule 606(b) except that it permits a juror to testify concerning drug or alcohol use by any juror upon an inquiry into the validity of a verdict or indictment.

SIGNIFICANT CASES

Tanner v. United States, 483 U.S. 107, 107 S. Ct. 2739, 97 L. Ed. 2d 90 (1987), *superseded by statute*, *United States v. Little*, 889 F.2d 1367 (5th Cir. Miss. 1989) (Federal Rule 606(b) prohibited juror testimony regarding drug and alcohol use during a criminal trial).

Rushen v. Spain, 464 U.S. 114, 104 S. Ct. 453, 78 L. Ed. 2d 267 (1983), *cert. denied*, 495 U.S. 910, 110 S. Ct. 1937, 109 L. Ed. 2d 300 (1990) (testimony of a juror regarding mental bias in matters not related to the specific issues juror was called upon to decide as admissible).

Henri v. Curto, 908 N.E.2d 196 (Ind. 2009) (the behavior of an alternate juror making noises and gestures and exercising on the floor do not expressly involve deliberation on the guilt of the accused and will not rise to the level of "gross misconduct" that prejudices a party in a degree sufficient to warrant impeachment of a verdict).

Williams v. State, 793 N.E.2d 1019 (Ind. 2003) (under Rule 606, a former juror may testify as to the validity of a verdict under very limited circumstances, such as when an allegation is made that an outside influence affected the verdict; the testimony of jurors themselves cannot be considered to impeach their verdict).

Majors v. State, 773 N.E.2d 231 (Ind. 2002) (juror affidavit indicating that jurors made comments during trial, about the physical characteristics of both state and defense attorneys and about the way a defense attorney questioned witnesses, was not a proper attempt to impeach the verdict in the murder trial).

Davis v. State, 770 N.E.2d 319 (Ind. 2002) (trial court's questioning of three jurors about potential outside influence on jury deliberations did not violate the rule governing the competency of juror as a witness).

Allen v. State, 749 N.E.2d 1158 (Ind. 2001) (while the general rule is that a jury's verdict may not be impeached by the testimony of the jurors who returned it, an exception to this rule occurs when there is evidence demonstrating that the jury was exposed to improper, extrinsic material and a substantial possibility exists that the defendant was prejudiced by that material).

Griffin v. State, 754 N.E.2d 899 (Ind. 2001) (alternate juror's opinion on defendant's guilt was an "outside influence" within meaning of evidentiary rule governing juror impeachment of verdicts).

Stephenson v. State, 742 N.E.2d 463 (Ind. 2001) (extrinsic or extraneous materials brought into jury deliberation may be grounds for impeaching a verdict where there is a substantial possibility that such extrinsic material prejudiced the verdict; defendant has the burden to prove that the material brought into the jury room was extrinsic, and then the burden shifts to the state to prove that it was harmless; a juror's extensive notebook that he prepared at home on his personal computer was not tainted by extrinsic influences and did not amount to extraneous material).

Huffman v. State, 543 N.E.2d 360 (Ind. 1989), *overruled*, *Street v. State*, 567 N.E.2d 102 (Ind. 1991) (jurors taking notes is a matter within the trial court's discretion).

Saperito v. State, 490 N.E.2d 274 (Ind. 1986) (juror testified that he examined the scene of the crime on his own but the court found that the testimony was not influential enough to have prejudiced the defendant).

State v. White, 474 N.E.2d 995 (Ind. 1985) (error to consider juror affidavit that verdict was based on matters not in evidence).

Bixler v. State, 471 N.E.2d 1093 (Ind. 1984) (juror affidavits or testimony may not be used to demonstrate improprieties in the method the verdict was reached).

Bean v. State, 460 N.E.2d 936 (Ind. 1984) (verdict could not be impeached by the jurors who returned it).

Fox v. State, 457 N.E.2d 1088 (Ind. 1984) (jurors may testify concerning improper extrinsic influences that the jury was exposed to).

Berman v. Cannon, 878 N.E.2d 836 (Ind. Ct. App. 2007) (statement from a juror that the jury was influenced by a party's absence from the trial was inadmissible under Rule 606(b)).

Evans v. Buffington Harbor River Boats, 799 N.E.2d 1103 (Ind. Ct. App. 2003) (when reviewing a denial of a request for a new trial, a court cannot consider a juror's comments about how an outside influence affected the decision; the prohibition against impeaching the validity of a verdict is greatest where the communication between jurors, not a communication by a nonjuror, creates the problem).

Sanchez v. State, 794 N.E.2d 488 (Ind. Ct. App. 2003) (an alternate juror is not a member of the jury, and he or she is considered an "outside influence" under Rule 606(b)).

Williams v. State, 757 N.E.2d 1048 (Ind. Ct. App. 2001) (the exception to the rule that a verdict may not be impeached by evidence from the jurors applies when jurors are exposed to improper extrinsic matters during deliberations and there is a substantial possibility that the extrinsic material prejudiced the verdict).

Johnson v. State, 700 N.E.2d 480 (Ind. Ct. App. 1998) (a juror's post-verdict affidavit stating that she was not inclined to find the defendant guilty but for psychological coercion by other jurors could not be used by defendant, because the juror was not improperly influenced by external factors outside of the jury).

Knight v. Parke, 595 N.E.2d 280 (Ind. Ct. App. 1992) (misconduct of jurors amounting to forming opinions before retiring to deliberate and discussing the case among themselves did not constitute extraneous influence).

Wagner v. Riley, 499 N.E.2d 1155 (Ind. Ct. App. 1986) (third party may not provide evidence concerning deliberation conduct that jurors themselves are prohibited from giving).

Schultz v. Valle, 464 N.E.2d 354 (Ind. Ct. App. 1984) (juror use of intoxicants during deliberations requires a new trial).

Chapter 607

Rule 607. Who May Impeach

Rule 607 reads as follows:

> The credibility of a witness may be attacked by any party, including the party calling the witness.

* * * * *

ANALYSIS

Witnesses Subject to Impeachment. Indiana Rule 607 provides that the credibility of a witness may be attacked by any party, including the party who called the witness. Rule 607 represents a change in preexisting Indiana law which prohibited the impeachment of a party's own witness.

Role of Rule 403. Potential abuse in the literal application of Rule 607 is subject to control by the trial judge where, for example, a witness is called for the purpose of introducing otherwise inadmissible evidence for the purpose of impeachment. Rule 403 may be applied in such situations to prevent admissibility.

Impeachment Techniques; Bias. The law of evidence has recognized several specific techniques that might be used to diminish the credibility of witnesses. These techniques include prior inconsistent statement impeachment (self-contradiction); contradiction; prior acts and convictions; character impeachment (propensity for lack of veracity); exposure of perceptual incapacity; the exposure of mental incapacity; and the introduction of evidence to expose bias, prejudice, interest, or motive to misrepresent. Although the Rules do not address each of these impeachment techniques explicitly, their absence in the Rules does not indicate any disfavor in their use. Rather the operation and limitation of these techniques remain guided by common law.

ADDITIONAL AUTHORITY

WEISSENBERGER'S FEDERAL EVIDENCE §§ 607.1–607.6

MCCORMICK §§ 45–47

4 WEINSTEIN 2d §§ 607.01–607.10

3 MUELLER & KIRKPATRICK §§ 256–259

WIGMORE §§ 896–918

WITNESSES

COMPARISON TO FEDERAL RULE

Indiana Rule 607 is identical to Federal Rule 607.

SIGNIFICANT CASES

Olden v. Kentucky, 488 U.S. 227, 109 S. Ct. 480, 102 L. Ed. 2d 513 (1988) (defendant's rights under the Confrontation Clause were violated when trial court refused to allow him to impeach the alleged rape victim's testimony on cross-examination with evidence revealing a motive to fabricate the alleged crime).

United States v. Gossett, 877 F.2d 901 (11th Cir. 1989) (impeachment by a prior inconsistent statement may not be permitted when used as a strategy to put before the jury otherwise inadmissible evidence).

United States v. Webster, 734 F.2d 1191 (7th Cir. 1984) (it is an abuse of the Rules of Evidence to permit a party to impeach his party with a prior statement simply to get hearsay evidence admitted).

Ingram v. State, 715 N.E.2d 405 (Ind. 1999) (it is clear that a witness's credibility may be attacked by any party, including the one who called the witness).

Edmond v. State, 790 N.E.2d 141 (Ind. Ct. App. 2003) (Rule 607, which allows a party to impeach his or her own witness, may not be used to introduce inadmissible evidence by calling a witness and impeaching that witness with a favorable extrajudicial statement previously made by a prior witness).

Impson v. State, 721 N.E.2d 1275 (Ind. Ct. App. 2000) (trial court did not err in allowing state to call reluctant victim and only witness of battery to testify even though she may not have given useful evidence; a party is authorized to impeach the credibility of its own witnesses, and if the state has a legitimate basis to call the witness, then the placement of otherwise inadmissible evidence before the jury is proper).

Rafferty v. State, 610 N.E.2d 880 (Ind. Ct. App. 1993) (state's impeachment of its own witness was proper even though the testimony elicited related to defendant's uncharged acts; state's purpose was not to place inadmissible evidence before jury, but to determine whether witnesses would corroborate material issues in the case).

DeMotte v. State, 555 N.E.2d 1336 (Ind. Ct. App. 1990) (refusal to permit defendant to impeach witness's credibility by attacking her ability to describe what happened without exaggeration held to be reversible error).

Chapter 608

Rule 608. Evidence of Character and Conduct of Witness

Rule 608 reads as follows:

(a) **Opinion and Reputation Evidence of Character.** The credibility of a witness may be attacked or supported by evidence in the form of opinion or reputation, but subject to these limitations: (1) the evidence may refer only to character for truthfulness, and (2) evidence of truthful character is admissible only after the character of the witness for truthfulness has been attacked by opinion or reputation evidence or otherwise.

(b) **Specific Instances of the Conduct of a Witness.** For the purpose of attacking or supporting the witness's credibility, other than conviction of a crime as provided in Rule 609, specific instances may not be inquired into or proven by extrinsic evidence. They may, however, in the discretion of the court, if probative of truthfulness or untruthfulness, be inquired into on cross-examination of the witness concerning the character for truthfulness or untruthfulness of another witness as to which character the witness being cross-examined has testified.

---

*   *   *   *   *

ANALYSIS

Impeachment Techniques Covered. Rule 608 governs the technique of impeaching and bolstering a witness through a distinct witness who testifies to the primary witness's character trait of veracity. Rule 608 changes pre-Rule Indiana law in two ways. First, under Rule 608(a), the character of a witness may be impeached using opinion testimony. Second, pre-Rule Indiana law permitted the admission of evidence of a witness's general moral character. Rule 608 is unlike Federal Rule 608, in that it does not authorize the impeachment of a witness by raising an inference of untruthful character arising from cross-examination of that witness concerning unconvicted prior acts of misconduct.

Impeachment Character Witness. The credibility or veracity of a witness who has taken the stand may be attacked by calling a character witness who is competent to testify to the reputation of the primary witness for untruthfulness. The format is as follows. The primary witness steps down from testifying. The proponent of the primary witness completes his case and rests. Then, the opponent of the primary witness, at a point later in the trial when he has an opportunity to call his own witnesses, calls a character witness. This character witness

then testifies in regard to the reputation of the primary witness sought to be impeached.

Qualifications; Testimony Permitted; Character Witness. The qualifications of an impeachment character witness are essentially the same as those qualifications applicable to a character witness under Rule 405. He must be a member of an appropriate community where the reputation of the person characterized is known. The character witness testifies to the reputation of the primary witness in regard to the character trait of veracity or truth-telling. The character witness may also be asked to state his personal opinion as to the veracity of the primary witness sought to be impeached. The character witness is not, however, permitted to testify to specific instances of untruthful conduct of the primary witness on direct examination. Specific acts of conduct of the primary witness may be elicited on cross-examination of the character witness in order to test the basis for his reputation or opinion testimony. It is unlikely that the cross-examiner will seek to elicit such information on cross-examination because the cross-examiner is the proponent of the primary witness. He, consequently, is not interested in the exposure of prior specific acts of untruthfulness of the witness which he has offered and which the character witness is seeking to impeach.

Illustration

Counsel: Mr. Johnson, an individual by the name of Jacob Rolfman testified during the plaintiff's case-in-chief. Are you acquainted with Mr. Rolfman?

Witness: Yes I am.

Counsel: Please state the basis of your acquaintance with Mr. Rolfman.

Witness: I have known Mr. Rolfman for 10 years. He is a neighbor of mine and lives two houses from me up the street.

Counsel: Do you know him personally? That is, have you socialized with him or had business dealings with him?

Witness: I know him casually. He is not a close friend, but I am acquainted with him. I have not had opportunity to have any business dealings with him or to socialize with him.

Counsel: Nevertheless, are you aware of Mr. Rolfman's reputation for truthfulness in your community?

Witness: Well, I know what everybody generally thinks about him, if that is what you mean.

Counsel: Yes. Please state what you understand to be the reputation of Mr. Rolfman for truth-telling.

Witness: Well, he generally has the reputation of being a liar. People in our community just do not think he is the sort of person who tells the truth.

Counsel: Have you heard of any instances of conduct which would justify this reputation?

Opposing Counsel: Objection. The response would be hearsay and it would violate

Rule 608(b).

Judge: Sustained.

Counsel: Have you ever observed Mr. Rolfman engaging in deceitful or untruthful conduct?

Opposing Counsel: Objection. The question calls for specific instances of conduct which are prohibited by Rule 608 on direct examination of the character witness.

Judge: Sustained.

Rule 608(a)(2) provides that reputation and opinion evidence tending to establish the truthful propensity of any witness may be admitted only after the principal witness's *character* has in fact been attacked by opinion or reputation evidence or by other impeachment evidence which represents an attack on character. The underlying theory provides that all witnesses under oath are presumed to be telling the truth and that the issue of a witness's truthfulness or credibility is collateral to the principal issues in the case. While every witness's credibility is an issue for the trier of fact, this does not, in the absence of an attack on character, authorize a party to bolster any witness through use of a character witness. The condition precedent for the use of a rehabilitation character witness is an attack on the character of the primary witness, and mere impeachment not involving the character of the primary witness is insufficient to authorize the calling of a positive character witness.

Practical Considerations

A witness merely discredited by evidence of bias not involving corruption has not been subjected to *character* impeachment. Also, where a prior inconsistent statement of a witness is introduced, where a witness is simply shown to be confused, or where a witness merely provides conflicting testimony, the witness's credibility may not be bolstered through a character witness attesting to the primary witness's good character for veracity. By comparison, however, where impeachment is effected by a negative character witness pursuant to Rule 608(a), by interrogation as to prior acts probative of untruthful character under Rule 608(b), or by evidence of a criminal conviction under Rule 609, the *character* of the primary witness is, in fact, attacked and, therefore, may be rehabilitated with a positive character witness. Beyond these presumptive attacks on character expressly addressed in the rules, the careful discretion of the trial judge must be exercised on a case-by-case basis to determine whether the form of impeachment employed effectively operates as an attack on character.

Impeachment by Cross-Examination Regarding Specific Instances of Conduct. Under Rule 608(b), a character witness may be impeached by cross-examination as to specific instances of conduct of the primary witness sought to be impeached. Such acts must be probative of truthfulness or untruthfulness and they may not be proven by "extrinsic evidence," that is, evidence introduced after the character witness steps down from testifying.

INCORPORATED STATUTES

Ind. Code § 35-37-4-2. [Credibility; general moral character]

In all questions affecting the credibility of a witness, his general moral character may be given in evidence.

Ind. Code § 34-45-4-1. [Impeachment by evidence of bad character]

(a) Except as provided in subsections (b) and (c), the party producing a witness shall not be allowed to impeach the credibility of the witness by evidence of bad character.

(b) The party producing a witness may impeach the credibility of the witness by evidence of bad character if:

    (1)   it was indispensable that the party produce the witness; or

    (2)   it is a case of manifest surprise.

(c) In all cases, the party producing the witness may contradict the witness:

    (1)   by other evidence; and

    (2)   by showing that the witness has made statements different from the present testimony of the witness.

Ind. Code § 34-45-2-12. [Effect of lack of religious belief; moral character]

Lack of belief in a supreme being or in the Christian religion does not render a witness incompetent. However, lack of religious belief may be shown upon the trial. In all questions affecting the credibility of a witness, the general moral character of the witness may be given in evidence.

Ind. Code § 35-37-4-15. [Child molestation; evidence of prior acts]

(a) In a prosecution for child molesting under IC 35-42-4-3, a prosecution for incest under IC 35-46-1-3, or a prosecution for an attempt or a conspiracy to commit child molesting or incest, evidence that the defendant has committed another crime or act of child molesting or incest or attempted or conspired to commit another crime or act of child molesting or incest:

    (1)   against the same victim; or

    (2)   that involves a similar crime or act of child molesting or incest against a different victim;

is admissible.

(b) If the state proposes to offer evidence described under subsection (a), the state must disclose the evidence to the defendant, including statements made by witnesses or a summary of the substance of any testimony that is expected to be offered at the defendant's trial:

    (1)   at least fifteen (15) days before the date the defendant's trial is scheduled to begin; or

    (2)   at a later date as determined by the court for good cause.

(c) The court shall hold a hearing out of the presence of the jury regarding the admissibility of the evidence described under subsection (a). Even if the court determines that the evidence is relevant, the evidence may be excluded if the probative value of the evidence is substantially outweighed by:

(1)   the danger of:

    (A)   unfair prejudice;

    (B)   confusion of the issues; or

    (C)   misleading the jury; or

(2)   considerations of:

    (A)   undue delay;

    (B)   waste of time; or

    (C)   needless presentation of cumulative evidence.

However, if the court finds that all or some of the evidence is admissible, the court shall enter an order stating what evidence may be introduced.

(d) This section may not be construed to limit the right to introduce evidence at a trial that would otherwise be admissible to prove any of the following:

(1)   Motive.

(2)   Opportunity.

(3)   Intent.

(4)   Plan.

(5)   Knowledge.

(6)   Identity.

(7)   Absence of mistake or accident.

ADDITIONAL AUTHORITY

WEISSENBERGER'S FEDERAL EVIDENCE §§ 608.1–608.10

McCORMICK § 41

4 WEINSTEIN 2d §§ 608.01–608.02, 608.10–608.15, 608.20–608.23, 608.30

3 MUELLER & KIRKPATRICK §§ 260–262

3 WIGMORE §§ 977–88

4 WIGMORE §§ 1100–1144

8 WIGMORE § 2276

COMPARISON TO FEDERAL RULE

Indiana Rule 608(a) and Federal Rule 608(a) are similar in substance. Federal Rule 608(b) and Indiana Rule 608(b) are dissimilar, however, in that pursuant to Federal Rule 608(b), a trial court has the discretion to allow inquiry into specific acts of the primary witness, not amounting to a conviction, on cross-examination of the witness. Federal Rule 608(b) further provides that the giving of testimony, whether by an accused or by any other witness, does

WITNESSES

not operate as a waiver of the accused's or the witness's privilege against self-incrimination when examined with respect to matters which relate only to credibility.

SIGNIFICANT CASES

Williams v. State, 749 N.E.2d 1139 (Ind. 2001) (defendant argued that a witness's prior drug use went not to her character but rather to her credibility; he said that it was more likely that she lied to her case officers about her continuing drug use, but he did not present any evidence that she lied to her case officers or anyone else about her past drug use. Even had there been evidence that she had lied, it appears that such evidence would have been inadmissible under Rule 608(b) as constituting extrinsic acts used to prove credibility).

Lambert v. State, 743 N.E.2d 719 (Ind. 2001) (prosecutor was not required to disclose possible impeachment evidence in the form of an application for substance abuse treatment in lieu of incarceration that described a prior bad act by showing that one had previously lied in order to reduce his sentence because Rule 608(b) prohibited using prior bad acts to attack credibility in this manner, and even if defendant had this evidence, he could not have introduced it; Rule 608(b) prohibits impeachment of a witness by evidence of prior bad acts unless the act is an "infamous" crime or a crime probative of credibility).

Bowles v. State, 737 N.E.2d 1150 (Ind. 2000) (there was an inadequate foundation for evidence of reputation in the community, and the trial court properly excluded such evidence based on the sparse information regarding the nature of the community, the basis for a reputation opinion, and the extent of the witness's contact with the community).

Hicks v. State, 544 N.E.2d 500 (Ind. 1989) (trial court properly denied defendant's discovery motion concerning information of a prosecution witness's prior acts of misconduct; evidence of the witness's acts not reduced to convictions held not to be admissible to impeach the witness).

Mueller v. State, 517 N.E.2d 788 (Ind. 1988), *overruled in part*, *Meriweather v. State*, 659 N.E.2d 133 (Ind. Ct. App. 1995) (trial court permitted witness to be cross-examined concerning false statements the witness made while making a sales pitch for magazines).

Johnston v. State, 517 N.E.2d 397 (Ind. 1988) (improper to permit cross-examination of a witness concerning prior bad acts to prove the witness's bad character).

Stonebraker v. State, 505 N.E.2d 55 (Ind. 1987) (improper to impeach a witness with evidence of specific acts of misconduct that did not result in criminal convictions).

Hansford v. State, 490 N.E.2d 1083 (Ind. 1986), *overruled*, *Richardson v. State*, 717 N.E.2d 32 (Ind. 1999) (witness may not be impeached by specific acts of misconduct that are not reduced to convictions).

Beaty v. State, 856 N.E.2d 1264 (Ind. Ct. App. 2006) (Rule 608(b) prohibits the introduction into evidence of specific instances of misconduct of a witness to impeach his character as a witness, though specific instances of conduct of a witness may be admissible to demonstrate bias by a witness; however, in this case, the bias of the witness was revealed sufficiently through other evidence, and the trial court did not err by limiting the cross-examination of the witness).

Saunders v. State, 848 N.E.2d 1117 (Ind. Ct. App. 2006), *transfer denied*, 860 N.E.2d 588 (Ind. 2006) (the trial court did not err in excluding evidence of a specific instance of conduct regarding a witness's truthfulness, as the Confrontation Clause exception to Rule 608 described in *State v. Walton*, 715 N.E.2d 824, 827 (Ind. 1999)—prior false accusations of rape—was inapplicable).

Norton v. State, 785 N.E.2d 625 (Ind. Ct. App. 2003) (under Rule 608, the nature of the "community" in which the reputation of a witness is being challenged or supported is not limited to the community at large; in some cases, one's family is deemed to be of sufficient size to provide the requisite reliability for an impeaching witness's testimony; in any event, such a determination is properly made by the trial court).

Rhodes v. State, 771 N.E.2d 1246 (Ind. Ct. App. 2002) (a witness may not be impeached by specific acts of misconduct that have not resulted in criminal convictions).

Simon v. Clark, 660 N.E.2d 634 (Ind. Ct. App. 1996) (in personal injury action, if trial court erred in preventing plaintiff from showing that defense expert had been paid by defendant-insurer in order to impeach expert's testimony that she was paid by other defendant's attorneys, such error was harmless; trial court's refusal to allow plaintiff to ask expert, about specific amount of compensation he received in past year for work for defense attorneys, was not error where proposed question was cumulative of expert's testimony).

Palmer v. State, 654 N.E.2d 844 (Ind. Ct. App. 1995) (trial court did not abuse its discretion by preventing defendant accused of cocaine dealing from impeaching testimony of police officer with evidence of officer's own drug use where such evidence did not demonstrate that officer was under influence of drugs either during trial or at time of event, or that officer's ability to perceive, remember, and testify was substantially affected by drug use).

Dietrich v. State, 641 N.E.2d 679 (Ind. Ct. App. 1994) (in prosecution for child molestation, testimony of victim's mother that she did not tell victim to lie about testimony was not impermissible vouching for truthfulness of victim where mother's testimony did not directly assert her belief in victim's testimony).

Pierce v. State, 640 N.E.2d 730 (Ind. Ct. App. 1994) (rule prohibiting impeachment of witnesses with prior bad acts prevents unfair prejudice to witness where evidence does not make witness's truthfulness less likely; Rules of Evidence permit impeachment of witness only by evidence of reputation or character, and forbid impeachment by prior bad acts evidence unless act is infamous crime or crime probative of credibility).

Turnbow v. State, 637 N.E.2d 1329 (Ind. Ct. App. 1994) (in reckless homicide prosecution, evidence that prosecution witness was in jail on charges of driving with a suspended license and failure to pay fine was inadmissible for purposes of impeachment; witness was jailed on charges which had not been reduced to convictions, and evidence was addressed only to witness's credibility and character).

Dynes v. Dynes, 637 N.E.2d 1321 (Ind. Ct. App. 1994) (in a custody action, trial court erred in excluding evidence of a wife's reputation for honesty in her workplace; evidence of reputation for veracity should not necessarily be limited to that within the person's community of residence).

WITNESSES

Chapter 609

Rule 609. Impeachment by Evidence of Conviction of Crime

Rule 609 reads as follows:

(a) **General Rule.** For the purpose of attacking the credibility of a witness, evidence that the witness has been convicted of a crime or an attempt of a crime shall be admitted but only if the crime committed or attempted is (1) murder, treason, rape, robbery, kidnapping, burglary, arson, criminal confinement or perjury; or (2) a crime involving dishonesty or false statement.

(b) **Time Limit.** Evidence of a conviction under this rule is not admissible if a period of more than ten years has elapsed since the date of the conviction or, if the conviction resulted in confinement of the witness then the date of the release of the witness from the confinement unless the court determines, in the interests of justice, that the probative value of the conviction supported by specific facts and circumstances substantially outweighs its prejudicial effect. However, evidence of a conviction more than ten years old as calculated herein, is not admissible unless the proponent gives to the adverse party sufficient advance written notice of intent to use such evidence to provide the adverse party with a fair opportunity to contest the use of such evidence.

(c) **Effect of Pardon, Annulment, or Certificate of Rehabilitation.** Evidence of a conviction is not admissible under this rule if (1) the conviction has been the subject of a pardon, annulment, certificate of rehabilitation, or other equivalent procedure based on a finding of the rehabilitation of the person convicted, and that person has not been convicted of a subsequent crime which was punishable by death or imprisonment in excess of one year, or (2) the conviction has been the subject of a pardon, annulment, or other equivalent procedure based on a finding of innocence.

(d) **Juvenile Adjudications.** Evidence of juvenile adjudications is generally not admissible under this rule. The court may, however, in a criminal case allow evidence of a juvenile adjudication of a witness other than the accused if conviction of the offense would be admissible to attack the credibility of an adult and the court is satisfied that admission in evidence is necessary for a fair determination of the issue of guilt or innocence.

(e) **Pendency of Appeal.** The pendency of an appeal therefrom does not render evidence of a conviction inadmissible. Evidence of the pendency of an appeal is

admissible.

* * * * *

ANALYSIS

Scope of Rule.   Rule 609 governs the impeachment of a witness by evidence of his or her prior criminal convictions. Rule 609(a) provides that for the purpose of attacking the credibility of a witness, evidence that the witness has been convicted of a crime or an attempt of a crime is admissible only for the following crimes: murder, treason, rape, robbery, kidnapping, burglary, arson, criminal confinement, perjury, or a crime involving dishonesty or false statement. The impeachment is effected by eliciting testimony from the witness that the conviction or attempt has occurred. The rule is limited to the function of impeachment, and it is not applicable to convictions that might be admissible because it is relevant to the substantive issues of the case. *See* Rule 404(b).

Methodology of Proof.   In a typical case, a prior conviction will sought to be introduced against an accused in a criminal case. When this occurs, the State must introduce into evidence proper certified and authenticated records of the defendant's prior felony conviction to prove the fact beyond a reasonable doubt. *See Dexter v. State*, 959 N.E.2d 235 (Ind. 2012). Direct inquiry concerning the prior conviction on cross-examination of the accused will generally not be allowed. However, if the accused decides to mention a prior conviction on direct examination, inquiry into the conviction on cross-examination may be permissible. Because the methodology of proof is limited to the public record, the only facts admitted surrounding an accused's prior convictions will generally be the date and place of the trial, jury's verdict, and final judgment.

Ten-Year Limit.   Under Rule 609(b), if more than 10 years have elapsed since the date of conviction, or the termination of confinement, probation or parole, the conviction is not admissible unless the court finds that the probative value of such evidence substantially outweighs its prejudicial effect.

Current Trends and New Developments

In *Dowdy v. State*, 672 N.E.2d 948 (Ind. Ct. App. 1996), evidence of robbery, defendant's previous conviction for robbery was admissible to impeach defendant because, even though defendant had been released on previous robbery conviction 12 years earlier, defendant had four convictions and several additional arrests for theft and robbery in the interim, and the prior robbery conviction was similar to the currently charged robberies.

Pardon, Annulment, Rehabilitation, etc.; Burden.   Rule 609(c) provides that evidence of the conviction is not admissible for the purpose of impeachment where a pardon, annulment, certificate of rehabilitation, or other equivalent procedure is based either upon a finding of innocence or a showing of rehabilitation, and where the witness has not subsequently been convicted of a felony. The burden of proving that a witness's prior conviction is inadmissible under Rule 609(c) rests with the party who opposes the use of the conviction. Pre-Rule Indiana law did not include a time limit after which a conviction was presumptively inadmissible.

Juvenile Adjudications. Under Rule 609(d) the admissibility of juvenile adjudications is left to the discretion of the trial judge. In a criminal case, the trial judge may allow evidence of a juvenile adjudication of a witness other than the accused as impeachment evidence if the judge determines that the evidence is necessary for a fair determination of the case.

Pendency of Appeal. Rule 609(e) provides that the pendency of an appeal from a conviction does not render evidence of the conviction inadmissible. The Rule provides, however, that where a witness is questioned about a prior conviction which has since been appealed, the fact that the appeal is pending is admissible. Consequently, the matter of appeal is left to the trier of fact in evaluating the weight of the conviction in regard to credibility.

ADDITIONAL AUTHORITY

WEISSENBERGER'S FEDERAL EVIDENCE §§ 609.1–609.11

McCORMICK § 43

3 WEINSTEIN 2d §§ 609.01–609.08, 609.20–609.25

3 MUELLER & KIRKPATRICK §§ 273–288

WIGMORE §§ 980–988

4 WIGMORE §§ 1106, 1116

Cooper, *Recent Developments in Indiana Evidence Law*, 32 IND. L. REV. 811 (1999)

COMPARISON TO FEDERAL RULE

Instead of enumerating specific crimes, Federal Rule 609 limits admissible crimes to crimes punishable by death or imprisonment in excess of one year. Federal Rule 609(a)(1) provides that a conviction for one of these crimes may be used to attack the accused's credibility as a witness only if the court determines that the probative value of the conviction outweighs its prejudicial effect. Evidence that a witness other than the accused has been convicted of such a crime is subject to Rule 403. Pursuant to Federal Rule 609(a)(2), evidence that any witness has been convicted of a crime involving dishonesty or false statement is admissible regardless of the punishment.

SIGNIFICANT CASES

Ohler v. United States, 529 U.S. 753, 120 S. Ct. 1851, 146 L. Ed. 2d 826 (2000) (a defendant who preemptively introduces evidence of a prior conviction on direct examination may not challenge the admission of such evidence on appeal).

Green v. Bock Laundry Mach. Co., 490 U.S. 504, 109 S. Ct. 1981, 104 L. Ed. 2d 557 (1989), *superseded by statute, Zola v. Kelley*, 149 N.H. 648, 826 A.2d 589 (2003) (under Federal Rule 609(a), prior to its 1990 amendment, a judge is required to permit impeachment of a civil witness with evidence of prior felony convictions regardless of unfair prejudice to the witness or the party offering the testimony).

Luce v. United States, 469 U.S. 38, 105 S. Ct. 460, 83 L. Ed. 2d 443 (1984) (trial court's motion in limine ruling under Federal Rule 609 is preserved for review only where accused actually testifies).

Dexter v. State, 959 N.E.2d 235 (Ind. 2012) (a certified and authenticated record of the defendant's prior felony convictions is the proper way to prove the existence of those prior convictions).

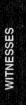

WITNESSES

Banks v. State, 761 N.E.2d 403 (Ind. 2002) (a defendant is not entitled on cross-examination to introduce details of a witness's prior conviction; only the fact of conviction was admissible).

Scalissi v. State, 759 N.E.2d 618 (Ind. 2001) (a party seeking to admit a conviction more than 10 years old must overcome the presumption in Rule 609, which generally excludes such convictions; accordingly, the party must support the argument for probative value with specific facts and circumstances upon which the trial court may base a finding of admissibility, and the trial court must balance the probative value against the prejudicial effect of the old convictions on the record).

Warren v. State, 757 N.E.2d 995 (Ind. 2001) (when a witness does nothing more than acknowledge the fact of a prior criminal conviction, the witness will not necessarily be subject to cross-examination concerning the details of the conviction).

Logan v. State, 729 N.E.2d 125 (Ind. 2000) (juvenile record of state's witness was properly excluded to attack credibility because juvenile adjudications are generally not admissible under Rule 609 and trial court found evidence was not necessary for a fair determination of defendant's guilt or innocence).

Rule 609(a)

Outback Steakhouse of Fla., Inc. v. Markley, 856 N.E.2d 65 (Ind. 2006) (wire fraud is a crime involving false statement because misrepresentation is an element of the crime).

Specht v. State, 734 N.E.2d 239 (Ind. 2000) (defendant's prior guilty plea to offense of confinement could be used to impeach him during a felony murder prosecution, even though the plea had not been reduced to a judgment because a guilty plea not yet reduced to judgment constitutes a conviction for impeachment purposes).

Williams v. State, 724 N.E.2d 1070 (Ind. 2000), *vacated*, *Aki-Khuam v. Davis*, 2003 U.S. App. LEXIS 15046 (7th Cir. Ind. July 28, 2003) (although evidence that the witness has been convicted of a crime or an attempt of a crime is admissible under certain circumstances, the evidence that witness had been convicted of criminal trespass and criminal mischief was inadmissible because the crimes are not contemplated as admissible under Rule 609(a)).

Brown v. State, 703 N.E.2d 1010 (Ind. 1998) (evidence of a prior conviction in another jurisdiction is not automatically admissible to impeach simply because the other jurisdiction uses a label for the crime that is found in Rule 609(a)(1); if the crime is not substantially equivalent to the Indiana crime listed, it does not qualify under Rule 609(a)(1)).

Cason v. State, 672 N.E.2d 74 (Ind. 1996) (trial court did not abuse its discretion by not allowing murder defendant to impeach identification witness with witness's conviction for assisting a criminal; crime of conviction was not impeachable offense, and even though witness was originally charged with robbery and pled guilty to lesser charge, court need not speculate about whether prosecutor might have proven robbery case).

In re Sheaffer, 655 N.E.2d 1214 (Ind. 1995) (in attorney disciplinary proceeding, exclusion of evidence of official misconduct charge against testifying officer and transcript of officer's guilty plea was not prejudicial error where officer admitted to underlying facts of charge and thus supplied full and accurate information about offense).

Moore v. State, 550 N.E.2d 318 (Ind. 1990) (witness was cross-examined concerning 10 prior convictions of theft or forgery; these constituted crimes involving honesty or false statement which is a proper method of impeaching a witness).

Roseberry v. State, 273 Ind. 179, 402 N.E.2d 1248 (1980) (a witness's credibility may be attacked by questioning him about his convictions for certain crimes).

Ashton v. Anderson, 258 Ind. 51, 279 N.E.2d 210 (1972) (for the purpose of impeaching the credibility of a witness only convictions of treason, murder, rape, arson, burglary, robbery, kidnapping, forgery, willful and corrupt perjury, and crimes involving dishonesty or false statement are admissible).

Brown v. Brown, 979 N.E.2d 684 (Ind. Ct. App. 2012) (Rule 609(a) permits evidence of a past criminal conviction to be admitted only for the purpose of attacking the credibility of a witness).

Wales v. State, 768 N.E.2d 513 (Ind. Ct. App. 2002) (unlike Rule 403, which favors the admissibility of evidence, Rule 609 presumes the exclusion of convictions more than 10 years old).

Newman v. State, 719 N.E.2d 832 (Ind. Ct. App. 1999) (witness did not place his own character into evidence at trial by claiming that he did not know car was stolen and there was no possibility that the jury could have been misled by the statement because it was elicited on cross-examination; therefore, door was not opened for state to introduce evidence of witness's prior juvenile adjudications for purposes of impeachment; furthermore, requirements of Rule 609(d) were not met to admit evidence of juvenile adjudications for theft because such evidence was not necessary for a fair determination of guilt or innocence).

Giles v. State, 699 N.E.2d 294 (Ind. Ct. App. 1998) (trial court improperly permitted state to introduce into evidence a stale conviction where the state did not provide defendant any advance written notice of its intent to use the conviction and where the state did not proffer any argument demonstrating that the probative value of the stale conviction outweighed its prejudicial effect).

Woods v. State, 654 N.E.2d 1153 (1995) (certified copies of judgments or commitments with same or prior offense conviction are admissible for purpose of habitual offender determination, but there must be supporting evidence to identify defendant as same person named in document).

Davis v. State, 654 N.E.2d 859 (Ind. Ct. App. 1995) (although prior crime was same as charged crime, reference to specific prior crime used to impeach defendant's credibility did not need to be deleted; however, reference generally as a "felony" would have invited speculation and suggested that conviction of any crime impeached a witness's truthfulness).

Palmer v. State, 654 N.E.2d 844 (Ind. Ct. App. 1995) (a witness may not be impeached by specific acts of misconduct if the misconduct did not result in a criminal conviction; defendant charged with cocaine dealing could not impeach police officer's testimony with evidence of officer's drug use or related suspension from police force because it was not opinion or reputation evidence regarding officer's veracity and was not offered to show that officer had been convicted of a crime).

Pierce v. State, 640 N.E.2d 730 (Ind. Ct. App. 1994) (where defendant was charged with attempted murder, trial court prohibited defendant from cross-examining a prosecution witness regarding his address because the witness was incarcerated on a cocaine charge at the time of trial; trial court had granted the prosecution's motion in limine prohibiting all references to the witness's cocaine conviction holding that dealing cocaine was not a crime probative of credibility; court of appeals held that defendant's right of confrontation was not violated).

Currin v. State, 638 N.E.2d 1319 (Ind. Ct. App. 1994), *vacated on other grounds*, 669 N.E.2d 976 (Ind. 1996) (trial court properly prohibited defendant from impeaching prosecution witness with evidence of the witness's prior conviction for aiding and abetting a battery because the conviction involved a crime of violence that did not necessarily reflect on the witness's credibility for truth and veracity).

Rule 609(b)

Stephenson v. State, 742 N.E.2d 463 (Ind. 2001) (trial court properly excluded evidence of witness's three robbery convictions that were more than 10 years old, which defendant sought to admit to impeach the witness, because the probative value of the evidence did not substantially outweigh its prejudicial effect and because defendant did not overcome the general rule that stale convictions are not admissible; trial court's application of Rule 609(b) did not prevent defendant from cross-examining the witness and attacking his credibility).

Schwestak v. State, 674 N.E.2d 962 (Ind. 1996) (trial court did not abuse its discretion by prohibiting defendant from impeaching witness with evidence of burglary conviction that was more than 10 years old, without showing of how probative value of conviction was great enough to defeat rule against admission of convictions; witness's testimony, although important to state's case, was not dispositive).

Whiteside v. State, 853 N.E.2d 1021 (Ind. Ct. App. 2006) (the date the witness testifies or the evidence is introduced, not the date of the charged crime or some other cutoff, is the most appropriate termination point for determining whether a conviction falls within the 10-year limit provided by Rule 609(b)).

Dowdy v. State, 672 N.E.2d 948 (Ind. Ct. App. 1996) (party wishing to overcome presumption of exclusion of a witness's old conviction must support argument with specific circumstances and facts; when balancing probative value of witness's old conviction against danger of unfair prejudice, court considers impeachment value of prior crime, time of conviction and witness's subsequent history, similarity between past crime and charged crime, importance of defendant's testimony, and centrality of credibility issue).

Rule 609(c)

Nunn v. State, 601 N.E.2d 334 (Ind. 1992) (trial court properly prevented impeachment by a criminal conviction that had been pardoned).

Rule 609(d)

Pope v. State, 737 N.E.2d 374 (Ind. 2000) (defendant's request for a jury instruction was properly denied because it was directed to the testimony of one witness who had a lengthy juvenile record (his accomplice) and intimated an opinion on the credibility of the witness or the weight to be given his testimony).

Martin v. State, 736 N.E.2d 1213 (Ind. 2000) (witness's juvenile record was not admissible to impeach him because his testimony did not provide the sole and crucial link against defendant, he freely revealed to the jury his status as a detainee, and defendant only offered the record as a general attack on the witness's credibility).

Rule 609(e)

Rowan v. State, 431 N.E.2d 805 (Ind. 1982) (permitting use of defendant's prior burglary conviction for impeachment purposes was not error though an appeal had been filed).

Craig v. State, 273 Ind. 361, 404 N.E.2d 580 (1980) (defendant was not denied a fair trial by permitting cross-examination as to prior possession of controlled substances conviction even though conviction was being appealed).

Lahr v. State, 640 N.E.2d 756 (Ind. Ct. App. 1994) (generally, evidence of juvenile delinquency proceedings is not admissible for impeachment purposes; trial court did not err in prohibiting defendant from cross-examining witness about juvenile record where witness was on probation for theft conviction as adult and defendant was permitted to cross-examine witness regarding conviction and probation).

Douglas v. State, 634 N.E.2d 811 (Ind. Ct. App. 1994), *opinion corrected on reh'g*, 640 N.E.2d 73 (juvenile records are not admissible for impeachment purposes; although evidence that defendant had been in Indiana Boys School was not admitted to impeach defendant, it was erroneously admitted where defendant had been in Boys School prior to commission of charged crime and jury was given impression that defendant had committed previous crimes; nevertheless, the error was harmless in view of overwhelming evidence, including defendant's confession).

Chapter 610

Rule 610. Religious Beliefs or Opinions

Rule 610 reads as follows:

> Evidence of the beliefs or opinions of a witness on matters of religion is not admissible for the purpose of showing that, by reason of their nature, the witness's credibility is impaired or enhanced.

*   *   *   *   *

ANALYSIS

Scope and Policy. Rule 610 generally prohibits the introduction of evidence or interrogation of witnesses as to religious beliefs or opinions for the purpose of impeaching or bolstering a witness's credibility. The principles of inadmissibility contained in Rule 610 rest primarily upon grounds of unfair prejudice and minimal probative value.

When Admissible. Rule 610 does not preclude the admission of evidence of religious beliefs where the evidence is relevant in a manner other than to show that the witness's trustworthiness is enhanced or diminished by virtue of the belief. Consequently, the rule does not prevent evidence tending to demonstrate bias or interest on the part of a witness, such as where the witness is affiliated with a church that is a party to the action.

ADDITIONAL AUTHORITY

WEISSENBERGER'S FEDERAL EVIDENCE §§ 610.1–610.2

4 WEINSTEIN 2d §§ 610.01–610.03

3 MUELLER & KIRKPATRICK §§ 289–290

McCORMICK § 48

3 WIGMORE § 936

COMPARISON TO FEDERAL RULE

Indiana Rule 610 is identical to Federal Rule 610.

SIGNIFICANT CASES

Pawlik v. Pawlik, 823 N.E.2d 328 (Ind. Ct. App. 2005), *transfer denied*, 831 N.E.2d 747 (Ind. 2005) (Rule 610 does not operate as an absolute bar to evidence about the religious beliefs of parties, but instead prohibits the use of such testimony only if it is offered for the purpose of buttressing or impugning the credibility of a witness; there may be practical, value-neutral reasons for the court to consider the parties' religious beliefs and practices that do not infringe on any of the parties' religious constitutional rights and liberties).

Chapter 611

Rule 611. Mode and Order of Interrogations and Presentations

Rule 611 reads as follows:

> **(a) Control by Court.** The court shall exercise reasonable control over the mode and order of interrogating witnesses and presenting evidence so as to (1) make the interrogation and presentation effective for the ascertainment of the truth, (2) avoid needless consumption of time, and (3) protect witnesses from harassment or undue embarrassment.
>
> **(b) Scope of Cross-Examination.** Cross-examination should be limited to the subject matter of the direct examination and matters affecting the credibility of the witness. The court may, in the exercise of discretion, permit inquiry into additional matters as if on direct examination.
>
> **(c) Leading Questions.** Leading questions should not be used on the direct examination of a witness except as may be necessary to develop the witness's testimony. Ordinarily, leading questions should be permitted on cross-examination. Whenever a party calls a hostile witness, an adverse party, or a witness identified with an adverse party, interrogation may be by leading questions.

*   *   *   *   *

ANALYSIS

Scope. Rule 611 governs the trial court's control over the mode and order of interrogating witnesses and presenting evidence, the scope of cross-examination, and the use of leading questions.

Judicial Discretion. Rule 611(a) accords the trial judge authority to control the examination of witnesses and the presentation of nontestimonial evidence. In the exercise of the trial court's discretion three guiding principles are indicated: (1) efficiency in ascertainment of the truth; (2) avoidance of needless consumption of time; and (3) protection of witnesses from harassment or undue embarrassment. Rule 611(a) seeks to advance goals similar to those underlying Rules 102 and 403, and consistent with the three objectives identified in Rule 611(a), the trial court has discretionary power over decisions such as whether and to what extent to allow re-direct and re-cross-examinations, whether a witness can be re-called, and whether a party may reopen its case. Judicial discretion in this regard will rarely be overturned on appeal; even in criminal cases, where the defendant is afforded

the greatest possible latitude in presenting a case, the judge may require that a criminal defendant testify at a certain point in the trial, rather than when the defendant wanted to testify.

Scope of Cross-Examination.   Under Indiana Rule 611(b), cross-examination is permitted on the subject matter covered in the direct examination and on matters affecting the credibility of the witness. Examination of a witness beyond the scope of direct inquiry is permissible only if authorized by the trial judge in the exercise of his or her discretion.

Recent Developments

In *Wallace v. State*, 836 N.E.2d 985 (Ind. Ct. App. 2005), *transfer denied*, 855 N.E.2d 995 (Ind. 2006), the court of appeals rejected the contention that a party may offer character evidence in response to a criminal defendant's appearance and demeanor at trial. In *Wallace*, the State argued that the defendant's denial that he shot the victim contradicted his respectful conduct during the trial, and thus "opened the door" to his character. The court of appeals disagreed, noting that rebuttal evidence is limited to evidence that explains, contradicts, or disproves evidence actually offered by the adverse party.

Leading Questions.   Rule 611(c) provides the court with discretion to control the use of leading questions. Leading questions suggest a particular answer by the form or substance of the interrogation. On direct examination, where the witness usually favors the calling party's case, leading questions are disapproved because the witness may readily accede to the version of the events stated in the examiner's question rather than describing the occurrence as he or she actually remembers it. On cross-examination, where the witness is likely aligned with the opposing party, leading questions are generally permissible because it is assumed that the witness is less susceptible to the question's suggestiveness.

Illustration

The following questions are likely to be held leading, depending upon the factual context in which they are asked:

Isn't it a fact that you were at home on January 19, 1988?

The light was green when you entered the intersection, isn't that true?

Was it 6 o'clock or was it some other time?

After the meeting with Mr. Johnson, did you go home?

(*Compare:* Where did you go after the meeting with Mr. Johnson?)

Am I correct in stating that you are a close friend of the accused?

When Leading Questions Permissible.   Leading questions may be allowed on direct examination but only when necessary to develop testimony or when used to elicit preliminary matters which are usually undisputed. Accordingly, leading questions are frequently permitted when interrogating a young child, or where the witness has temporarily forgotten relatively undisputed facts. Leading questions are expressly authorized by the rule when a party calls a hostile witness, an adverse party, or a witness identified with an adverse party.

Hostile Witnesses.   A hostile witness is one who is so evasive or uncooperative on examination that his testimony is impeded. Usually, counsel asks the trial judge to have the witness declared hostile, thereby permitting counsel to proceed with a leading question form. The term "witness identified with an adverse party" is intended to apply broadly to an identification based upon employment by the party or by virtue of a demonstrated connection to an opposing party.

Constitutional Considerations

The U.S. Supreme Court has examined constitutional limitations on the degree to which witnesses can be protected in criminal trials. In *Coy v. Iowa*, 487 U.S. 1012, 108 S. Ct. 2798, 101 L. Ed. 2d 857 (1988), the Court determined that the Confrontation Clause of the Sixth Amendment was violated by allowing minor victims to testify behind a large screen which prevented the victim from seeing the defendant. The Court interpreted a confrontation "as requiring face-to-face meeting." In *Maryland v. Craig*, 497 U.S. 836, 110 S. Ct. 3157, 111 L. Ed. 2d 666 (1990), however, the Supreme Court emphasized that the right to confront witnesses was not absolute. The Court found that the Confrontation Clause was not violated by allowing a child witness to testify via a one-way, closed-circuit television where necessary to further important public policy such as protecting that particular child from emotional trauma and where "other elements of confrontation—oath, cross-examination and observation of witness's demeanor" were present.

ADDITIONAL AUTHORITY

WEISSENBERGER'S FEDERAL EVIDENCE §§ 611.1–611.6

MCCORMICK §§ 5, 6, 19–31

4 WEINSTEIN 2d §§ 611.01–611.06

3 MUELLER & KIRKPATRICK §§ 291–322

3 WIGMORE §§ 768–780

5 WIGMORE §§ 1390–1394

6 WIGMORE §§ 1884–1894

8 WIGMORE § 2276

Cooper, *Recent Developments in Indiana Evidence Law*, 32 IND. L. REV. 811 (1999)

COMPARISON TO FEDERAL RULE

Indiana Rule 611 and Federal Rule 611 are functionally identical.

WITNESSES

SIGNIFICANT CASES

Maryland v. Craig, 497 U.S. 836, 110 S. Ct. 3157, 111 L. Ed. 2d 666 (1990) (Confrontation Clause was not violated by allowing a child witness to testify via one-way, closed-circuit television where necessary to further important public policy such as protecting that particular child from emotional trauma and where "other elements of confrontation—oath, cross-examination, and observation of witness's demeanor" were present).

Coy v. Iowa, 487 U.S. 1012, 108 S. Ct. 2798, 101 L. Ed. 2d 857 (1988), *superseded by statute, United States v. Moses*, 137 F.3d 894 (6th Cir. Mich. 1998) (Confrontation Clause was violated by allowing a child victim to testify from behind a screen; the Confrontation Clause provides a criminal defendant with the right to confront, face-to-face, the witnesses giving evidence against him).

Rule 611(a)

Clark v. State, 668 N.E.2d 1206 (Ind. 1996) (whether to allow recall of witness is within trial court's discretion; murder defendant did not have right to recall defense witness to testify that he had not been coached by defense counsel, where proposed testimony was not essential to defense and defendant had chance to elicit that testimony on redirect and chose not to).

Isaacs v. State, 659 N.E.2d 1036 (Ind. 1995) (trial court was within its discretion to prohibit murder defendant from recalling defense pathologist witness where defendant's own inaction and refusal to comply with discovery rules delayed victim's blood test results until after pathologist testified, and defendant could have presented same testimony through another witness; decision on whether to recall witness may be partly based on trial court's evaluation of moving party's behavior and compliance with pretrial orders).

Pigg v. State, 603 N.E.2d 154 (Ind. 1992) (trial court limited defendant's cross-examination of an informant regarding the informant's address on the grounds of relevance; court held that, in cases where the trial court limits cross-examination of a witness, prejudice is presumed when an informant is the sole witness to a controlled buy with defendant and there has been no in-camera hearing at which defendant had an opportunity to show prejudice).

McQuay v. State, 566 N.E.2d 542 (Ind. 1991) (trial court's limitation of defense counsel's cross-examination of the victim was not error because defense counsel had been given sufficient opportunity to impeach victim by pointing out inconsistencies between her testimony at the deposition and at trial).

Atkins v. State, 561 N.E.2d 797 (Ind. Ct. App. 1990) (defense counsel need not engage in extended questioning to preserve a defendant's right of confrontation; the critical inquiry is whether the opportunity to do so was given).

Jackson v. State, 535 N.E.2d 1173 (Ind. 1989) (trial court has the discretion to determine the manner in which a party questions a young witness).

Pitman v. State, 436 N.E.2d 74 (Ind. 1982) (in exercising control over proceedings, the trial court has wide discretion in the manner of taking testimony to ensure adherence to the rules of evidence and procedure).

Book v. State, 880 N.E.2d 1240 (Ind. Ct. App. 2008) (trial court's requirement that a criminal defendant testify at a certain point in the trial, rather than when the defendant wanted to testify, did not violate his right against self-incrimination and his right to counsel; the right to due process does not necessarily include the right to determine the order of witnesses and the timing and manner of the defendant's own testimony).

Estate of Lee v. Lee & Urbahns Co., 876 N.E.2d 361 (Ind. Ct. App. 2007) (the trial court did not abuse its discretion in denying a party permission to recall a witness because the estate repeatedly failed to exercise due diligence).

Pierce v. State, 640 N.E.2d 730 (Ind. Ct. App. 1994) (where defendant was charged with attempted murder, trial court granted the prosecution's motion in limine prohibiting all references to a prosecution witness's cocaine conviction finding that dealing cocaine was not a crime probative of credibility; at trial, court prohibited defendant from cross-examining the witness regarding his address because such questioning would have revealed that the witness was incarcerated; court of appeals held that defendant's right of confrontation was not violated by the limitation).

Robinson v. State, 634 N.E.2d 1367 (Ind. Ct. App. 1994) (at defendant's drug trial, defendant wanted to cross-examine a prosecution witness regarding the witness's involvement in unrelated drug transactions and witness's knowledge of drugs; defendant's right of confrontation was not violated when the trial court limited the cross-examination upon the witness's invocation of his right against self-incrimination).

Rule 611(b)

Saylor v. State, 765 N.E.2d 535 (Ind. 2002) (cross-examination questions that exceed the scope of direct or redirect examination are improper and may be prohibited).

Fayson v. State, 726 N.E.2d 292 (Ind. 2000) (testimony about cousin being in the house claimed to be outside the scope established only that the cousin was in the house at some time and not necessarily the night of the murder; trial court ruling as to the scope of cross-examination will be reversed only for an abuse of discretion).

Marcum v. State, 725 N.E.2d 852 (Ind. 2000) (trial court correctly limited cross-examination where witness repeatedly denied memory of prior statements).

Hobbs v. State, 548 N.E.2d 164 (Ind. 1990) (trial court has the discretion to determine whether to allow cross-examination to test the credibility of a witness).

Mullins v. State, 504 N.E.2d 570 (Ind. 1987) (defendant opened the door to questions concerning his previous purchases of drugs from a dealer after he testified on cross-examination that he had never sold drugs to the dealer).

Hudson v. State, 496 N.E.2d 1286 (Ind. 1986) (scope of cross-examination includes any matter that tends to modify, explain, or rebut the witness's testimony on direct).

Newman v. State, 485 N.E.2d 58 (Ind. 1985) (scope of cross-examination is within the discretion of the trial court).

Wallace v. State, 836 N.E.2d 985 (Ind. Ct. App. 2005), *transfer denied*, 855 N.E.2d 995 (Ind. 2006) (rejecting the argument that a party "opens the door" to his character through his choice of clothing and demeanor at trial, against which the opposing party may offer evidence of the defendant's character).

Lyles v. State, 834 N.E.2d 1035 (Ind. Ct. App. 2005), *transfer denied*, 841 N.E.2d 191 (Ind. 2005) (during its cross-examination of a witness and rebuttal, questions concerning the consistency of the testimony with a prior statement were directed to the subject matter of the direct examination and the credibility of the witness; accordingly, the trial court properly allowed the party to conduct its cross-examination and rebuttal).

Witte v. M.M., 800 N.E.2d 185 (Ind. Ct. App. 2003), *superseded*, 820 N.E.2d 128 (Ind. 2005) (trial judges retain wide latitude to impose reasonable limits based on concerns about harassment, prejudice, confusion of the issues, the witness's safety, or interrogation that is repetitive or only marginally relevant).

Tawdul v. State, 720 N.E.2d 1211 (Ind. Ct. App. 1999) (defense counsel opened the door on direct examination to prosecution's cross-examining defendant about a traffic offense that occurred 10 years prior to trial for resisting arrest; state was entitled to attempt to clarify defendant's direct examination testimony for the jury).

Lycan v. State, 671 N.E.2d 447 (Ind. Ct. App. 1996) (state was entitled to cross-examine detective

about weapons purchased by murder defendant, after defendant elicited testimony on direct examination that defendant had purchased weapon similar to weapon that killed victim but with different serial number; scope of cross-examination is within trial court's discretion and is reversible only for abuse of discretion; scope of cross-examination is not restricted to those parts specifically included in direct examiner's questions).

Hopkins v. State, 668 N.E.2d 686 (Ind. Ct. App. 1996) (if party introduces subject on cross-examination, opposing party may pursue that subject on redirect examination; defendant may not open and close issue at his convenience).

Reeves v. Boyd & Sons, 654 N.E.2d 864 (Ind. Ct. App. 1995) (because testimony of plaintiff's witnesses could leave the jury with the false impression that plaintiff would not drive while intoxicated, that testimony opened the door to an inquiry on cross-examination leading to evidence that plaintiff had been convicted of operating under the influence).

Whitehair v. State, 654 N.E.2d 296 (Ind. Ct. App. 1995) (state was entitled to cross-examine witness about defendant's less than honorable discharge from military because defense introduced subject by repeatedly referring to defendant's time in service in "apparent attempt" to suggest to jury defendant's good character).

Small v. State, 632 N.E.2d 779 (Ind. Ct. App. 1994) (in trial for resisting law enforcement, defendant was not entitled to mistrial after prosecutor asked defendant on cross-examination if he had prior resisting arrest conviction and trial court referred to "other offenses" in ruling on objection to question, as defendant's direct examination revealed another inadmissible conviction and prosecutor made no further attempts to admit evidence of other crimes; court's admonishment sufficed to cure any error).

White v. State, 630 N.E.2d 215 (Ind. Ct. App. 1994) (trial court did not abuse its discretion by limiting scope of defendant's cross-examination of police officer on his familiarity with victim's address, where subject was not raised in direct examination and it was not apparent how that line of questioning would have elucidated, modified, explained, contradicted, or rebutted any testimony given during direct examination).

Rule 611(c)

Lampkins v. State, 778 N.E.2d 1248 (Ind. 2002) (the use of leading questions during direct examination generally rests within the trial court's discretion).

Williams v. State, 733 N.E.2d 919 (Ind. 2000) (leading questions to 20-year-old witness, who was fearful of her own safety and that of her children, in a murder prosecution case were improper because the apprehensive and vulnerable emotional state of the witness may have well increased her susceptibility to suggested questions and impaired the accuracy of the resulting questions; however the court did not reverse the trial court's action in permitting the leading questions, even if they were erroneous, because they were not inconsistent with substantial justice and did not affect defendant's substantial rights).

Bussey v. State, 536 N.E.2d 1027 (Ind. 1989) (court permitted leading questions during the direct examination of a 16-year-old rape victim; proper to use leading questions to guide a witness in testifying where the witness was young, inexperienced, and frightened).

Edwards v. State, 500 N.E.2d 1209 (Ind. 1986) (trial court has the discretion to permit a party to treat a witness as a hostile witness if circumstances surrounding the examination indicate such treatment is necessary).

Goodman v. State, 479 N.E.2d 513, 515 (Ind. 1985) ("A leading question is one that suggests to the witness the answer desired.").

Chapter 612

Rule 612. Writing or Object Used to Refresh Memory

Rule 612 reads as follows:

(a) **While Testifying.** If, while testifying, a witness uses a writing or object to refresh the witness's memory, an adverse party is entitled to have the writing or object produced at the trial, hearing, or deposition in which the witness is testifying.

(b) **Before Testifying.** If, before testifying, a witness uses a writing or object to refresh the witness's memory for the purpose of testifying and the court in its discretion determines that the interests of justice so require, an adverse party is entitled to have the writing or object produced, if practicable, at the trial, hearing, or deposition in which the witness is testifying.

(c) **Terms and Conditions of Production and Use.** A party entitled to have a writing or object produced under this rule is entitled to inspect it, to cross-examine the witness thereon, and to introduce in evidence those portions which relate to the testimony of the witness. If production of the writing or object at the trial, hearing, or deposition is impracticable, the court may order it made available for inspection. If it is claimed that the writing or object contains matters not related to the subject matter of the testimony, the court shall examine the writing or object in camera, excise any portions not so related, and order delivery of the remainder to the party entitled thereto. Any portion withheld over objections shall be preserved and made available to the appellate court in the event of an appeal. If a writing or object is not produced, made available for inspection, or delivered pursuant to order under this rule, the court shall make any order justice requires, but in criminal cases if the prosecution elects not to comply, the order shall be one striking the testimony or, if the court in its discretion determines that the interests of justice so require, declaring a mistrial.

---

*   *   *   *   *

ANALYSIS

Refreshing Recollection Generally; Writing Need Not Be Admissible.   According to Rule 612, the recollection of a witness may be refreshed through the use of a document. The writing is used to revive the memory of the witness, and it must provide sufficient stimulus that the witness has a present, independent recollection of the matter. In order to apply the

WITNESSES

Rule properly, it is imperative to recognize that the writing is not the evidence. It is the refreshed recollection in the form of testimony that is the evidence. As a consequence, it is important to appreciate that the writing need not be admissible under the rules. There is no necessity of compliance with the best evidence rule, the authentication rule, or the hearsay rule. Frequently, however, a document used to refresh recollection is marked for the purposes of the record, even though it is not being offered as evidence.

Procedure.   Utilizing the technique of present recollection refreshed, the witness at trial must be incapable of recalling all of the pertinent facts as to which he or she has first-hand knowledge and as to which he or she has been called to testify. The witness is then handed the writing by trial counsel. The proponent of the witness then asks the witness to read the writing silently in order to refresh his or her recollection. The witness is then asked if his or her recollection is refreshed, and if he or she then has a present recollection, the witness provides testimony from revived memory.

Disclosure to Opponent.   When a writing is used as a memory jogging device, the writing must be shown to opposing counsel on request. Rule 612 also expands the traditional rule by permitting production of a writing within the judge's discretion even if the writing was only used prior to trial to stimulate the witness's memory. The existence of such a document used prior to trial would normally be exposed during the course of cross-examination of the witness by the witness's opponent. A recess may be requested where the pretrial memory jogging document is not readily available for production.

Practical Application of Rule 612

It should be noted that when a document is used at trial in an effort to refresh the recollection of a witness, the document must be produced for adverse counsel. Where, however, the document is used prior to testifying in order to refresh the witness's recollection, the document is subject to production in the discretion of the trial judge subject to the interests of justice. Accordingly, documents used at trial to refresh recollection must be delivered to adverse counsel on request. In this context, Rule 612 does not provide for discretion. The discretion provided by Rule 612 applies only to those documents used prior to trial to refresh recollection.

Writing Containing Unrelated Matters; Failure to Produce.   Where a claim is made that the writing used to refresh recollection contains matters that are unrelated to the litigation and that have not affected the witness's testimony, the court has the duty to inspect the writing in camera to excise any unrelated or irrelevant portions. The remainder is delivered to the adverse party. Where a party fails to produce documents in compliance with the trial court's order, the court may make any further order necessitated by the ends of justice, including in criminal cases, ordering a mistrial where the prosecution fails to comply.

Failure to Revive Recollection.   Where a document fails to revive the recollection of a witness, the document may be admissible as "past recollection recorded" under Rule 803(5). *See* Analysis to Rule 803(5). In this regard, it should be appreciated that the Rules of Evidence essentially provide for a three-tiered preference. First, the unaided testimony of a witness is preferred. Second, if the unaided testimony is not available, the law then prefers refreshed recollection. Third, if the witness's recollection cannot be revived, the recorded recollection exception to the hearsay rule may be available to admit the document that contains the witness's prior knowledge of the facts in question.

Practical Considerations

The technique of refreshing a witness's recollection must be distinguished from the hearsay exception, "past recollection recorded," the subject of Rule 803(5). Under the technique of refreshing recollection, the witness reviews the writing to revive his or her memory of the material event and then proceeds to testify on the basis of present, personal knowledge. The writing itself is not offered as evidence. It merely serves as a memory jogging device, and compliance with the hearsay rule, the authentication rule, or the so-called best evidence rule is not required. In contrast, under the "past recollection recorded" exception to the general proscription against hearsay, the document itself is offered as the evidence. Rule 803(5) may operate to admit written hearsay in certain instances where the witness's present recollection remains absent or incomplete and cannot be refreshed by the writing. Under Rule 803(5), the witness's trial testimony establishes the foundational fact that recollection was complete at the time of writing and that the facts were accurately recorded in the document. Obviously, where a writing is offered into evidence, it must comply with all the rules regarding the admissibility of documentary evidence, one of which is the hearsay rule. Where a writing is offered, one of the hearsay exceptions available to admit the out-of-court statement is Rule 803(5). Of course, other exceptions might be available as well.

ADDITIONAL AUTHORITY

WEISSENBERGER'S FEDERAL EVIDENCE §§ 612.1–612.7

4 WEINSTEIN 2d §§ 612.01–612.09

3 MUELLER & KIRKPATRICK §§ 323–328

MCCORMICK § 9

3 WIGMORE §§ 758–765

COMPARISON TO FEDERAL RULE

Indiana Rule 612 is similar in substance to Federal Rule 612.

SIGNIFICANT CASES

Gault v. State, 878 N.E.2d 1260 (Ind. 2008) (trial court improperly refused to allow defendant access to report used to refresh arresting officer's recollection during cross-examination; defendant's interests were potentially harmed by the report, and defendant was thus an "adverse party" under Rule 612 who should have been permitted access to the report; however, the error was harmless).

Young v. State, 746 N.E.2d 920 (Ind. 2001) (state's use of a transcript to refresh the brother's recollection that he had reported he heard screams coming from the bedroom during defendant's attack on the victim was appropriate).

WITNESSES

Joyner v. State, 736 N.E.2d 232 (Ind. 2000) (trial court did not err in excluding police report to refresh an officer's recollection because nothing in the officer's direct, cross, or redirect examinations suggested that he testified contrary to the information defendant alleged was contained in the police report; thus, the predicate for refreshing the officer's recollection was not met in the first instance).

Thompson v. State, 728 N.E.2d 155 (Ind. 2000) (it was harmless error for the trial court to prevent defendant from using a deposition to refresh witness's memory on the theory that the witness did not prepare the deposition; a writing used to refresh a witness's memory can be prepared by the witness or another person; state was entitled to introduce statement relating to incident defendant attempted to use to refresh witness's recollection but trial court committed harmless error in admitting remainder of statement over defendant's objection).

Evans v. State, 563 N.E.2d 1251 (Ind. 1990) (although a written memorandum may be used to refresh the recollection of a witness, the memorandum may not be substituted for the witness's memory).

Trotter v. State, 559 N.E.2d 585 (Ind. 1990) (written memorandum may be used to refresh a witness's recollection).

Mitchem v. State, 503 N.E.2d 889 (Ind. 1987) (where prosecution witness examined a document on the stand and proceeded to testify from his refreshed memory, defense counsel was entitled to see the document and use it in cross-examination).

Gault v. State, 861 N.E.2d 728 (Ind. Ct. App. 2007), *superseded in part*, 878 N.E.2d 1260 (Ind. 2008) (the party who refreshes a witness's recollection is not the opposing party for Rule 612 purposes even though that party did not call that witness to the stand; refreshing the recollection of a witness on cross-examination does not give that party the right to have the document introduced into evidence).

Mroz v. Harrison, 815 N.E.2d 551 (Ind. Ct. App. 2004) (Rule 612 does not require that the writing used to refresh a witness's memory be prepared by the witness).

Chapter 613

Rule 613. Prior Statements of Witnesses

Rule 613 reads as follows:

> **(a) Examining Witness Concerning Prior Statement.** In examining a witness concerning a prior statement made by the witness, whether written or not, the statement need not be shown nor its contents disclosed to the witness at that time, but on request the same shall be shown or disclosed to opposing counsel.
>
> **(b) Extrinsic Evidence of Prior Inconsistent Statement of Witness.** Extrinsic evidence of a prior inconsistent statement by a witness is not admissible unless the witness is afforded an opportunity to explain or deny the same and the opposite party is afforded an opportunity to interrogate the witness thereon, or the interests of justice otherwise require. This provision does not apply to statements of a party-opponent as defined in Rule 801(d)(2).

* * * * *

ANALYSIS

Function of Rule. Under Rule 613, a witness may be impeached through the introduction of evidence of a statement made by that witness prior to trial that is inconsistent with the testimony he has provided at trial.

Extrinsic Evidence Defined; Judicial Discretion; Statements of Opponent. Under Rule 613(b), a witness may be impeached by "extrinsic evidence," that is, evidence admitted after the primary witness has stepped down from testifying. Where such evidence is introduced, the witness must be given an opportunity to explain or deny the inconsistent statement and the opposing party must have an opportunity to interrogate the witness concerning the statement. It should be noted that Rule 613(b) affords the trial judge discretion to permit the introduction of extrinsic evidence in the absence of the specified requirements of Rule 613(b) where "the interests of justice require." It also should be noted that the requirements of Rule 613(b) do not apply to out-of-court statements of a party-opponent that are admissible as substantive evidence under Rule 801(d)(2).

Showing of Written Statement. Rule 613(a) dispenses with the foundational necessity of showing the witness a written prior inconsistent statement before interrogating the witness about any discrepancy between the prior written statement and his trial testimony. Opposing

counsel (the proponent of the witness), however, has the right to be shown a copy of the document upon request.

Practical Application of Rule 613

Extrinsic evidence is testimony or documentary evidence that is submitted to the trier of fact after the conclusion of the testimony of the witness sought to be impeached. Usually, it involves the calling of a distinct witness to provide the testimony as to the prior inconsistent statement or to authenticate the document containing the prior contradictory statement. Where a witness is sought to be impeached while he or she is still testifying, the requirements of Rule 613(b) are not applicable.

Limited Purpose; Limiting Instruction.   Where a prior inconsistent statement is offered for the purpose of impeachment, the jury may only consider the prior statement as substantive evidence where the prior statement is admissible hearsay. Hearsay may be admissible pursuant to an exception to either the basic definition or the exclusionary rule. *See* Article VIII. Where the prior inconsistent statement does not conform to a hearsay exception, opposing counsel (the proponent of the witness sought to be impeached) may wish to seek a limiting instruction under Rule 105. The limiting instruction would advise the jury that it may consider the prior inconsistent statement solely for the purpose of evaluating the credibility of the witness sought to be impeached.

Constitutional Considerations

When a defendant exercises his right to testify at trial, statements ordinarily subject to the exclusionary rule and constitutionally inadmissible in the prosecution's case-in-chief are often admissible to impeach the defendant's inconsistent testimony. The U.S. Supreme Court has held that the exclusionary rule is not "a license to use perjury by way of defense." *See Harris v. New York*, 401 U.S. 222, 226, 91 S. Ct. 643, 646, 28 L. Ed. 2d 1, 5 (1971). The possibility that this impeachment exception will encourage police misconduct is merely "speculative" and therefore outweighed by the furtherance of the truthseeking function of the court. The impeachment exception, however, may not be extended beyond the defendant's own testimony to include other defense witnesses. *See James v. Illinois*, 493 U.S. 307, 110 S. Ct. 648, 107 L. Ed. 2d 676 (1990).

In *Michigan v. Harvey*, 494 U.S. 344, 110 S. Ct. 1176, 108 L. Ed. 2d 293 (1990), statements obtained in violation of the accused's Sixth Amendment right to counsel were admitted at trial for impeachment purposes. The U.S. Supreme Court held that, although these statements may not be used as substantive evidence, they may be used to impeach the defendant's inconsistent trial testimony.

Practical Considerations

Rule 613 does not contain a test that determines when a statement is inconsistent, and the degree of necessary inconsistency will be governed by prior case law. A general test endorsed by McCormick is: "It is enough if the proffered testimony, taken as a whole, either by what it says or by what it omits to say, affords some indication that the fact was different from the testimony of the witness whom it sought to contradict." MCCORMICK § 34.

ADDITIONAL AUTHORITY

WEISSENBERGER'S FEDERAL EVIDENCE §§ 613.1–613.8

4 WEINSTEIN 2d §§ 613.01–613.05

3 MUELLER & KIRKPATRICK §§ 329–333

MCCORMICK §§ 34–39

3A WIGMORE §§ 1017–1046

COMPARISON TO FEDERAL RULE

Indiana Rule 613 is identical in substance to Federal Rule 613.

SIGNIFICANT CASES

Michigan v. Harvey, 494 U.S. 344, 110 S. Ct. 1176, 108 L. Ed. 2d 293 (1990) (statements taken in violation of defendant's Sixth Amendment right to counsel were admissible to impeach the defendant's testimony).

James v. Illinois, 493 U.S. 307, 110 S. Ct. 648, 107 L. Ed. 2d 676 (1990) (the impeachment exception to the exclusionary rule may not be extended beyond the defendant's own testimony to include other defense witnesses).

Harris v. New York, 401 U.S. 222, 91 S. Ct. 643, 28 L. Ed. 2d 1 (1971) (statement obtained in violation of defendant's *Miranda* rights admissible to impeach defendant's testimony).

Dunlap v. State, 761 N.E.2d 837 (Ind. 2002) (a statement at trial of "I am not sure" or "I don't remember" is not necessarily inconsistent with an earlier statement that provides the answer to the question being asked).

LeFlore v. State, 823 N.E.2d 1205 (Ind. Ct. App. 2005), *transfer denied*, 831 N.E.2d 744 (Ind. 2005) (Rule 613 does not require that a prior statement be authenticated before it can be used for impeachment purposes).

Martin v. State, 779 N.E.2d 1235 (Ind. Ct. App. 2002) (a party is forbidden from placing a witness on the stand when the sole purpose for doing so is to present otherwise inadmissible evidence under the guise of impeachment).

Young v. State, 746 N.E.2d 920 (Ind. 2001) (ordinarily, prior inconsistent statements are used to impeach, not as substantive evidence on the matter report; brother's prior statement to the police that he had heard screams was admissible under Rule 613 to impeach his denial at trial that he had heard screams).

Appleton v. State, 740 N.E.2d 122 (Ind. 2001) (state's witness denied defendant's presence at the scene of the charged crime; prosecution improperly attempted to impeach witness by reading line-by-line a prior inconsistent statement in which the witness described defendant's

participation—permissible impeachment was limited to making witness aware of specific portions of his testimony that were inconsistent with his statements made prior to trial and giving him an opportunity to explain the inconsistencies).

Martin v. State, 736 N.E.2d 1213 (Ind. 2000); *Small v. State*, 736 N.E.2d 742 (Ind. 2000) (after witness claimed that she did not tell police where to look for a gun, the trial court properly admitted witness's prior inconsistent statement to police to attack the witness's credibility).

Jackson v. State, 728 N.E.2d 147 (Ind. 2000) (trial court did not err in excluding witness's prior inconsistent statement that he thought murder was accidental for impeachment purposes because statement of belief was a collateral matter and irrelevant).

Owens v. State, 659 N.E.2d 466 (Ind. 1995) (in murder trial, admission of investigating officer's testimony that witness's two taped pretrial statements were consistent was harmless error where central issue was whether defendant was too intoxicated to have necessary *mens rea* and jury could only have inferred mental state from defendant's words and acts).

Hilton v. State, 648 N.E.2d 361 (Ind. 1995), *overruled in part, State v. Wilson*, 836 N.E.2d 407 (Ind. 2005) (defendant did not establish basis for impeachment of witness with his alleged admission that he shot victim; defendant did not cross-examine witness about admission and, thus, witness made no statement that might be inconsistent with regard to remembering the person who would have testified about witness's alleged prior inconsistent statement).

Wrencher v. State, 635 N.E.2d 1095 (Ind. 1994) (shooting victim's original identification of codefendant as trigger man did not make later identification of defendant as trigger man inadmissible where earlier statement was made while victim was confused and in critical condition in hospital).

Stubbs v. State, 560 N.E.2d 528 (Ind. 1990) (trial court did not err in refusing to admit in evidence a prosecution witness's prior statement where the statement was not directly inconsistent with the witness's testimony at trial and where defense counsel was permitted to read part of the statement in front of the jury during cross-examination).

Maynard v. State, 513 N.E.2d 641 (Ind. 1987) (a proper foundation must be laid to impeach a witness with a prior statement).

Hutcherson v. State, 507 N.E.2d 969 (Ind. 1987) (in pre-Rule case, defendant was not permitted to impeach a witness with prior inconsistent statements where the statements were found not to be inconsistent).

Gray v. State, 982 N.E.2d 434 (Ind. Ct. App. 2013) (under Rule 613, a prior inconsistent statement may be admitted to impeach a witness, and when used in this manner, the statement is not hearsay).

Stoltmann v. State, 793 N.E.2d 275 (Ind. Ct. App. 2003) (a witness's prior inconsistent unsworn statement is not admissible as substantive evidence, but may be used for the limited purpose of impeaching that witness).

Kendall v. State, 790 N.E.2d 122 (Ind. Ct. App. 2003) (a witness who has admitted an inconsistent prior statement has impeached herself and further evidence of impeachment is unnecessary).

Chapter 614

Rule 614. Calling and Interrogation of Witnesses by Court and Jury

Rule 614 reads as follows:

(a) Calling by Court. The court may not call witnesses except in extraordinary circumstances or except as provided for court-appointed experts, and all parties are entitled to cross-examine witnesses thus called.

(b) Interrogation by Court. The court may interrogate witnesses, in an impartial manner, whether called by itself or by a party.

(c) Objections. Objections to the calling of witnesses by the court or to interrogation by it may be made at the time or at the next available opportunity when the jury is not present.

(d) Interrogation by Juror. A juror may be permitted to propound questions to a witness by submitting them in writing to the judge who will decide whether to submit the questions to the witness for answer, subject to the objections of the parties, which may be made at the time or at the next available opportunity when the jury is not present. Once the court has ruled upon the appropriateness of the written questions, it must then rule upon the objections, if any, of the parties prior to submission of the questions to the witness.

---

* * * * *

ANALYSIS

Scope of Rule. Rule 614 applies in civil and criminal cases and permits the trial judge to call and interrogate witnesses only in extraordinary circumstances or in situations involving court-appointed experts. Where the trial judge elects to call a witness, all parties are allowed to cross-examine that witness using leading question form. The power of the trial court to interrogate witnesses is, of course, subject to the restriction that the trial judge must maintain his or her status as an impartial arbiter.

Recent Developments

In *Ashba v. State*, 816 N.E.2d 862 (Ind. Ct. App. 2004), an Indiana court set forth guidelines to be used by courts in ensuring that juries are provided with an opportunity to ask questions of a witness under Rule 614 and Jury Rule 20. The Court held that, to avoid any confusion in the minds of the jurors about the procedure, courts should explain to jurors what the questioning procedure will entail and how it will work. Judges may use a variety of methods to actually obtain jury questions, but the court must ensure that jurors know when they will be given an opportunity to ask such questions. Permissible procedures include: (1) informing the jurors that it will be glancing at the jury to see if any questions exist after a witness's testimony; (2) instructing jurors to verbally or physically indicate if they have any questions; or (3) informing the jurors that it will specifically ask for questions after each witness.

Objections. Rule 614(c) permits trial counsel to make objections to either the court's calling of its own witness or the court's questioning of any witness. If the party appears pro se and the court interrogates that party while testifying, the party must object to the question while on the stand. A party need not make an immediate objection in a jury trial; Rule 614(c) provides that such objection is timely if it is made at the earliest opportunity outside of the hearing of the jury.

Unlike its federal counterpart, Indiana Rule 614 expressly provides for the interrogation of witnesses by jurors. Specific procedures for such interrogation are provided in Rule 614(d).

ADDITIONAL AUTHORITY

WEISSENBERGER'S FEDERAL EVIDENCE §§ 614.1–614.4

4 WEINSTEIN 2d §§ 614.01–614.05

3 MUELLER & KIRKPATRICK §§ 334–337

MCCORMICK § 8 at 12–14

3 WIGMORE § 784

9 WIGMORE § 2484

COMPARISON TO FEDERAL RULE

Federal Rule 614 permits a judge to call and interrogate witnesses in civil and criminal cases and, consequently, does not limit the practice as does Indiana Rule 614. Additionally, Federal Rule 614 does not provide for interrogation of witnesses by jurors.

SIGNIFICANT CASES

Isaac v. State, 605 N.E.2d 144 (Ind. 1992) (judge may intervene and question witnesses in fact-finding process to promote clarity and dispel obscurity so long as questioning is conducted in an impartial manner and defendant is not prejudiced).

White v. State, 547 N.E.2d 831 (Ind. 1989) (trial court may intervene and interrogate a witness in order to promote clarity).

McVey v. State, 531 N.E.2d 458 (Ind. 1988) (a trial judge can properly interrogate a witness providing the interrogation does not improperly influence the jury).

Fox v. State, 497 N.E.2d 221 (Ind. 1986) (court is permitted to question witnesses to develop the truth or present facts overlooked by the party).

Rosendaul v. State, 864 N.E.2d 1110 (Ind. Ct. App. 2007) (in a bench trial, a defendant is required to lodge a contemporaneous objection to the trial court's interrogation of him to preserve the issue for appeal; this is a function of Rule 614's requirement that a party object to interrogation by the court at the time or at the next available opportunity when the jury is not present), *transfer denied*, 878 N.E.2d 204 (Ind. 2007).

Burks v. State, 838 N.E.2d 510 (Ind. Ct. App. 2005) (the procedure used for asking questions from the jury for a witness under Rule 614 should also be used under Ind. Jury R. 20: (1) the trial court should initially determine whether the juror questions are appropriate; (2) questions that are deemed appropriate are then subject to the trial court's ruling when the parties object; the decision whether to propound a question submitted by a juror is a determination that rests within the discretion of the trial court).

Howard v. State, 818 N.E.2d 469 (Ind. Ct. App. 2004) (the holding in *Ashba v. State*, 816 N.E.2d 862 (Ind. Ct. App. 2004), does not require the trial court to ask the jury if it has questions after excusing each witness; accordingly, the judge may instruct jurors that they may put their question in writing and submit it to the court, with a physical gesture or "eye check" used to determine if the jury has any questions).

Ashba v. State, 816 N.E.2d 862 (Ind. Ct. App. 2004) (detailing the procedure for asking questions from the jury to a witness; a trial court should explain to jurors what the questioning procedure will entail, and a variety of methods to obtain jury questions may be used, but the court must ensure that jurors know when they will be given an opportunity to ask such questions; permissible methods include: (1) informing the jurors that it will be glancing at the jury to see if any questions exist after a witness's testimony; (2) instructing jurors to verbally or physically indicate if they have any questions; or (3) informing the jurors that it will specifically ask for questions after each witness).

In re Roberts, 723 N.E.2d 474 (Ind. Ct. App. 2000) (in civil commitment hearing to the bench, trial court did not err in calling and examining witnesses; trial judge in civil commitment hearings are given wide latitude to ensure that the statutory criteria for commitment are met and that the rights of the person facing commitment are fully protected).

Dowdy v. State, 672 N.E.2d 948 (Ind. Ct. App. 1996) (trial court properly instructed jury that jurors could submit questions to witnesses to elucidate their testimony; decision to propound juror's question to witness is within discretion of trial court and it properly excluded juror's question to witness about whether defendant had been previously charged with same charges as in current trial).

Lawson v. State, 664 N.E.2d 773 (Ind. Ct. App. 1996) (trial court did not commit error in asking the jury if it had any questions prior to excusing each witness).

WITNESSES

Chapter 615

Rule 615. Separation of Witnesses

Rule 615 reads as follows:

At the request of a party, the court shall order witnesses excluded so that they cannot hear the testimony of or discuss testimony with other witnesses, and it may make the order on its own motion. This rule does not authorize the exclusion of (1) a party who is a natural person, or (2) an officer or employee of a party that is not a natural person designated as its representative by its attorney, or (3) a person whose presence is shown by a party to be essential to the presentation of the party's cause.

---

*   *   *   *   *

ANALYSIS

When Separation Mandatory; Parties Excepted; Party Defined.   Under Rule 615, a party has the right to the separation of witnesses, frequently called sequestration, upon timely request. Where the request is made, the trial court lacks the discretion to deny the request except in regard to certain necessary witnesses expressly identified in the Rule. A party may not be subject to the exclusion order.

Under the Rule, a *party* is defined as a natural person, an employee or agent of a party who is not a natural person and designated by its attorney, or another person whose presence is shown to be necessary to the presentation of the cause (*e.g.*, an expert witness). In some cases, an expert witness will base her testimony on evidence actually admitted at trial, thus mandating their presence. Rule 703 authorizes such a procedure.

The Rule is obviously designed to minimize the risk of cross-witness bias and influence by ensuring that a witness's testimony is, as much as possible, a product of his own independent recollection. Similarly, the exceptions to the Rule are designed around several ancillary purposes. In criminal cases, the presence of a party is an essential component of the Confrontation Clause rights guaranteed to the defendant. A party has an adequate opportunity to confront the accusers. The Rule also provides a mechanism for permitting a legal entity to participate in a trial to the same extent as a natural person.

Finally, the Rule also provides counsel with the flexibility to present the case effectively. For example, a prosecutor may need a police officer in attendance to hear testimony and assist in proving the case. A parent of a child witness may also need to be present to suggest

WITNESSES

alternate phrasing for confusing questions, or interpreters may be required for parties whose command of English is questionable.

Non-Witnesses. It should be noted that this Rule relates to persons at counsel table who may also be witnesses, and it does not apply to persons who will not be witnesses, for example, co-counsel, investigators, clerks, or secretaries.

Violation of Sequestration Order—Practical Considerations

The question of whether a separation order has been violated is typically a highly-nuanced fact-specific determination, and the trial court is granted the customary discretion in determining which corrective measures, if any, should be taken. *See Wisner v. Laney,* 984 N.E.2d 1201 (Ind. 2012). Accidental violations, such as casual witness-to-witness encounters, are usually not subject to sanction. Remedial measures include citing the witness for contempt, refusing to permit him to testify, striking his testimony, or permitting the transgression to reflect upon the witness's credibility.

ADDITIONAL AUTHORITY

WEISSENBERGER'S FEDERAL EVIDENCE §§ 615.1–615.3

4 WEINSTEIN 2d §§ 615.01–615.07

3 MUELLER & KIRKPATRICK §§ 338–341

6 WIGMORE §§ 1837–1841

COMPARISON TO FEDERAL RULE

Indiana Rule 615 is identical to Federal Rule 615 except that Indiana Rule 615 seeks to prevent witnesses from discussing testimony with other witnesses as well as hearing the testimony of other witnesses. Federal Rule 615 also prohibits exclusion of a person authorized by statute to be present; Indiana Rule 615 does not.

SIGNIFICANT CASES

Wisner v. Laney, 984 N.E.2d 1201 (Ind. 2012) (a trial court's determination regarding a violation of a separation of witnesses order will be upheld absent a showing of a clear abuse of discretion; in this case, the interaction between witnesses was accidental and the communication between the witnesses did not involve trial-related matters).

K.S. v. State, 849 N.E.2d 538 (Ind. 2006) (because Indiana juvenile law designates a child's parent as a party to the proceedings and grants the parent "all rights of parties provided under the Indiana Rules of Trial Procedure," K.S.'s mother was a party not subject to the order for a separation of witnesses).

Jiosa v. State, 755 N.E.2d 605 (Ind. 2001) (after an order separating witnesses for trial has been violated, courts may issue contempt citations, permit evidence of witnesses' noncompliance to impeach their credibility, exclude the testimony of the witnesses if the party is at fault or the testimony does not directly affect the party's ability to present its case).

Osborne v. State, 754 N.E.2d 916 (Ind. 2001) ("party representative" exception from the rule requiring separation of witnesses allows only one representative to remain in the courtroom during trial).

Anderson v. State, 743 N.E.2d 1273 (Ind. Ct. App. 2001) (although a motion for separation of witnesses is ideally made before any witnesses testify, a motion sometime afterwards may be permissible as long as the basic notions of fundamental fairness are not offended; trial court's erroneous denial of defendant's motion to separate witnesses was harmless where there was no evidence that any other witnesses were in the courtroom during the testimony of any other witnesses).

Long v. State, 743 N.E.2d 253 (Ind. 2001) (trial court did not err in permitting (1) an FBI agent (a testifying witness) to remain in the courtroom throughout trial as a person essential to the presentation of the state's case under Rule 615(3) and (2) a police trooper to remain in the courtroom throughout trial as an officer of the state under Rule 615(2) after it ordered a separation of witnesses because the FBI agent's presence was essential to the case where he and the police trooper divided many of the responsibilities of the investigation).

Jordan v. State, 656 N.E.2d 816, 818 (Ind. 1995) (a trial court is provided with considerable discretion in fashioning sequestration orders, determining whether they have been violated, and imposing a sanction for their violation).

Bell v. State, 495 N.E.2d 526 (Ind. 1986) (purpose of separating witnesses is to prevent the testimony of one witness from influencing the testimony of another witness).

Clark v. State, 480 N.E.2d 555 (Ind. 1985) (court found that where two witnesses had a discussion prior to either of them being called as witnesses, there was no danger of prejudice; primary purpose of a separation order is to prevent witnesses from hearing questions posed to, and answers given by, another witness).

Hayden v. State, 830 N.E.2d 923 (Ind. Ct. App. 2005), *transfer denied*, 841 N.E.2d 184 (Ind. 2005) (although police officers and detectives are officers or employees of a party and thus exempt from witness separation orders under Rule 615, other officers or employees working for the State of Indiana, such as the superintendent of a facility within the Department of Correction, as is the case here, may also be designated as the State's representative and thus permitted to be seated at the counsel table with the attorney for the State).

Julian v. State, 811 N.E.2d 392 (Ind. Ct. App. 2004) (an investigating detective was properly permitted to remain in the courtroom after sequestration of witnesses was ordered because the detective fell within the exception in Rule 615(2)).

Anderson v. State, 774 N.E.2d 906 (Ind. Ct. App. 2002) (a trial court has the discretion to allow a witness to testify after the violation of a separation order).

Kirby v. State, 774 N.E.2d 523 (Ind. Ct. App. 2002) (a party seeking an exception to the rule requiring the separation of witnesses on the basis that his witness is essential to the presentation of his case must convince the trial court that the witness has such specialized expertise or intimate knowledge of the facts of the case that counsel could not function effectively without the presence and aid of the witness).

Corley v. State, 663 N.E.2d 175 (Ind. Ct. App. 1996) (the purpose of witness separation order is to prevent influence of one witness's testimony on another, and, unless there is collusion or connivance by prosecutor, court has discretion to permit witness to testify after violation of separation order; appellate court will only disturb ruling for prejudice amounting to abuse of discretion).

Heeter v. State, 661 N.E.2d 612 (Ind. Ct. App. 1996) (although police officer assisting in prosecuting the case clearly qualifies under the Rule's second exemption from exclusion, the better practice would be for the state to designate the officer as its representative prior to the presentation of evidence).

Fourthman v. State, 658 N.E.2d 88 (Ind. Ct. App. 1995) (rule requiring court to exclude certain witnesses at party's request does not give court unbridled discretion to decide which witnesses will be excluded; trial court must grant request of party for witness separation order except for those witnesses who by rule are not subject to exclusion; whether witness is exempt from

exclusion is within trial court's discretion, but once witness is granted exempt status, court has no discretion to exclude witness).

Chapter 616

Rule 616. Bias of Witness

Rule 616 reads as follows:

> For the purpose of attacking the credibility of a witness, evidence of bias, prejudice, or interest of the witness for or against any party to the case is admissible.

* * * * *

ANALYSIS

Overview. Indiana Rule 616 provides that evidence of bias, prejudice, or interest of a witness for or against any party in an action is admissible to attack the witness's credibility. There is no cognate federal Rule although witnesses may be impeached on the basis of bias in federal court.

Function of Bias; Impeachment. Where a party seeks to demonstrate a witness is biased or interested, that party is essentially seeking to demonstrate that certain types of relationships may affect the witness's testimony, and as a result, the accuracy of the truth-finding process may be compromised. Bias, interest, prejudice, or motive to misrepresent may be proven by conduct or words of a witness. In addition, almost all types of interpersonal relationships will facially establish some potential bias or interest.

ADDITIONAL AUTHORITY

Weissenberger's Federal Evidence § 607.4

McCormick § 40 at 85

3 Mueller & Kirkpatrick §§ 256–259

3 Wigmore §§ 901, 948–953

COMPARISON TO FEDERAL RULE

There is no comparable federal rule, *but see generally* Federal Rule 607.

SIGNIFICANT CASES

United States v. Abel, 469 U.S. 45, 105 S. Ct. 465, 83 L. Ed. 2d 450 (1984) (impeachment of a witness for bias is proper, notwithstanding the lack of a specific rule).

Ingram v. State, 715 N.E.2d 405 (Ind. 1999) (while Rules of Evidence allow for the admission of evidence showing bias or prejudice of a witness without any qualifications, the provision should be read in conjunction with the separate rule requiring a balancing of probative value of evidence against the danger of unfair prejudice).

Jarrett v. State, 498 N.E.2d 967 (Ind. 1986) (error to prevent a defendant from impeaching the prosecution's witnesses with evidence of bias or motive).

Hossman v. State, 467 N.E.2d 416 (Ind. 1984) (trial court prevented party from impeaching a prosecution witness with evidence of her dependency on drugs, and evidence that the witness was allegedly involved in the murder of her husband and feared that the state would bring charges against her).

Reynolds v. State, 797 N.E.2d 864 (Ind. Ct. App. 2003) (evidence of bias, prejudice, or ulterior motives, on the part of a witness, is relevant at trial because it may discredit the witness or affect the weight of the witness's testimony and is thus admissible under Rule 616).

Kirk v. State, 797 N.E.2d 837 (Ind. Ct. App. 2003) (a party's intention to introduce a prior refusal to lie for a witness as evidence that the witness was biased against that party is relevant to the witness's partiality and is thus a proper subject to explore at trial).

Zawacki v. State, 753 N.E.2d 100 (Ind. Ct. App. 2001) (evidence that the victim requested permission from defendant and his wife to engage in a sexual relationship with defendant's daughter and wrote defendant's daughter letters that demonstrated victim's sexual feelings for defendant's daughter was admissible in sexual misconduct trial as impeachment evidence showing victim's bias, prejudice, or ulterior motive, where victim testified that she had not requested permission to engage in a sexual relationship with defendant's daughter).

Bell v. State, 655 N.E.2d 129 (Ind. Ct. App. 1995) (the defendant's interest in educating jury of any and all inducements that a witness receives in exchange for testimony is of utmost importance and outweighs any harm to state in drug conspiracy trial, even though informant's plea agreement did not require his testimony, jury should be told full extent of penalties that informer avoided in exchange for testifying).

Domangue v. State, 654 N.E.2d 1 (Ind. Ct. App. 1995) (in criminal trial where witness has financial motive to give certain testimony, jury should learn of those motives because they are relevant evidence of credibility and affect how much weight jury gives to testimony).

Barber v. Cox Communication, 629 N.E.2d 1253 (Ind. Ct. App. 1994) (in personal injury action, evidence of loan receipt agreement is admissible to impeach settling party/lender's credibility, although loan amount and any statements in agreement drafted only for purpose of manufacturing evidence should first be deleted; settling party's credibility was put in issue when plaintiff elicited favorable testimony from settling party's employers during their cross-examination).

Fullenkamp v. Newcomer, 508 N.E.2d 37 (Ind. Ct. App. 1987) (permissible to impeach a witness with evidence that the witness has a financial interest in the outcome of the case).

Chapter 617

Rule 617. Unrecorded Statements During Custodial Interrogation

Rule 617 reads as follows:

(a) In a felony criminal prosecution, evidence of a statement made by a person during a Custodial Interrogation in a Place of Detention shall not be admitted against the person unless an Electronic Recording of the statement was made, preserved, and is available at trial, except upon clear and convincing proof of any one of the following:

(1) The statement was part of a routine processing or "booking" of the person; or

(2) Before or during a Custodial Interrogation, the person agreed to respond to questions only if his or her Statements were not Electronically Recorded, provided that such agreement and its surrounding colloquy is Electronically Recorded or documented in writing; or

(3) The law enforcement officers conducting the Custodial Interrogation in good faith failed to make an Electronic Recording because the officers inadvertently failed to operate the recording equipment properly, or without the knowledge of any of said officers the recording equipment malfunctioned or stopped operating; or

(4) The statement was made during a custodial interrogation that both occurred in, and was conducted by officers of, a jurisdiction outside Indiana; or

(5) The law enforcement officers conducting or observing the Custodial Interrogation reasonably believed that the crime for which the person was being investigated was not a felony under Indiana law; or

(6) The statement was spontaneous and not made in response to a question; or

(7) Substantial exigent circumstances existed which prevented the making of, or rendered it not feasible to make, an Electronic Recording of the Custodial Interrogation, or prevent its preservation and availability at trial.

(b) For purposes of this rule, "Electronic Recording" means an audio-video recording that includes at least not only the visible images of the person being interviewed but also the voices of said person and the interrogating officers; *Custodial Interrogation* means an interview conducted by law enforcement during which a reasonable person would consider himself or herself to be in custody; *Place of Detention* means a jail, law enforcement agency station house, or any other stationary or mobile building owned or operated by a law enforcement agency at

WITNESSES

which persons are detained in connection with criminal investigations.

(c) The Electronic Recording must be a complete, authentic, accurate, unaltered, and continuous record of a Custodial Interrogation.

(d) This Rule is in addition to, and does not diminish, any other requirement of law regarding the admissibility of a person's statements.

*   *   *   *   *

ANALYSIS

Overview. Following the national trend, Indiana adopted Rule 617, effective January 1, 2011, to provide for mandatory recording of all interrogations in felony cases. The Rule operates to exclude any such statement admitted in a felony case that was not recorded, with exceptions noted in subrules (a)(1)–(7). The Rule applies only to custodial interrogations in stationary buildings, as defined in subrule (b), so routine police questioning during traffic stops is not required to be recorded. The Rule requires both video and audio recording of an interrogation, and a complete and unchanged recording is required.

Rationale. Recording of interrogations is considered beneficial for both law enforcement and criminal defendants. Recordings help to protect police against claims of abuse of coercion during interrogations and provide first-hand evidence that confessions met the "knowing, intelligent, and voluntary" standards for admission. They may also ward off claims that Miranda warnings and the likes were not provided, thus saving courts and law enforcements time and resources that would otherwise be spent defending against such claims. Of course, recordings will also constitute overwhelming evidence when such claims are true, thus benefitting defendants as well. The judicial opinion adopting the Rule also noted that recording allows the police to focus on a criminal suspect's answers and body language rather than on taking notes; the recording can be reviewed for any overlooked details. The recording can also serve as a training tool for effective interrogation techniques. Because recordings are likely to lead to a decrease in factual disputes, they should reduce the number of motions to suppress evidence, court hearings to resolve such motions, and appellate litigation challenging the resulting rulings.

Electronically recorded interrogations can also help to resolve claims of false confessions. A suspect's tone of voice, facial expressions, and body language can be important in determining the likelihood of a false confession, and the interrogator's questions, tone, and manner of questioning provide invaluable context that can assist experts and courts in evaluating the accuracy of the suspect's statements. These recordings will undoubtedly supplement the growing field of DNA testing in sorting through claims of "actual innocence" by defendants.

Exceptions. Exceptions to the recording requirement are listed in subrule (a), and they capture the circumstances in which recording would be either impracticable or undesirable. They also allow for waiver of the recording requirement by the defendant or accidental malfunction of the recording equipment. In such cases, any statements made during interrogation will be admissible notwithstanding the fact that they weren't recorded.

In accordance with the parallel application for statements taken in violation of *Miranda*, statements that do not comply with Rule 617 may nonetheless be admissible against the defendant for purposes of impeachment.

Other Evidentiary Requirements. Subrule (d) makes clear that the recording requirement does not obviate the need to comply with other evidentiary doctrines, such as relevance, hearsay, authentication, and the "best evidence" rule. Where an oral confession is sought to be admitted, for example, the recording of the confession itself should constitute the "best evidence" of the confession under Rule 1002. However, when the confession is reduced to writing, the videotaped interrogation leading to the confession should not be admitted as original evidence of the confession. However, it will remain available, of course, for use in challenging the circumstances leading to the written confession.

ADDITIONAL AUTHORITY

COMPARISON TO FEDERAL RULE

There is no comparable federal rule.

SIGNIFICANT CASES

Cutler v. State, 983 N.E.2d 217, 219 (Ind. Ct. App. 2013) (statements that do not comply with Rule 617 may nonetheless be admissible against the defendant for purposes of impeachment).

Gasper v. State, 833 N.E.2d 1036, 1041 (Ind. Ct. App. 2005) ("There can be little doubt that the electronic recording of a custodial interrogation benefits all parties involved.").

Stoker v. State, 692 N.E.2d 1386, 1390 (Ind. Ct. App. 1998) (strongly recommending the adoption of a Rule such as Rule 617).

WITNESSES

VII
OPINIONS AND EXPERT TESTIMONY

Chapter 701

Rule 701. Opinion Testimony by Lay Witnesses

Rule 701 reads as follows:

> If the witness is not testifying as an expert, the witness's testimony in the form of opinions or inferences is limited to those opinions or inferences which are (a) rationally based on the perception of the witness and (b) helpful to a clear understanding of the witness's testimony or the determination of a fact in issue.

* * * * *

ANALYSIS

Requirements for Admission. Rule 701 governs the admissibility of opinion testimony from a lay witness. Before an opinion from a lay witness is permitted, two circumstances must exist. First, consistent with Rule 602, the opinion must be rationally based upon first-hand perceptions by the witness, and second, the opinion must facilitate an understanding of the witness's testimony.

Examples. Some things simply cannot be expressed in terms other than an opinion. Obvious examples would be testimony about color, speed of a vehicle, and the like. Opinion testimony is permitted in more complex circumstances where the opinion will facilitate a more complete understanding of the witness's testimony. Such circumstances might include the identity of a person, elements of a person's health, age, or appearance. Another area in which a lay witness is permitted to give opinion testimony under controlled circumstances relates to sanity or intoxication. In either case, a foundation is necessary to establish that the witness has had sufficient perceptions to form an opinion based upon those perceptions of the witness. The degree to which a witness may give an opinion, of course, is predicated in part upon whether and the extent to which the witness has sufficient life experiences that would permit making a judgment as to the matter involved.

Several Indiana cases refer to "skilled witnesses," or lay witnesses who possess the characteristics sufficient to qualify them as expert witnesses under Rule 702 but who are actually testifying to what they have observed or know through first-hand knowledge. *See, e.g., Farrell v. Littell,* 790 N.E.2d 612 (Ind. Ct. App. 2003). These cases imply that such "skilled witnesses" may provide opinions or inferences based on their observations. However, Rule 701 is clear that any lay witness may provide an opinion or inference if the requirements of the rule are satisfied, that is, if the opinion or inference is rationally based on the perception of the witness and the testimony is helpful to a clear understanding of the testimony or a fact in issue. Nonetheless, the skills, training, or experience of a lay witness will be relevant to the court's determination of whether an opinion or inference may be offered, and lay witnesses who possess these characteristics in greater degrees may be permitted greater latitude in their testimony.

Helpfulness Required; Judicial Discretion; Rule 403 Considerations. It is important to note that lay opinions may be determined to be not "helpful" under the rule whenever the jury can readily draw the necessary inferences and conclusions without the aid of the opinion. Likewise, such opinions are not helpful when they are confusing or excessively time consuming. Accordingly, the rule vests considerable discretion in the trial court and mandates care in determining whether the jury will be aided by lay opinion testimony in reaching a just result. Furthermore, in a proper case, lay opinion testimony otherwise admissible may be excluded by the trial court if the probative value of the testimony is sufficiently outweighed by the considerations set forth in Rule 403.

Practical Application of Rule 701

Any question that asks a lay witness to speculate as to certain facts will likely be "not helpful" under Rule 701. Consequently, a question such as "What would have happened if your son had survived the accident?" is likely to be subject to objection based upon its speculative nature.

ADDITIONAL AUTHORITY

WEISSENBERGER'S FEDERAL EVIDENCE §§ 701.1–701.4

McCORMICK § 11

4 WEINSTEIN 2d §§ 701.01–701.08

3 MUELLER & KIRKPATRICK §§ 342–347

7 WIGMORE §§ 1917–1929

COMPARISON TO FEDERAL RULE

Federal Rule 701 was amended in December 2000 to read as follows:

Rule 701. Opinion Testimony by Lay Witnesses

If the witness is not testifying as an expert, the witness's testimony in the form of opinions or inferences is limited to those opinions or inferences which are (a) rationally based on the perception of the witness, and (b) helpful to a clear understanding of the witness's testimony or the determination of a fact in issue, and (c) not based on scientific, technical or other specialized knowledge within the scope of Rule 702.

The Advisory Committee Notes to Federal Rule 701 make clear that it was amended to eliminate the risk that the reliability requirements set forth in Federal Rule 702 would be evaded through the proffering of an expert as a lay witness. The amendment distinguishes between expert and lay testimony; the focus is no longer on the status of the witnesses. Under the amendment to Federal Rule 701, a witness's testimony must now be scrutinized under the rules regulating expert opinion to the extent that the witness is providing testimony based on scientific, technical, or other specialized knowledge within the scope of Federal Rule 702. The amendment to Federal Rule 701 ensures that expert testimony will be channeled to Federal Rule 702 and prevent a party from evading the expert witness disclosure requirements of Federal Rule of Civil Procedure 26 and Federal Rule of Criminal Procedure 16 by simply calling an expert witness in the guise of a lay person.

SIGNIFICANT CASES

Stroud v. State, 809 N.E.2d 274 (Ind. 2004) (police officer may provide lay opinion that Reebok shoes run smaller than Nike shoes, based on his personal experience purchasing those brands of shoes; however, prosecution should have laid a proper foundation for the lay opinion testimony by asking the police officer whether he had ever purchased Nike or Reebok shoes and whether his opinion on their sizings could be rationally based on his perception of those shoes).

Love v. State, 761 N.E.2d 806 (Ind. 2002) (an inference gleaned from a witness's testimony cannot be based upon evidence which is uncertain or speculative or which raises merely a conjecture or possibility).

Dickens v. State, 754 N.E.2d 1 (Ind. 2001) (rule requiring that opinion testimony of a lay witness be rationally based on his perception simply means that the opinion must be one that a reasonable person normally could form from the perceived facts).

Stephenson v. State, 742 N.E.2d 463 (Ind. 2001) (crime scene technician's opinion that he found no hair, blood, or fiber in defendant's vehicle because someone cleaned the vehicle was properly admitted because his testimony was rationally based on his experience of observing other vehicles and his perceptions that it was unusual to find nothing in the vehicle and that the floorboard was damp).

Vasquez v. State, 741 N.E.2d 1214 (Ind. 2001) (defendant was convicted of glue sniffing; police officers properly opined that a bottle of clear liquid and a rag found at defendant's apartment was soaked with toluene because they were sufficiently experienced with the drug and the inference was rationally related to their perceptions).

Warren v. State, 725 N.E.2d 828 (Ind. 2000) (trial court did not err in allowing police officer who identified himself as "crime scene specialist" to testify regarding what "appeared to be blood" on a t-shirt even though he was not a serologist and no foundation laid for expert witness; witness is permitted to testify concerning the appearance of an object observed).

Cutter v. State, 725 N.E.2d 401 (Ind. 2000) (witness's testimony that the size of partner's genitals in autopsy photograph were unusually large was admissible as lay opinion because it was rationally based on the perception of the witness and helpful to a clear understanding of the witness's testimony or determination of a fact in issue).

Butler v. State, 658 N.E.2d 72 (Ind. 1995) (opinion testimony on issue of law is not properly admissible; if prejudice does not result, error is harmless).

Weaver v. State, 643 N.E.2d 342 (Ind. 1994) (in trial for attempted murder, court could exclude lay opinion testimony of defendant's girlfriend, the crime victim, regarding her beliefs about what caused defendant to beat her and whether he intended to kill her, even though she was uniquely placed to observe defendant's actions and may have had insightful opinions on defendant's motivations).

Hawkins v. State, 626 N.E.2d 436 (Ind. 1993) (Indiana Rule 701 consistent with prior case law; lay witness opinion testimony requires no particular quantum of knowledge; extent of lay witness's knowledge goes to weight, not admissibility).

Kimp v. State, 546 N.E.2d 1193 (Ind. 1989) (speculation by witnesses who lack personal knowledge of the underlying facts is inadmissible).

Shepherd v. State, 538 N.E.2d 242 (Ind. 1989) (witness cannot offer an opinion on whether a claim of innocence was believable).

Mitchell v. State, 535 N.E.2d 498 (Ind. 1989) (lay witness may not offer legal conclusion).

Kirby v. State, 481 N.E.2d 372 (Ind. 1985) (witness could properly give opinion based on first-hand knowledge that defendant was faking crying).

Hartlerode v. State, 470 N.E.2d 716 (Ind. 1984) (trial court permitted witnesses to testify concerning footprints found; each witness's testimony was helpful to the jury and properly admitted).

Gerrick v. State, 451 N.E.2d 327 (Ind. 1983) (lay witness's testimony that noises sounded like gunshots was admissible opinion).

Poe v. State, 445 N.E.2d 94 (Ind. 1983) (lay witness's opinion on identity of a person was properly admitted).

Meyer v. Marine Builders, Inc., 797 N.E.2d 760 (Ind. Ct. App. 2003) (an opinion is rationally based under Rule 701, if it is one that a reasonable person normally could form from the perceived facts; an opinion is helpful, for purposes of Rule 701, if the testimony gives substance to facts that were difficult to articulate).

Davis v. State, 791 N.E.2d 266 (Ind. Ct. App. 2003) (a *skilled* witness is defined as "a person with a degree of knowledge short of that sufficient to be declared an expert under Rule 702, but somewhat beyond that possessed by the ordinary juror").

Farrell v. Littell, 790 N.E.2d 612 (Ind. Ct. App. 2003) (qualification as an expert under Rule 702 is required only if the witness's opinion is based on information received from others under Rule 703 or through a hypothetical question; the testimony of an observer, who may have the qualifications of an expert, may act as a lay witness and simply provide a report of what the witness observed; such witnesses are "skilled witnesses" and may testify about their observations, opinions, or inferences that are based solely on facts within their own personal knowledge).

Gibson v. State, 709 N.E.2d 11 (Ind. Ct. App. 1999) (lay opinion testimony by a person who is not an eyewitness to the crimes charged concerning the identity of a person who is depicted in a surveillance videotape may be admissible if the testimony would be helpful to the jury).

Hanson v. State, 704 N.E.2d 152 (Ind. Ct. App. 1999) (opinion testimony must be rationally based on perception such that the opinion must be one that a reasonable person normally could form from the perceived facts; moreover, the opinion should be helpful so that the testimony gives substance to facts which are difficult to articulate).

Ackles v. Hartford Underwriters Ins. Corp., 699 N.E.2d 740 (Ind. Ct. App. 1998) (because lay witness opinion testimony must be rationally based on the personal perception of the witness, speculation or testimony based on improper inferences is inadmissible).

Reeves v. Boyd & Sons, 654 N.E.2d 864 (Ind. Ct. App. 1995) (lay witness is allowed to give opinion of another's intoxication).

Warner Trucking v. Hall, 653 N.E.2d 1057 (Ind. Ct. App. 1995), *superseded*, *Warner Trucking v. Carolina Cas. Ins. Co.*, 686 N.E.2d 102 (Ind. 1997) (in personal injury action against employer based on theory of respondent superior, truck driver's statements about his reasons for taking and driving employer's truck were inadmissible speculation, where driver acknowledged that he could not remember what happened or why he was driving truck).

Robinson v. State, 634 N.E.2d 1367 (Ind. Ct. App. 1994) (lay witness's memory could be refreshed with a police report).

Chapter 702

Rule 702. Testimony by Experts

Rule 702 reads as follows:

> (a) If scientific, technical, or other specialized knowledge will assist the trier of fact to understand the evidence or to determine a fact in issue, a witness qualified as an expert by knowledge, skill, experience, training, or education, may testify thereto in the form of an opinion or otherwise.
>
> (b) Expert scientific testimony is admissible only if the court is satisfied that the scientific principles upon which the expert testimony rests are reliable.

* * * * *

ANALYSIS

Functions of Rule. Rule 702 governs the admissibility of testimony by experts and it performs four distinct functions. First, it expressly authorizes the use of expert testimony. Second, the rule establishes standards to be applied in determining whether expert testimony should be admitted in a particular case. Third, the rule provides criteria to be applied in determining whether an individual qualifies as an expert. Fourth, the rule governs the form of expert testimony.

Lay and Expert Witnesses Distinguished. In understanding expert testimony, it should be appreciated that there are essentially two types of witnesses at the trial of a lawsuit. First, a lay witness testifies because he or she has first-hand knowledge of relevant facts. Second, an expert may testify, not because he or she has first-hand knowledge of relevant facts, but rather because of special expertise which will assist the trier of fact in interpreting the facts of the case.

Aids Trier of Fact; Judicial Discretion. While the test for the use of expert testimony requires that the trier of fact be aided by the testimony, the standard is a relative one which will depend upon the particular subject, the particular witness, and the facts of the litigation. By necessity, the trial court has a substantial degree of discretion in determining whether to permit expert testimony in a particular case. This discretion should also extend to the trial court's determination of whether the state of the art in the particular discipline permits a rational and reliable opinion to be asserted by an expert.

Qualifications. Rule 702 addresses the qualifications necessary to accord a witness expert status. Under the rule, a witness may qualify as an expert by reason of his or her knowledge, skill, experience, training, or education. It is important to note that any one of these characteristics may qualify an individual as an expert, although in the usual case, more than one of these factors will be present. For a witness who qualifies as an expert through her knowledge of the subject matter in question, the issue of qualification will typically be demonstrated through the expert's own testimony. *See Bennett v. Richmond*, 960 N.E.2d 782 (Ind. 2012).

Rule 702 does not contain any bright line rules regarding specific qualifications of an expert in certain cases, and Indiana courts have been reluctant to impose any such restrictions. For example, Indiana courts have allowed expert testimony regarding medical causation from witnesses without medical degrees if the witnesses prove their expertise in a manner satisfactory to the court. *See Person v. Shipley*, 962 N.E.2d 1192 (Ind. 2012).

New Developments Under Federal Law

In *Daubert v. Merrell Dow Pharms.*, 509 U.S. 579, 113 S. Ct. 2786, 125 L. Ed. 2d 469 (1993), the U.S. Supreme Court held that under the Federal Rules of Evidence, the so-called *Frye* test (Frye v. United States, 293 F. 1013, 54 App. D.C. 46 (D.C. Cir. 1923)) does not apply to determine whether expert testimony may be offered on a particular subject. The *Frye* test, or the "general acceptance test" provides that an expert opinion based on a scientific technique is admissible only where the technique is generally accepted as reliable in the relevant scientific community. The court held that the express language of the pertinent Federal Rules of Evidence places appropriate limits on the admissibility of purportedly scientific evidence by requiring the trial judge to ensure that an expert's testimony rests on a reliable foundation. It should be noted that the *Daubert* opinion interprets Federal Rule 702. The extent to which the *Daubert* opinion has been followed by Indiana courts is discussed in greater detail below.

GE v. Joiner, 522 U.S. 136, 118 S. Ct. 512, 139 L. Ed. 2d 508 (1997), reaffirmed the idea that it is the responsibility of the trial court to determine the admissibility of evidence. The Supreme Court held that abuse of discretion is the proper standard of appellate review regarding trial court's decisions on the admission of evidence, including expert scientific testimony. Hence, the trial court's decision to admit or exclude expert scientific testimony based on the sufficiency of the foundation for that evidence will only be overturned if the trial court abused its discretion in making that decision. The *Joiner* decision thus preserves the role of the trial court as "gatekeeper" by leaving to it the task of screening all evidence prior to admission to ensure that the evidence is both relevant and reliable.

In 1999, the U.S. Supreme Court expanded the reach of *Daubert* in the case of *Kumho Tire Co. v. Carmichael*, 526 U.S. 137, 119 S. Ct. 1167, 143 L. Ed. 2d 238 (1999). On its surface, *Kumho* extends the core principle of *Daubert*—the "gatekeeping" obligation of trial courts to ensure the reliability of expert testimony—to expert testimony based on "technical" or "other specialized" knowledge, not simply expert testimony based on "scientific" testimony. The *Kumho* Court clarified that the function of the trial court with respect to expert witnesses is the same, regardless of the underlying nature of the testimony: To determine the "reliability" of the testimony and to admit proffered testimony when, in the court's discretion, it meets a sufficient threshold of reliability (in addition to meeting the threshold of relevance). *Kumho* may thus be viewed by some as a tightening of the standards under which expert testimony is admissible, but the significance of the case should not be confined to such a restricted view.

A closer examination of the reasoning in *Kumho*, however, reveals limits to the applicability of the more specific holdings in *Daubert* to nonscientific expert testimony. The Court declined to limit the trial court's determination of the reliability of expert testimony to the celebrated (or notorious, depending upon one's adversarial posture) list of factors set forth in *Daubert*, and the Court also stated that an application of those factors was not necessary in every case. After *Kumho*, it is clear that factors other than those listed in *Daubert* may be considered by trial courts in determining the reliability of proffered testimony, and certain *Daubert* factors may simply be inapplicable to certain kinds of expert testimony.

Although portions of *Kumho* appear to disclaim any distinction between the trial court's admissibility determination for scientific expert testimony and that for "technical, or other specialized" expert testimony, the reasoning of the Court implicitly acknowledges differences in the essence of the underlying subject matter of proffered testimony, which, in turn, impacts the course of court's admissibility determination. In each case, the function of the court in determining the "reliability" of the testimony remains the same, though the analysis used in so doing will vary depending upon the subject matter of the testimony.

"Does *Daubert* apply in Indiana?" Rule 702(b) provides that scientific expert testimony is admissible only where the court is satisfied that the scientific principles upon which the expert testimony rests are "reliable." The *Daubert* case and its progeny, discussed above, were also based on the Federal Rules' requirement that expert testimony be "reliable," thus begging the question of the extent to which *Daubert* applies in Indiana as well. The answer does not appear to be clear cut, though it is perhaps accurate to say that Indiana slouches toward *Daubert*, at least for testimony based on scientific knowledge, though it has not adopted the case wholesale.

Under Indiana practice, it is clear that, pursuant to Rule 702(b), the "general acceptance" test is not the exclusive means of establishing the threshold reliability of expert testimony. *See Davidson v. State*, 580 N.E.2d 238 (Ind. 1991). The Indiana Supreme Court has noted that *Daubert* concerns "coincide with the express requirement of Indiana Rule of Evidence 702(b) that the trial court be satisfied of the reliability of the scientific principles involved." *Malinski v. State*, 794 N.E.2d 1071, 1084 (Ind. 2003) (quoting *McGrew v. State*, 682 N.E.2d 1289, 1290 (Ind. 1997)). However, though the *Daubert* factors may be used in determining reliability, "there is no specific 'test' or set of 'prongs' which must be considered in order to satisfy Indiana Evidence Rule 702(b)." *Carter v. State*, 766 N.E.2d 377, 380 (Ind. 2002) (quoting *McGrew v. State*, 682 N.E.2d 1289, 1292 (Ind. 1997)). In other words, the Indiana Supreme Court has found *Daubert* to be "helpful, but not controlling, when analyzing testimony under Indiana Evidence Rule 702(b)." *See Turner v. State*, 953 N.E.2d 1039 (Ind. 2011).

Additionally, the *Turner* Court purported to re-establish a non-*Daubert* style of analysis to non-scientific expert testimony, noting that "Indiana's Rule 702 is not intended 'to interpose an unnecessarily burdensome procedure or methodology for trial courts.'" *Turner v. State*, 953 N.E.2d 1039 (Ind. 2011) (citing *Sears Roebuck & Co. v. Manuilov*, 742 N.E.2d 453, 460 (Ind. 2001)). The *Turner* Court went on to explain why the subject matter of the expert testimony in that case, tool mark analysis, would not be appropriate for a full-throated *Daubert* critique. Of course, this is precisely the message in the *Kumho Tire* opinion, but the *Turner* Court disclaimed a reliance on that case.

In addition to the *Daubert* factors, "reliability" may be also established by judicial notice that the scientific principles are sufficiently indisputable to satisfy Rule 201.

It is critical to appreciate that the reliability requirement addresses the methodology of an expert's analysis, not the expert's conclusions or even the assumptions upon which an expert bases an opinion. An expert may make assumptions about the conditions which may have existed at the time in forming an opinion, and so long as there is evidence to support a finding that those facts may have existed, the opinion will be admitted. *See Person v. Shipley*, 962 N.E.2d 1192 (Ind. 2012). Any questions about the existence of those facts, or the underlying expert opinion, can be weighed by the factfinder in its final determination, but it should not affect the opinion's admissibility.

Current Trends and New Developments

Once the trial court has determined that a particular scientific technique is capable of producing reliable results, any questions regarding reliability of the testing procedure, or its results, go to weight of the scientific testimony and not its admissibility. In *McGrew v. State*, 682 N.E.2d 1289, 1292 (Ind. 1997), the trial court did not abuse its discretion in admitting testimony of microscopic hair analysis because the evidence was more a "matter of observations of persons with specialized knowledge" than a "matter of 'scientific principles' governed by Indiana Evidence Rule 702(b)."

"Opinion or Otherwise." Traditionally, the primary purpose for qualifying a witness as an expert has been to enable that individual to express his or her opinion on a central matter in issue. Rule 702 authorizes expert testimony in the form of opinion "or otherwise." The "or otherwise" language of Rule 702 is designed to permit an expert to provide relevant scientific, professional, technical, or other principles as a basis for an application of those principles to the relevant issues by the trier of fact.

Indiana courts have sanctioned the use of charts, models, or other aids that will assist an expert in presenting a complete and accurate description of their testimony. Such aids will constitute demonstrative evidence, and so long as they are offered for illustrative or descriptive purposes, they should be routinely admitted.

Subject Matter. Caution should be exercised in assuring that the subject matter of the expert witness's testimony relates to the expertise the witness brings to the courtroom.

Illustration

In a criminal prosecution, *X* is prosecuted for possession of marijuana and a police chemist is qualified as an expert in identifying the marijuana. The chemist testifies that he thought the substance was marijuana because the container the substance was in looked like ones he saw used in Mexico. Such opinion is suspect because the basis of the opinion is not directly related to his qualification as a police chemist.

Practical Considerations

As noted in *Rynerson v. City of Franklin*, 669 N.E.2d 964 (Ind. 1996), polygraph examinations are generally inadmissible unless a valid stipulation exists between parties before giving such exam that it may be used as evidence by either party. Even if such a stipulation exists, the admission of polygraph tests is within discretion of trial court.

New Developments Under Federal Law

In *United States v. Scheffer*, 523 U.S. 303, 118 S. Ct. 1261, 140 L. Ed. 2d 413 (1998), the Supreme Court held that expert testimony regarding polygraph test results can be excluded from trial without violating a defendant's Sixth Amendment rights. In the course of its opinion, the Court also implied that such expert testimony should not be admissible in any jury trial.

The Court was faced with the issue of whether Military Rule of Evidence 707, which excludes polygraph evidence in court-martial proceedings, violated a defendant's constitutional right to present a defense. The Court found that the restriction contained in Rule 707 was a reasonable restriction on a defendant's right to present his case, and did not in any way preclude the defendant from introducing factual evidence or providing the court members with his perspective on the relevant details of the charged offense. According to the majority, Rule 707 served the legitimate purpose of ensuring that only reliable evidence is admitted at trial, as "there is simply no consensus that polygraph evidence is reliable." The Court also stated that the *per se* exclusion on the admission of polygraph evidence imposed by Military Rule 707 was a permissible and proportionate means to avoid the collateral litigation that would be involved in determining whether polygraph evidence was admissible in a particular case.

The Court went on to explain that excluding expert testimony regarding polygraph results also preserves the jury's role as "the lie detector" of the criminal justice system. Traditionally, the question of witness credibility has been a question for the jury, and expert testimony is only allowed when the expert testifies about matters outside the knowledge or competency of the jury. Allowing polygraph experts to provide an opinion as to whether a witness was telling the truth, in the Court's view, would diminish the jury's role in making credibility determinations.

INCORPORATED STATUTES

Ind. Code § 34-45-3-2. [Witness compelled to appear and testify]

A witness described in section 1 of this chapter may be compelled to appear and testify in:

(1)   any court in the county of the residence of the witness; or

(2)   any court in an adjoining county;

to an opinion as an expert in relation to any matter whenever the opinion is material evidence relevant to an issue on trial before a court or jury.

Ind. Code § 34-45-3-4. [Expert witness subject to same rules as nonexpert witnesses]

The same rules and regulations apply to witnesses described in section 1 [IC 34-45-3-1] of this chapter as apply to a witness who can be compelled to appear and testify to knowledge the witness has of facts relevant to the same issue.

Ind. Code § 35-37-4-13. ["Forensic DNA analysis" defined; admissibility]

(a) As used in this section, *forensic DNA analysis* means an identification process in which the unique genetic code of an individual that is carried by the individual's deoxyribonucleic acid (DNA) is compared to genetic codes carried in DNA found in bodily substance samples obtained by a law enforcement agency in the exercise of the law enforcement agency's investigative function.

(b) In a criminal trial or hearing, the results of forensic DNA analysis are admissible in evidence without antecedent expert testimony that forensic DNA analysis provides a trustworthy and reliable method of identifying characteristics in an individual's genetic material.

ADDITIONAL AUTHORITY

WEISSENBERGER'S FEDERAL EVIDENCE §§ 702.1–702.5

McCORMICK § 13

4 WEINSTEIN 2d §§ 702.01–702.08

3 MUELLER & KIRKPATRICK §§ 348–353

COMPARISON TO FEDERAL RULE

Federal Rule 702 was amended in December 2000 to read as follows:

Rule 702. Testimony by Experts

If scientific, technical, or other specialized knowledge will assist the trier of fact to understand the evidence or to determine a fact in issue, a witness qualified as an expert by knowledge, skill, experience, training, or education, may testify thereto in the form of an opinion or otherwise, if (1) the testimony is based upon sufficient facts or data, (2) the testimony is the product of reliable principles and methods, and (3) the witness has applied the principles and methods reliably to the facts of the case.

Federal Rule 702 was amended in response to *Daubert v. Merrell Dow Pharms.*, 509 U.S. 579, 113 S. Ct. 2786, 125 L. Ed. 2d 469 (1993), which charged trial judges with the responsibility of acting as gatekeeper to exclude unreliable expert testimony, and *Kumho Tire Co. v. Carmichael*, 526 U.S. 137, 119 S. Ct. 1167, 143 L. Ed. 2d 238 (1999), which clarified that the gatekeeper function applied to all expert testimony and not just testimony based in science.

The amendment to Federal Rule 702 affirms the trial court's role as gatekeeper and provides general standards that a trial court must use to assess the reliability and helpfulness of any expert testimony.

While no attempt has been made to codify the standards a trial court must use, courts have found the following factors relevant in determining whether expert testimony is sufficiently reliable to be considered by the trier of fact:

(1)   Whether the expert's technique or theory can be or has been tested.

(2)   Whether the technique or theory has been subject to peer review and publication.

(3)   Whether the rate of error of the technique or theory is known when applied.

(4)   Whether there are the existence and maintenance of standards and controls.

(5)   Whether the technique or theory has been generally accepted in the scientific community.

(6)   Whether experts are proposing to testify about matters growing naturally and directly out of research conducted independent of the litigation, or whether they have developed their opinions expressly for testifying.

(7)   Whether the expert has unjustifiably extrapolated from an accepted premise to an unfounded conclusion.

(8)   Whether the expert has adequately accounted for obvious alternative explanations.

(9)   Whether the expert is being as careful as he would be in his regular professional work outside of paid consulting for litigation.

(10)   Whether the field of expertise claimed by the expert is known to reach reliable results for the type of opinion the expert would give.

These factors are neither exclusive nor dispositive.

The amendment to Federal Rule 702 does not alter the practice of using expert testimony to educate the factfinder on general principles for which the expert does not attempt to apply the principles to the specific facts of the case. For generalized testimony, Federal Rule 702 merely requires that (1) the expert be qualified, (2) the testimony address a subject matter on which the factfinder can be assisted by an expert, (3) the testimony be reliable, and (4) the testimony fit the facts of the case.

Experience is still a sufficient basis for expert testimony under the amendment to Federal Rule 702. Federal Rule 702 expressly contemplates that an expert may be qualified on the basis of experience. However, if the witness is relying solely or primarily on experience, then the witness must explain how that experience leads to the conclusion reached, why that experience is a sufficient basis for the opinion, and how that experience is reliably applied to the facts. The trial court must do more than just take the expert's word in its gatekeeping function.

SIGNIFICANT CASES

Weisgram v. Marley Co., 528 U.S. 440, 120 S. Ct. 1011, 145 L. Ed. 2d 958 (2000) (in light of *Daubert*'s exacting standards for the reliability of expert evidence, parties will not likely present less than their best expert evidence at trial, so a court of appeals may direct the entry of judgment as a matter of law against a party whose expert evidence was erroneously admitted at trial and whose remaining evidence is insufficient to support the jury's verdict).

Kumho Tire Co. v. Carmichael, 526 U.S. 137, 119 S. Ct. 1167, 143 L. Ed. 2d 238 (1999) (the Court extended its holding in *Daubert* to all fields of expert knowledge, and arguably clarified or refined its holding in *Daubert* by characterizing the factors set forth in that case as flexible ones, and not as a definitive checklist).

United States v. Scheffer, 523 U.S. 303, 118 S. Ct. 1261, 140 L. Ed. 2d 413 (1998) (holding that a rule excluding expert testimony regarding polygraph results did not violate a defendant's Sixth Amendment rights and suggesting that polygraph experts should not be allowed to testify regarding whether an individual has lied as such testimony would invade the province of the jury).

GE v. Joiner, 522 U.S. 136, 118 S. Ct. 512, 139 L. Ed. 2d 508 (1997) (holding that abuse of discretion is the proper standard of appellate review regarding trial court's decisions on the admission of evidence, including expert scientific testimony).

Daubert v. Merrell Dow Pharms., 509 U.S. 579, 113 S. Ct. 2786, 125 L. Ed. 2d 469 (1993) (U.S. Supreme Court, interpreting Federal Rule 702, held that the Rules of Evidence provide the standard for the admission of expert scientific evidence, rather than the *Frye* test).

Person v. Shipley, 962 N.E.2d 1192 (Ind. 2012) (to the extent that an expert used his knowledge and experience to make reasonable estimates of speed and weight upon which to base his opinion, and then used reliable methods about those facts to form an opinion about the plaintiff's injury, the opinion will be admissible).

Bennett v. Richmond, 960 N.E.2d 782 (Ind. 2012) (neither the criteria for qualifying under Rule 702 (knowledge, skill, experience, training, or education) nor the purpose for which expert testimony is admitted (to assist the trier of fact) supports a *per se* rule banning psychologists' testimony on the cause of a brain injury).

Turner v. State, 953 N.E.2d 1039 (Ind. 2011) (admitting expert testimony within the tool mark examination field even though there was no showing that the expert's theory or technique was testable, whether the theory has been subjected to peer review and publication, whether there is a known or potential error rate, and whether the theory has been generally accepted within the relevant field of study).

TRW Vehicle Safety Sys. v. Moore, 936 N.E.2d 201 (Ind. 2010) (trial court properly held that an expert witness qualified as a biomedical engineer could not offer testimony concerning the nature and timing of plaintiff's death, as the testimony was outside her expertise).

Diaz v. State, 934 N.E.2d 1089, 1093–1094 (Ind. 2010) (expert witness in foreign language translation should have been allowed to present a chart summarizing the errors she believed occurred during the guilty plea hearing; the chart was not hearsay but functioned as a demonstrative exhibit prepared to facilitate a complete and accurate summary of the conclusions reached by the expert).

Raess v. Doescher, 883 N.E.2d 790 (Ind. 2009) (a trial court objection to the qualification of an expert witness was not sufficient to preserve a claim of error relating to the lack of reliability of the underlying expert testimony; no reference to an objection under Rule 702 or scientific reliability was made).

Overstreet v. State, 783 N.E.2d 1140 (Ind. 2003) (DNA testimony becomes admissible as evidence when the trial court is satisfied that (1) the scientific principles upon which the expert testimony rests are reliable, (2) the witness is qualified, and (3) the testimony's probative value is not substantially outweighed by the dangers of unfair prejudice; Indiana does not recognize a test or specific set of elements to satisfy reliability of a process under the rules of evidence).

Malinski v. State, 794 N.E.2d 1071 (Ind. 2003) (the concerns in *Daubert* by the U.S. Supreme Court under Fed. R. Evid. 702 coincide with the express requirement of Ind. R. Evid. 702 regarding those rules' "reliability" requirement; thus, *Daubert* is helpful, but not controlling in Indiana Courts; in addition, the "reliability" of the methodology underlying novel expert witness may be established by judicial notice as well as by a party).

Kubsch v. State, 784 N.E.2d 905 (Ind. 2003) (under Rule 702, only one characteristic is necessary to qualify an individual as an expert, and a witness may qualify as an expert on the basis of practical experience alone; although the appellate court may doubt whether a police detective with experience investigating homicide scenes and attending seminars exploring victim-suspect relationships qualifies as an expert in an area involving rather complex behavioral and social science issues, the determination of whether a witness qualifies as an expert is within the trial court's sound discretion, and the appellate courts should decline to substitute their judgment for that of the trial court; nonetheless, appellate courts should appropriately rule on the reliability of expert witness testimony, and it was erroneous for the trial court to allow testimony by the detective outside the scope of his expertise).

Troxell v. State, 778 N.E.2d 811 (Ind. 2002) (under Rule 702, no specific test is required to establish the reliability of a scientific process).

Carter v. State, 766 N.E.2d 377 (Ind. 2002) (in determining the reliability of expert testimony for purposes of admissibility, there is no specific test that must be considered).

West v. State, 755 N.E.2d 173 (Ind. 2001) (the reliability of scientific evidence may be established by judicial notice or by a sufficient foundation from the proponent of the evidence to convince the trial court that the scientific principles are reliable).

Stephenson v. State, 742 N.E.2d 463 (Ind. 2001) (admission of coroner's testimony who testified that he was not qualified to give an "expert" opinion on the timing of death but nevertheless opined on the time of death was harmless error because it was merely cumulative of other properly admitted evidence concerning the time of death).

Sears Roebuck & Co. v. Manuilov, 742 N.E.2d 453 (Ind. 2001) (medical testimony, from a doctor that treated the customer in the emergency room but not in the intervening period of nearly 10 years to the time of trial and from a psychiatrist, that the customer's fall in the department store caused post-concussion syndrome that disabled him from returning to work as a circus high-wire performer was properly admitted because it explained the basis for the medical diagnosis and the medical diagnosis was scientifically reliable).

Cook v. State, 734 N.E.2d 563 (Ind. 2000) (trial court did not abuse its discretion by refusing to allow defendant's expert witness to testify on the reliability of eyewitness identification because there were several eyewitnesses and defendant did not present this case as one of mistaken identity).

Creasy v. Rusk, 730 N.E.2d 659 (Ind. 2000) (expert witness may be qualified as an expert by virtue of only one of the following characteristics: Knowledge, skill, experience, training, or education and may qualify on the basis of practical experience alone).

Cutter v. State, 725 N.E.2d 401 (Ind. 2000) (trial court did not err in allowing expert witness to give opinion on whether victim's vagina appeared unusually dilated at death, to estimate the extent of dilation, and to explain what would cause it; expert had performed between 1,000 and 1,200 autopsies and testimony regarding dilated state of vagina and the effects of death on the appearance of the body falls into the area of specialized knowledge within his scope of expertise and beyond knowledge generally held by laypersons).

Doe v. Shults-Lewis, 718 N.E.2d 738 (Ind. 1999) (fraudulent concealment places a burden squarely on the plaintiff to point to the fraudulent or wrongful acts of the defendant; in a repressed memory case, the expert opinion alone is not enough to trigger the fraudulent concealment exception—an expert opinion cannot be used as proof of the defendant's actions themselves, but can only be used to aid the jury in understanding conclusions drawn from these actions if taken as true; memory repression is a phenomenon beyond the ability of the average juror to understand and requires expert testimony to explain it to the jury; expert scientific testimony is only admissible if the scientific principles on which it rests are reliable).

Wooley v. State, 716 N.E.2d 919 (Ind. 1999) (whether or not an expert witness meets the requirements of knowledge, skill, experience, education, or training and should be allowed to testify is within the trial court's discretion; trial court did not abuse its discretion in concluding that the experience of an emergency room nurse was insufficient to qualify witness as an expert on the standard of care for a doctor).

Harris v. Raymond, 715 N.E.2d 388 (Ind. 1999) (not all medical malpractice cases are so technical that they require expert testimony, and when no reasonable jury could reach any conclusion other than that a specific standard of care is applicable and was breached, the questions of what specific standard is applicable and whether that standard was breached are questions of law for the court).

Taylor v. State, 710 N.E.2d 921 (Ind. 1999) (pathologist who had served a four-year residency in pathology, practiced in the area for nearly 20 years, and performed approximately 700 autopsies was qualified to offer an opinion with respect to the position of the shooter who killed the victim regardless of whether he was certified as a "forensic pathologist" or merely a pathologist).

Carter v. State, 706 N.E.2d 552 (Ind. 1999) (state established sufficient evidentiary foundation for admission of laboratory technician's testimony concerning urinalysis results even though technician could not explain the scientific basis for the test because neither *Frye* nor Rule 702 were applicable in defendant's probation revocation hearing).

McGrew v. State, 682 N.E.2d 1289 (Ind. 1997) (the proponent of scientific evidence has the burden to prove the reliability of the scientific test before the results are admissible; trial court did not abuse its discretion in admitting evidence of a state police analyst's physical microscopic comparison of hairs because the comparison was sufficiently reliable).

Rynerson v. City of Franklin, 669 N.E.2d 964 (Ind. 1996) (polygraph examinations are inadmissible unless valid stipulation exists between parties before giving such exam that it may be used as evidence by either party and even then admissibility of polygraph results is within discretion of trial court).

Newhart v. State, 669 N.E.2d 953 (Ind. 1996) (Indiana law does not recognize the *Frye* test, which concerns validity of scientific evidence, as a requirement under Indiana Rules of Evidence).

Fleener v. State, 656 N.E.2d 1140 (Ind. 1995) (trial court should not have allowed testimony of psychotherapist about child sexual abuse syndrome after defense's objection where no foundational showing of reliability was made).

Steward v. State, 652 N.E.2d 490 (Ind. 1995) (expert scientific testimony is only admissible if its reliability is demonstrated; if child sexual abuse syndrome evidence is shown to be reliable enough for admission into evidence as expert testimony its probative value must still outweigh risk of unfair prejudice).

In re Adoption of L.C., 650 N.E.2d 726 (Ind. Ct. App. 1995) (in contested adoption proceeding, trial court did not abuse its discretion in qualifying licensed social workers and appointed counsel who had represented child in prior proceedings as expert witnesses; trial court only abuses its discretion in qualifying witness as expert if decision is obviously contrary to logic and effect of facts and circumstances before court or probable, reasonable and actual deductions to be drawn therefrom).

Stidham v. State, 637 N.E.2d 140 (Ind. 1994) (in murder trial, officer's testimony about blood spatters found at crime scene was admissible even though chemical analysis of the splatters was not done to determine that they were human blood; lack of chemical analysis affected only weight of evidence not its admissibility).

Jenkins v. State, 627 N.E.2d 789 (Ind. 1993) (DNA tests held to be admissible; expert witness may base his opinion on hearsay reports of lab technicians).

Lockhart v. State, 609 N.E.2d 1093 (Ind. 1993) (trial court did not err in permitting a pathologist who had conducted more than 4000 autopsies and testified as an expert in more than 200 trials to testify as an expert witness concerning cause of death).

Davidson v. State, 580 N.E.2d 238 (Ind. 1991) (scientific evidence "capable of producing reliable results" is admissible).

Hopkins v. State, 579 N.E.2d 1297 (Ind. 1991) (the reliability of scientific evidence may be proved by showing general acceptance of the principles in the scientific community).

Clark v. State, 562 N.E.2d 11 (Ind. 1990) (an expert witness must limit opinions to areas of the witness's expertise).

Wissman v. State, 540 N.E.2d 1209 (Ind. 1989) (pathologist with 25 years' experience permitted to offer expert testimony on angle of the gun that caused the wound).

Brackens v. State, 480 N.E.2d 536 (Ind. 1985) (fingerprint expert with 18 years of experience but no formal training was properly qualified as an expert witness).

Gambill v. State, 479 N.E.2d 523 (Ind. 1985) (determination of whether a witness is qualified to testify as an expert witness is within the discretion of the trial court).

Grimes v. State, 450 N.E.2d 512 (Ind. 1983) (expert testimony permitted on homosexual and sado-masochistic sexual practices).

Noblesville Casting Div. of TRW, Inc. v. Prince, 438 N.E.2d 722 (Ind. 1982) (expert testimony is admissible where it will aid the jury in determining material issues).

Gresser v. Dow Chem. Co., 2013 Ind. App. LEXIS 204 (Apr. 30, 2013) (Rule 702 provides scientific testimony is admissible only if the court is satisfied that the methodology, or the scientific principles used to generate the expert's conclusions, is reliable).

Shafer & Freeman Lakes Envtl. Conservation Corp. v. Stichnoth, 877 N.E.2d 475 (Ind. Ct. App. 2007) (expert testimony offered by vocational economic analyst was sufficiently reliable, as the opinions were based on personal interviews and data sets from the United States Bureau of Labor Statistics and used the data reliably to arrive at an opinion).

Dyer v. Doyle (In re Estate of Dyer), 870 N.E.2d 573 (Ind. Ct. App. 2007), *transfer denied*, 878 N.E.2d 221 (Ind. 2007) (although Rule 803(4) will operate to admit statements contained within medical records, the actual medical opinions and diagnoses must satisfy the requirements for expert opinions set out in Rule 702).

Shady v. Shady, 858 N.E.2d 128 (Ind. Ct. App. 2006) (an expert was properly qualified as such because of her knowledge, training, and experience; the fact that she lacked a formal education did not prevent her from being qualified as an expert).

Prewitt v. State, 819 N.E.2d 393 (Ind. Ct. App. 2004), *superseded*, 878 N.E.2d 184 (Ind. 2007) (challenges to the validity of an expert's statistical methodology speak to the weight of the evidence, not its admissibility).

Smith v. Yang, 829 N.E.2d 624 (Ind. Ct. App. 2005) (expert testimony on "faked left syndrome" in the field of accident reconstruction was inadmissible, where the party presented no evidence that the theory can or has been tested, subjected to substantial peer review, the rate of error or the standards controlling the application of the syndrome, or whether the expert has been trained in the application of this theory or whether he has ever applied the theory before doing so in this case, and no evidence concerning the theory's general acceptance in the field other than the statement of the expert himself).

Burnett v. State, 815 N.E.2d 201 (Ind. Ct. App. 2004) (the admissibility of scientific evidence under Rule 702(b) is considered in light of *Daubert v. Merrell Dow Pharms.*, 509 U.S. 579, 113 S. Ct. 2786, 125 L. Ed. 2d 469 (1993), and the federal evidence law of *Daubert* and its progeny are helpful in applying Rule 702; although the reliability of ACE-V methodology has not been established in Indiana state courts, the federal courts in Indiana have determined that the methodology is reliable under Federal Rule of Evidence 702; furthermore, it was established that the methodology is generally accepted within the expert's relevant field of study and it is more likely than not that the scientific principles upon which the testimony rests are reliable).

Mitchell v. State, 813 N.E.2d 422 (Ind. Ct. App. 2004) (exclusion of expert witness on the grounds that she was married to the defendant was improper, as there is no requirement that an expert be unbiased; however, the error was harmless, as the wife testified as a fact witness about matters she would have testified to as an expert).

Walker v. Cuppett, 808 N.E.2d 85 (Ind. Ct. App. 2004) (although Rule 106 embodies what was known as the "completeness doctrine," which was designed to avoid misleading impressions caused by taking a statement out of its proper context or otherwise conveying a distorted picture by the introduction of only selective parts of the statement, the redacted portions of a document are still subject to normal rules of admissibility before they may be admitted; because the party offering medical records did not prove the expert qualifications of the doctors who rendered opinions or made statements in the redacted portions of the records, the trial court properly allowed the redactions to stand).

State v. Lloyd, 800 N.E.2d 196 (Ind. Ct. App. 2003) (a party who fails to lay a proper foundation establishing that a witness had any knowledge or expertise as to how shattered automobile glass might be when a car window is broken cannot introduce expert testimony from that witness because the witness has not been qualified as such).

Fulton County Comm'rs v. Miller, 788 N.E.2d 1284 (Ind. Ct. App. 2003) (in determining the reliability of an expert witness in Indiana, there is no specific test or set of prongs which must be considered in order to satisfy Rule 702(b); the admissibility of expert testimony under Rule 702 is a matter within the broad discretion of the trial court and will be reversed only for abuse of that discretion).

Farrell v. Littell, 790 N.E.2d 612 (Ind. Ct. App. 2003) (qualification as an expert under Rule 702 is required only if the witness's opinion is based on information received from others under Rule 703 or through a hypothetical question; the testimony of an observer, who may have the qualifications of an expert, may act as a lay witness and simply provide a report of what the witness observed; such witnesses are "skilled witnesses" and may testify about their observations, opinions, or inferences that are based solely on facts within their own personal knowledge).

Thayer v. Vaughan, 798 N.E.2d 249 (Ind. Ct. App. 2003) (an expert opinion affidavit must state the reasoning or methodologies upon which the opinion is based in addition to asserting admissible underlying facts).

Hobson v. State, 795 N.E.2d 1118 (Ind. Ct. App. 2003) (a witness may qualify as an expert on the basis of practical experience alone; it is within the trial court's sound discretion to decide whether a person qualifies as an expert witness).

Suell v. Dewees, 780 N.E.2d 870 (Ind. Ct. App. 2002) (once the trial court is satisfied that an expert's general methodology is based on reliable scientific principles, then the accuracy, consistency, and credibility of the expert's opinions may properly be left to vigorous cross-examination, presentation of contrary evidence, argument of counsel, and resolution by the trier of fact).

Hartford Steam Boiler Inspection & Ins. Co. v. White, 775 N.E.2d 1128 (Ind. Ct. App. 2002) (witness was qualified to testify as expert based on licensure in other states).

Brooks v. Friedman, 769 N.E.2d 696 (Ind. Ct. App. 2002) (medical opinions and diagnoses in hospital records must meet the requirements for expert opinions to be admitted into evidence).

Cansler v. Mills, 765 N.E.2d 698 (Ind. Ct. App. 2002), *overruled in part*, *Schultz v. Ford Motor Co.*, 857 N.E.2d 977 (Ind. 2006) (a witness may qualify as an expert on the basis of practical experience alone).

Schaefer v. State, 750 N.E.2d 787 (Ind. Ct. App. 2001) (hospital records of victim of child molestation could not be excluded simply because they contained opinions or diagnosis, but for the medical opinions or diagnosis to be admitted into evidence, they must meet the requirements of Rule 702 for expert opinions).

Ford Motor Co. v. Ammerman, 705 N.E.2d 539 (Ind. Ct. App. 1999) (once the proponent of expert testimony establishes that the requirements of Rule 702(b) have been met, the burden shifts to the opponent of the evidence who then must attack the basis for receipt of the evidence, usually through the use of preliminary questions).

Schloot v. Guinevere Real Estate Corp., 697 N.E.2d 1273 (Ind. Ct. App. 1998) (although hospital records may not be excluded as hearsay simply because they include opinions or diagnoses, to be admitted into evidence, they must meet the requirements for expert opinions set forth in Rule 702).

Lytle v. Ford Motor Co., 696 N.E.2d 465 (Ind. Ct. App. 1998) (trial court did not err in excluding expert testimony not based on scientific principles where the record did not reveal that the expert possessed knowledge or experience that would assist the trier of fact, nor did it err in excluding expert testimony based on scientific principles where uncontroverted evidence revealed that the basis of the expert's opinion is scientifically unreliable).

Ross v. State, 665 N.E.2d 599 (Ind. Ct. App. 1996) (witness was qualified as expert on DNA identification in rape case as he was forensic scientist specializing in forensic serology and DNA analysis and supervising police crime lab, held several degrees and attended FBI training sessions in DNA analysis, published several academic articles, taught courses in subject, and had served as expert witness in over 300 cases).

Hottinger v. Trugreen Corp., 665 N.E.2d 593 (Ind. Ct. App. 1996) (when expert scientific testimony is offered, court must first determine whether reasoning or methodology on which testimony would be based is scientifically valid and whether that reasoning or methodology can properly be applied to facts in issue; to be admissible, expert testimony must have valid scientific connection to relevant inquiry, and while testimony need not be known to certainty, any inference or assertion must be arrived at by scientific method).

Koziol v. Vojvoda, 662 N.E.2d 985 (Ind. Ct. App. 1996) (in negligence action arising from car accident, police officer was qualified to give expert opinion, where officer had eight years of experience as accident investigator, had attended several training sessions and seminars on accident reconstruction, had investigated over 3,000 accidents, and, arrived on scene of accident at issue a few minutes after it happened and spoke with drivers).

Edgin v. State, 657 N.E.2d 445 (Ind. Ct. App. 1995) (witnesses, whether lay or expert witnesses, are not allowed to testify about the credibility of another witness; police detective's testimony that alleged child molestation victims "seemed very credible" was improper vouching).

Reeves v. Boyd & Sons, 654 N.E.2d 864 (Ind. Ct. App. 1995) (in personal injury action arising from car accident, it was harmless error at most to admit emergency room medical record which included plaintiff's blood alcohol content test result without defendant meeting four-prong foundation requirement alleged to apply in criminal cases; testimony of emergency room physician and his explanation of medical records did not indicate any untrustworthiness in test result that would make it inadmissible under business records exception to hearsay rule, and physician's conclusion as expert witness that plaintiff was intoxicated could be based on inadmissible records; finally, test result was cumulative to other evidence of intoxication).

Simms v. Schweikher, 651 N.E.2d 348 (Ind. Ct. App. 1995) (due to complexity of medical diagnosis and treatment, expert testimony is usually needed to establish applicable standard of care in medical malpractice case).

Randolph County Hosp. v. Livingston, 650 N.E.2d 1215 (Ind. Ct. App. 1995) (affidavit stating that purported expert attended school in Indiana and is currently licensed and practicing in Indiana suffices to establish expert's competence; in medical malpractice action, plaintiff's expert witness was qualified to testify about standard of care where he was familiar with standard of care for abdominal surgery in area, had reviewed pertinent medical records of patient and deposition, and concluded that defendant provided substandard care which was a cause of patient's death).

Sanchez v. State, 650 N.E.2d 734 (Ind. Ct. App. 1995), *vacated on other grounds*, 675 N.E.2d 306 (Ind. 1996) (stipulations that polygraph examination results are admissible must be signed by both defendant and prosecuting attorney's office in order to be valid).

Nasser v. State, 646 N.E.2d 673 (Ind. Ct. App. 1995) (police officer who testified about her involvement in investigation of traffic accident and her administration of breath test to defendant was not subject to cross-examination by defendant regarding the pharmacology of alcohol absorption, where direct examination brought forth no information on alcohol absorption, and state did not present officer as expert in breath testing or alcohol absorption).

Harlan Sprague Dawley, Inc. v. S.E. Lab Group, 644 N.E.2d 615 (Ind. Ct. App. 1994) (expert opinion must be preceded by foundational evidence demonstrating witness's credentials as expert: (1) subject matter must be connected to a scientific field beyond average lay person's knowledge; and (2) witness must be shown to have sufficient skill in that area that trier of fact in its search for truth will probably find witness's opinion helpful; trial court has wide discretion in deciding if expert is qualified and if foundation for opinion evidence is sufficient).

Hudson v. McClaskey, 641 N.E.2d 36 (Ind. Ct. App. 1994) (witness's work experience and formal training sufficed to make witness "expert"; witness was able to aid trier of fact in assessing property value, where witness was auctioneer, real estate broker, and appraiser, had taken appraisal courses, and had experience as agent buying and selling real estate).

Smith v. Beaty, 639 N.E.2d 1029 (Ind. Ct. App. 1994) (opinion of expert that something is "possible" or "could have been" may suffice to sustain verdict or award when opinion is given together with other probative evidence establishing material factual question to be proved).

Wine v. State, 637 N.E.2d 1369 (Ind. Ct. App. 1994) (trial court has discretion to admit results of polygraph examination where parties have stipulated to their admissibility).

Martin v. State, 636 N.E.2d 1268 (Ind. Ct. App. 1994), *superseded*, 760 N.E.2d 597 (Ind. 2002) (although not qualified as expert witness, dentist was qualified to testify about physical identity of murder victim's skeletal remains, where dentist was licensed and had personally treated patient thought to be victim; that dentist had been out of school only three months when he compared patient's X-rays and victim's teeth, and had never made such comparison before, affected testimony's weight not its admissibility).

Landau v. Bailey, 629 N.E.2d 264 (Ind. Ct. App. 1994) (expert may be qualified by practical experience as well as by formal training, and determinations of whether expert is qualified are within discretion of trial court).

Mundy v. Angelicchio, 623 N.E.2d 456 (Ind. Ct. App. 1993) (in medical malpractice action, expert's opinion that surgeon was not negligent was admissible).

Chapter 703

Rule 703. Bases of Opinion Testimony by Experts

Rule 703 reads as follows:

> The facts or data in the particular case upon which an expert bases an opinion or inference may be those perceived by or made known to the expert at or before the hearing. Experts may testify to opinions based on inadmissible evidence, provided that it is of the type reasonably relied upon by experts in the field.

* * * * *

ANALYSIS

Permissible Bases of Opinion or Inference.   Rule 703 identifies permissible sources of facts or data upon which the expert may base his or her opinion or inference. The expert may predicate his or her opinion on first-hand knowledge, or in the alternative, the expert may draw upon facts or data made known to the expert at or before the hearing. Additionally, the rule provides that if the facts or data are of the type reasonably relied upon by experts in the field, they are a permissible source of information even if they would not be admissible in evidence.

Personal Knowledge.   Where an expert has personal knowledge of the facts or data underlying his or her opinion, this basis is a permissible predicate for his or her testimony. For example, an attending physician who treated an injured plaintiff would have first-hand knowledge of the facts which could permissibly support expert opinion testimony as to the permanence of plaintiff's disability. In this case, the expert is aware of the supporting data by reason of his or her first-hand experience.

Alternative bases for expert testimony are sources in regard to which the expert does not have personal knowledge. For example, the expert may base his or her opinion on reports prepared by others. If such material is inadmissible, it nevertheless is an appropriate basis for expert testimony provided it is the type of information reasonably relied upon by experts in the field.

When an expert testifies to otherwise inadmissible facts and data that are used in formulating an opinion, the inadmissible facts and data may be used only for the purpose of evaluating the appropriateness of the expert's opinion. They are not admissible as substantive evidence. Accordingly, the more appropriate procedure in admitting expert testimony is to restrict the introduction of the otherwise inadmissible underlying facts or data to cross-

235

examination; an expert should not generally be permitted to testify on *direct examination* that the expert relied on consultations with colleagues or other experts in reaching his or her opinion. The fact that consultations were made may be brought out on cross-examination.

If brought out on direct examination, the risk is that the expert's testimony regarding the consultation serves only to bolster his or her opinion on the issue to which the expert is testifying. Such evidence is subject to exclusion on Rule 403 grounds by motion of opposing counsel, but if the evidence is admitted, a limiting instruction under Rule 107 is always appropriate. The trial judge must be alert to ensure that this section is not used merely as a pretext for getting inadmissible and prejudicial evidence before the jury. Because the otherwise inadmissible materials relied upon by the expert are not admitted as exhibits, they should never be shown to the jury, either as records or by being projected onto a screen inside the courtroom.

Constitutional Considerations—Bases of Expert Opinion and the Confrontation Clause

The use of otherwise inadmissible information by experts may implicate the Confrontation Clause. In *Crawford v. Washington*, 541 U.S. 36, 124 S. Ct. 1354, 158 L. Ed. 2d 177 (2004), the United States Supreme Court held that the Confrontation Clause is concerned only with the admission of "testimonial" evidence; such evidence absolutely requires both the unavailability of the declarant and a prior opportunity for cross-examination. In *Williams v. Illinois*, ___ U.S. ___, 132 S. Ct. 2221, 183 L. Ed. 2d 89 (2012), the Supreme Court made a sudden left turn into Rule 703, thereby complicating what most had seen as the Confrontation Clause's interaction with the hearsay rules.

In *Williams*, the Supreme Court addressed the use of surrogate expert witnesses, or expert testimony that discloses the contents of laboratory reports by non-testifying witnesses. The DNA comparison expert in *Williams* based her testimony on a lab report authored by a non-testifying witness. The important difference between *Williams* and the evidence in *Bullcoming v. New Mexico*, 564 U.S. ___, 131 S. Ct. 2705, 180 L. Ed. 2d 610 (2011), another case involving the testimony of surrogate lab analysts, was the actual evidence sought to be admitted. In *Bullcoming*, the report itself was admitted into evidence. In *Williams*, on the other hand, the DNA report itself was not sought to be admitted, but rather used as the primary basis of the expert's testimony.

Although the *Williams* Court upheld the use of this kind of expert DNA comparison testimony, it did so under through a majority cobbled together by distinct rationales. The plurality conceptualized the case as a Rule 703 question rather than a hearsay question. In other words, the expert testimony did not violate the Confrontation Clause because it does not apply to non-hearsay statements, i.e., statements not offered to prove the truth of the matter asserted. Because Illinois Rule of Evidence 703 (like Federal Rule of Evidence 703 and other state cognate rules, including Michigan Rule 703) authorizes an expert to base an opinion on out-of-court regardless of whether those statements may themselves be admissible, the out-of-court statement (in this situation, the lab report) is relevant for the limited purpose of explaining the expert's conclusion, not for its truth. In such a case, the credibility of the expert testimony, not the lab report, is ultimately at issue.

This decision was joined by Justice Thomas, who clearly rejected this line of reasoning but nonetheless determined that the Confrontation Clause was not implicated because the lab report lacked the requisite degree of formality needed to trigger constitutional scrutiny. No other member of the Court has signed on to Justice Thomas's Confrontation Clause approach, but as the tiebreaking vote, his opinion is controlling. The dissent, composed of the *Melendez-Diaz* and *Bullcoming* majority, characterized the plurality reasoning that the expert's summary of the lab report was not offered for its truth a "prosecutorial dodge" depending on a "simple abdication to state-law labels." *Williams*, 132 S. Ct. at 2265, 2272 (Kagan, J., dissenting). Instead, the dissent continued its pragmatic approach to out-of-court statements, describing the question as whether the Confrontation Clause allows a State to "introduce[] the results of Cellmark's testing through an expert witness who had no idea how they were generated." *Id.* at 2265.

Williams will surely generate confusion among lower courts and practitioners attempting to discern a rule of decision in similar kinds of Confrontation Clause challenges. However, a majority of the Court who would prohibit the kind of expert testimony in *Williams* appears to be intact, even if the testimony was actually upheld in *Williams* itself.

ADDITIONAL AUTHORITY

WEISSENBERGER'S FEDERAL EVIDENCE §§ 703.1–703.5

McCORMICK § 15

4 WEINSTEIN 2d §§ 703.01–703.06

3 MUELLER & KIRKPATRICK §§ 354–359

3 WIGMORE § 687

COMPARISON TO FEDERAL RULE

Federal Rule 703 was amended in December 2000. Federal Rule 703 now reads as follows:

Rule 703. Bases of Opinion Testimony by Experts

The facts or data in the particular case upon which an expert bases an opinion or inference may be those perceived by or made known to the expert at or before the hearing. If of a type reasonably relied upon by experts in the particular field in forming opinions or inferences upon the subject, the facts or data need not be admissible in evidence in order for the opinion or inference to be admitted. Facts or data that are otherwise inadmissible shall not be disclosed to the jury by the proponent of the opinion or inference unless the court determines that their probative value in assisting the jury to evaluate the expert's opinion substantially outweighs their prejudicial effect.

Federal Rule 703 was amended to emphasize that when an expert reasonably relies on inadmissible information to form an opinion or inference, the underlying information is not admissible simply because the opinion or inference is admitted. Federal Rule 703 provides a presumption against disclosure to the jury of information used as the basis of an expert's opinion and not admissible for any substantive purpose, when that information is offered by the proponent of the expert.

When information is reasonably relied upon by an expert and yet is admissible only for the purpose of assisting the jury in evaluating an expert's opinion, a trial court must consider the information's probative value in assisting the jury to weigh the expert's opinion and the risk of prejudice resulting from the jury's potential misuse of the information for substantive purposes. The information may be disclosed to the jury, upon objection, only if the trial court finds that the probative value of the information in assisting the jury to evaluate the expert's opinion substantially outweighs its prejudicial effect. However, the balancing test is not applicable to facts or data that are admissible for any other purpose but have not been offered for such a purpose at the time the expert testifies. Nevertheless, if the evidence is admitted under the balancing test, the trial judge must give a limiting instruction upon request, informing the jury that the underlying information must not be used for substantive purposes.

SIGNIFICANT CASES

Williams v. Illinois, ___ U.S. ___, 132 S. Ct. 2221, 183 L. Ed. 2d 89 (2012) (the Confrontation Clause does not prohibit an expert from expressing an opinion based on facts that have been made known to the expert but about which the expert is not competent to testify) (plurality opinion).

Bullcoming v. New Mexico, 564 U.S. ___, 131 S. Ct. 2705, 180 L. Ed. 2d 610 (2011) (the certification of an analyst who did not sign a DUI report or personally observe the test does not satisfy the Confrontation Clause).

Melendez-Diaz v. Massachusetts, 557 U.S. 305, 129 S. Ct. 2527, 174 L. Ed. 2d 314 (2009) (drug lab reports constitute affidavits which fall within the "core class of testimonial statements" covered by the Confrontation Clause; accordingly, the prosecution must produce the analysts who prepared the report for cross-examination or the report will not be admissible).

Delaware v. Fensterer, 474 U.S. 15, 106 S. Ct. 292, 88 L. Ed. 2d 15 (1985) (admission of an expert opinion did not violate criminal defendant's rights under the Confrontation Clause of the Sixth Amendment, even though the expert could not recall the method whereby he arrived at his opinion).

Vaughn v. Daniels Co., 841 N.E.2d 1133 (Ind. 2006) (an expert may form an opinion on inadmissible documents provided that the documents are of a type that other experts use in forming such opinions).

In re Adoption of L.C., 650 N.E.2d 726 (Ind. Ct. App. 1995) (expert may base opinion on hearsay or otherwise inadmissible evidence, provided that evidence is of type reasonably relied on by experts in the field).

Harrison v. State, 644 N.E.2d 1243 (Ind. 1995), *opinion after remand*, 659 N.E.2d 480 (Ind. 1995) (in capital murder trial, pretrial *Frye* hearing was necessary to decide admissibility of DNA test results used in polymerase chain reaction (PCR) test).

Jenkins v. State, 627 N.E.2d 789 (Ind. 1993) (expert may base opinion on hearsay reports of non-testifying lab technician; no confrontation violation).

Lockhart v. State, 609 N.E.2d 1093 (Ind. 1993) (expert could properly base his opinion regarding the similarity of two homicides on two autopsy reports conducted by other pathologists).

Miller v. State, 575 N.E.2d 272 (Ind. 1991) (where an expert bases an opinion on information that is inadmissible, the information is admissible to help the jury evaluate the expert's credibility if the expert's credibility has been disputed).

Gambill v. State, 479 N.E.2d 523 (Ind. 1985) (expert may base an opinion on reports prepared by others if the sources are usually relied on by members of that profession).

Wilber v. State, 460 N.E.2d 142 (Ind. 1984) (pathologist permitted to rely on the medical reports of the treating physicians in forming opinion as to cause of death).

Wickliffe v. State, 424 N.E.2d 1007 (Ind. 1981) (expert opinion based on the autopsy report prepared by another pathologist and not admitted into evidence at trial was proper).

Gresser v. Dow Chem. Co., 2013 Ind. App. LEXIS 204 (Apr. 30, 2013) (Rule 703 provides that experts may testify to opinions based on inadmissible evidence, provided that the evidence is of a type reasonably relied upon by experts in the field).

Mills v. Berrios, 851 N.E.2d 1066 (Ind. Ct. App. 2006) (an expert's affidavit was not legally insufficient because the medical records upon which the expert's opinion was based was not attached to the affidavit; an expert's opinion may be based on inadmissible evidence under certain circumstances).

A.J. v. Marion County Dep't of Child Servs., 877 N.E.2d 805 (Ind. Ct. App. 2007) (expert may rely on opinions based, in part, on otherwise inadmissible polygraph results; the results of the polygraph results were not specifically reported, and there was evidence that the use of polygraphs as a treatment tool was widely accepted in his field).

M.M. v. Clarian Health Partners, 826 N.E.2d 90 (Ind. Ct. App. 2005), *transfer denied*, 841 N.E.2d 183 (Ind. 2005) (although an expert witness may consider inadmissible hearsay in formulating an opinion regarding a patient's mental condition, the information may not be used as substantive evidence to support an involuntary commitment).

Schmidt v. State, 816 N.E.2d 925 (Ind. Ct. App. 2004) (expert testimony may be based on otherwise inadmissible facts that are "of the type reasonably relied upon by experts in the field"; however, courts have shown considerable reluctance to find reasonable reliance on information not prepared by persons with specialized training; accordingly, the trial court's determination that statements by the defendant do not fall within the purview of the types of information or data contemplated by Rule 703 is not erroneous).

Marlatt v. State, 715 N.E.2d 1001 (Ind. Ct. App. 1999) (before results of scientific tests are admissible, the proponent of the evidence must lay a proper foundation establishing the reliability of the procedure that is used; to lay a proper foundation for the admission of radar test results, the state must establish that the radar device was properly operated and regularly tested; it is not necessary to offer an expert to explain the use or theory of a radar gun).

Buzzard v. State, 669 N.E.2d 996 (Ind. Ct. App. 1996) (expert opinion is generally not admissible to prove defendant's character for particular trait, even if opinion is based on personality profile; admissibility of such testimony is within discretion of trial court).

Faulkner v. Markkay of Ind., 663 N.E.2d 798 (Ind. Ct. App. 1996) (trial court did not abuse its discretion by not permitting chiropractor testifying for plaintiff in slip-and-fall action to state opinions of plaintiff's treating physicians which were indicated in medical records, or by not admitting into evidence a compilation of records; expert witness may give opinion based partly on reports not in evidence and on inadmissible hearsay, provided that expert is qualified to judge accuracy and reliability of information, report is of the kind normally found reliable and information is of the type customarily relied on by expert in practice of profession; expert witness's reliance on hearsay may not be used as means to place hearsay before jury, and expert must rely on own expertise to reach opinion and may not merely repeat others' opinions).

Scott v. City of Seymour, 659 N.E.2d 585 (Ind. Ct. App. 1995) (unlike lay witnesses, experts may testify to opinions based on inadmissible evidence, provided that it is of the type reasonably relied on by experts in the field; expert witness's opinion in affidavit was admissible and sufficed to establish genuine issue of material fact regarding City's negligence, thus precluding summary judgment).

Meisberger v. State, 640 N.E.2d 716 (Ind. Ct. App. 1994) (trial court did not err in permitting expert witness to identify the victim's body using dental records not admitted into evidence at trial).

Prange v. Martin, 629 N.E.2d 915 (Ind. Ct. App. 1994) (opinion of police officer about cause of motor vehicle accident, which was based on hearsay statements of three drivers involved, should not have been admitted if defendant's counsel had objected on that basis because officer was testifying as lay person at that time; but defense counsel made no such objection and same or similar evidence was admitted without objection; therefore, testimony on direct examination was harmless).

Mundy v. Angelicchio, 623 N.E.2d 456 (Ind. Ct. App. 1993) (expert witness may base opinion on hearsay evidence if witness has sufficient expertise to evaluate the reliability of the evidence, if the evidence is the type normally found reliable, and if the evidence is the type customarily relied on by an expert in his or her professional practice).

Conner v. First Nat'l Bank, 118 Ind. App. 173, 77 N.E.2d 598 (1948) (expert may base an opinion solely on first-hand knowledge of the facts).

Chapter 704

Rule 704. Opinion on Ultimate Issue

Rule 704 reads as follows:

> (a) Testimony in the form of an opinion or inference otherwise admissible is not objectionable merely because it embraces an ultimate issue to be decided by the trier of fact.
>
> (b) Witnesses may not testify to opinions concerning intent, guilt, or innocence in a criminal case; the truth or falsity of allegations; whether a witness has testified truthfully; or legal conclusions.

* * * * *

ANALYSIS

Scope. Rule 704 provides that testimony in the form of an opinion is not subject to exclusion solely because it addresses the ultimate issue in the case. The rule applies both to expert and lay testimony.

"Otherwise Admissible" Lay Opinion. Rule 704 provides that ultimate issue testimony "otherwise admissible" is not subject to exclusion, and consequently, the testimony at issue must minimally satisfy the requirements of all Rules of Evidence. For example, Rule 701 governs opinions offered by a lay witness. The ultimate issue testimony of a lay person must be rationally based on facts perceived by the witness in order to be admissible. Moreover, under Rule 701 the opinion or inference is not admissible if it does not assist the trier of fact in the determination of a factual issue. When the jury can easily draw the inference from a simple recitation of facts by the witness, the witness's opinion on the ultimate issue might be subject to exclusion under Rule 701 even though Rule 704 would not afford a basis for exclusion.

Expert Opinion. Under Rule 702 the expert's special body of knowledge must assist the trier of fact in determining a fact in issue or in understanding the evidence. It is the inability of the unaided jury to reach the ultimate opinion that renders the expert opinion vital. For this reason, an ultimate issue opinion from a properly qualified expert should not be excluded except in the extreme case where the expert opinion is inherently misleading or unfairly prejudicial.

Current Trends and New Developments

For many years, Indiana remained in a minority of jurisdictions in permitting a limited form of child witness "vouching" testimony in child molestation cases. In *Hoglund v. State*, the Indiana Supreme Court joined the majority of jurisdictions in holding that Rule 704(b)'s prohibition on testimony concerning whether a witness has testified truthfully prohibits this practice as well. *Hoglund v. State*, 962 N.E.2d 1230, 1232–1237 (Ind. 2012) (*overruling Lawrence v. State*, 464 N.E.2d 923, 925 (Ind. 1984); *Head v. State*, 519 N.E.2d 151, 153 (Ind. 1988)). Included in this prohibition is testimony concerning whether an alleged child victim may be prone to exaggeration or fantasies about sexual matters, which the *Hoglund* Court noted was "an indirect but nonetheless functional equivalent of saying the child is 'telling the truth.'" *Hoglund v. State*, 962 N.E.2d 1230, 1232–1237 (Ind. 2012).

The *Hoglund* Court further refused to carve out an exception to the prohibition of Rule 704(b) for child victims of alleged sexual abuse. It pointed out that the "shift in public attitudes concerning allegations of child sex abuse undermines the necessity to carve out an exception to Rule 704(b)," thus bringing Indiana in accord with the modern trend. *Hoglund v. State*, 962 N.E.2d 1230 (Ind. 2012).

Subsection (b) of Rule 704 is designed to preserve pre-Rule Indiana law by providing that witnesses may not testify to certain specified subjects, that is, opinions as to intent, guilt, or innocence in a criminal case; the truth or falsity of allegations; whether a witness has testified truthfully; or legal conclusions.

Practice Point

The line separating inadmissible opinions concerning criminal intent, guilt, or innocence from admissible ones is not as clear as one might hope. Indiana courts have not operationalized this standard in a satisfactory manner, relying instead on the exclusion of opinions that seem "problematic." Examples of statements that have been excluded under Rule 704(b) include: (1) "It happened. And you were there, you were there and we know it, and you know it, or we wouldn't be up here", *see Wilkes v. State*, 917 N.E.2d 675 (Ind. 2009); (2) "I thought it was you", *see Smith v. State*, 721 N.E.2d 213, 217 (Ind. 1999); and (3) "Something stinks. So basically all we've got is your word that Boogie shot this guy. Is that what you're telling us . . . I think you was looking out for Boogie," *see Lampkins v. State*, 778 N.E.2d 1248, 1251 (Ind. 2002).

ADDITIONAL AUTHORITY

WEISSENBERGER'S FEDERAL EVIDENCE §§ 704.1–704.5

MCCORMICK § 12

4 WEINSTEIN 2d §§ 704.01–704.06

3 Mueller & Kirkpatrick §§ 360–362

7 Wigmore §§ 1920–1921

COMPARISON TO FEDERAL RULE

Indiana Rule 704(a) is distinguished from Federal Rule 704(a) by the clarifying addition of the word "merely" following the word "objectionable." Federal Rule 704(b) provides that an expert witness is prohibited from testifying in a criminal case with respect to whether the defendant had the necessary mental state. Indiana Rule 704(b) specifies several subjects inappropriate for opinion testimony.

SIGNIFICANT CASES

Barefoot v. Estelle, 463 U.S. 880, 103 S. Ct. 3383, 77 L. Ed. 2d 1090 (1983), *superseded by statute*, *Treesh v. Bagley*, 2007 U.S. Dist. LEXIS 28985 (N.D. Ohio Mar. 31, 2007) (testimony of psychiatrists in response to hypothetical questions regarding future dangerousness of defendant was admissible, where psychiatrists had not personally examined defendant).

Hoglund v. State, 962 N.E.2d 1230, 1232–1237 (Ind. 2012) (indirect vouching testimony is functionally identical to testimony that a child witness is telling the truth, and thus prohibited under Rule 704(b); furthermore, the Court declined to carve out an exception to the rule for sex abuse cases).

TRW Vehicle Safety Sys. v. Moore, 936 N.E.2d 201 (Ind. 2010) (Rule 704(b) provides, in part, that witnesses may not testify to opinions concerning intent, guilt, or innocence in a criminal case).

Wilkes v. State, 917 N.E.2d 675 (Ind. 2009) (a statement made by a detective during an interrogation was an opinion of defendant's guilt and should have been excluded).

Ritchie v. State, 875 N.E.2d 706, 728–729 (Ind. 2007) (when facts sufficient to demonstrate deficient performance by an attorney are undisputed, whether those facts show ineffective assistance of counsel constitute a question of law to which an expert may not provide an opinion).

Vaughn v. Daniels Co., 841 N.E.2d 1133 (Ind. 2006) (an expert's opinions relating to reasonable care and proximate cause are admissible because they speak to ultimate issues to be decided by the trier of fact, not legal conclusions).

McManus v. State, 814 N.E.2d 253 (Ind. 2004) (expert's testimony was in response to a question calling for a legal conclusion, which is rendered inadmissible under Rule 704).

Miller v. State, 770 N.E.2d 763 (Ind. 2002) (when jurors are faced with evidence that falls outside common experience, the Supreme Court allows specialists to supplement the jurors' knowledge and interpretation of the evidence).

Jackson v. State, 728 N.E.2d 147 (Ind. 2000) (trial court did not err in excluding witness's prior inconsistent statement that he thought murder was accidental for impeachment purposes because statement of belief was an expression of opinion as to intent and was barred by Rule 704(b)).

Smith v. State, 721 N.E.2d 213 (Ind. 1999) (police officer's statement, "I thought it was you," to defendant during out-of-court interview was improperly admitted; the same reasoning underlying Rule 704(b)'s prohibition of opinions of guilt during live in-court testimony applies to statements offered at trial that were made at another time or place).

Bufkin v. State, 700 N.E.2d 1147 (Ind. 1998) (police officer's testimony concerning the credibility of another witness violated Rule 704(b) which prohibits witnesses from testifying to opinions concerning, among other things, whether a witness has testified truthfully).

Fleener v. State, 656 N.E.2d 1140 (Ind. 1995) (testimony of psychologist that child sexual abuse victim was "in touch with reality" and psychologist's testimony about victim's propensity to exaggerate or fantasize about sexual matters did not improperly invade jury's province, although it may have indirectly supported victim's credibility, where questions and psychologist's answer involved no direct statement regarding whether psychologist believed victim was telling truth; evidentiary foundation was established for propounding hypotheticals and psychologist was asked about typical victim not particular victim and neither asked for direct opinion about victim's truthfulness nor defendant's guilt or innocence).

Weaver v. State, 643 N.E.2d 342 (Ind. 1994) (trial court can exclude lay opinion testimony of defendant's girlfriend, who was the victim of attempted murder with which defendant was charged, regarding what she believed caused defendant to beat her and whether defendant intended to kill her, although girlfriend was uniquely situated to observe actions of defendant and may have had insight into his motivations).

Marks v. Gaskill, 563 N.E.2d 1284 (Ind. 1990) (expert in accident reconstruction not permitted to give opinion as to who was at fault).

Shepherd v. State, 538 N.E.2d 242 (Ind. 1989) (trial court erred in permitting a prosecution witness to testify on whether she believed defendant's denials of murder).

Head v. State, 519 N.E.2d 151 (Ind. 1988) (psychologist's opinion that a child victim's allegations were true impermissibly invaded the province of the jury).

Freed v. State, 480 N.E.2d 929 (Ind. 1985) (psychiatrist's opinion that defendant was legally sane was not error because the opinion involved a mixture of expert opinion and legal conclusion).

Brown v. State, 448 N.E.2d 10 (Ind. 1983) (fireman permitted to give an opinion that a burning home presented conditions dangerous to human life; admission of the opinion was upheld although the opinion involved one of the elements of the crime of *arson*).

De Vaney v. State, 259 Ind. 483, 288 N.E.2d 732 (1972) (expert opinion is admissible even though it embraces an ultimate fact in issue).

Shelby v. State, 986 N.E.2d 345 (Ind. Ct. App. 2013) (experts may testify on the general subjects of coercive police interrogation and false or coerced confessions and regarding the techniques the police used in a particular interrogation; however, Rule 704(b) limits such testimony to general matters, and experts may not comment about the specific interrogation in controversy in a way that may be interpreted by the jury as the expert's opinion that the confession in that particular case was coerced or false).

Guzik v. Town of St. John, 875 N.E.2d 258 (Ind. Ct. App. 2007) (under Rule 704(b), witnesses may not testify to opinions concerning legal conclusions).

Lumbermens Mut. Cas. Co. v. Combs, 873 N.E.2d 692 (Ind. Ct. App. 2007) (the trend under the Indiana Rules of Evidence embodied in Rule 704 is to allow expert opinion testimony on the ultimate issue of the case so long as the testimony concerns matters which are not within the common knowledge and experience of ordinary persons and the testimony will aid the jury).

Rose v. State, 846 N.E.2d 363 (Ind. Ct. App. 2006) (although limited testimony is admissible concerning a particular child's tendency to exaggerate or fantasize about sexual matters, an expert's repeated testimony about how "convincing" the child was when she described what had happened to her constituted improper vouching prohibited by Rule 704).

Weis v. State, 825 N.E.2d 896 (Ind. Ct. App. 2005) (a police officer who merely explained the course of the investigation after speaking with a witness and did not specifically state that she believed the witness's testimony did not violate Rule 704(b)).

Farris v. State, 818 N.E.2d 63 (Ind. Ct. App. 2004) (testimony by an expert questioning the veracity of prior witnesses was prohibited expert testimony under Rule 704).

Carew v. State, 817 N.E.2d 281 (Ind. Ct. App. 2004) (although Rule 704 prohibits opinion testimony that a specific individual's confession was false, Rule 704 does not prohibit general opinion testimony that coercive police techniques could increase the likelihood of a false confession from an individual with diminished intellectual functioning).

Witte v. M.M., 800 N.E.2d 185 (Ind. Ct. App. 2003), *superseded, Witte v. Mundy*, 820 N.E.2d 128 (Ind. 2005) (Rule 704 permits expert opinion testimony on the ultimate issue of the case, so long as the testimony concerns matters which are not within the common knowledge and experience of lay persons and the testimony will aid the jury).

Krumm v. State, 793 N.E.2d 1170 (Ind. Ct. App. 2003) (although Rule 704 prohibits "vouching," or the admission into evidence of expert testimony concerning whether a witness has testified truthfully in a case, a special case exists for the credibility of children who are called upon as witnesses to describe sexual conduct; in some cases, the court may allow opinion testimony by parents, teachers, and others having adequate experience with the child to establish that the child is not prone to exaggerate or fantasize about sexual matters; as long as the opinions do not comment on the truth or falsity of child witness's testimony directly, they may be admitted in the court's discretion).

Vaughn v. Daniels Co., 777 N.E.2d 1110 (Ind. Ct. App. 2002), *superseded*, 841 N.E.2d 1133 (Ind. 2006) (statements constituting legal conclusions relating to proximate cause and reasonable care in a summary judgment affidavit should be stricken; though the trend is to allow expert opinion testimony on the ultimate issue of a case, experts are not permitted to offer legal conclusions as part of their testimony).

Meyer v. Burke (In re Estate of Meyer), 747 N.E.2d 1159 (Ind. Ct. App. 2001) (trial court did not abuse its discretion in denying a motion to strike an attorney's opinion testimony because the testimony merely recounted the attorney's business dealings with the clients and did not contain any impermissible legal conclusions under Rule 704(b)).

Major v. OEC-Diasonics, Inc., 743 N.E.2d 276 (Ind. Ct. App. 2001) (the trend is to allow expert opinion testimony even on the ultimate issue of the case, so long as the testimony concerns matters which are not within the common knowledge and experience of ordinary persons and will aid the trier-of-fact; trial court did not abuse its discretion in permitting expert opinion testimony on the ultimate issue in the case because the judge felt free to ignore the expert on a legal conclusion if it disagreed with the expert because ultimately it was the judge's call).

Koziol v. Vojvoda, 662 N.E.2d 985 (Ind. Ct. App. 1996) (in negligence action arising from car accident, police officer was entitled to give expert opinion about fault of nonparty driver although testimony embraced ultimate issue because officer had special knowledge helpful to jury in understanding evidence surrounding accident and deciding factual issues; officer spoke with parties to accident, examined lighting conditions in area, wrote thorough accident report, and observed intersection and grade of roadway).

In re Annexation Proposed by Ordinance No. X-01-93., 654 N.E.2d 284 (Ind. Ct. App. 1995) (in landowner's action for remonstrance against city annexation, testimony that city sewer agreements were recorded in chain of title to landowner's property was not impermissible testimony as to legal conclusion; testimony concerning property's chain of title is not legal conclusion requiring determination by court since process of determining chain of title for particular tract of land is not complex).

Osmulski v. Becze, 638 N.E.2d 828 (Ind. Ct. App. 1994) (expert testimony that accident was caused by motorist's failure to yield to a pedestrian in a crosswalk was properly admissible).

City of Columbia City v. Indiana Util. Regulatory Comm'n, 618 N.E.2d 21 (Ind. Ct. App. 1993) (expert witness's opinion on what facts might be relevant to defendant in deciding on proposed utility territorial realignment was acceptable testimony on ultimate factual issues, rather than improper opinion on legal conclusions).

Chapter 705

Rule 705. Disclosure of Facts or Data Underlying Expert Opinion

Rule 705 reads as follows:

> The expert may testify in terms of opinion or inference and give reasons therefor without first testifying to the underlying facts or data, unless the court requires otherwise. The expert may in any event be required to disclose the underlying facts or data on cross-examination.

* * * * *

ANALYSIS

Scope; Hypothetical Question. Rule 705 sets forth the procedure governing the disclosure of the facts or data used by an expert in formulating his or her opinion. Under the rule, the expert need not first disclose the underlying basis for his or her opinion unless the court in its discretion requires such a sequence. Consequently, the rule is designed to provide flexibility in the presentation of expert testimony. Moreover, the rule implicitly rejects the necessity of a hypothetical question.

Reasons Supporting Opinions. Rule 705 provides that the expert may give reasons for the opinion. It is normally during this stage of the interrogation that the expert witness provides a thorough explanation for the opinions and inferences that have been stated. The expert systematically explains his or her reasoning, or provides the jury with an elucidation of the application of his or her expertise to the identified operative facts supporting the opinion.

ADDITIONAL AUTHORITY

WEISSENBERGER'S FEDERAL EVIDENCE §§ 705.1–705.5

McCORMICK § 14

4 WEINSTEIN 2d §§ 705.01–705.08

3 MUELLER & KIRKPATRICK §§ 363–365

2 WIGMORE §§ 672–686

COMPARISON TO FEDERAL RULE

Indiana Rule 705 is identical to Federal Rule 705.

SIGNIFICANT CASES

Henson v. State, 535 N.E.2d 1189 (Ind. 1989) (court discussed the proper way to use hypothetical questions in examining expert).

Decker v. State, 528 N.E.2d 1119 (Ind. 1988), *overruled*, *Wright v. State*, 658 N.E.2d 563 (Ind. 1995) (fingerprint expert testified to facts and details underlying her opinion).

Ashby v. State, 486 N.E.2d 469 (Ind. 1985) (hypothetical questions are not required during expert testimony).

Dahlberg v. Ogle, 268 Ind. 30, 373 N.E.2d 159 (1978) (when examining an expert witness using a hypothetical question, the attorney should include sufficient facts to form a reliable basis for the expert's opinion).

Prewitt v. State, 819 N.E.2d 393 (Ind. Ct. App. 2004), *superseded*, 878 N.E.2d 184 (Ind. 2007) (an expert is not required to explain the source of statistics used to support a theory to render the expert's testimony admissible, as Rule 705 indicates).

Krumm v. State, 793 N.E.2d 1170 (Ind. Ct. App. 2003) (the admissibility of expert testimony does not hinge on the expert's disclosure of the facts and reasoning that support the opinion, but the absence of facts and reasoning may be elicited on cross-examination of the expert and impacts the weight of the testimony, but it does not affect its admissibility).

VIII
HEARSAY

Chapter 801

Rule 801. Definitions

Rule 801 reads as follows:

The following definitions apply under this Article:

(a) Statement. A *statement* is (1) an oral or written assertion or (2) nonverbal conduct of a person, if it is intended by the person as an assertion.

(b) Declarant. A *declarant* is a person who makes a statement.

(c) Hearsay. *Hearsay* is a statement, other than one made by the declarant while testifying at the trial or hearing, offered in evidence to prove the truth of the matter asserted.

(d) Statements Which are Not Hearsay. A statement is not hearsay if:

(1) *Prior statement by witness.* The declarant testifies at the trial or hearing and is subject to cross-examination concerning the statement, and the statement is (A) inconsistent with the declarant's testimony and was given under oath subject to the penalty of perjury at a trial, hearing, or other proceeding, or in a deposition; or (B) consistent with the declarant's testimony, offered to rebut an express or implied charge against the declarant of recent fabrication or improper influence or motive and made before the motive to fabricate arose; or (C) one of identification of a person made shortly after perceiving the person;

(2) *Statement by party-opponent.* The statement is offered against a party and is (A) the party's own statement, in either an individual or a representative capacity; or (B) a statement of which the party has manifested an adoption or belief in its truth; or (C) a statement by a person authorized by the party to make a statement concerning the subject; or (D) a statement by the party's agent or servant concerning a matter within the scope of the agency or employment, made during the existence of the relationship; or (E) a statement by a coconspirator of a party during the course and in furtherance of the conspiracy.

* * * * *

ANALYSIS

Definition of "Statement," "Declarant," and "Hearsay"

Overview. The hearsay rules govern the admissibility of out-of-court statements, that is, statements that are made by a person other than while testifying at the trial at which the statement is offered into evidence. The law of evidence has developed a system of exclusion which rejects the admission of certain out-of-court statements that fail to satisfy accepted standards of reliability. Usually, testimony received at trial is accompanied by the safeguards of cross-examination, oath, and the opportunity to observe the demeanor of the witness. Hearsay is inherently unreliable because it is lacking in these safeguards. The general hearsay exclusionary Rule is codified in Rule 802, and it will operate on statements defined as hearsay pursuant to the definitions contained in Rule 801.

"Statement" Defined. Rule 801(a) provides the definition of a "statement" and must be considered in conjunction with the definition of hearsay in Rule 801(c), which comprehends out-of-court "statements." Evidence not meeting the definition of a "statement" will not be considered hearsay under the basic definition. For example, in *Steen v. State*, 987 N.E.2d 159, 162 (Ind. Ct. App. 2013), the Indiana Court of Appeals correctly held that labels attached to articles of clothing were not admitted for the truth of the matter asserted, but instead as circumstantial evidence showing that because the tags were attached to the clothing, it made it more likely than not that the clothing belonged to H & M Stores.

Rule 801(a) provides that a "statement" may be either an oral or a written assertion, or conduct of a person that is intended by that person to be an assertion. Accordingly, documentary evidence almost inevitably contains out-of-court statements. Likewise, any oral statement made outside of the courtroom, subsequently reported by a distinct individual or the same individual as a witness on the stand, is a statement under the definitional scheme of Rule 801. It should nevertheless, be noted, that not all oral or written out-of-court statements are inadmissible hearsay. Whether an out-of-court statement is hearsay is determined by the application of Rule 801(c), which requires a determination of whether the out-of-court statement is offered for its truth.

Nonverbal Conduct. According to Rule 801(a), certain nonverbal conduct may be a statement for the purposes of the hearsay system. Certain nonverbal signals are obviously the equivalent of words for the purposes of communication. Such signals would include nodding, pointing, and the sign language of the hearing impaired. Such conduct may be hearsay if the conduct is intended as assertive and if the intended assertion is offered for its truth. Other types of cognitive nonverbal conduct are more difficult to analyze. In certain situations, the conduct of a person may reflect his or her belief, and in certain situations a person's belief that is established by his or her conduct might be relevant in a particular case. Under Rule 801, the question of whether conduct may be a statement is resolved exclusively by the determination of whether the actor subjectively intended to make a cognitive assertion. Where evidence of conduct is offered on a theory that it is not intended by the actor as an assertion, and consequently not subject to exclusion under the hearsay system, the burden of showing that an assertion is intended should logically fall on the party objecting to the admission of the evidence on hearsay grounds.

"Declarant" Defined. Rule 801(b) defines *declarant* as a person who makes a statement. Consequently, in conjunction with Rule 801(a), a declarant is a person who makes an oral or written statement or who engages in intentionally assertive nonverbal conduct. It should be noted that the definition of declarant employs the term "person." Under the hearsay system,

only a person may make a statement, and as a result, machine, or animal statements cannot be hearsay.

"Hearsay" Defined.   Rule 801(c) codifies the generally accepted definition of hearsay. *Hearsay* is defined as a statement, other than the one made by the declarant while testifying at the trial or hearing, offered in evidence to prove the truth of the matter asserted. Two key components should be identified in applying the definition of hearsay. The first component of the hearsay definition relates to statements that are made outside of the courtroom. Hearsay potentially involves any statement made outside the courtroom by any person, even a prior statement made by a witness who later testifies. The second element of the hearsay definition provides that the out-of-court statement must be "offered in evidence to prove the truth of the matter asserted." Applying this element requires an examination of whether the statement is offered to prove the substance of its contents. Where an out-of-court statement is offered for its truth and determined to be hearsay, the evidence is presumptively inadmissible, and admissibility may only be achieved through the vehicle of the exception to the basic definition, an exception to the exclusionary rule, or some other basis identified in Rule 802.

Nonhearsay Out-of-Court Statements.   Not all out-of-court statements are relevant in a manner that relies upon their truthfulness, and when an out-of-court statement is relevant in a manner that does not depend upon the truth of the statement, the out-of-court statement is not hearsay under the definition. Such a statement will not be excluded by the hearsay system, because the exclusionary rule contained in Rule 802 only operates on statements defined as hearsay. Statements that are not offered for their truth, and consequently are nonhearsay out-of-court statements, generally fall into certain patterns. These patterns include: (1) statements offered for the effect on a listener; (2) verbal acts or operative facts; (3) state of mind; and (4) prior inconsistent statements used for impeachment. It should be recognized that there is no requirement to fit a particular out-of-court statement within one of these classes to qualify it as admissible nonhearsay. Nevertheless, these traditionally recognized categories are helpful in discerning whether a particular statement should be classified as nonhearsay.

Statements of the Witness—Inconsistent Statements

Impeachment.   Rule 801(d)(1)(A) contains vehicles for the admission of prior out-of-court statements of a witness, that is, a person who testifies at the trial at which the out-of-court statement is offered. Rule 801(d)(1)(A) relates exclusively to prior inconsistent statements used in conjunction with the impeachment technique of self-contradiction. *See* Rule 613. Where the out-of-court statement is inconsistent with the witness's trial testimony and was given under the penalty of perjury at a trial, hearing or like proceeding, the prior statement may be considered for its truth. It may be considered as substantive evidence, and the jury may base its verdict upon it. Where the prior inconsistent statement conforms to the exception, the opponent of the witness sought to be impeached is not entitled to a limiting instruction requiring the jury to consider the prior statement only for impeachment. The prior statement has a dual purpose; it may be considered for impeachment as well as substantive evidence.

Statements of the Witness—Prior Consistent Statements

Rehabilitation.   Rule 801(d)(1)(B) applies to prior statements used to rehabilitate a witness. No oath or cross-examination attending the prior statement is necessary for the prior consistent statement to be considered as substantive evidence. This subdivision has very narrow application. The exception is only triggered where there has been an inference of fabrication, fraud, or improper motive of such a nature that a prior consistent statement would be probative to negate such an inference.

Current Trends and New Developments

In *Tome v. United States*, 513 U.S. 150, 115 S. Ct. 696, 130 L. Ed. 2d 574 (1995), the U.S. Supreme Court ruled that, under Federal Rule 801(d)(1)(A), the party offering the prior consistent statement must show that it was made before a motive to fabricate existed or improper influence was exercised over the declarant, rejecting the argument that the pre-motive requirement is a function of the relevance rules, not the hearsay rules. The Court noted the absence of any indication in the legislative history or Advisory Committee Notes rejecting the prevailing common law rule that a prior consistent statement be made before the motive or improper influence arose.

Statements of the Witness—Prior Identification

Subject to Cross-Examination. Rule 801(d)(1)(C) does not apply in the context of impeachment or rehabilitation. Rather, it applies to the situation where a witness is present at trial and a prior out-of-court identification made by that witness is offered into evidence. This exception is available where a witness testifies to earlier statements made as to the identity of a particular person. The identification may have been a line-up identification, a street identification, or even a photographic array identification. It is imperative, however, that the person who made the out-of-court identification be a witness at trial and be subject to cross-examination.

Constitutional Considerations: Eyewitness Identifications and Due Process

Out of court identifications are most often sought to be admitted, of course, in criminal cases. In those instances, Rule 801(d)(1)(c) may not be the only basis for exclusion, as the Constitutional guarantees of due process also provide protection to criminal defendants.

For years, due process protection was understood to apply in cases in which witness identifications were made under suggestive circumstances that were orchestrated by the police. *See Neil v. Biggers*, 409 U.S. 188, 93 S. Ct. 375, 34 L. Ed. 2d 401 (1972); *Manson v. Brathwaite*, 432 U.S. 98, 97 S. Ct. 2243, 53 L. Ed. 2d 140 (1977). In those cases, the court was required to review the identification to determine whether police conduct resulted in a "substantial likelihood of misidentification."

In *Perry v. New Hampshire*, ___ U.S. ___, 132 S. Ct. 716, 181 L. Ed. 2d 694 (2012), the Supreme Court declined to extend due process protection beyond those cases of alleged police impropriety. As the *Perry* Court noted, however, numerous other

mechanisms for screening out unreliable identifications exist: (1) the presence of counsel at post indictment lineups; (2) vigorous cross-examination; (3) protective rules of evidence; (4) jury instructions on both the fallibility of eyewitness identification; and (5) the requirement that guilt be proved beyond a reasonable doubt.

Perry illustrates the common ground that can underlie the rule excluding hearsay (and the Rules of Evidence generally) and the due process clause. However, each analysis is distinct, as the objectives of each area of law do not overlap completely. Although both are concerned with ensuring that only reliable evidence be used to convict a criminal defendant, the due process clause targets a specific source of potential unreliability: police misconduct. As the *Perry* Court noted, "A primary aim of excluding identification evidence obtained under unnecessarily suggestive circumstances is to deter law enforcement use of improper procedures in the first place." Rules of evidence, on the other hand, use a brush that sweeps more broadly, but less specifically, in targeting unreliable testimony for exclusion.

Although jury instructions are beyond the scope of this manual, the Court of Appeals decision in *United States v. Telfaire*, 469 F.2d 552 (D.C. Cir. 1972) has been a leading model for drafting instructions governing eyewitness identifications where the suggestibility of the identification has been argued by the defense. The four *Telfaire* factors should be incorporated in any standard jury instruction: (1) whether the "witness had the capacity and an adequate opportunity to observe the offender"; (2) whether "the identification made by the witness subsequent to the offense was the product of his own recollection"; (3) whether the witness made an inconsistent identification; and (4) the credibility of the witness.

Statement by Party-Opponent

Foundation Generally. Rule 801(d)(2)(A) provides for the admissibility of statements by a party opponent. Hearsay offered through this exception must involve an out-of-court statement by a party where the out-of-court statement is offered against the party at trial. Consequently, as foundational testimony, the witness who heard the party make a statement must be prepared to testify that he had firsthand knowledge of the statement and that the statement was made by the party against whom it is offered.

Adoption. Under Rule 801(d)(2)(B) an out-of-court statement may be attributable to a party through express or implied adoption. In a number of jurisdictions, this very limited principle has been misapplied and enlarged to create the erroneous notion that if a statement is made in the presence of the parties it is not hearsay, or at least is admissible hearsay by virtue of the parties' presence alone.

Authorized Statements and Statements of Agents or Servants

Authorized Statement—Foundation. Under Rule 801(d)(2)(C), a statement by a person that is authorized by a party will be attributed to that party. The statement is imputed to the party and considered to be his or her statement for the purposes of the hearsay rule. Foundational evidence is necessary to establish that the declarant was an agent of the party opponent, and that the declarant had "speaking authority" to make declarations on behalf of the party opponent. Rule 801(d)(2)(D) authorizes the admission of a statement by a party's agent or servant concerning a matter within the scope of the agency or employment. To utilize this hearsay exception, the proponent of evidence must establish a foundation that the declarant was an employee or agent of the party against whom the statement is offered. Second, the statement must merely "concern" a matter within the scope of the agency or employment. No express or implied speaking authority need be given to the agent or employee. Finally, it must be established that the statement was made while the employment or the agency existed. Statements made after the employment or agency has terminated do not qualify under this exception.

Coconspirator Statements

Foundation. Rule 801(d)(2)(E) provides for the admission of coconspirator statements. The statement of a member of a conspiracy is attributed to the coconspirator party against whom the statement is offered at trial. To utilize this exception, the proponent must establish that there was a conspiracy, that both the declarant and the party against whom the statement is offered were members of the conspiracy, and that the statement, in fact, furthered or advanced the conspiracy. In regard to the last element, common sense dictates that a confession to the police does not advance a conspiracy.

Constitutional Considerations: Hearsay and the Confrontation Clause

The hearsay rules provide, subject to various exceptions, that a party may ordinarily object to evidence about things that were said or written by anyone outside of the courtroom. When that objecting party is the accused in a criminal case, the exclusion of such evidence may also be required by the Confrontation Clause of the Sixth Amendment, which provides: "In all criminal prosecutions, the accused shall enjoy the right . . . to be confronted with the witnesses against him."

For nearly a quarter of a century after its decision in *Ohio v. Roberts*, 448 U.S. 56, 100 S. Ct. 2531, 65 L. Ed. 2d 597, 17 Ohio Op. 3d 240 (1980), the Supreme Court interpreted the Confrontation Clause as imposing only a minimal constraint on a prosecutor's use of hearsay that would otherwise be admissible under the hearsay rules. As interpreted in *Roberts*, the Sixth Amendment allowed the admission of any unavailable witness's out-of-court statement against a defendant, even though that would deny him any opportunity to literally confront the witness, as long as the statement was determined by the Court to bear "adequate indicia of reliability," a test that was routinely met if the evidence either fell within "a firmly rooted hearsay exception" or had "particularized guarantees of trustworthiness." As a practical matter, this test rendered the Confrontation Clause largely duplicative of the hearsay rules, and greatly minimized the incentive for criminal defense attorneys to object on constitutional grounds to the admission of hearsay.

A quarter century of constitutional law based on *Roberts* has now been completely overturned, however, beginning with the Supreme Court's recent decision in *Crawford v. Washington*, 541 U.S. 36, 124 S. Ct. 1354, 158 L. Ed. 2d 177 (2004). In that landmark case, the Court abrogated *Roberts* almost in its entirety, created a new constitutional standard for the admission of hearsay against a criminal defendant, and established for the first time in decades that the Sixth Amendment requires the exclusion of many extrajudicial statements that would otherwise be admissible under the hearsay rules (for example, in a civil case).

Under *Crawford* and its progeny cases, such as, *Davis v. Washington*, 547 U.S. 813, 126 S. Ct. 2266, 165 L. Ed. 2d 224 (2006) and *Michigan v. Bryant*, ___ U.S. ___, 131 S. Ct. 1143, 179 L. Ed. 2d 93 (2011), the admission of hearsay statements at a criminal trial no longer turns on whether the trial judge believes the evidence to be "reasonably reliable," "contains guarantees of trustworthiness," or would be admitted under a "firmly rooted" hearsay exception. As the Supreme Court stated in *Crawford* with evident disdain: "Dispensing with confrontation because testimony is obviously reliable is akin to dispensing with jury trial because a defendant is obviously guilty." *Crawford v. Washington*, 541 U.S. 36, 62, 124 S. Ct. 1354, 1371 (2004). Instead, the Court adopted a new, and seemingly elegant, standard: Whether the out-of-court statement is testimonial. The Court concluded that the Confrontation Clause, construed in light of its history and text, applies only to statements by "witnesses," which would only be true of those who give the functional equivalent of "testimony" against the accused. Stated simply, if an out-of-court statement of a witness is testimonial, it may not be admitted against the accused to prove the truth of what that witness said unless that witness is unavailable to testify and the defendant had a prior opportunity to cross-examine that witness. Other than statements admitted under the "former testimony" exception in Rule 804(b)(1), these two conditions will rarely be satisfied. On the other hand, if a statement is nontestimonial, it simply is not subject to the Confrontation Clause, and its admission is now regulated entirely by the traditional rules governing hearsay evidence. It simply no longer matters, as it did under *Roberts*, whether the statement is deemed to be reliable by the trial judge. If the statement is testimonial, it must satisfy the "unavailability" and "prior opportunity to cross-examine" requirements. If the statement is not testimonial, no Confrontation Clause issue is presented.

In *Davis v. Washington*, 547 U.S. 813, 126 S. Ct. 2266, 165 L. Ed. 2d 224 (2006), the United States Supreme Court expanded upon its *Crawford* decision and clarified the definition of "testimonial" for purposes of determining whether the Confrontation Clause applies to a particular statement. Under *Davis*, a statement will be considered "testimonial" when an objective consideration of the circumstances indicate that the statement was not elicited for the purpose of responding to an emergency and that the primary purpose of the interrogation is to establish or prove past events potentially relevant to later criminal prosecution. Such a finding is most likely if, for example, the witness was describing events some time after they happened, especially if the witness was already separated from her assailant, speaking at the station house or otherwise under police protection, or responding calmly to structured police questioning.

Conversely, a statement will be considered "nontestimonial" when an objective consideration of the circumstances indicates that the interrogation was emergency related or that the interrogation had a primary purpose other than to establish its value for future litigation. Such a finding is most likely if the witness was describing events as they were actually happening; if the witness faced an ongoing emergency; or if the conversation was not tranquil but frantic, perhaps over the phone, especially if the caller

was unprotected by the police and apparently still in possible immediate danger. The Court made clear that the existence of police interrogation was not dispositive of the issue one way or another: Statements to questions made in the context of police interrogations could be either "testimonial" or "nontestimonial," as could statements made outside of a formal interrogation context.

Although the *Davis* opinion may seem to imply a somewhat dichotomous nature for statements subsequently challenged under the Confrontation Clause as either being made for the purpose of future litigation or to respond to an emergency, the holding of the case should be rather easily applied to non-emergency statements. Under the Court's reasoning, the Confrontation Clause was designed to protect against the admission of prior testimony or other statements under oath, or functionally equivalent statements, without being subject to cross-examination. A statement can be made for a virtually infinite number of motivations, and the Confrontation Clause excludes only those statements made for one—its use in a future criminal prosecution. The remainder of the universe of motivations surrounding the making of a statement—a universe within which resides the making of a statement to allow police to respond to an emergency— are not encompassed within the protections of the Confrontation Clause.

In *Michigan v. Bryant*, ___ U.S. ___, 131 S. Ct. 1143, 179 L. Ed. 2d 93 (2011), the United States Supreme Court continued to refine its Confrontation Clause analysis revolutionized in *Crawford*. Specifically, the Court expanded its thinking begun in the *Davis* case and provided greater guidance for statements made in the context of police questioning.

Most importantly, the *Bryant* Court clarified that the fundamental issue is not whether an "ongoing emergency" exists, but whether the "primary purpose" of the police questioning is for a reason other than to establish or prove past events potentially relevant to later criminal prosecution. Certainly, the former is important to a determination of the latter, but perhaps not necessarily so. In other words, "the existence *vel non* of an ongoing emergency is [not] dispositive of the testimonial inquiry. As *Davis* made clear, whether an ongoing emergency exists is simply one factor—albeit an important factor—that informs the ultimate inquiry regarding the 'primary purpose' of an interrogation." *Bryant*, 131 S. Ct. at 1160.

The *Bryant* Court stressed the objective evaluation of the circumstances in which the encounter between the individual and the police occurs; the inquiry is not a subjective one. However, an examination of the statements and actions of the police and the victim, as well as other individuals involved while the questioning occurred, should be considered. The Court also noted that the formality of the interaction between the police and the victim is a factor that should be considered.

The *Bryant* case may be seen by some as a partial retreat from the cut-and-dried "testimonial-or-not" approach adopted in *Crawford* and *Davis*, as the *Bryant* majority opinion provoked a strong dissent from Justice Scalia, who originally authored the *Crawford* and *Davis* opinions. Justice Scalia would have held that the inquiry is a subjective one, determined entirely by the intent of the person making the statement. To be sure, the approach of the *Bryant* majority will have the practical effect of rendering slightly more declarant statements admissible in court and thus may be regarded as pro-law enforcement. However, a careful reading of Justice Scalia's dissent suggests that his views are driven by intellectual consistency and historical accuracy rather than consequentialist concerns.

Finally, it should be appreciated that testimonial hearsay is only barred by the Sixth Amendment if the statement is offered as evidence of the truth of what was said by that witness, and only if that witness does not testify about the statement at trial. Regardless of whether a statement is testimonial, therefore, its exclusion is not required by the Confrontation Clause if the one who made the statement is present at trial to defend or explain it, even if the witness has only a very limited ability to answer questions about the statement. The Confrontation Clause is also not implicated if a statement is admitted "for purposes other than establishing the truth of the matter asserted" in that statement. Courts must take care, however, to ensure that *Crawford* is not circumvented by allowing police officers to relate incriminating reports about the accused for the supposed purpose of giving the jury so-called "background" evidence about the initiation of their investigation, especially when the reasons for the police activities can be explained without exposing the jury to the details of incriminating reports received by the police.

Despite *Crawford*'s likely inapplicability to statements in furtherance of a conspiracy, the full impact of the case must await further developments. In *Bourjaily v. United States*, 483 U.S. 171, 107 S. Ct. 2775, 97 L. Ed. 2d 144 (1987), *superseded by statute*, **United States v. Kemp**, 2005 U.S. Dist. LEXIS 2072 (E.D. Pa. Feb. 10, 2005), the Supreme Court analyzed the constitutional application of the federal coconspirator exception with regard to independent indicia of reliability as to the out-of-court statement. The Court held that no independent inquiry into reliability is required because the co-conspirator exception is a "firmly rooted" hearsay exception. As noted, *Crawford* abolishes this reasoning, while nonetheless suggesting that statements in furtherance of a conspiracy are "nontestimonial" in any event. The *Bourjaily* Court further held that when the proponent of the coconspirator statement has made a preponderant case of conspiracy, this aspect of the foundation for use of the exception is satisfied. Moreover, the Court in *Bourjaily* concluded that a trial court may consider the offered hearsay statement itself in making the preliminary factual determination of whether the conspiracy existed and whether the statement was made in furtherance of the conspiracy.

On the other hand, the *Crawford/Davis/Bryant* line of cases clearly indicate that prior testimony and at least some statements made during police interrogations fall into the "testimonial" category, which require both unavailability and a prior opportunity for cross-examination. With respect to other hearsay exceptions, such as the "excited utterance" exception in Rule 803(2) and the "medical diagnosis or treatment" exception in Rule 803(4), the clarification provided in *Davis* makes relatively clear that such statements would not be "testimonial" in nature.

In addition to the body of case law surrounding statements ultimately determined to be "nontestimonial" in nature, case law concerning "testimonial" hearsay statements to which an opportunity for cross-examination has been provided should also survive

Crawford. Accordingly, earlier holdings that delayed cross-examination of a declarant concerning his or her prior hearsay statement may satisfy the Sixth Amendment and should remain good law. *See United States v. Owens,* 484 U.S. 554, 108 S. Ct. 838, 98 L. Ed. 2d 951 (1988); *California v. Green,* 399 U.S. 149, 90 S. Ct. 1930, 26 L. Ed. 2d 489 (1970). Likewise, cross-examination of the declarant at the time of the making of the out-of-court statement may satisfy the Sixth Amendment where, for example, the statement was made at a preliminary hearing.

The status of Indiana case law under *Crawford*'s new Confrontation Clause framework must await an analysis on a case-by-case basis. However, the Confrontation Clause protections under *Crawford* may ultimately turn out to be consistent with those under existing Indiana case law.

The Indiana Constitution provides criminal defendants with a right to "face to face confrontation" with an accuser—a right that the Indiana Supreme Court intended to reach further than both the right to mere "confrontation" under the Indiana Constitution and the Federal Constitution under pre-*Crawford* federal case law. *See* Ind. Const. art. I, § 13; *Brady v. State,* 575 N.E.2d 981 (Ind. 1991); *State v. Owings,* 622 N.E.2d 948 (Ind. 1993). Accordingly, Indiana already provided criminal defendants with greater protection than that under the pre-*Crawford* framework.

Accordingly, Indiana courts have held that prior testimony from an unavailable witness is admissible at a subsequent trial, provided that the defendant had the opportunity to confront the witness when the testimony was originally given. *See, e.g., Atkins v. State,* 561 N.E.2d 797, 801 (Ind. Ct. App. 1990) (testimony given at bail hearing); *Ingram v. State,* 547 N.E.2d 823, 826 (Ind. 1989) (deposition testimony). On the other hand, Indiana courts have refused to admit statements contained in prior testimony where a defendant has never had the opportunity to cross-examine a witness and meet him face to face, on the ground that it violates the Indiana constitutional right of a fact-to-face confrontation. *See, e.g., Brady v. State,* 575 N.E.2d 981 (Ind. 1991) (videotaped testimony taken outside the presence of defendant and used at trial); *Miller v. State,* 517 N.E.2d 64 (Ind. 1987) (videotaped statement of child where defendant received no notice).

Although the full reach of *Crawford* is not yet known, Indiana's prior ruling on its state constitutional right of face-to-face confrontation may turn out to be co-extensive with the principles and framework announced in *Crawford,* and may thus represent a model for interpreting *Crawford* nationally.

In *Hendricks v. State,* 809 N.E.2d 865 (Ind. Ct. App. 2004), an Indiana Court of Appeals intimated that certain statements of child victims admitted under Ind. Code § 35-37-4-6 would violate the rule announced in *Crawford.* However, resolution of the issue was considered to be unnecessary by the court of appeals, as the case involved the right of confrontation before *Crawford* had been decided. Nonetheless, under the Indiana case law discussed above, it is difficult to see how statements of child victims that are testimonial in nature would satisfy the "face-to-face" confrontation right contained in Ind. Const. art. I, § 13.

ADDITIONAL AUTHORITY

WEISSENBERGER'S FEDERAL EVIDENCE §§ 801.1–801.25

MCCORMICK §§ 246, 248–250

5 WEINSTEIN 2d §§ 801.01–801.02, 801.10–801.11, 801.20–801.23, 801.30–801.34

4 MUELLER & KIRKPATRICK §§ 368–430

2 WIGMORE § 267

5 WIGMORE § 1361

6 WIGMORE § 1766

COMPARISON TO FEDERAL RULE

Federal Rule 801(d)(1)(B) differs from Indiana Rule 801(d)(1)(B), in that the Federal Rule does not require that the witness's statement be made before the motive to fabricate arose. Additionally, Federal Rule 801(d)(2) refers to "admissions" by a party-opponent, instead of "statements."

Federal Rule 801(d)(2) was altered by the 1997 amendments to the Federal Rules of Evidence that address the issues raised by the Supreme Court in *Bourjaily v. United States*, 483 U.S. 171, 107 S. Ct. 2775, 97 L. Ed. 2d 144 (1987), *superseded by statute*, **United States v. Kemp**, 2005 U.S. Dist. LEXIS 2072 (E.D. Pa. Feb. 10, 2005), and codify the Court's holding in that case.

Under amended Federal Rule 801(d)(2), a court can consider the contents of a coconspirator's statement in making the preliminary determination as to the existence of a conspiracy between the declarant and the party against whom the statement is offered. The trial court should consider circumstances surrounding the statement, such as the identity of the speaker and evidence corroborating the contents of the statement, in addition to the contents of the statement itself, in determining whether the proponent has proven the existence of a conspiracy by a preponderance of the evidence, as required under Federal Rule 104(a). The Advisory Committee Note explains that every court of appeals that has resolved this issue has also required evidence beyond the mere contents of the statement to establish the existence of the conspiracy.

The amendment also serves to extend the reasoning of *Bourjaily* to subdivisions (C) and (D) of Rule 801(d)(2). Thus, under the revised Rule, the contents of the offered statement can be used to help establish that the declarant was authorized to make the statement by the party against whom the statement is offered, pursuant to subdivision (C), or to establish that the declarant was the agent or employee of the party against whom the statement is offered, and that the statement concerned a matter within the scope of that agency or employment and was made within the duration of the relationship, as required under subdivision (D). As with the subdivision (E) coconspirator exception, the contents of the statement alone will not be sufficient to establish either authorization or an agency relationship, but should be considered in connection with other evidence, including the circumstances surrounding the statement, in determining whether the particular exception applies.

SIGNIFICANT CASES

Perry v. New Hampshire, ___ U.S. ___, 132 S. Ct. 716, 181 L. Ed. 2d 694 (2012) (declining to extend due process protection beyond those cases in witness identifications made under suggestive circumstances were orchestrated by the police).

Michigan v. Bryant, ___ U.S. ___, 131 S. Ct. 1143, 179 L. Ed. 2d 93 (2011) (in cases involving police questioning, the fundamental issue in the Confrontation Clause analysis is not whether an "ongoing emergency" exists, but whether the "primary purpose" of the police questioning is for a reason other than to establish or prove past events potentially relevant to later criminal prosecution).

Davis v. Washington, 547 U.S. 813, 126 S. Ct. 2266, 165 L. Ed. 2d 224 (2006) (a statement will be considered "testimonial" for Confrontation Clause purposes when an objective consideration of the circumstances indicate that the statement was not elicited for the purpose of responding to an emergency and that the primary purpose of the interrogation is to establish or prove past events potentially relevant to later criminal prosecution).

Crawford v. Washington, 541 U.S. 36, 124 S. Ct. 1354, 158 L. Ed. 2d 177 (2004) (where testimonial evidence is at issue, the Confrontation Clause of the Sixth Amendment requires both the unavailability of the declarant and a prior opportunity for cross-examination; overruling *Ohio v. Roberts*, 448 U.S. 56, 100 S. Ct. 2531, 65 L. Ed. 2d 597, 17 Ohio Op. 3d 240 (1980), in part).

Lilly v. Virginia, 527 U.S. 116, 119 S. Ct. 1887, 144 L. Ed. 2d 117 (1999) (confession of criminal accomplice admitted into evidence under Virginia's "statement against penal interest" exception to the rule excluding hearsay was not "firmly rooted" under *Ohio v. Roberts* and thus did not satisfy the requirements of the Confrontation Clause on that basis).

Tome v. United States, 513 U.S. 150, 115 S. Ct. 696, 130 L. Ed. 2d 574 (1995) (Federal Rule 801(d)(1)(A) requires a showing that consistent statement was made prior to the motive to fabricate).

White v. Illinois, 502 U.S. 346, 112 S. Ct. 736, 116 L. Ed. 2d 848 (1992) (where hearsay statement is admitted pursuant to a firmly rooted exception, the prosecution does not have to make a good faith effort to produce the witness or account for his or her unavailability).

Idaho v. Wright, 497 U.S. 805, 110 S. Ct. 3139, 111 L. Ed. 2d 638 (1990), (admission of child's hearsay statements violated the defendant's Confrontation Clause rights since the statements did not have "particularized guarantees of trustworthiness").

Beech Aircraft Corp. v. Rainey, 488 U.S. 153, 109 S. Ct. 439, 102 L. Ed. 2d 445 (1988) (a judge advocate report regarding the crash of a military aircraft was admissible under Federal Rule 803(8) where portions of the report contained opinions and the author's statement as to probable cause of crash).

Coy v. Iowa, 487 U.S. 1012, 108 S. Ct. 2798, 101 L. Ed. 2d 857 (1988), *superseded by statute*, *United States v. Moses*, 137 F.3d 894 (6th Cir. 1998) (defendant's right to face-to-face confrontation was violated where a screen was placed between child sexual assault victims and defendant during their testimony).

United States v. Owens, 484 U.S. 554, 108 S. Ct. 838, 98 L. Ed. 2d 951 (1988) (admission of prior out-of-court identification statement did not violate the Confrontation Clause of the Sixth Amendment or Federal Rule 801, where the witness testified he was unable to explain the basis for the identification because of memory loss).

Bourjaily v. United States, 483 U.S. 171, 107 S. Ct. 2775, 97 L. Ed. 2d 144 (1987), *superseded by statute*, *United States v. Kemp*, 2005 U.S. Dist. LEXIS 2072 (E.D. Pa. Feb. 10, 2005) (under Federal Rule 801(d)(2)(E) the trial court may examine hearsay statements sought to be admitted in making a preliminary factual determination of whether a conspiracy existed).

United States v. Inadi, 475 U.S. 387, 106 S. Ct. 1121, 89 L. Ed. 2d 390 (1986) (Confrontation Clause does not require a showing of unavailability as a condition to admission of the out-of-court statements of a nontestifying coconspirator).

Tennessee v. Street, 471 U.S. 409, 105 S. Ct. 2078, 85 L. Ed. 2d 425 (1985) (under Federal Rule

801(c), an accomplice's confession was not considered a hearsay statement where offered to rebut defendant's testimony that his own confession was a coerced "copy" of the accomplice's confession).

Mason v. Duckworth, 74 F.3d 815 (7th Cir. 1996) (new Indiana Rule of Evidence for admission of prior inconsistent statements by witness, which added requirement that prior statement be made under oath in judicial or quasi-judicial proceeding, was not of "federal constitutional magnitude" and, therefore, did not apply retroactively to cases pending when rule was announced).

Stone v. Farley, 877 F. Supp. 1246 (N.D. Ind. 1995) (state law hearsay restrictions on substantive use of witness's prior statements are not constitutionally mandated; in homicide trial, out-of-court statements of accomplice were properly admitted, in so far as hearsay and Sixth Amendment considerations were relevant, especially since accomplice was in court under oath on witness stand and subject to cross-examination).

HEARSAY

Turner v. State, 953 N.E.2d 1039, 1049–1053 (Ind. 2011) (a police officer's testimony offered to explain why a witness was not present for trial was not hearsay, as the statement was not offered for its truth).

Clark v. State, 915 N.E.2d 126 (Ind. 2009) (an entry on the defendant's MySpace page constituted statements to be analyzed under the hearsay rules rather than acts to be analyzed as prior acts under Rule 404(b)).

Lewis v. State, 904 N.E.2d 290 (Ind. Ct. App. 2009) (in the context of a criminal investigation, an out-of-court statement introduced to explain a particular course of action does not constitute hearsay because it is not offered to prove the truth of the matter asserted in the statement).
Stroud v. State, 809 N.E.2d 274 (Ind. 2004) (affidavit introduced into evidence for the purpose of demonstrating the source of a witness's knowledge about information contained in the affidavit is not offered for its truth, and thus not rendered inadmissible by the rule excluding hearsay).

Garner v. State, 777 N.E.2d 721 (Ind. 2002) (generally, deposition testimony of an absent witness offered in court to prove the truth of the matter asserted constitutes classic hearsay).

Carter v. State, 766 N.E.2d 377 (Ind. 2002) (for purposes of the rule excluding hearsay, an utterance that is in the form of a question can contain an assertion of fact).

Maxey v. State, 730 N.E.2d 158 (Ind. 2000) (police officer's statements regarding defendant's flight from jurisdiction after the crime were hearsay despite state's argument that it was offered merely to describe the course of the investigation; any error regarding admission of the statements was harmless in light of police officer's personal observation of defendant in Tennessee).

Brown v. State, 725 N.E.2d 823 (Ind. 2000) (out-of-court statement was not hearsay because it was not used to prove the truth of the matter asserted but rather to show prearrangement by defendant and other coconspirators).

Jester v. State, 724 N.E.2d 235 (Ind. 2000) (hearsay testimony regarding prior statements by defendant's wife that she believed defendant was having an affair, and that she had considered leaving defendant was improperly admitted but harmless error in prosecution of defendant for murder of wife, where testimony was merely cumulative of other properly admitted evidence that defendant and wife had often argued, and that defendant had in fact had an affair).

Smith v. State, 721 N.E.2d 213 (Ind. 1999) (police questions and comments in an interview may be designed to elicit responses from the defendant, and if so, are not offered as proof of the facts asserted therein; however, statements "half of the people at the jail's [*sic*] called me wanting to tell me that you did it" and "[Lampley] said you did it because it was over [Riggs] ripping you off your dope, your stash" made by police officer during questioning were inadmissible hearsay because (1) statements appeared to be assertions of fact by police officer, not mere questions, and (2) trial court did not admonish jury that the statements were not to be used to prove the truth of the matter asserted—other statement by police officer was designed to elicit a response and was admissible).

Miller v. State, 720 N.E.2d 696 (Ind. 1999) (out-of-court statement was not hearsay because it was not used to prove the truth of the matter asserted but rather to show defendant's state of mind in his self-defense claim; however, trial court's erroneous exclusion was harmless).

Anderson v. State, 718 N.E.2d 1101 (Ind. 1999) (out-of-court statements as to why witness was concerned about victim were not inadmissible on the basis of hearsay because they were not offered for their truth).

McIntyre v. State, 717 N.E.2d 114 (Ind. 1999) (state's hearsay evidence offered to prove something other than truth of matter asserted was improperly admitted because it was only marginally relevant and the probative effect of the statement was outweighed by its prejudicial value; however, error was found to be harmless in light of confession and thumbprint found at crime scene).

Barber v. State, 715 N.E.2d 848 (Ind. 1999) (in context of prosecution's question, "Why did they want to find out [if the men who robbed them were at Love's house]?" the answer, "to get them" was an assertion of motive that is susceptible of being true or false and is, therefore, inadmissible hearsay).

Spencer v. State, 703 N.E.2d 1053 (Ind. 1999) (admission of a victim's statements through the testimony of a police officer is improper when the sole purpose was claimed to be showing the steps in the investigative process, although the state may offer testimony to show the steps of an investigation, the testimony of the officers should be limited to that specific purpose; accordingly, if statements made by the police are actually used only to prove the truth of the matter asserted, they constitute hearsay).

Craig v. State, 630 N.E.2d 207 (Ind. 1994) (Indiana Supreme Court held that an out-of-court statement admitted for a nonhearsay purpose must meet the requirements of relevance and the statement's relevance must not be outweighed by the danger of unfair prejudice).

State v. Owings, 622 N.E.2d 948 (Ind. 1993) (discussion of the use of hearsay statements against criminal defendant; Indiana Constitution requires a showing of unavailability of declarant and indicia of reliability surrounding the statement).

Pinkerton v. State, 258 Ind. 610, 283 N.E.2d 376 (1972) (defendant's confrontation rights were not violated simply because an expert relied on evidence not admitted at trial in forming his opinion; defendant was entitled to examine the evidence for cross-examination purposes).

Steen v. State, 987 N.E.2d 159, 162 (Ind. Ct. App. 2013) (store security tags and labels are not hearsay, as they were not admitted for their truth but as circumstantial evidence that belonged to the store).

Lampitok v. State, 817 N.E.2d 630 (Ind. Ct. App. 2004) (although true requests, commands, and questions are not assertions, and evidence regarding such utterances will not be excluded as hearsay because they are not offered for the truth of the facts asserted, an assertion can nonetheless be found in a question or command; an utterance that is in the form of a question can in substance contain an assertion of a fact, and in this case, the command or request to find the gun and dispose of it is the factual assertion that there was, in fact, a gun used in the course of the offense, which was a contested issue of fact at trial).

Meisberger v. State, 640 N.E.2d 716 (Ind. Ct. App. 1994) (trial court did not err in permitting expert witness to identify the victim's body using dental records not admitted into evidence at trial; court held that absent some question as to the accuracy of the identification, it was competent for the doctor to rely upon hearsay information as to identity and to offer an expert opinion regarding the victim's identity).

Ortiz v. State, 741 N.E.2d 1203 (Ind. 2001) (police officer's testimony in a murder prosecution that defendant's girlfriend told the officer that she had argued with defendant before the murder, and that he had left with a knife was not hearsay because it was not offered for the truth of the statements made but rather to prove that the girlfriend said the things to which the officer was an eyeball witness; however, the evidence was inadmissible because it was not relevant).

Sylvester v. State, 698 N.E.2d 1126 (Ind. 1998) (in a prosecution for murder in which the defendant claimed that the act was manslaughter, the trial court erred in not allowing the defendant to offer evidence of statements made by the victim, his wife, during conversation concerning the defendant's belief that his wife was having an affair; the statements were not hearsay as they were offered not to show that his wife had an affair, but to demonstrate their effect on the listener. However, the error was harmless, in that the excluded evidence was cumulative of other evidence showing that the defendant believed his wife was having an affair).

HEARSAY

Grund v. State, 671 N.E.2d 411 (Ind. 1996) ("hearsay" is out-of-court statement offered to prove truth of matter asserted, and same statement if offered for a different purpose would not be hearsay; testimony of defendant's sister about conversation she had with defendant and defendant's children was offered not to prove truth of matter asserted but to prove defendant was attempting to coerce child into changing her memory, which was relevant to show defendant's consciousness of guilt).

Williams v. State, 669 N.E.2d 956 (Ind. 1996) (statements made and questions asked by police informant during conversation in which defendant boasted of involvement in murder of another police informant were not hearsay, and thus, their admission at murder trial did not violate defendant's Sixth Amendment right to confrontation, because purpose of statements was to induce defendant to speak and they were not admitted to prove the truth of matters asserted).

Isaacs v. State, 659 N.E.2d 1036 (Ind. 1995) ("hearsay" is testimony or written evidence of statement made out of court that is offered in court to prove truth of matters asserted by statement).

Owens v. State, 659 N.E.2d 466 (Ind. 1995) ("hearsay" is statement made out of court that is offered to prove facts asserted in statement).

Matusky v. Sheffield Square Apartments, 654 N.E.2d 740 (Ind. 1995) (where no exception applies, hearsay is inherently unreliable for use in plenary actions and may not be considered by trier of fact).

Bonner v. State, 650 N.E.2d 1139 (Ind. 1995) (where out-of-court statements received by police during investigation is challenged as hearsay and state offers that evidence for purpose other than proving facts asserted therein, court must consider whether a fact to be proved under state's suggested purpose is relevant and whether risk of prejudice outweighs probative value).

Mullins v. State, 646 N.E.2d 40 (Ind. 1995) (printout results of alcohol breath test are hearsay).

Arndt v. State, 642 N.E.2d 224 (Ind. 1994) (out-of-court statements made by child-molestation victim and which were repeated at trial by victim's parents to prove facts asserted in statement that defendant molested victim were inadmissible hearsay).

Buie v. State, 633 N.E.2d 250 (Ind. 1994), *overruled, Richardson v. State*, 717 N.E.2d 32 (Ind. 1999) (in trial for conspiracy to commit murder, statement of alleged coconspirator that he and defendant were going to car to talk was not offered to prove truth of matter asserted and thus was not hearsay; coconspirator's intent to go to car to talk with defendant was relevant to prove conspiracy whether or not coconspirator and defendant actually talked).

Craig v. State, 630 N.E.2d 207 (Ind. 1994) (where defendant was charged with molesting his son, trial court erred by admitting a hearsay statement made by the victim's mother to a police officer; the statement had no relevance except to prove the facts asserted in the statement; error held to be harmless in light of other evidence; court discussed the interplay of Rules 401 and 403 when a hearsay objection is made at trial).

Modesitt v. State, 578 N.E.2d 649 (Ind. 1991) (court adopted the language of Federal Rule

801(d)(1)(A)–(C); specifies circumstances in which an out-of-court statement will not be hearsay).

Heck v. State, 552 N.E.2d 446 (Ind. 1990) (police officer properly testified concerning statements made to him to show why he conducted the investigation; statements were not offered for their truth).

Williams v. State, 544 N.E.2d 161 (Ind. 1989) (trial court erred in permitting a police officer to testify to a tip that identified defendant as the robber to explain why the officer put a photo of defendant in a photo array shown to the victim; Supreme Court held that, in admitting out-of-court statements, it "requires a reasonable assurance that such testimony was not offered by the proponent nor received by the trier of fact as evidence of the truth of the third party's statement").

Mayhew v. State, 537 N.E.2d 1188 (Ind. 1989) (a statement that is in the form of a command or a request is not an assertion of fact and is not hearsay).

Johnston v. State, 530 N.E.2d 1179 (Ind. 1988) (trial court did not err in allowing a police officer to testify regarding an informant's out-of-court statement incriminating defendant because the statement was admitted to show why the police commenced an undercover investigation of defendant).

Chinn v. State, 511 N.E.2d 1000 (Ind. 1987) (letter admitted to compare handwriting, not for the truth of the matter asserted in the letter).

Vertner v. State, 793 N.E.2d 1148 (Ind. Ct. App. 2003) (where testimony does not explicitly contain a statement made by anyone other than the testifying witness, even though the statement strongly suggests the allegation of a robbery was made by the person to whom the officer was speaking, the statement will not be regarded as hearsay).

Kendall v. State, 790 N.E.2d 122 (Ind. Ct. App. 2003) (the requirement that a prior statement be made under oath applies only to Rule 801(d)(1)(A), not to Rule 801(d)(1)(C)).

Stoltmann v. State, 793 N.E.2d 275 (Ind. Ct. App. 2003) (a witness's prior inconsistent unsworn statement is not admissible as substantive evidence, but may be used for the limited purpose of impeaching that witness).

Allen v. State, 787 N.E.2d 473 (Ind. Ct. App. 2003) (the exception from the definition from the rule excluding hearsay for statements of a party-opponent applies in criminal cases to statements by government employees concerning matters within the scope of their agency or employment).

City of Indianapolis v. Taylor, 707 N.E.2d 1047 (Ind. Ct. App. 1999) (witness's statement in wrongful death action that a police officer told him that decedent was a "punk" and "got what he deserved" was not hearsay, because the statement was not offered in evidence to prove the truth of the matter asserted but was instead offered to show the attitude of the police and/or a possible motivation for the police to have shot decedent).

Greer v. State, 669 N.E.2d 751 (Ind. Ct. App. 1996), *vacated on other grounds*, 685 N.E.2d 700 (Ind. 1997) (hearsay rule is applicable in probation revocation hearing).

Owensby v. Lepper, 666 N.E.2d 1251 (Ind. Ct. App. 1996) (because hearsay depends on credibility of out-of-court declarant who is not available for cross-examination, hearsay statements are usually inadmissible).

Potter v. State, 666 N.E.2d 93 (Ind. Ct. App. 1996), *vacated on other grounds*, 684 N.E.2d 1127 (Ind. 1997) (when hearsay objection is made, court should first ask whether testimony describes out-of-court statement asserting fact susceptible of being true or false; if statement asserts such a fact, then court should ask what evidentiary purpose the statement serves; if the purpose is to prove asserted fact, and such purpose is not proper under applicable evidentiary rule, then hearsay objection should be sustained unless statement falls within exception to hearsay rule).

Utley v. Healy, 663 N.E.2d 229 (Ind. Ct. App. 1996) ("hearsay" is statement made out of court that is offered to prove truth of matter asserted, and is not admissible unless it falls within one of enumerated exceptions; statement offered not to prove truth of matter asserted but for some other relevant purpose is admissible).

Malone v. State, 660 N.E.2d 619 (Ind. Ct. App. 1996) ("hearsay" is statement made out of court but offered in court to prove truth of matter asserted in statement; "hearsay" depends on credibility of declarant who is not in court and not available for cross-examination).

Storrjohann v. State, 651 N.E.2d 294 (Ind. Ct. App. 1995) (results of breath test are inadmissible hearsay unless within statutorily or judicially defined exception such as for blood alcohol content analysis).

Clark v. State, 648 N.E.2d 1187 (Ind. Ct. App. 1995) (out-of-court statements of police officer were not hearsay where they were not offered to prove truth of matter asserted but to explain how defendant became robbery suspect).

Whited v. State, 645 N.E.2d 1138 (Ind. Ct. App. 1995) (out-of-court statements of rape victim to defendant about her dating status, offered to show defendant's state of mind in concluding that victim had consented to sex, rather than to prove truth of victim's dating status, were not "hearsay" and should have been admitted).

Robinson v. State, 634 N.E.2d 1367 (Ind. Ct. App. 1994) (statement by witness that someone had told him that defendant previously participated in drug transaction before the currently charged transactions amounted to hearsay).

Levi v. State, 627 N.E.2d 1345 (Ind. Ct. App. 1994) (where professor's conversation with defendant as professor was leaving building that defendant was charged with burglarizing was offered only to show professor had opportunity to speak with defendant and thus could identify him at trial, testimony was not inadmissible hearsay).

Rule 801(d)(1)—Prior Statement by Witness

Treadway v. State, 924 N.E.2d 621 (Ind. 2010) (under Rule 801(d)(1)(c), the declarant must testify and be subject to cross-examination, but the witness may testify out of sequence and connect up the prior testimony).

Clark v. State, 808 N.E.2d 1183 (Ind. 2004) (witness's written statement was admissible as a prior inconsistent statement, as it was given under oath subject to penalties for perjury and the declarant's availability for recall for cross-examination satisfies the requirement that he be available for cross-examination, even though the defendant chose to cross-examine the declarant).

Holsinger v. State, 750 N.E.2d 354 (Ind. 2001) (declarant's trial testimony was consistent with the second statement that she gave to police, which shifted blame for killing of robbery victim from other accomplice to defendant; whether a motive to fabricate has arisen is a fact-sensitive issue, and a reviewing court will not automatically find that a participant in a crime had a motive to fabricate, even where the police were inquiring into the declarant's involvement in the crime; declarant's statement was admissible because she had no motive to fabricate, especially where she implicated herself in the crimes).

Young v. State, 746 N.E.2d 920 (Ind. 2001) (because the statement of defendant's brother to police was not made under oath, it was not admissible under Rule 801(d)(1)(A)).

Stephenson v. State, 742 N.E.2d 463 (Ind. 2001) (eyewitness's out-of-court statements were properly admitted under the prior consistent statement rule in order to rebut defendant's charge that the eyewitness had an improper motive to shift the blame on defendant; eyewitness was impeached on cross-examination because he admitted that he lied in his deposition to officers by telling them that he did not discuss the murders with his friend, and the state sought to rehabilitate the eyewitness by calling a friend who provided the prior consistent statements, had no motive to fabricate, and had a limited role in the circumstances surrounding the murders).

Appleton v. State, 740 N.E.2d 122 (Ind. 2001) (by permitting admission of a prior statement under oath as substantive evidence, the witness is notified of the solemnity and importance of his statements and any dishonesty may result in a perjury indictment; trials should principally proceed on the basis of testimony given in court, not on statements or affidavits obtained before trial; therefore, line-by-line recitation of a witness's prior inconsistent statement in which the witness described defendant's participation was improper).

Martin v. State, 736 N.E.2d 1213 (Ind. 2000) (witness's prior statement to police regarding where they should search for a gun was not made under oath and the exception to the hearsay rule for a prior inconsistent statement was not available).

Chambers v. State, 734 N.E.2d 578 (Ind. 2000) (trial court did not abuse its discretion by refusing to give a proposed jury instruction that the jury had the right to reject the uncorroborated testimony of witnesses whose credibility had been impeached by prior inconsistent statements).

Cline v. State, 726 N.E.2d 1249 (Ind. 2000) (a prior statement does not have to be completely consistent to meet the requirements of Rule 801(d)(1)(B) but need only be sufficiently consistent to be admissible; trial court did not err in admitting witness's prior consistent statement as the statement was sufficiently consistent with trial testimony and witness had little motive to lie at the time he gave the statement because he was not charged with victim's death).

Mitchell v. State, 726 N.E.2d 1228 (Ind. 2000) (trial court did not abuse discretion in allowing social worker to testify as to prior consistent statement made by nine-year-old child nine months before trial because prior consistent statement was sufficiently consistent with trial testimony, defendant implied that child had fabricated her trial testimony, and child made statement to social worker before any motive for fabrication would have arisen).

Sturgeon v. State, 719 N.E.2d 1173 (Ind. 1999) (in cases where declarant is defendant or co-defendant, a motive to fabricate is likely to arise immediately upon commission of the crime but the role of timing is not so clear when the declarant becomes involved after the crime was committed leaving motive to fabricate a fact-sensitive issue; therefore, prior consistent statement by declarant regarding events before and after murder to rebut charge of recent fabrication was properly admitted because no evidence implicated declarant in murder, and there was no evidence he had motive to lie about defendant's involvement when questioned by police).

Bouye v. State, 699 N.E.2d 620 (Ind. 1998) (holding that trial court erred in allowing prosecution to introduce evidence of a prior consistent statement made by a testifying accomplice; although the prosecution sought to introduce the statement only after the witness's credibility had been challenged, the prior statement was made after the witness developed a motive to fabricate the statement and shift culpability to the defendant).

Yamobi v. State, 672 N.E.2d 1344 (Ind. 1996) (testimony that murder victim named defendant in answer to police officer's question about who shot him, offered by state to prove defendant was the assailant, was inadmissible hearsay).

Brown v. State, 671 N.E.2d 401 (Ind. 1996) (right to confrontation is not violated where testimony of witness at former hearing or trial on same case is reproduced and admitted; where defendant either cross-examined witness or had the opportunity to do so, witness is now unavailable).

Willoughby v. State, 660 N.E.2d 570 (Ind. 1996) (testimony to facts about which the witness possesses personal knowledge is not hearsay; witness's initial statement to police was admissible as a prior consistent statement offered to rebut charge of recent fabrication, where witness in his statement admitted driving truck, that co-defendant fired weapon at defendant's husband, and that witness and defendant had been out together the night before the murder; the statement was sufficiently consistent with witness's trial testimony to rebut inference that witness fabricated story to receive leniency from prosecutor; once object of conspiracy is attained, subsequent statements by coconspirator are not admissible under the coconspirator exclusion to the hearsay rule).

Evans v. State, 643 N.E.2d 877 (Ind. 1994) (prior inconsistent statements are admissible to rebut charges that witness had improper motive if they are made before the alleged improper motive occurred).

Splunge v. State, 641 N.E.2d 628 (Ind. 1994), *superseded by statute*, **Wheeler v. State**, 749 N.E.2d 1111 (Ind. 2001) (trial court properly sustained state's objection to officer's testimony; while witness could be called to prove prior inconsistent statements, defense counsel possessed prior statements and used them for extensive cross-examination of accomplice; therefore, officer's hearsay testimony contributed nothing further).

Modesitt v. State, 578 N.E.2d 649 (Ind. 1991) (prior statement of a witness is admissible if the declarant testifies at trial, is subject to cross-examination, and the statement is offered to rebut a charge of recent fabrication).

Samuels v. State, 267 Ind. 676, 372 N.E.2d 1186 (1978), *overruled in part, Modesitt v. State*, 578 N.E.2d 649 (Ind. 1991) (prior inconsistent statements used solely to impeach a witness are not offered for their truth).

Moreland v. State, 701 N.E.2d 288 (Ind. Ct. App. 1998) (when prior statements are used to impeach and rehabilitate a witness, they are not hearsay because they are not used to prove the truth of the matter asserted; thus, where a witness is impeached by evidence of statements made out of court contradictory to those made in court on the witness stand, it is permissible on rebuttal to introduce evidence of statements made at or about the time of the impeaching statements and in harmony with the statements or testimony given on the witness stand).

Johnston v. State Farm Mut. Auto. Ins. Co., 667 N.E.2d 802 (Ind. Ct. App. 1996) (because insured's testimony about alleged opinion of attorney that insurer had breached duty to deal in good faith would be inadmissible under hearsay rule, insured's sworn answer to interrogatory containing such hearsay could not be considered on motion for summary judgment).

Caley v. State, 650 N.E.2d 54 (Ind. Ct. App. 1995) (out-of-court statements by witnesses testifying at trial and subject to cross-examination about those statements are admissible under some circumstances, including when statement is consistent with declarant's trial testimony and is offered to rebut express or implied charge of recent fabrication).

Fleener v. State, 648 N.E.2d 652 (Ind. Ct. App. 1995), *aff'd in part and vacated in part*, 656 N.E.2d 1140 (Ind. 1995) (testimony of child sexual abuse victim's mother, regarding whether she divorced defendant because victim told her that defendant had "done something to her," which was offered in rebuttal, was not hearsay but a legitimate attempt to show course of action after defendant suggested that victim fabricated story with mother's encouragement and that he never knew why he was thrown out of house; nor was testimony by physician concerning statements made by victim hearsay where offered to support validity of physician's professional conclusion).

Marshall v. State, 643 N.E.2d 957 (Ind. Ct. App. 1994) (to be admissible to rebut charge of recent fabrication, prior consistent statement must have been made before alleged motive to fabricate occurred).

Kiner v. State, 643 N.E.2d 950 (Ind. Ct. App. 1994) (evidence of out-of-court identification is not admissible when the identification procedure was impermissibly suggestive and created very substantial likelihood of misidentification; just as identification evidence is not allowed from the prosecution if the identification procedure was impermissibly suggestive, court will not permit defendant to misrepresent facts to a witness in order to produce misidentification).

Hall v. State, 634 N.E.2d 837 (Ind. Ct. App. 1994) (witness's testimony that she indicated in her deposition that she had told police that child informed her of defendant's molestation was not hearsay in so far as state offered it to prove witness's inconsistent testimony).

Anderson v. Scott, 630 N.E.2d 226 (Ind. Ct. App. 1994) (where prior inconsistent statements of witness were not made under oath they were inadmissible as substantive evidence).

HEARSAY

Kielblock v. State, 627 N.E.2d 816 (Ind. Ct. App. 1994) (audiotape of welfare worker's interview with alleged child victim, in which victim discussed sexual molestation, and transcript of tape were admissible despite defendant's hearsay objection; tape was offered to rebut defendant's expressed or implied charge against victim of recent fabrication or improper influence or motive, and worker did not testify about contents of interview but only that interview occurred and she recorded it; although victim had already testified in prosecution's case-in-chief, she was still under subpoena and was subject to recall and defendant never expressed wish to recall her).

Brim v. State, 624 N.E.2d 27 (Ind. Ct. App. 1993) (prior statement made to the police by a beating victim was properly admitted into evidence where the victim could not remember the beating at trial; victim was available for cross-examination because she testified at trial under oath and responded willingly to questions).

Rule 801(d)(2)—Statements by Party-Opponent

Lander v. State, 762 N.E.2d 1208 (Ind. 2002) (the state must introduce independent evidence of a conspiracy before the statements of a coconspirator during the course and in furtherance of the conspiracy are sought to be admitted as nonhearsay; accordingly, the state must show: (1) the existence of a conspiracy between the declarant and the party against whom the statement is offered; and (2) that the statement was made in the course and in furtherance of this conspiracy).

Smith v. State, 721 N.E.2d 213 (Ind. 1999) (responses by defendant during police questioning were exempt from hearsay definition as statements by a party-opponent).

Barber v. State, 715 N.E.2d 848 (Ind. 1999) (for statement to be admissible under 801(d)(2)(E), the state must demonstrate that (1) a conspiracy existed between the declarant and the party against whom the statement is offered and (2) the statement was made during the course and in furtherance of the conspiracy; trial court erred in admitting hearsay because there was no independent evidence of conspiracy—such error was harmless in light of the significant, uncontested evidence of defendant's guilt).

Wright v. State, 690 N.E.2d 1098 (Ind. 1997), *overruled in part*, *Fuller v. State*, 875 N.E.2d 326 (Ind. Ct. App. 2007) (holding that statements made to recruit potential coconspirators are admissible under Rule 801(d)(2)(E) provided the court first determines that a conspiracy exists).

Edgecomb v. State, 673 N.E.2d 1185 (Ind. 1996) (at trial for aiding in felony murder, defendant only objected to portions of witness's testimony about conversation overheard between defendant and principal concerning statements made by principal; thus he was precluded on appeal from contesting the admission of that portion of the witness's testimony pertaining to defendant's statements).

Neal v. State, 659 N.E.2d 122 (Ind. 1995), *overruled*, *Atchely v. State*, 730 N.E.2d 758 (Ind. Ct. App. 2000), and *Richardson v. State*, 717 N.E.2d 32 (Ind. 1999) (threat by defendant against potential witness is not introduced as prior act of misconduct to impeach credibility or attach dependant's character, but is offered to show attempt to conceal or suppress implicating evidence and is admissible as relevant to defendant's guilty knowledge).

Hilton v. State, 648 N.E.2d 361 (Ind. 1995), *overruled in part*, *State v. Wilson*, 836 N.E.2d 407 (Ind. 2005) (defendant failed to establish a proper foundation for impeaching witness, where defendant did not cross-examine witness about alleged admission, and witness therefore made no statement that might be inconsistent with failure to recollect person who would have testified about prior inconsistent statement).

Mayhew v. State, 537 N.E.2d 1188 (Ind. 1989) (Supreme Court summarized the circumstances under which statements by accomplices qualify coconspirators' admissions).

Page v. State, 518 N.E.2d 1089 (Ind. 1988) (defendant's flight from the scene and attempt to dispose of the victim's body qualified as an admission).

Chinn v. State, 511 N.E.2d 1000 (Ind. 1987) (letter from the alleged murderer to defendant, demanding payment for the killing was admissible).

Shackelford v. State, 498 N.E.2d 382 (Ind. 1986) (incriminating statement made by one other than the party may be admissible as an admission if the party concedes its truth).

Cooper v. State, 461 N.E.2d 1119 (Ind. 1984) (witness properly permitted to testify concerning a telephone call in which defendant admitted breaking into the witness's home and asked the witness to drop the charges).

Roush v. State, 875 N.E.2d 801 (Ind. Ct. App. 2007) (before a statement is admitted under Rule 801(d)(2)(E), it must be proved that there is "independent evidence" of the conspiracy; in other words, there must be proof, by a preponderance of the evidence: (1) of the existence of a conspiracy between the declarant and the party against whom the statement is offered; and (2) that the statement was made in the course and in furtherance of the conspiracy).

Davis v. Washington, 547 U.S. 813, 126 S. Ct. 2266, 165 L. Ed. 2d 224 (2006) (a statement will be considered "testimonial" for Confrontation Clause purposes when an objective consideration of the circumstances indicate that the statement was not elicited for the purpose of responding to an emergency and that the primary purpose of the interrogation is to establish or prove past events potentially relevant to later criminal prosecution).

Jones v. State, 834 N.E.2d 167 (Ind. Ct. App. 2005) (the statement of a coconspirator is not "testimonial" under *Crawford v. Washington*, 541 U.S. 36, 124 S. Ct. 1354, 158 L. Ed. 2d 177 (2004) and thus its admission does not violate the Confrontation Clause).

Banks v. State, 839 N.E.2d 794 (Ind. Ct. App. 2005) (the exception to the rule defining hearsay for statements of a party-opponent in Rule 801(d)(2) applies to statements by government employees concerning matters within the scope of their agency or employment in criminal cases as well as civil cases).

Collins v. State, 826 N.E.2d 671 (Ind. Ct. App. 2005), *transfer denied*, 841 N.E.2d 185 (Ind. 2005), *cert. denied*, 546 U.S. 1108, 126 S. Ct. 1058, 163 L. Ed. 2d 885 (2006) (a criminal defendant did not manifest adoption of a statement when he first admitted the shooting but later changed his story and claimed that the shooting did not occur as a witness who later described it; the trial court therefore erred when it admitted the statement as one of a party-opponent under Rule 801(d)(2)(B)).

Murrell v. State, 747 N.E.2d 567 (Ind. Ct. App. 2001) (even though a formal charge of conspiracy had not been filed, a nephew's statement about the "business" he shared with defendant showed that defendant was involved in an ongoing conspiracy to sell drugs, and was admissible nonhearsay as a statement of a coconspirator).

Cockrell v. State, 743 N.E.2d 799 (Ind. Ct. App. 2001) (for a statement to be admissible under Rule 801(d)(2)(E), the state must demonstrate both that a conspiracy existed between the declarant and the party against whom the statement is offered, and that the statement was made during the course of and in furtherance of the conspiracy; independent evidence of a conspiracy is required—other than the statement itself; trial court abused its discretion in admitting hearsay statements into evidence under Rule 801(d)(2)(E) because there was not sufficient evidence of a conspiracy where there was no evidence that declarant and defendant made contact with one another).

Leslie v. State, 670 N.E.2d 898 (Ind. Ct. App. 1996) (state must establish evidentiary foundation showing existence of conspiracy in order to introduce evidence of coconspirator's statement under the coconspirator exception to hearsay rule; such proof may be direct or circumstantial and does not have to be strong; trial court has discretion to decide if evidence is sufficient to establish conspiracy).

Houser v. State, 661 N.E.2d 1213 (Ind. Ct. App. 1996) (statements by witness who was project manager of check-issuing corporation before and during conspiracy to present false invoices for alleged equipment rental from defendant's company were admissible under coconspirators exception to hearsay rule; there was circumstantial evidence of existence of conspiracy between defendant and project manager, independent of project manager's statements to the corporation's accounting manager, and those statements were in furtherance of conspiracy).

Loman v. State, 640 N.E.2d 745 (Ind. Ct. App. 1994) (in trial for obtaining controlled substances by fraud or deceit, contents of telephone call between caller and physician were admissible despite hearsay objection; caller identified himself as defendant, falsely claimed to be patient of one of physician's partners, and requested something "to get by" for toothache).

Simpson v. State, 628 N.E.2d 1215 (Ind. Ct. App. 1994) (after state makes prima facie showing of existence of conspiracy, those acts or declarations that occurred between beginning and ending of conspiracy and in furtherance of its objectives are admissible against alleged coconspirator who did not make the declarations).

Chapter 802

Rule 802. Hearsay Rule

Rule 802 reads as follows:

Hearsay is not admissible except as provided by law or by these rules.

---

*　*　*　*　*

ANALYSIS

Overview.　The hearsay rule is a general rule of exclusion of statements falling within the definition of hearsay under Rule 801. Once having established that the evidence is hearsay, it is inadmissible unless the proponent of the declaration can bring it within an exception to the basic definition under Rule 801(d), within an exception under either Rule 803 or Rule 804, or within some other basis identified in Rule 802.

Analysis of Hearsay.　Hearsay issues are subject to systematic analysis. The analysis may be made in the following manner:

(1)　Is the witness testifying to an out-of-court "statement" for purposes of the hearsay rule? (*See* Rule 801(a)).

(2)　If so, is the out-of-court statement being offered to prove the truth of the matter asserted in the statement? (*See* Rule 801(c).) It may be offered to prove only that the statement was made, not that the statement is true. In such cases the statement is not hearsay, and if otherwise admissible, may be subject to a limiting instruction under Rule 105.

(3)　If the statement is offered to prove the truth of the statement, is it exempted under Rule 801(d)(1), "Prior statements of a witness," or Rule 801(d)(2), "Statements of a party opponent"?

(4)　If the statement is not exempted by Rule 801(d), is it subject to an exception under Rule 803? The availability of the declarant is not a material requisite to the Rule 803 exceptions.

(5)　Is the declarant unavailable as defined by Rule 804(a)? If so, does the statement fit within one of the exceptions under Rule 804(b)? Each of these exceptions has as a prerequisite the unavailability of the declarant.

(6)　Is the statement admissible pursuant to a statute or rule of procedure?

(7)   If it is a criminal case, does the prosecution's use of a hearsay exception pass constitutional muster relative to rights of confrontation and due process? Hearsay otherwise admissible may be inadmissible under the Constitution in criminal cases if offered against the accused.

(8)   Again, in a criminal case even if a statement is hearsay and not subject to a specific exception, is it offered by the defendant and would the defendant be denied due process by its exclusion?

ADDITIONAL AUTHORITY

WEISSENBERGER'S FEDERAL EVIDENCE § 802.1

5 WEINSTEIN 2d §§ 802.01–802.07

4 MUELLER & KIRKPATRICK §§ 431–432

COMPARISON TO FEDERAL RULE

Indiana Rule 802 is parallel to Federal Rule 802.

SIGNIFICANT CASES

Tyler v. State, 903 N.E.2d 463 (Ind. 2009) (Indiana's Protected Person Statute (PPS), Ind. Code Ann. § 35-37-4-6 does not conflict with the rule excluding hearsay in Rule 802, as the statute is a provision of "law" that Rule 802 specifically excludes from its operation).

Carpenter v. State, 786 N.E.2d 696 (Ind. 2003) (Indiana's "protected person statute," Ind. Code § 35-37-4-6, sets forth a detailed set of conditions under which evidence that is "not otherwise admissible" will be allowed in cases involving crimes against children and individuals with certain disabilities; accordingly, prior videotaped statements are admissible if, inter alia: (1) the trial court found, in a hearing attended by the child, that the time, content, and circumstances of the statement or videotape provided sufficient indications of reliability; and (2) the child was available for cross-examination at the hearing).

Kubsch v. State, 784 N.E.2d 905 (Ind. 2003) (evidence that would constitute inadmissible hearsay must both satisfy an exception to the rule excluding such evidence and the general rule of relevance).

Martin v. State, 736 N.E.2d 1213 (Ind. 2000) (hearsay testimony is excluded from judicial proceedings because its admission defeats a defendant's right to confront and cross-examine witnesses against him).

Smith v. State, 721 N.E.2d 213 (Ind. 1999) (statements may be admitted to prove identity or motive, but if to establish a collateral issue the statements must first prove the truth of the matter asserted, it remains hearsay).

Grund v. State, 671 N.E.2d 411 (Ind. 1996) (even if testimony of defendant's sister about conversation she had with defendant and defendant's children about events on night murder weapon was stolen constituted hearsay, its admission was harmless, since testimony was merely cumulative of testimony of one of defendant's children).

Williams v. State, 669 N.E.2d 956 (Ind. 1996) (statements made and questions asked by police informant during conversation in which defendant boasted about role in murder of another police informant were not hearsay, and thus, their admission at murder trial was not a violation of defendant's Sixth Amendment right to confrontation because statements of informant were meant to prompt defendant to speak and were not admitted for truth of matters asserted therein).

Smith v. State, 668 N.E.2d 661 (Ind. 1996) (even if hearsay statement given by defendant to police concerning his presence in victim's home and car on night before murder was not admission by party opponent, defendant suffered no disadvantage from the statement's admission and its admission was not grounds for reversal, where defendant claimed statement was not contrary to position he took at trial).

Taylor v. State, 659 N.E.2d 535 (Ind. 1995) (admission of hearsay statement of murder victim to police, that defendant had threatened to kill her if she accused him of sexual abuse, was harmless error where there was considerable evidence from other sources that defendant murdered victim because she accused him of sexual abuse and where probable impact of statement on jury was minor).

Owens v. State, 659 N.E.2d 466 (Ind. 1995) (in murder trial, admission of investigating officer's testimony about witness's statements concerning crime scene events, although hearsay, was harmless error and did not prejudice defendant's substantial rights, where witness testified to same events and court admonished jury that investigating officer's statements were offered not for their truth but to explain investigative procedure).

Greenlee v. State, 655 N.E.2d 488 (Ind. 1995) (in attempted murder trial, where defense counsel's objection to eyewitness's testimony as inadmissible hearsay was sustained and jury was admonished to disregard it, there was no error for review).

Jones v. State, 655 N.E.2d 49 (Ind. 1995) (whether to admit hearsay is within discretion of trial judge and only constitutes a due process violation where defendant is deprived of a fair trial).

Mitchell v. State, 644 N.E.2d 102 (Ind. 1994) (any error in admitting hearsay testimony concerning whereabouts of defendant on evening in question was harmless where evidence clearly established defendant's presence at scene of altercation and defendant's whereabouts was not at issue).

Powell v. State, 644 N.E.2d 82 (Ind. 1994) (at sentencing hearing in murder case, sworn statement given to police by friend of defendant, concerning telephone conversation with defendant in which he told her she should have reason to fear him, was admissible because it carried some indicia of reliability and defendant had opportunity to indicate to court any inaccuracies).

Craig v. State, 630 N.E.2d 207 (Ind. 1994) (error in the admission of two hearsay statements was harmless, and reversal was not required).

Miller v. State, 575 N.E.2d 272 (Ind. 1991) (court erred in admitting testimony by the victim's physician consisting of statements made by another physician; statements did not come within an exception to the hearsay rule and were, therefore, inadmissible).

Lock v. State, 567 N.E.2d 1155 (Ind. 1991) (hearsay evidence is generally inadmissible because it deprives a criminal defendant of the right to confront and cross-examine the declarant).

C. T. S. Corp. v. Schoulton, 270 Ind. 34, 383 N.E.2d 293 (1978) (hearsay evidence is not admissible unless it falls within a specific exception).

Wells v. State, 254 Ind. 608, 261 N.E.2d 865 (1970) (hearsay evidence is inadmissible unless it falls within an exception).

McGrew v. State, 673 N.E.2d 787 (Ind. Ct. App. 1996), *aff'd in part, vacated in part on other grounds*, 682 N.E.2d 1289 (Ind. 1997) (admission of post-incident hearsay statements by victim of criminal deviate conduct was harmless error because testimony of witnesses on issue was brief and consistent with victim's later testimony).

Owensby v. Lepper, 666 N.E.2d 1251 (Ind. Ct. App. 1996) (hearsay statements, which depend on credibility of out-of-court declarant unavailable for cross-examination, are generally inadmissible; in appeal of dissolution of marriage proceeding, wife waived hearsay objection even though her counsel referred to contents of exhibit as hearsay, where substance of wife's objection at trial was to lack of proper authentication).

Potter v. State, 666 N.E.2d 93 (Ind. Ct. App. 1996), *vacated on other grounds*, 684 N.E.2d 1127 (Ind. 1997) (in rape and battery prosecution, police officer's testimony about his interview with victim, her children, and neighbors, was inadmissible hearsay but its admission was harmless

error where testimony of victim, her children, and neighbors also described their statements to police and defendant was able to cross-examine each witness; tendency of officer's statements to bolster their credibility had only minor impact on jury).

Faulkner v. Markkay of Ind., 663 N.E.2d 798 (Ind. Ct. App. 1996) (hearsay is inadmissible unless it falls within one of judicially or statutorily created exceptions to hearsay rule).

Williams v. State, 658 N.E.2d 598 (Ind. Ct. App. 1995) (even if detective's testimony about amount of money given to informant to purchase controlled drug was hearsay, its admission did not warrant reversal of conviction, where detective's statement would not have substantially affected jury verdict).

Lucre Corp. v. County of Gibson, 657 N.E.2d 150 (Ind. Ct. App. 1995) (in condemnation case, any error in refusal to admit newspaper articles discussing demand for landfill sites was harmless where owner's expert was permitted to testify about matters discussed in newspaper articles and it was not disputed that publication occurred).

Kotsopoulos v. State, 654 N.E.2d 44 (Ind. Ct. App. 1995) (hearsay evidence was admissible at sentencing to determine amount of restitution).

Showalter v. Brubaker, 650 N.E.2d 693 (Ind. Ct. App. 1995) (in dissolution of marriage proceeding, appraisal of marital business was not inadmissible hearsay although valuation of production machinery was conducted by third party who did not testify; husband testified that his appraisal was the same with one exception which went to weight and credibility, not to admissibility).

Caley v. State, 650 N.E.2d 54 (Ind. Ct. App. 1995) (error in admitting hearsay warrants remedial action on appeal only where error prejudices substantial rights of defendant; defendant may open door to otherwise inadmissible evidence by introducing issue into trial).

Whited v. State, 645 N.E.2d 1138 (Ind. Ct. App. 1995) (if challenged evidence is hearsay and does not fit within one of exceptions to hearsay rule, it is inadmissible).

Robinson v. State, 634 N.E.2d 1367 (Ind. Ct. App. 1994) (admitting witness's statement that he had been informed that defendant previously participated in drug transaction prior to charged transactions was harmless error, where substantial independent evidence established defendant's predisposition to deliver illegal drugs; where defense counsel had referred to deposition questioning witness's personal knowledge of defendant, it was cumulative and not reversible error to allow state on redirect to read another deposition question regarding witness's knowledge of defendant's drug dealing to provide context for first question and answer).

Chapter 803

Rule 803. Hearsay Exceptions; Availability of Declarant Immaterial

Rule 803 reads as follows:

The following are not excluded by the hearsay rule, even though the declarant is available as a witness.

(1) *Present sense impression.* A statement describing or explaining a material event, condition or transaction, made while the declarant was perceiving the event, condition or transaction, or immediately thereafter.

(2) *Excited utterance.* A statement relating to a startling event or condition made while the declarant was under the stress of excitement caused by the event or condition.

(3) *Then Existing Mental, Emotional, or Physical Condition.* A statement of the declarant's then existing state of mind, emotion, sensation, or physical condition (such as intent, plan, motive, design, mental feeling, pain, and bodily health), but not including a statement of memory or belief to prove the fact remembered or believed unless it related to the execution, revocation, identification, or terms of declarant's will.

(4) *Statements for purposes of medical diagnosis or treatment.* Statements made by persons who are seeking medical diagnosis or treatment and describing medical history, or past or present symptoms, pain, or sensations, or the inception or general character or the cause or external source thereof insofar as reasonably pertinent to diagnosis or treatment.

(5) *Recorded recollection.* A memorandum or record concerning a matter about which a witness once had knowledge but now has insufficient recollection to enable the witness to testify fully and accurately, shown to have been made or adopted by the witness when the matter was fresh in the witness's memory and to reflect that knowledge correctly. If admitted, the memorandum or record may be read into evidence but may not itself be received as an exhibit unless offered by an adverse party.

(6) *Records of regularly conducted business activity.* A memorandum, report, record, or data compilation, in any form, of acts, events, conditions, opinions, or diagnoses, made at or near the time by, or from information transmitted by, a

person with knowledge, if kept in the course of a regularly conducted business activity, and if it was the regular practice of that business activity to make the memorandum, report, record, or data compilation, all as shown by the testimony or affidavit of the custodian or other qualified witness, unless the source of information or the method or circumstances of preparation indicate a lack of trustworthiness. The term "business" as used in this rule includes business, institution, association, profession, occupation, and calling of every kind, whether or not conducted for profit.

(7) *Absence of entry in records kept in accordance with the provisions of paragraph (6).* Evidence that a matter is not included in the memoranda, reports, records, or data compilations, in any form, kept in accordance with the provisions of paragraph (6), to prove the nonoccurrence or nonexistence of the matter, if the matter was of a kind of which a memorandum, report, record, or data compilation was regularly made and preserved, unless the sources of information or other circumstances indicate lack of trustworthiness.

(8) *Public records and reports.* Unless the sources of information or other circumstances indicate lack of trustworthiness, records, reports, statements, or data compilations in any form, of a public office or agency, setting forth its regularly conducted and regularly recorded activities, or matters observed pursuant to duty imposed by law and as to which there was a duty to report, or factual findings resulting from an investigation made pursuant to authority granted by law. The following are not within this exception to the hearsay rule: (a) investigative reports by police and other law enforcement personnel, except when offered by an accused in a criminal case; (b) investigative reports prepared by or for a government, a public office, or an agency when offered by it in a case in which it is a party; (c) factual findings offered by the government in criminal cases; and (d) factual findings resulting from special investigation of a particular complaint, case, or incident, except when offered by an accused in a criminal case.

(9) *Records of vital statistics.* Records or data compilations in any form, of births, fetal deaths, deaths, or marriages, if the report thereof was made to a public office pursuant to requirements of law.

(10) *Absence of public record or entry.* To prove the absence of a record, report, statement, or data compilation in any form, or the nonoccurrence or nonexistence of a matter of which a record, report, statement, or data compilation in any form was regularly made and preserved by a public office or agency, evidence in the form of a certification in accordance with Rule 902, or testimony, that a diligent search failed to disclose the record, report, statement, or data compilation, or entry.

(11) *Records of religious organizations.* Statements of births, marriages, divorces, deaths, legitimacy, ancestry, relationship by blood or marriage, or other similar facts of personal or family history, contained in a regularly kept record of a religious organization.

(12) *Marriage, baptismal, and similar certificates.* Statements of fact contained in a certificate that the maker performed a marriage or other ceremony or administered a sacrament, made by a clergyman, public official, or other person

authorized by the rules of practices of a religious organization or by law to perform the act certified, and purporting to have been issued at the time of the act or within a reasonable time thereafter.

(13) *Family records.* Statements of fact concerning personal or family history contained in family Bibles, genealogies, charts, engravings on rings, inscriptions on family portraits, engravings on urns, crypts, or tombstones, or the like.

(14) *Records of documents affecting an interest in property.* The record of a document purporting to establish or affect an interest in property, as proof of the content of the original recorded document and its execution and delivery by each person by whom it purports to have been executed, if the record is a record of a public office and an applicable statute authorized the recording of documents of that kind in that office.

(15) *Statements in documents affecting an interest in property.* A statement contained in a document purporting to establish or affect an interest in property if the matter stated was relevant to the purposes of the document, unless dealings with the property since the document was made have been inconsistent with the truth of the statement or the purport of the document.

(16) *Statements in ancient documents.* Statements in a document in existence thirty years or more, the authenticity of which is established.

(17) *Market reports, commercial publications.* Market quotations, tabulations, lists, directories, or other published compilations, generally used and relied upon by the public or by persons in particular occupations.

(18) *Learned treatises.* To the extent called to the attention of an expert witness upon cross-examination or relied upon by the expert witness in direct examination, statements contained in published treatises, periodicals, or pamphlets that contradict the expert's testimony on a subject of history, medicine, or other science or art, established as a reliable authority by the testimony or admission of the witness or by other expert testimony or by judicial notice. If admitted, the statements may be read into evidence but may not be received as exhibits.

(19) *Reputation concerning personal or family history.* Reputation among members of a person's family by blood, adoption, or marriage, or among a person's associates, or in the community, concerning a person's birth, adoption, marriage, divorce, death, legitimacy, relationship by blood, adoption, or marriage, ancestry, or other similar fact of a person's personal or family history.

(20) *Reputation concerning boundaries or general history.* Reputation in a community, arising before the controversy, as to boundaries of or customs affecting lands in the community, and reputation as to events of general history important to the community or state or nation in which located.

(21) *Reputation as to character.* Reputation of a person's character among associates or in the community.

(22) *Judgment of previous conviction.* Evidence of a final judgment entered after a trial or upon a plea of guilty (but not upon a plea of nolo contendere) adjudging a person guilty of a crime punishable by death or imprisonment in

excess of one year, to prove any fact essential to sustain the judgment, but not including, when offered by the government in a criminal prosecution for purposes other than impeachment, judgments against persons other than the accused. The pendency of an appeal may be shown but does not affect admissibility.

(23)   *Judgment as to personal, family, or general history, or boundaries.* Judgments as proof of matters of personal, family or general history, or boundaries, essential to the judgment, if the same would be provable by evidence of reputation.

* * * * *

ANALYSIS

Hearsay Exceptions; Availability of Declarant Immaterial

(1) Present Sense Impression

Requirement for Admissibility.   In order for an out-of-court statement of a declarant to be admissible as a present sense impression, the statement must be made while the declarant is perceiving the facts in question or immediately thereafter. There is no necessity of a startling event. Consequently, the foundational requirement for application of this exception requires establishing that the declarant had firsthand knowledge of the event perceived, and that the statement made by the declarant described the event or condition. It must be established that the statement was made contemporaneously with the event or immediately after the event. The out-of-court statement must describe the event, and any expansion beyond what is perceived would not be admissible as a statement of present sense impression.

Illustration

If Norb testifies that Ralph said, "There goes that Acme Service truck through the red light. I saw that truck getting its brakes repaired yesterday," the second sentence is not admissible under Rule 803(1). The sentence involves a recollection of past events and is not a report of the immediate sense impression.

---

(2) Excited Utterance

Startling Event; Scope of Statement.   An excited utterance is an admissible out-of-court statement that is made in response to a startling event during the trauma or stress of the event. In order for the exception to apply, there must be an extremely startling or shocking event. Foundational evidence as to the existence of the event may be established through the out-of-court statement of the declarant. It must further be established as a foundation that the declarant had personal knowledge of the event, and that, as a subjective matter, the declarant was under extreme stress when he or she made the statement. Because stress can continue for a period of time after a startling event, the statement need not be made immediately after the startling event has occurred. Compare Rule 803(1), *above*. The statement must also "relate" to the startling event in question and the term "relate" is broader than the term "describe," which is operative in the context of Rule 803(1). The excited utterance may expand upon a description of the event as long as the statement in some way relates to the startling event.

Illustration

Bystander observing an accident states to a companion, "Look at that blue car crash that red car!" Immediately after the accident, before the dust has yet settled, a passenger in the car says of the driver, "Oh my God, why did he drink those three beers before we left work?"

In the first statement, the present sense impression exception limits the scope of statement to a description of the event. Under the excited utterance exception, Rule 803(2), if the reflective processes remain stilled, the declaration is admissible as to a matter pertinent to the event even if it relates to an occurrence at another time. Therefore, what the passenger said with regard to events affecting his ability to drive would be admissible even though it pertained to events occurring at another time.

Constitutional Considerations: Excited Utterances and the Confrontation Clause

The hearsay rules provide, subject to various exceptions, that a party may ordinarily object to evidence about things that were said or written by anyone outside of the courtroom. When that objecting party is the accused in a criminal case, the exclusion of such evidence may also be required by the Confrontation Clause of the Sixth Amendment, which provides: "In all criminal prosecutions, the accused shall enjoy the right . . . to be confronted with the witnesses against him."

For nearly a quarter of a century after its decision in *Ohio v. Roberts*, 448 U.S. 56, 100 S. Ct. 2531, 65 L. Ed. 2d 597, 17 Ohio Op. 3d 240 (1980), the Supreme Court interpreted the Confrontation Clause as imposing only a minimal constraint on a prosecutor's use of hearsay that would otherwise be admissible under the hearsay rules. As interpreted in *Roberts*, the Sixth Amendment allowed the admission of any unavailable witness's out-of-court statement against a defendant, even though that would deny him any opportunity to literally confront the witness, as long as the statement was determined by the court to bear "adequate indicia of reliability," a test that was routinely met if the evidence either fell within "a firmly rooted hearsay exception" or had "particularized guarantees of trustworthiness." As a practical matter, this test rendered the Confrontation Clause largely duplicative of the hearsay rules, and greatly minimized the incentive for criminal defense attorneys to object on constitutional grounds to the admission of hearsay.

A quarter century of constitutional law based on *Roberts* has now been completely overturned, however, with the Supreme Court's recent decision in *Crawford v. Washington*, 541 U.S. 36, 124 S. Ct. 1354, 158 L. Ed. 2d 177 (2004), and its progeny. In that landmark case, the Court abrogated *Roberts* almost in its entirety, created a new

HEARSAY

constitutional standard for the admission of hearsay against a criminal defendant, and established for the first time in decades that the Sixth Amendment requires the exclusion of many extrajudicial statements that would otherwise be admissible under the hearsay rules (for example, in a civil case).

Under *Crawford*, the admission of hearsay statements at a criminal trial no longer turns on whether the trial judge believes the evidence to be "reasonably reliable," "contains guarantees of trustworthiness," or would be admitted under a "firmly rooted" hearsay exception. As the Supreme Court stated in *Crawford* with evident disdain: "Dispensing with confrontation because testimony is obviously reliable is akin to dispensing with jury trial because a defendant is obviously guilty." *Crawford v. Washington*, 541 U.S. 36, 62, 124 S. Ct. 1354, 1371 (2004). Instead, the Court adopted a new, and seemingly elegant, standard: Whether the out-of-court statement is *testimonial*. The Court concluded that the Confrontation Clause, construed in light of its history and text, applies only to statements by "witnesses," which would only be true of those who give the functional equivalent of "testimony" against the accused. Stated simply, if an out-of-court statement of a witness is testimonial, it may not be admitted against the accused to prove the truth of what that witness said unless that witness is unavailable to testify and the defendant had a prior opportunity to cross-examine that witness. Other than statements admitted under the "former testimony" exception in Rule 804(b)(1), these two conditions will rarely be satisfied. On the other hand, if a statement is nontestimonial, it simply is not subject to the Confrontation Clause, and its admission is now regulated entirely by the traditional rules governing hearsay evidence. It simply no longer matters, as it did under *Roberts*, whether the statement is deemed to be reliable by the trial judge. If the statement is testimonial, it must satisfy the "unavailability" and "prior opportunity to cross-examine" requirements. If the statement is not testimonial, no Confrontation Clause issue is presented.

In *Davis v. Washington*, 547 U.S. 813, 126 S. Ct. 2266, 165 L. Ed. 2d 224 (2006), the United States Supreme Court expanded upon its *Crawford* decision and clarified the definition of "testimonial" for purposes of determining whether the Confrontation Clause applies to a particular statement. Under *Davis*, a statement will be considered "testimonial" when an objective consideration of the circumstances indicate that the statement was not elicited for the purpose of responding to an emergency and that the primary purpose of the interrogation is to establish or prove past events potentially relevant to later criminal prosecution. Such a finding is most likely if, for example, the witness was describing events some time after they happened, especially if the witness was already separated from her assailant, speaking at the station house or otherwise under police protection, or responding calmly to structured police questioning.

Conversely, a statement will be considered "nontestimonial" when an objective consideration of the circumstances indicates that the interrogation was emergency related or that the interrogation had a primary purpose other than to establish its value for future litigation. Such a finding is most likely if the witness was describing events as they were actually happening; if the witness faced an ongoing emergency; or if the conversation was not tranquil but frantic, perhaps over the phone, especially if the caller was unprotected by the police and apparently still in possible immediate danger. The

Court made clear that the existence of police interrogation was not dispositive of the issue one way or another: Statements to questions made in the context of police interrogations could be either "testimonial" or "nontestimonial," as could statements made outside of a formal interrogation context.

In *Michigan v. Bryant*, ___ U.S. ___, 131 S. Ct. 1143, 179 L. Ed. 2d 93 (2011), the United States Supreme Court continued to refine its Confrontation Clause analysis revolutionized in *Crawford*. Specifically, the Court expanded its thinking begun in the *Davis* case and provided greater guidance for statements made in the context of police questioning.

Most importantly, the *Bryant* Court clarified that the fundamental issue is not whether an "ongoing emergency" exists, but whether the "primary purpose" of the police questioning is for a reason other than to establish or prove past events potentially relevant to later criminal prosecution. Certainly, the former is important to a determination of the latter, but perhaps not necessarily so. In other words, "the existence *vel non* of an ongoing emergency is [not] dispositive of the testimonial inquiry. As *Davis* made clear, whether an ongoing emergency exists is simply one factor—albeit an important factor—that informs the ultimate inquiry regarding the 'primary purpose' of an interrogation." *Bryant*, 131 S. Ct. at 1160.

The *Bryant* Court stressed the objective evaluation of the circumstances in which the encounter between the individual and the police occurs; the inquiry is not a subjective one. However, an examination of the statements and actions of the police and the victim, as well as other individuals involved while the questioning occurred, should be considered. The Court also noted that the formality of the interaction between the police and the victim is a factor that should be considered.

The *Bryant* case may be seen by some as a partial retreat from the cut-and-dried "testimonial-or-not" approach adopted in *Crawford* and *Davis*, as the *Bryant* majority opinion provoked a strong dissent from Justice Scalia, who originally authored the *Crawford* and *Davis* opinions. Justice Scalia would have held that the inquiry is a subjective one, determined entirely by the intent of the person making the statement. To be sure, the approach of the *Bryant* majority will have the practical effect of rendering slightly more declarant statements admissible in court and thus may be regarded as pro-law enforcement. However, a careful reading of Justice Scalia's dissent suggests that his views are driven by intellectual consistency and historical accuracy rather than consequentialist concerns.

The application of the *Crawford/Davis/Bryant* triumvirate to statements admitted under the "excited utterance" exception should be routine: The statements will be admissible in all but the most unlikely of cases. In identifying the line between testimonial and nontestimonial statements, the distinguishing criterion has much to do with the formality of the statement, since "formality is . . . essential to testimonial utterance." *Davis v. Washington*, 547 U.S. 813, 126 S. Ct. 2266, 2278 n.5, 165 L. Ed. 2d 224 (2006). Because this requisite formality is highly unlikely to be present for statements qualifying as "excited utterances," the statements will not be regarded as "testimonial," thus indicating that the Confrontation Clause poses no impediment to admissibility.

Of course, the statement must still satisfy the requirements of the hearsay exception itself under Rule 803(2). Some courts have stretched the limits of the Rule, allowing statements made days or weeks after the startling event or condition to be admitted under the exception. If such statements are made with an eye toward future criminal prosecution, the Confrontation Clause would become implicated. Hopefully, the re-examination of the purposes of the Confrontation Clause will curb further expansion of the exception along these lines.

(3) Then Existing Mental, Emotional, or Physical Condition

Scope of Rule.   Rule 803(3) provides for the admissibility of statements made by the declarant concerning his state of mind, emotions, sensations, or physical condition. The out-of-court statement must refer to then existing subjective qualities of the declarant. The out-of-court statement may not refer to qualities that existed at a prior point in time. For example, the statement "I felt ill yesterday" would not qualify under the exception.

Statements of Intent.   An out-of-court statement that looks forward to some act and expresses an intent or plan to do some act in the future is admissible under Rule 803(3). Intent is considered to be a mental condition under the exception, and consequently, the statement "I intend to go to Boston" would be comprehended by the exception.

Declarations may also be admitted not only as proof of the declarant's then-existing state of mind, but also as circumstantial evidence of the declarant's future conduct. *See Mutual Life Ins. Co. v. Hillmon*, 145 U.S. 285, 12 S. Ct. 909, 36 L.Ed. 706 (1892). A jury may infer from the declarant's past state of mind that the declarant held the same mental state at a future time and acted on it. Courts permit this sub-category of evidence because it lacks many of the dangers traditionally associated with hearsay: a jury's connecting a declarant's expressed mental state to their actions requires inferring only that one generally does what they intend, with no need to appraise memory, perception, or testimonial qualities. However, when admitted as circumstantial proof of the fact believed, the evidence is no longer a statement of the declarant's state of mind but rather a statement of expectation of another person's actions, and one which lacks a foundation about the basis for that expectation. The statement is thus no more reliable than any other classic form of hearsay, and this unreliability erodes the basis for admitting state-of-mind declarations in the first place. *See Camm v. State*, 908 N.E.2d 215 (Ind. 2009).

Statements Regarding Wills.   The Rule specifically provides that out-of-court statements relating to the execution, revocation, identification, or terms of the declarant's will are admissible. Such statements of belief must be made by the testator in regard to his or her own will. The Rule otherwise, however, does not comprehend statements of belief when such statements are used to prove the fact believed.

Illustration

   The following statements, if relevant, would generally satisfy Rule 803(3) depending upon the context in which the out-of-court statement is made:

I am ill.

I am tired.

I have a pain in my chest.

I feel dizzy.

I am afraid.

I like Norb.

I am depressed.

I am happy.

I plan to sell my house.

I don't plan to go on any trips this year.

(4) Statements for Purposes of Medical Diagnosis or Treatment

Overview. Rule 803(4) provides for the admissibility of certain statements made in subjective contemplation of medical treatment or diagnosis. The out-of-court declarant must subjectively believe that the statement is being made in anticipation of treatment or diagnosis. The statement usually will be made to a physician, but the out-of-court statement may be made to someone other than a physician where the out-of-court declarant subjectively believes that he or she is making the statement in contemplation of receiving treatment or diagnosis. For example, the statement could be made to a nurse, clinical social worker, an ambulance attendant, or even to a member of the declarant's family.

The subjective contemplation of treatment or diagnosis is the significant foundational requirement that must be established to utilize the exception, as the reasonable expectation of proper medical treatment, which depends on an accurate diagnosis, provides the requisite motivation for the person to tell the truth. As the Indiana Supreme Court put it, "Rule 803(4) reflects the idea that people are unlikely to lie to their doctors because doing so might jeopardize their opportunity to be made well." *VanPatten v. State*, 986 N.E.2d 255, 260 (Ind. 2013).

With respect to statements made by children, the Indiana Supreme Court has held that additional foundational evidence that the child understood the nature of the interaction and the professional's role is required. *VanPatten*, at 261. Additional indicia of reliability are warranted with child declarants, whose impressionability may make them susceptible to making untrue statements and who may not recognize the consequences of an inaccurate diagnosis.

Practical Application

Physicians and health care professionals should be aware of the additional foundation required before statements by children are admitted under Rule 803(4). The *VanPatten* case indicated that the physical manifestations of the setting—the appearance of the building, the exam room, the clothing worn by the examiner, and the examiner's job title—may be sufficient to provide the requisite foundation, especially for older children. However, for younger children, a routine pre-examination description by the examiner may not be sufficient. The Court indicated that asking a few simple questions would have been very helpful in establishing whether the child understood the nature of the visit and why it was important to tell the truth:

"Have you been to a doctor's office before?"

"Have you been seen by a nurse before?"

"Do you know what nurses do?"

"What do they do?"

"Do you know the difference between the truth and a lie?"

"Do you tell nurses and doctors the truth?"

"Do you know why you tell the nurses and doctors the truth?"

"Did you know why you were seeing Nurse []?"

"Reasonably Pertinent to Diagnosis or Treatment."   Rule 803(4) conditions admissibility of statements made for the purpose of obtaining medical treatment or diagnosis upon the objective standard that such hearsay declarations must be "reasonably pertinent" to the treatment or diagnosis sought. The exception consequently operates as a vehicle for the admission of statements of medical history, past and present symptoms and conditions, past and present pain or sensations, the inception or cause of the medical condition or illness, and the external source, if any, of the medical condition, injury, or illness. The fact that a doctor solicited or took the information should be sufficient evidence that the statement is reasonably pertinent to diagnosis or treatment. Nevertheless, the requirement of pertinency to diagnosis and treatment does, of course, impose a real limitation in certain cases.

Statements Made by Victim. Rule 803(4) was amended in 2012 to clarify that the exception applies only to patients, i.e., statements made by persons seeking medical treatment. Prior to the amendment, Rule 803(4) has been read by some courts as allowing statements from a physician concerning a patient's diagnosis and prognosis under the rationale that the language of the exception of does not explicitly state whose statements fall within the exception. This interpretation was rejected in *Sibbing v. Cave*, 922 N.E.2d 594 (Ind. 2010), which held that the Rule applies only to statements made by persons who are actually seeking medical diagnosis or treatment. The *Sibbing* Court accurately reasoned that the justification for the exception relies on the declarant's self-interest in obtaining a correct medical diagnosis and treatment, a motivation not present when the physician responds to the patient regarding a diagnosis and course of treatment. To be sure, physicians have an interest in making correct diagnoses and providing accurate information to patients—the avoidance of malpractice liability and disciplinary regulation by medical boards—but this added indicia of reliability has not been traditionally accepted as sufficient under the Rule 803(4) exception. The amendment to Rule 803(4) codifies the holding in *Sibbing* and resolves the question definitively: the exception applies for statements made by the patient alone.

Statements Attributing Fault.   Statements concerning fault or guilt are not reasonably pertinent to diagnosis or treatment. A declarant's out-of-court statements that his or her injury resulted, for example, from the defendant's negligent driving, refusing to provide a safe work environment, or failing to maintain a reasonably safe condition or diagnosis and treatment of an injury, will fall outside the scope of the exception.

Expert Opinion Considerations. The distinction between declarations by the patient for purposes of treatment or for purposes of diagnosis has been abandoned. This exception may be invoked even as to statements made for purposes of medical evaluation in preparation for trial. *See* Rule 703 with regard to the requisites of disclosure of the basis for an expert opinion. However, Rule 803(4) will operate only to admit statements contained within medical records and not the actual medical opinions and diagnoses themselves. When admitted for their truth, medical opinions and diagnoses must still satisfy the requirements for expert opinions set out in Rule 702.

Constitutional Considerations: Statements for Medical Diagnosis or Treatment and the Confrontation Clause

The admission into evidence of statements made for purposes of medical diagnosis or treatment against a criminal defendant may involve an additional analysis concerning the violation of the defendant's Confrontation Clause rights under the United States and Indiana Constitutions. In *White v. Illinois*, 502 U.S. 346, 112 S. Ct. 736, 116 L. Ed. 2d 848 (1992), the United States Supreme Court held that the Confrontation Clause does not require the prosecution to produce the declarant at trial or show that the declarant is unavailable before a trial court admits testimony under the "medical diagnosis or treatment" exception to the rule excluding hearsay.

The reasoning in *White*, however, was based largely on the Court's prior framework for analyzing the Confrontation Clause implications of admitting hearsay statements against a criminal defendant in *Ohio v. Roberts*, 448 U.S. 56, 100 S. Ct. 2531, 65 L. Ed. 2d 597, 17 Ohio Op. 3d 240 (1980). Under *Roberts*, a hearsay statement did not violate a criminal defendant's Confrontation Clause rights if it was "firmly rooted," as *White* subsequently held. This framework was abolished by the United States Supreme Court in *Crawford v. Washington*, 541 U.S. 36, 124 S. Ct. 1354, 158 L. Ed. 2d 177 (2004), which held that, with respect to "testimonial" evidence, the Confrontation Clause requires both unavailability and a prior opportunity for cross-examination.

In *Davis v. Washington*, 547 U.S. 813, 126 S. Ct. 2266, 165 L. Ed. 2d 224 (2006), the United States Supreme Court expanded upon its *Crawford* decision and clarified the definition of "testimonial" for purposes of determining whether the Confrontation Clause applies to a particular statement. Under *Davis*, a statement will be considered "testimonial" when an objective consideration of the circumstances indicate that the statement was not elicited for the purpose of responding to an emergency and that the primary purpose of the interrogation is to establish or prove past events potentially relevant to later criminal prosecution. Such a finding is most likely if, for example, the witness was describing events some time after they happened, especially if the witness was already separated from her assailant, speaking at the station house or otherwise under police protection, or responding calmly to structured police questioning.

Conversely, a statement will be considered "nontestimonial" when an objective consideration of the circumstances indicates that the interrogation was emergency related or that the interrogation had a primary purpose other than to establish its value for future litigation. Such a finding is most likely if the witness was describing events as they were actually happening; if the witness faced an ongoing emergency; or if the conversation was not tranquil but frantic, perhaps over the phone, especially if the caller was unprotected by the police and apparently still in possible immediate danger. The Court made clear that the existence of police interrogation was not dispositive of the issue one way or another: Statements to questions made in the context of police interrogations could be either "testimonial" or "nontestimonial," as could statements made outside of a formal interrogation context.

In *Michigan v. Bryant*, ___ U.S. ___, 131 S. Ct. 1143, 179 L. Ed. 2d 93 (2011), the United States Supreme Court continued to refine its Confrontation Clause analysis revolutionized in *Crawford*. Specifically, the Court expanded its thinking begun in the *Davis* case and provided greater guidance for statements made in the context of police questioning.

Most importantly, the *Bryant* Court clarified that the fundamental issue is not whether an "ongoing emergency" exists, but whether the "primary purpose" of the police questioning is for a reason other than to establish or prove past events potentially relevant to later criminal prosecution. Certainly, the former is important to a determination of the latter, but perhaps not necessarily so. In other words, "the existence *vel non* of an ongoing emergency is [not] dispositive of the testimonial inquiry. As *Davis* made clear, whether an ongoing emergency exists is simply one factor—albeit an important factor—that informs the ultimate inquiry regarding the 'primary purpose' of an interrogation." *Bryant*, 131 S. Ct. at 1160.

The *Bryant* Court stressed the objective evaluation of the circumstances in which the encounter between the individual and the police occurs; the inquiry is not a subjective one. However, an examination of the statements and actions of the police and the victim, as well as other individuals involved while the questioning occurred, should be considered. The Court also noted that the formality of the interaction between the police and the victim is a factor that should be considered.

The *Bryant* case may be seen by some as a partial retreat from the cut-and-dried "testimonial-or-not" approach adopted in *Crawford* and *Davis*, as the *Bryant* majority opinion provoked a strong dissent from Justice Scalia, who originally authored the *Crawford* and *Davis* opinions. Justice Scalia would have held that the inquiry is a subjective one, determined entirely by the intent of the person making the statement. To be sure, the approach of the *Bryant* majority will have the practical effect of rendering slightly more declarant statements admissible in court and thus may be regarded as pro-law enforcement. However, a careful reading of Justice Scalia's dissent suggests that his views are driven by intellectual consistency and historical accuracy rather than consequentialist concerns.

The application of the *Crawford/Davis/Bryant* triumvirate to statements admitted under the "medical diagnosis or treatment" exception should be routine: The statements will be admissible in all but the most unlikely of cases. In identifying the line between testimonial and nontestimonial statements, the distinguishing criterion has much to do with the formality of the statement, since "formality is . . . essential to testimonial utterance." *Davis v. Washington*, 547 U.S. 813, 126 S. Ct. 2266, 2278 n.5, 165 L. Ed. 2d 224 (2006). Because this requisite formality is highly unlikely to be present for statements made for purposes of medical diagnosis or treatment, the statements will not be regarded as "testimonial," thus indicating that the Confrontation Clause poses no impediment to admissibility.

(5) Recorded Recollection

Comparison to Refreshing Recollection. In contrast to the device of refreshing a witness's recollection under Rule 612, Rule 803(5) provides for the admission of a written document that contains a recorded recollection. The use of this exception is only appropriate where a document fails to revive the recollection of a witness. Consequently, the proper foundation for the use of this exception must comprehend the technique of refreshing recollection. *See* Rule 612. First, it must be established that the memorandum or record containing the witness's past recollection concerns a matter of which the witness once had personal knowledge. Second, the document must have been prepared when the matter was fresh in the memory of the witness, although, of course, at the time of trial the witness has no independent recollection of the matter. Third, the witness must testify that after reading the document, he has no independent recollection of the events preserved in that writing. According to Rule 803(5), the document will be admissible where the present recollection of the witness is insufficient to enable the witness to testify "fully and accurately." Consequently, it is not necessary for the witness to have forgotten all of the facts preserved in the writing. Of course, if the witness does have a complete and independent recollection of the event recorded in the document, the document is not admissible pursuant to this exception. The witness merely provides testimony as to his or her refreshed recollection.

Read into Evidence. If a writing qualifies as a past recollection recorded, it is read into evidence and is not received as an exhibit. The purpose of this limitation is to avoid elevating this type of declaration above testimonial evidence. It ought to be afforded no greater opportunity for scrutiny than is afforded testimonial evidence unless the party against whom the writing is offered desires that it be subjected to closer scrutiny.

(6) Records of Regularly Conducted Business Activity

Business Records. Rule 803(6) is commonly referred to as the "business record exception" but its application goes far beyond business entities, and records of associations, clubs, or other organizations may qualify under this exception.

Recent Developments

In *In re Termination of the Parent-Child Rel. of E.T.*, 808 N.E.2d 639 (Ind. 2004), the Indiana Supreme Court had the opportunity to review Rule 803(6) as it applies to records and reports of organizations prepared for the benefit of government agencies. After reviewing the common law foundations of the "business record exception," the Court held that Rule 803(6) is consistent with this common law foundation. With respect to the specific records—reports of a social service agency describing home visits and supervised visitations—the Court held that, although the reports may have furthered the mission of the agency, they were not prepared for the systematic conduct of the agency as a nonprofit corporation. Accordingly, the reports did not qualify as business records and thus were not admissible under Rule 803(6).

Foundation.   In order for an out-of-court statement to be admitted under this exception, there must be a business record or writing. As a general proposition, an oral business record does not qualify under this exception.

First-Hand Knowledge.   In order to establish the proper foundation for the admission of a business record, testimony, or an affidavit from an appropriate foundation witness must be used. The witness must have firsthand knowledge of the method by which the business in question prepares, stores, and maintains its records. Generally, the foundation witness is a custodian or records librarian, but any witness with the requisite first-hand knowledge of the business's record-keeping procedures may qualify. The foundation witness testifies that the record in question was prepared by an employee of the business in question who had a duty to report the information. The foundation witness further testifies that the person preparing the record or contributing information to the record had personal knowledge of the facts or events reported, and that the report was prepared at or near the time of the event that is recorded. The witness must also testify that it is the regular practice or custom of the business in question to make and retain the type of record involved.

Third-Person Statements.   It is important to recognize that the preparer of the document must have had a business duty to report the information, and likewise he or she or must have relied upon reports made to him or her by persons who also have a business duty to report the information. A business document that records information that is not within the personal knowledge of individuals with a business duty to report the information is not admissible under this exception as to the information provided by third persons.

Record Prepared in Contemplation of Litigation.   An opponent of a business record may seek to exclude the record because it was a document prepared in subjective contemplation of litigation. The operative language in Rule 803(6) is "unless the source of information or the method or circumstances of preparation indicate a lack of trustworthiness."

"Palmer Doctrine." Even though complying with all the parameters of the business records exception, documents prepared for use in litigation are excludable within the discretion of the trial judge. The case of *Palmer v. Hoffman*, 318 U.S. 109, 63 S. Ct. 477, 87 L. Ed. 645 (1943), held that such litigation-oriented documents are not prepared in the "regular course of business."

Practical Application

Quite frequently, business records contain statements of persons who are not employees of the business that keeps the record and who do not have a business duty to report accurately to that business. Such third party statements recorded in business records are not comprehended by this particular exception, whereas all statements of persons who have a business duty to report to the business that keeps the records are encompassed by the exception. Statements of third persons are only admissible when contained in a business record where they satisfy the multiple hearsay requirements of Rule 805. Under Rule 805, the third party statement must have an independent basis of admissibility pursuant to an exception to the basic definition, a hearsay exception, a nonhearsay basis, or some other basis identified in Rule 802.

Constitutional Considerations: Business Records and the Confrontation Clause

In *Crawford v. Washington*, 541 U.S. 36, 124 S. Ct. 1354, 158 L. Ed. 2d 177 (2004), the Supreme Court asserted, albeit in dictum, that the admission of "business records" does not implicate the Confrontation Clause. Furthermore, in *Davis v. Washington*, 547 U.S. 813, 126 S. Ct. 2266, 165 L. Ed. 2d 224 (2006), the Court clarified that out-of-court statements do not implicate the Confrontation Clause unless they are "testimonial," which would ostensibly exclude business records under Rule 803(6), so long as they were not prepared in anticipation of trial or a criminal prosecution. The records may be admissible even if they were prepared by law enforcement agents or other government officials. *See United States v. Bahena-Cardenas*, 411 F.3d 1067, 1075 (9th Cir. 2005).

Some lower courts had even extended this logic so far as to cover affidavits and other documents created in actual preparation for the criminal trial as long as those documents merely record "unambiguous factual matter," *See United States v. Weiland*, 420 F.3d 1062, 1077 (9th Cir. 2005). However, those cases appear to be effectively overruled as the result of the Supreme Court's decision in *Melendez-Diaz v. Massachusetts*, 557 U.S. 305, 129 S. Ct. 2527, 174 L. Ed. 2d 314 (2009), in which the Supreme Court held that drug lab reports constitute affidavits which fall within the "core class of testimonial statements" covered by the Confrontation Clause. Accordingly, the prosecution must produce the analysts who prepared the report for cross-examination or the report will not be admissible. In so holding, the Court rejected a slew of arguments which would have brought lab reports outside the scope of *Crawford* and its progeny: that only "accusatory" witnesses are subject to the Confrontation Clause, that the reports were "nearly contemporaneous" with the observations of the analysts, that the absence of interrogation is relevant, that a voluntary witness is somehow exempt from Confrontation Clause scrutiny, that the reports qualify as public or business records, and that reports resulting from neutral scientific testing constitute an exception to requirement of face-to-face confrontation contained in the Sixth Amendment.

As the majority in *Melendiaz-Diaz* concedes, the effect of the decision is that some criminal prosecutions will be more burdensome. It is likely that criminal defendants can now insist that the prosecution call to the stand those technicians who are at least more than minimally involved in analyzing drug samples and preparing the reports based on those analyses. On the other hand, the defendant must have a valid reason for calling those witnesses to the stand; the majority notes that defense attorneys typically refrain from wasting time by calling prosecution witnesses whose testimony they cannot effectively challenge because they do not wish to antagonize the judge or jury. However, whether the majority or dissent proves correct in their assessment of the impact of the decision does not appear to have influenced the majority's reasoning in the case, which is built upon a historical and textual foundation rather than a utilitarian outcome-determinative approach. Thus, prosecutors should accept the reality of occasional challenges to drug lab reports and be prepared to call lab analysts and technicians to the stand.

What about DUI lab reports? Questions about whether the Supreme Court actually intended to be taken seriously on this question were answered in *Bullcoming v. New Mexico*, ___ U.S. ___, 131 S. Ct. 2705, 180 L. Ed. 2d 610 (2011). In *Bullcoming*, the Court addressed the question of whether a surrogate analyst would satisfy the Confrontation Clause. Many lab technicians are qualified as expert witnesses with respect to the laboratory equipment and protocols used. Are they sufficient? The *Bullcoming* Court responded with a definitive "No": The accused's right is to be confronted with the analyst who made the certification, unless that analyst is unavailable at trial, and the accused had an opportunity, pretrial, to cross-examine that particular scientist. The certification of an analyst who did not sign the document or personally observe the test is inadequate.

The Court rejected the contention that the testimony of the actual analyst was a "hollow formality." Instead his certification represented that "he received Bullcoming's blood sample intact with the seal unbroken; that he checked to make sure that the forensic report number and the sample number corresponded; that he performed a particular test on Bullcoming's sample, adhering to a precise protocol; and that he left the report's remarks section blank, indicating that no circumstance or condition affected the sample's integrity or the analysis' validity."

The *Bullcoming* decision is at odds with the Indiana Supreme Court's decision in *Pendergrass v. State*, 913 N.E.2d 703 (Ind. 2009), in which the Court wrestled with substantially the same problem: Of all those individuals who may be involved in the laboratory testing sought to be admitted, exactly who is required to testify? In *Pendergrass*, the Indiana Supreme Court found it sufficient that the prosecution supplied a supervisor with direct involvement in the laboratory's technical processes and an expert who interpreted the results and reached an opinion based in part on the results. The Court noted that if the defendant wanted to explore any systemic problems with the laboratory processes, the supervisor would be an ideal witness to respond to such questions. This pragmatic approach to satisfying the Confrontation Clause was rejected in *Bullcoming*, which requires the testimony of the person who actually conducted the laboratory testing, and not a functional surrogate.

Anticipation that the Crawford era may be drawing to a close was rejected in *Williams v. Illinois*, ___ U.S. ___, 132 S. Ct. 2221, 183 L. Ed. 2d 89 (2012), in which the Supreme Court issued a decidedly indecisive opinion. In *Williams*, the Supreme Court addressed the use of surrogate expert witnesses, or expert testimony that discloses the contents of laboratory reports by non-testifying witnesses. The DNA comparison expert in *Williams* based her testimony on a lab report authored by a non-testifying witness. The important difference between *Williams* and the evidence in *Bullcoming* was the actual evidence sought to be admitted. In *Bullcoming*, the report itself was admitted into evidence. In *Williams*, on the other hand, the DNA report itself was not sought to be admitted, but rather used as the primary basis of the expert's testimony.

Although the *Williams* Court upheld the use of this kind of expert DNA comparison testimony, it did so under through a majority cobbled together by distinct rationales. The plurality conceptualized the case as a Rule 703 question rather than a hearsay question. In other words, the expert testimony did not violate the Confrontation Clause because it does not apply to non-hearsay statements, i.e., statements not offered to prove the truth of the matter asserted. Because Illinois Rule of Evidence 703 (like Federal Rule of Evidence 703 and other state cognate rules, including Indiana Rule 703) authorizes an expert to base an opinion on out-of-court regardless of whether those statements may themselves be admissible, the out-of-court statement (in this situation, the lab report) is relevant for the limited purpose of explaining the expert's conclusion, not for its truth. In such a case, the credibility of the expert testimony, not the lab report, is ultimately at issue.

This decision was joined by Justice Thomas, who clearly rejected this line of reasoning but nonetheless determined that the Confrontation Clause was not implicated because the lab report lacked the requisite degree of formality needed to trigger constitutional scrutiny. No other member of the Court has signed on to Justice Thomas's Confrontation Clause approach, but as the tiebreaking vote, his opinion is controlling. The dissent, composed of the *Melendez-Diaz* and *Bullcoming* majority, characterized the plurality reasoning that the expert's summary of the lab report was not offered for its truth a "prosecutorial dodge" depending on a "simple abdication to state-law labels." *Williams*, 132 S. Ct. at 2265, 2272 (Kagan, J., dissenting). Instead, the dissent continued its pragmatic approach to out-of-court statements, describing the question as whether the Confrontation Clause allows a State to "introduce[] the results of Cellmark's testing through an expert witness who had no idea how they were generated." *Id.* at 2265.

Williams will surely generate confusion among lower courts and practitioners attempting to discern a rule of decision in similar kinds of Confrontation Clause challenges. However, a majority of the Court who would prohibit the kind of expert testimony in *Williams* appears to be intact, even if the testimony was actually upheld in *Williams* itself.

(7) Absence of Entry in Records Kept in Accordance with the Provisions of Paragraph (6)

Overview.   Rule 803(7) serves the purpose of permitting a fact to be proven by the absence of an entry in the same manner and under the same conditions as Rule 803(6) permits facts to be proven by the existence of an entry. Of course, where an entry is absent, evidence to that effect may not represent hearsay at all, since the preparer of the record (the declarant) may intend to make no assertion about matters not mentioned. Where no assertion is subjectively intended, there can be no out-of-court statement and, consequently, no hearsay.

Foundational Requirements. The foundational requirements for evidence offered pursuant to Rule 803(7) are, with obvious adjustments, substantially similar to those for evidence offered under Rule 803(6). Instead of demonstrating that a record is of the type routinely kept by a business, the proponent of evidence under Rule 803(7) must demonstrate that such a business routinely kept records of matters like the entry not made. In similar fashion, instead of showing a contemporaneous recording, the proponent must be prepared to demonstrate that the matter not mentioned was of such a nature that had it occurred, it would have alerted the record-keeper and been promptly recorded.

Examples. Proof that payments have not been made as indicated by the absence of notations on account ledger, or proof that the patient has not reported a claimed injury to his doctor by reference to absence of notation on the medical chart, could be established by use of this exception. In such cases, special attention should be given in qualifying the record to establish that it would be customary for those responsible to make such notations had information been provided to them.

(8) Public Records and Reports

Proof of Activities of Agency. Rule 803(8) permits proof of the activities of a public office or agency by means of its records. Foundational requirements for this exception are easily satisfied, and where the record is properly authenticated pursuant to Article IX, it will be presumed that responsible persons, acting in the course of their official duties, prepared and maintained accurate entries based upon reliable information.

Examples of evidence admissible as proof of the activities of official agencies include:

- Accounting records of governmental agencies
- Documents and journal entries of courts, legislative bodies, and administrative tribunals
- Certificates of title, registry, death, and birth
- Records of licensing agencies
- Records of deeds and conveyances

Proof of Matters; Observed Foundation. Rule 803(8) also provides for the admission of matters that are observed and reported under a legal duty and that are external to the agency or public office. The admissibility of reports of matters observed is conditioned on three requirements. First, the governmental employer's agent who is the source of the information must have personal knowledge of the event or condition described in the report, as the qualifying phrase "matters observed" clearly imports. Second, the source must be under a legal duty to report the information. Third, the official agency must be legally required to prepare and maintain the record, as the term "duty" implies.

Factual Findings. Finally, Rule 803(8) provides for the admissibility of factual findings resulting from an investigation made pursuant to authority granted by law. The admissibility of investigative reports is parallel to federal practice. *See Beech Aircraft Corp. v. Rainey*, 488 U.S. 153, 109 S. Ct. 439, 102 L. Ed. 2d 445 (1988). Such reports may contain opinions or evaluations resulting from an investigation.

Reports Not Admissible.   The Rule explicitly prohibits the introduction of public reports in the following situations: (1) investigative reports by police and other law enforcement personnel, except when offered by the defendant in a criminal case; (2) investigative reports prepared by or for the government, when offered by the government in a case in which it is a party; (3) factual findings offered by the government in a criminal case; and (4) factual findings resulting from the special investigation of a particular complaint, case, or incident, unless offered by the defendant in a criminal case. These restrictions should apply to any record qualifying under Rule 803(8) but offered pursuant to Rule 803(6).

Trustworthiness Compromised.   In similar fashion to the exception provided for business records in Rule 803(6), Rule 803(8) contains a clause authorizing exclusion where trustworthiness is demonstrably compromised. Accordingly, an official record otherwise satisfying the requirements of the Rule, may be excluded on the basis that the circumstances surrounding the source of the information or the manner of its recording indicate an unusual degree of unreliability.

Current Trends and New Developments

In *Ealy v. State*, 685 N.E.2d 1047 (Ind. 1997), the Indiana Supreme Court undertook an extensive analysis to determine when Rule 803(8)(c) would operate to exclude certain evidence from admission in a criminal case. The Court undertook an extensive analysis of similar provisions in federal and other state judicial systems, and concluded that Rule 803(8) served two functions. The first is to serve as "a watch guard against reports made in an adversarial setting because there is a possible motive to fabricate the contents of the report, and, therefore, the preparer of the report must be in court for cross-examination purposes." Secondly, the Rule addresses the concern that "factual findings that pertain to a critical and contested issue in the case are worrisome without the presence of the author in court for cross-examination."

The Supreme Court explained that a series of inquiries is appropriate to determine whether evidence should be excluded by Rule 803(8)(c).

To determine whether a piece of evidence is inadmissible under Rule 803(8)(c), the trial court must consider first whether the "findings" objected to address a materially contested issue in the case. If the findings are not directed at a material issue, the evidence is admissible; the safeguards contained in the Rule, including the requirement that the evidence evince trustworthiness in all respects, sufficiently protect the defendant. If, however, the contested evidence does or may contain "findings" that are relevant to a material issue, the court must then consider the nature of what is objected to. If the evidence does not contain factual findings—for example, if it contains simple listings or a recordation of numbers—then the evidence is not made inadmissible by Rule 803(8). Finally, if the evidence does contain actual factual findings that are relevant to a material issue in the case, the court must determine whether the report was prepared in anticipation of litigation. If not, then the evidence is admissible. Again, the Court believed that the other safeguards of Rule 803(8) served to adequately protect the defendant.

Recent Developments

In *Napier v. State*, 820 N.E.2d 144 (Ind. Ct. App. 2005), *reaff'd*, 827 N.E.2d 565 (Ind. Ct. App. 2005), an Indiana Court of Appeals ruled on the admission of breath test results by certification documents and a BAC DataMaster Evidence Ticket (BAC ticket) under the Confrontation Clause analysis set forth in *Crawford v. Washington*, 541 U.S. 36, 124 S. Ct. 1354, 158 L. Ed. 2d 177 (2004). The opinion is significant for two reasons. First, the court ruled that, because the information contained in the certificates did not pertain to the ultimate issue of the defendant's guilt, but instead only to the proper functioning of the equipment, a defendant's inability to cross-examine the information contained in the certificates was not similar to the kind of testimonial evidence at issue in *Crawford*. Accordingly, the admission of the breath test instrument certification documents at issue here did not violate the Confrontation Clause. Second, the court ruled that the documents were inadmissible nonetheless, as the State had not presented any foundational evidence, through witness testimony or otherwise, for the certificates. In other words, the court appeared to rule that the certificates were not self-authenticating under Rule 902, but instead required extrinsic authentication as provided in Rule 901.

(9) Records of Vital Statistics

Rule 803(9) creates a hearsay exception for public records relating to births, fetal deaths, deaths, and marriages. It allows the contents of such records to be introduced as substantive evidence, thereby facilitating the proof of a wide variety of information contained in such records.

(10) Absence of Public Record or Entry

Rule 803(10) admits evidence of the absence of a public record or entry in order to prove either the absence of certain documents or the nonexistence or nonoccurrence of a matter regarding which there would normally be a public record. The rule is similar in effect to the provisions of Rule 803(7), which governs proof of the absence of an entry in the records of a regularly conducted business activity. *See* Analysis to Rule 803(7).

(11), (12), (13) Records of Religious Organizations; Marriage, Baptismal, and Similar Certificates; Family Records

Overview. These three exceptions relate to proof of births, marriages, divorces, deaths, legitimacy, relationships, and ancestry. The circumstantial guarantee of trustworthiness of such records and certificates lies in the lack of motivation to fabricate inherent in the information recording process and in the opportunity for scrutiny of the information by others who may be in a position to verify or protest the data recorded. Requirements of authentication of Article IX must be met.

Tombstones, etc. An interesting problem of the best evidence rule, Article X, arises where an inscription on an urn, crypt, or tombstone is being introduced under this exception.

Since the tombstone is being offered to prove its written contents, a photograph of the tombstone or testimony of the inscription would be secondary evidence. Nevertheless, the requisite showing of the unavailability of the original would be easily met in such a case. Since the best evidence rule requires only a showing that the original is not available, any evidence of the tombstone inscription would be admissible. This might be a tombstone rubbing, photograph, or even one testifying as to what he saw on the stone. Any concerns of reliability of such evidence go to the credibility and probative value, not to its admissibility.

(14), (15) Records of Documents Affecting an Interest in Property; Statements in Documents Affecting an Interest in Property

Rule 803(14) recognizes a hearsay exception for all statements contained in a properly recorded deed establishing the interest in the property. Rule 803(15) creates a similar exception for statements relevant to the property interest so long as the dealings with respect to the property since execution of the document are consonant with the statement.

Illustration 1

X offers an unrecorded deed to Blackacre to prove that at the time of execution grantor was an unmarried person.

Objection: Hearsay.

Court: Overruled.

The ruling is correct so long as the instrument is recordable and it was properly recorded.

Illustration 2

A offers an unrecorded lease to Blackacre to prove the existence of a described monument used as part of the property description.

Objection: Hearsay.

Court: Overruled.

The ruling is correct as long as it was established by way of foundation that dealings with respect to the property since execution of the lease were consonant with the declaration.

It should be noted that Rule 803(15) does not require the document to have been recorded or to be subject to recordation. Also, documents affecting personal property as well as real property are within the scope of Rule 803(15), for example, contracts, bills of sale, security agreements, wills, estate inventories, and other documents that establish or affect an interest in property.

Authentication.   Documents embraced by the exception may be self-authenticating under Rule 902(1), concerning domestic public documents, or Rule 902(9), concerning certified domestic records of regularly conducted activity, or they may qualify as ancient documents under Rule 901(b)(8).

(16) Statements in Ancient Documents

Overview.   The "ancient document" hearsay exception applies to documents that are more than 30 years old and whose authenticity can be established. The ancient document hearsay exception, Rule 803(16), directly complements Rule 901(b)(8), which provides for the authentication of a document that is in excess of 30 years old, which is found in its proper repository, and which manifests no indications of suspicion as to the document's authenticity. Consequently, utilizing the ancient document authentication technique will simultaneously satisfy the hearsay exception.

Writings Only.   The ancient document hearsay exception applies only to writings, but it contains no restriction as to the type of writing that will qualify. Consequently, Rule 803(16) may be applied to documents of formal nature, such as wills and deeds as well as other types of writings, such as letters, leases, powers of attorney, receipts, maps, and public surveys.

(17) Market Reports, Commercial Publications

Rule 803(17) authorizes the admission of certain books and reports as substantive proof of the information contained in such sources. The exception applies to market quotations, tabulations, lists, directories, or other published compilations. These reports and publications are admissible where the proponent by way of foundation shows that the publication is one that is both generally used and generally relied upon either by the public or by persons in particular occupations.

Data that is admissible under this exception should include:

- Weather data, either in the meteorological reports or even in the almanac
- Stock market reports as evidence of value of securities on a given day
- Telephone directories to prove telephone numbers (e.g., as part of evidence of authentication of a telephone conversation under Rule 901(b)(6))
- Mail order catalogues to establish value
- City directories to establish addresses
- Blue or red books to prove automobile values
- Membership lists to prove enrollment or membership in institutions or organizations

The admissibility of bottles and other containers with labels or trade inscriptions is frequently mistakenly analyzed under Rule 803(17). For example, a drug possession charge is sometimes proved by possession of an unopened bottle with an ingredient label listing a prohibited or controlled substance. Strictly speaking, this is not a hearsay issue, as the label or trade inscription is being introduced to prove the truth of an underlying fact (presence of the substance in question), rather than to prove the truth of the label or trade inscription itself. Although the distinction is subtle, the question is not properly a hearsay issue. Instead, the issue becomes the self-authenticating status of the exhibit under Rule 902(5).

Authentication.   Many of the writings falling within this exception would be self-authenticating under Rule 902(3) "Official publications," Rule 902(4) "Newspapers and periodicals," or Rule 902(5) "Trade inscriptions and the like." Others would be easily authenticated under Rule 901(b)(7) "Public records or reports," or Rule 901(b)(8) "Ancient documents or data compilations."

(18) Learned Treatises

Rule 803(18) creates a hearsay exception for statements contained in published treatises, periodicals, or pamphlets on a subject of history, medicine, or other science or art established as a reliable authority to the extent that such statements are called to the attention of an expert witness upon cross-examination or relied upon by him or her in direct examination. The reliability of the authority may be established by the testimony or admission of the witness, by other expert testimony, or by judicial notice. Once the authority is established as reliable, statements contained in treatises and the like that are addressed on direct or cross-examination may be considered as substantive evidence. To prevent the possibility of misuse of the evidence by the jury, however, statements contained in books and articles may not be offered as substantive evidence independent of expert testimony.

(19), (20), (21) Reputation Exceptions

Overview.   These exceptions reflect the essential hearsay nature of reputation evidence. Reputation is simply the composite of a large number of out-of-court declarations evincing belief in a particular fact or set of facts. These exceptions permit proof of matters relating to personal or family history, boundaries or general history, or a person's character by reputation evidence. The reputation concerning boundaries or general history must have arisen prior to the matter in controversy.

Relation to Other Rules.   Rule 803(21) serves to reenforce other rules that allow the introduction of reputation testimony in specific situations. For example, under Rule 404(a)(1), an accused in a criminal trial may authorize evidence of his or her character and if he or she does so, the prosecution may offer character evidence in rebuttal. In addition, under Rule 404(a)(2), the accused and the prosecution may, under certain circumstances, offer evidence relating to the character of the victim. In these instances, and also in situations where character itself is "in issue," Rule 405 permits proof of character to be established by testimony as to reputation. The function of Rule 803(21) is to ensure that where reputation evidence is admissible, it may be received for the truth of the matter asserted. Moreover, the reference to "associates" and "community" in Rule 803(21) refers to a variety of settings such as business, church, or social groups, and the only prerequisite to use of the exception is a showing that the person characterized is sufficiently known in the group in question to have permitted others to have become acquainted with him or her such that a reputation has developed.

(22) Judgment of Previous Conviction

Purpose of Rule Limitations.   Subject to express restrictions, Rule 803(22) authorizes the admission of felony convictions in subsequent civil and criminal actions in order to prove any fact essential to the previous criminal judgment. The evidence offered must be that of a final judgment, entered after a trial or guilty plea, but not upon a plea of *nolo contendere*. Additional limitations provide that the previous conviction must relate to a crime punishable by death or imprisonment in excess of one year and that in criminal prosecution, the government may not utilize the prior conviction of persons other than the accused for a purpose other than impeachment. It should be noted that the evidence offered pursuant to Rule 803(22) is merely probative, rather than conclusive, of the fact sought to be proved. In other words, it merely serves as evidence as to the consequential fact sought to be proven.

Facts Provable.   Subject to the limitations of the Rule, this hearsay exception admits evidence of previous convictions in criminal and civil actions as proof of any fact essential to sustain the conviction. Consequently, the proponent must establish not only the conviction itself through, for example, introduction of a certified record, but he or she must also establish that the fact sought to be proved was essential to sustain the prior judgment. Accordingly, the trial judge must determine that issue as a preliminary matter, based upon an examination of the entire record of the prior case, if necessary. Admissibility of a prior conviction to prove a fact essential to that determination also depends upon its relevance in the litigation in which it is offered. In this respect, the proponent may not run afoul of the forbidden inference of Rule 404(b).

Finally, it should be noted that this exception does not impinge upon *res judicata* or collateral estoppel, but it merely makes a felony conviction evidence of the facts underlying the conviction. Moreover, the exception does not give rise either to a shifting of the burden of persuasion or the shifting of the burden of production by establishing a rebuttable presumption.

(23) Judgment as to personal, family, general history, or boundaries

Function of Rule Limitations.   Rule 803(23) authorizes the admissibility of a judgment as substantive proof of certain matters in a subsequent action. The matters that may be proved by this method are limited to those of personal, family, or general history, or boundaries. The exception is further circumscribed by the requirements that the facts sought to be proved must have been essential to the prior judgment and that the matter must be one that would be provable by reputation evidence. The exception is consequently limited in application.

Res Judicata, Collateral Estoppel Distinguished.   The doctrines of *res judicata* and collateral estoppel must be distinguished from the principles reflected in Rule 803(23). The hearsay exception permits the use of judgments as evidence. Nevertheless, such evidence is not conclusive and may be rebutted in the same fashion as any other evidence. This use of a judgment is distinct from the concept of *res judicata*, in which a judgment operates as a bar to further litigation between the same parties concerning the same subject matter. It is also distinguishable from collateral estoppel, which operates as a bar to re-litigation of facts previously litigated between the same parties. A judgment offered under Rule 803(23), then, is merely probative of the fact to which it is relevant.

The elements of this exception are:

- The judgment pertains to matters of personal, family, general history, or boundaries;
- The matter was essential to the judgment;
- *Res judicata* or collateral estoppel do not take the matter out of the realm of proof; and
- The matter is one that could also be proved by the reputation exceptions Rules 803(19) or 803(20).

See Analysis to Rule 803(22), Judgment of previous conviction.

ADDITIONAL AUTHORITY

WEISSENBERGER'S FEDERAL EVIDENCE §§ 803.1–803.88

McCORMICK §§ 254–420

5 WEINSTEIN 2d §§ 803.01–803.30

4 MUELLER & KIRKPATRICK §§ 433–478

5 WIGMORE §§ 1420–1684

6 WIGMORE §§ 1690–1764

COMPARISON TO FEDERAL RULE

Indiana Rule 803(6) permits the foundation for a business record to be established by affidavit.

Federal Rule 803(6) was amended in December 2000. It now states:

(6) *Records of regularly conducted activity.* A memorandum, report, record, or data compilation, in any form, of acts, events, conditions, opinions, or diagnoses, made at or near the time by, or from information transmitted by, a person with knowledge, if kept in the course of a regularly conducted business activity, and if it was the regular practice of that business activity to make the memorandum, report, record or data compilation, all as shown by the testimony of the custodian or other qualified witness, or by certification that complies with Rule 902(11), Rule 902(12), or a statute permitting certification, unless the source of information or the method or circumstances of preparation indicate lack of trustworthiness. The term "business" as used in this paragraph includes business, institution, association, profession, occupation, and calling of every kind, whether or not conducted for profit.

The amendment now allows the foundational requirements to be satisfied through certification and without the expense and inconvenience of producing time-consuming foundation witnesses.

Federal Rule 803(8) prohibits in criminal cases the use of public records containing matters observed by police officers or by other law enforcement personnel. Additionally, Federal Rule 803(8) limits the use of factual findings from an investigation to civil proceedings and to criminal cases in which they are used against the government. Indiana Rule 803(8) contains distinct limitations.

Federal Rule 803(16) establishes 20 years, rather than 30, as the age of ancient documents.

Federal Rule 803(24) provided a separate exception called "Other exceptions" for a statement not covered by other exceptions but having equivalent circumstantial guarantees of trustworthiness. This provision was transferred to Federal Rule 807, effective December 1, 1997.

SIGNIFICANT CASES

Rule 803—In General

Beach v. State, 816 N.E.2d 57 (Ind. Ct. App. 2004) (the State should avoid introducing hearsay statements without calling the declarant to testify in cases where the declarant is in fact available to testify; the discussion of whether *Crawford v. Washington*, 541 U.S. 36, 124 S. Ct. 1354, 158 L. Ed. 2d 177 (2004) completely exempts the State from demonstrating declarant unavailability before admitting "nontestimonial" hearsay statements against a defendant was not required to be decided).

Rule 803(1)—Present Sense Impression

Jones v. State, 780 N.E.2d 373 (Ind. 2002) (a murder victim's statement, identifying a person as her landlord was a contemporaneous description of the person driving by, and thus was admissible under hearsay exception for present sense impressions; however, her statement that she was afraid of her landlord did not describe or explain an event, condition, or transaction that she was perceiving as she spoke, and thus was not admissible under hearsay exception for present sense impressions).

Mullins v. State, 646 N.E.2d 40 (Ind. 1995) (prosecution need not fit breath test results into judicially or statutorily created hearsay exception until defense objects on hearsay grounds to admission of results).

Harrison v. State, 644 N.E.2d 1243 (Ind. 1995), *superseded by statute, Kroegher v. State*, 774 N.E.2d 1029 (Ind. Ct. App. 2002) (Supreme Court rules of procedure, including rules of evidence, prevail over any statute).

Powell v. State, 644 N.E.2d 82 (Ind. 1994) (at sentencing hearing in murder case, sworn statement to police given by friend of defendant, about telephone conversation with defendant in which he told her she should have reason to fear him, was admissible, where statement carried some indicia of reliability and defendant had chance to notify court of any inaccuracies).

Arndt v. State, 642 N.E.2d 224 (Ind. 1994) (admission of three-year-old victim's out-of-court statements did not violate federal constitutional rights of defendant where victim lacked motive to falsify, victim and defendant got along well, victim made statements during bath time while crying and in pain, victim used language appropriate to child his age, and victim repeated statements to more than one person he trusted, even though victim could not understand nature and obligation of oath and thus was unavailable for trial).

Truax v. State, 856 N.E.2d 116 (Ind. Ct. App. 2006) (the contemporaneous nature of a police officer's notes with his telephone negotiations makes the notes admissible as a present sense impression under Rule 803(1)).

Rule 803(2)—Excited Utterances

Hammon v. State, 829 N.E.2d 444 (Ind. 2005), *cert. granted, motion granted*, 546 U.S. 976, 126 S. Ct. 552, 163 L. Ed. 2d 459 (2005) (concluding that the crucial question facing a court analyzing whether a statement violates a criminal defendant's rights under the Confrontation Clause is whether the statement was made with a principal motive of either the person making the statement or the person or organization receiving it to preserve it for future use in legal proceedings), *on remand, remanded*, 853 N.E.2d 477 (Ind. 2006).

Fowler v. State, 829 N.E.2d 459 (Ind. 2005) (trial court determination that statement made 15 minutes after domestic disturbance qualified as excited utterance; defendant's right to challenge admissibility of statement on Confrontation Clause grounds was waived because the defendant allowed the witness to leave the witness stand without challenging her refusal to answer questions on cross-examination and then choosing to not recall her to the stand after her statement was admitted through third-person testimony).

Michigan v. Bryant, ___ U.S. ___, 131 S. Ct. 1143, 179 L. Ed. 2d 93 (2011) (in cases involving police questioning, the fundamental issue in the Confrontation Clause analysis is not whether an "ongoing emergency" exists, but whether the "primary purpose" of the police questioning is for a reason other than to establish or prove past events potentially relevant to later criminal prosecution).

Davis v. Washington, 547 U.S. 813, 126 S. Ct. 2266, 165 L. Ed. 2d 224 (2006) (a statement will be considered "testimonial" for Confrontation Clause purposes when an objective consideration of the circumstances indicate that the statement was not elicited for the purpose of responding to an emergency and that the primary purpose of the interrogation is to establish or prove past events potentially relevant to later criminal prosecution).

Crawford v. Washington, 541 U.S. 36, 124 S. Ct. 1354, 158 L. Ed. 2d 177 (2004) (where testimonial evidence is at issue, the Confrontation Clause of the Sixth Amendment requires both the unavailability of the declarant and a prior opportunity for cross-examination; overruling *Ohio v. Roberts*, 448 U.S. 56, 100 S. Ct. 2531, 65 L. Ed. 2d 597, 17 Ohio Op. 3d 240 (1980), in part).

White v. Illinois, 502 U.S. 346, 112 S. Ct. 736, 116 L. Ed. 2d 848 (1992) (the Confrontation Clause does not require the production of the declarant at trial or a finding of unavailability in order to admit statement under the spontaneous declaration exception).

Davenport v. State, 749 N.E.2d 1144 (Ind. 2001) (in determining whether evidence falls under the "excited utterance" exception of the hearsay rule, the trial court merely determines whether the evidence is sufficient to allow the trier of fact to find, by a preponderance of evidence, that the speaker was under the stress of the startling event or condition; trial court properly admitted 911 call of five-year-old boy as an excited utterance because he experienced a startling event—finding the body of his mother—and then called 911 to report this finding, he did not have time to reflect, and the police officers who arrived at the house a few minutes later confirmed this when they described him as confused, in shock, upset, and fidgety).

Noojin v. State, 730 N.E.2d 672 (Ind. 2000) (although not specifically stated in the Rule, it is assumed that an excited utterance must be based on the declarant's personal knowledge; thus, it was error to admit declarant's statement that defendant "killed [the victims]" as an excited utterance because she did not actually witness the acts, however, error was harmless in view of its lack of persuasive force).

Jenkins v. State, 725 N.E.2d 66 (Ind. 2000) (declarant's statements regarding consensual sex versus rape made 2½ hours after arrest did not constitute excited utterances under the hearsay rule because declarant had ample time free of any ongoing effects of the arrest and his learning of the charges against him to reflect and compose a statement).

Yamobi v. State, 672 N.E.2d 1344 (Ind. 1996) (murder victim's identification of defendant as his assailant was admissible under excited utterance exception even though it was in response to police officer's question and as late as one hour after the shooting; officer did not interrogate victim or suggest a specific answer but only asked who shot him, and given that victim was lying prostrate and suffering from what would be life-ending injury, court could reasonably conclude victim was still under stress of shooting when officer arrived; amount of time that passed after startling event is not dispositive, and declaration does not lack spontaneity merely because it was response to a question).

Williams v. State, 546 N.E.2d 1198 (Ind. 1989), *superseded*, 716 N.E.2d 897 (Ind. 1999) (excited utterance by a three-year-old child held to be admissible although the child was not competent to testify as a witness).

Matthews v. State, 515 N.E.2d 1105 (Ind. 1987) (where there was no evidence presented as to when the incident occurred during a two-day time period, the trial court could not determine the length of time between the charged offense and the child's declarations; statements not admitted as excited utterances).

King v. State, 508 N.E.2d 1259 (Ind. 1987) (proof of startling event sufficient to still the declarant's reflective faculties required for statement to qualify as an excited utterance).

Holmes v. State, 480 N.E.2d 916 (Ind. 1985) (spontaneous statements made by bystanders are admissible as excited utterances).

Reburn v. State, 421 N.E.2d 604 (Ind. 1981) (court held that statement made three hours after the event was not admissible as an excited utterance).

Frye v. State, 850 N.E.2d 951 (Ind. Ct. App. 2006), *transfer denied*, 860 N.E.2d 592 (Ind. 2006) (witness's statement occurred when she was distraught, crying, and hysterical, and her statement related to the event that was occurring or had occurred immediately beforehand; statement in the present case fits within the nontestimonial definition provided by the Supreme Court in *Davis v. Washington*, 547 U.S. 813, 126 S. Ct. 2266, 165 L. Ed. 2d 224 (2006)).

Fowler v. State, 809 N.E.2d 960 (Ind. Ct. App. 2004), *superseded*, 829 N.E.2d 459 (Ind. 2005) (wife's "excited utterance" not "testimonial" under the holding of *Crawford v. Washington*, 541 U.S. 36, 124 S. Ct. 1354, 158 L. Ed. 2d 177 (2004) because it was not given during any type of pretrial hearing or deposition and it was not contained within a "formalized" document of any kind).

Hammon v. State, 809 N.E.2d 945 (Ind. Ct. App. 2004), *rev'd, Davis v. Washington*, 547 U.S. 813, 126 S. Ct. 2266, 165 L. Ed. 2d 224 (2006) (wife's "excited utterance" not "testimonial" under the holding of *Crawford v. Washington*, 541 U.S. 36, 124 S. Ct. 1354, 158 L. Ed. 2d 177 (2004) because it was not given during any type of pretrial hearing or deposition and it was not contained within a "formalized" document of any kind), *on remand, remanded, Hammon v. State*, 853 N.E.2d 477 (Ind. 2006).

Jones v. State, 800 N.E.2d 624 (Ind. Ct. App. 2003) (the test for determining whether a statement qualifies as an excited utterance is not mechanical in nature; instead, the admissibility of the statement turns on whether it was inherently reliable because the witness was under the stress of the event and unlikely to make deliberate falsifications; the heart of the inquiry is whether the declarant was incapable of thoughtful reflection).

Williams v. State, 782 N.E.2d 1039 (Ind. Ct. App. 2003) (when considering whether a statement qualifies as an excited utterance, the amount of time that has passed is not dispositive, and the court must look at the underlying question of whether the statement is inherently reliable; a declaration does not lack spontaneity simply because it was an answer to a question but must be unrehearsed and made while still under the stress of excitement from the startling event).

Marcum v. State, 772 N.E.2d 998 (Ind. Ct. App. 2002) (the test of whether a statement satisfies the excited utterance exception to the Rule excluding hearsay involves the determination of whether the statement was inherently reliable because the witness was under stress of event and unlikely to make deliberate falsifications; lapse of time between event and statement is one focus of court in deciding whether statement is excited utterance).

Gordon v. State, 743 N.E.2d 376 (Ind. Ct. App. 2001) (in defendant's trial for battery, the victim's statements to the police officer that defendant had hit her were admissible as excited utterances because she spoke to the officer five minutes after placing a 911 call and was still visibly distressed).

Impson v. State, 721 N.E.2d 1275 (Ind. Ct. App. 2000) (police officer's testimony regarding victim's statements at the time of battery were admissible as substantive evidence under the excited utterances exception to the hearsay rule and for impeachment purposes).

City of Indianapolis v. Taylor, 707 N.E.2d 1047 (Ind. Ct. App. 1999) (the excited utterance exception applies only where the declarant personally witnessed the event about which he speaks, although direct evidence of the personal observation where the personal observation can be proven by circumstantial evidence; thus, it is sufficient if it can be inferred that the declarant personally observed the event, and there is nothing to make the inference that he did not observe the event more probable).

Carter v. State, 683 N.E.2d 631 (Ind. Ct. App. 1997) (holding that trial court did not err in allowing neighbors to testify that the defendant's child had stated that the defendant "took the gun and went bang"; although the excited utterance exception requires that the declarant have personal knowledge of the event he is describing and there was no direct evidence that the declarant personally observed the shooting, the evidence did lead to the inference that the child witnessed the shooting, rendering the statement admissible).

Rule 803(3)—Then Existing Mental, Emotional, or Physical Condition

White v. Illinois, 502 U.S. 346, 112 S. Ct. 736, 116 L. Ed. 2d 848 (1992) (the Confrontation Clause does not require the production of the declarant at trial or a finding of unavailability in order to admit statement under the medical examination exception).

United States v. Levine, 5 F.3d 1100 (7th Cir. 1993), *vacated*, 1997 U.S. App. LEXIS 34124 (7th Cir. Dec. 3, 1997) (statements that murder victims made in months preceding their deaths regarding alleged embezzlement by defendant from victims' businesses were admissible as evidence to show defendant's state of mind and defendant's motive for hiring an assassin).

Camm v. State, 908 N.E.2d 215 (Ind. 2009) (the out-of-court statement by the defendant's wife that that "she was expecting her husband home between 7:00 and 7:30" was sought to be admitted as circumstantial proof of the fact believed, and thus was not a statement of the declarant's state of mind but rather was a statement of her expectation of the defendant's actions).

Lasater v. House, 841 N.E.2d 553 (Ind. 2006) (although a statement may be admissible to prove a testator's state of mind, the question of whether the statements are admissible for the purpose of proving undue influence is not covered by the hearsay analysis).

Bassett v. State, 795 N.E.2d 1050 (Ind. 2003) (it was erroneous to admit testimony concerning the victim's prior declarations that she feared the defendant or that the defendant had threatened her because the victim's fear was not relevant to a determination of a fact at issue in the case).

Hatcher v. State, 735 N.E.2d 1155 (Ind. 2000) (witness's testimony that she heard the victim tell police that she was scared that defendant was going to kill her was inadmissible under the exception to the hearsay rule for statements of declarant's then existing state of mind; the court refused to extend the list of admissibility (i.e., intent of victim to act in a particular way, when defendant puts the victim's state of mind in issue, and to explain physical injuries suffered by victim) to include the admissibility of a victim's state of mind to show the nature of a relationship between the victim and defendant; although the nature of the relationship may be relevant to motive, motive does not constitute an exception to the hearsay rule).

Monegan v. State, 721 N.E.2d 243 (Ind. 1999) (statement, "I told you not to f**k with me, mother f**ker," which witness heard a few seconds after hearing a gunshot, was not admissible in murder prosecution under excited utterance exception to the hearsay rule, where witness did not see defendant utter the incriminating words).

Smith v. State, 721 N.E.2d 213 (Ind. 1999) (declarant's statements regarding what victim said on day of murder were not admissible under state of mind exception to hearsay rule because state failed to identify any issue in the case that turned on victim's state of mind).

Spencer v. State, 703 N.E.2d 1053 (Ind. 1999) (statements by murder victim made hours or days after beatings inflicted by defendant do not constitute statements of the victim's then existing state of mind, because the statements were not sufficiently contemporaneous with the victim's mental emotions).

Ford v. State, 704 N.E.2d 457 (Ind. 1998) (witness's testimony that victim stated she wanted to leave her husband, the defendant, but was afraid that he would kill her if she did so constituted a statement of declarant's then-existing statement of mind and was admissible, because it indicated that victim was fearful of defendant and was offered to controvert directly evidence presented by the defendant to show that victim acted aggressively toward him and provoked his actions).

Montgomery v. State, 694 N.E.2d 1137 (Ind. 1998) (trial court did not err by allowing officers who arrived at the scene several minutes after the victim had been shot four times to testify as to the victim's response when asked who had shot him; the court explained that being shot is clearly a traumatic event sufficient for the purposes of the excited utterance exception, and that there was no evidence that either the officers or other bystanders had suggested that the victim identify the defendant as his assailant).

Wrinkles v. State, 690 N.E.2d 1156 (Ind. 1997) (in a prosecution for murder, it was error, although harmless, to allow a witness to testify as to the contents of telephone conversations she had with the victim a few days prior to the murder; although the court recognized that the calls related to the victim's then-existing state of mind, namely that she was fearful of the defendant, the court stated that the victim's state of mind was not relevant to any issues in the case).

Lock v. State, 567 N.E.2d 1155 (Ind. 1991) (where victim's fear of defendant was put at issue by defendant, declarations of victim were admissible to show her state of mind).

Light v. State, 547 N.E.2d 1073 (Ind. 1989) (victim's statement expressing fear of defendant not admissible where victim's state of mind was not a material issue in the case).

Simmons v. State, 746 N.E.2d 81 (Ind. Ct. App. 2001) (stepmother's testimony about child's statement that she was putting her hands between her legs because defendant was hurting her was a statement of what caused her pain and was, therefore, inadmissible under the then existing mental, emotional, or physical condition for hearsay).

Rule 803(4)—Statements for Purposes of Medical Diagnosis or Treatment

VanPatten v. State, 986 N.E.2d 255, 261 (Ind. 2013) (when a statement of a child declarant is sought to be admitted under Rule 803(4), additional foundational evidence is required that demonstrates that the child understood the professional's role in order to trigger the motivation to provide truthful information).

Jackson v. State, 925 N.E.2d 369 (Ind. 2010) (although statements by close family members may qualify for the Rule 803(4) medical treatment exception to the rule excluding hearsay, an unidentified bystander does not enjoy the close relationship necessary to impute any indicia of reliability).

Sibbing v. Cave, 922 N.E.2d 594 (Ind. 2010) (Rule 803(4) applies only to statements made by persons who are seeking medical diagnosis or treatment, not to statements made by physicians or others providing treatment).

Cleveland, C., C. & I. R. Co. v. Newell, 104 Ind. 264, 3 N.E. 836 (1885) (a physician may testify concerning statements made by the declarant describing an existing physical condition when the information was necessary for treatment).

Gaddie v. Manlief (In re H.R.M.), 864 N.E.2d 442 (Ind. Ct. App. 2007) (before a statement may be admitted under the medical records exception to the Rule excluding hearsay, there must be evidence that the person making the statement was aware that the statement was being made for that reason; a child's statement made to a social worker was inadmissible because the child was unaware that the interview during which the statement was made was for diagnostic purposes).

Dyer v. Doyle (In re Estate of Dyer), 870 N.E.2d 573 (Ind. Ct. App. 2007) (although Rule 803(4) will operate to admit statements contained within medical records, the actual medical opinions and diagnoses must satisfy the requirements for expert opinions set out in Rule 702), *transfer denied*, 878 N.E.2d 221 (Ind. 2007).

Miles v. State, 777 N.E.2d 767 (Ind. Ct. App. 2002) (victim's statements to nurse and physician were admissible under exception to hearsay rule governing statements made for the purpose of diagnosis and treatment).

Bartrum v. Grant County Office of Family & Children (In re W.B.), 772 N.E.2d 522 (Ind. Ct. App. 2002) (statements made for purposes of medical diagnosis or treatment are permitted as an exception to the hearsay rule based upon the belief that a declarant's self-interest in seeking medical treatment renders it unlikely that declarant will mislead the person he wants to treat him; however, any facts within a medical history given by the patient are not admissible as substantive evidence).

McGrew v. State, 673 N.E.2d 787 (Ind. Ct. App. 1996), *aff'd in part, vacated in part on other grounds* 682 N.E.2d 1289 (Ind. 1997) (hearsay statements offered to demonstrate victim's mental state before crime are admissible if legally relevant under state of mind exception to hearsay rule; statement by victim of criminal deviate conduct that she was forced by defendant to perform oral sex was not admissible over hearsay objection to demonstrate victim's mental state after incident, since victim's state of mind was not probative as to whether defendant acted knowingly or intentionally, and even if victim's state of mind was relevant to issue of whether defendant "forced" her to engage in sexual act, defendant did not raise issue of consent; victim's statement that defendant pulled her hair recounted painful experience in past and did not describe pain she was presently experiencing so as to be admissible under hearsay exception for statements concerning declarant's then-existing physical condition).

Taylor v. State, 659 N.E.2d 535 (Ind. 1995) (murder victim's statement to police officer, that she had been afraid to come forward with sexual abuse allegations at earlier time, was admissible despite hearsay objection because it reflected her then present state of mind).

Fleener v. State, 648 N.E.2d 652 (Ind. Ct. App. 1995), *aff'd in part and vacated in part*, 656 N.E.2d 1140 (Ind. 1995) (statement by child sexual abuse victim that her "bottom was sore," made to victim's grandmother while she gave victim a bath, was admissible under hearsay exception as statement of then-existing sensation or physical condition).

Rule 803(5)—Recorded Recollection

Kubsch v. State, 866 N.E.2d 726 (Ind. 2007) (the recorded recollection exception applies when a witness has insufficient memory of the event recorded, but the witness must be able to vouch for the accuracy of the prior statement; in this case, the witness testified twice that she had no memory of being interviewed by the police as a child in 1998, and the statement was properly excluded).

Clark v. State, 808 N.E.2d 1183 (Ind. 2004) (statement was not properly admitted under Rule 803(5) because the statement was introduced as an exhibit, which the Rule prohibits).

Small v. State, 736 N.E.2d 742 (Ind. 2000) (state properly read portions of a witness's deposition into evidence because she could not recall the exact answers she previously gave during her deposition and could not recall making the specific statements documented in her deposition even after careful review).

Baran v. State, 639 N.E.2d 642 (Ind. 1994) (admission of a probable cause affidavit prepared by a state trooper was not error because affidavit constituted a past recollection recorded).

Gee v. State, 271 Ind. 28, 389 N.E.2d 303 (1979) (where the witness's memory is completely exhausted and cannot be refreshed, accurate written documents prepared by the witness at or near the time of the event may be admissible as a past recollection recorded).

Ballard v. State, 877 N.E.2d 860 (Ind. Ct. App. 2007) (under Rule 803(5), a party failed to lay a proper foundation for the introduction of a prior recorded statement because the person making the statement did not remember making it and could not vouch for it).

Impson v. State, 721 N.E.2d 1275 (Ind. Ct. App. 2000) (prosecutor did not commit prosecutorial misconduct in calling attention to battery affidavit because it falls within hearsay exception for recorded recollection, victim had insufficient memory of attack, victim signed affidavit on day of attack, and the affidavit was consistent with victim's statements to police officer and others indicating that it reflected her knowledge correctly).

Smith v. State, 719 N.E.2d 1289 (Ind. Ct. App. 1999) (trial court did not err in allowing security report from seven years ago to be read into record under recorded recollection exception to the hearsay rule; complete exhaustion of the witness's memory is not required to introduce evidence under this exception).

Mejia v. State, 702 N.E.2d 794 (Ind. Ct. App. 1998) (police officer's handwritten asterisks and notations on list of serial numbers of money given to confidential informant and photocopy of actual currency given to informant were admissible as recorded recollections where the police officer had personal knowledge of the serial numbers of the currency given to him when he made those notations).

Flynn v. State, 702 N.E.2d 741 (Ind. Ct. App. 1998) (for a past recollection recorded to be admissible as a hearsay exception, a witness must have personal knowledge of the event that she contemporaneously recorded or adopted, if recorded by another, while she retained a clear memory of it; also, the party offering the recording must establish that the witness has no present recollection of the events to be proven).

Woodworth v. Estate of Yunker, 673 N.E.2d 825 (Ind. Ct. App. 1996) (testimony of claimant, who sought to recover from testator's estate under alleged oral contract for care services, regarding statement of testator creating contract was not admissible as excited utterance or *res gestae* exception to dead man's statute, insofar as no such exceptions existed to alter claimant's incompetence, under statute, as a witness; further, testator's purported statement was not excited utterance since statement did not relate to startling event or condition).

McGrew v. State, 673 N.E.2d 787 (Ind. Ct. App. 1996), *aff'd in part, vacated in part on other grounds*, 682 N.E.2d 1289 (Ind. 1997) (admission of hearsay statement under excited utterance exception is not precluded because statement was made in response to questions from witnesses; the fact that victim left crime scene and travelled some distance to report crime does not preclude excited utterance exception; here, statements made by victim of criminal deviate conduct, that defendant forced her to perform oral sex and pulled her hair were not admissible under excited utterance exception where victim traveled some distance after accident, ordered a drink, and calmed herself before making statements).

Thomas v. State, 656 N.E.2d 819 (Ind. Ct. App. 1995) (attack victim's statements to physician concerning cause of injuries were admissible under hearsay exception, since they were made for purpose of diagnosis and treatment of injuries).

Coffey v. Coffey, 649 N.E.2d 1074 (Ind. Ct. App. 1995) (in dissolution action, letter from husband's physician about husband's medical condition and diagnosis was admissible under hearsay exception, as statements were made for purposes of medical diagnosis or treatment).

Fleener v. State, 648 N.E.2d 652 (Ind. Ct. App. 1995), *aff'd in part and vacated in part*, 656 N.E.2d 1140 (Ind. 1995) (statements by child sexual abuse victim to psychologist were admissible under hearsay exception as statements made for purposes of medical diagnosis or treatment even though psychologist was not physician; statements made to someone other than physician may be admissible under hearsay exception where declarant subjectively believes he is making statement in contemplation of receiving medical diagnosis or treatment; victim's statements concerned her inability to exclude thoughts of molestation from her mind, and statements were basis for psychologist's diagnosis of post-traumatic stress syndrome).

Blinn v. State, 487 N.E.2d 462 (Ind. Ct. App. 1986) (in order to admit a document under the past recollection recorded exception to the hearsay rule, it must be shown that the witness lacks present recollection).

Rule 803(6)—Business Records

Williams v. Illinois, ___ U.S. ___, 132 S. Ct. 2221, 183 L. Ed. 2d 89 (2012) (the Confrontation Clause does not prohibit an expert from expressing an opinion based on facts that have been made known to the expert but about which the expert is not competent to testify) (plurality opinion).

Bullcoming v. New Mexico, ___ U.S. ___, 131 S. Ct. 2705, 180 L. Ed. 2d 610 (2011) (the certification of an analyst who did not sign a DUI report or personally observe the test does not satisfy the Confrontation Clause).

Melendez-Diaz v. Massachusetts, 557 U.S. 305, 129 S. Ct. 2527, 174 L. Ed. 2d 314 (2009) (drug lab reports constitute affidavits which fall within the "core class of testimonial statements" covered by the Confrontation Clause; accordingly, the prosecution must produce the analysts who prepared the report for cross-examination or the report will not be admissible).

Weir v. Crown Equip. Corp., 217 F.3d 453 (7th Cir. 2000) (merely asserting that reports were a report of events, conditions, opinions, or diagnosis, made at a time or near the time by a person with knowledge and kept in the course of a regularly conducted business activity and that it was the regular practice of that business activity to make the report was insufficient to satisfy the business records exception to the hearsay rule).

Pendergrass v. State, 913 N.E.2d 703 (Ind. 2009) (it was sufficient for Confrontation Clause purposes for the prosecution to supply a supervisor with direct involvement in a laboratory's technical processes and the expert who rendered an opinion based on the lab results).

In re Termination of the Parent-Child Rel. of E.T., 808 N.E.2d 639 (Ind. 2004) (concluding that reports compiled by a social services agency describing home visits and supervised visitations do not qualify as business records and thus are inadmissible under Rule 803(6)).

Games v. State, 743 N.E.2d 1132 (Ind. 2001) (defendant's disciplinary record from the Department of Correction was properly admitted as rebuttal evidence under the business records exception to the hearsay rule; in any event, a trial court may consider hearsay in a sentencing proceeding).

Holmes v. State, 671 N.E.2d 841 (Ind. 1996) (in prosecution for capital murder of restaurant's night shift manager, notes by night shift manager to day shift manager about defendant's problems with fellow employee on day defendant was fired were admissible under hearsay exception for business records).

Humbert v. Smith, 664 N.E.2d 356 (Ind. 1996) (statute permitting blood and genetic test results to be admitted without establishing a foundation if party opposing admission fails to file written objection at least 30 days before hearing at which test results may be offered has no force and effect insofar as it conflicts with evidence rule requiring foundation for admission of reports under the business records exception to the hearsay rule).

Campbell v. State, 500 N.E.2d 174 (Ind. 1986) (in admission of documents as business records, witness must testify the records were made at or near the time of the event or transaction).

Landers v. State, 464 N.E.2d 912 (Ind. 1984) (entry must be made in the routine course of business).

Brandon v. State, 272 Ind. 92, 396 N.E.2d 365 (1979) (in a business record, entry must be made by employee who was under a duty to make such an entry and who had personal knowledge of the transaction).

Dyer v. Doyle (In re Estate of Dyer), 870 N.E.2d 573 (Ind. Ct. App. 2007) (medical opinions and diagnoses contained within medical or hospital records historically have not been admissible under the business records exception to the Rule excluding hearsay because their accuracy cannot be evaluated without the safeguard of cross-examination of the person offering the opinion), *transfer denied*, 878 N.E.2d 221 (Ind. 2007).

Rolland v. State, 851 N.E.2d 1042 (Ind. Ct. App. 2006) (the fact that information could be amended or changed within the Bank's computer records does not change the fact that the Customer Information Screen (CIS) is a business record kept in the normal course of business).

Wilkinson v. Swafford, 811 N.E.2d 374 (Ind. Ct. App. 2004) (medical opinions and proposed treatment plan produced by a doctor after examination of a patient memorializes the examination and are prepared in the regular course of business within the physicians' practice; statement by another doctor that his personal practice was to dictate a report immediately after seeing the patient, in addition to the fact that the report was dated the same day as the examination, was sufficient to establish the reliability of the record).

J.L. v. State, 789 N.E.2d 961 (Ind. Ct. App. 2003) (Rule 803(6) applies to "data compilation, in any

HEARSAY

form," a category sufficiently broad to include computer-stored records electronically printed on demand; the proponent of an exhibit under Rule 803(6) may authenticate the evidence by calling a witness who has a functional understanding of the record-keeping process of the business with respect to the specific entry, transaction, or declaration contained in the document, and by establishing that the data compilation or record is regularly made).

Schaefer v. State, 750 N.E.2d 787 (Ind. Ct. App. 2001) (hospital records of victim of child molestation could not be excluded simply because they contained opinions or diagnosis, but for the medical opinions or diagnosis to be admitted into evidence, they must meet the requirements of Rule 702 for expert opinions).

Jennings v. State, 723 N.E.2d 970 (Ind. Ct. App. 2000) (in child molestation case, profile report of defendant was admissible under the public records exception to the hearsay rule to prove defendant's age).

Ground v. State, 702 N.E.2d 728 (Ind. Ct. App. 1998) (rebuttable presumption that entries in business records were made by a person who had a duty to make the record and who had personal knowledge of the event represented by the entry; thus, absent rebuttal evidence to the contrary, it may be presumed that someone with personal knowledge prepared the bank documents).

Schloot v. Guinevere Real Estate Corp., 697 N.E.2d 1273 (Ind. Ct. App. 1998) (holding that hospital records are admissible under the business records exception only if their contents are otherwise admissible under the Rules of Evidence, and that expressions of medical opinion contained within hospital records are not admissible because their accuracy cannot be evaluated without the safeguard of cross-examination of the person offering the opinion).

Fowler v. Napier, 663 N.E.2d 1197 (Ind. Ct. App. 1996) (DNA test results were admissible in paternity proceeding under business record exception to hearsay rule, where testing lab's report was prepared by lab's director, testing accorded to lab's standard protocol, and director's report was notarized).

Faulkner v. Markkay of Ind., 663 N.E.2d 798 (Ind. Ct. App. 1996) (in slip-and-fall action against store, customer's claim that trial court erred in refusing to admit orthopedic surgeon's report under business records exception to hearsay rule was deemed waived, where each time customer offered report objection to its admission was sustained but customer never introduced report under business records exception or brought exception to attention of trial court).

Payne v. State, 658 N.E.2d 635 (Ind. Ct. App. 1995) (in habitual offender phase of felony robbery prosecution, prior arrest records of defendant were admissible, where witness testified to being police department's record keeper and testified that arrest records were under his custody, police department kept those records in normal course of business, and persons with business duty to do so kept and recorded arrest information at or near time transactions represented in record occurred; unavailability of witness with firsthand knowledge should not affect business records exception in absence of evidence indicating record is not authentic).

Carmichael v. Kroger Co., 654 N.E.2d 1188 (Ind. Ct. App. 1995) (exhibit including affidavit from custodian of records and report from physician about plaintiff's physical examination after slip-and-fall injury met requirements of hearsay exception for records of routine business activity and was self-authenticating).

D.W.S. v. L.D.S., 654 N.E.2d 1170 (Ind. Ct. App. 1995) (Department of Public Welfare reports, based on accounts by people with no business duty to observe and report facts of alleged child abuse, did not fall within business record exception except insofar as parts of reports established that incident was reported by child's mother and her therapist and properly attested to or authenticated report is admissible only if hearsay statements within report are also admissible under an exception to the hearsay rule).

Reeves v. Boyd & Sons, 654 N.E.2d 864 (Ind. Ct. App. 1995) (in personal injury action arising from car accident, any error in admission of emergency room medical record with plaintiff's blood alcohol content test result without opposing party's satisfaction of four-pronged foundation requirement was harmless, where emergency room doctor's testimony and explanation of medical records did not suggest that report of test result was untrustworthy, and thus inadmissible under business records exception, doctor's conclusion as expert witness that plaintiff was intoxicated could be based on inadmissible records, and test result was cumulative to other evidence of intoxication).

Donaldson v. Indianapolis Pub. Transp. Corp., 632 N.E.2d 1167 (Ind. Ct. App. 1994) (harmless error where trial court admitted police report that contained statements of various witnesses and a diagram of the accident scene because the statements and diagram were cumulative of other evidence already admitted).

Williams v. Hittle, 629 N.E.2d 944 (Ind. Ct. App. 1994) (financial statements prepared by an accountant to assist plaintiff in preparing taxes were admissible under the business records exception in a breach of lease action against defendant).

Rule 803(8)—Public Records and Reports

Beech Aircraft Corp. v. Rainey, 488 U.S. 153, 109 S. Ct. 439, 102 L. Ed. 2d 445 (1988) (a judge advocate report regarding the crash of a military aircraft was admissible under Federal Rule 803(8) where portions of the report contained opinions and the author's statement as to probable cause of the crash).

Joyner v. State, 736 N.E.2d 232 (Ind. 2000) (information in police investigative reports may be admissible if it meets the requirements of Rule 803(8) and is offered by the accused; however, defendant did not challenge the trial court's exclusion of the police report on the basis of Rule 803).

Thompson v. State, 728 N.E.2d 155 (Ind. 2000) (autopsy reports that do not address a materially contested issue in the case are admissible under the public records exception to the hearsay rule; as the only contested issue in the case was who shot the victim, the autopsy report did not address the contested issue and was admissible).

Bartlett v. State, 711 N.E.2d 497 (Ind. 1999) (documents were used to prove that defendant had committed two previous felonies in other states were admissible where both sets of documents were public records maintained by agencies that regularly keep criminal records).

Wisehart v. State, 693 N.E.2d 23 (Ind. 1998) (noting that, in a criminal case, investigative reports by police and other law enforcement personnel are not rendered admissible by Rule 803(8) except when offered by the accused).

Ealy v. State, 685 N.E.2d 1047 (Ind. 1997) (to determine whether a piece of evidence is inadmissible under Rule 803(8)(c), the trial court must consider: (1) whether the "findings" objected to address a materially contested issue in the case; (2) whether the evidence does actually contain "factual findings"; and (3) whether the report was prepared for advocacy purposes or in anticipation of litigation; if any of these questions are answered in the negative, then the evidence is not made inadmissible by Rule 803(8)).

Collins v. State, 567 N.E.2d 798 (Ind. 1991) (duty to make a public record must be expressly imposed by statute).

Mott v. State, 547 N.E.2d 261 (Ind. 1989) (where the appropriate public official testifies that a document is a true and accurate copy of an original public record, authentication is complete).

Starkey v. State, 266 Ind. 184, 361 N.E.2d 902 (1977) (party offering a public record must show that the document is the written statement of a public official who had a legal duty to make the record, and personal knowledge of the facts within the record).

Napier v. State, 820 N.E.2d 144 (Ind. Ct. App. 2005), *reaff'd*, 827 N.E.2d 565 (Ind. Ct. App. 2005) (concluding that the admission of breath test results by certification documents and a BAC DataMaster Evidence Ticket (BAC ticket) does not violate the Confrontation Clause under

Crawford v. Washington, 541 U.S. 36, 124 S. Ct. 1354, 158 L. Ed. 2d 177 (2004)).

Rhone v. State, 825 N.E.2d 1277 (Ind. Ct. App. 2005), *transfer denied*, 841 N.E.2d 183 (Ind. 2005) (under Rule 803(8), the exception pertaining to "factual findings offered by the government in criminal cases" does not operate to admit an affidavit for probable cause, as the affidavit was prepared for advocacy purposes).

Mazza v. Merkler (In re P.E.M.), 818 N.E.2d 32 (Ind. Ct. App. 2004) (the exception in Rule 803(8) allowing the introduction of investigative reports by police and other law enforcement personnel when offered by an accused in a criminal case does not apply to a defendant in a civil case, and the reports are thus rendered inadmissible under Rule 803(8)).

Serrano v. State, 808 N.E.2d 724 (Ind. Ct. App. 2004) (the trial court improperly admitted a police officer's arrest report as the only evidence of defendant's age, which was a specific element of the charged crime, as the arrest report was inadmissible hearsay under Rule 803(8) and the testifying officer had no personal knowledge of the information contained in the report).

State v. Lloyd, 800 N.E.2d 196 (Ind. Ct. App. 2003) (self-authentication under Rule 902 does not provide an exception to the hearsay rule; however, a certification may also satisfy the public records exception of Rule 803(8) and thus be admissible).

In re E.T., 787 N.E.2d 483 (Ind. Ct. App. 2003), *vacated in part*, 808 N.E.2d 639 (Ind. 2004) (investigative police reports are specifically excluded from the business records hearsay exception because eyewitness statements taken by a police officer are not given in the usual course of the witness's business).

Pitman v. State, 749 N.E.2d 557 (Ind. Ct. App. 2001) (although hearsay is admissible in probation proceedings, the court noted that the court docket and charging information are items of public record that would be admissible as exceptions to the hearsay rule at a proceeding where the rules of evidence were applicable).

Sparkman v. State, 722 N.E.2d 1259 (Ind. Ct. App. 2000) (certified, sealed copy of surveyor's map showing 1,000-foot radius marking did not fall within the public records exception to hearsay because it did not evince the requisite trustworthiness; surveyor's maps typically do not have 1,000-foot radius markings and there was no evidence presented as to who placed it on the map).

Rule 803(16)—Statements in Ancient Documents

Payne v. State, 658 N.E.2d 635 (Ind. Ct. App. 1995) (in habitual offender phase of felony robbery prosecution, court documents demonstrating defendant previously entered guilty plea to robbery and to theft were self-executing and properly admitted as official record, both exhibits included required official certification stamp and clerk of court's signature indicating they were official certified copies of court records).

Nasser v. State, 646 N.E.2d 673 (Ind. Ct. App. 1995) (attestation page with stamped signature of director of Department of Toxicology on document listing police officers certified as breath test operators was not hearsay and was admissible to demonstrate proper certification of officer as breath test operator; attestation was on Department of Toxicology stationery, indicated that officers met operator requirements for breath test machines and included effective dates of recertification).

Steele v. Fowler, 111 Ind. App. 364, 41 N.E.2d 678 (1942) (ancient document is a written document that is at least 30 years old, has been kept in proper custody, has not been altered, and is free of suspicion).

Rule 803(17)—Market Reports, Commercial Publications

Reemer v. State, 835 N.E.2d 1005 (Ind. 2005) (labels of commercially marketed drugs are properly admitted into evidence under Rule 803(17) to prove the composition of the drug, as the contemporary nature of pharmaceutical practice exemplifies the inherent trustworthiness of the labels on cold medication, and federal and state regulations require that drug labels be accurate and trustworthy).

Robertson v. State, 877 N.E.2d 507 (Ind. Ct. App. 2007) (exhibits did not satisfy the market reports hearsay exception under Rule 803(17) because the exhibits were opened and did not meet the second foundational requirement of *Reemer*, which requires some evidence that the contents of the product remained as the manufacturer packaged them; the two unopened, shrink-wrapped heat source canisters were properly admitted under the exception in Rule 803(17) because they were in the same condition as when the manufacturer packaged them) (question should instead be analyzed under Rule 902(5)).

Forler v. State, 846 N.E.2d 266 (Ind. Ct. App. 2006) (because there was a sufficient foundation for the finding that a label on a bottle of starting fluid still contained its original contents, the label is admissible as proof of its contents and for the fact that the defendant possessed those contents).

Rule 803(18)—Learned Treatises

Stallings v. State, 232 Ind. 646, 114 N.E.2d 771 (1953) (in the cross-examination of an expert witness, it may be permissible to read from books not relied on by the expert, if the cross-examiner can establish them as recognized authorities).

Rule 803(20)—Reputations Concerning Boundaries or General History

Roser v. Silvers, 698 N.E.2d 860 (Ind. Ct. App. 1998) (reputation evidence as to customs affecting land applies only to reputation or general consensus evidence and does not permit the admission of specific statements or assertions made by the predecessor in interest regarding a boundary).

Rule 803(22)—Judgment of Previous Conviction

Kimberlin v. DeLong, 637 N.E.2d 121 (Ind. 1994) (prior criminal judgment admissible in civil case if relevance requirements are met).

Lepucki v. Lake County Sheriff's Dep't, 801 N.E.2d 636 (Ind. Ct. App. 2003) (Rule 803(22), which concerns judgments after conviction, is similar in substance to Ind. Code § 34-39-3-1, which provides that evidence of certain final judgments entered after a trial or upon a plea of guilty (but not upon a plea of nolo contendere) is not subject to Rule excluding hearsay; convictions for misdemeanors or traffic offenses are not within the scope of the Rule).

HEARSAY

Chapter 804

Rule 804. Hearsay Exceptions; Declarant Unavailable

Rule 804 reads as follows:

(a) Definition of Unavailability. "Unavailability as a witness" includes situations in which the declarant:

(1) is exempted by ruling of the court on the ground of privilege from testifying concerning the subject matter of the declarant's statement; or

(2) persists in refusing to testify concerning the subject matter of the declarant's statement despite an order of the court to do so; or

(3) testifies to a lack of memory of the subject matter of the declarant's statement; or

(4) is unable to be present or to testify at the hearing because of death or then existing physical or mental illness or infirmity; or

(5) is absent from the hearing and the proponent of a statement has been unable to procure the declarant's attendance by process or other reasonable means.

A declarant is not unavailable as a witness if exemption, refusal, claim of lack of memory, inability, or absence is due to the procurement or wrongdoing of the proponent of a statement for the purpose of preventing the witness from attending or testifying.

(b) Hearsay Exceptions. The following are not excluded by the hearsay rule if the declarant is unavailable as a witness.

(1) *Former Testimony.* Testimony given as a witness at another hearing of the same or a different proceeding, or in a deposition taken in compliance with law in the course of the same or another proceeding, if the party against whom the testimony is now offered, or, in a civil action or proceeding, a predecessor in interest, had an opportunity and similar motive to develop the testimony by direct, cross, or redirect examination.

(2) *Statement Under Belief of Impending Death.* A statement made by a declarant while believing that the declarant's death was imminent, concerning the cause or circumstances of what the declarant believed to be impending death.

(3) *Statement Against Interest.* A statement that was at the time of its making so far contrary to the declarant's pecuniary or proprietary interest, or so far tended to subject the declarant to civil or criminal liability, or to render invalid a claim by

the declarant against another, that a reasonable person in the declarant's position would not have made the statement unless believing it to be true. A statement or confession offered against the accused in a criminal case, made by a codefendant or other person implicating both the declarant and the accused, is not within this exception.

(4) *Statement of Personal or Family History.* (A) A statement concerning the declarant's own birth, adoption, marriage, divorce, legitimacy, relationship by blood, adoption, or marriage, ancestry, or other similar fact of personal or family history, even though declarant had no means of acquiring personal knowledge of the matter stated; or (B) a statement concerning the foregoing matters, and death also, of another person, if the declarant was related to the other by blood, adoption, or marriage or was so intimately associated with the other's family as to be likely to have accurate information concerning the matter declared.

*   *   *   *   *

ANALYSIS

(a) Definition of Unavailability

Overview. Rule 804 establishes a principle of preference for the admissibility of certain types of hearsay. The preference is for in-court testimony over hearsay, and, further, for certain forms of hearsay over a total loss of the evidence. In contrast to the Rule 803 exceptions, the admissibility of the Rule 804 exceptions is dependent upon laying a foundation satisfactory to the court that the declarant is unavailable as a witness. As to the standard of proof for the foundation, *see* Analysis to Rule 104.

Rule 804(a) identifies five types of situations in which a declarant is determined to be unavailable as a witness and in which the condition to the use of the Rule 804(b) exceptions is satisfied. Although the language of Rule 804(a) emphasizes the unavailability of the declarant, the significant issue is whether the declarant's testimony is unavailable. In each of the first three types of situations identified in Rule 804(a), the declarant may be physically present in the courtroom, but hearsay is admissible because his or her testimony is not available. Also, it should be noted that Rule 804(a) provides that if the proponent of the hearsay statement procured the unavailability of the declarant, the declarant is not considered to be unavailable.

Burden of Proving Unavailability. Rule 804 places the burden of establishing the unavailability of a declarant on the proponent of the hearsay and the court must determine whether the declarant is unavailable as a witness. While Rule 804 treats all types of unavailability uniformly, consistent with the Sixth Amendment, there may be a more stringent application of the unavailability standard in criminal cases where the evidence is offered against the accused. *See* Analysis to Rule 801.

Privilege. Rule 804(a)(1) provides that a witness's valid assertion of privilege, exempting him from testifying, satisfies the unavailability requirement of Rule 804. The witness's mere assertion of the privilege, however, is not sufficient to make the witness unavailable. Rather, the court must rule that the assertion of the privilege is justified.

Refusal to Testify.   Rule 804(a)(2) extends the definition of unavailability to include situations in which a witness refuses to testify. The Rule requires that the proponent of the hearsay show more than an indication by the potential witness of an unwillingness to testify. Specifically, the witness must disobey a court order to testify, and this disobedience by the witness in the face of a court order distinguishes a refusal to testify from an assertion of privilege. Without the requirement of disobedience of a court order, the mistaken assertion of a privilege would satisfy the requirement of unavailability.

Lack of Memory.   Rule 804(a)(3) extends prior law by providing that a hearsay declarant is unavailable if he or she testifies to a lack of memory as to the content of the out-of-court declaration. The Rule adopts the modern position that the value of the hearsay outweighs the danger arising from the potential for perjury.

Death or Infirmity.   Rule 804(a)(4) follows the long established tradition in treating as unavailable a declarant who is determined to be dead. As in other instances of unavailability, the burden for demonstrating the death of the declarant is upon the proponent of the hearsay. Rule 804(a) also provides that a witness is unavailable where he or she is subject to a mental or physical infirmity. An obvious difference between infirmity and death is that an infirmity may not be permanent. If an infirmity is temporary, the trial can be continued in the court's discretion until the witness is available.

Absence.   Rule 804(a)(5) provides that if a person is absent and his or her testimony cannot be procured by process or other reasonable means, the witness is not available. The Rule imposes on the proponent of the hearsay an obligation to employ "reasonable means" in attempting to procure the witness.

Constitutional Considerations: Hearsay and the Confrontation Clause

The U.S. Supreme Court's Confrontation Clause jurisprudence rules took a dramatic turn in 2004 with its decision in *Crawford v. Washington*, 541 U.S. 36, 124 S. Ct. 1354, 158 L. Ed. 2d 177 (2004). In *Crawford*, the Supreme Court took a decidedly marked turn, holding that, with respect to "testimonial" evidence, the Confrontation Clause requires both unavailability and a prior opportunity for cross-examination. In this sense, *Crawford* reverses *Ohio v. Roberts*, 448 U.S. 56, 100 S. Ct. 2531, 65 L. Ed. 2d 597, 17 Ohio Op. 3d 240 (1980), and its two-part "firmly rooted" or "particularized guarantees of trustworthiness" Confrontation Clause framework for admitting statements against a criminal defendant.

The Supreme Court's holding in *Lilly v. Virginia*, 527 U.S. 116, 119 S. Ct. 1887, 144 L. Ed. 2d 117 (1999), appears to be affected by *Crawford*. In that case, the Court discussed whether the admission of statements under the "statement against penal interest" exception to the Rule excluding hearsay under state law was sufficiently "firmly rooted" to satisfy the requirements of the Confrontation Clause. In examining the "firmly rooted" hearsay exception doctrine, a plurality of the Court concluded that the reason that such statements were constitutionally permissible under the Confrontation Clause was that they carry "'special guarantees of credibility' essentially equivalent to, or greater than, those produced by the Constitution's preference for cross-examined trial testimony." *See Lilly v. Virginia*, 527 U.S. 116, 128, 119 S. Ct. 1887, 144 L. Ed. 2d 117 (1999) (*citing **White v. Illinois***, 502 U.S. 346, 356, 112 S. Ct. 736, 116 L. Ed. 2d 848 (1992)).

The plurality then discussed whether the "statement against penal interest" hearsay exception under Virginia state evidence law satisfied this constitutional requirement. It noted that such statements are typically admitted in criminal cases under three different sets of circumstances: (1) as inculpatory evidence offered by the government against the declarant; (2) as exculpatory evidence offered by the defendant; and (3) as inculpatory evidence offered by the government against an alleged accomplice of the declarant. Statements in the first category enjoy a "distinguishing heritage" as voluntary admissions of a criminal party-opponent, and the admissibility of statements in the second category are guaranteed under the Due Process Clause if there are considerable assurances of the statements' reliability. *See Chambers v. Mississippi*, 410 U.S. 284, 300, 93 S. Ct. 1038, 35 L. Ed. 2d 297 (1973). The Confrontation Clause is not implicated, however, in these circumstances because either the "accuser" who must be confronted is the defendant himself (the former case) or the statements are being offered by the defendant himself (the latter case).

However, inculpatory statements made by persons other than criminal defendants, the plurality explained, constitute statements triggering classical Confrontation Clause scrutiny. This category also encompasses statements that are inherently unreliable and thus were held to be inadmissible under the Federal Rules of Evidence in *Williamson v. United States*, 512 U.S. 594, 114 S. Ct. 2431, 129 L. Ed. 2d 476 (1994), with respect to the non-self-inculpatory portions of the statements. Though the holding in *Williamson* does not, of course, require the states to construe their own rules of evidence in similar fashion, the *Lilly* plurality reasoned that *Williamson*, read within the context of federal Confrontation Clause jurisprudence, supports the view that the "statement against penal interest" hearsay exception is not sufficiently "firmly grounded" to satisfy the requirements of the Confrontation Clause under the first prong of *Roberts*.

This analysis in *Lilly*, of course, is abrogated in light of the *Crawford* case. Accordingly, inculpatory statements made by persons other than criminal defendants may not be admitted under the Confrontation Clause because they have not been subject to cross-examination, not because, as the *Lilly* Court explained, they do not constitute a "firmly rooted" hearsay exception. The implication in *Lilly* that a "statement against penal interest" may be admissible under the alternative "residual admissibility" test set forth in *Roberts*, which requires a demonstration that the circumstances surrounding the making of the statements bear particularized guarantees of inherent trustworthiness of the statement, has been overruled by *Crawford*. The status of Indiana case law under *Crawford*'s new Confrontation Clause framework must await an analysis on a case-by-case basis. However, the Confrontation Clause protections under *Crawford* may ultimately turn out to be consistent with those under existing Indiana case law.

The Indiana Constitution provides criminal defendants with a right to "face to face confrontation" with an accuser—a right that the Indiana Supreme Court intended to reach farther than both the right to mere "confrontation" under the Indiana Constitution and the Federal Constitution under pre-*Crawford* federal case law. *See* Ind. Const. art. I, § 13; *Brady v. State*, 575 N.E.2d 981 (Ind. 1991); *State v. Owings*, 622 N.E.2d 948 (Ind. 1993). Accordingly, Indiana already provided criminal defendants with greater protection than that under the pre-*Crawford* framework.

Accordingly, Indiana courts have held that prior testimony from an unavailable witness is admissible at a subsequent trial, provided that the defendant had the opportunity to confront the witness when the testimony was originally given. *See, e.g., Atkins v. State*, 561 N.E.2d 797, 801 (Ind. Ct. App. 1990) (testimony given at bail hearing); *Ingram v. State*, 547 N.E.2d 823, 826 (Ind. 1989) (deposition testimony). On the other hand, Indiana courts have refused to admit statements contained in prior testimony where a defendant has never had the opportunity to cross-examine a witness and meet him face to face, on the ground that it violates the Indiana constitutional right of a fact-to-face confrontation. *See, e.g., Brady v. State*, 575 N.E.2d 981 (Ind. 1991) (videotaped testimony taken outside the presence of defendant and used at trial); *Miller v. State*, 517 N.E.2d 64 (Ind. 1987) (videotaped statement of child where defendant received no notice).

In *Hendricks v. State*, 809 N.E.2d 865 (Ind. Ct. App. 2004), an Indiana court of appeals intimated that certain statements of child victims admitted under Ind. Code § 35-37-4-6 would violate the rule announced in *Crawford*. However, resolution of the issue was considered to be unnecessary by the court of appeals, as the case involved the right of confrontation before *Crawford* had been decided. Nonetheless, under the Indiana case law discussed above, it is difficult to see how statements of child victims that are testimonial in nature would satisfy the "face-to-face" confrontation right contained in Ind. Const. art. I, § 13.

(b) Hearsay Exceptions

(1) Former Testimony

Conditions for Admissibility. Rule 804(b)(1) creates a hearsay exception for former testimonial statements by an unavailable declarant where two conditions are satisfied: (1) the statement must have been made while the declarant was testifying as a witness in a proceeding and (2) the party against whom the statement is offered, or in civil cases a predecessor in interest, must have had an opportunity and similar motive to develop the declarant's testimony by direct, re-direct, or cross-examination at the time the statement was made.

Exception Qualified. Several qualifications of this exception should be noted. First, the Rule addresses the hearsay issue only, and it does not affect an objection to the prior testimony evidence based upon some other ground where the live testimony of like content or effect would be objectionable. Second, Rule 804(b)(1) is not the only basis for the admission of a transcript or a deposition. A transcript or a deposition could conceivably satisfy numerous other hearsay exceptions. Third, Rule 804(b)(1) does not dictate the manner in which the former testimony must be proved at trial. Customarily, however, when evidence is admitted pursuant to this hearsay exception, the transcript is merely read into the record in the presence of the trier of fact. Finally, where only a portion of the former testimony or deposition is introduced, the adverse party is entitled to introduce other portions that should in fairness be construed by the trier of fact. *See* Rule 106.

Circumstances. In applying Rule 804(b)(1), it should be noted that the declarant's statements must have been made at a deposition, hearing, or a proceeding. The term "proceeding" should, absent any statutory definition, be broadly interpreted so as to encompass any form of official inquiry conducted in accordance with law, including judicial, administrative, and legislative forms. The term "testimony" should be restricted to only those statements that are sworn, subject to perjury, and on the record.

Tests Focus on Identity of Party. Two key tests must be satisfied in order to admit hearsay pursuant to this exception. These tests are "the opportunity test" and "the similar motive test." It should be noted that these tests focus on the party against whom the hearsay, that is, the transcript, is offered. Focusing on the party against whom the hearsay is offered facilitates the fairness rationale that underpins this exception. "The opportunity test" provides that the party against whom the hearsay is offered must have had an opportunity to examine the declarant at the former hearing. The party against whom the hearsay is offered, must have effectively been present at the former hearing and had an opportunity to conduct some type of examination of that declarant when he or she provided testimony at the former hearing. Only an opportunity is necessary. No actual examination need have taken place. The examination in question could be a cross-examination, a direct examination, or a re-direct examination. It should be noted that in a civil case, the party's "predecessor in interest" will qualify if that predecessor had an opportunity to examine the declarant.

Current Trends and New Developments

The exact purport of the "predecessor in interest" language in the Rule is less than clear. While an expansive reading of this language would appear to reduce the opportunity requirement to a nullity, some federal courts interpreting the identical language in the cognate Federal Rule have read the language broadly to include virtually anyone who would satisfy the similar motive requirement. *See Lloyd v. American Export Lines, Inc.*, 580 F.2d 1179 (3d Cir. 1978), *cert. denied sub nom. Alvarez v. American Export Lines, Inc.* 439 U.S. 969, 99 S. Ct. 461, 58 L. Ed. 2d 428 (1978). In contrast, the same language in the Federal Rule has been subjected to strict application, and it has been held that only a predecessor in privity in the property sense will qualify under the Rule. *See In re IBM Peripheral EDP Devices Antitrust Litigation*, 444 F. Supp. 110 (N.D. Cal. 1978). While reliability and fairness may not be sacrificed by the broader interpretation of the predecessor in interest requirement, the stricter reading more logically comports with the customary meaning of the term "predecessor in interest," and moreover, it preserves the obvious intent of the rule to require more than simply a similarity in motive as between the party developing the testimony at the prior proceeding and the party against whom it is offered at the instant proceeding.

"Similar Motive Test." Under the "similar motive test," the party against whom the hearsay is offered must have had a motive at the former proceeding in examining the

declarant that is similar to the motive this party would have in examining the declarant if the declarant were now available at the instant trial. The motive in question pertains to the motive to develop or refute facts. It should be noted that an identical motive is not required.

Illustration

Assume that *D* is charged with two distinct crimes of murder and robbery involving one occurrence, and further that the crimes are the subject of two distinct trials. The murder case is tried first and at this trial an occurrence witness, *X* who was present at the scene testifies to all the pertinent facts on behalf of the prosecution. The occurrence witness, *X*, dies before the trial of the second case, the robbery case, and is, consequently, unavailable. At the robbery trial, the prosecution may seek to introduce the transcript of *X*'s testimony given at the murder trial. The transcript may be admissible under the prior testimony exception to the hearsay rule because *D*, the defendant, had the opportunity at the earlier trial to cross-examine the occurrence witness, and also, the defendant presumably had a motive at the earlier trial in cross-examining the occurrence witness that is similar to the motive he would have if the witness were available for testimony at the instant robbery trial.

Constitutional Considerations: Showing of Unavailability and the Confrontation Clause

As a general constitutional principle, the state bears the burden in criminal cases to produce the declarant regarding hearsay made at a prior judicial hearing, or to establish that the declarant is unavailable to testify. *See Ohio v. Roberts*, 448 U.S. 56, 100 S. Ct. 2531, 65 L. Ed. 2d 597, 17 Ohio Op. 3d 240 (1980). The prosecution must satisfy this burden in order to utilize hearsay made at the prior judicial proceeding.

The right of confrontation under the Ind. Const. art. I, § 13, is discussed in *Brady v. State*, 575 N.E.2d 981 (Ind. 1991) and *State v. Owings*, 622 N.E.2d 948 (Ind. 1993).

---

(2) Statement Under Belief of Impending Death

"Dying Declaration." The exception contained in Rule 804(b)(2) is traditionally known as the "dying declaration." The exception for deathbed statements, which developed in the common law well before the development of the hearsay system, originally derived its assumed guarantee of trustworthiness from the religious belief that no person would purposefully meet his maker with a lie on his lips. In the more secular world, however, this rationale for the exception has largely been supplanted by the theory that the powerful psychological forces bearing on the declarant at the moment of death engender an impulse to speak truthfully.

Foundation. Rule 804(b)(2) expressly provides that before a dying declaration may be admitted, foundational evidence must be established that the declarant possessed a subjective

belief in the certainty of his or her death. There is no standard rule here as to the adequacy of the foundation, and the requisite consciousness of death may be obtained from many sources, including: The declarant's own words; the opinions of his attending physicians; the nature and extent of his or her wounds or illness; the fact that he or she received last rites; the statements made to the declarant about his or her condition, and any other similar circumstantial factual source.

Subject Matter of Statement. It should be noted that Rule 804(b)(2) requires that the statement concern the cause or circumstances of what the declarant believed to be his impending death.

Illustration

In a homicide case against Jackson, the witness is a physician.

Q: Did you see the declarant (victim) prior to his death?

A: Yes.

Q: How long before he died did you arrive on the scene?

A: Five minutes.

Q: Was there anyone else present?

A: The ambulance attendant.

Q: Did the victim say anything to you?

Objection: Hearsay. The foundation has not been laid for a dying declaration.

Court: Sustained.

Q: *(On voir dire of witness)* Did the ambulance attendant say anything to you?

A: Yes. He said the victim told him that he knew he had only a few minutes to live and hoped that a priest would come before he died.

Q: How soon after you arrived did the victim die?

A: About five minutes.

Q: What did the victim say to you prior to his death?

A: He said, "Jackson shot me. And now I have got to die."

Objection: Move to strike the answer; hearsay.

Court: Overruled.

The rulings by the court are correct. The point of the first objection is that there had been no foundation established that the declarant was aware of his impending death. The statement by the ambulance driver established on voir dire, while probably not admissible under any exceptions to the hearsay rule, would be sufficient under Rule 102 to establish the foundation for a dying declaration. *See* Analysis to Rule 102. There is evidence from which the court could conclude that the victim was under a belief of impending death, and his declaration was made concerning the cause of that death. Therefore, the requirements of the dying declaration have been met.

(3) Statement Against Interest

Scope of Rule; Penal Interest.   Rule 804(b)(3) codifies the historical exception to the hearsay rule for statements against interest. The Rule encompasses the traditional exception for statements against the financial or proprietary interests of the declarant and statements that tend to subject the declarant to civil liability. It significantly expands the traditional exception, however, to include statements that tend to subject the declarant to criminal punishment, that is, statements against penal interest.

Foundation.   The foundational requirements for statements against interest under Rule 804(b)(3) are as follows:

- The declarant must be unavailable as defined in Rule 804(a);

- The declarant must have first-hand knowledge as contemplated by Rule 602;

- The nature of the statement must be such that a reasonable person would not have uttered it unless he or she believed it to be true;

- The statement must be contrary to a pecuniary, proprietary, or penal interest at the time of its utterance; and

- The Rule expressly provides that a statement or confession offered against the accused in a criminal case, made by a co-defendant or other person, implicating the declarant and the accused, is not within the exception.

Statement of Party-Opponent Distinguished.   It is critical to appreciate the distinction between declarations constituting statements against interest, identified in Rule 804(b)(3), and those that are statements of a party-opponent as defined in Rule 801(d)(2). Statements of a party opponent are excluded from the hearsay definition under the Rule's evidentiary scheme without regard to (1) whether the declarant is unavailable; (2) whether the statement was against any particular interest when made; (3) whether the party had any first-hand knowledge of the underlying events; or (4) whether any sort of reasonable person test is satisfied.

Practical Considerations

A statement that would be admissible under the statement against interest hearsay exception will not be admissible where protected by privilege or other exclusionary principle. *See, for example, Mayberry v. State,* 670 N.E.2d 1262 (Ind. 1996).

---

(4) Statements of Personal or Family History

Scope of Rule.   Rule 804(b)(4)(A) admits statements concerning an unavailable declarant's own personal or family history, embracing such topics as "birth, adoption, marriage, divorce, legitimacy, relationship by blood." Rule 804(b)(4)(B) admits declarations concerning these subjects pertaining to another person if the declarant was related by blood, adoption, or marriage, or "was so intimately associated with the other's family as to be likely to have accurate information concerning the matter declared."

The conditions to the admission of statements of personal or family history are threefold:

- Unavailability of the declarant as defined in Rule 804(a) must be established;

- The statement must be restricted to the subject matters described in the Rule; and

- An appropriate relation to or association with the family in question must be shown.

(5) Forfeiture by Wrongdoing

Scope of Rule. Paralleling and perhaps prompted by an Indiana Court of Appeals' adoption of variant of the "forfeiture by wrongdoing" exception to the rule excluding hearsay, *see Roberts v. State*, 894 N.E.2d 1018 (Ind. Ct. App. 2008), Rule 804(b)(5) was added in 2009, and is patterned on the federal rule adopted in 1997. Under the exception, the offering party must show that the party engaged in wrongdoing that resulted in the witness's unavailability and that one purpose was to cause the witness to be unavailable at trial. This requirement distinguishes the variation of the exception adopted in Roberts, which simply made the hearsay exclusion inapplicable for statements made a person rendered unavailable for cross-examination through a criminal act, such as homicide. In this regard, the *Roberts* version of the exception was similar to that rejected by the United States Supreme Court in *Giles v. California*, 554 U.S. 353, 128 S. Ct. 2678, 171 L. Ed. 2d 488 (2008). Under the common law of most states, the "wrongdoing" need not consist of a criminal act, though the issue has not been addressed by Indiana courts.

The Rule does not address the standard of proof to be used in determining whether the conditions for the application of Rule 804(b)(5) have been satisfied. However, the preponderance of the evidence standard is applicable under the analogous Federal Rule, and there is no reason to believe that the result would be different under the Indiana version of the Rule.

Constitutional Considerations: Forfeiture by Wrongdoing and the Confrontation Clause

In *Giles v. California*, 554 U.S. 353, 128 S. Ct. 2678, 171 L. Ed. 2d 488 (2008), the United States Supreme Court struck down California's forfeiture by wrongdoing exception to the rule excluding hearsay. The California hearsay exception was unusual in that it did not require the accused to cause the unavailability of the declarant for the express purpose of preventing the witness from being able to testify at trial. In other words, the hearsay exception did not require any finding of the defendant's intent or purpose in causing that unavailability. In this respect, California's hearsay exception was similar to that established in *Roberts v. State*, 894 N.E.2d 1018 (Ind. Ct. App. 2008), which paralleled the adoption of Indiana's hearsay exception by Rule. However, under the Supreme Court's reasoning in *Giles*, because this kind of exception was not established at the time the Sixth Amendment was passed, statements admitted under the exception will be deemed to have violated the Confrontation Clause in the absence of an opportunity for actual confrontation. The hearsay exception set out in Rule 804(b)(5) is distinguishable from California's hearsay exception and the one established in *Roberts*, and thus should not pose any serious Confrontation Clause issue. The holding of *Roberts*, on the other hand, must be limited to non-testimonial statements, or else it risks a Confrontation Clause violation.

ADDITIONAL AUTHORITY

WEISSENBERGER'S FEDERAL EVIDENCE §§ 804.1–804.34

MCCORMICK §§ 253–261, 276–287, 322

5 WEINSTEIN 2d §§ 804.01–804.08

4 MUELLER & KIRKPATRICK §§ 479–507

5 WIGMORE §§ 1370, 1371, 1386–1389, 1402–1415, 1430–1452, 1455–1477, 1480–1503, 1660–1669

7 WIGMORE §§ 2098–2099

COMPARISON TO FEDERAL RULE

Federal Rule 804(a) provides that a declarant is not "unavailable" where satisfaction of the express provisions of Rule 804(a) is due to procurement or wrongdoing of the proponent of the statement. Federal Rule 804(b)(2) differs from Indiana Rule 804(b)(2), in that the Federal Rule is limited in criminal cases to homicide cases only. Additionally, Federal Rule 804(b)(3) contains a corroboration requirement for statements offered to exculpate the accused in a criminal case.

The 1997 amendments to the Federal Rules of Evidence worked two changes to Rule 804. The first removed Federal Rule 804(b)(5) and transferred its contents to Rule 807. The second added new Federal Rule 804(b)(6); there is no corresponding rule in the Indiana Rules of Evidence.

Under Federal Rule 804(b)(6), a party cannot object to, as hearsay, the admission of statements made by an individual declarant whose unavailability for trial resulted from some deliberate wrongdoing engaged or acquiesced in by that party. The Rule was designed to thwart those who wrongly attempt to keep an adverse witness from testifying from trial. All parties are subject to this Rule, including the government.

In order to overcome an objection under this Rule, the party offering the declarant's statement(s) must establish the following by a preponderance of the evidence:

- The declarant is unavailable, as defined in Rule 804(a)

- The declarant's unavailability was brought about either by some deliberate wrongdoing or acquiescence therein by the objecting party (note that this wrongdoing need not consist of a criminal act)

SIGNIFICANT CASES

Giles v. California, 554 U.S. 353, 128 S. Ct. 2678, 171 L. Ed. 2d 488 (2008) (indicating that the forfeiture by wrongdoing exception requires a showing of intent or purpose by the defendant to prevent a witness from testifying; without such a showing, the statements of the unavailable witness are inadmissible under this Confrontation Clause).

Crawford v. Washington, 541 U.S. 36, 124 S. Ct. 1354, 158 L. Ed. 2d 177 (2004) (where testimonial evidence is at issue, the Confrontation Clause of the Sixth Amendment requires both the unavailability of the declarant and a prior opportunity for cross-examination; overruling *Ohio v. Roberts*, 448 U.S. 56, 100 S. Ct. 2531, 65 L. Ed. 2d 597, 17 Ohio Op. 3d 240 (1980), in part).

Lilly v. Virginia, 527 U.S. 116, 119 S. Ct. 1887, 144 L. Ed. 2d 117 (1999) (confession of criminal accomplice admitted into evidence under Virginia's "statement against penal interest" exception to the Rule excluding hearsay was not "firmly rooted" under *Ohio v. Roberts* and thus did not satisfy the requirements of the Confrontation Clause on that basis).

Rule 804(a)—Unavailability

Ohio v. Roberts, 448 U.S. 56, 100 S. Ct. 2531, 65 L. Ed. 2d 597, 17 Ohio Op. 3d 240 (1980), (reliability of hearsay statements of an unavailable declarant can be inferred where the evidence falls within a "firmly rooted hearsay exception").

Howard v. State, 853 N.E.2d 461 (Ind. 2006) (because opposing party had a full, fair, and adequate opportunity to confront and cross-examine a witness when her pretrial deposition was taken, the Confrontation Clause does not prohibit the introduction of the deposition transcript into evidence; the Indiana Rules of Criminal Procedure do not distinguish between discovery depositions and testimonial depositions, which other jurisdictions have found significant in analyzing the Confrontation Clause issue; nonetheless, the witness was not found to be "unavailable" for trial under applicable statutory law, so the transcript was improperly admitted).

Garner v. State, 777 N.E.2d 721 (Ind. 2002) (for purposes of determining whether the state made a good faith effort to obtain an absent witness's attendance at trial, the good faith obligation may demand effectuation; reasonableness is the test that limits the extent of alternatives the state must exhaust).

Lowery v. State, 640 N.E.2d 1031 (Ind. 1994) (in an action for postconviction relief, witness was unavailable where he refused to testify at trial after being held in contempt by trial judge; at defendant's second trial, no error where trial court admitted a transcript of the witness's sworn testimony from defendant's first trial where defendant had full opportunity for cross-examination).

Stidham v. State, 637 N.E.2d 140 (Ind. 1994) (accomplice's refusal to testify at defendant's second trial made him an "unavailable witness," and thus, transcript of his testimony at first trial was admissible).

State v. Owings, 622 N.E.2d 948 (Ind. 1993) (Indiana Supreme Court, interpreting Indiana Constitution, held that prosecution may use a deposition of an unavailable witness if the deposition bears indicia of reliability).

Ingram v. State, 547 N.E.2d 823 (Ind. 1989) (witness was unavailable where reasonable, but unsuccessful efforts were made to locate the witness).

Diggs v. State, 531 N.E.2d 461 (Ind. 1988) (witness who asserts Fifth Amendment is unavailable).

Abner v. State, 479 N.E.2d 1254 (Ind. 1985) (witness who refused to testify despite the threat of contempt was unavailable).

Johnson v. State, 881 N.E.2d 10 (Ind. Ct. App. 2008) (a requirement of the "protected person" statute is that a hearing must be conducted outside the presence of the jury and that the trial court must find that the hearsay statement is sufficiently reliable; under *Pierce v. State*, 677 N.E.2d 39, 44 (Ind. 1997), the Indiana Supreme Court has articulated the following factors that a court should consider in determining the reliability of a statement being offered at trial: (1) time and circumstances of the statement; (2) whether there was opportunity for coaching; (3) whether there was a motive to fabricate; (4) use of age-appropriate terminology; (5) spontaneity; and (6) repetition).

Proctor v. State, 874 N.E.2d 1000 (Ind. Ct. App. 2007) (the "unavailability" doctrine of Rule 804(a) cannot be imported wholesale into the Confrontation Clause analysis under *Crawford*; accordingly, even if a witness is determined to be "unavailable" under Rule 804(a) because the declarant is unable to recall the events in question, that determination does not render the person unavailable for cross-examination for purposes of the Confrontation Clause; as long as the declarant testifies, the Confrontation Clause is satisfied, even if the declarant is unable to recall the events in question).

Purvis v. State, 829 N.E.2d 572 (Ind. Ct. App. 2005), *transfer denied*, 841 N.E.2d 180 (Ind. 2005) (under the Indiana Protected Persons Statute, Ind. Code § 34-37-4-6, the cross-examination requirement is satisfied when a child, judged incompetent to testify, is available to be cross-examined at a hearing under the statute, even if the child's testimony at the hearing is not coherent).

Bass v. State, 797 N.E.2d 303 (Ind. Ct. App. 2003) (evidence of service of a subpoena should be submitted in support of an allegation that a witness was "unavailable" to testify after being so served; in addition, the statement must also satisfy one of the exceptions listed in subdivision (b) of Rule 804 for an exception to the Rule excluding hearsay to be applicable).

Swanigan v. State, 720 N.E.2d 1257 (Ind. Ct. App. 1999) (trial court did not abuse discretion in excluding letters written by inmate and partner in the crime that tended to incriminate him and exculpate defendant because the letters were not reliable based on trial court's note that letters contained references to drug and alcohol addiction, mental illness, and direct contradictory information regarding culpability).

Kellems v. State, 651 N.E.2d 326 (Ind. Ct. App. 1995) (witnesses who invoked Fifth Amendment privilege against self-incrimination were "unavailable" for purposes of hearsay rule exception).

Crider v. Crider, 635 N.E.2d 204 (Ind. Ct. App. 1994) (in action to set aside conveyance from father to son, hearsay statements allegedly made by father about intentions regarding disposition of property were inadmissible to show truth of matter asserted, as son failed to establish father's unavailability as witness; father's status as residential patient in health care facility did not make him unavailable).

Rule 804(b)(1)—Former Testimony

United States v. Salerno, 505 U.S. 317, 112 S. Ct. 2503, 120 L. Ed. 2d 255 (1992), *vacated*, *United States v. DiNapoli*, 8 F.3d 909 (2d Cir. 1993) (the Court held that former testimony may not be admitted under Federal Rule 804(b)(1) without a showing of satisfaction of the "similar motive" requirement. The Court determined that each of the rule's express elements had to be satisfied before admission of prior testimony).

Garner v. State, 777 N.E.2d 721 (Ind. 2002) (depositions that comport with the principal purposes of cross-examination provide sufficient indicia of reliability to be admissible under hearsay exceptions for prior recorded testimony).

Kidd v. State, 738 N.E.2d 1039 (Ind. 2000) (even though witnesses were only on vacation and were, therefore, unavailable, their depositions were admissible at trial because defense counsel cross-examined the witnesses at their deposition).

Jackson v. State, 735 N.E.2d 1146 (Ind. 2000) (trial court erred in admitting polygraph examiner's deposition because although it comported with the principal purposes of cross-examination and provided sufficient indicia of reliability, the examiner was not unavailable within the meaning of the hearsay exception because the state did not make any effort to obtain his attendance at trial; such error, however, was harmless).

Brown v. State, 671 N.E.2d 401 (Ind. 1996) (former testimony of witness who is presently unavailable but who testified under oath at previous judicial proceeding where available for cross-examination may be admissible).

Lowery v. State, 640 N.E.2d 1031 (Ind. 1994) (at defendant's second trial, no error where trial court admitted a transcript of the witness's sworn testimony from defendant's first trial where defendant had full opportunity for cross-examination).

Stidham v. State, 637 N.E.2d 140 (Ind. 1994) (decision to admit former testimony of unavailable witness is within trial court's discretion; prior recorded testimony is admissible if testimony was given under oath at prior judicial proceeding, if party against whom testimony is offered had chance to cross-examine witness at prior proceeding, and if witness is unavailable at time of later proceeding).

Johnston v. State, 517 N.E.2d 397 (Ind. 1988) (deposition admitted where deponent could not be found for trial).

Moore v. State, 467 N.E.2d 720 (Ind. 1984) (prior testimony admitted where witness died after the hearing but before the trial).

Howard v. State, 816 N.E.2d 948 (Ind. Ct. App. 2004), *superseded*, 853 N.E.2d 461 (Ind. 2006) (the introduction of pretrial testimony into evidence in lieu of live testimony did not violate defendant's Confrontation Clause rights, as the deposition was given under oath and at defendant's request; the fact that defendant was not personally present at the deposition is without merit).

Rhea v. State, 814 N.E.2d 1031 (Ind. Ct. App. 2004) (testimony of a co-defendant at a prior trial was inadmissible at a subsequent trial, as the defendant was not provided with an opportunity to cross-examine the co-defendant at the prior trial and the co-defendant was unavailable as a witness in the subsequent trial).

Hagerman Constr. v. Copeland, 697 N.E.2d 948 (Ind. Ct. App. 1998) (holding that Indiana law does not recognize any distinction between a discovery deposition and a trial deposition, and that testimony from a discovery deposition is admissible pursuant to Rule 804(b)(1) where the party opposing admission had the opportunity to cross-examine the deponent; the court noted that although the adverse party may have expected that the deponent would testify at trial and be subject to further cross-examination at that time, it did not believe that the party's motive to cross-examine at trial would be any different than its motive was during the deposition).

L.K.I. Holdings v. Tyner, 658 N.E.2d 111 (Ind. Ct. App. 1995) (in action by passenger against city and real estate developer for injuries sustained in car accident, driver's deposition was inadmissible at summary judgment hearing even though deposition may have been admissible as hearsay testimony of unavailable witness, where real estate developer and passenger were not parties to action in which deposition was taken, and passenger did not receive notice of deposition and was neither present nor represented by counsel at driver's deposition).

Kellems v. State, 651 N.E.2d 326 (Ind. Ct. App. 1995) (depositions of defendant's alibi witnesses were admissible where witnesses were unavailable, prosecutor had chance to examine witnesses regarding their alibi testimony, and prosecutor had same opportunity and similar motive to develop alibi witnesses' testimony during depositions as he would have at trial; just because evidence is in deposition form rather than live testimony does not affect its admissibility).

Rule 804(b)(2)—Statement Under Belief of Impending Death

Sisk v. State, 736 N.E.2d 250 (Ind. 2000) (defendant argued that the state did not lay an adequate foundation to show that the victim believed death was imminent to admit hearsay testimony; however, the court did not reach the issue because the substance of the officer's testimony regarding the victim's statement was separately received in evidence from two other witnesses without objection).

Anderson v. State, 471 N.E.2d 291 (Ind. 1984) (declarant's statements did not fall within the dying declaration exception where declarant stated that she was all right and did not need an ambulance).

Dean v. State, 432 N.E.2d 40 (Ind. 1982) (declarant must possess the belief that he is going to die for a statement to be admissible as a dying declaration).

Wallace v. State, 836 N.E.2d 985 (Ind. Ct. App. 2005), *transfer denied,* 855 N.E.2d 995 (Ind. 2006) (under the dying declaration exception to the Rule excluding hearsay, a statement will be admissible when made by the declarant under an expectation that death is imminent, regardless of whether death actually occurs; accordingly, the trial court may consider the general statements, conduct, manner, symptoms, and condition of the declarant which flow as the reasonable and natural results from the extent and character of his wound, or state of his illness).

Thompson v. State, 796 N.E.2d 834 (Ind. Ct. App. 2003) (a statement that did not relate to the circumstances giving rise to the imminent death is not admissible under the "dying declaration" exception to the Rule excluding hearsay).

Rule 804(b)(3)—Statement Against Interest

Williamson v. United States, 512 U.S. 594, 114 S. Ct. 2431, 129 L. Ed. 2d 476 (1994) (statement against interest exception should be read narrowly to apply only to those statements that are individually self-inculpatory; exception does not apply to parts of statements that are actually self-exculpatory or to collateral statements that are neutral).

Mayberry v. State, 670 N.E.2d 1262 (Ind. 1996) (statement by victim to paralegal is protected by attorney-client privilege after paralegal spoke of it to police officer, even if officer's testimony regarding statement was otherwise admissible under hearsay exception for statement against interest).

Washburn v. State, 499 N.E.2d 264 (Ind. 1986), *overruled, Ludy v. State,* 784 N.E.2d 459 (Ind. 2003) (statement must have been against the interest of the declarant).

Bryant v. State, 794 N.E.2d 1135 (Ind. Ct. App. 2003) (Rule 804(b)(3) has removed the requirement of corroborative evidence and, as such, is not identical to its federal counterpart; nevertheless, trial courts should evaluate the overall reliability of the proffered statement, and an implicit requirement of reliability is embodied within the Rule).

Newby v. State, 701 N.E.2d 593 (Ind. Ct. App. 1998) (declarant's statements that he had purchased the cocaine and marijuana from defendant, that he owed defendant money for the two ounces of cocaine recovered from his vehicle, and that he expected to purchase five pounds of marijuana from defendant the following night were not statements against penal interest where the declarant had already been caught with drugs in his possession, neither the declarant's decision to reveal his source to the police nor his statement concerning intent to purchase marijuana subjected him to any additional criminal liability, and police officer informed declarant that his cooperation might lessen the chances of his own prosecution).

Davis v. State, 635 N.E.2d 1117 (Ind. Ct. App. 1994) (requirements of Rule 804(b)(3) discussed).

McGraw v. Horn, 134 Ind. App. 645, 183 N.E.2d 206 (1962) (statements contrary to the pecuniary and proprietary interests of the now unavailable declarant are admissible).

Rule 804(b)(4)—Statement of Personal or Family History

In re Paternity of Thompkins, 542 N.E.2d 1009 (Ind. Ct. App. 1989) (witness could testify to declarant's statements concerning declarant's child's parentage).

Emberry Community Church v. Bloomington Dist. Missionary & Church Extension Soc., 482 N.E.2d 288 (Ind. Ct. App. 1985) (witness testified to identity of great grandparents and other family history; "testimony more closely resembles personal knowledge than mere hearsay").

Rule 804(b)(5)—Forfeiture by Wrongdoing

Roberts v. State, 894 N.E.2d 1018 (Ind. Ct. App. 2008) (with respect to non-testimonial statements, a party who has made a witness unavailable for cross-examination through a criminal act, including homicide, may not object to the introduction of hearsay statements by the witness as being inadmissible under the Indiana Rules of Evidence).

Chapter 805

Rule 805. Hearsay Within Hearsay

Rule 805 reads as follows:

> Hearsay included within hearsay is not excluded under the hearsay rule if each part of the combined statements conforms with an exception to the hearsay rule provided in these rules.

ANALYSIS

Multiple Hearsay; Statement of Personal or Family History. Rule 805 expressly authorizes the admission of multiple hearsay where each element or level of hearsay conforms to an exception to the hearsay rule. While this is not explicitly set forth in the language of the Rule, Rule 805 implicitly authorizes the admission of multiple levels of out-of-court statements offered for their truth where each level conforms to either a hearsay exception or to an exception to the definition of hearsay. These latter exceptions are set forth in Rules 801(d)(1) and 801(d)(2).

Illustration 1

Where an admission of a party admissible under Rule 801(d)(2) is contained within a business record admissible under Rule 803(6), the entire document is admissible.

Illustration 2

Where a party's prior inconsistent statement not under oath offered only for its impeachment value is contained within a public record admissible under Rule 803(8), both levels of out-of-court statement may be received.

Illustration 3

Negligence action, *P v. D.*   *P* is injured and is taken to the emergency room. Statement in the hospital record by emergency room nurse:

"*P* brought in by his brother *B*. Observed severe laceration of head, *P* appears unconscious. *B* states *P* was struck by *D* in the crosswalk."

Objection: Self-serving.

Court: Sustained.

The ruling is correct for the wrong reason.

The record could come in under Rule 803(6) upon adequate authentication and qualification. The statement by *B* is not part of the business record, and it is admissible as an observation of the emergency room nurse only if *B*'s statement qualifies under some other hearsay exception since he is under no duty to the hospital to report incidents accurately. If *B*'s statement as to *P*'s condition qualified under Rule 803(4), it might be admissible. Otherwise, *B*'s statement should be excised. The fact that *B*'s statement serves *P*'s interests is not the reason for exclusion. The reason is that it is multiple hearsay and no exception applies to the second-level declaration.

Reliability.   Rule 805 does not limit admissibility to double, that is, two-level, hearsay. Rather, multiple hearsay exceeding two levels of out-of-court statements is admissible as long as each level of out-of-court statement satisfies an exception to the hearsay rule. One difficulty with multiple hearsay is that the reliability of the evidence is diminished by each additional layer of hearsay. In this context, Rule 403 may operate to authorize the court to exclude multiple hearsay where the court determines the reliability of the evidence has been diminished to an unacceptable extent.

ADDITIONAL AUTHORITY

Weissenberger's Federal Evidence §§ 805.1–805.2

McCormick § 313

5 Weinstein 2d §§ 805.01–805.06

4 Mueller & Kirkpatrick §§ 508–509

5 Wigmore §§ 1361–1363

COMPARISON TO FEDERAL RULE

Indiana Rule 805 is identical to Federal Rule 805.

SIGNIFICANT CASES

Hardiman v. State, 726 N.E.2d 1201 (Ind. 2000) (trial court properly excluded police report containing statements from bystanders who were not present at trial that they heard unnamed members of a crowd say someone other than defendant killed the victim; when faced with multiple hearsay, each part of the combined statement must conform with a hearsay exception; although the police report would fall under the exception for investigative reports by police personnel (Rule 803(8)(a)), the bystanders' statements do not fall within any exception to the hearsay rule, including the exception for an excited utterance).

Davis v. State, 635 N.E.2d 1117 (Ind. Ct. App. 1994) (where multiple levels of hearsay exist, an exception must be found for each level before the hearsay is admissible).

Davis v. Eagle Products, Inc., 501 N.E.2d 1099 (Ind. Ct. App. 1986) (where a spoken hearsay statement contains another spoken hearsay statement, the proponent must establish an exception for each of the statements).

Keramida v. Zachmanoglou, 470 N.E.2d 769 (Ind. Ct. App. 1984) (where a document contains statements made by a person other than the person who prepared the document, the party offering the document must establish an applicable exception for both levels of hearsay).

HEARSAY

Chapter 806

Rule 806. Attacking and Supporting Credibility of Declarant

Rule 806 reads as follows:

> When a hearsay statement, or a statement defined in Rule 801(d)(2)(C), (D), or (E), has been admitted in evidence, the credibility of the declarant may be attacked, and if attacked may be supported, by any evidence which would be admissible for those purposes if declarant had testified as a witness. Evidence of a statement or conduct by the declarant at any time, inconsistent with the declarant's hearsay statement, is not subject to any requirement that the declarant may have been afforded an opportunity to deny or explain. If the party against whom a hearsay statement has been admitted calls the declarant as a witness, the party is entitled to examine the declarant on the statement as if under cross-examination.

* * * * *

ANALYSIS

Function of Rule; Policy. Rule 806 delineates the procedure for attacking and supporting the credibility of declarant's hearsay statements. Recognizing that admissions by authorized persons, agents, or coconspirators are technically not hearsay under an exception to the basic definition, Rule 806 treats such admissions as hearsay for the purposes of impeaching or rehabilitating the declarant. *See* Rule 801(d).

Rule 806 authorizes the admissibility of any evidence that would be used to impeach or rehabilitate a declarant of hearsay if that declarant had testified as a witness. The Rule reflects the position that justice is best served by the presentation of all evidence relevant to the reliability of statements made out of court. Where a party calls as a witness the declarant whose hearsay has been admitted against him, Rule 806 provides that the party may examine the declarant on the hearsay as if on cross-examination. Rule 806 complements Rule 611(c), which provides for cross-examination of hostile and adverse witnesses by the proponent of the witness, Rule 607, which allows a party to impeach his or her own witness.

Illustration

Impeachment evidence would be permitted, for example, in attacking the credibility of a declarant whose statement qualified under the dying declaration exception even though the court had found that the requisites of the dying declaration had been met. Such requisites are predicated upon the assumption that the person will not meet his maker with a lie on his lips. Impeachment might take the form of establishing that the declarant had a bad reputation for veracity through a character witness. Also, a witness might be called who would testify that the declarant had an extreme bias against the defendant. None of this evidence would affect the admissibility of the evidence in the first instance, but it would affect the credibility to be attached to the declarant's hearsay statement.

ADDITIONAL AUTHORITY

WEISSENBERGER'S FEDERAL EVIDENCE §§ 806.1–806.4

MCCORMICK § 37

5 WEINSTEIN 2d §§ 806.01–8061.07

4 MUELLER & KIRKPATRICK §§ 510–511

3A WIGMORE §§ 1025–1039

COMPARISON TO FEDERAL RULE

Indiana Rule 806 is essentially identical to Federal Rule 806.

IX

AUTHENTICATION AND IDENTIFICATION

AUTHENTICATION

Chapter 901

Rule 901. Requirement of Authentication or Identification

Rule 901 reads as follows:

(a) **General Provision.** The requirement of authentication or identification as a condition precedent to admissibility is satisfied by evidence sufficient to support a finding that the matter in question is what its proponent claims.

(b) **Illustrations.** By way of illustration only, and not by way of limitation, the following are examples of authentication or identification conforming with the requirements of this rule:

(1) *Testimony of witness with knowledge.* Testimony of a witness with knowledge that a matter is what it is claimed to be.

(2) *Nonexpert opinion on handwriting.* Nonexpert opinion as to the genuineness of handwriting, based upon familiarity not acquired for purposes of the litigation.

(3) *Comparison by trier or expert witness.* Comparison by the trier of fact or by expert witnesses with specimens which have been authenticated.

(4) *Distinctive characteristics and the like.* Appearance, contents, substance, internal patterns, or other distinctive characteristics, taken in conjunction with circumstances.

(5) *Voice identification.* Identification of a voice, whether heard firsthand or through mechanical or electronic transmission or recording, by opinion based upon hearing the voice at any time under circumstances connecting it with the alleged speaker.

(6) *Telephone conversations.* Telephone conversations, by evidence that a call was made to the number assigned at the time by the telephone company to a particular person or business, if (i) in the case of a person, circumstances, including self-identification, show the person answering to be the one called, or (ii) in the case of a business, the call was made to a place of business and the conversation related to business reasonably transacted over the telephone.

(7) *Public records or reports.* Evidence that a writing authorized by law to be recorded or filed and in fact recorded or filed in a public office, or a purported public record, report, statement, or data compilation, in any form, is from the public office where items of this nature are kept.

AUTHENTICATION

(8) *Ancient documents or data compilation.* Evidence that a document or data compilation, in any form, (i) is in such condition as to create no suspicion concerning its authenticity, (ii) was in a place where it, if authentic, would likely be, and (iii) has been in existence 30 years or more at the time it is offered.

(9) *Process or system.* Evidence describing a process or system used to produce a result and showing that the process or system produces an accurate result.

(10) *Methods provided by statute or rule.* Any method or authentication or identification provided by the Supreme Court of this State or by a statute or as provided by the Constitution of this State.

* * * * *

ANALYSIS

(a) General provision

Overview. Authentication and identification are terms that apply to the process of laying a foundation for the admission of such nontestimonial evidence as documents and objects. Authentication and identification may also refer to foundational evidence that identifies a person's voice on a tape recording or in a telephone conversation. Conceptually, the function of authentication or identification is to establish, by way of preliminary evidence, a connection between the evidence offered and the relevant facts of the case. Authentication and identification involve laying a foundation, which establishes the "connective relevance" of the evidence.

Sufficiency of Evidence. The standard of authentication as provided in Rule 901(a) operates to screen out certain evidence that cannot meet a threshold test of connective relevance. Rule 901(a) provides that "the requirement of authentication or identification as a condition precedent to admissibility is satisfied by evidence sufficient to support a finding that the matter in question is what its proponent claims." The "sufficient to support a finding" standard merely means that foundational evidence must be sufficient to constitute a rational basis for a jury decision that the primary evidence is what its proponent claims it to be. If the proponent claims the object to be a murder weapon taken from the scene of a crime, the proponent must submit sufficient preliminary evidence to support such a finding. Likewise, if a proponent offers a letter that he claims to have been executed by the plaintiff, he must submit sufficient foundational evidence to support such a finding.

Two key points should be recognized in conjunction with the threshold standard for authentication. First, the foundational evidence need not be absolutely conclusive as to whether the evidence in question connects to the facts of the case. Only evidence sufficient to support a finding need be submitted as a foundation. Second, once the judge determines the threshold test of authentication or identification has been met, and has submitted the evidence to the jury, the jury need not accept the foundational evidence as truthful. The jury need not believe that the primary evidence is in any way connected to the facts of the case. The jury may reject the authenticity of the evidence and decline to believe the foundational witness's testimony.

(b) Illustrations

Rule 901(b) provides illustrations of authentication and identification that may be used to meet the threshold standard of authentication or identification provided in Rule 901(a). The illustrations set forth in Rule 901(b) should not be considered as directives to use particular types of foundations. Rather, the illustrations are suggestive of the means by which the threshold standard of Rule 901(a) may be satisfied.

(1) Testimony of a Witness with Knowledge

Custody.   Most frequently, the illustration contained in Rule 901(b)(1) will be used. Rule 901(b)(1) provides that any person who has first-hand knowledge that a matter is what its proponent claims may testify to such facts and establish the foundation for connective relevance. For example, custody authentication falls within the category of authentication through testimony. Under this technique, the authenticating witness or witnesses account for the precise whereabouts of an object from the time it was found in connection with the relevant facts of the case until the moment it is offered into evidence. Where more than one person has had custody of an item, a chain of custody may be accounted for. The use of chain of custody authentication is usually required in the discretion of the trial judge where identification of an object would be difficult because of a lack of distinctive characteristics such as a serial number or signature.

Recent Developments

In *Napier v. State*, 820 N.E.2d 144 (Ind. Ct. App. 2005), *reaff'd*, 827 N.E.2d 565 (Ind. Ct. App. 2005), an Indiana Court of Appeals ruled on the admission of breath test results by certification documents and a BAC DataMaster Evidence Ticket (BAC ticket) under the Confrontation Clause analysis set forth in *Crawford v. Washington*, 541 U.S. 36, 124 S. Ct. 1354, 158 L. Ed. 2d 177 (2004). The opinion is significant for two reasons. First, the court ruled that, because the information contained in the certificates did not pertain to the ultimate issue of the defendant's guilt, but instead only to the proper functioning of the equipment, a defendant's inability to cross-examine the information contained in the certificates was not similar to the kind of testimonial evidence at issue in *Crawford*. Accordingly, the admission of the breath test instrument certification documents at issue here did not violate the Confrontation Clause. Second, the court ruled that the documents were inadmissible nonetheless, as the State had not presented any foundational evidence, through witness testimony or otherwise, for the certificates. In other words, the court appeared to rule that the certificates were not self-authenticating under Rule 902, but instead required extrinsic authentication as provided in Rule 901.

Execution of Document.   Another illustration of Rule 901(b)(1) would be the testimony provided by an authenticating witness regarding the execution of a document. Where connective relevance involves attributing authorship or execution to a particular individual, a person who has had first-hand knowledge of the execution may testify that the document offered at trial is the same one executed by a particular individual. Such foundational testimony connects the document offered at trial with the actual execution by a particular person.

Illustration

Counsel: Did you have occasion on February 12, 1990 to meet with the defendant and Mr. Johnstone?

Witness: Yes I did.

Counsel: Please describe the nature of that occasion.

Witness: I happened to attend a meeting at Mr. Johnstone's office which involved the review and execution of certain documents.

Counsel: I hand you now what has been marked as Plaintiff's Exhibit No. 3 and ask you if you recognize that document.

Witness: Yes, it was one of the documents that was reviewed on that date.

Counsel: I direct your attention to the signature at the bottom of the page. Were you present at the time that signature was executed?

Witness: Yes, I actually saw the defendant execute that document at the meeting. That is the signature I saw the defendant put at the bottom of the page.

Counsel: Your Honor, we now would like to offer this exhibit into evidence based on the authentication provided by this witness.

Judge: Is there an objection?

Opposing Counsel: No, Your Honor.

Judge: Then it will be received into evidence and it may be published to the jury.

Photograph.   The authentication of a photograph may also be established through the testimony of a witness. The foundational witness testifies that the photograph being offered at trial is a faithful and accurate representation of the object or scene depicted. The authenticating witness, through his testimony, connects the photograph offered at trial with the relevant facts of the case where the relevant facts are related to the scene, event, or object depicted.

(2) Nonexpert Opinion on Handwriting

The authenticity of a document may also be established through nonexpert opinion on handwriting. Rule 901(b)(2) codifies the principle that nonexpert foundational opinion may be used to attribute the handwriting on an offered exhibit to a particular individual. Under this technique, a person familiar with the handwriting of an individual provides foundational testimony that, based on his knowledge of the individual's handwriting, the document was written by the individual in question. The document is being connected to a particular individual who authored it where such execution or authorship is a relevant fact of the case. Obviously, the authenticating witness must have sufficient familiarity with the handwriting of the document's author to render a valuable opinion as to authorship. The burden is on the proponent of the document to establish, as part of the foundation, that the authenticating witness has the requisite familiarity.

Illustration

Q:	Mr. Johnson, how do you know the plaintiff, Mr. Murphy?
A:	I have been his business partner for five years. We operate a car rental agency.
Q:	During those five years, have you had an opportunity to observe Mr. Murphy sign his name?
A:	Yes, I see him sign his name several times a day.
Q:	Would you know his signature if you were to see it?
A:	I am certain I would.
Q:	I hand you now what has been marked as Plaintiff's Exhibit Number 16. Please look at the signature at the bottom of page 3. Do you recognize that signature?
A:	Yes.
Q:	Whose signature is it?
A:	Mr. Murphy's.

---

(3) Comparison by Trier or Expert Witness

Authentication or identification of a document may be established through the device of comparison of an offered document with specimens or exemplars which have been authenticated. Rule 901(b)(3) provides for the authentication device of comparison to be used to attribute authorship to a particular individual. Where an expert makes the comparison between the offered exhibits and the authenticated specimen, the expert must be qualified as provided in Article VII of the rules. *See* Analysis to Rule 702. Regardless of whether an expert is utilized, the specimen used for the basis of comparison must be authenticated through the normal authentication process. In order to avoid confusion, it is helpful to use a specimen or exemplar that is unquestionably authentic. A signature card from a bank is often used. Alternately, in order to avoid confusion, a stipulation may be sought to establish the conclusive authenticity of the specimen or exemplar. It should be noted that a lay witness is not qualified to render an opinion as to the similarity between the specimen and the handwriting on the offered exhibit. Only opinion testimony from an expert is appropriate. When no expert is utilized for the purpose of rendering an opinion as to authenticity, the exemplar and the offered exhibit are both tendered to the jury for their consideration in determining whether or not the offered exhibit is authentic.

Constitutional Considerations

A handwriting or voice specimen of a defendant in a criminal case may be obtained by compulsion without violating the defendant's Fifth or Sixth Amendment rights. *Gilbert v. California*, 388 U.S. 263, 87 S. Ct. 1951, 18 L. Ed. 2d 1178 (1967).

---

(4) Distinctive Characteristics and the Like

Distinctive contents of a document may be the basis for authentication under Rule 901(b)(4). For example, a letter might be authenticated and attributed to a particular author where the letter reveals knowledge that only one individual would possess. This technique is occasionally referred to as the reply doctrine technique where the unique information revealed in the letter indicates that the author is replying to prior correspondence.

Many documents may be authenticated by virtue of their custody. Custody, considered in conjunction with appearance, contents, and substance may be used to authenticate a business record under Rule 901(b)(4). In addition to requiring the foundation to satisfy the hearsay rule, business records must also be authenticated. Custodial authentication is established by a foundation witness who testifies that he has personal knowledge of the business's system of maintaining records. *See* Rule 901(b)(1). The foundational witness further provides testimony that the record or writing being offered at trial was removed from the business's files prior to trial and brought to the courtroom by the witness. Alternately, the witness may testify that he or she recognizes the document offered at trial as one which was removed from the business's files by virtue of its distinctive characteristics or contents. Usually, a witness qualified to establish the foundation for Rule 803(6) will also be qualified to establish the foundation for authentication of the business record under Article IX. A similar technique is used for public records and reports pursuant to Rule 901(b)(7).

(5) Voice Identification

Just as the authentication of a document involves attributing authorship to a particular individual, the authentication of an oral statement involves identifying the individual who made the statement. Rules 901(b)(5) and (6) illustrate methods by which oral statements may be attributed to a particular speaker where the identification of the speaker is relevant in a case.

Voice identification is established by opinion evidence, that is, by testimony of a witness that, based upon his or her familiarity with a speaker's voice, it is the witness's belief that the voice sought to be identified or authenticated is that of the specific speaker. It is clear from the provisions of Rule 901(b)(5) that anyone who has heard the voice of the alleged speaker, at any time, may offer opinion testimony sufficient to identify the voice. Such a witness need not offer conclusive proof on the issue of identity, but must merely offer testimony sufficient to establish a finding of identity.

The proponent of voice identification testimony must establish by way of foundation that the witness has some familiarity with the alleged speaker's voice. Pursuant to the rule, this foundation may be established by showing that the witness has heard the voice sought to be identified under circumstances connecting it with the alleged speaker. Accordingly, the requisite familiarity may arise from exposure to the alleged speaker's voice prior to or subsequent to the conversation or communication sought to be authenticated. In the typical situation, however, a witness offering an opinion on voice identification will do so based upon his prior familiarity with the voice in question.

(6) Telephone Conversations

Rule 901(b)(6) provides for authentication of telephone conversations. The Rule is designed to apply specifically to calls initiated by the person who offers the foundational evidence. In other words, it pertains to outgoing calls. The Rule applies to telephone calls to both individuals and business establishments, and a slightly different foundational requirement is indicated for each. The Rule provides a method for attributing oral statements to a particular speaker or to a person who speaks for a particular business establishment where the identity of the speaker is relevant to an issue in the case.

In order to utilize this provision, there must be evidence that a call was placed to a number assigned at the time by the telephone company to a particular person or business. This evidence may consist of testimony or other proof such as, for example, telephone company records. In regard to an individual, there must be circumstantial evidence that identifies the person who answered the call as the one who was intended to be called. This requirement may be satisfied by the testimony that the recipient identified himself or herself, or by other circumstances that are probative of identity. In regard to a call to a business, the foundation must include evidence that the call was made to a place of business and that the conversation related to business reasonably transacted over the phone. If the answering person has purported to speak for the business, it is not necessary that his or her individual identity be established, as long as the conversation is circumstantially probative of the identity of the place of business.

(7) Public Records or Reports

Rule 901(b)(7) provides for the authentication of public records based upon a preliminary showing that the records are from a public office where records of that type are kept. Accordingly, a party may authenticate public records by foundational evidence that, prior to the trial, such records were in the custody of an appropriate public office. It should be noted that the Rule includes within its scope writings that are authorized by law to be recorded or filed in a public office and that are in fact so recorded or filed.

Authentication of public records pursuant to Rule 901(b)(7) contemplates that the original record itself will be offered into evidence. Due to the inconvenience or impossibility of producing the original record in court, the proponent may seek to introduce a copy. If the copy is certified, it may be authenticated pursuant to Rule 902. If the copy is not certified, it may also be offered into evidence and authenticated pursuant to Rule 901(b)(7). In this case, however, the proponent must also satisfy the best evidence requirements identified in Rule 1005. *See* Analysis to Rule 1005.

The Rule will apply to such writings as judicial records, legislative records, records of administrative agencies, records of correctional institutions and law enforcement agencies, coroner's records and reports, tax returns, selective service files, weather reports, patent office reports, military records, and any other official records from an office of any level of government, domestic as well as foreign.

(8) Ancient Documents or Data Compilation

Rule 901(b)(8) provides a method for authenticating any document or data compilation on the combined bases of age and corroborating circumstances as to genuineness. The threshold standard of admissibility may be satisfied by showing that a document or data compilation is at least 30 years old, that its condition creates no suspicion as to its genuineness, and that it was kept or found in a place where, if authentic, it would likely be retained.

Authentication of an ancient document or data compilation under Rule 901(b)(8) simultaneously satisfies the hearsay requirements of Rule 803(16). Nevertheless, the proponent may need to address best evidence considerations and must address general relevance principles in order to ensure the admissibility of the document or data compilation.

(9) Process or System

Rule 901(b)(9) provides a method for authenticating the resulting product of a process or system. Authentication under this Rule is established by foundational evidence that describes the process or system and that shows that the process or system produces an accurate result.

While the method of establishing authenticity provided by the Rule may be utilized in connection with any process or system, Rule 901(b)(9) will frequently be used to authenticate computer results. It should be noted that there is no requirement under Rule 901(b)(9) that printouts have been produced in the regular course of business, although this factor may be significant if Rule 803(6) is used as a basis for satisfying the hearsay system. The Rule will, of course, be utilized for authenticating results from processes or systems other than computer systems, such as X-ray films, motion pictures, audio recordings, police radar systems, medical tests such as electrocardiograms, and certain out-of-court experiments, polls, and surveys.

(10) Methods Provided by Statute or Rule

Rule 901(b)(10) is in effect a clarifying provision, and the Rule preserves methods of authentication or identification provided by certain legislative provisions and by rules promulgated by the Supreme Court of Indiana.

ADDITIONAL AUTHORITY

WEISSENBERGER'S FEDERAL EVIDENCE §§ 901.1–901.43

MCCORMICK §§ 205, 218, 220–221, 223–226, 228

5 WEINSTEIN 2d §§ 901.01–901.12

5 MUELLER & KIRKPATRICK §§ 512–539

2 WIGMORE §§ 570, 658, 660, 666, 694–697

5 WIGMORE §§ 1638(a), 1651, 1672–1684

7 WIGMORE §§ 1997–2015, 2128–2135, 2138–2146, 2148–2154, 2158–2160, 2162, 2164, 2167

COMPARISON TO FEDERAL RULE

Indiana Rule 901 is identical in substance to Federal Rule 901.

SIGNIFICANT CASES

Kidd v. State, 738 N.E.2d 1039 (Ind. 2000) (deputy clerk who provided one page at the end of each of three exhibits of properly certified evidence of defendant's prior convictions because certification does not have to take a particular form and each exhibit was a complete, individual document that stated the number, caption, and summary disposition).

Thomas v. State, 734 N.E.2d 572 (Ind. 2000) (a letter was properly admitted into evidence because there was a sufficient foundation laid to justify the admission of evidence where the envelope contained defendant's address, was postmarked near his prison, was mailed during the time he was incarcerated, and the letter itself contained sufficient evidence to support a finding that defendant authored the letter; an inculpatory telephone conversation was also properly admitted into evidence because a sufficient foundation was laid to justify its admission where defendant identified himself, gave a detailed statement of events, and made reference to other interviews).

Craig v. State, 730 N.E.2d 1262 (Ind. 2000) (redacting or removing portions from a certified document does not render the documents uncertified and inadmissible; admission of documentary evidence merely requires the proponent to show that the evidence is what its proponent claims).

Lewis v. State, 730 N.E.2d 686 (Ind. 2000) (witness who was a firearms expert properly authenticated X-ray by testifying that he was present when the X-ray was taken, identified the six-shot standard included in the X-ray, and marked the X-ray envelope with the identifying information; X-ray authentication only requires the sponsoring witness to establish that the X-ray is a true and accurate representation of the evidence portrayed).

Young v. State, 696 N.E.2d 386 (Ind. 1998) (generally, the identities of both parties must be authenticated before admitting a telephone call, and this may be accomplished by circumstantial evidence and need not be proven beyond a reasonable doubt; however, a telephone call to a 911 system may not always require such authentication where the point of submitting it as evidence is not really to establish the identification of the caller, for example, where the purpose was to demonstrate where the call originated and how the police discovered the crime scene).

Napier v. State, 820 N.E.2d 144 (Ind. Ct. App. 2005), *reaff'd*, 827 N.E.2d 565 (Ind. Ct. App. 2005) (concluding that certification documents and a BAC DataMaster Evidence Ticket (BAC ticket) showing the results of breath test results were not self-authenticating documents, but instead foundational evidence concerning their authenticity as provided in Rule 901).

Rule 901(a)

Jenkins v. State, 627 N.E.2d 789 (Ind. 1993) (chain of custody of DNA samples was sufficiently demonstrated although lab technician did not testify; party offering challenged evidence need only supply reasonable assurance that item was undisturbed in chain of custody and supply evidence strongly suggesting exact whereabouts of evidence at all times).

Rolland v. State, 851 N.E.2d 1042 (Ind. Ct. App. 2006) (the testimony of a witness who demonstrated an understanding of a bank's recordkeeping process and the creation of the record generating the Customer Information Screen (CIS) was sufficient authentication of a CIS printout).

Bone v. State, 771 N.E.2d 710 (Ind. Ct. App. 2002) (testimony of police officer sufficiently authenticated images copied from defendant's computer; officer testified that he removed hard drive, made an image of it, write-protected floppy disks, viewed both, and generated and printed images, and that copied images "fairly and accurately" depicted images on computer).

Clenna v. Marion County Office of Family & Children (In re A.C.), 770 N.E.2d 947 (Ind. Ct. App. 2002) (to establish a proper foundation for the admission of exhibits, there must be a reasonable probability that the exhibit is what it purports to be and that its condition is substantially unchanged as to any material feature; absolute proof of authenticity is not necessary).

Robinson v. State, 724 N.E.2d 628 (Ind. Ct. App. 2000) (trial court did not err in excluding results of urine screen for marijuana taken on the night of collision because defendant could not testify regarding administration of the test or the reliability of the equipment).

Dumes v. State, 718 N.E.2d 1171 (Ind. Ct. App. 1999), *as clarified on reh'g*, 723 N.E.2d 460 (Ind. Ct. App. 2000) (when an item of evidence is offered as proof, its relevance depends on a finding that it is what its sponsor purports it to be; prosecutor, as party to the case, cannot certify and authenticate documents because it effectively defeats the purposes of the authentication requirement imposed by the Trial Rules, Rules of Evidence, and Indiana Statutes).

Lockhart v. State, 671 N.E.2d 893 (Ind. Ct. App. 1996) (item is admissible if evidence establishes reasonable probability that item is what it is claimed to be).

Owensby v. Lepper, 666 N.E.2d 1251 (Ind. Ct. App. 1996) (on appeal of marriage dissolution proceeding, wife waived argument that documents were inadmissible for lack of authenticity, where she did not raise claim in her appellate brief).

Salone v. State, 652 N.E.2d 552 (Ind. Ct. App. 1995) (before documents may be admitted, proof of authentication is required).

Nasser v. State, 646 N.E.2d 673 (Ind. Ct. App. 1995) (defendant's objection to admission of breath test results based upon lack of foundation did not preserve for review issues of whether testing officer checked print record to ensure accuracy or attached new mouthpiece to breath tube; failure to specify reasons why evidentiary foundation is inadequate constitutes waiver of issue for appeal).

Collins v. State, 645 N.E.2d 1089 (Ind. Ct. App. 1995), *aff'd in part, vacated in part*, 659 N.E.2d 509 (Ind. 1995) (physical evidence has proper foundation if witness can identify item and it is relevant to case's disposition).

Lahr v. State, 640 N.E.2d 756 (Ind. Ct. App. 1994) (authenticity must be proved to establish proper foundation for admission of document, but absolute proof of authenticity is not necessary, only evidence showing reasonable probability that exhibit is what it is claimed to be and that its condition is substantially unchanged regarding any material feature).

Columbian Rope Co. v. Todd, 631 N.E.2d 941 (Ind. Ct. App. 1994) (under common law, generally, item is admissible if evidence establishes reasonable probability that item is what it is claimed to be and that its condition is materially unchanged; any inconclusiveness about connection of item with events goes only to weight of exhibit).

Underwood v. State, 644 N.E.2d 108 (Ind. 1994) (subsequent testimony cured any deficiency in foundation for picture of initialed money clip owned by robbery victim, where victim and another witness testified that during robbery defendant demanded that victim surrender money clip, victim testified he surrendered it, victim identified picture as photograph of his money clip, and detective testified that picture was of money clip that he removed from defendant after he was taken into custody).

Evans v. State, 643 N.E.2d 877 (Ind. 1994) (physical evidence is admissible if witness can testify that exhibit is "like" something associated with crime and there is showing that exhibit is connected to defendant and commission of crime; party offering evidence need not conclusively identify item, and lack of positive identification affects weight, not admissibility of evidence).

Rule 901(b)(1)—Testimony of Witness with Knowledge

Bonnes v. Feldner, 642 N.E.2d 217 (Ind. 1994) (trial court admitted into evidence an uncertified copy of a doctor's opinion from a panel that had considered whether defendant had met the standard of care; no error because a certified copy of the same document had already been submitted to the trial court).

Underwood v. State, 535 N.E.2d 507 (Ind. 1989) (witness testified that an exhibit possessing identifiable characteristics was the same item as the one involved in a material event).

Starks v. State, 517 N.E.2d 46 (Ind. 1987), *vacated on other grounds*, 523 N.E.2d 735 (Ind. 1988) (although the prosecution must establish a continuous chain of custody for evidence, it is not required to eliminate every possibility of tampering).

McAnalley v. State, 514 N.E.2d 831 (Ind. 1987) (chain of custody requires an adequate foundation to be laid showing the continuous whereabouts of the exhibit beginning with the time it came into the possession of the police).

Warriner v. State, 435 N.E.2d 562 (Ind. 1982) (a unique exhibit is admissible if a witness testifies that the exhibit is the item in question and that it was substantially unchanged).

Jones v. State, 425 N.E.2d 128 (Ind. 1981) (in a criminal case, the proponent of an exhibit must present evidence to trace the possession of the exhibit from the time it was acquired to the time it was introduced at trial).

Owens v. State, 263 Ind. 487, 333 N.E.2d 745 (1975) (where an item is unique and readily identifiable, it is authenticated when a witness identifies it as the item he recognizes).

Herrera v. State, 710 N.E.2d 931 (Ind. Ct. App. 1999) (handwritten documents describing three witnesses, where they lived, where they worked, and what kind of cars they drove were properly authenticated by coconspirator's testimony that he had seen defendant prepare the documents and that they were in substantially the same condition as when coconspirator received them; thus, trial court did not abuse its discretion in admitting the documents).

Collins v. State, 645 N.E.2d 1089 (Ind. Ct. App. 1995), *aff'd in part and vacated in part*, 659 N.E.2d 509 (Ind. 1995) (officer's search of confidential informant before controlled purchase, observation of informant from time of search until he returned, and unobstructed view of transaction between informant and defendant provided reasonable assurance that drug evidence was not disturbed while it passed from defendant to informant to officer, thus supplying adequate foundation under chain of custody doctrine for exhibit's admission).

Curry v. State, 643 N.E.2d 963 (Ind. Ct. App. 1994) (chain of custody rule seeks to ensure that while evidence is in law enforcement authority's possession, there is no substitution or alteration of the evidence; rule applies with decreasing strictness as exhibits become less susceptible to alteration, tampering, or substitution, and if offered item has fairly unique characteristics, is readily identifiable, and is composed of substance relatively impervious to change, trial court has broad discretion to admit evidence simply on basis of testimony that item is the one in question and is substantially unchanged; state is not required to show perfect chain of custody, and any gaps affect weight, not admissibility of evidence).

Lahr v. State, 640 N.E.2d 756 (Ind. Ct. App. 1994) (proof of chain of custody not necessary to prove authenticity of note written by defendant while in prison on charge for which he was tried, where prison trustee who gave note to authorities identified note and testified to recognizing handwriting and that note was written by defendant).

Grimes v. State, 633 N.E.2d 262 (Ind. Ct. App. 1994) (at defendant's drug trial, prosecution introduced audiotapes of a drug deal recorded by a confidential informant; trial court did not err in permitting the jury to use transcripts to assist them in listening to the audiotapes; police officer who monitored the taping testified to the accuracy of the tapes and verified the voices on the tape).

Scott v. State, 632 N.E.2d 761 (Ind. Ct. App. 1994) (two showings are necessary to establish adequate foundation for admission of physical evidence: Witness must be able to testify that item is "like" item associated with crime, and it must be shown that item is connected to defendant and commission of crime; witness's uncertainty about whether item is same item associated with crime affects weight, not admissibility of physical evidence).

Levi v. State, 627 N.E.2d 1345 (Ind. Ct. App. 1994) (testimony of police officer who identified computer equipment in photographs as that found in burglary defendant's car trunk and in the apartment of defendant's girlfriend, and testimony of university officials that computer equipment depicted in exhibits was property taken from university, supplied sufficient foundation to authenticate photographs for admission into evidence).

AUTHENTICATION

Ruth v. First Federal Sav. & Loan Asso., 492 N.E.2d 1105 (Ind. Ct. App. 1986) (witness present at the signing was a witness with knowledge).

Rule 901(b)(2)—Nonexpert Opinion on Handwriting

Brooks v. State, 497 N.E.2d 210 (Ind. 1986) (witness identified the handwriting in letters as that of defendant; she recognized the handwriting and identified certain phrases in the letters as those used frequently by defendant).

Wolfe v. State, 426 N.E.2d 647 (Ind. 1981) (police officer authenticated letter by comparing a letter with defendant's signature authorizing release of automobile).

Rule 901(b)(3)—Comparison by Trier or Expert Witness

Kindred v. State, 524 N.E.2d 279 (Ind. 1988) (chain of custody of film after its removal from camera had to be established).

Lockhart v. State, 671 N.E.2d 893 (Ind. Ct. App. 1996) (trial court's admission of handwriting exemplar, even if improper, did not require reversal, where jury was instructed to only use exemplar in evaluating weight of handwriting expert's testimony, and admission of exemplar and expert's testimony were cumulative).

Schnitz v. State, 650 N.E.2d 717 (Ind. Ct. App. 1995), *aff'd*, 666 N.E.2d 919 (Ind. 1996) (in prosecution for cocaine dealing within 1,000 feet of school, state supplied sufficient foundation for admission of aerial photomap of area surrounding cocaine delivery, in support of city engineer's testimony that delivery location was 246 feet from school, although engineer did not physically measure distance or have personal knowledge about map's preparation or verification, engineer testified that he determined distance by measuring map with engineer's scale, that he physically observed area represented in map, and that observations confirmed scale and map-based distance measurement).

Columbian Rope Co. v. Todd, 631 N.E.2d 941 (Ind. Ct. App. 1994) (in product liability suit initiated prior to the adoption of the Indiana Rules of Evidence, foundation for admitting rope samples to demonstrate manufacturer's identity was established although ropes were not in unchanged condition and samples were not to be considered evidence of defect; jury was instructed to regard samples only for identification purpose).

Rule 901(b)(4)—Distinctive Characteristics and the Like

In re Sheaffer, 655 N.E.2d 1214 (Ind. 1995) (incriminating tape met foundational requirements in attorney disciplinary proceeding, despite claim that alteration of tape made it unauthentic; officer had marked tape as original, initialed and dated it, officer and sergeant monitored entire conversation at time of taping and each affirmed that recording reflected conversation accurately, other participant in conversation verified recording's accuracy, experts found no evidence of filtering, alteration, masking, dubbing, or additional background noise).

Tingle v. State, 632 N.E.2d 345 (Ind. 1994) (admission of defendant's taped confession was not error although detective testified that tape and transcript were not identical, where detective testified that recording was authentic and transcript accurate, and that transcript was not identical to tape only where portions of tape were inaudible, and jury was instructed to disregard transcript and focus on tape in event of discrepancies).

Brooks v. State, 497 N.E.2d 210 (Ind. 1986) (letters held to be admissible where witness identified characteristics in the letters: Return address was on the envelopes, the letters contained a smiley face insignia, and the letters referred to family matters confirmed by defendant's mother).

Kern v. State, 426 N.E.2d 385 (Ind. 1981) (letter identified by its contents, which indicated it came from defendant).

Salone v. State, 652 N.E.2d 552 (Ind. Ct. App. 1995) (authenticity of defendant's letter to victims, written while defendant was incarcerated awaiting trial for criminal deviate conduct, was established by one addressee's testimony that letter arrived in envelope with red-stamped inscription stating that the letter had been mailed by incarcerated offender, that it described in detail and demanded return of certain personal possessions of defendant's left in victims' homes, and that it was signed with defendant's nickname).

Scott v. State, 632 N.E.2d 761 (Ind. Ct. App. 1994) (state supplied sufficient foundation for introduction of defendant's tennis shoes, based on defendant's admission that red spots on shoes were blood from battery victim).

Rule 901(b)(5)—Voice Identification

Huspon v. State, 545 N.E.2d 1078 (Ind. 1989) (witness, who was an acquaintance of defendant's, testified concerning the voice on the victim's answering machine).

Ashley v. State, 493 N.E.2d 768 (Ind. 1986) (testimony from a witness that he was familiar with a voice and recognized it was sufficient for Rule 901).

Rule 901(b)(6)—Telephone Conversations

Williams v. State, 669 N.E.2d 956 (Ind. 1996) (in murder trial, taped conversations between defendant and police informant made with body microphone under police supervision were sufficiently authenticated to be admissible; where police detective and state trooper who helped informant both testified to having conversed with informant and defendant and to recognizing their voices on tapes; arguments that officers were not voice recognition experts and their experience in hearing voice of defendant was too limited affected weight of evidence, not admissibility).

Lock v. State, 567 N.E.2d 1155 (Ind. 1991) (evidence that a caller possessed knowledge of facts that only a certain person would know is sufficient for authentication purposes).

King v. State, 560 N.E.2d 491 (Ind. 1990) (trial court refused to permit a witness to testify to the contents of a phone conversation where insufficient evidence was offered concerning the identity of the caller).

Reed v. State, 491 N.E.2d 182 (Ind. 1986), *aff'd*, Reed v. Farley, 512 U.S. 339, 114 S. Ct. 2291, 129 L. Ed. 2d 277 (1994) (testimony that a caller identified himself is not sufficient by itself).

Rule 901(b)(7)—Public Records or Reports

Donahoo v. State, 640 N.E.2d 702 (Ind. 1994) (in rape prosecution, record showing samples were sealed and placed in locked containers until delivery to police lab established sufficient chain of custody).

Spencer v. State, 660 N.E.2d 359 (Ind. Ct. App. 1996) (where defendant failed to object to admission of certified copies to establish his prior record for habitual offender purposes, defendant waived any error in their admission; even though actual language of certification appeared to be copied, separate case numbers were typed and deputy clerk's signature was written in ink).

Payne v. State, 658 N.E.2d 635 (Ind. Ct. App. 1995) (foundation for business record exception to hearsay rule can be established by testimony of any person with functional understanding of business's record-keeping process regarding specific entry, transaction, or declaration included in document).

Rule 901(b)(9)—Process or System

Kindred v. State, 524 N.E.2d 279 (Ind. 1988) (where an automatic camera was involved, there had to be evidence as to how the camera operated).

AUTHENTICATION

Chapter 902

Rule 902. Self-Authentication

Rule 902 reads as follows:

Extrinsic evidence of authenticity as a condition precedent to admissibility is not required with respect to the following:

(1) *Domestic public documents.* The original or a duplicate of a domestic official record proved in the following manner: An official record kept within the United States, or any state, district, commonwealth, territory, or insular possession thereof, or within the Panama Canal Zone, the Trust Territory of the Pacific Islands, or the Ryukyu Islands, or an entry therein, when admissible for any purpose, may be evidenced by an official publication thereof or by a copy attested by the officer having the legal custody of the record, or by his deputy. Such publication or copy need not be accompanied by proof that such officer has the custody. Proof that such officer does or does not have custody of the record may be made by the certificate of a judge of a court of record of the district or political subdivision in which the record is kept, authenticated by the seal of the court, or may be made by any public officer having a seal of office and having official duties in the district or political subdivision in which the record is kept, authenticated by the seal of his office.

(2) *Foreign public documents.* The original or a duplicate of a foreign official record proved in the following manner: A foreign official record, or an entry therein, when admissible for any purpose, may be evidenced by an official publication thereof; or a copy thereof, attested by a person authorized to make the attestation, and accompanied by a final certification as to the genuineness of the signature and official position:

(a) of the attesting person; or

(b) of any foreign official whose certificate of genuineness of signature and official position relates to the attestation or is in a chain of certificates of genuineness of signature and official position relating to the attestation. A final certification may be made by a secretary of embassy or legation, consul general, consul, vice consul, or consular agent of the United States, or a diplomatic or consular official of the foreign country assigned or accredited to the United States. If reasonable opportunity has been given to all parties to investigate the authenticity and accuracy of the documents, the court may, for good cause shown:

    (i) admit an attested copy without final certification; or

    (ii) permit the foreign official record to be evidenced by an attested summary with or without a final certification.

(3) *Official publications.* Books, pamphlets, or other publications issued by public authority.

(4) *Newspapers and periodicals.* Printed materials purporting to be newspapers or periodicals.

(5) *Trade inscriptions and the like.* Inscriptions, signs, tags, or labels purporting to have been affixed in the course of business and indicating ownership, control, or origin.

(6) *Acknowledged documents.* Original documents accompanied by a certificate of acknowledgment executed in the manner provided by law by a notary public or other officer authorized by law to take acknowledgments.

(7) *Commercial paper and related documents.* Commercial paper, signatures thereon, and documents relating thereto to the extent provided by general commercial law.

(8) *Presumptions created by law.* Any signature, document, or other matter declared by any law of the United States or of this state, to be presumptively or prima facie genuine or authentic.

(9) *Certified domestic records of regularly conducted activity.* Unless the source of information or the circumstances of preparation indicate a lack of trustworthiness, the original or a duplicate of a domestic record of regularly conducted activity within the scope of Rule 803(6), which the custodian thereof or another qualified person certifies under oath (i) was made at or near the time of the occurrence of the matters set forth, by or from information transmitted by, a person with knowledge of those matters; (ii) is kept in the course of the regularly conducted activity, and (iii) was made by the regularly conducted activity as a regular practice. A record so certified is not self-authenticating under this subsection unless the proponent makes an intention to offer it known to the adverse party and makes it available for inspection sufficiently in advance of its offer in evidence to provide the adverse party with a fair opportunity to challenge it.

(10) *Certified foreign records of regularly conducted activity.* Unless the source of information or the circumstances of preparation indicate lack of trustworthiness, the original or a duplicate of a foreign record of regularly conducted activity within the scope of Rule 803(6), which is accompanied by a written declaration by the custodian thereof or another qualified person that the record (i) was made at or near the time of the occurrence of the matters set forth, by or from information transmitted by, a person with knowledge of those matters; (ii) is kept in the course of the regularly conducted activity; and (iii) was made by the regularly conducted activity as a regular practice. The record must be signed in a foreign country in a manner which, if falsely made, would subject the maker to criminal penalty under

the laws of that country, and the signature certified by a government official in the manner provided in subsection (2) above. The record is not self-authenticating under this subsection unless the proponent makes his or her intention to offer it known to the adverse party and makes it available for inspection sufficiently in advance of its offer in evidence to provide the adverse party with a fair opportunity to challenge it.

*   *   *   *   *

ANALYSIS

The theory of self-authentication is that certain documents are self-evidently genuine on their face, and consequently, the proponent of the document is relieved of the obligation of meeting the threshold test of proving that the document is what he claims it to be. Self-authentication relieves the proponent from submitting foundational testimony regarding connective relevance. In considering self-authenticating documents, two factors should not be overlooked. First, while self-authentication does relieve the proponent of the document from submitting foundational testimony as to authenticity, it does not guarantee admissibility of the document.

Other issues, such as best evidence and hearsay, must be addressed in considering the admissibility of the document. Second, it is important to recognize that a self-authenticating document is not conclusively genuine. While self-authentication does relieve the proponent of submitting authentication evidence, the jury may still determine in rendering its final decision that the document is not genuine, that is, it is not what its proponent claims it to be.

AUTHENTICATION

Recent Developments

In *Napier v. State*, 820 N.E.2d 144 (Ind. Ct. App. 2005), *reaff'd*, 827 N.E.2d 565 (Ind. Ct. App. 2005), an Indiana Court of Appeals ruled on the admission of breath test results by certification documents and a BAC DataMaster Evidence Ticket (BAC ticket) under the Confrontation Clause analysis set forth in *Crawford v. Washington*, 541 U.S. 36, 124 S. Ct. 1354, 158 L. Ed. 2d 177 (2004). The opinion is significant for two reasons. First, the court ruled that, because the information contained in the certificates did not pertain to the ultimate issue of the defendant's guilt, but instead only to the proper functioning of the equipment, a defendant's inability to cross-examine the information contained in the certificates was not similar to the kind of testimonial evidence at issue in *Crawford*. Accordingly, the admission of the breath test instrument certification documents at issue here did not violate the Confrontation Clause. Second, the court ruled that the documents were inadmissible nonetheless, as the State had not presented any foundational evidence, through witness testimony or otherwise, for the certificates. In other words, the court appeared to rule that the certificates were not self-authenticating under Rule 902, but instead required extrinsic authentication as provided in Rule 901.

(1) Domestic Public Documents

Amendments to Rule 902(1) in 2004 transferred the self-authentication provisions for domestic public documents from Indiana Rule of Trial Procedure 44(A)(2) to the Indiana Rules of Evidence to consolidate the self-authentication provisions for all evidence within a single rule. It should be noted that certain laws may also be subject to judicial notice under Rule 201(b)—this method of proof may also be available to counsel who desire an easier method of proof. The procedure for authenticating public documents located within the United States or the territories specified in the rule is described in greater detail below.

An original or a duplicate of a domestic official record may be authenticated either through an official publication of the record or through a copy of the record to which an official having legal custody of the record or a person designated by the official has attested its validity. Under the rule, there is no need for the proponent of the evidence to prove that the official or designated person had actual custody. Instead, the party opposing the evidence is provided with the opportunity to demonstrate the absence of custody through two methods. First, the party may submit a certificate of a judge of a court of record of the district or political subdivision in which the record is kept, authenticated by the seal of the court, verifying the lack of custody or other evidence that the document is not authentic. Alternatively, the party opposing the introduction of the document into evidence may submit an affidavit of any public officer having a seal of office and having official duties in the district or political subdivision in which the record is kept, authenticated by the seal of his office, attesting to the conditions demonstrating the document's lack of authenticity.

(2) Foreign Public Documents

A companion amendment to Rule 902(2) in 2004 transferred the self-authentication provisions for foreign public documents from Indiana Rule of Trial Procedure 44(A)(2) to the Indiana Rules of Evidence. A foreign public document is any document not regarded as a domestic public document under Rule 902(1).

Under the rule, an original or a duplicate of a foreign official record may be authenticated either through an official publication of the record or through a copy of the record to which a proper attestation has been made. The attestation must be made by a person authorized to make the attestation and must be accompanied either by a "final certification" concerning the genuineness of the attesting person's signature and official position or by a "final certification" of any foreign official whose certificate of genuineness of signature and official position relates to the attestation or is in a chain of certificates of genuineness of signature and official position relating to the attestation. The "final certification" must be made by a secretary of embassy or legation, consul general, consul, vice consul, or consular agent of the United States, or a diplomatic or consular official of the foreign country assigned or accredited to the United States.

The rule dispenses with the need for the "final certification" requirement if all parties have been provided with a reasonable opportunity to investigate the authenticity and accuracy of the documents and good cause is shown. The rule also provides the court with the discretion to permit a summary of the foreign record, with proper attestation, and with or without a final certification.

(3) Official Publications

Rule 902(3) applies the doctrine of self-authentication to books, pamphlets, and other publications issued by a public authority. The rule relieves the proponent from establishing an extrinsic foundation that the publication was actually printed or issued by public authority.

(4) Newspapers and Periodicals

Rule 902(4) makes the doctrine of self-authentication applicable to nonofficial printed materials purporting to be newspapers or periodicals. The rule also by its express terms includes notices and advertisements contained in the identified publications. This provision may be used to prove the contents of newspapers or periodicals, for example, in a libel action, or in an action involving deceptive advertising. Periodicals and newspapers may also be used as proof of collateral matters such as the date and place of publication. Finally, it must be remembered that Rule 902 only provides for authentication, and other issues such as best evidence and hearsay must be addressed before admissibility is attained.

(5) Trade Inscriptions and the Like

Rule 902(5) accords self-authenticating status to trade inscriptions, signs, tags or labels, as long as they purport to have been affixed in the course of business and are indicative of ownership, control, or origin. Generally, this type of evidence will be introduced to prove ownership or control, for example, in a products liability action.

The Rule is justified because there is only a slight risk of forgery of items within the purview of the Rule due to the difficulty of reproduction and because trademark infringement involves serious penalties. Substantial efforts are devoted to inducing the public to buy and otherwise acquire items in reliance on brand names, and substantial protection is given by the law. The Rule requires that the inscription, label, or the like purport to have been affixed in the course of "business." The term "business" should be interpreted liberally to include any ongoing enterprise or institution regardless of its commercial or noncommercial nature, including, for example, a private university or social organization that uses an identifying inscription or symbol.

(6) Acknowledged Documents

Rule 902(6) provides that documents accompanied by a certificate of acknowledgement are self-authenticating and, consequently, do not require an extrinsic foundation. The certificate of acknowledgement serves as prima facie evidence that the document is what it purports to be. Rule 902(6) is not limited to title documents, and it applies to any type of document that is properly acknowledged. The acknowledgement required is a certificate executed by a notary public or other officer authorized to take acknowledgements in the jurisdiction where the certificate is executed. In addition, the certificate must be executed in the manner provided by law.

(7) Commercial Paper and Related Documents

Rule 902(7) expressly adopts the principles of general commercial law in applying the doctrine of self-authentication to commercial paper, signatures on commercial paper, and documents relating to commercial paper.

(8) Presumptions Created by Law

Rule 902(8) confers self-authenticating status to any signature, document, or other matter

that is declared to be authentic by the law of any state or by federal law. By its express terms, the rule incorporates any federal or state law that declares a matter to be presumptively or prima facie genuine or authentic. It should be noted that statutes that grant "presumptive" authenticity to a matter go beyond the doctrine of self-authentication in the sense that the trier of fact is bound by the presumption in the absence of evidence sufficient to support a finding to the contrary. *See* Analysis to Rule 301.

(9) Certified Domestic Records of Regularly Conducted Activity

Rule 902(9) provides that certified domestic records of regularly conducted activity, or copies, are self-authenticating. The Rule sets forth specific requirements that must be included in the certification, including certification or verification by the custodian or other qualified person. Also, a notice provision must be satisfied as set forth in the Rule.

(10) Certified Foreign Records of Regularly Conducted Activity

Rule 902(10) provides that certified foreign records of regularly conducted acts are self-authenticating. The Rule sets forth specific requirements that must be included in the certification. Significantly, the Rule requires the certification of the record by a government official. Under a corrective amendment made in 2005, the certification must be made under the consolidated provisions of subdivision (2), instead of under the former procedure set forth in Indiana Rule of Trial Procedure 44. Also, a notice provision must be satisfied as set forth in the Rule.

ADDITIONAL AUTHORITY

WEISSENBERGER'S FEDERAL EVIDENCE §§ 902.1–902.19

McCORMICK §§ 218, 283, 308

5 WEINSTEIN 2d §§ 902.01–902.12

5 MUELLER & KIRKPATRICK §§ 538–548

4 WIGMORE § 1234

5 WIGMORE §§ 1677, 1680, 1684

7 WIGMORE §§ 2129–2130, 2150, 2152, 2161–2165

COMPARISON TO FEDERAL RULE

As noted in the Analysis, Indiana Rule 902(1) and (2) were amended in 2004, and now provide for the self-authentication of domestic and foreign public records. The provisions are similar to those under the Federal Rules of Evidence. Additionally, Indiana Rule 902(9) and (10) provide for the self-authentication of certified foreign and domestic business records. A corrective amendment to Rule 902(10) was made in 2005, rendering the government certification subject to the procedures in Rule 902(2).

Federal Rule 902 was amended in December 2000. Two additional types of documents can now be self-authenticated—certified domestic records of regularly conducted activity and certified foreign records of regularly conducted activity—thereby eliminating the need for testimony of foundation witnesses. The notice requirement in the two new sections are intended to give the opponent of the evidence a full opportunity to test the adequacy of the foundation set forth in the declaration.

Federal Rule 902(11) and (12) now state:

(11) *Certified domestic records of regularly conducted activity.* The original or a duplicate of a domestic record of regularly conducted activity that would be admissible under Rule 803(6) if accompanied by a written declaration of its custodian or other qualified person, in a manner complying with any Act of Congress or rule prescribed by the Supreme Court pursuant to statutory authority, certifying that the record—

    (A)   was made at or near the time of the occurrence of the matters set forth by, or from information transmitted by, a person with knowledge of those matters;

    (B)   was kept in the course of the regularly conducted activity; and

    (C)   was made by the regularly conducted activity as a regular practice.

A party intending to offer a record into evidence under this paragraph must provide written notice of that intention to all adverse parties, and must make the record and declaration available for inspection sufficiently in advance of their offer into evidence to provide an adverse party with a fair opportunity to challenge them.

(12) *Certified foreign records of regularly conducted activity.* In a civil case, the original or a duplicate of a foreign record of regularly conducted activity that would be admissible under Rule 803(6) if accompanied by a written declaration by its custodian or other qualified person certifying the record—

    (A)   was made at or near the time of the occurrence of the matters set forth by, or from information transmitted by, a person with knowledge of those matters;

    (B)   was kept in the course of the regularly conducted activity; and

    (C)   was made by the regularly conducted activity as a regular practice.

The declaration must be signed in a manner that, if falsely made, would subject the maker to criminal penalty under the laws of the country where the declaration is signed. A party intending to offer a record into evidence under this paragraph must provide written notice of that intention to all adverse parties, and must make the record and declaration available for inspection sufficiently in advance of their offer into evidence to provide an adverse party with a fair opportunity to challenge them.

RECENT SIGNIFICANT CASES

Craig v. State, 730 N.E.2d 1262 (Ind. 2000) (redacting or removing portions from a certified document does not render the remaining documents uncertified and inadmissible where remaining documents bear identification that appears on the certification page).

Hernandez v. State, 716 N.E.2d 948 (Ind. 1999) (each page of a multi-page exhibit neither have to be separately certified nor do the pages have to be numbered and incorporated by reference on the certification document; the certification on a single page of a multi-page exhibit provides adequate certification for the entirety of the exhibit as certification placement does not cause confusion as to the authenticity of the paper).

Bartlett v. State, 711 N.E.2d 497 (Ind. 1999) (documents showing that defendant had committed two previous felonies in other states were self-authenticating, were compiled and kept by public officers in their respective states, and were authenticated by a seal of office).

Brown v. State, 650 N.E.2d 304 (Ind. 1995) (testimony by record-keeper was not necessary to authenticate records of defendant's prior felony convictions; the fact that copies of court records had been separated from clerk's certifications did not make records of prior convictions inadmissible as validity of records from foreign jurisdictions does not depend on sturdiness of binder; matching case numbers and case names on documents attached to clerk's certification to those listed on certification provides sufficient reliability for admission of exhibit to prove defendant's prior felony convictions in habitual offender proceeding).

Armstead v. State, 538 N.E.2d 943 (Ind. 1989) (docket sheets certified by the clerk of courts held to be admissible).

Luttrull v. State, 499 N.E.2d 1139 (Ind. 1986) (properly certified public records are self-authenticating).

Connell v. State, 470 N.E.2d 701 (Ind. 1984) (official records certified by the clerk of court are self-authenticating).

Gross v. State, 444 N.E.2d 296 (Ind. 1983) (suggestion that a judge or notary public must certify that the record keeper certifying the record is the proper custodian).

B.J.R. v. C.J.R., 984 N.E.2d 687 (Ind. Ct. App. 2013) (a domestic official record is self-authenticating provided that it is attested by the officer having the legal custody of the record, and there is no mandate that the certification take a particular form).

Robertson v. State, 877 N.E.2d 507 (Ind. Ct. App. 2007) (exhibits did not satisfy the market reports hearsay exception under Rule 803(17) because the exhibits were opened and did not meet the second foundational requirement of *Reemer*, which requires some evidence that the contents of the product remained as the manufacturer packaged them; the two unopened, shrink-wrapped heat source canisters were properly admitted under the exception in Rule 803(17) because they were in the same condition as when the manufacturer packaged them) (question should instead be analyzed under Rule 902(5)).

Speybroeck v. State, 875 N.E.2d 813 (Ind. Ct. App. 2007) (bank affidavit that was merely a boilerplate recitation unconnected to the underlying documents lacked trustworthiness and did not comply with Rule 902(9), as none of the documents were created by a bank employee with personal knowledge of the matters set forth in the documents).

Gaddie v. Manlief (In re H.R.M.), 864 N.E.2d 442 (Ind. Ct. App. 2007) (the Rule 902(9) requirement that an affiant "certify under oath" statements made in an affidavit is substantially the same as requiring the person to "verify" his or her statements).

Napier v. State, 820 N.E.2d 144 (Ind. Ct. App. 2005), *reaff'd*, 827 N.E.2d 565 (Ind. Ct. App. 2005) (concluding that certification documents and a BAC DataMaster Evidence Ticket (BAC ticket) showing the results of breath test results were not self-authenticating documents, but instead foundational evidence concerning their authenticity as provided in Rule 901).

Smith v. State, 839 N.E.2d 780 (Ind. Ct. App. 2005) (the fact that a business record is created by an individual who is not an employee of the business subject to subpoena does not bar its self-authenticating nature as a record of that business).

State v. Lloyd, 800 N.E.2d 196 (Ind. Ct. App. 2003) (self-authentication under Rule 902 does not provide an exception to the hearsay rule; however, a certification may also satisfy the public records exception of Rule 803(8) and thus be admissible).

Berry v. State, 725 N.E.2d 939 (Ind. Ct. App. 2000) (driving records obtained on the Internet and certified by paralegal employed by prosecutor's office were improperly admitted into evidence because the prosecutor's office was not the appropriate entity to certify driving records as true and complete).

Dumes v. State, 718 N.E.2d 1171 (Ind. Ct. App. 1999), *as clarified on reh'g*, 723 N.E.2d 460 (Ind. Ct. App. 2000) (certification of public records by the custodian of records is sufficient evidence that the records are what the sponsor purports them to be, and thus, there is no need for foundational testimony or the introduction of the "original document"; the custodian of driving records is the

BMV and the certification of public records must be made by the custodian of records).

Lucre Corp. v. County of Gibson, 657 N.E.2d 150 (Ind. Ct. App. 1995) (authentication for admission of official record necessitates officer with custody of record attest through testimony or certification that it is the official original record or true and accurate copy; in condemnation case, refusal to admit mine map prepared by state agency as self-authenticated document was not error, as document was not self-authenticated merely by being official publication).

Carmichael v. Kroger Co., 654 N.E.2d 1188 (Ind. Ct. App. 1995) (exhibit including affidavit from records custodian and doctor's report of plaintiff's physical examination after alleged slip-and-fall injury qualify as self-authenticating business records).

Coates v. State, 650 N.E.2d 58 (Ind. Ct. App. 1995) (while self-authenticating documents make it unnecessary to provide foundational testimony about authenticity, admissibility is not automatic but depends on other issues such as hearsay).

Chapter 903

Rule 903. Subscribing Witness's Testimony Unnecessary

Rule 903 reads as follows:

> The testimony of a subscribing witness is not necessary to authenticate a writing unless required by the laws of the jurisdiction whose laws govern the validity of the writing.

*   *   *   *   *

ANALYSIS

Rule 903 provides that authentication of a writing need not involve the testimony of a subscribing witness unless such testimony is required by the laws of the jurisdiction whose laws govern the validity of the writing. Consequently, where there is no applicable statutory or common law provision requiring testimony of a subscribing witness, authentication of a document may be established in accordance with the provisions of Rules 901 or 902.

INCORPORATED STATUTES

Ind. Code § 29-1-5-3.2. [Use of videotape messages]

Subject to the applicable Indiana Rules of Trial Procedure, a videotape may be admissible as evidence of the following:

(1)   The proper execution of a will.

(2)   The intentions of a testator.

(3)   The mental state or capacity of a testator.

(4)   The authenticity of a will.

(5)   Matters that are determined by a court to be relevant to the probate of a will.

ADDITIONAL AUTHORITY

WEISSENBERGER'S FEDERAL EVIDENCE §§ 903.1–903.3

MCCORMICK § 220

5 WEINSTEIN 2d §§ 903.01–903.02

5 MUELLER & KIRKPATRICK §§ 549–550

4 WIGMORE §§ 1287–1321

COMPARISON TO FEDERAL RULE

Indiana Rule 903 is identical in substance to Federal Rule 903.

X

CONTENTS OF WRITINGS, RECORDINGS, AND PHOTOGRAPHS

WRITINGS

Chapter 1001

Rule 1001. Definitions

Rule 1001 reads as follows:

> For purposes of this article the following definitions are applicable:
>
> (1) *Writings and recordings.* "Writings" and "recordings" consist of letters, words, sounds, or numbers, or their equivalent, set down by handwriting, typewriting, printing, photostating, photographing, magnetic impulse, mechanical or electronic recording, or other forms of data compilation.
>
> (2) *Photographs.* "Photographs" include still photographs, x-ray films, video-tapes, and motion pictures.
>
> (3) *Original.* An "original" of a writing or recording is the writing or recording itself or any counterpart intended to have the same effect by a person executing or issuing it. An "original" of a photograph includes the negative or any print therefrom. If data are stored in a computer or similar device, any printout or other output readable by sight, shown to reflect the data accurately, is an "original."
>
> (4) *Duplicate.* A "duplicate" is a counterpart produced by the same impression as the original, or from the same matrix, or by means of photography, including enlargements and miniatures, or by mechanical or electronic rerecording, or by chemical reproduction, or by facsimile transmission, or video tape, or by other equivalent techniques which accurately reproduce the original.

* * * * *

ANALYSIS

Overview. The collection of rules contained in Article X were historically known as the "best evidence rule." The best evidence rule has frequently been criticized as a misnomer, because the rule does not require the best evidence as a general proposition of law. Rather, the rule in certain instances requires original evidence. The essence of the best evidence rule, as it is applied in Article X, provides that in proving the contents of a writing, recording, or photograph, the original is preferentially required. The rule further provides that if the original is unavailable through no fault of the proponent of the evidence, secondary evidence may be admitted. It should be noted that the best evidence rule does not apply to proving the contents of physical objects or things other than writings, recordings, or photographs, and there is no general requirement that the most probative evidence be used to prove a fact in every instance. Evidence need only be relevant under Rule 401 to satisfy the threshold qualification of admissibility under Rule 402.

"Secondary Evidence." Article X contains no express definition of "secondary evidence." Nevertheless, it is clear that *secondary evidence* may be defined as any evidence that is probative of the contents other than the original itself. Consequently, secondary evidence of the contents of a document could be testimony of a person with firsthand knowledge of the contents or it could be a hand-transcribed copy. It should be noted that, except in regard to Rule 105 governing public records, Article X does not erect a hierarchy of secondary evidence such that, for example, a hand-transcribed copy is preferred to oral testimony. Once an exception to the requirement for the original is established, any secondary evidence may be used to prove contents.

"Writings and Recordings." Rule 1001(1) defines "writings and recordings" in their broadest sense, to include any setting down of "letters, words, sounds, or numbers or their equivalent" by virtually any means constituting a writing or recording. Moreover, a writing or recording is not only a setting down or inscription of letters and numbers, but also any compilation or recording of data such as might be produced by a computer, modern electronic device or other newly developed machine or technique.

Practical Application of the "Best Evidence Rule"

Article X of the Rules of Evidence, the so-called best evidence rule, applies only where the contents of a writing, recording, or photograph are sought to be proven. Generally, if a party is seeking to establish the terms of a dispositive document such as a contract, lease, will, or trust, the so-called best evidence rule will apply and will require the original if it is available. If, however, some other fact concerning a document is sought to be proven, for example, its delivery, the best evidence rule does not apply. Moreover, the best evidence rule is a rule of mandatory preference. It prefers the original if it is available. Secondary evidence may be used, however, to establish the contents of a writing, recording, or photograph where it is authorized under Rule 1002.

Photographs. Rule 1001(2) defines photographs to include "still photographs, x-ray films, videotapes, and motion pictures." It should be noted that offering a photograph at trial will only involve the best evidence rule where the contents of the photograph itself are at issue. In the case of an allegedly obscene film, for example, the film's contents must be proved in order to establish the purported obscenity. Nevertheless, where a photograph of an item (itself not a writing, recording, or photograph) is available to prove the appearance of the item, the best evidence rule does not operate to prefer the photograph over other evidence. Proof of the appearance of the object of the photograph is not subject to the best evidence rule. Consequently, where the appearance of a particular individual is sought to be established, the best evidence rule is not invoked.

X-rays. X-rays and X-ray films may invoke the operation of the best evidence rule. Where the object of proof is the physical condition of the person who has been x-rayed, the best evidence rule does not necessarily operate to prefer the X-ray over the testimony of the medical expert. The physical condition of the person in question is not a writing, recording, or photograph. The testimony and the X-ray are both admissible to prove facts that are not within the scope of the rule. Where, however, the X-ray is offered to establish a fact that may be derived only from the contents of the X-ray, the best evidence rule is invoked.

"Original." The definition of an "original" is provided in Rule 1001(3). The Rule provides that an original writing or recording is the writing or recording itself and any counterpart intended by the person executing it or issuing it to be an original. Accordingly, a contract that is signed by the parties is an original even though the parties may not have initially distinguished that writing for execution. Multiple originals arise in the situation where, by virtue of intent, there is more than one original, for example, where parties to a bilateral contract intend that each should have an executed original.

Original of Photograph. Rule 1001(3) provides that an original of a photograph is either "a negative or any print therefrom." In accordance with this Rule, either the negative or the print made from the negative is equally admissible in evidence as an original. The Rule also provides that any printout or other output readable by sight from a computer or electronic device is an original if the printout accurately reproduces the data that is stored. In addition to the printout, the computer data cards and magnetic tape should also be admissible as originals.

"Duplicate" Generally. Rule 1001(4) provides a general definition of a duplicate that includes any counterpart that accurately reproduces the original. Accurate reproduction may be achieved by any of a variety of ways designated in the Rule, that is, by the same impression, as in the case of a carbon copy; from the same matrix, as in the case of a published book; by means of photography, as in the case of photostats, enlargements, or reductions; by mechanical or electronic recording, as in the case of a tape recording; by chemical reproduction, as in the case of a thermofax copy; or by facsimile transmission or videotape; or by any equivalent techniques or means.

ADDITIONAL AUTHORITY

WEISSENBERGER'S FEDERAL EVIDENCE §§ 1001.1–1001.16

McCORMICK §§ 214, 229–231, 235

6 WEINSTEIN 2d §§ 1001.01–1001.11

5 MUELLER & KIRKPATRICK §§ 551–566

3 WIGMORE §§ 790, 792–798

4 WIGMORE §§ 1173–1180, 1230, 1232–1241

COMPARISON TO FEDERAL RULE

Federal Rule 1001(1) does not include "sounds" in the definition of "writings" and "recordings." Additionally, Federal Rule 1001(4) does not include facsimile transmission or videotape in the definition of "duplicate."

SIGNIFICANT CASES

King v. State, 540 N.E.2d 1203 (Ind. 1989) (the foundation required for the admission of an audio recording is the same as for a document).

Wade v. State, 490 N.E.2d 1097 (Ind. 1986) (best evidence of a conversation is a tape recording;

WRITINGS

where the recording is lost, a transcript may be read to the jury if the accuracy of the transcript is established).

Morris v. State, 273 Ind. 614, 406 N.E.2d 1187 (1980), *superseded by statute*, **Havens v. State**, 429 N.E.2d 618 (Ind. 1981) (carbon copies considered originals).

Brandon v. State, 272 Ind. 92, 396 N.E.2d 365 (1979) (computer printouts considered originals).

Sutherlin v. State, 784 N.E.2d 971 (Ind. Ct. App. 2003) (a computer-generated array containing the same six photographs as the actual array is an "original" under Rule 1001(3) and is thus admissible).

Grimes v. State, 633 N.E.2d 262 (Ind. Ct. App. 1994) (at defendant's drug trial, prosecution introduced audiotapes of a drug deal recorded by a confidential informant; trial court did not err in permitting the jury to use transcripts to assist them in listening to the audiotapes).

Harwood v. State, 555 N.E.2d 513 (Ind. Ct. App. 1990), *aff'd*, 582 N.E.2d 359 (Ind. 1991) (holding that a document was not inadmissible simply because it was a facsimile copy of the original).

Chapter 1002

Rule 1002. Requirement of Original

Rule 1002 reads as follows:

> To prove the content of a writing, recording, or photograph, the original writing, recording, or photograph is required, except as otherwise provided in these rules or by statute. An electronic record of the Indiana Bureau of Motor Vehicles obtained from the Bureau that bears an electronic or digital signature, as defined by statute, is admissible in a court proceeding as if the signature were an original.

* * * * *

ANALYSIS

Overview. Rule 1002 restates the traditional best evidence rule in modern terms. The Rule requires that in proving the contents of a writing, recording, or photograph, the original must be offered as evidence unless a foundation is established to justify its nonproduction. In addition, the Rule expressly provides that its application may be limited by statute or by other Rules of Evidence. It should be noted that the scope of Rule 1002 is in large part determined by the definition set forth in Rule 1001. *See* Analysis to Rule 1001, *above.*

Recent Development

In *Romo v. State*, 941 N.E.2d 504 (Ind. 2011), the Indiana Supreme Court wrestled with the question of whether to permit an English language translation of a transcripted recording between a criminal defendant and a police informant to be admitted as substantive evidence. The Court ultimately allowed the translation, reasoning that the transcripts, not the original recording, constituted the source of the relevant information. Accordingly, the best evidence rule did not apply to the original recording.

Conditions. In applying Rule 1002, it should be recognized that the Rule is only applicable where two conditions occur: (1) the evidence involves a writing, recording, or photograph; and (2) the object of proof is the contents of that writing, recording, or photograph. The first condition indicates that Rule 1002 is inapplicable in proving the nature of uninscribed physical objects or a fact which is subsequently memorialized in a writing.

Consequently, the best evidence rule codified in Rule 1002 does not require that a confiscated substance be introduced into evidence to prove the nature, identity, or status of the substance. The second condition for application of the best evidence rule provides that the rule is only applicable where a party offering evidence seeks to prove the contents of that writing, recording, or photograph. A party is seeking to prove the contents of a writing, recording, or photograph only where the issue is what the writing or recording says or what the photograph depicts.

Illustration 1

Where the issue is whether a written contract obligates a party to perform in a certain way, the best evidence rule is triggered because the contract, being embodied in the writing, is established by proving the content of the writing.

Illustration 2

Where a motion picture is offered to prove an external fact, such as the mobility of the plaintiff, the best evidence rule is not implicated because the contents of the film are not at issue, only the mobility of the plaintiff. In comparison, however, the best evidence rule is triggered in an obscenity trial at which the film is claimed to be obscene. In this case, the best evidence rule applies because the object of proof is the contents of the film.

The second sentence of Indiana Rule 1002 was added in 2002. It clarifies the situation in which an electronic or digital signature appearing on a Bureau of Motor Vehicles record is sought to be admitted. In such cases, the original signature need not be admitted, and the admission of the electronic signature will satisfy the "best evidence" rule.

ADDITIONAL AUTHORITY

WEISSENBERGER'S FEDERAL EVIDENCE §§ 1002.1–1002.4

McCORMICK §§ 229–233

6 WEINSTEIN 2d §§ 1002.01–1002.05

5 MUELLER & KIRKPATRICK §§ 567–571

4 WIGMORE §§ 1171–1183

COMPARISON TO FEDERAL RULE

The first sentence of Indiana Rule 1002 is parallel to Federal Rule 1002. The second sentence of Indiana Rule 1002 was added in 2002 and does not contain a parallel provision under the Federal Rules of Evidence.

SIGNIFICANT CASES

Romo v. State, 941 N.E.2d 504 (Ind. 2011) (trial court did not err in allowing the State to introduce into evidence an English language translation of a transcripted recording of a conversation between the defendant and a police informant).

Jones v. State, 780 N.E.2d 373 (Ind. 2002) (an effective objection must identify an actual dispute over the accuracy of the secondary evidence to preserve the issue of the improper use of secondary evidence for appeal).

Moore v. State, 498 N.E.2d 1 (Ind. 1986) (best evidence rule was inapplicable where the document was not central to the litigation).

Lilly v. State, 482 N.E.2d 457 (Ind. 1985) (best evidence rule inapplicable where the photograph of the gun was used to prove the existence of the gun).

Jackson v. State, 274 Ind. 297, 411 N.E.2d 609 (1980) (best evidence rule applied to videotape).

Pinkerton v. State, 258 Ind. 610, 283 N.E.2d 376 (1972) (best evidence rule held inapplicable because X-rays contain scientific evidence that must be explained to the jury).

Sutherlin v. State, 784 N.E.2d 971 (Ind. Ct. App. 2003) (a computer-generated array containing the same six photographs as the actual array is an "original" under Rule 1001(3) and is thus admissible).

Belcher v. State, 797 N.E.2d 307 (Ind. Ct. App. 2003) (when addressing whether it would be unfair to admit the duplicate in lieu of the original, the court should look primarily to circumstances affecting the trustworthiness of the duplicate for the purpose for which it is offered; because the duplicate is not fully legible in the two major portions of the document relevant to facts at issue in the case, the duplicate should not have been admitted).

Laughner v. State, 769 N.E.2d 1147 (Ind. Ct. App. 2002) (printouts of online instant message chats were the "best evidence" of conversations and thus admissible despite the fact that the text was not an original preserved by the Internet provider's logging feature but a copy of the conversation pasted into a word processing program, where a witness testified that he saved the conversations with defendant after they were concluded, and that the printout accurately reflected the content of those conversations).

Grimes v. State, 633 N.E.2d 262 (Ind. Ct. App. 1994) (in prosecution for marijuana possession and dealing, use of transcripts of tape recording to help jury was not error although it was not clear who transcribed the tapes; jury was admonished to rely on tapes over transcripts and resolve differences in favor of tapes, court instructed jury that transcripts were only to be used as assistance, and police officer who monitored conversations testified to tapes' and transcripts' accuracy and verified voices on tape as those labeled in transcripts).

WRITINGS

Chapter 1003

Rule 1003. Admissibility of Duplicates

Rule 1003 reads as follows:

> A duplicate is admissible to the same extent as an original unless (1) a genuine question is raised as to the authenticity of the original or (2) in the circumstances it would be unfair to admit the duplicate in lieu of the original.

*   *   *   *   *

ANALYSIS

Overview; Definition. Rule 1003 provides that duplicates are generally admissible as originals in all cases except where there is a genuine question of authenticity of the original, or where admission of the duplicate instead of the original would be unfair. The term "duplicate" is defined in Rule 1001(4). *See* Analysis to Rule 1001, *above*.

It should be noted that Rule 1003 does not create a "second best" evidence rule. In no case does it actually require the use of a duplicate. Nor does it create a hierarchy of secondary evidence in which a duplicate is preferred over some other type of secondary evidence. Rather, the rule provides that a duplicate may be used interchangeably with an original, unless the opponent of the evidence challenges the use of the duplicate on one of the grounds specified in the rule. Consequently, use of a duplicate does not require laying a foundation as to why the use of the original is excused. The duplicate is merely used in lieu of the original and will operate as the original unless appropriately challenged under the rule.

Examples. Where there is a question as to whether the original has been altered after the reproduction has been made, whether accidentally, negligently, or fraudulently, production of the original should be required where the opponent raises the appropriate objection under the rule. Likewise, where a duplicating process fails to produce some of the most essential parts of an original, fairness may require production of the original.

It should also be observed that a duplicate, as defined by Rule 1001(4), may be used as "other evidence of the contents," even if Rule 1003 does not apply, so long as the requisites of Rule 1004 are met.

ADDITIONAL AUTHORITY

WEISSENBERGER'S FEDERAL EVIDENCE §§ 1003.1–1003.3

MCCORMICK §§ 229, 231, 235, 236

6 WEINSTEIN 2d §§ 1003.01–1003.05

5 MUELLER & KIRKPATRICK §§ 572–574

4–5 WIGMORE §§ 1177–1180, 1190, 1198, 1229, 1232–1241, 1249

COMPARISON TO FEDERAL RULE

Indiana Rule 1003 is identical to Federal Rule 1003.

SIGNIFICANT CASES

Owensby v. State, 467 N.E.2d 702 (Ind. 1984) (a photocopy of a document is as admissible as the original).

Belcher v. State, 797 N.E.2d 307 (Ind. Ct. App. 2003) (when addressing whether it would be unfair to admit the duplicate in lieu of the original, the court should look primarily to circumstances affecting the trustworthiness of the duplicate for the purpose for which it is offered; because the duplicate is not fully legible in the two major portions of the document relevant to facts at issue in the case, the duplicate should not have been admitted).

Seattle Painting Co. v. Commissioner of Labor, 661 N.E.2d 596 (Ind. Ct. App. 1996) (photocopy of agency's original final order fulfilled evidentiary requirement).

Levi v. State, 627 N.E.2d 1345 (Ind. Ct. App. 1994) (copies are admissible to same extent as original unless genuine issue is raised as to authenticity of original or under such circumstances that it would be unfair to admit duplicate as original; defendant's speculative claim that original may have included notations not apparent on photocopy of consent to search form was not sufficient to overcome general rule regarding admissibility of copies).

Stuckey v. State, 560 N.E.2d 88 (Ind. Ct. App. 1990) (photocopy of carbon copy of a business record was admissible).

Wilson v. State, 169 Ind. App. 297, 348 N.E.2d 90 (1976) (a duplicate is admissible as an original unless a genuine issue is raised as to the accuracy of the duplicate).

Chapter 1004

Rule 1004. Admissibility of Other Evidence of Contents

Rule 1004 reads as follows:

The original is not required, and other evidence of the contents of a writing, recording, or photograph is admissible if:

(1) *Originals lost or destroyed.* All originals are lost or have been destroyed, unless the proponent lost or destroyed them in bad faith;

(2) *Original not obtainable.* No original can be obtained by any available judicial process or procedure;

(3) *Original in possession of opponent.* At a time when an original was under the control of the party against whom offered, such party was put on notice, by the pleadings or otherwise, that the contents would be a subject of proof at the hearing, and such party does not produce the original at the hearing;

(4) *Collateral matters.* The writing, recording, or photograph is not closely related to a controlling issue.

---

*   *   *   *   *

ANALYSIS

Overview; Secondary Evidence. Rule 1004 lists four general situations in which originals are not required to be produced and in which secondary evidence may be used to prove the contents of a writing, recording, or photograph. If one of the Rule 1004 exceptions applies, a party may prove the contents of a writing, recording, or photograph with any secondary evidence. Rule 1004 rejects the concept of degrees of secondary evidence, and the Rule allows any form of secondary evidence to be used to prove the contents of the original where an exception is satisfied.

Secondary evidence may consist of any of the following illustrations without ranking as to priority:

- A duplicate original as defined in Rule 1001(4), even if Rule 1003 is not applicable

- A carbon or photocopy not otherwise admissible under Rule 1003

- Testimony of a witness who recalls the content of the writing, photograph, or recording

377

- Circumstantial evidence from which an inference could be made as to what the contents were

Rule 1005 Considerations. It should be noted that Rule 1004 is superseded in certain situations by Rule 1005, and in effect, Rule 1005 does create a hierarchy of secondary evidence for the proof of contents of public records.

(1) Originals Lost or Destroyed

Rule 1004(1) codifies the principle that where an original is lost or destroyed, secondary evidence of the contents of the original is admissible providing the party offering the secondary evidence has not lost or destroyed the original in bad faith. Courts have traditionally placed the burden for proof of loss or destruction on the party offering the secondary evidence, and the party offering the secondary evidence must justify use of the secondary evidence by establishing a foundation satisfactory to the court to show that the original cannot be produced. Where the proponent is relying upon loss as a basis for nonproduction of the original, he or she must show that a reasonable or diligent search was undertaken. Destruction may be proven by direct or circumstantial evidence.

Rule 1004(1) does not absolutely bar a proponent from introducing secondary evidence to prove the contents of the original where the party lost or destroyed the original. The Rule only prohibits a party from introducing secondary evidence where the party has lost or destroyed the original in bad faith. While the Rule does not define bad faith, it is clear that the term applies to the destruction of an original with the intent of preventing its use as evidence or with the intent of perpetrating a fraud.

(2) Original Not Obtainable

Rule 1004(2) relieves the proponent from using the original to prove contents where the original is not obtainable by available judicial process. Although the rule does not define the circumstances under which an original is unobtainable, case law generally provides that an original is unavailable where it is merely shown that the original is outside the court's jurisdiction. It should be noted that where the original at issue is a public record of a foreign jurisdiction, Rule 1004(2) is preempted by Rule 1005, which requires a certified copy to be used where the original cannot be produced. Rule 1004(2) is applicable where a third party within the jurisdiction refuses to produce a document, and where the object in question cannot be readily produced in the court, such as in the situation where the writing is inscribed on a tombstone.

Although no showing of an effort to produce the original is required where the original is outside the court's jurisdiction, such an effort must be shown where the original is within the jurisdiction. In essence, the effort required is that of serving a writ of subpoena *duces tecum* on the party possessing the original. Secondary evidence should be admitted where the possessor of the original refuses to obey the subpoena.

(3) Original in Possession of Opponent

Rule 1004(3) provides that if an adverse party (1) possesses or controls an original; (2) has received notice that the contents of the original will be an issue at the hearing; and (3) fails to produce the original, then secondary evidence of the original's contents will be admissible if offered by the opponent of the party in possession of the original. It should be noted that this Rule operates as a justification for the admission of secondary evidence. It does not have any compulsory force to produce the original. Also, it should be noted that satisfactory notice under the Rule may be effected through the pleading or through other means. The Rule does not require any formal notice.

Illustration

Q: Did you send a letter on or about July 10 to the defendant concerning the contract?

A: Yes.

Q: Do you have the letter?

A: No, the defendant has it.

Counsel: Your Honor, the defendant was notified by pleadings in this case that the contents of this letter would be the subject of proof at this trial today and defendant has failed to bring the original to court, today.

Court: Yes, counselor, you have met the requirements of Evidence Rule 1004(3). You may proceed.

Q: Do you recall the contents of that letter?

Q: *(or)*

Q: Have you brought with you a carbon copy of that letter?

---

(4) Collateral Matters

Rule 1004(4) provides that proof of the contents of writings, recordings, or photographs may be established by secondary evidence where the contents are not closely related to a central or controlling issue in the litigation. The trial court has wide discretion in determining whether proof of the contents is collateral to the matter at issue.

ADDITIONAL AUTHORITY

WEISSENBERGER'S FEDERAL EVIDENCE §§ 1004.1–1004.12

McCORMICK §§ 234–239

6 WEINSTEIN 2d §§ 1004.01–1004.13, 1004.20–1004.21, 1004.30–1004.32, 1004.40–1004.42

5 MUELLER & KIRKPATRICK §§ 575–580

4 WIGMORE §§ 1188, 1189, 1192–1217, 1252–1254, 1264–1275

COMPARISON TO FEDERAL RULE

Indiana Rule 1004 is identical to Federal Rule 1004.

SIGNIFICANT CASES

Romo v. State, 941 N.E.2d 504 (Ind. 2011) (Rule 1004 does not allow transcripts to be used in place of an original recording).

Wade v. State, 490 N.E.2d 1097 (Ind. 1986) (best evidence of a conversation is a tape recording;

WRITINGS

where the recording is lost, a transcript may be read to the jury if the accuracy of the transcript is established).

Vega v. Allen County Dep't of Family & Children Servs. (In re J.V.), 875 N.E.2d 395 (Ind. Ct. App. 2007) (although an original is required under the best evidence rule, an exception exists that allows for the admission of evidence of the contents of a writing, recording, or photograph where the original is lost or destroyed unless the proponent lost or destroyed the original in bad faith; the proponent of the evidence must demonstrate that the original was lost or destroyed by showing that a diligent but unsuccessful search has been made in the place or places where the original was most likely to be found).

Weisman v. Hopf-Himsel, Inc., 532 N.E.2d 29 (Ind. Ct. App. 1989) (secondary evidence is admissible only after a diligent search was made to locate the original document).

Chapter 1005

Rule 1005. Public Records

Rule 1005 reads as follows:

> The contents of an official record, or of a document authorized to be recorded or filed and actually recorded or filed, including data compilations in any form, if otherwise admissible, may be proved by copy, certified as correct in accordance with Rule 902, or testified to be correct by a witness who has compared it with the original. If a copy complying with the foregoing cannot be obtained by the exercise of reasonable diligence, other evidence of the contents may be given.

* * * * *

ANALYSIS

Overview. Rule 1005 provides that a copy of the public record may be used to prove contents of the original where the copy is certified as correct in accordance with Evidence Rule 902 or authenticated as correct by testimony from a witness who has compared the copy with the original. The Rule also provides that if a copy cannot be obtained by the exercise of reasonable diligence, "other evidence of the contents may be given."

Degrees of Secondary Evidence; Rules 1003, 1004 Preempted. By establishing a preference for certified copies of official records and filed or recorded documents, Rule 1005 introduces into the rules the concept of degrees of secondary evidence for documents within its purview. Copies of official records that are authenticated by the stipulated requirements are preferred to any other secondary evidence that might be offered to prove the contents of a public record. Accordingly, Rule 1005 preempts Rule 1003's general provision that duplicates are admissible as originals. In addition, the Rule supersedes Rule 1004 insofar as it allows the use of a copy certified or testified to be correct without any showing that the original is lost, destroyed, unobtainable, or pertinent to a collateral matter. It further supersedes Rule 1004 by creating a mandatory preference for the use of certified copies over other types of secondary evidence.

Documents Covered. It should be noted that Rule 1005 applies to public documents as well as to documents authorized to be filed or recorded and actually filed or recorded. It thereby authorizes the proof of the contents of such recorded documents as deeds, leases, or mortgages.

Secondary Evidence Examples. Rule 1005 provides that if, by the reasonable exercise of

WRITINGS

diligence, a copy that satisfies Rule 1005 cannot be obtained, other evidence of the contents of the public record may be admitted. Where this provision is satisfied, any otherwise admissible secondary evidence may be offered to prove the contents of the document. Secondary evidence might include, for example, an uncertified copy of the document, testimony by somebody familiar with the contents of the document, or other documentary evidence.

Obvious examples of the application of this Rule would be:

- Birth and death certificates, marriage records
- Recorded deeds
- Police records
- Workers' compensation files
- Rolls of the Supreme Court, Medical Board, or other licensing agencies
- Records of the Treasurer's and Auditor's office to show amount of taxes or assessments
- U.S. Veterans' Bureau records
- Statistical data
- Court files
- Reports or returns required by law to be filed with a government agency

Any report or document falling within this Rule must be otherwise admissible. This Rule only establishes the method by which the best evidence rule is satisfied.

ADDITIONAL AUTHORITY

WEISSENBERGER'S FEDERAL EVIDENCE §§ 1005.1–1005.4

McCORMICK § 240

6 WEINSTEIN 2d §§ 1005.01–1005.06

5 MUELLER & KIRKPATRICK §§ 581–582

4 WIGMORE §§ 1215–1218

COMPARISON TO FEDERAL RULE

Indiana Rule 1005 is identical to Federal Rule 1005.

SIGNIFICANT CASES

Meredith v. State, 503 N.E.2d 880 (Ind. 1987) (commitment papers containing photographs and descriptions of defendant were sufficient to identify defendant as the person committed).

Russell v. State, 489 N.E.2d 955 (Ind. 1986) (certified copies of judgment along with other circumstantial evidence are sufficient to prove defendant's prior convictions).

Walker v. State, 246 Ind. 386, 204 N.E.2d 850 (1965) (copies admitted to prove the contents of public records).

Chapter 1006

Rule 1006. Summaries

Rule 1006 reads as follows:

> The contents of voluminous writings, recordings, or photographs which cannot conveniently be examined in court may be presented in the form of a chart, summary, or calculation. The originals, or duplicates, shall be made available for examination or copying, or both, by other parties at a reasonable time and place. The court may order that they be produced in court.

* * * * *

ANALYSIS

Rule 1006 codifies an exception to the best evidence rule in providing that where writings are voluminous, summaries, abstracts, or schedules may be admitted into evidence. For a summary, calculation, or chart to be admissible under Rule 1006, three conditions must be satisfied. First, the writings, recordings, or photographs must be voluminous. This is a question for the court. Second, a proper foundation must be established for the introduction of the summary. As part of this requirement, the originals must be admissible in order that the summaries, calculations, or charts based on those originals be admissible. In addition, the charts, summaries, or calculations may not include information not contained in or computed from the originals. Third, the originals or duplicates must be made available to all litigants for examination or copying at any reasonable time and place.

Illustration

Defendant has compiled a summary of all property transactions with regard to farm lands in the county within the past three years from records maintained by the county auditor's office and proposes to use the summary in lieu of specific records of the said auditor's office. Copies of all data are available for inspection or copying by the opposing party on request. The summary complies with Rule 1006.

ADDITIONAL AUTHORITY

WEISSENBERGER'S FEDERAL EVIDENCE §§ 1006.1–1006.4

WRITINGS

McCormick § 240

6 Weinstein 2d §§ 1006.01–1006.08

5 Mueller & Kirkpatrick §§ 583–585

4 Wigmore § 1230

COMPARISON TO FEDERAL RULE

Indiana Rule 1006 is identical to Federal Rule 1006.

SIGNIFICANT CASES

DesJardins v. State, 759 N.E.2d 1036 (Ind. 2001) (videotapes constitute "writings" or "recordings" for purposes of Rule 1006, which requires admission of other parts of written or recorded statements in the interest of fairness).

Crawford v. State, 401 N.E.2d 715 (Ind. Ct. App. 1980) (voluminous records may be summarized if the underlying records are admissible and available to the opposing party).

Cleveland, C. C. & S. L. R. Co. v. Woodbury Glass Co., 80 Ind. App. 298, 120 N.E. 426 (1918) (where books or documents are voluminous, an expert may be used to summarize them).

Chapter 1007

Rule 1007. Testimony or Written Admissions of Party

Rule 1007 reads as follows:

> Contents of writings, recordings, or photographs may be proved by the testimony or deposition of the party against whom offered or by a written admission, without accounting for the nonproduction of the original.

* * * * *

ANALYSIS

Rule 1007 shortcuts the best evidence requirement in certain cases where the opponent has admitted to the contents of the subject writing, photograph, or recording. In other words, the best evidence rule can be satisfied by offering an opponent's admission either in writing, or by testimony, or deposition. Under Rule 1007 there is no necessity of accounting for the nonproduction of the original. The admission itself is sufficient to establish contents.

It should be emphasized that the contents of the writing, recording, or photograph sought to be proven through Rule 1007 need not have been prepared by the party whose admission is offered as a means of proof. For example, this exception to the best evidence rule may be used to prove the contents of a writing originally prepared by a person other than the party whose written or testimonial admission is used to prove contents.

Illustration

Action for slander. Defendant called to prove publication.

Q: *(To defendant by plaintiff's counsel)* Did you state in your deposition of September 24 that *X* had written a letter to you in which he acknowledged your telephone conversation with him?

A: Yes.

Q: And did you also state that *X* said in his letter that he was surprised to hear you say in your telephone conversation with him that plaintiff was a liar and a cheat?

Objection: Best evidence and hearsay.

> **Court:** Overruled.
>
> The best evidence rule is satisfied because the testimony established that defendant admitted the contents of a writing (*X*'s letter to *D*) in his deposition. The best evidence rule is satisfied under the provisions of Rule 1007 by such admission. Alternately the deposition could be read into evidence to establish the admission.
>
> The letter of *X* is not offered to prove the truth of *D*'s assertion but only to prove the slander was published by *D* to *X*. Therefore, the letter is not hearsay. *See* Rule 801.

ADDITIONAL AUTHORITY

WEISSENBERGER'S FEDERAL EVIDENCE §§ 1007.1–1007.3

McCORMICK § 242

6 WEINSTEIN 2d §§ 1007.01–1007.07

5 MUELLER & KIRKPATRICK §§ 586–587

4 WIGMORE § 1255

COMPARISON TO FEDERAL RULE

Indiana Rule 1007 is identical to Federal Rule 1007.

SIGNIFICANT CASES

Mark v. Indianapolis, 247 Ind. 511, 219 N.E.2d 434 (1966) (contents of a writing proved by opposing party's testimony).

Chapter 1008

Rule 1008. Functions of Court and Jury

Rule 1008 reads as follows:

> When the admissibility of other evidence of contents of writings, recordings, or photographs under these rules depends upon the fulfillment of a condition of fact, the question whether the condition has been fulfilled is ordinarily for the court to determine in accordance with the provisions of Rule 104. However, when an issue is raised whether (1) the asserted writing ever existed, or (2) another writing, recording, or photograph produced at the trial is the original, or (3) other evidence of contents correctly reflects the contents, the issue is for the trier of fact.

*   *   *   *   *

ANALYSIS

Rule 1008 allocates responsibility for deciding preliminary questions of fact involving the admissibility of evidence other than originals to prove the contents of writings, records, or photographs. Factual questions otherwise respecting admissibility, which in reality are determinative issues in the case, and which generally turn on questions of credibility or the weight to be accorded certain evidence, are allocated to the trier of fact. Other preliminary questions of fact that relate to the admissibility of secondary evidence are within the province of the trial court. Under Rule 1008, the trial judge is not permitted to make a preliminary determination as to the appropriateness of secondary evidence and thereby exclude the secondary evidence based on a finding which embraces the conclusion that the original never existed, that some other writing, recording, or photograph is the original, or that the offered secondary evidence is not a faithful reproduction of the original. These issues may not be taken from the trier of fact.

This rule implicitly allows the trier of fact to disregard evidence in which the conditional relevancy question is not adequately established. The trier of fact should place no probative value on evidence which it believes did not exist, which it believes was not the correct writing, or which it believes was inaccurate as to content. For example, the trier of fact may decline to attach probative value to a writing it believes was forged, or a writing or other evidence that it believes does not accurately reflect the contents of the original.

ADDITIONAL AUTHORITY

WEISSENBERGER'S FEDERAL EVIDENCE §§ 1008.1–1008.3

MCCORMICK § 53 at 135–136

6 WEINSTEIN 2d §§ 1008.01–1008.05

5 MUELLER & KIRKPATRICK §§ 588–590

4 WIGMORE § 1192

COMPARISON TO FEDERAL RULE

Indiana Rule 1008 is similar in substance to Federal Rule 1008.

SIGNIFICANT CASES

Marksill Specialties, Inc. v. Barger, 428 N.E.2d 65 (Ind. Ct. App. 1981) (whether the party has made an adequate showing of diligence in the search for the original document is a question of fact for the judge to decide).

XI
MISCELLANEOUS RULES

MISC. RULES

Chapter 1101

Rule 1101. Evidence Rules Review Committee

Rule 1101 reads as follows:

A. The Supreme Court Committee on Rules of Practice and Procedure, as constituted under Ind. Trial Rule 80, shall serve as the Evidence Rules Review Committee.

B. The Evidence Rules Review Committee shall conduct a continuous study of the Indiana Rules of Evidence and shall submit to the Supreme Court from time to time recommendations and proposed amendment to such rules. The Committee shall follow the procedure set forth in Ind. Trial Rule 80(D) in the amendment of the Rules of Evidence. Amendments or additions may be suggested by the Supreme Court of Indiana in current case law or the Indiana General Assembly through enactment of legislation. Proposed amendments or comment on published amendments offered by the Bench, Bar, and Public, shall be delivered in writing to the Committee's Executive Secretary, 30 South Meridian Street, Suite 500, Indianapolis, Indiana 46204.

*   *   *   *   *

ANALYSIS

Rule 1101 provides for the creation of a permanent Evidence Rules Review Committee to review and recommend changes of evidence rules to the Supreme Court of Indiana. The Evidence Rules Review Committee has not played an important role in the development of Indiana evidence law through amendments to the Rules, allowing for growth and refinement in evidence law through common law. Only a handful of individual Rules have been amended since their adoption in 1994.

Appendix

COMMENTARY

Below are the committee commentaries for the Indiana Rules of Evidence. In some cases the text, as supplied by the Supreme Court of Indiana, contained typographical inaccuracies. We have elected to reproduce the text in its entirety without correction.

This is a modification of Uniform Rule of Evidence ("URE") 101 and 1101. URE 1101 is deleted; its content is included herein. Nine other states have merged URE 1101 with URE 101.

In small claims, the rules do not strictly apply. Small Claims Rule 8 only retains privileges and offers to compromise.

Rule 101(a) identifies the types of court proceedings to which these rules apply. The Indiana Supreme Court has the authority to adopt the Rules of Evidence which apply to judicial proceedings in the State of Indiana, and, in so doing, the adopted rules of evidence will control the laws of evidence even if contradicted by statutory law. *See Hawkins v. Auto-Owners (Mut.) Ins. Co.* (1993), Ind., 608 N.E.2d 1358; *Matter of Public Law No. 305 and Public Law No. 309* (1975), 263 Ind. 506, 334 N.E.2d 659. If these rules do not cover a specific evidentiary issue, other applicable common or statutory law should apply.

In bench trials there may be a less strict application of the rules of evidence. The court is not required to rule promptly on evidence questions, and is presumed to be able to disregard inadmissible evidence. *Pinkston v. State* (1982), Ind., 436 N.E.2d 306; *Courtney v. Luce* (1936), 101 Ind.App. 622, 200 N.E.501.

The rules are not strictly enforced; for example, at certain pre- and post-trial hearings. *Payne v. State* (1987), Ind., 515 N.E.2d 1141 (probation revocation hearing); *Dillon v. State* (1986), Ind., 492 N.E.2d 661 (sentencing); *Lindsey v. State* (1985), Ind., 485 N.E.2d 102 *reh'g. denied with opinion* 491 N.E.2d 191 (suppression hearing); *Ray v. State* (1986), Ind.App., 496 N.E.2d 93 (Post Conviction Relief hearing); and *Clemons v. State* (1974), 162 Ind.App. 50, 317 N.E.2d 859, *cert. denied* 423 U.S. 859 (1975).

In juvenile fact finding hearings under Ind.Code § 31-6-4-14, rules of evidence have been applicable. *In re B.M.P. v. State* (1983), Ind.App., 446 N.E.2d 17 (admissibility of prior statement of witness); Simmons v. State (1978), Ind.App., 371 N.E.2d 1316 (hearsay rule and business record exception). Rule 104(a) is not intended to change the applicability of Rules of Evidence to these proceedings.

The party asserting that these Rules of Evidence do not apply has the burden of establishing that with the court.

This is URE and Federal Rules of Evidence ("FRE") 102. Twenty-six states adopted this rule verbatim; three states varied the language; two states deleted it. Some judges use this rule as authority to deviate from more specific rules of evidence in order "to achieve fairness." This rule is not intended as a license to ignore the requirements or limitations of other specific rules of evidence.

This is URE and FRE 103, with a substitution of "proper offer of proof" in (a)(2) for "offer."

Although there is no provision for a motion in limine, such motions are encouraged by Rule 103(c) in both civil and criminal cases. Also, it is recommended that where pre-trial evidentiary disputes are anticipated, the dispute should be addressed in the Pre-Trial Order under Indiana Trial Rule 16.

A ruling on a motion in limine is not final and preserves no issue for appeal. If the motion is denied, the objection must be renewed at trial or any claimed error is waived. *Harris v. State* (1985), Ind., 480 N.E.2d 932. If granted, the excluded evidence must be offered at trial (out of the jury's hearing) to preserve the issue for appeal. *Bieghler v. State* (1985), Ind., 481 N.E.2d 78, *cert. denied*, 475 U.S. 1031 (1986).

Rule 103(a)(1) is consistent with the doctrine that failure to timely object waives any error in the admission of evidence. *Scott v. State* (1973), 260 Ind. 67, 292 N.E.2d 252. It is consistent with Indiana Criminal Rule 6. The grounds of the objection must be specific or apparent from the context of the questioning.

In Indiana, an objection must be specific in order for the issue to be preserved for appellate review. *Willis v. State* (1987), Ind., 510 N.E.2d 1354, *cert. denied*, 484 U.S. 1015 (1988). Concerning the specificity of an objection, Rule 103(a)(1) provides that a general objection is sufficient if a specific ground is "apparent from the context". There is Indiana authority that if the grounds for the objection are obvious from the context, the specific grounds need not be stated. *Kinsman v. State* (1881), 77 Ind. 132; *McVey v. Blair* (1856), 7 Ind. 590; *see also Robert Lowell Miller, Jr., Indiana Practice*, § 103.501 (1984) (hereinafter *"Miller, Indiana Practice"*).

Where an improper or unresponsive answer is given, a timely motion to strike is required to preserve error. This practice is unaltered by Rule 103(a)(1).

Rule 103(a)(2) concerns the necessity of offers of proof when the offered testimony or evidence is excluded. This rule is consistent with Criminal Rule 6 and Indiana Trial Rule 43(C). Nothing in this rule is intended to change the current practice regarding offers of proof.

Rule 103(b) adds to Indiana law; currently, there is no Indiana case law on the trial court's authority to direct that the offer of proof be by question and answer. Miller, *supra*, §§ 103.111, 103.201.

Rule 103(c) requires holding proceedings on contested evidentiary issues outside the jury. Prior Indiana law viewed this as the better practice, but did not mandate it. *Bryant v. State* (1979), 270 Ind. 268, 385 N.E.2d 415; *Stephenson v. State* (1932), 205 Ind. 141, 186 N.E. 293.

Rule 103(d) addresses fundamental errors. A fundamental error in a civil case is an error which, if not rectified, would deny the litigant "fundamental due process." This results where a statement is made or an act is done which results in prejudicial error that goes to the very heart of a party's case and where the statement or act is wholly outside of the preventive or corrective powers of that litigant. *United Farm Bureau Family Life Ins. v. Fultz* (1978), 176 Ind.App. 217, 375 N.E.2d 601. A similar rule exists in criminal proceedings. In *Malo v. State* (1977), 266 Ind. 157, 361 N.E.2d 1201, the Supreme Court described fundamental error in a criminal case to be error which, if not corrected, would deprive the accused of fundamental due process. *See also Webb v. State* (1972), 259 Ind. 101, 284 N.E.2d 812.

Rule 103 is consistent with Trial Rule 61 on harmless error. Rule 103 does not address the issue of standard of review for harmless error, and the committee makes no recommendation upon this issue. A review of case law suggests that various standards have been applied. Some federal appeals courts have held that the standard of review is whether the substantial rights of the parties were "more probably than not untainted by the error." *See, e.g., United States Industries v. Touche Ross & Co.*, 854 F.2d 1223 (10th Cir. 1988); *Smith v. Chesapeake & Ohio Railroad*, 778 F.2d 384 (7th Cir. 1985); *Haddad v. Lockheed Cal Corp.*, 720 F.2d 1454 (9th Cir. 1983). In contrast, other federal appeals courts have held that an error is not harmless unless it affects substantial rights. *Williams v. United States Elevator Corp.*, 920 F.2d 1019 (D.C. Cir. 1990); *McQueeney v. Wilmington Trust Co.*, 779 F.2d 916 (3rd Cir. 1985); *O'Rear v. Fruehauf Corp.*, 554 F.2d 1304 (5th Cir. 1977).

The Indiana Supreme Court, in *Bowman v. State* (1991), Ind., 577 N.E.2d 569, held that to find an error in the admission of evidence harmless, there must be "no substantial likelihood that the evidence contributed to the verdict." However, the Indiana Court of Appeals applied a different standard in *Sierp v. Vogel* (1992), Ind.App., 592 N.E.2d 1253. In that case, the court held that where incompetent evidence is admitted on a material point in favor of the party who offered it, a presumption exists that such evidence is influential. If the erroneously admitted evidence does not bear on a material issue, prejudice is not presumed.

In *Chapman v. California*, 386 U.S. 18 (1967), the Court stated that a criminal case must be reversed if a constitutional violation occurs unless the error is shown to be harmless, beyond a reasonable doubt.

Only four states have adopted URE 104 verbatim. Others have adopted the rule, with only minor changes. Like many states, Indiana has omitted "in the Court's discretion" in subsection (b). *See* Unif.R.Evid. § 104, 13A U.L.A. 50–52 (1986) for a listing of other states deleting the same phrase. Indiana's rule is the same as FRE 104 except as noted below.

Rule 104(a) and (b) retain current Indiana law. *Miller, Indiana Practice,* § 104.601. Rule 104(a) says that in preliminary hearings on admissibility of evidence the court is not bound by the Rules of Evidence except those with respect to privileges. Indiana has already permitted relaxation of strict evidence rules in certain proceedings. *See, e.g., Lindsey v. State* (1985), Ind.App., 485 N.E.2d 102 (pre-trial suppression hearing). *See* Commentary to Rule 101.

This rule does not mention the standard to be applied by the trial court in determining admissibility of evidence. In *United States v. Franco*, 874 F.2d 1136, 1139 (7th Cir. 1989) the court used a "preponderance of the evidence" standard to determine the admissibility of evidence under a hearsay exception, and considered hearsay and other evidence normally inadmissible at trial in so ruling. This is contrasted with *Cardin v. State* (1989), Ind.App., 540

N.E.2d 51, which specifically stated Indiana has not adopted the federal approach of allowing circumstantial evidence derived from the document itself, without the testimony of the custodian or another qualified person, to support admission. Rule 104 now gives the court discretion to contravene the *Cardin* holding.

Before a confession is admissible, the State must prove beyond a reasonable doubt that it was voluntary. *Coates v. State* (1989), Ind., 534 N.E.2d 1087. In Indiana criminal cases, challenges to a confession, identifications and searches must be held outside the presence of the jury. *Grimm v. State* (1990), Ind., 556 N.E.2d 1327; *Quarles v. State* (1965), 247 Ind. 32, 211 N.E.2d 167. Although the Federal Rule states, "outside the hearing of the jury," the Indiana rule has added out of the "presence" of the jury. This continues existing Indiana law. The better practice is to present motions addressing matters in the rule before trial and, if necessary, renew an objection during trial. Otherwise, disruption and delay may occur. Moreover, an informed decision to proceed to trial may depend upon the trial court's ruling.

Rule 104(c) continues the procedure of allowing objections to be made outside the hearing of the jury so that jury members are not exposed to prejudicial information.

Indiana does not have any decisions directly relating to the matters addressed in Rule 104(d), but it appears that a defendant's cross-examination is limited to the subject matter of the direct testimony. The testimony of a defendant at a preliminary hearing cannot be admitted against him at trial. *Simmons v. United States*, 390 U.S. 377 (1966). It can be used to impeach him if his trial testimony is different. *Harris v. New York*, 401 U.S. 222 (1971).

Twenty-four states have adopted URE 105 verbatim, and others have made only minor modifications. Indiana's Rule 105 is identical to the URE and FRE. Empirical studies unanimously show that a limiting instruction does not prevent spill-over prejudice. American Bar Association Section of Litigation, *Study of Emerging Problems Under the Federal Rules of Evidence* (David A. Schleuter ed., 2d ed. 1991) (hereinafter "A.B.A. Study"). In criminal cases the classic "Bruton" problem is an example. *See Bruton v. United States*, 391 U.S. 123 (1968). Indiana follows redaction as a solution, but it is still to the trial court's discretion.

Indiana refers to instructions contemplated by Rule 105 which are given during trial as "admonitions." These are not currently required in Indiana. The rule is intended to require the trial court to give an immediate admonition, if requested, as well as applicable final instructions.

Eighteen states have adopted URE 106 verbatim. Five states have added "acts, declarations and conversations." Two states allow the opponent the right to introduce the remaining portion of the item immediately.

URE 106 is limited to writings and recorded statements. The present language expands the rule to come closer to current Indiana law. Additionally, the term "recording" is intended to include video tapes.

URE 106 does not specify that the evidence admitted under this rule must also be admissible. This rule and the rule in some other states includes the "otherwise admissible" provision. The requirement of "otherwise admissible" should be used to exclude inadmissible evidence from being admitted as a "remainder."

Indiana's "completeness doctrine" provides that when a conversation for transaction is put into evidence, the other party may call for the entire conversation or transaction to be admitted. *Saperito v. State* (1986), Ind., 490 N.E.2d 274. Generally when one part of an item of evidence is introduced, the balance is admissible if it (1) is relevant to the portion introduced, and (2) is not incompetent evidence. *Ascherman v. State* (1991), Ind.App., 575 N.E.2d 277. *Davis v. State* (1985), Ind., 481 N.E.2d 387, holds that one party cannot introduce part of a conversation, transaction, deposition or other evidentiary material without allowing the remainder to come in to explain or illustrate the context from which the excerpted evidence was taken or to mitigate the prejudice caused by only admitting part of the evidence. Irrelevant portions of the document or conversation may be omitted because they relate to a different topic. *Johnston v. State* (1988), Ind., 517 N.E.2d 397; *Ryans v. State* (1988), Ind.App., 518 N.E.2d 494.

In *United States v. LeFevour*, 798 F.2d 977, 982 (7th Cir. 1986), the court wrote "[t]he purpose of the (completeness) rule codified in [Federal] Rule 106 is merely to make sure that a misleading impression created by taking matters out of context is corrected on the spot, because of the 'inadequacy of repair work when delayed to a point later in the trial.' " Because the federal rule appears to be aimed at addressing the immediate impact of an incomplete presentation, any omitted portion that would only be helpful to the jury is not sufficient under 106. *United States v. Sweiss*, 814 F.2d 1208 (7th Cir. 1987). Thus, 106 changes the timing of the introduction of the remainder of the item. Current law in Indiana would delay it until cross-examination, but Rule 106 allows introduction at that time.

The impact of this rule must be considered in conjunction with Rule 613 and the use of prior statements of a witness. Rule 106 is not aimed at determining the admissibility issue addressed in Rule 613. Since *Modesitt v. State* (1991), Ind., 578 N.E.2d 649, overruled *Patterson v. State* (1975), 263 Ind. 55, 324 N.E.2d 482, the approach on the use of prior consistent statements as set forth in Rule 613 and 801 should carry out the Indiana Supreme Court's approach in *Modesitt*.

Ten states have adopted URE 201 verbatim. Seven states have adopted FRE 201 which has a different treatment of whether a judicially-noticed fact in a criminal case is conclusive or permissive. Because Indiana's constitution provides that a jury in a criminal case may determine the law and the facts, it would appear that any judicially-noticed fact must only be permissive. The above rule is a modification of URE 201. Twelve states have added provisions on judicial notice of law.

FRE 201 is limited to adjudicative facts, and does not address legislative facts. In Indiana, some legislative facts have been judicially noticed. *Roeschlein v. Thomas* (1972), 258 Ind. 16, 280 N.E.2d 581 (legislative history); *State ex rel. White v. Grant Super. Ct.* (1930), 202 Ind. 197, 172 N.E. 897 (country's history); *Williams v. State* (1878), 64 Ind. 553 (topography and conditions). *O'Laughlin v. Barton* (1991), Ind., 582 N.E.2d 817, holds it is error to judicially notice affidavits of two former legislators as to their intent in passing a certain statute because the intent or motive of the individual sponsors of the bill could not be imputed to the Legislature. A modified New Hampshire version of 201 is adopted here and is not intended to change existing Indiana treatment of legislative facts. Uncodified municipal ordinances are not judicially noticed, *In the Matter of Public Law 305 and 309* (1975), 263 Ind. 506, 334 N.E.2d 659, and must be proven or established by stipulation, *Viccaro v. City of Fort Wayne* (1983), Ind.App., 449 N.E.2d 1161. The trial court reviews the

COMMENTARY

matter under the general guidelines set forth in Rule 201(a).

City of Hammond v. Doody (1990), Ind.App., 553 N.E.2d 196, 198, holds that "facts that are judicially noted must be generally known or capable of accurate determination by resort to sources whose accuracy cannot reasonably be questions." Rule 201(a) reflects no change in current Indiana law.

Current Indiana law allows the trial court to judicially notice its records in the proceedings before it. *Miller v. State* (1990), Ind., 563 N.E.2d 578 (judicial notice of defendant's testimony at bail hearing). However, courts may not take judicial notice of evidence in a different case, even if the evidence was presented to the same trial court. *Smith v. State* (1983), Ind., 443 N.E.2d 1187. Rule 201 is not intended to alter this law. Note the admissibility of public records under Rule 803(8).

Current Indiana law limits judicial notice of reasonable attorney fees to routine claims involving a modest sum. *Kahn v. Cundiff* (1989), Ind.App., 543 N.E.2d 164, *adopted* Ind., 543 N.E.2d 627. Rule 201 is not intended to alter this law.

Rule 201(d) modifies current Indiana law by making judicial notice mandatory. Formerly the court was free to deny the request for judicial notice, unless required by statute. *Miller, Indiana Practice*, §§ 201.301, 201.401. Examples of statutes requiring judicial notice include rules and regulations of agencies in *Ind.Code* § 4-22-2-11; uniform traffic control devices manual, *Ind.Code* § 9-4-1-125(f); the law of another state, *Ind.Code* § 34-3-2-1, and the law of a foreign country, Trial Rule 44.1(A).

Rule 201(g) is substantially different from current Indiana law in civil cases. Under URE 201(g) and FRE 201(g), a judicially noticed fact is conclusive in civil cases, but the jury reserves the right to reject a judicially-noticed fact in criminal cases. Thus, currently, a judicially-noticed fact is a rebuttable presumption, which disappears when competent evidence is produced tending to disprove the noticed fact. *Sumpter v. State* (1974), 261 Ind. 471, 306 N.E.2d 95, appeal after remand (1976), 264 Ind. 117, 340 N.E.2d 764, *cert. denied*, 425 U.S. 952 (1976). Rule 201(e) attempts to resolve this problem by giving a party the opportunity to be heard if there is a request for judicial notice. Under this rule, if the trial court does take judicial notice of a fact, it is conclusively found. Clearly, there is a difference between admitting evidence on a fact that may be contested and judicially noticing that fact. If there is a legitimate dispute as to judicial notice of a fact, the matter should be left to the determination of the jury.

This rule is substantially the same as FRE 301. States are split between adopting the FRE which holds that once contrary evidence is produced, the presumption disappears and the URE rule which provides for a continuing effect. Four states have allowed common law to control.

This commentary is not intended to list the numerous presumptions in Indiana created by common law or statute. For example, proof of violation of a safety regulation creates a rebuttable presumption of negligence. *Thornton v. Pender* (1978), 268 Ind. 540, 377 N.E.2d 613. It would appear that Indiana's current common law treatment is very close to FRE 301. *Young v. State* (1972), 258 Ind. 246, 280 N.E.2d 595; *Miller, Indiana Practice*, § 301.102.

The rule does not state the quantum of evidence required to defeat a presumption in a civil case. Common law should be relied upon to resolve this on an individual case-by-case basis. *See Miller, supra,* § 301.102, for discussion of the strength of different presumptions in Indiana.

Presumptions in criminal cases do not have the same effect as in civil cases. A presumption is unconstitutional if it is conclusive against the accused, or if it shifts the burden of persuasion. *Sandstrom v. Montana,* 442 U.S. 510 (1979); *Reid v. State* (1988), Ind., 529 N.E.2d 1309. A presumption may shift the burden of going forward with evidence. *Chilcutt v. State* (1989), Ind.App., 544 N.E.2d 856. The results of a blood alcohol test do not create a conclusive presumption of intoxication in a criminal case. *Hall v. State* (1990), Ind.App., 560 N.E.2d 561.

Few states have adopted URE 303 dealing with presumptions in criminal cases. There is a sufficient body of federal and state court decisions to prevent the improper use of presumptions in criminal cases. *Carella v. California,* 491 U.S. 263 (1989) (error to instruct that intent to commit theft if presumed); *Reid v. State* (1988), Ind., 529 N.E.2d 1309 (giving Sandstrom instruction was error, but harmless); *Sturgeon v. State* (1991), Ind.App., 575 N.E.2d 679 (error to instruct jury that it must infer intoxication if blood alcohol content is .10%).

URE 401 has been adopted by thirty-four states. This rule is identical to the FRE 401 and appears consistent with current Indiana law. *Valinet v. Eskew* (1991), Ind., 574 N.E.2d 283; *State v. Hall* (1982), Ind., 432 N.E.2d 679.

This rule has been criticized because litigants have been permitted to spend a great deal of time proving uncontested, but emotionally-sympathetic facts. American Bar Association Section of Litigation, *Study of Emerging Problems Under the Federal Rules of Evidence* (David A. Schleuter ed., 2d ed. 1991) (hereinafter "A.B.A. Study"). The rule does not address the relevancy standard for scientific evidence. For example, Indiana has specific statutes on blood tests for paternity determinations and D.N.A. test results. *Ind.Code* § 35-37-4-13.

This rule makes no changes to URE 402, which has been adopted by all states considering it, and is substantially the same as FRE 402. This rule does not change current Indiana law. *Lake Co. Council v. Arredondo* (1977), 266 Ind. 318, 363 N.E.2d 218; *Rust v. Watson* (1966), 141 Ind.App. 59, 215 N.E.2d 42, *on reh'g.,* 217 N.E.2d 859.

The determination of relevancy is fact sensitive and made on a case-by-case basis. *Hancock Truck Lines v. Butcher* (1950), 229 Ind. 36, 94 N.E.2d 537.

This rule authorizes the trial court to exclude relevant evidence that will do more harm than good to the truth-finding process and to the efficiency of the trial process. Because of the balance required by the rule, the higher the probative value of evidence, the less likely it is to be excluded. Probative value must be *substantially* outweighed and, since most evidence is prejudicial to the opponent, the danger referred to must be caused by unfair prejudice, i.e., a tendency to suggest decision on an improper basis such as an emotional one.

Although cases refer to "unfair surprise" and "remoteness," Indiana has followed an approach similar to Rule 403. *See, e.g., Greathouse v. Armstrong* (1992), Ind.App., 601 N.E.2d 419, (remoteness); *Indiana Ins. v. Plummer Power Mower* (1992), Ind.App., 590 N.E.2d 1085 (remoteness); *Andrews v. State* (1988), Ind.App., 529 N.E.2d 360, *cert. denied,*

COMMENTARY

493 U.S. 919 (1989) (remoteness); *McClamroch v. McClamroch* (1985), Ind.App., 476 N.E.2d 514 (witness not listed on final witness list was properly excluded). Remoteness is obviously a factor in applying the balance required by Rule 403. Unfair surprise is not included in the rule because, even though it may still be a problem despite the rules of discovery, generally granting a continuance is a more appropriate remedy than exclusion of the evidence. *Thompson v. State* (1986), Ind., 492 N.E.2d 264 (continuance to interview undisclosed witness). The choice of remedy is within the discretion of the trial court. *Rhone v. State* (1986), Ind., 492 N.E.2d 1063. In criminal cases exclusion is a proper remedy when the State's failure to disclose is flagrant and deliberate. *Wagner v. State* (1985), Ind., 474 N.E.2d 476. In civil cases, the pre-trial order under Indiana Trial Rule 16 may be used to exclude "surprise" evidence.

In criminal cases, application of this rule to evidence offered by the defendant must take into account the constitutional right to present a defense. *See Olden v. Kentucky* (1988), 488 U.S. 227; Edward J. Imwinkelried, Exculpatory Evidence, 155–169 (1990). Also, the right to present a defense must be considered when a defendant's evidence is to be excluded as a sanction for violating a discovery order. *Taylor v. Illinois*, 484 U.S. 400 (1988).

Rule 404(a) has been adopted verbatim by twelve states; eight have added a reference to their rape shield law in (2). Two states include civil action in (2). A.B.A. Study, *supra*, at 47–51, questions the extent the rule is applicable to civil cases.

Indiana has expanded criminal discovery. The advantages are obvious. The State and a criminal defendant can only make informed decisions in negotiating pleas when both know what evidence is going to be presented at trial. Trial by ambush is avoided. The procedures contained in these rules suggest pre-trial determinations of the admissibility of evidence. Both the state and the defense should know, prior to trial, the kind of evidence to be presented under Rules 201, 404, 405, 412 and others.

Rule 404(a)(2) is not intended to conflict with Rule 412, which is the current Indiana Rape Shield law, *Ind.Code* § 35-37-4-4. Rule 412 establishes a general prohibition to introduction of the victim's past sexual history.

Rule 404(b) is the federal version of the rule which was adopted by the Indiana Supreme Court in *Lannan v. State* (1992), Ind., 600 N.E.2d 1334. Rule 404(b) including the accused's ability to request notice, is in accord with present discovery policy in Indiana. *See Schumpert v. State* (1992), Ind.App., 603 N.E.2d 1339, applying 404(b) (issue of identity). This rule will enable the trial court to resolve evidentiary disputes prior to trial. *Lannan* also overturned the "depraved sexual instinct" rule. 600 N.E.2d at 1338.

Rule 404(b) does not contain standards as to the required foundation for admission of prior crimes. Prior Indiana law required that the evidence of other crimes be substantial and amount to at least a prima facie case. *Kindred v. State* (1970), 254 Ind. 127, 258 N.E.2d 411; *Miller, Indiana Practice*, § 404.203. The United States Supreme Court in reviewing 404(b) has determined that evidence of uncharged misconduct need not be proven by a preponderance. *Huddleston v. United States* (1988), 485 U.S. 681. In *Huddleston*, the Court stated that four protections are available to a defendant to prevent the admission of such evidence. First, under 404(b) the conduct must be offered for one of the purposes listed in the rule. Second, the trial court must determine under Rule 402 whether the evidence is relevant and that determination is made under Rule 104(b). Third, there should be a Rule 403 evaluation of undue prejudice. Fourth, the trial court should give a jury instruction, if requested, that such evidence is only admitted to show the purpose of its admission. If offered to show intent, the jury must limit its consideration to the intent issue. *Id.* at 1502.

Rule 404(b) evidence must be evaluated as to whether it is unfairly prejudicial and therefore excludible applying Rule 403. Current Indiana law allows a trial court to consider whether the prejudicial impact of the uncharged crimes outweighs its probative value. *Brewer v. State* (1990), Ind., 562 N.E.2d 22. Evidence of other criminal activity must be weighed against unfair prejudice to the defendant, even if admissible under some exception to the rule. *Johnson v. State* (1989), Ind.App., 544 N.E.2d 164. Rule 404(b) is in accord with Indiana law.

Before the trial court admits evidence under a 404(b) exception, the court must make the determination that the issue is disputed and that the probative value of the evidence outweighs the risk of unfair prejudice. If intent is in dispute, the other crime or act may be admissible to prove that intent. *See United States v. Johnson*, 634 F.2d 735, (4th Cir. 1980), *cert. denied*, 451 U.S. 907 (1981); *United States v. Grimes*, 620 F.2d 587, (6th Cir. 1980). This evidence may be presented in the State's case-in-chief. *United States v. Alessi*, 638 F.2d 466 (2d Cir. 1980). If intent is not at issue, it may be preferable for other crime or act evidence to be reserved for rebuttal and offered only if intent becomes an issue. *See United States v. Figueroa*, 618 F.2d 934 (2d Cir. 1980). As a general rule, evidence of matters not disputed, especially prejudicial evidence, should not be readily admitted under 404(b). *See* A.B.A. Study, *supra* at 48–51.

The notice requirement of the Indiana battery statute, *Ind.Code* § 35-37-4-14, is in conformity with Rule 404(b). This 1991 statute allows the introduction of evidence of the defendant's previous battery on the victim in the State's case-in-chief. This evidence is admissible for the purpose of proving motive, intent, identity, or common scheme and design. The statute requires the filing of a written notice thereof and an opportunity for a hearing outside the presence of the jury on whether the evidence is admissible.

Eighteen states have adopted the URE verbatim; six states prohibit proof by opinion. This rule is identical to FRE 405 except for the addition of the third sentence in (a).

Generally, a character witness cannot be asked on cross-examination whether knowledge that the defendant committed the instant crime would change the witness's opinion. *United States v. Williams*, 738 F.2d 172 (7th Cir. 1984); *United States v. Polsinelli*, 649 F.2d 793 (10th Cir. 1981); *United States v. Palmere*, 578 F.2d 105 (5th Cir. 1978). A character witness's knowledge of prior specific acts of misconduct by the defendant whose reputation is at issue may be asked on cross-examination. *Lineback v. State* (1973), 260 Ind. 503, 296 N.E.2d 788. The evidence is not admitted to prove the prior acts, but to affect weight of the reputation evidence. *Michelson v. United States*, 335 U.S. 469 (1948); *United States v. Alvarez*, 860 F.2d 801 (7th Cir. 1988); *Miller, Indiana Practice*, § 405.103. Because the inquiry is considered collateral, the cross-examiner is bound by the answer. The cross-examiner may not introduce extrinsic proof of the misconduct. 1 *Kenneth S. Brown, et al., McCormick on Evidence*, § 191 (John W. Strong, ed., 4th ed. 1992); *Miller, Indiana Practice*, § 405.103, 607.106.

In order to ask a character witness a question during cross-examination which refers to a prior act of misconduct by the defendant, there must be a reasonable basis. By asking the question, counsel impliedly represents that he is prepared to dispute a denial. *United States v. Elizondo*, 920 F.2d 1308 (7th Cir. 1990) (cross-examination question improper for want of good faith basis); *United States v. Jungles*, 903 F.2d 468, (7th Cir. 1990); *Haynes v. State* (1980), Ind.App., 411 N.E.2d 659.

The requirement that the State give notice of its intent to cross-examine a character witness regarding prior acts of misconduct allows the defendant the opportunity to argue that such prior acts of misconduct did not occur or that mention of the act would be unduly prejudicial under 402. The notice requirement is consistent with the notice obligations for judicial notice, Rule 201; Rape Shield, Rule 412; previous batteries, *Ind.Code* § 35-37-4-14; and other crimes, wrongs or acts, Rule 404(b).

This is the FRE verbatim. Twenty states have adopted this rule verbatim; five adopted the URE. The URE allows habit or routine to be proven by opinion or by specific instances of conduct sufficient in number to warrant a finding that the habit existed. Habit or custom may not be proven by opinion.

While there is commentary on the admissibility of habit, there is no clear Indiana precedent concerning evidence of an individual's habits. *Miller, Indiana Practice*, § 406.101. Indiana and the federal rules are the same regarding customs or routine business practices. *Id.* at 406.102. See cases on custom of speed of a train on a particular occasion. *Id.* at § 406.102, n. 7. Admission of evidence of similar acts or occurrences is within the discretion of the trial court. *Bottoms v. B & M Coat Corp.* (1980), Ind.App., 405 N.E.2d 82; *In Re: The Adoption of Dove* (1977), 174 Ind.App. 464, 368 N.E.2d 6.

Fourteen states have adopted URE 407 verbatim, which is identical to FRE 407 which Indiana has adopted. Nine states made stylistic changes. Four admit such evidence in product liability cases, while one state excludes it.

See Bruce I. McDaniel, Annotation, *Admissibility of Evidence of Subsequent Repairs or Other Remedial Measures in Products Liability Cases*, 74 A.L.R.3d 1001 (1976), for treatment of this topic in product liability cases. In strict liability cases, the rule may not be applicable in Indiana. *Ortho Pharmaceutical Corp. v. Chapman* (1979), 180 Ind.App. 33, 388 N.E.2d 541. *See also Ragsdale v. K-Mart Corp.* (1984), Ind.App., 468 N.E.2d 524 (the fact that a revision in design was made in a defective design case would not be admissible unless feasibility was contested). Rule 407 does not address the issue of admission of remedial measures in strict liability cases under *Restatement (Second) of Torts* § 402A (1965).

The firing of the employee at fault has been treated as a subsequent remedial measure. *Dukett v. Mausness* (1989), Ind.App., 546 N.E.2d 1292, 1294.

The admission or exclusion of evidence of subsequent remedial measures is within the discretion of the trial court. The evidence is inadmissible unless its need outweighs the danger inherent in its misuse. *Welch v. Railroad Crossing, Inc.* (1986), Ind.App., 488 N.E.2d 383.

If the plaintiff's contributory negligence is raised as a defense, evidence of subsequent remedial safety measures may become admissible on the issue of contributory negligence. *Rimkus v. Northwest Colorado Ski Corp.*, 706 F.2d 1060 (10th Cir. 1983).

Seventeen states adopted URE 408 verbatim, eleven with minor stylistic changes. This rule is FRE 408 except for the addition of the last sentence. *See New Burnham Prairie Homes, Inc. v. Village of Burnham*, 910 F.2d 1474, (7th Cir. 1990), as an example of the federal rule.

It appears that the first and second to the last sentences of 408 are not in conflict with Indiana law. The middle sentences abrogate Indiana common law. *Miller, Indiana Practice*, § 408.104 (Miller does not explain the conflict).

This rule encourages settlements. "The fear is that settlement negotiations will be inhibited if the parties know that their statements may later be used as admissions of liability." *Kritikos v. Palmer Johnson, Inc.*, 821 F.2d 418 (7th Cir. 1987), *quoting Central Soya Co., Inc. v. Epstein Fisheries, Inc.*, 676 F.2d 939 (7th Cir. 1982). Alternate Dispute Resolution Rule 2.12 is almost identical to 408. This rule is not intended to apply to criminal proceedings.

Twenty-two states adopted verbatim URE 409; two made stylistic changes; and five expanded the rule to include any kind of expense. The Indiana rule has added "paying" in the first sentence and extended the coverage to property damage. Rule 409 does not change Indiana law.

Ind.Code § 34-3-2.5-1 excludes the introduction of evidence of advance payments by a defendant or its insurer. Indiana law, beyond the statute, is unclear. *Miller, Indiana Practice*, § 409.102. *See Karl H. Larsen, Annotation, Admissibility of Evidence Showing Payment, or Offer or Promise of Payment, of Medical, Hospital, and Similar Expenses of Injured Party by Opposing Party*, 65 A.L.R.3d 932 (1975).

Seven states adopted the URE verbatim; eight have adopted the URE in substance. Some states have adopted the federal rule, which is substantially different; three have deleted the "completeness" exception; three have deleted the "perjury" exception. Seven states have added an "impeachment" exception. The rule adopted here is the URE with the second paragraph taken from the federal rule. The rule retains Indiana law on admissibility of plea negotiations and discourages a defendant from committing perjury in open court.

Current Indiana law is found at *Ind.Code* §§ 35-35-1-4 and 35-35-3-4. Ind.Code § 35-35-1-4(d) states that "A plea of guilty, or guilty but mentally ill at the time of the crime, which is not accepted by the Court or is withdrawn, shall not be admissible as evidence in any criminal, civil, or administrative proceeding." *See also Ind.Code* § 35-35-3-4.

Plea bargaining is an important tool of the criminal justice system and is encouraged. Both sides are free to make disclosures without the fear of hearing them repeated at a trial if negotiations are unsuccessful. The fact that the defendant engaged in plea discussions or made a plea agreement should not be received in evidence in any criminal, civil or administrative hearing unless the defendant enters a plea of guilty or nolo contendere which is not withdrawn. *Moulder v. State* (1972), 154 Ind.App. 248, 289 N.E.2d 522. In order to be inadmissible, the communication must have as its ultimate purpose the reduction of punishment or other favorable treatment to the defendant. *Id.* However, pre-charge statements made by the defendant to a police officer who does not have authority to enter into a binding plea agreement are admissible. *Martin v. State* (1989), Ind., 537 N.E.2d 491; *Chase*

COMMENTARY

v. State (1988), Ind., 528 N.E.2d 784. *But see Messer v. State* (1987), Ind.App., 509 N.E.2d 249 (statements made by a defendant attempting to plea bargain are inadmissible and trial counsel was ineffective for not objecting). A defendant's statement establishing a factual basis made at a guilty plea hearing is inadmissible when the guilty plea is later withdrawn. *Tyree v. State* (1988), Ind.App., 518 N.E.2d 814. Whether the communications are actually plea negotiations is a factual determination left to the trial court.

Indiana's current rule also applies to sentencing hearings. A sentencing court may not consider "clean-up" statements of the defendant made during plea negotiations which did not result in a plea agreement accepted by the Court, *Hensley v. State* (1991), Ind.App., 573 N.E.2d 913, 917. *But see Williams v. State* (1992), Ind.App., 601 N.E.2d 347 (no error where a clean-up statement of a withdrawn plea used to impeach defendant when the impeaching evidence was not a substantial part of the State's case).

The rule creates an exception for perjury or false statements. The rule has been applied in Indiana although that court did not adopt the Federal Rule of Criminal Procedure. *See State v. Wolff* (1989), Ind.App., 545 N.E.2d 39 (perjury charge allowed when defendant entered a guilty plea and made misrepresentations as to his past driving record).

Twenty states have adopted the URE verbatim; all others made only stylistic changes. Indiana's rule is identical to URE and FRE 411. A.B.A. Study, *supra*, at 68–69, states the rule fails to specify a balancing test for admissibility of insurance when offered for "other purposes."

A plaintiff may not introduce evidence of insurance coverage for a compensatory damage claim after the defendant testified to his minimal net worth on a punitive damage claim. *Osborne v. Wenger* (1991), Ind.App., 572 N.E.2d 1343.

Rule 411 does not change Indiana law. *See Miller, Indiana Practice*, § 411.104.

Evidence of insurance coverage is not relevant to the amount of damages. It has been recognized that if a jury is cognizant that a defendant will not bear the incidents of the judgment, the jury may be prejudiced in favor of an excessive verdict. *Rust v. Watson* (1966), 141 Ind.App. 59, 215 N.E.2d 42; *Miller, Indiana Practice*, § 411.101; 2 *John H. Wigmore, Wigmore on Evidence*, § 282a (Chadbourn rev. 1979).

URE 412 deals directly with a Rape Shield approach. Rule 412 is used seldom because there are few federal rape cases. Only one state has adopted the federal rule. The current Indiana Rape Shield law, *Ind.Code* § 35-37-4-4, is adopted as Rule 412.

If the Indiana Supreme Court adopts Rules of Evidence that contravene existing statutory law in Indiana, the Court adopted Rules of Evidence will control. *Hawkins v. Auto-Owners (Mut.) Ins. Co.* (1993), Ind., 608 N.E.2d 1358; *Matter of Public Law No. 305 and Public Law No. 309* (1975), 263 Ind. 506, 334 N.E.2d 659.

There are a number of cases interpreting Indiana's current Rape Shield law. Under the current statute, the defendant has the opportunity to argue that exclusion of such evidence violates the constitutional right to present a defense. *Chambers v. Mississippi*, 410 U.S. 284 (1973); *Washington v. Texas*, 388 U.S. 14 (1967). *See also Doe v. United States*, 666 F.2d 43, 48, n. 9 (4th Cir. 1981) (and cases cited therein); Joel E. Smith, Annotation, *Constitutionality of "Rape Shield" Statute Restricting Use of Evidence of Victim's Sexual Experience*, 1 A.L.R.

4th 283 (1980). The determination of a constitutional violation is fact sensitive, and is best resolved on a case-by-case basis. *See Roberts v. State* (1978), 268 Ind. 127, 373 N.E.2d 1103 (rule is not direct violation of constitutional right). *See* Edward J. Imwinkelried, Exculpatory Evidence, § 9-4 (1990); Churchwell, *The Constitutional Right to Present Evidence: Progeny of Chambers v. Mississippi*, 19 CrimL.Bul. 131, 132 (1983).

Rule 412 balances the defendant's constitutional right to present relevant evidence with encouraging a victim to report the crime without fear that her sexual history will become public. *Harris v. State* (1987), Ga., 362 S.E.2d 211 (public policy statement); *Olden v. Kentucky*, 488 U.S. 227; (1988) (when consent was the issue in a rape case, it was error in not admitting a black defendant's evidence that the white rape victim was living with another black man, and the rape claim may have been to protect that relationship); *Imwinkelried, Exculpatory Evidence*, Sec. 5-2, pp. 118–121 (1990); Sec. 9-4, pp. 222–223.

Rule 412 is not applicable to civil cases. *Barnes v. Barnes* (1992), Ind., 603 N.E.2d 1337. Prior and subsequent sexual conduct of a plaintiff may be admissible if relevant to liability or damage issues. *Id.* at 1345.

Article V—Privileges—Commentary

Regional Committee's Note

The committee recommends the adoption of URE 501 as modified to include URE 510–512 and a notice provision, but unanimously and strongly recommends that no further rules concerning privilege be adopted as part of Article V of the Indiana Rules of Evidence. The Supreme Court's adoption of rules concerning specific privileges would (1) contravene general views concerning the creation of privileges, (2) contravene prior Indiana law, and (3) create significant uncertainty in the state's trial courts.

1. Identification of relationships entitled to protection of a privilege generally is a matter of public policy. While courts are well-equipped to gauge matters such as the privilege's impact on the fact-finding process and whether a privilege has been asserted or waived, courts are more poorly suited than the legislature to identify the "interests and relations which, rightly or wrongly, are regarded as of sufficient social importance to justify some sacrifice of availability of evidence relevant to the administration of justice." 1 *Kenneth S. Brown, et al., McCormick on Evidence*, § 72 (John W. Strong, ed., 4th ed. 1992); *see also* 23 Charles A. Wright and Kenneth W. Graham, Jr., *Federal Practice and Procedure:* Evidence § 5422, at 673–675 (1980) ("In a society with egalitarian pretensions, the creation and justification of a privilege to refuse to respond to a judicial inquiry is essentially a political question; i.e., it is an allocation of power as between various components of the society. . . . Given the political nature of privileges, it is not surprising that in most states the allocation of these exemptions tends to follow the distribution of political power in contemporary society.").

The committee believes that the commentary to the Washington Rules of Evidence applies with equal force to Indiana:

> Much of the law of privileged communications in Washington is statutory. Although the statutes lack the detail codified in other jurisdictions, many details can be determined by reference to decisional law. These statutes and decisions interpreting

them remain in law under the Washington Rules of Evidence. The drafters of the Washington rules felt that privileges are established in order to protect a specific relationship or interest as a matter of public policy. Evidentiary privileges pertaining to confidential communications foster interests or relationships determined to be of sufficient social importance that nondisclosure of the communication is considered an acceptable cost even though consideration of the testimony would aid in the determination of the truth in the course of litigation. The legislature is equipped to make the policy determinations underlying the creation of evidentiary privileges. Thus privileges are ordinarily more appropriately created by statute than by procedural rule.

5 Karl B. Teglund, *Washington Practice:* Evidence, at 359 (1982).

2. Consistent with this view, Indiana long has held that privileges are statutory in nature and that it is within the power of the legislature to create them. *Terre Haute Regional Hospital v. Trueblood* (1992), Ind., 600 N.E.2d 1358. With very few exceptions, Indiana's courts have complied with this stricture. *See, e.g., Hunter v. State* (1977), 172 Ind.App. 397, 360 N.E.2d 588, *cert. denied*, 434 U.S. 906 (1977). While the General Assembly has seen fit to create many statutory privileges, discussed in greater detail below, the courts have adopted privileges only for voters' ballots, *McArtor v. State* (1925), 196 Ind. 460, 148 N.E. 477, and police informants, *Beverly v. State* (1989), Ind., 543 N.E.2d 1111. The court's adoption of rules creating privileges would constitute a dramatic break with this history. The committee believes it would be a mistake for the Supreme Court, through court-adopted rules, to change course and undertake a task long left to the legislative branch of government.

3. The committee initially believed that placement of Indiana's law of privilege in the Indiana Rules of Evidence would be an attractive proposition, allowing the bench and bar a ready reference to succinct, court-approved statements of the law of privilege. Based on comments received at the public hearing, this appears to be a universal initial reaction. Further investigation led the committee to a different conclusion, even apart from the traditional roles of the judicial and legislative branches with respect to privileges.

The URE addresses eight privileges. Four of those are the traditional common law privileges for communications to lawyers, physicians, spouses, and clergy, found in *Ind.Code* § 34-1-14-5; a fifth, the informant's privilege, is of more recent vintage. The remaining three address privileges with which Indiana has little or no experience: the political vote, trade secrets, and official government information. Adoption of those eight rules would leave unmentioned a considerable number of privileges presently recognized in Indiana. The URE do not provide:

   a. an accountant-client privilege, *see Ind.Code* § 25-2-1-23;

   b. a hospital peer review privilege, *see Ind.Code* § 34-4-12.6-2(c);

   c. a newsperson's source privilege, *see Ind.Code* § 34-3-5-1;

   d. a school counselor's privilege, *see Ind.Code* § 20-6.1-6-15;

   e. privileges for social workers and clinical social workers, *see Ind.Code* § 25-23.6-6, or certified marriage and family therapists, *see Ind.Code* § 25-23.6-9;

   f. a potential privilege concerning child abuse reports to juvenile authorities, *see*

Ind.Code § 31-6-11-18, or others, *see Ind.Code* § 31-6-11-22;

g.   a potential privilege concerning certain juvenile proceedings, *see Ind.Code* §§ 31-6-8-1.3, 3-4-1A-15, 31-6-8-1, 31-6-11-18;

h.   a privilege concerning a patient's AIDS diagnosis, *see Ind.Code* §§ 16-1-9.7-7, 16-1-10.5-11;

i.   a privilege for battered spouse and child abuse centers, *see Ind.Code* § 35-37-6-9(b);

j.   a privilege for communications concerning the Commission on Judicial Qualifications, *see Ind.Code* § 32-2.1-5-4;

k.   a privilege for certain hospital records, *see Ind.Code* § 16-4-3-1; 34-3-15.5-6, or mental health records, *see Ind.Code* § 16-4-8.3-1;

l.   a privilege concerning prescription records, *see Ind.Code* § 25-26-13-15;

m.   a privilege for accident reports mandated by law, *see Ind.Code* § 9-26-3-4;

n.   a privilege for aircraft accident reports to the transportation department, *see Ind.Code* § 8-21-3-6;

o.   a privilege for communicable disease information for semen donors, *see Ind.Code* § 16-8-7.5-15;

p.   a privilege for records of traffic violations, *see Ind.Code* § 9-14-3-7(e);

q.   a privilege for mandatory reports by railroad companies concerning accidents, *see Ind.Code* § 8-3-1-21;

r.   a potential privilege for reports to environmental agencies, *see Ind.Code* § 13-7-16-3;

s.   a potential privilege for reports by medical personnel to a fire marshall, *see Ind.Code* § 35-47-7-3;

t.   a potential privilege for appraisal and relocation of documents prepared by or for the highway department, *see Ind.Code* § 8-9.5-4-8;

u.   a potential privilege for records of the Bureau of Motor Vehicles concerning an undercover officer, *see Ind.Code* § 9-14-3-9;

v.   a potential privilege concerning bond issues, *see Ind.Code* § 5-1-15-5;

w.   a potential privilege concerning commercial feed, *see Ind.Code* § 15-5-3-23;

x.   a potential privilege concerning the communicable disease registry, *see Ind.Code* § 16-1-10.5-11.6;

y.   a potential privilege concerning complaints to the consumer protection division, *see Ind.Code* § 4-6-9-4(b);

z.   a potential privilege for complaints concerning regulated professions, *see Ind.Code* § 25-17-10;

aa.   a potential privilege for certain information concerning controlled substances, *see Ind.Code* § 35-48-6-9;

ab.   a potential privilege concerning criminal histories, *see Ind.Code* § 5-2-5-1;

ac.   a potential privilege concerning licensing examinations, *see Ind.Code* § 5-14-3-4;

ad.   a potential privilege concerning certain records of life insurance companies, *see Ind.Code* § 27-8-8-10; or

ae.   a potential privilege concerning property taxes, *see Ind.Code* § 6-1.1-35-12.

Adoption of URE 502 through 509 would leave these statutory privileges in limbo and create confusion within Indiana's tribunals in light of the doctrine that evidentiary statutes are void if they conflict with rules adopted by the Indiana Supreme Court. *Hawkins v. Auto-Owners (Mut.) Ins. Co.* (1993), Ind., 608 N.E.2d 1358; *Matters of Public Law No. 305 and Public Law No. 309* (1975), 263 Ind. 506, 334 N.E.2d 659.

The committee considered expanding the number of specific privileges to be contained in the rules of evidence to reflect existing privileges. As the foregoing subparagraphs demonstrate, however, the provisions on privilege would become unwieldy, and little more would be gained than merely to transfer existing statutes into court rules. The committee also doubts that any researcher can claim to have uncovered every statutory privilege in Indiana.

The committee gave strong consideration to adopting the URE as to the privileges most commonly claimed (communications to attorneys, physicians, spouses and clergy, and communication by informants) and stating, either in Rule 501 or in the official commentary, that the rules are not intended to abrogate other existing privileges. Vermont added such a provision to its version of Rule 501, while Delaware did so in its commentary.

The committee rejected that approach for two reasons. First, any such provision carries a risk of misinterpretation and disputes that will cause delay and expense in litigation. Second, and more important, Indiana statutes also contain exceptions to privileges, including the privileges most commonly claimed. Adoption of a variant of the URE without including the statutory exceptions casts doubt upon the exceptions' existence. *See Hawkins v. Auto-Owners (Mut.) Ins. Co.* (1993), Ind., 608 N.E.2d 1358; *Matter ofPublic Law No. 305 and Public Law No. 309* (1975), 263 Ind. 506, 334 N.E.2d 659.

For example, URE 503(d) provides three exceptions to the physician-patient privilege: hospitalization proceedings, court-ordered examinations, and conditions placed at issue through claim or defense. Indiana statutes also provide that a trial court has discretion to abrogate the privilege with respect to certified psychologists in homicide cases, *Ind.Code* § 23-33-1-17(1); that the privilege is inapplicable in cases of child abuse and neglect, Ind.Code § 31-6-11-8; that a trial court may abrogate the privilege as to communications by patients receiving mental health services or developmental disability services, *Ind.Code* § 16-4-8.3-11; that there is no privilege for blood samples, test results, or disclosures in criminal cases in which the result of a chemical test is relevant, *Ind.Code* § 9-30-6-6; and that the privilege is inapplicable in workmen's compensation proceedings, *Ind.Code* § 22-3-3-6. These exceptions could be written into an Indiana Rule 503(d), but to do so would preclude legislative change. To decline to include them would leave the state's courts and adminis-trative agencies uncertain as to the continuing effect of the legislative exceptions. The committee does not believe there should be indefinite uncertainty before learning whether the physician-patient privilege continues to apply in workmen's compensation cases.

More than half the states that have adopted variants on the URE and FRE have declined to adopt rules on specific privileges. Ten states—Arizona, Colorado, Iowa, Louisiana, Michigan, Minnesota, Montana, North Carolina, Ohio, Utah—adopted URE 501 or a variant on it, but adopted no further rules on privilege. Rhode Island Rule 501 simply states, "Nothing in these rules shall be deemed to modify or supersede existing law relating to privilege." Utah Rule 501 is quite similar, as is West Virginia's. Oregon's rule simply declares that all existing privileges shall continue to exist until changed or repealed, and the commentary contained a "partial list" of such privileges with statutory citation. Wyoming's rule looks much like FRE 501, with no further privilege rules. Louisiana and Washington did not even adopt a Rule 501.

The committee agrees with the approach taken by that majority, with some variation. Although the Indiana rules should not attempt to define specific privileges—a legislative task—the rules should articulate a standard approach to issues of waiver, comment and instructions, and should provide a notice requirement. In other words, creation of privileges is a legislative task, but enforcement of privileges is a matter as to which the judiciary can adopt a standardized approach.

Privileges Recognized Only as Provided; Waiver; Comment; Instruction; Notice

Regional Committee's Note   **Section (a).** Rule 501(a) is identical to URE 501, with two modifications. The phrase, "as enacted or interpreted by the courts of this State" is inserted after "statute" to make clear that the case law interpreting statutory privileges remains authoritative. The phrase, "or by principles of common law in light of reason and experience," is designed to preserve for the courts the right to recognize privileges in the future without amending these rules. Although Indiana's courts traditionally have been disinclined to create new privileges, adoption of a rule that would foreclose the option forever is imprudent.   **Section (b).** Rule 501(b) is identical to URE 510, which is quite consistent with present Indiana law. While each of the various statutory privileges has unique methods of waiver, state law holds that a privilege is irrevocably waived to the extent of any voluntary disclosure of privileged matter by the holder of the privilege. *Lindsey v. State* (1985), Ind., 485 N.E.2d 102, *on reh'g.*, 491 N.E.2d 191 (client's privilege); *Hunt v. State* (1956), 235 Ind. 276, 133 N.E.2d 48 (spousal privilege); *In Re Estate of Beck* (1968), 143 Ind.App. 291, 240 N.E.2d 88 (patient's privilege).

Rule 501(b) might change Indiana law in one minor respect. In *Nordyke & Marmon Co. v. Whitehead* (1914), 183 Ind. 7, 106 N.E. 867, the court held that presentation of other evidence of a communication to a physician does not waive the privilege as to the physician's testimony. No other case has followed this rule, and this eighty-year-old rule is inconsistent with other forms of privileged communications.   **Section (c).** Rule 501(c) is identical to URE 511. Research disclosed no Indiana cases on involuntary disclosure of privileged material, but this provision seems to be a logical and necessary corollary to Rule 501(b).   **Section (d).** Rule 501(d), except for the introductory clause, is identical to URE 512. Research disclosed no Indiana case that is inconsistent with this rule. Indiana courts have held comment on the exercise of an evidentiary privilege to be improper, *Pinkerton v. State* (1972), 258 Ind. 610, 283 N.E.2d 376, and that invocation of the Fifth Amendment in a criminal case should be done outside the jury's presence, *Tucker v. State* (1989), Ind., 534 N.E.2d 1110. Although no case considers a party's entitlement to such an instruction, it has been held to be proper to instruct the jury not to draw any inference from the exercise of an

evidentiary privilege. *Mortimer v. Daub* (1912), 52 Ind.App. 30, 98 N.E. 845. The addition of the introductory clause, rendering the rule inapplicable to civil cases in which a claim of the privilege against self-incrimination is raised, brings the rule into conformity with prior Indiana law, *Gash v. Kohm* (1989), Ind.App., 476 N.E.2d 910, and federal law. *Brink's, Inc. v. City of New York*, 717 F.2d 700 (2nd Cir. 1983); *see also Baxter v. Palmigiano*, 425 U.S. 308 (1976).   **Section (f).** The committee believes that a provision for notice to the court and opposing counsel of a witness's known intent to claim a privilege is consistent with other rules and appropriate for the sound administration of justice. Other rules requiring such notice include 201 (judicial notice), 404(b) (extrinsic acts), 405 (character), and 412 (rape shield). Provision of notice reduces the likelihood of a claim that a state-created privilege has violated a criminal defendant's constitutionally protected right to present a defense, *Washington v. Texas*, 388 U.S. 14 (1967), and also should assist trial preparation and judicial administration in civil cases. The last sentence, which protects the privilege for that which is disclosed in a hearing that results in sustaining the claim of privilege, insures that those who lawfully claim a privilege will not be penalized.

The addition of the language "or by act of the Indiana General Assembly" to the URE, is intended to preserve the statutory classifications of persons not competent as witnesses under Indiana law. This would include insane persons, intoxicated witnesses and persons whose testimony is governed by *Ind.Code* §§ 34-1-14-6 through 31-1-14-11 (the Dead Man's Statutes).

The sentence, "A witness does not have personal knowledge, . . ." preserves existing law with regard to hypnosis.

Rule 602 changes the law in Indiana. Previously, a witness was presumed to have personal knowledge when called to the witness stand and the party opposing the witness had the obligation to raise lack of personal knowledge. Rule 602 requires that the proponent of a witness lay a foundation as to the personal knowledge of the witness.

Rule 603 is identical to *Ind.Code* § 35-1-14-2. No particular form of oath is required. The mode of administering an oath or affirmation, however, must be "such as may be most consistent with, and binding upon, the conscience of the person to whom such oath or affirmation may be administered." *Ind.Const.* art. I, § 8.

Whenever, under the trial rules or any statute, an oath is required to be taken, a solemn affirmation may be accepted in lieu of the oath. Ind.Trial Rule 43(D).

The object of requiring the witness to state that he will tell the truth in his testimony is two-fold. First, it is to affect the conscience of the witness in order to impress upon them the duty to speak the truth. Second, the witness is cautioned that if he willfully falsifies his testimony, he can be punished for perjury under *Ind.Code* § 35-44-2-1.

Rule 603 does not require the witness to possess a level of responsibility or sense of responsibility to tell the truth. The witness is not required to believe in God. Rule 603 functions as a mere stimulus to tell the truth, and does not function to exclude competent witnesses on other grounds.

Whether a witness has sufficiently declared by oath or affirmation that he will testify truthfully is a determination to be made by the court. The determination, however, is not required by Rule 603. The court may explore whether a witness is capable of understanding his obligation to tell the truth and may inquire whether the witness can distinguish between the truth and a lie. In determining credibility, the court may consider Rule 104(a) regarding the qualifications of an individual to be a witness. *United States v. Haro*, 573 F.2d 661, (10th Cir. 1978), *cert. denied*, 439 U.S. 851.

Upon proper objection, the court's failure to administer the required oath or affirmation is prejudicial error. *Tomlin v. State* (1966), 247 Ind. 277, 215 N.E.2d 190. The requirement, however, that testimony be given under oath or affirmation is waived upon failure to object. *United States v. Perez*, 651 F.2d 268 (5th Cir. 1981); *Sweet v. State* (1986), Ind., 498 N.E.2d 924; *Pooley v. State* (1945), 116 Ind.App. 199, 62 N.E.2d 484.

In *United States v. Fowler*, 605 F.2d 181 (5th Cir. 1979), cert. denied, 445 U.S. 950 (1980), Fowler complained that the District Court erred in refusing to allow him to testify when he refused to either swear or affirm that he would tell the truth or submit to cross-examination. The court found his contention frivolous, stating that no witness has the right to testify but on the penalty of perjury and subject to cross-examination.

Rule 604 specifically requires that the interpreter meet the qualifications for an expert witness contained in Rule 702. Rule 702 requires that the interpreter, by reason of knowledge, skill, experience, training, or education, is capable of providing a true translation.

Rule 604 requires that the interpreter be administered an oath or affirmation to make a "true translation". This requires the interpreter to communicate exactly what the witness expresses in his testimony. An interpreter appointed for a criminal defendant is required to interpret everything said in the courtroom; whether by a witness, an attorney, or the court. Federal law requires the interpreter to be at the defendant's side continuously in federal cases. *See* 28 USC § 1827.

The Indiana Court provides a statutory right to an interpreter in a civil case for a party or a witness who cannot speak or understand the English language, or who suffers a hearing impairment. *Ind.Code* § 34-1-14-3 states:

> (a) Every person who cannot speak or understand the English language or who because of hearing, speaking, or other impairment has difficulty in communicating with other persons, and who is a party to any civil proceeding or a witness therein, shall be entitled to an interpreter to assist such person throughout the proceeding.

> (b) Such an interpreter may be retained by such party or witness himself, or may be appointed by the court before which the action is pending. If an interpreter is appointed by the court, the fee for the services of the interpreter shall be set by the court and shall be paid in such manner as the court may determine.

> (c) Any court may inquire into the qualifications and integrity of any interpreter, and may disqualify any person from serving as an interpreter.

> (d) Every interpreter for another person who is either a party or a witness in a court proceeding as referred to herein shall take the following oath: Do you solemnly swear (or affirm) that you will justly, truly and impartially interpret to _____ the oath about to be administered to him (her), and the questions which may be asked him (her), and the answers that he (she) shall give to such questions, relative to the

cause now under consideration before this court, so help you God (or under the pains and penalties for perjury)?

The interpreter may be retained by a party or witness or appointed by the court. The fee for the services of a court-appointed interpreter shall be set by the court and paid as the court may determine. Indiana Trial Rule 43(F) also provides that the court may appoint an interpreter and order compensation for the interpreter be paid by one of the parties and may be taxed as costs.

Previously a state provided a right to an interpreter in criminal cases, but the statute was repealed and has not been replaced. The Indiana Supreme Court, however, has held that an indigent defendant who cannot speak or understand English has a right to have his proceedings simultaneously translated to allow for effective participation. *Martinez Chevez v. State* (1989), Ind., 534 N.E.2d 731. Although Indiana courts have not considered the issue, the failure to provide an interpreter to a criminal defendant has been held to violate the Due Process Clause of the Fourteenth Amendment to the United States Constitution. *United States ex rel. Negron v. New York*, 434 F.2d 386 (2d Cir. 1970).

In all criminal cases where there is no provision made under Title 35, the Indiana Trial Rules govern pursuant to *Ind.Code* § 35-35-2-2. Additionally, where there is no procedure provided by Title 35, the court may proceed in any manner consistent with applicable statutes or court rules. *Id.*

The court may appoint and select an interpreter and may fix a reasonable compensation for the interpreter. The rule does not state when an interpreter must be appointed; thus, the matter is determined on a case-by-case basis. Interpreters, however, are generally required where (1) a witness does not speak English or not well enough to testify fully; (2) a witness speaks in sign language; and (3) a criminal defendant does not speak English or not well enough to communicate with counsel and understand the proceedings. *See 3 John H. Wigmore, Wigmore on Evidence*, § 811 (Chadbourn rev. 1970).

A court-appointed interpreter should be free from any appearance of interest or favor towards either party. *Bielich v. State* (1920), 189 Ind. 127, 126 N.E. 220. Additionally, the oath the interpreter takes requires the interpreter to be impartial. *See Ind.Code* § 24-1-14-3(d). Because the court has authority to appoint a particular interpreter against the wishes of the person being assisted, the interpreter cannot be considered the agent of the person for whom he interprets. *Schearer v. Harber* (1871), 36 Ind. 536. However, in light of the statutory right to an interpreter in civil cases, and the due process right of a criminal defendant to an interpreter, a trial court should exercise caution in appointing a particular interpreter over the objection of the person for whose benefit the appointment is being made, if an alternate interpreter is reasonably available. The trial court also has authority to appoint as many interpreters in a case as necessary to permit the presentation of the evidence. *Skaggs v. State* (1886), 108 Ind. 53, 8 N.E. 695.

This Rule effectively makes the sitting judge incompetent to testify as a witness as to any matter arising in a trial before that judge. Rule 605 changes Indiana law by making a type of witness, the presiding judge, who would otherwise be competent to testify under *Ind.Code* § 34-1-14-4 and § 34-1-14-5, incompetent to testify.

Many of the situations in which a judge may be called as a witness are avoided by the

Indiana Code of Judicial Conduct which requires a judge to disqualify himself if the judge "is to the judge's knowledge likely to be a material witness in the proceeding." Ind. Judicial Conduct Canon 3(E)(1)(d)(iv). Rule 605 is a blanket rule of "general incompetency" that makes no distinction between "material" or "immaterial" matters. Therefore, Rule 605 is broader than Canon 3 because Rule 605 prohibits any testimony by the presiding judge and Rule 605 is not dependent upon the judge's knowledge of what is "likely" to occur in a trial.

Rule 605 has a narrow application. It prevents the presiding judge from taking the stand or otherwise providing "witness-like" testimony in the trial in which that judge is presiding. Whether a judge may testify in a subsequent proceeding or in any other proceeding in which the judge is not presiding is solely a matter of Indiana common law and not within the scope of Rule 605. *Cf. Hindman v. State* (1903), 159 Ind. 586, 65 N.E. 911; *Cornett v. Johnson* (1992), Ind.App., 571 N.E.2d 572. Rule 605 applies if the judge testifies without being formally called as a witness. 3 *Jack B. Weinstein & Margaret A. Berger, Weinstein's Evidence* ¶ 605[04] (1988). Thus, Rule 605 prevents a presiding judge from engaging in off-the-record fact gathering because the activity provides the judge with substantive evidence without the benefits accorded evidence provided on the record. *Lillie v. United States*, 953 F.2d 1188, 1191 (10th Cir. 1992) (improper for judge to take a view of the accident scene outside the record).

Rule 605 does not prevent a judge from controlling the presentation of evidence; *United States v. Maceo*, 947 F.2d 1191 (5th Cir. 1991), *cert. denied*, 112 S.Ct. 1510 (1992) (judge did not impermissibly testify as to fact issue when he stated that attorney was misstating the law); *United States v. Sliker*, 751 F.2d 477 (2d Cir. 1984), *cert. denied*, 470 U.S. 1058 (1985) (Rule 605 does not address judge's preliminary determination of admissibility). It does not prohibit the judge from asking questions of a witness or from summarizing a witness' testimony. *United States v. Paiva*, 892 F.2d 148, 159 (1st Cir. 1989). Rule 605 does not prohibit the judge from giving the jury an instruction about a defendant's flight from authority. *United States v. Sanchez*, 790 F.2d 245, 252 (2d Cir. 1986), *cert. denied*, 479 U.S. 989 (instruction is not implied testimony).

Two policies are served by a rule prohibiting testimony from the presiding judge. First, if the presiding judge were to become a witness, the judge would be required to abdicate the rule of courtroom referee or would be required to wear the dual hats of witness and referee. Second, aside from the obvious problems of procedure associated with such a dual role, the judge's testimony would likely provide the appearance of partiality regarding one side. For these two reasons, Rule 605 requires the presiding judge at all times to remain the referee of evidence and at no time to be the source of substantive evidence.

Rule 606(b) comports with Indiana common law providing that the testimony or affidavits of jurors may not be received to impeach their verdict. *See, e.g., State v. White* (1985), Ind., 474 N.E.2d 995; *Bixler v. State* (1984), Ind., 471 N.E.2d 1093, *cert. denied*, 474 U.S. 834 (1985); *Bean v. State* (1984), Ind., 460 N.E.2d 936; *Knight v. Parke* (1992), Ind.App., 595 N.E.2d 280; *Harrison v. State* (1991), Ind.App., 575 N.E.2d 642. However, as with existing Indiana common law, Rule 606(b) allows jurors to provide evidence of their deliberative process for a limited purpose. The evidence may be offered to show that the jury was exposed to extraneous prejudicial information or improper extrinsic influences during their deliberations. *Fox v. State* (1984), Ind., 457 N.E.2d 1088; *Knight*, 595 N.E.2d at 280; *Harrison*, 575

N.E.2d at 646. Thus, a juror's testimony or affidavit regarding the prejudicial misconduct of a third person, like a bailiff, may be considered to determine the truth of that allegation. *Cf. Wallace v. State* (1977), Ind., 363 N.E.2d 956. While a juror may provide evidence about the misconduct of a third person, a third person, like a bailiff, may not provide evidence about the deliberation conduct of the jurors. *Wagner v. Riley* (1986), Ind.App., 499 N.E.2d 1155 (cannot allow third party to provide evidence secondhand that jurors themselves are prohibited from providing).

Indiana's adherence to the traditional rule that prohibits impeaching one's own witness is abandoned. If enforced in accord with its clear language, however, Rule 607 is subject to prejudicial abuse. A party should not be permitted to call a witness for the sole purpose of admitting in the guise of impeachment otherwise inadmissible evidence. A trial court should prevent a party from impeaching the party's own witness if the court finds the proponent of impeachment has an improper motive. *United States v. Gossett*, 877 F.2d 901 (11th Cir. 1989) (per curiam), *cert. denied*, 493 U.S. 1082 (1990); *United States v. Webster*, 734 F.2d 1191 (7th Cir. 1984); *United States v. Miller*, 664 F.2d 94 (5th Cir. 1982), *cert. denied*, 459 U.S. 854; *United States v. Morlang*, 531 F.2d 183 (4th Cir. 1975).

(a) **Section (a).** Rule 608(a) changes existing Indiana law by permitting opinion testimony to be used to establish character for purposes of impeachment and rehabilitation. It also limits the inquiry to the character trait of truthfulness and untruthfulness. Permitting opinion testimony to be used to establish character recognizes that most testimony relating to general reputation is in reality merely an expression of the testifying witness's opinion. Limiting character testimony for purposes of impeachment or rehabilitation to the trait of truthfulness or untruthfulness is appropriate as that is the trait most relevant to credibility.

(b) **Section (b).** Rule 608(b) codifies prior Indiana law. Unlike URE 608(b) and FRE 608(b), the Rule does not permit a witness to be impeached by an inference of untruthful character arising from cross-examination concerning unconvicted acts of misconduct. Although the Indiana Rule is a minority position, it has been strongly supported. In commenting on the minority rule Professor McCormick stated:

> Finally, a number of courts prohibit altogether cross-examination as to acts of misconduct for impeachment purposes. This latter view is arguably the fairest and most expedient practice because of the dangers otherwise of prejudice (particularly if the witness is a party), or distraction and confusion, of abuse by the asking of unfounded questions and of the difficulties, as demonstrated in the cases on appeal, of ascertaining whether particular acts relate to character for truthfulness.

1 *Kenneth S. Brown, et al., McCormick on Evidence*, § 41 (John W. Strong, ed., 4th ed. 1992). Rule 608 does not deal with or limit impeachment of a witness by evidence demonstrating bias, prejudice, or interest.

(a) **Section (a).** Rejecting both the FRE and URE, this section preserves prior Indiana law. *See Roseberry v. State* (1986), 273 Ind. 179, 402 N.E.2d 1248; *Ashton v. Anderson* (1972), 258 Ind. 51, 279 N.E.2d 210; *Adams v. State* (1989), Ind.App., 542 N.E.2d 1362; *Mayes v. State* (1974), 162 Ind.App. 186, 318 N.E.2d 811; *Lessig v. State* (1986), Ind.App., 489 N.E.2d 978.

(b)   Section (b). The rule adopts the FRE's use of stale convictions for impeachment. It modifies prior Indiana law which did not presume passage of time rendered a criminal conviction of no probative value for impeachment. The presumption of inadmissibility may be rebutted only if the proponent of the conviction's use gives "sufficient written notice of intent to use such evidence" to the adverse party, and the trial court determines "in the interests of justice, that the probative value of the conviction . . . substantially outweighs its prejudicial effect."

The proponent of a conviction otherwise inadmissible under Rule 609(b) must meet a heavy burden if he desires to use the conviction for impeachment. If contested, a hearing may be required to determine "specific facts and circumstances" which permits a stale conviction to be used for impeachment. The written notice of intent to use a stale conviction should contain: (1) the date of the conviction, (2) the jurisdiction, (3) the offense, and (4) the specific facts and circumstances alleged to justify admission.

(c)   Section (c). Adopting the language of the FRE, this section excludes from use for impeachment convictions that were the subject of a "pardon, annulment, certificate of rehabilitation" if the pardon, etc., was based upon a "finding of rehabilitation or a finding of innocence." If a pardon, certificate of rehabilitation, etc., was predicated upon a finding of rehabilitation and the witness is subsequently convicted of a felony, the preclusive effect of the pardon is removed. The Indiana Supreme Court first adopted Federal Rule 609(c) in *Nunn v. State* (1992), Ind., 601 N.E.2d 334 (proper to prevent impeachment by a conviction which has been pardoned after a finding of rehabilitation).

(d)   Section (d). Rule 609(d) adopts the language of the FRE, and makes a minor change in prior Indiana law. In a criminal case, the court has discretion to admit evidence of a juvenile adjudication of a witness other than the accused as impeachment evidence if the court "is satisfied that admission is necessary for a fair determination of guilt or innocence." The URE does not permit the use of a juvenile adjudication for impeachment. The FRE recognizes that refusal to permit a criminal defendant to use a juvenile adjudication to impeach a prosecution witness may, in some circumstances, violate due process. *See Davis v. Alaska*, 415 U.S. 308 (1974).

(e)   Section (e). Rule 609(e) adopts language found in both the FRE and URE. It does not change prior Indiana law. *See Rowan v. State* (1982), Ind., 431 N.E.2d 805; *Craig v. State* (1980), 273 Ind. 361, 404 N.E.2d 580; *Snelling v. State* (1975), 167 Ind.App. 70, 337 N.E.2d 829. It does make clear, however, that a witness impeached by evidence of a conviction has the right to inform the jury that the conviction is under appeal. Prior Indiana law was silent on this issue.

This rule is inconsistent with *Ind.Code* § 35-1-14-13, which states,

> No want of a belief in a Supreme Being, or in the Christian religion shall render a witness incompetent. But the want of such religious belief may be shown upon the trial. In all questions affecting the credibility of a witness, his general moral character may be given in evidence.

The statute, while affirming the fact that a witness would not be rendered incompetent regarding "matters of religion," contains the additional language, "but the want of such

COMMENTARY

religious belief may be shown upon the trial."

Rule 611(a). Control by court. Indiana Trial Rule 43(A) states that evidence "shall be presented according to the most convenient method prescribed in any of the statutes or rules to which reference is herein made." The Indiana Supreme Court in *Pittman v. State* (1982), Ind., 436 N.E.2d 74, held the trial court has the responsibility to manage and control the proceedings and is given wide latitude in the taking of testimony in a manner to insure that the rules of procedure and evidence will be adhered to.

In criminal proceedings, the trial court's discretion will be affected by the defendant's confrontation rights. In upholding the constitutionality of the major provisions of *Ind.Code* § 35-37-4-8, the Indiana Supreme Court in *Brady v. State* (1991), Ind., 575 N.E.2d 981, held that the purpose of the statute was to protect child witnesses from the potentially traumatic experience of having to testify in open court before the person they are accusing, and approved the use of a two-way closed circuit television which made the witness and accused visible to each other. *See also Maryland v. Craig*, 110 S.Ct. 3157 (1991), which upheld at Maryland statute nearly identical to *Ind.Code* § 35-37-4-8.

The appellate tribunals in Indiana have held the following to be within the discretion and control of the trial court: repetitive testimony, cumulative testimony, narrative testimony, number of witnesses called, the time permitted to examine a witness, the order of proof (within the parameters of Indiana Trial Rule 43(G)), conditional admission of documents and testimony, demonstrations, experiments, and questions posed by jurors during the proceedings.

Rule 611(b). Scope of cross-examination. The trial court has the discretion to determine the scope of cross-examination. *See Newman v. State* (1985), Ind., 485 N.E.2d 58. A party may not establish their defense by cross-examining a witness beyond the scope of direct examination. *Solomon v. State* (1982), Ind., 439 N.E.2d 570.

The scope of permissible cross-examination generally extends to all phases of the subject matter covered in direct examination and may include any matter which tends to elucidate, modify, explain, contradict, or rebut testimony given in chief by the witness. *Hudson v. State* (1986), Ind., 496 N.E.2d 1286.

Whether to permit cross-examination to test the credibility of a witness is within the trial court's discretion. *Hobbs v. State* (1990), Ind., 548 N.E.2d 164; *Huffman v. State* (1989), Ind., 543 N.E.2d 360, *cert. denied* 497 U.S. 1011 (1990).

Rule 611(c). Leading questions. A leading question has been most often defined as one that suggests to the witness the answer desired, embodies a material fact and admits of a conclusive answer in the form of a simple "yes" or "no." *Goodman v. State* (1985), Ind., 479 N.E.2d 513.

Unique facts may justify inquiring of a witness by leading questions. A witness may be treated in the same manner as a hostile witness if the peculiar circumstances attending the examination, such as the age of the witness, his lack of understanding, or the demeanor of the witness so indicate. *Edwards v. State* (1986), Ind., 500 N.E.2d 1209.

Note also that Indiana Trial Rule 43(B), sets forth conditions which when met permit the questioning of unwilling or hostile witnesses and adverse parties by leading questions.

Based on FRE 612, the Indiana rule differs only in grammatical form, and its gender-neutral style, rather than in any of the substance found in URE 612. Indiana Rule 612 addresses the same dangers and concerns and, likewise, includes the identical safeguards as URE and FRE 612. The adoption of Rule 612 represents a significant change in Indiana law.

Indiana Rule 612 is in accord with the basic premise of FRE 612, "to promote the search of credibility and memory." *See* Fed. R. Evid. 612 Advisory Committee's Note on 1972 Proposed Rules.

Rule 612 authorizes opposing counsel to inspect, cross-examine, and introduce written memoranda into evidence used to refresh a witness's memory prior to testifying, when the court determines that it is in "the interest of justice." When a document used to refresh a witness's memory contains unused portions that are irrelevant, prejudicial or harmful to one side of a dispute, the court has discretionary power under the rule to conduct *in camera* review of written memoranda and limit the use of such writings to those portions used, when necessary, to refresh a witness's memory. These rights and safeguards effectively promote and protect the ability of the trier of fact to determine truth from the relevant facts in admissible evidence.

Indiana Trial Rule 26(B)(3), provides that materials which qualify as work product are discoverable only upon a showing that the party seeking discovery has substantial need of the materials in preparation of their case and that the party is unable without undue hardship to obtain the substantial equivalent of the materials by other means. When a witness has used such materials to actually refresh their recollection prior to testifying, Rule 612 weights the balance in favor of finding that the "substantial need" exists, because of the policy in favor of effective cross-examination. *See In re Comair Air Disaster Litigation*, 100 F.R.D. 350 (E.D. Ky. 1983).

When the requirement of this rule to disclose materials used to refresh recollection conflicts with the protections afforded by the attorney-client privilege and the work-product doctrine, the weight of authority holds that Rule 612 prevails. *S & A Painting Co., Inc. v. O.W.B. Corp.*, 103 F.R.D. 407 (W.D. Pa. 1984).

Indiana Rule 613 adopts in major part the text and grammatical style of FRE 613, and its precursor in the URE 613. As adopted, Rule 613 represents a substantial change in Indiana law as reflected in the common law. Rule 613 moves away from the formalistic, and sometimes mechanical, approach to the impeachment process, and provides greater flexibility to the practitioner and the trial court in utilizing and regulating the use of prior statements during witness testimony.

See J. Schmertz, Jr., The First Decade, 30 Vill. L. Rev. 1367; *S. Saltzburg & K. Redden, Federal Rules of Evidence Manual* 595–96 (4th ed. 1986); *Michael H. Graham, Federal Practice and Procedure* § 7683 (interim ed. 1992).

The most significant portion of Rule 614 provides jurors a procedure for questioning witnesses.

Rule 615 should also include conversations conducted outside the courtroom. Witnesses should be restricted from not only being in the courtroom at the same time, but also from discussing the substance of testimony which is being presented to the trier of fact.

A. Does the Rule change current Indiana law?

Rule 701 is consistent with existing Indiana law governing lay witness opinions.

B. Differences between IRE, FRE and URE.

None.

C. State variations.

None. All states adopted this rule.

D. Committee commentary.

None.

E. Consistent existing law.

The opinion rule requires testimony to be as concrete and factual as practicable, bars speculation and conjecture, and bars legal conclusions. Trial courts are given broad discretion to permit opinion testimony whenever it will be helpful to the jury. *See Hartlerode v. State* (1984), Ind., 470 N.E.2d 716.

In general, a lay witness may state an opinion reasonably based on first hand knowledge whenever the underlying facts are difficult to express. *See Kirby v. State* (1985), Ind., 481 N.E.2d 372 (defendant was faking crying); *Gerrick v. State* (1983), Ind., 451 N.E.2d 327 (noises sounded like gunshots). Opinions routinely are admitted on the following topics: (1) Mental condition, if the witness has known and personally observed a person over a period of time, *Healey v. Healey* (1952), 123 Ind.App. 155, 109 N.E.2d 101, including the defendant's sanity in a criminal case. *Montano v. State* (1984), Ind., 468 N.E.2d 1042. (2) Physical condition, if based on personal observation, including identity, resemblance, bodily condition, intoxication, state of health, appearance and age. *Poe v. State* (1983), Ind., 445 N.E.2d 94. (3) Value, if the witness is familiar with the property or services being valued. *C.F. Broughton v. Riehle* (1987), Ind.App., 512 N.E.2d 1133 (value of services); *City of Lake Station v. Rogers* (1986), Ind.App., 500 N.E.2d 235 (property). (4) Speed and distance, if the witness observed the vehicle or object. *Gates v. Rosenogle* (1983), Ind.App., 452 N.E.2d 467.

However, some kinds of opinions are generally not admitted: (1) Speculation and conjecture by witnesses who lack personal knowledge of the underlying facts. *Kimp v. State* (1989), Ind., 546 N.E.2d 1193. (2) Legal conclusions of the witness. *Mitchell v. State* (1989), Ind., 535 N.E.2d 498. (3) Credibility of witnesses, and whether the witness believed an accusation, *Head v. State* (1988), Ind., 519 N.E.2d 151, or claim of innocence. *Shepard v. State* (1989), Ind., 538 N.E.2d 242.

In some cases, an opinion offered by a lay witness cannot be said to be "rationally based on the perception of the witness" unless the witness possesses specialized knowledge. Such witnesses are often called "skilled lay observers." Both the URE and Indiana law have recognized this category of opinion. *See Wagner v. State* (1985), Ind., 474 N.E.2d 476 (police officer could state opinion concerning what other officers were doing at crime scene because of his experience as member of investigation team); *Almodovar v. State* (1984), Ind., 464 N.E.2d 906 (witness familiar with guns could give opinion of caliber of gun he observed).

A. Does the Rule change current Indiana law?

The Rule clarifies Indiana law. It makes expert testimony admissible whenever it will "assist" the jury. Prior Indiana case law sometimes stated a more restrictive standard that expert testimony was admissible only when the subject was "beyond the knowledge" of the average juror. It also makes "reliability" the standard for admitting scientific evidence. Prior Indiana case law sometimes applied the more restrictive "general acceptance" standard.

B. Differences between IRE, FRE and URE.

Part (a) is taken verbatim from URE 702 which is identical to FRE 702 and consistent with existing Indiana law. Part (b) is not found in either URE or FRE 702. It is based on existing Indiana law governing the admissibility of scientific evidence.

C. State variations.

None. All states adopted this rule.

D. Committee commentary.

Part (a): The rule does not require a formal tender of the witness as an expert. The committee believes that judges normally should not announce their ruling that a witness is qualified as an expert, because the jurors may misinterpret such a ruling as an endorsement of the witness's testimony.

Part (b): FRE 702 has been criticized for failing to address the continuing validity of the "general acceptance" standard of *Frye v. United States*, 293 Fed. 1013 (D.C. Cir. 1923). Judge Edward R. Becker of the United States Court of Appeals for the Third Circuit calls this failure to clarify the standard for admitting novel scientific evidence "the greatest single oversight in the rules." *Edward R. Becker and Aviva Orenstein, Is the Evidence All In? A Proposal for Revising the Federal Rules*, A.B.A.J., October 1992, at 84. Part (b) clarifies that standard for Indiana.

For novel scientific evidence, the usual procedure will be for the judge to hold a separate hearing on the reliability of the proposed scientific evidence.

In part (b), we adopted the "reliability" standard in preference to the *Frye* test because it is more consistent with existing Indiana law governing the admissibility of novel scientific evidence, and because it is the test preferred by scholarly commentators. *See Becker & Orenstein, supra*, at 84; *J. Alexander Tanford et al., Novel Scientific Evidence of Intoxication: Acoustic Analysis of Voice Recordings from the Exxon Valdez*, 82 J. Crim. L. & Criminology 579, 591–95 (1991).

We rejected two alternatives to part (b). The Advisory Committee on Civil Rules has proposed that expert testimony be admissible if it is "reasonably" reliable. We agree with Judge Becker & Prof. Orenstein, *supra* at 84, that adding the undefined word "reasonably" before "reliable" invites a return to the ill-advised *Frye* test. We also rejected Judge Becker's proposal that the test for admissibility include a determination concerning "the likelihood that introduction of the testimony may overwhelm or mislead the jury." *Id.* at 84. The fear that scientific evidence may overwhelm jurors is dubious. Social psychologists have shown that jurors tend to undervalue science, under-utilize statistics, and reject science if it conflicts with intuition, emotion and personal experiences. *See Tanford et al., supra*, at 596–97.

E. Consistent existing law.

Part (a): An expert is one who, by reason of formal training or practical experience, has

COMMENTARY

special knowledge of a subject that is not a matter of common knowledge to the jury. An expert may testify and give opinions whenever it will aid the jury in determining material issues. *Noblesville Casting Div. of TRW v. Prince* (1982), Ind., 438 N.E.2d 722. The qualifications of an expert may be established by formal training and education, or by practical experience. *Epps v. State* (1977), 267 Ind. 177, 369 N.E.2d 404. Only minimal training must be proved. *See Balfour v. State* (1981), Ind., 427 N.E.2d 1091 (only four hours of formal training). An expert does not need both training and experience; either will suffice. *Brackens v. State* (1985), Ind., 480 N.E.2d 536 (fingerprint expert with no formal training but 18 years of experience); *Gambill v. State* (1985), Ind., 479 N.E.2d 523 (pathologist with education and training but no experience with stabbings). Whether a proposed expert witness has been sufficiently qualified is for the trial court's determination based on the witness' testimony; there is no fixed standard. *See Wissman v. State* (1989), Ind., 540 N.E.2d 1209 (no precise quantum of knowledge required); *Willis v. State* (1987), Ind.App., 512 N.E.2d 871 (whether witness qualified as expert is for trial court's discretion). The background and knowledge of the witness must relate to the specific subject in question. *McCraney v. Kuechenberg* (1969), 144 Ind.App. 629, 248 N.E.2d 171. An expert may not render an opinion beyond their area of expertise. *See Clark v. State* (1990), Ind., 562 N.E.2d 11, *cert. denied*, 112 S.Ct. 425 (1991). There is no requirement that the expert be licensed to practice in Indiana. *State v. Willian* (1981), Ind.App., 423 N.E.2d 668.

The old rule was that expert testimony was allowed only when the subject matter was beyond the knowledge of the average juror. If the jurors could draw inferences from the facts as well as the expert, or if the subject was a matter of common knowledge, expert opinions were not allowed. *Brunker v. Cummins* (1892), 133 Ind. 443, 32 N.E. 732; *Snow v. Cannelton Sewer Pipe Co.* (1965), 138 Ind.App. 119, 210 N.E.2d 118. The modern trend is to permit expert testimony whenever it will assist the jury in resolving a difficult issue. Even when the subject is not beyond the knowledge of the average juror, an expert may nevertheless testify within the expert's field of specialty if the opinion will be helpful to the jury. *See Grimes v. State* (1983), Ind., 450 N.E.2d 512 (expert testimony on homosexual, sado-masochistic sexual practices permitted).

Part (b): Scientific evidence "capable of producing reliable results" is admissible. *Davidson v. State* (1991), Ind., 580 N.E.2d 238. The court may determine scientific reliability in any one of three ways:

(1) Courts may take judicial notice of simple scientific principles which are well known or indisputable to all people of ordinary understanding and intelligence. *See, e.g., Highshew v. Kushto* (1956), 126 Ind.App. 584, 131 N.E.2d 652.

(2) The reliability of established scientific evidence is normally proved by showing that the principles on which it is based have achieved general acceptance in the scientific community. *See Hopkins v. State* (1991), Ind., 579 N.E.2d 1297.

(3) The reliability of new scientific procedures will have to be established at a pretrial hearing by the testimony of properly qualified expert witnesses. *See Cornett v. State* (1983), Ind., 450 N.E.2d 498 (to establish the reliability of a new scientific procedure, a party must call neutral expert witnesses from a number of related scientific fields). In addition to the expert's testimony that the procedure is reliable,

the court can look to cases in other jurisdictions to see if they admit such evidence. *Jones v. State* (1982), Ind., 425 N.E.2d 128 (neutron activation analysis).

A. *Does the Rule change current Indiana law?*

No.

B. *Differences between IRE, FRE and URE.*

The differences are semantic. The URE and FRE are reprinted below, with the differences highlighted:

> The facts or data in the particular case upon which an expert bases an opinion or inference may be those perceived by or made known to the expert at or before the hearing. If ~~Experts may testify to opinions based on inadmissible evidence, provided that it is~~ of a type reasonably relied upon by experts in the <u>particular</u> field <u>in forming opinions or inferences upon the subject, the facts or data need not be admissible in evidence.</u>

C. *State variations.*

Two states did not adopt this rule, preferring the traditional hypothetical question format of expert testimony.

D. *Committee commentary.*

The committee felt that the second sentence of the Federal Rule was incomprehensible. We rewrote the sentence to make it clearer without changing the meaning, following the suggestion of Edward Becker and Aviva Orenstein, *The Federal Rules of Evidence After Sixteen Years—The Effect of "Plain Meaning" Jurisprudence, the Need for an Advisory Committee on the Rules of Evidence, and Suggestions for Selected Revision of the Rules,* 60 GEO. WASH. L. REV. 857, 894 (1992).

Normally, any inadmissible evidence used in forming an opinion would remain inadmissible on direct examination, but might be inquired into on cross-examination. If an expert relies on hearsay, however, it is admissible, not for its truth, but to help the jury evaluate the credibility of the expert's opinion if the issue of credibility is controverted.

E. *Consistent existing law.*

(1) An expert may testify to an opinion based solely on personal knowledge of the facts, as in the case of an examining physician. In such a case a hypothetical question need not be used. *Conner v. First Nat'l. Bank* (1948), 118 Ind.App. 173, 77 N.E.2d 598.

(2) Experts also may state opinions based on information gathered from sources other than personal observation. A consulting expert may examine files and reports prepared by others and base an opinion on them if those sources are of a type usually reliable and customarily relied upon in that profession. *Gambill v. State* (1985), Ind., 479 N.E.2d 523; *Public Service Indiana v. Nichols* (1986), Ind.App., 494 N.E.2d 349. If all or much of the information relied on by the expert is hearsay or otherwise inadmissible, the expert may nonetheless give an opinion based on it. The underlying hearsay is not admissible for its truth, *Gambill*, 479 N.E.2d at 528; *Indiana & Mich. Elec. Co. v. Hurm* (1981), Ind.App., 422 N.E.2d 371, but it is admissible to help the jury evaluate the credibility of the expert's opinion if the issue of

credibility is controverted. *Miller v. State* (1991), Ind., 575 N.E.2d 272.

(3) Speculative opinions. The expert must base an opinion on concrete information of some sort, whether personally observed or learned from reliable sources. Experts may not speculate in the absence of information.

A. *Does the Rule change current Indiana law?*

No.

B. *Differences between IRE, FRE and URE.*

All three rules are slightly different. The URE is reprinted below, with the differences highlighted:

(a) Testimony in the form of an opinion or inference otherwise admissible is not objectionable merely because it embraces an ultimate issue to be decided by the trier of fact.

(b) Witnesses may not testify to opinions concerning guilt or innocence in a criminal case, liability in a civil case, the truth or falsity of allegations, whether a witness has testified truthfully, or legal conclusions.

FRE 704 reads as follows (differences highlighted):

(a) Except as provided in subdivision (b), testimony in the form of an opinion or inference otherwise admissible is not objectionable merely because it embraces an ultimate issue to be decided by the trier of fact.

(b) Witnesses may not testify to opinions concerning guilt or innocence in a criminal case, liability in a civil case, the truth or falsity of allegations, whether a witness has testified truthfully, or legal conclusions.

(b) No expert witness testifying with respect to the mental state or condition of a defendant in a criminal case may state an opinion or inference as to whether the defendant did or did not have the mental state or condition constituting an element of the crime charged or of a defense thereto. Such ultimate issues are matters for the trier of fact alone.

C. *State variations.*

Most states have adopted URE 704 verbatim. Only one state has adopted the criminal case limitation in FRE 704. Seven states have added the word "merely" or "solely" immediately after the word "objectionable."

D. *Committee commentary.*

In part (a), the committee has modified the language of the URE 704 by inserting the word "merely" after the word "objectionable," to make the language clearer.

The committee rejected the FRE 704 exception for issues of mental state in criminal cases. We could see no principled reason for carving out an exception, especially one that prevents experts, but not lay witnesses, from giving opinions on mental state. We also thought that issues concerning a defendant's mental state were matters on which expert testimony would usually be helpful.

The committee added part (b) to reflect current Indiana law and to clear up an ambiguity in URE 704.

E. Consistent existing law.

An expert opinion is admissible even though it embraces an ultimate fact in issue or invades the province of the jury. *De Vaney v. State* (1972), 259 Ind. 483, 288 N.E.2d 732 (explicitly overruling prior contrary authority); *Public Service Indiana v. Nichols* (1986), Ind.App., 494 N.E.2d 349. However, experts may not testify to purely legal conclusions. *Harman v. C.E. & M., Inc.* (1986), Ind.App., 493 N.E.2d 1319 (whether defendant owed plaintiff a duty); *Breese v. State* (1982), Ind.App., 449 N.E.2d 1098 (whether a hospital had duty to protect suicidal patient). *Cf. Freed v. State* (1985), Ind., 480 N.E.2d 929 (psychiatrist could testify defendant was "legally sane" because issue involved a mixed legal and expert opinion). *But see Head v. State* (1988), Ind., 519 N.E.2d 151 (psychologist's opinion that child's allegations were true impermissibly invaded province of jury).

Similarly, lay witnesses may give their opinions on ultimate issues if the court finds them to be helpful and rationally based on perception. *See State v. Bouras* (1981), Ind.App., 423 N.E.2d 741. *See also Brown v. State* (1983), Ind., 448 N.E.2d 10 (opinion by fireman that a burning home presented conditions dangerous to human life, one of the elements of the crime of arson; admission upheld). However, witnesses may not state their opinions that specific allegations made by crime victims are true or that they believe the defendant to be guilty. *Head v. State* (1988), Ind., 519 N.E.2d 151.

A. Does the Rule change current Indiana law?

Rule 705 represents a change in emphasis (though not in substance) from existing Indiana common law governing the form of expert testimony.

B. Differences between IRE, FRE and URE.

None.

C. State variations.

Most states adopted the URE verbatim. Four states added a voir dire procedure for determining whether there is a sufficient factual basis for an opinion before it is admitted. Four states added a requirement of adequate pretrial disclosure. Three states rejected this rule altogether, in favor the traditional requirement that the facts must be proved first.

D. Committee commentary.

The language "without prior disclosure" refers to the proper procedure for direct examination, and has nothing to do with the discovery rules. An expert may give an opinion on the witness stand without first testifying to the underlying facts or being asked a hypothetical question.

E. Consistent existing law.

Hypothetical questions are not required. *Ashby v. State* (1985), Ind., 486 N.E.2d 469.

If an attorney uses a hypothetical question, the facts it assumes must be shown to exist by the evidence or by reasonable inferences from the evidence. *Henson v. State* (1989), Ind., 535 N.E.2d 1189 (excellent opinion summarizing proper way of asking hypothetical questions).

COMMENTARY

Facts upon which it is based may be proved by subsequent witnesses. *Ecker v. Ecker* (1975), 163 Ind.App. 339, 323 N.E.2d 683. It need not include all potentially relevant facts, only sufficient facts to form a reliable basis for an opinion. *Dahlberg v. Ogle* (1978), 268 Ind. 30, 373 N.E.2d 159. Generally, if the opponent objects to the facts contained in the hypothetical, the remedy is to ask a question on cross examination that contains what he feels to be the necessary facts. *City of Indianapolis v. Robinson* (1981), Ind.App., 427 N.E.2d 902. However, if the question assumes facts which are so clearly exaggerated or unsupported by inferences from the evidence as to be misleading or confusing, the question should not be allowed. *Chicago, I. & L.R. v. Freeman* (1972), 152 Ind.App. 492, 284 N.E.2d 133.

F. Inconsistent Indiana law.

Old Indiana common law stated that an expert who bases an opinion on personal knowledge, as in the case of an examining physician, usually must first state the facts, and then give an opinion. *See Mutual Life Ins. Co. of N.Y. v. Jay* (1942), 112 Ind.App. 383, 44 N.E.2d 1020. For experts relying on second-hand information, the old procedure was to first prove the underlying facts through the testimony of witnesses, and then interrogate the expert using hypothetical questions, *Snow v. Cannelton Sewer Pipe Co.* (1965), 138 Ind.App. 119, 210 N.E.2d 118; although it was permissible to prove some of the underlying facts after the expert had testified. *Howard v. State* (1976), 264 Ind. 275, 342 N.E.2d 604; *Automobile Underwriters Inc. v. Smith* (1960), 131 Ind.App. 454, 166 N.E.2d 341, *on reh'g.* 167 N.E.2d 882. Under Rule 705, these preferences are abrogated.

A. Differences between FRE and URE.

The URE 706 is identical to FRE 706 in substance. Rule 706 reads as follows:

(a) Appointment. The court, on motion of any party or its own motion, may enter an order to show cause why expert witnesses should not be appointed, and may request the parties to submit nominations. The court may appoint any expert witness agreed upon by the parties, and may appoint witnesses of the court's own selection. An expert witness shall not be appointed by the court unless the witness consents to act. A witness so appointed shall be informed of the witness' duties by the court in writing, a copy of which shall be filed with the clerk, or at a conference in which the parties shall have the opportunity to participate. A witness so appointed shall advise the parties of the witness' findings, if any; the witness' deposition may be taken by any party; and the witness may be called to testify by the court or any party. The witness shall be subject to cross-examination by each party, including a party calling the witness.

(b) Compensation. Expert witnesses so appointed are entitled to reasonable compensation in whatever sum the court may allow. The compensation thus fixed is payable from funds which may be provided by law in criminal cases and civil actions and proceedings involving just compensation for the taking of property. In other civil actions and proceedings the compensation shall be paid by the parties in such proportion and at such time as the court directs, and thereafter charged in like manner as other costs.

(c) Disclosure of appointment. In the exercise of its discretion, a court may authorize disclosure to the jury of the fact that the court appointed the expert witness.

(d) Parties' experts of own selection. Nothing in this rule limits the parties in calling expert witnesses of their own selection.

B. State variations.

The states are split about evenly. Only five states adopted the URE verbatim, although another ten or so adopted it in substance, disagreeing on the method of payment. However, nine states rejected it altogether, and another three limited it to cases in which the parties agree to the appointment of an expert.

C. Committee commentary.

The committee recommends against adopting URE 706. The rule is unnecessary, and the committee believes the matter of appointing expert witnesses should be left to the discretion of the trial judge. The rule implicates local funding issues. Unless the legislature appropriates money for court-appointed expert witnesses, a state-wide rule may be unworkable, as the availability of funds may vary from county to county.

Part One: The Definition of Hearsay

A. Does the Rule change current Indiana law?

No.

B. Differences between IRE, FRE and URE.

None.

C. State variations.

None. All states have enacted this definition.

D. Committee commentary.

None.

E. Consistent existing law.

Hearsay is testimony by a witness, or a written document, offered in court, that communicates the content of an out-of-court written or oral declaration by another person, if it is offered to prove the truth of the facts asserted therein. If the declarant is present and available for cross-examination, the out-of-court statements are still hearsay if offered for their truth, except in those circumstances outlined in *Modesitt v. State* (1991), Ind., 578 N.E.2d 649.

Only extra-judicial declarations that are offered to prove the truth of the facts asserted by the declarant are hearsay. *Trustees of Ind. Univ. v. Williams* (1969), 252 Ind. 624, 251 N.E.2d 439. Proof of out-of-court utterances and writings may be made for an almost infinite variety of other purposes which do not depend upon the veracity of the out-of-court declarant. *Morse v. State* (1980), Ind., 413 N.E.2d 885. If a document or declaration is not being offered for its truth, the offering party must state for what relevant purpose it is being offered. The common response that "I am just offering it to show that the statement was made," is not usually sufficient. Rarely will it be a contested material issue whether a statement was made. *See Connell v. State* (1984), Ind., 470 N.E.2d 701. Legitimate non-hearsay purposes include:

(1) The testimony of a police officer about information he received during an

investigation, offered to show why he conducted that investigation. *See Heck v. State* (1990), Ind., 552 N.E.2d 446, *cert. denied*, 113 S.Ct. 1308 (1993). However, statements made to a police officer during the course of his investigation that amount to assertions that the defendant is guilty are not admissible even though they provide important leads. *See Williams v. State* (1989), Ind., 544 N.E.2d 161. This exception must be narrowly construed; statements to police that are detailed and contain an accusation are likely to be used by the jury as evidence of the defendant's guilt and are not admissible.

(2) A prior inconsistent statement used to impeach a witness. *Samuels v. State* (1978), 267 Ind. 676, 372 N.E.2d 1186.

(3) Threats made to the accused to show his state of mind in a self-defense case, *Shepard v. State* (1983), Ind.App., 451 N.E.2d 1118; and threats communicated to a witness showing witness's state of mind at the time he made a prior inconsistent statement. *Fox v. State* (1986), Ind., 497 N.E.2d 221.

(4) A letter used as a handwriting exemplar for the purpose of comparing handwriting. *Chinn v. State* (1987), Ind., 511 N.E.2d 1000.

Only utterances capable of being true or false can be classified as hearsay. Questions, commands, and requests are not assertions of fact, and therefore cannot be objected to as hearsay. *Mayhew v. State* (1989), Ind., 537 N.E.2d 1188.

Part Two: Prior Statements of Available Witnesses

A. Does the Rule change current Indiana law?

No.

B. Differences between IRE, FRE and URE.

The Rules are different on whether a prior inconsistent statement must have been made under oath, whether a prior consistent statement must have been made before the motive to fabricate arose, and whether a statement of identification must have been made while still fresh in the declarant's mind. URE 801(d)(1) is reprinted below, with the differences highlighted:

(1) Prior statement by witness. The declarant testifies at the trial or hearing and is subject to cross-examination concerning the statement, and the statement is (A) inconsistent with the declarant's testimony and, if offered in a criminal proceeding, was given under oath subject to the penalty of perjury at a trial, hearing or other proceeding, or in a deposition, or (B) consistent with the declarant's testimony, offered to rebut an express or implied charge against the declarant of recent fabrication or improper influence or motive, *and made before the motive to fabricate arose;* or (C) one of identification of a person made shortly after perceiving the person.

FRE 801(d)(1) provides:

(1) Prior statement by witness. The declarant testifies at the trial or hearing and is subject to cross-examination concerning the statement, and the statement is (A) inconsistent with the declarant's testimony and, *if offered in a criminal proceeding,* was given under oath subject to the penalty of perjury at a trial, hearing or other

proceeding, or in a deposition, or (B) consistent with the declarant's testimony, offered to rebut an express or implied charge against the declarant of recent fabrication or improper influence or motive, *and made before the motive to fabricate arose*; or (C) one of identification of a person made shortly after perceiving the person.

C. State variations.

States split about evenly on whether a prior statement must have been under oath. Two states did not enact part (A), two states did not enact part (B), and two states did not enact part (C).

D. Committee commentary.

The committee recommends the URE distinction between civil and criminal cases, permitting prior inconsistent statements to be admitted for their truth in civil cases if the declarant is available to explain them. In criminal cases, however, the Confrontation Clause limits the use of prior inconsistent statements against a defendant. The committee also adopted the URE's limitation to statements of identification made "shortly" after the witness perceived the person. Statements made other than shortly after the event may be unreliable. The Confrontation Clause prohibits using unreliable hearsay against criminal defendants. The rule is compatible with Indiana Trial Rule 32(A)(1), which permits depositions to be used to impeach.

The committee recommends adding the requirement that a prior consistent statement must have been made before the motive to fabricate arose. That makes it relevant. Consistent statements made after the motive arises are redundant bolstering. Judge Edward Becker writes that the ambiguity of the FRE on this point has led to inconsistent decisions. Edward Becker and Aviva Orenstein, *The Federal Rules of Evidence After Sixteen Years—The Effect of "Plain Meaning" Jurisprudence, the Need for an Advisory Committee on the Rules of Evidence, and Suggestions for Selected Revision of the Rules*, 60 GEO. WASH. L. REV. 857, 896–97 (1992).

Adopting this rule answers an open question in Indiana law. Under the *Patterson* rule, prior statements of identification were fully admissible. This rule was abrogated in *Modesitt v. State* (1991), Ind., 578 N.E.2d 649, at least as far as general prior consistent statements were concerned, but the Supreme Court has not specifically addressed the problem of prior statements of identification.

E. Consistent existing law.

Prior inconsistent statements used to impeach a witness are generally not offered for their truth, and therefore are not hearsay. *Samuels v. State* (1978), 267 Ind. 676, 372 N.E.2d 1186. Only if they were made under oath are they admissible for their truth. *Modesitt*, 578 N.E.2d 649. Under *Modesitt*, the prior statement of an available witness is admissible only if the declarant testifies at trial, is subject to cross-examination, and the statement is offered to rebut a charge of recent fabrication or improper motive. No prior Indiana law exists specifically addressing the admissibility of prior statements of identification. Dictum in *Modesitt*, suggests that the Supreme Court approves of the language of Rule 801(d)(1)(c).

Part Three: Statements by Party-Opponent

A. Does the Rule change current Indiana law?

Under Indiana law, statements by party-opponents (sometimes called admissions) are considered an exception to the hearsay rule, rather than being excluded from the definition. However, it is a distinction without a difference. The committee included this rule in Rule 801 because most other states do and FRE do so.

The major difference concerns statements by agents. Under the FRE and URE, the statements of agents are considered statements of the principal as long as they are made within the scope of that agency. Indiana has followed the older rule limiting agent statements to those made while the agent was carrying out the job.

B. Differences between IRE, FRE and URE.

The FRE and URE call this exception "admissions by party-opponent" instead of statements by party-opponent. This has caused needless confusion over whether a statement by the opposing party needs to be against interest to be admissible. Calling it a "statement" clarifies that any statement by the adverse party is admissible.

> (2) ~~Statement~~ Admission by party-opponent. The statement is offered against a party and is (A) the party's own statement, in either an individual or representative capacity or (B) a statement of which the party has manifested an adoption or belief in its truth, or (C) a statement by a person authorized by the party to make a statement concerning the subject, or (D) a statement by the party's agent or servant concerning a matter within the scope of the agency or employment, made during the existence of the relationship; or (E) a statement by a co-conspirator of a party during the course and in furtherance of the conspiracy.

C. State variations.

Most states adopted URE 801(d)(2) verbatim. Two states made it a hearsay exception. Two states broadened the scope of admissible statements by agents; one narrowed it. Several states require independent evidence of conspiracy as a foundation for the co-conspirator exception.

D. Committee commentary.

The Rule does not specify what kind of foundation is required for a co-conspirator admission. We believe the foundation rule of *Mayhew v. State* (1989), Ind., 537 N.E.2d 1188 should continue to be valid. In *Mayhew*, the Supreme Court stated that this rule is easily subject to abuse and must be strictly limited to situations where a foundation has been clearly established by other than hearsay evidence that a conspiracy genuinely existed. The court must rule on whether the foundation has been satisfied; the matter may not be sent to the jury to decide if a conspiracy existed, with instructions to ignore the hearsay if it decides there was no conspiracy.

E. Consistent existing law.

The rule is compatible with Indiana Trial Rule 32(A)(2), which permits depositions to be used against the adverse party.

Any act or statement made by or attributable to the opposing party is an admission and admissible against that party. The statements may be made either personally or through agents. *Jethroe v. State* (1974), 262 Ind. 505, 319 N.E.2d 133. An admission does not have to be against the interest of the party when it is made. *Indiana State Hwy. Comm'n v. Vanderbur* (1982), Ind.App., 432 N.E.2d 418; 4 *John H. Wigmore, Wigmore on Evidence* § 1048 (Chadbourn rev. 1972). The only limitation is that the statement must be introduced on a material issue; a statement by the opponent offered only for its prejudicial effect is not admissible. *Beresford v. Starkey* (1990), Ind.App., 563 N.E.2d 116. The party making the admission need not have had personal knowledge of the fact admitted. *Hebel v. Conrail, Inc.* (1985), Ind., 475 N.E.2d 652.

An incriminating statement made by someone other than the party may be admissible as a tacit admission if the party concedes it to be true through words or conduct, *Shackelford v. State* (1986), Ind., 498 N.E.2d 382, or fails to deny accusations made in the party's presence. *James v. State* (1985), Ind.App., 481 N.E.2d 417. However, silence by a defendant in police custody who has been told of his right to remain silent is not admissible. *Doyle v. Ohio*, 426 U.S. 610 (1976).

Declarations made by one partner while engaged in partnership business are admissible against the partnership but not the partners as individuals. *See Puzich v. Pappas* (1974), 161 Ind.App. 191, 314 N.E.2d 795. Statements by one spouse are not admissions of the other spouse unless agency can be proved. *Owen County State Bank v. Guard* (1940), 217 Ind. 75, 26 N.E.2d 395.

Conduct that shows a guilty conscience may be an admission. Evidence of flight, concealment, assumption of a false name, resisting arrest, and attempts to escape custody are all admissible acts that show a consciousness of guilt. *See Page v. State* (1988), Ind., 518 N.E.2d 1089 (flight from scene and attempt to dispose of body); *Serano v. State* (1990), Ind.App., 555 N.E.2d 487 (giving false name). A person's refusal to submit to a chemical test is admissible in a prosecution for driving while intoxicated. *Ind.Code* § 9-30-6-3. However, some conduct which could be viewed as an admission is inadmissible on public policy grounds, for example, subsequent repairs as an admission of antecedent negligence. See Rules 407–411.

The statements of a co-conspirator made in the course of and in furtherance of the conspiracy are admissible, whether or not a conspiracy has been charged, as long as there is independent evidence of the existence of the conspiracy. *See Chinn v. State* (1987), Ind., 511 N.E.2d 1000. In *Mayhew v. State* (1989), Ind., 537 N.E.2d 1188, the court summarized the circumstances under which accomplice statements qualify as co-conspirator admissions, pointing out that this is an extreme rule easily subject to abuse, and stating that it must be strictly limited to situations where the foundation is clearly established. The conspiracy does not necessarily end when the crime is committed, but may continue through escape or the splitting up of proceeds. However, the conspiracy usually will not extend to statements made after arrest. *See Mayhew*, 537 N.E.2d 1188.

A. *Does the Rule change current Indiana law?*

No.

B. *Differences between IRE, FRE and URE.*

None.

C. State variations.

None. All states adopted this rule.

D. Committee commentary.

The hearsay rule is designed to restrict unreliable evidence, and thus continues to be justified despite some scholarly argument that it should be abandoned. In criminal cases, the admissibility of hearsay is controlled in part by the Sixth Amendment of the United States Constitution. Under the Confrontation Clause, hearsay is not admissible against a defendant unless it is both reliable and firmly rooted in a traditional hearsay exception. *See Idaho v. Wright*, 497 U.S. 805 (1990). Under the Compulsory Process Clause, hearsay is admissible on behalf of a defendant if it falls within a traditional exception and is of a type that other parties are permitted to introduce. *See Washington v. Texas*, 388 U.S. 14 (1967).

E. Consistent existing law.

Hearsay is not admissible unless it falls within a specific exception provided by law. The trial court does not have the discretion to admit "reliable" hearsay that does not fall within one of the exceptions. *C.T.S. Corp. v. Schoulton* (1978), 270 Ind. 34, 383 N.E.2d 293.

Part One: General Rule

A. Does the Rule change current Indiana law?

Current Indiana law is ambiguous on whether the identity of the declarant must be known.

B. Differences between IRE, FRE and URE.

The URE and FRE are identical. Neither specifies whether the identity of the declarant must be known. The URE is reprinted below, with the differences highlighted:

> The following are not excluded by the hearsay rule, even though the declarant is available as a witness. ~~The identity of the declarant need not be known in order for the declarant's statement to be admitted under this Rule.~~

C. State variations.

None. All states adopted this rule.

D. Committee commentary.

There is no requirement under this rule that the identity of the declarant must always be known. Whether knowledge of the identity of the declarant is relevant must be left to the discretion of the court in individual cases.

Part Two: Present Sense Impression

A. Does the Rule change current Indiana Law?

Maybe. Indiana cases have occasionally invoked the *"res gestae"* concept to permit statements accompanying and explaining a litigated event or transaction, and have occasionally rejected the concept.

B. Differences between IRE, FRE and URE.

The FRE and URE do not limit admissible present sense impressions to those explaining and accompanying material events. The URE is reprinted below with the differences highlighted:

(1) Present sense impression. A statement describing or explaining an a material event ~~or~~ condition ~~or transaction~~, made while the declarant was perceiving the event ~~or~~ condition ~~or transaction~~, or immediately thereafter.

C. State variations.

Five states declined to adopt this exception.

D. Committee commentary.

Under the rubric of res gestae, statements accompanying and describing or explaining a litigated event have probably always been admissible. This exception gives concrete definition to this concept. For a present sense impression to be admissible, it must describe or explain a material event, act, condition, or transaction at the heart of a case. The event being described should be more than minimally relevant and not collateral.

E. Consistent existing law.

Older cases grouped a number of different evidence rules together under the vague concept "res gestae." Statements accompanying and explaining a material event were probably included in this concept, although the term res gestae is so vague as to be essentially useless and confusing. *Ferrier v. State* (1977), 266 Ind. 117, 361 N.E.2d 150. Indiana law is therefore ambiguous on whether this type of hearsay is admissible. *See Spears v. State* (1980), Ind., 401 N.E.2d 331.

Part Three: Excited Utterance

A. Does the Rule change current Indiana Law?

No.

B. Differences between IRE, FRE and URE.

None.

C. State variations.

None. All states adopted this rule.

D. Committee commentary.

This is a traditional, firmly rooted exception to the hearsay rule.

E. Consistent existing law.

When a startling event occurs, the spontaneous unplanned statements of participants, witnesses or bystanders, made without thinking or reflection are admissible. *See Holmes v. State* (1986), Ind., 480 N.E.2d 916. To qualify as an excited utterance, there must have been a startling or unusual event sufficient to overcome the reflective faculties of the declarant, *King v. State* (1987), Ind., 508 N.E.2d 1259 (proof of startling event required), the statement must relate to the startling event, *Tenta v. Guraly* (1966), 140 Ind.App. 160, 221 N.E.2d 577, and must have been spontaneously given, and may not be responses to questions. *Anderson v. State* (1984), Ind., 471 N.E.2d 291. The statement must have been sufficiently contemporaneous with the event so that there was no time for reflection. There is no fixed time limit. Compare *Reburn v. State* (1981), Ind., 421 N.E.2d 604 (statement three hours after event not admissible) and *Cauldwell, Inc. v. Patterson* (1961), 133 Ind.App. 138, 177 N.E.2d 490

COMMENTARY

(statements thirty minutes later not admissible), with *Choctaw v. State* (1979), 270 Ind. 545, 387 N.E.2d 1305 (statement made within one hour admissible).

In *Williams v. State* (1989), Ind., 546 N.E.2d 1198, the court held that an excited utterance by a three-year-old child was admissible even though the child was incompetent to testify. All that matters is the spontaneity of the statement, not the speaker's general competence as a witness.

Part Four: Then Existing Mental, Emotional, or Physical Condition

A. *Does the Rule change current Indiana Law?*

No, but it clarifies it. Indiana's case law is ambiguous about whether a statement of intent to do an act with another person is admissible to prove what the other person did.

B. *Differences between IRE, FRE and URE.*

The FRE and URE are identical, but different from the proposed IRE. The URE is reprinted below with those differences highlighted.

> (3) A statement of the declarant's then existing state of mind, emotion, sensation, or physical condition (such as intent, plan, motive, design, mental feeling, pain and bodily health), but not including a statement of memory or belief to prove the fact remembered or believed unless it related to the execution, revocation, identification, or terms of declarant's will. ~~A statement of intent to do an act with another person is not admissible to prove that the other person did the act.~~

C. *State variations.*

Most adopted the FRE verbatim. Several states prohibit statements of intent to prove the conduct of another.

D. *Committee commentary.*

(1) State of mind. This exception is one of the traditional, firmly rooted hearsay exceptions. However, it must be applied cautiously. Every statement tells us something about the state of mind of the speaker. Therefore, the declarant's state of mind must be a contested, material issue for this exception to apply. Otherwise, it eviscerates the hearsay rule. Rarely will the state of mind of anyone other than the parties be material. Particular caution should be employed in criminal cases where the state of mind will be material (e.g., self-defense cases, robbery by putting the victim in fear). In most cases, however, the victim's state of mind will not be a material element of a claim or defense.

Whether statements of intent by one person should be admissible to prove that another person did an act has always been controversial. The usual context is a statement by a crime victim that the victim is going out to meet the defendant, offered to prove that the victim in fact met the defendant. The committee fails to see the connection, because the victim has no control over what the defendant does, and therefore the victim's intent cannot influence the defendant.

(2) Physical condition. Statements of then-existing physical condition are also a firmly rooted hearsay exception. To qualify under this exception, the statement must reflect then-existing pain or symptoms, and may not repeat medical history. The statements may be made to anyone; they do not need to be made to medical personnel.

E. Consistent existing law.

(1) State of mind. Statements expressing a then-existing state of mind are admissible if state of mind is in issue, as in a determination of domicile, where intent to remain in the state is a necessary element. *Brittenham v. Robinson* (1897), 18 Ind.App. 502, 48 N.E. 616. In criminal cases, the state of mind of the victim is rarely a material issue, so the victim's hearsay statements expressing fear of the defendant are not admissible. *Light v. State* (1989), Ind., 547 N.E.2d 1073. *See also Komyatti v. State* (1986), Ind., 490 N.E.2d 279 (murder victim's state of mind not an issue; therefore his reasons for changing will inadmissible hearsay); *Lock v. State* (1991), Ind., 567 N.E.2d 1155, *cert. denied*, 112 S.Ct. 1686 (1992) (victim's state of mind must be relevant: declarations of decedent admissible to show her state of mind (fear of defendant) when victim's fear of defendant put in issue by defendant).

A declaration of intent to do an act is admissible as circumstantial evidence that the declarant later committed the act, if the statement and the act occur reasonably close together and the declarant had the capacity to do the act. *American Sec. Co. v. Minard* (1948), 118 Ind.App. 310, 77 N.E.2d 762; *Koenig v. Bryce* (1932), 94 Ind.App. 689, 180 N.E. 682.

(2) Physical condition. Statements made by a person that express or describe the person's present existing physical condition are admissible if physical condition is a material issue. Such statements can be made to anyone; they do not have to be made to a physician. *Cleveland, C.C. & L. Ry. v. Newell* (1885), 104 Ind. 264, 3 N.E. 836; *Indianapolis Traction & Terminal Co. v. Gillaspy* (1914), 56 Ind.App. 332, 105 N.E.242; *Treschman v. Treschman* (1901), 28 Ind.App. 206, 61 N.E. 961.

Part Five: Statements for Purposes of Medical Diagnosis or Treatment

A. Does the Rule change current Indiana Law?

Yes. Prior Indiana law admitted statements of medical history to support a physician's diagnosis only, not for their truth.

B. Differences between IRE, FRE and URE.

None.

C. State variations.

Most states adopted this rule in substance. Three states deleted the reference to "inception or cause." Three adopted a version that distinguished between treating physicians and those retained just for rendering opinions.

D. Committee commentary.

Statements to a physician which recite past suffering and symptoms are admissible in most jurisdictions. In Indiana, however, they have heretofore been admissible only to show the basis for a doctor's opinion, and not for their truth. This rule draws no distinction between treating and examining physicians. The statement must be made in order to obtain medical assistance, but need not be made directly to medical personnel. If a declaration includes a statement describing the cause of an injury or naming the person responsible, it will be admissible only if reasonably pertinent to obtaining proper medical care, i.e., that it would help a doctor diagnose or treat the patient to know this information. The phrase "reasonably pertinent" is intended to place limits on the kind of medical history information that is admissible. Irrelevant and prejudicial information without an obvious connection to the medical problem should usually be excluded by the judge as not reasonably pertinent to diagnosis.

E. Consistent existing law.

None.

F. Inconsistent existing law.

In Indiana, statements for diagnosis or treatment are not admissible for their truth but only to show the basis for a doctor's opinion. A physician may testify to a statement given by a patient when the information was necessary either for treatment or for formulating an expert opinion. *Cleveland, M.C. & L. Ry. v. Newell* (1885), 104 Ind. 264, 3 N.E. 836. *See also Spillers v. Tri-State Glass Lined Storage, Inc.*, 325 F.2d 322; (7th Cir. 1963).

Part Six: Recorded Recollection

A. Does the Rule change current Indiana Law?

Yes. Indiana law currently requires complete exhaustion of memory before past recollection is admissible; the FRE and URE require only that the witness have "insufficient" recollection.

B. Differences between IRE, FRE and URE.

The FRE and URE contain a limitation that a hearsay document admitted under this exception may be read to the jury but may not be introduced as an exhibit. The URE is reprinted below, with the differences highlighted:

> (5) A memorandum or record concerning a matter about which a witness once had knowledge but now has insufficient recollection to enable the witness to testify fully and accurately, shown to have been made or adopted by the witness when the matter was fresh in the witness' memory and to reflect that knowledge correctly. <u>If admitted, the memorandum or record may be read into evidence but may not itself be received as an exhibit unless offered by an adverse party.</u>

C. State variations.

Five states rejected this rule. Five states permit the document to be received as an exhibit at the discretion of the trial judge.

D. Committee commentary.

The traditional exception permitted records of past recollection only if a witness' memory was completely exhausted. This rule relaxes that foundation. It should therefore be cautiously applied in criminal cases, because it implicates the Confrontation Clause. To permit records of past recollection when the witness' memory is insufficient to allow full cross-examination runs afoul of the Supreme Court's standards that hearsay used against the defendant must usually fall into a traditional, firmly rooted exception. *See Idaho v. Wright*, 110 S.Ct. 3139 (1990). However, such records may be admitted upon a showing that the circumstances of their preparation make them particularly reliable.

The document used must have been prepared near the time of the event while the witness's memory was still fresh.

At least in civil cases, the trial court should have discretion to either admit the document or require that it be read. For example, a judge should have the discretion to decide that a lengthy document on a tangential issue be admitted as an exhibit rather than read to the jury.

E. Consistent existing law.

Accurate written documents prepared by the witness at or near the time of the event may be admissible under the hearsay exception for past recollection recorded. *Gee v. State* (1979), 271 Ind. 28, 389 N.E.2d 303. The writing must have been prepared or adopted by the witness, contemporaneously with the event while the witness had a clear memory. The witness must vouch for the accuracy of the writing when it was made, and must have had personal knowledge of the facts recorded. The written record may be either read by the witness or introduced into evidence itself. *Id.*

F. Inconsistent existing law.

The memory of the witness must be completely exhausted and cannot be refreshed. *Gee v. State* (1979), 271 Ind. 28, 389 N.E.2d 303.

Part Seven: Records of Regularly Conducted Business Activity

COMMITTEE NOTE

The committee was seriously divided on whether the foundation for business records should be provable by affidavit (bracketed language). The modern trend is to allow it. Members of the bar at the public hearings were uniformly opposed to it. The committee was unable to reach consensus. A related disagreement is found in Rule 902(9)–(10).

A. Does the Rule change current Indiana Law?

It depends. If the bracketed language is enacted, it would permit laying essentially uncontested business record foundations by affidavit, eliminating the need for time-consuming foundation witnesses.

B. Differences between IRE, FRE and URE.

Neither the FRE nor the URE permits the foundation to be laid by affidavit, although there is a pending proposal to amend FRE 803(6) to permit the procedure.

C. State variations.

Most states adopted 803(6) verbatim, but a substantial minority permit laying the foundation by affidavit or certification. Four states require the source to be under a business duty to report the information. All but one state adopted 803(7) verbatim.

D. Committee commentary.

The business record exception is one of the oldest. This rule continues the modern trend of defining "business" broadly to include all regularly conducted activity, and of dropping the common law requirement that the record be an "original." Computer data and print-outs in all forms are considered business records.

Permitting proof of the business records foundation by affidavit is the modern trend. *See, e.g.,* Texas Rule of Civil Evidence 803(6).

Any report prepared by law enforcement personnel and offered against a criminal

defendant that would be excluded as a public record under 803(8) should also be excluded if offered as a business record.

E. Consistent existing law.

A document is admissible as a business record if it is identified by someone who is familiar with the business' activities and record keeping system generally, *Darnell v. State* (1982), Ind., 435 N.E.2d 250; *Wilson v. Jenga Corp.* (1986), Ind.App., 490 N.E.2d 375, who testifies that the entry was made in the routine course of business, *Landers v. State* (1984), Ind., 464 N.E.2d 912, at or near the time of the event or transaction, *Campbell v. State* (1986), Ind., 500 N.E.2d 174, by or on information from an employee under a business duty to make such entries who had personal knowledge of the transaction. *Brandon v. State* (1979), Ind., 396 N.E.2d 365. Thus, the inclusion of statements made by students to welfare workers rendered their case reports inadmissible because the students were under no business duty to observe and report the facts of the incident. *Hinkle v. Garrett-Keyser-Butler School District* (1991), Ind.App., 567 N.E.2d 1173. There is no requirement that the proponent of a business record prove the actual entrant to be unavailable. *See Getha v. State* (1988), Ind.App., 524 N.E.2d 325.

The term "business" has been broadened to include every business, bank, industry, profession, occupation, and calling of every kind. *Wells v. State* (1970), 254 Ind. 608, 261 N.E.2d 865 (1970) (police department records).

As part of the foundation, it is generally said that the person who made the entry into the permanent records of the business must have had direct personal knowledge of the transaction being recorded. In one case this requirement was carried to an extreme, excluding hospital records that were dictated to a nurse for inclusion in the files because the nurse made the entry and it was the physician who had the personal knowledge. *Espenlaub v. State* (1936), 210 Ind. 687, 2 N.E.2d 979. The personal knowledge requirement should not be read quite so literally. If information is transmitted from one employee with personal knowledge to another employee who makes the entry, this requirement is satisfied if both employees were operating under a business duty. *See Jones v. State* (1977), 267 Ind. 205, 369 N.E.2d 418, overruled on other grounds by *Elmore v. State* (1978), Ind., 382 N.E.2d 893. *See also Landers v. State* (1984), Ind., 464 N.E.2d 912 (personal knowledge may be passed along a chain of business employees).

Machine-created original entries such as audit tape produced by an automatic teller machine are admissible as business records if it can be shown that: (1) the electronic equipment is standard; (2) the entries are made in the regular course of business at or near the time the transaction occurred; and (3) the testimony regarding the creation and storage of the records is adequate to indicate their accuracy and authenticity. *Stark v. State* (1986), Ind., 489 N.E.2d 43; *Brandon v. State* (1979), 272 Ind. 92, 396 N.E.2d 365.

Testimony that a search of business records showed no entry was made concerning an alleged transaction, offered to show that the transaction never took place, is admissible. *Brandon v. State*, 272 Ind. 92, 396 N.E.2d 365.

As in the case of the best evidence rule, a duplicate (carbon or photocopy) is admissible if there is no genuine issue as to its accuracy. *See Ind.Code* §§ 34-3-15-2, 34-3-15.5-2; *Wilson v. State* (1976), 169 Ind.App. 297, 348 N.E.2d 90. If the business keeps in its permanent files summaries of transactions, rather than the records of those transactions themselves, the summaries are the original business records. *Weismen v. Hopf-Himsel, Inc.* (1989), Ind.App., 535 N.E.2d 1222 (tractor repair shop kept invoices that were compiled based on mechanics' individual labor tickets, but that merely summarized those tickets; summary invoices were business records).

Hospital records, if of a kind regularly maintained by the hospital, are admissible as business records. *See Ind.Code* § 34-3-15.5-5 (certified copies admissible without sponsoring witness). Most hospitals now keep records on electronic data processing equipment. *Ind.Code* § 34-3-15.5-3 provides a method for authenticating such records:

(1)   The data processing equipment is standard hospital equipment;

(2)   Entries were made in the regular course of business, at or near the time of the event or diagnosis;

(3)   The system is shown to be secure from unauthorized access; and

(4)   Records of entries and access to information are separately maintained.

F. Inconsistent existing law.

Older cases state that the record must be the original. The original is understood to mean the one kept by the business as a permanent record, or a print-out if the business' records are stored in a computer. *See Brandon v. State* (1979), Ind., 396 N.E.2d 365. This requirement was already breaking down. *See*, J. Alexander Tanford and Richard M. Quinlan *Indiana Trial Evidence Manual* §§ 20.3, 20.8 (2d ed. 1987).

Part Eight: Public Records

A. Does the Rule change current Indiana Law?

The rule clarifies Indiana law rather than actually changing it. Police reports are not admissible against defendants. Records of vital statistics are clearly admissible.

B. Differences between IRE, FRE and URE.

The FRE is different. It is reprinted below, with the differences highlighted.

(8) Public records and reports. ~~Unless the sources of information or other circumstances indicate lack of trust-worthiness,~~ records, reports, statements, or data compilations in any form, of a public offices or agencies, setting forth (a) ~~its regularly conducted and regularly recorded~~ the activities <u>of the office or agency</u>, or (B) matters observed pursuant to duty imposed by law and as to which <u>matters</u> there was a duty to report, <u>excluding, however, in criminal cases matters observed by police officers and other law enforcement personnel</u>, or (C) <u>in civil actions and proceedings and against the Government in criminal cases</u>, factual findings resulting from an investigation made pursuant to authority granted by law <u>unless the sources of information or other circumstances indicate lack of trustworthiness.</u> ~~The following are not within this exception to the hearsay rule, (i) investigative reports by police and other law enforcement personnel, except when offered by an accused in a criminal case; (ii) investigative reports prepared by or for a government, a public office, or an agency when offered by it in a case in which it is a party; (iii) factual findings offered by the government in criminal cases; and (iv) factual findings~~

~~resulting from special investigation of a particular complaint, case, or incident, except when offered by an accused in a criminal case.~~

C. State variations.

Most states adopted all three rules verbatim. Three require notice to the adverse party sufficient to give them time to investigate the authenticity of the record. Four states do not permit the results of factual investigations to be admitted.

D. Committee commentary.

The rule is compatible with *Ind.Code* § 9-26-2-3 (police accident reports not confidential), and *Ind.Code* § 9-26-3-4 (driver accident reports confidential).

Any report prepared by law enforcement personnel and offered against a criminal defendant that would be excluded under 803(8) should also be excluded if offered under 803(6).

To qualify as an official record, the source of the information must be a government official.

E. Consistent existing law.

Properly certified copies of records maintained in public and governmental offices are admissible as an exception to the hearsay rule. *McGraw v. State* (1981), Ind., 426 N.E.2d 1290. In *Starkey v. State* (1977), 266 Ind. 184, 361 N.E.2d 902, the court stated that the proponent must show that the document is the written statement of a public official, the official had a legal duty to make the record, and the official had personal knowledge of the facts. In *Collins v. State* (1991), Ind., 567 N.E.2d 798, the court overruled several prior cases holding that the duty to make the record be expressly imposed by statute. The court held that the specific duty to make the record could be inferred from relevant statutory provisions. *Ind.Code* § 34-1-17-7 provides that copies of records kept in any public office in this State shall be admitted as legal evidence if properly certified.

In *Mott v. State* (1989), Ind., 547 N.E.2d 261, the court held that official documents could be authenticated if an appropriate public official appeared in person and testified that the documents were true and accurate copies of the original public records.

Part Nine: Pedigree

A. Does the Rule change current Indiana law?

Yes. Records of religious organizations that did not qualify as business records were not previously admissible. Marriage and similar certificates that did not qualify as public records were not previously admissible. Indiana required that the declarant be dead, and that the statement have been made before the controversy arose.

B. Differences between IRE, FRE and URE, and state variations.

None.

D. Committee commentary.

None.

E. Inconsistent existing law.

Prior Indiana law required that the declarant must be dead. *See In re Paternity of Tompkins* (1989), Ind.App., 542 N.E.2d 1009.

Part Ten: Records Affecting an Interest in Real Property

A. Does the Rule change current Indiana law?

No substantive change. Current Indiana law recognizes only the exception for ancient documents. However, documents affecting a legal interest in property are not hearsay at all, but "operative legal facts," therefore excluded from the hearsay rule anyway.

B. Differences between IRE, FRE and URE.

The FRE and URE version establishes 20 years, rather than 30, as the age of ancient documents. It is reprinted below, with the differences highlighted:

(16) Statements in ancient documents. Statements in a document in existence 30 20 years or more, the authenticity of which is established.

C. State variations.

The only variation is the period of time necessary for a document to become an "ancient" document. It ranges from 15 to 30 years.

D. Committee commentary.

None.

E. Consistent existing law.

An ancient document is defined as a written document that is at least thirty years old, has been kept in proper custody, and is unblemished by alterations and otherwise free from suspicion. *Steele v. Fowler* (1942), 111 Ind.App. 364, 41 N.E.2d 678.

Part Eleven: Commercial Directories

A. Does the Rule change current Indiana law?

Yes. It expands current Indiana law, which excepts only market reports and television schedules from the hearsay rule.

B. Differences between IRE, FRE and URE.

None.

C. State variations.

None. All states adopted this rule.

D. Committee commentary.

Although the rule changes Indiana law, it will have little impact. Documents generally used and relied upon by the public could have been judicially noticed anyway under existing law. Obviously, this exception assumes that the directory in question comes from an unbiased source, is found in public libraries as a general reference, or is widely used by persons for purposes having nothing to do with law or litigation. For example, a directory of television programs distributed every week by a local newspaper qualifies under this exception, a "directory" of television programs promoting good family values prepared by a coalition of ministers would not.

E. Consistent existing law.

Whenever the prevailing price of goods regularly bought and sold in an established commodity market is an issue, reports in trade journals, official publications, or newspapers that show such market price are admissible as an exception to the hearsay rule. *Ind.Code* § 26-1-2-724.

Part Twelve: Learned Treatises

A. Does the Rule change current Indiana law?

Yes. Current Indiana law admits learned treatises for impeachment purposes only, not for their truth.

B. Differences between IRE, FRE and URE.

None.

C. State variations.

Most states adopted the rule; six rejected it.

D. Committee commentary.

The committee recommends adopting the majority view that learned treatises are fully admissible. We doubt the efficacy of instructions designed to limit a jury's use of this evidence to impeachment purposes only. *See J. Alexander Tanford, The Law and Psychology of Jury Instructions, 69 Neb. L. Rev. 71, 86–87 (1990).*

F. Inconsistent existing law.

If the expert claims to have relied on a certain treatise, passages from that book may be read which contradict the opinion given. These excerpts are still hearsay and may not be argued for their truth. *Miller v. Griesel* (1973), Ind.App., 297 N.E.2d 463 *trans. granted on other grounds* (1974), 261 Ind. 604, 308 N.E.2d 701; *Hess v. Lowery* (1889), 122 Ind. 225, 23 N.E. 156. It also may be possible to read from books not relied on by the expert, if the cross-examiner can establish them as recognized authorities. *See Stallings v. State* (1953), 232 Ind. 646, 114 N.E.2d 771.

Part Thirteen: Reputation

A. Does the Rule change current Indiana law?

Hard to say. Although there was no previous exception for reputation testimony, evidence of reputation has never been considered hearsay at all because it does not depend on any particular declarant's credibility. Evidence of reputation concerning property boundaries, however, probably would previously have been excluded as hearsay.

B. Differences between IRE, FRE and URE.

None.

C. State variations.

None. All states adopted this rule.

D. Committee commentary.

The committee doubts that reputation constitutes hearsay in the first place, even if offered for the truth of what people say about a person. The most likely reason is that it does not depend upon the veracity of any one individual. *See generally Graeter v. State* (1886), 105

Ind. 271, 4 N.E. 461. However, the rule should resolve any doubts about the matter.

Part Fourteen: Judgments

A. *Does the Rule change current Indiana law?*

No substantive change. Under Indiana law, a judgment constitutes "operative legal facts" and is not hearsay to begin with.

B. *Differences between IRE, FRE and URE.*

None.

C. *State variations.*

Most states adopted these rules in substance, but the details vary. Five states adopted both rules. Four states admit evidence of *nolo contendere* pleas. Three states rejected them.

D. *Committee commentary.*

The committee doubts that judgments are hearsay in the first place. Under the operative legal facts/verbal acts doctrine, words that have independent legal significance are not considered hearsay. *See generally Resnover v. State* (1978), 267 Ind. 597, 372 N.E.2d 457.

E. *Consistent existing law.*

Under *Ind.Code* § 34-3-18-1, a judgment of a felony conviction entered in a criminal case is not hearsay.

Part One: Definition of Unavailability

A. *Does the Rule change current Indiana law?*

The rule differs in two ways. Subdivision (5) creates a requirement that a party attempt to depose an absent declarant before other forms of hearsay may be used, which requirement applies to criminal cases as well as civil. For dying declarations, Indiana previously recognized only death as unavailability.

B. *Differences between IRE, FRE and URE.*

The FRE and URE are ambiguous on whether under definition (5) the proponent of hearsay must first attempt to depose the declarant. FRE/URE 804(a)(5) is reprinted below, with the differences highlighted:

> (5) is absent from the hearing and the proponent of a statement has been unable to procure the declarant's attendance (or in the case of a hearsay exception under subdivision (b)(2), (3), or (4), the defendant's attendance or testimony) by process or other reasonable means, ~~or obtain the declarant's testimony by deposition.~~

C. *State variations.*

All states adopted parts (1) through (4) in substance. Most rewrote part (5) to require the proponent to attempt to depose an absent declarant before the declarant is considered unavailable.

D. *Committee commentary.*

The definition of unavailability presents few problems. The only subdivision that may need explanation is 804(a)(5). Under this rule, only reasonable efforts must be made to

produce the declarant. The committee believes that it is not reasonable to expend large sums of money to locate or transport declarants. However, it is reasonable in most civil cases to expect that the proponent will first attempt to depose the declarant. However, the committee has doubts that it will always be reasonable to expect the parties in a criminal case to take depositions. Few prosecuting attorneys or public defenders have the time or resources to take depositions of anyone except the most important witnesses. In important cases and for important witnesses, judges should impose the deposition requirement in criminal cases. In unimportant cases or witnesses, however, the requirement should usually be waived. Because the accused is entitled under the Compulsory's Process Clause to produce evidence in his favor, this rule cannot constitutionally be used to prevent a criminal defendant from producing favorable material evidence merely because the defendant did not take the declarant's deposition.

E. Consistent existing law.

The following constitute unavailability: death, insanity or physical disability of the witness, *New York Cent. R.R. v. Pinnell* (1942), 112 Ind.App. 116, 40 N.E.2d 988; asserting the Fifth Amendment and refusing to testify, *Diggs v. State* (1989), Ind., 531 N.E.2d 461, *cert. denied*, 490 U.S. 1038(witness who asserts Fifth Amendment is unavailable); unsuccessful, reasonable efforts to locate and produce the witness if still alive, *Ingram v. State* (1989), Ind., 547 N.E.2d 823; refusal of the witness to testify despite the threat of contempt, *Abner v. State* (1985), Ind., 479 N.E.2d 1254; *Drummond v. State* (1984), Ind., 467 N.E.2d 742; or absence from the jurisdiction caused by the opposing party. *Lowery v. State* (1985), Ind., 478 N.E.2d 1214, *cert. denied*, 475 U.S. 1098 (1986). In civil cases, if witnesses are out of the state for legitimate reasons and it is economically difficult to fly them back, they are unavailable. *Rambend Realty Corp. v. Backstreet Band* (1985), Ind.App., 482 N.E.2d 741. *See Freeman v. State* (1989), Ind., 541 N.E.2d 533 (witness is unavailable when outside state and unable to attend because of age, sickness, infirmity or imprisonment). The jury normally should not be told why the witness is unavailable. *Moore v. State* (1982), Ind., 440 N.E.2d 1092, *appeal after remand* (1984), Ind., 467 N.E.2d 720.

Part Two: Former Testimony

A. Does the Rule change current Indiana law?

It expands the scope of prior proceedings that qualify; otherwise, the rule is consistent with recent Indiana cases.

B. Differences between IRE, FRE and URE.

None.

C. State variations.

Most states adopted the rule. Six expanded this exception to include former testimony elicited by or against an unrelated party with a similar motive to develop the testimony.

D. Committee commentary.

This proposed rule takes a middle ground. It liberally allows the proponent to use prior testimony from a variety of proceedings, hearings and depositions, but protects the adverse party by restricting it to situations in which the adverse party personally (or a legal predecessor or interest) had the opportunity to cross-examine. The committee believes it would be unfair to deprive the party personally of some reasonable opportunity for cross-examination.

The rule is compatible with Indiana Trial Rule 32(A)(3), permitting the use of depositions if the deponent is unavailable at trial.

E. Consistent existing law.

The former testimony of unavailable witnesses given under oath at a deposition or former trial of the same cause, Trial Rule 32(A)(3); *Wabash R.R. v. Miller* (1901), 158 Ind. 174, 61 N.E. 1005, or one involving similar issues, *Spence v. State* (1979), 182 Ind.App. 62, 393 N.E.2d 277, is admissible. *Moore v. State* (1982), Ind., 467 N.E.2d 720. The proponent need not have been involved in the prior proceeding, but the party against whom it is offered must have had the opportunity and a similar motive to cross-examine the witness at the prior proceeding. *Johnston v. State* (1988), Ind., 517 N.E.2d 397. A deposition may be used if the party was present or had reasonable notice of it. Ind.Trial Rule 32(A)(3).

In criminal cases, if a new trial is ordered and the defendant does not take the stand, the State may use his testimony from a former trial against him. However, if the defendant attempts to use his own prior testimony rather than take the stand, it is not admissible under this exception. Since the State cannot compel him to testify, he would be unavailable to the prosecution for cross-examination. He cannot himself claim to be unavailable since he has the option to testify. *See Bryant v. State* (1979), 270 Ind. 539, 385 N.E.2d 415. The state may use the former testimony of unavailable witnesses against the defendant. *Kimble v. State* (1979), 270 Ind. 539, 387 N.E.2d 64.

Although the case law is unclear, former testimony may probably be proved by a witness who heard it and can now repeat the substance, by having the former stenographer testify from his or her notes, *see generally Meyer v. Garvin* (1941), 110 Ind.App. 403, 37 N.E.2d 291; *Houk v. Branson* (1896), 17 Ind.App. 119, 45 N.E. 78, or by the attorney reading from or introducing a certified transcript. Ind.Trial Rule 74(A) and (E); Ind.Crim.Rule 5; *City of Indianapolis v. Parker* (1981), Ind.App., 427 N.E.2d 456.

F. Inconsistent existing law.

By statute, all agents of corporations have been granted limited immunity in civil antitrust cases, and must testify. However, that testimony may not later be used against them in a criminal antitrust case, even if such former testimony otherwise would qualify under this hearsay exception. *Ind.Code* § 24-1-2-11.

Part Three: Dying Declarations

A. Does the Rule change current Indiana law?

Yes. Under Indiana law, the declarant must have died, and the statement is admissible only in criminal homicide cases.

B. Differences between IRE, FRE and URE.

The URE/FRE is limited in criminal cases to homicide cases only. It is reprinted below, with the differences highlighted:

(2) *Statement under belief of impending death.* <u>In a prosecution for homicide or in</u>

a civil action or proceeding, a statement made by a declarant while believing that the declarant's death was imminent, concerning the cause or circumstances of what the declarant believed to be impending death.

C. State variations.

Most states adopted the broader exception permitting dying declarations in all cases. A sizeable minority adhered to the FRE restriction to homicide and civil cases.

D. Committee commentary.

The committee saw no valid justification for limiting dying declarations to homicide and civil cases. If the hearsay is reliable enough to be admitted in those cases, it is reliable enough to be admitted in other kinds of cases.

Courts must bear in mind that part of the foundation for this exception is that the declarant must have believed he or she was dying and would not recover. If the declarant believed they would survive, then the presumption of "deathbed reliability" vanishes. In this age of fancy health care, it will be a rare case in which the proponent will be able to prove that the declarant had given up hope that modern medicine would save him.

E. Consistent existing law.

Before a dying declaration is admissible, the proponent must show that the declarant knew his death was imminent and had abandoned all hope of recovery. *Dean v. State* (1982), Ind., 432 N.E.2d 40; *Montgomery v. State* (1881), 80 Ind. 338. The declarant need not say directly that he expects to die. *Morgan v. State* (1869), 31 Ind. 193. The trial court can consider statements, conduct, manner, and symptoms of the declarant and the nature of the wound. *Williams v. State* (1907), 168 Ind. 87, 79 N.E. 1079. *See, e.g., Anderson v. State* (1984), Ind., 471 N.E.2d 291 (statements made by stabbing victim could not be dying declarations when she had stated to onlookers that she thought she was all right). The statement must relate to the circumstances of the declarant's death, *Montgomery*, 80 Ind. at 347, the identity of the killer, and facts connected to the alleged crime. *Stephenson v. State* (1932), 205 Ind. 141, 179 N.E. 633. Dying declarations do not have to be spontaneous. They may be in writing or may be made in response to the questions of another. *Anderson v. State* (1933), 205 Ind. 607, 186 N.E. 316; *Boyle v. State* (1884), 97 Ind. 322.

F. Inconsistent existing law.

Declarant must have died. *Montgomery v. State* (1881), 80 Ind. 338. Dying declarations are admissible only in criminal homicide cases. *Id.* They are not admissible in civil cases. *Duling v. Johnson* (1869), 32 Ind. 155.

Part Four: Statement Against Interest

A. Does the Rule change Indiana law?

No.

B. Differences between IRE, FRE and URE.

The URE is reprinted below, with the differences highlighted:

(3) *Statement against interest.* A statement which was at the time of its making so far contrary to the declarant's pecuniary or proprietary interest, or so far tended to

subject the declarant to civil or criminal liability, or to render invalid a claim by the declarant against another, <u>or to make the declarant an object of hatred, ridicule, or disgrace</u>, that a reasonable person in the declarant's position would not have made the statement unless believing it to be true. <u>A statement tending to expose the declarant to criminal liability and offered to exculpate the accused is not admissible unless corroborating circumstances clearly indicate the trustworthiness of the statement.</u> <u>A statement or confession offered against the accused in a criminal case, made by a codefendant or other person implicating both the declarant and the accused, is not within this exception.</u>

The FRE is reprinted below, with the differences highlighted:

(3) Statement against interest. A statement which was at the time of its making so far contrary to the declarant's pecuniary or proprietary interest, or so far tended to subject the declarant to civil or criminal liability, or to render invalid a claim by the declarant against another, that a reasonable person in the declarant's position would not have made the statement unless believing it to be true. <u>A statement tending to expose the declarant to criminal liability and offered to exculpate the accused is not admissible unless corroborating circumstances clearly indicate the trustworthiness of the statement.</u> ~~A statement or confession offered against the accused in a criminal case, made by a co-defendant or other person implicating both the declarant and the accused, is not within this exception.~~

C. State variations.

Most states adopted the FRE verbatim. Six states adopted the URE version that includes statements against societal interest, and excludes statements jointly implicating both declarant and accused.

D. Committee commentary.

The FRE and URE contain a limitation that prevents the defendant in a criminal case from using this exception to prove that another person confessed to the crime. This anti-defendant provision has been uniformly criticized by evidence scholars. Wigmore rejected the argument that it was necessary because of the danger of perjury, since that danger is one that attends all human testimony for both sides. He pointed out that the far greater danger was that it prevents an innocent defendant from exonerating himself. 5 *John H. Wigmore, Wigmore on Evidence* § 1477 (Chadbourn rev. 1974).

The committee believes that basic fairness requires that both sides be treated the same—either both sides must prove the statement trustworthy, or neither. We prefer that the requirement be imposed on neither. It is redundant, being already implicit in the requirement that "a reasonable person in the declarant's position would not have made the statement unless believing it to be true." We know of no evidence that suggests that a criminal defendant's friends are more likely to commit perjury than the victim's friends. Our experience is that there are just as many "false confessions" implicating the defendant as there are exculpating the defendant. Any rule that presumes to the contrary conflicts with both the presumption of innocence and the compulsory process clause. At a minimum, the compulsory process clause teaches that the defendant must be entitled to introduce any evidence of the same type as that used against him.

The limitation on statements that jointly inculpate the declarant and the accused is probably constitutionally required. If the declarant is unavailable, the accused does not have the opportunity to cross-examine. That violates the Confrontation Clause unless the hearsay exception is reliable and firmly rooted. *See Idaho v. Wright*, 497 U.S. 805 (1990). Declarations against penal interest were traditionally *not* admissible, 1 *Kenneth S. Broun, et al., McCormick on Evidence* § 318 (John W. Strong, ed., 4th ed. 1992), and have traditionally been considered unreliable (see the special corroboration requirement in the FRE).

Nothing in this rule prevents the admission of a co-conspirator's statement that qualifies for admission under Rule 801(d)(2)(E).

E. Consistent existing law.

Because people are not likely to make statements against their own interests unless they are true, a hearsay statement that was contrary to the declarant's interest when made is admissible if the declarant is now unavailable. *McGraw v. Horn,* (1962), 134 Ind.App. 645, 183 N.E.2d 206.

The statement must have been obviously against the interest of the declarant, and the declarant must have had personal knowledge of the facts stated. *Washburn v. State*, (1986), Ind., 499 N.E.2d 264.

F. Inconsistent existing law.

Prior Indiana law required that there must have been no probable motive to testify falsely, determined from the circumstances against penal interest. *Taggart v. State (1978)*, 269 Ind. 667, 382 N.E.2d 916.

Part Five: Pedigree

A. Does the Rule change current Indiana law?

Yes. Indiana law limited admissibility to statements made by family members.

B. Differences between IRE, FRE and URE.

None.

C. State variations.

None. All states adopted this rule.

D. Committee commentary.

None.

E. Consistent existing law.

Statements made by family members offered to prove matters of family history are admissible on issues of descent, relationship, birth, marriage, and death, and the dates on which these events occurred may all be proved through this exception. *De Haven v. De Haven* (1881), 77 Ind. 236; *In re Paternity of Thompkins* (1989), Ind.App., 542 N.E.2d 1009 (declarant must be family member). The statement should have been made before the controversy arose. *DeHaven*, 77 Ind. 236. There is no requirement that the declarant must have had personal knowledge of the matter. *See, e.g., DeHaven*, 77 Ind. 236. Declarations of pedigree may be either oral, *e.g., DeHaven*, 77 Ind. 236, or written. *Collins v. Grantham*

(1859), 12 Ind. 440 (written entry in hymnal).

F. Inconsistent existing law.

Prior law held that the declarant must be a family member, either by blood or marriage, and must now be dead. *See, In re Paternity of Thompkins* (1989), Ind.App., 542 N.E.2d 1009.

This is a traditional principle of hearsay law, *see Kenneth S. Broun, et. al., McCormick on Evidence* § 324.2 (John W. Strong, ed., 4th ed. 1992), although it does not appear to have been previously articulated in Indiana law.

The committee fails to see the reason for including a non-binding list of illustrations on how the authentication rule is to be interpreted in the rule itself. We believe it is more appropriately placed in the commentary. Thus, by way of illustration only, and not by way of limitation, the following are examples of authentication or identification conforming with the requirements of this rule:

(1) *Testimony of witness with personal knowledge.* Testimony by a witness with personal knowledge that an exhibit possessing identifiable characteristics is the same item as the one involved in a material event, *Warriner v. State* (1982), Ind., 435 N.E.2d 562; *Owens v. State* (1975), 263 Ind. 487, 333 N.E.2d 745, that a document was prepared by a particular person if the witness was present at the signing, *Ruth v. First Fed. Sav. & Loan Assoc.* (1986), Ind.App., 492 N.E.2d 1105; that a diagram is a fair and accurate representation of what the witness observed, *Underwood v. State* (1989), Ind., 535 N.E.2d 507 *cert. denied* 493 U.S. 900 (1989).

(2) *Chain of custody.* A chain of custody that traces the possession of the exhibit from the time it was acquired to the time it is introduced, establishing by the testimony of each possessor that this is the same object and that it was not tampered with. *McAnnalley v. State* (1987), Ind., 514 N.E.2d 831; *Jones v. State* (1981), Ind., 425 N.E.2d 128.

(3) *Nonexpert opinion on handwriting.* Nonexpert opinion as to the genuineness of handwriting which is based upon familiarity not acquired for purposes of the litigation. *Wolfe v. State* (1981), Ind., 426 N.E.2d 647.

(4) *Comparison by trier or expert witness.* Comparison of the writing in a document to genuine specimens, either by an expert witness, *Kindred v. State* (1988), Ind., 524 N.E.2d 279, or by the trier of fact, *Ind.Code* § 34-3-6-1.

(5) *Distinctive characteristics and the like.* Appearance, contents, substance, internal patterns, or other distinctive characteristics, taken in conjunction with circumstances. *See Kern v. State* (1981), Ind., 426 N.E.2d 385 (a letter was authenticated by its contents, which contained references indicating a likelihood it came from the defendant).

(6) *Reliability of the process or system producing the evidence.* Evidence showing that a technological system, such as a computer or a videotape recorder, probably produces accurate results or output, either through expert testimony or circumstantial evidence. *See, e.g., Kindred v. State* (1988), Ind., 524 N.E.2d 279 (when case involves automatic cameras, there should be evidence as to how and when the camera was loaded, how frequently it was activated, when the pictures were taken,

COMMENTARY

and the chain of custody and processing of the film after its removal from the camera).

(7) *Voice identification.* Identification of a voice heard firsthand, or on tape, by direct testimony by a witness that he is familiar with and recognized the voice, *Ashley v. State* (1986), Ind., 493 N.E.2d 768, or met the caller after the conversation and recognized the voice, *Allison v. State* (1960), 240 Ind. 556, 166 N.E.2d 171, *cert. denied*, 365 U.S. 608; or by circumstantial evidence. *Starks v. State* (1987), Ind., 517 N.E.2d 46 *reh'g. granted on other grounds* (1988) 523 N.E.2d 735.

(8) *Telephone conversations.* Telephone conversations, by evidence that a call was made to the number assigned at the time by the telephone company to a particular person or business, if circumstances, including self-identification, show the person answering to be the one called, or the call was made to a place of business and the conversation related to business reasonably transacted over the telephone. *See Epperson v. Rostatter* (1929), 90 Ind.App. 8, 168 N.E. 126. Testimony that the caller identified himself is not sufficient by itself. *Reed v. State* (1986), Ind., 491 N.E.2d 182.

(9) *Demonstrations.* Proof that the demonstration can be conducted under conditions sufficiently similar to those existing at the time of the original event. *O'Connor v. State* (1988), Ind., 529 N.E.2d 331.

The committee was seriously divided on whether the foundation for business records should be provable by affidavit (bracketed language). The modern trend is to allow it. Members of the bar at the public hearings were uniformly opposed to it. The committee was unable to reach consensus. A related disagreement is found in Rule 803(6).

A. Does the Rule change current Indiana law?

Yes. It makes government publications and newspapers and periodicals self-authenticating.

B. Differences between IRE, FRE and URE.

The URE is reprinted below, with differences highlighted:

(1) Domestic public documents. ~~The original or a duplicate of a domestic official record proved in manner provided by Trial Rule 44(A)(1).~~

~~(2) Foreign public documents. The original or a duplicate of a foreign official record proved in the manner provided by Trial Rule 44(A)(2).~~ A document bearing a seal purporting to be that of the United States, or of any State, district, Commonwealth, territory, or insular possession thereof, or the Panama Canal Zone, or the Trust Territory of the Pacific Islands, or of a political subdivision, department, officer, or agency thereof, and a signature purporting to be an attestation or execution.

(2) Domestic public documents are not under seal. A document purporting to bear the signature in the official capacity of an officer or employee of any entity included in paragraph (1) hereof, having no seal, if a public officer having a seal and having official duties in the district or political subdivision of the officer or employee certifies under seal that the signer has the official capacity and that the signature is genuine.

2)(3) Foreign public documents. ~~The original or a duplicate of a foreign official record proved in the manner provided by Trial Rule 44(A)(2).~~ A document purporting to be executed or attested in an official capacity by a person authorized by the laws of a foreign country to make the execution or attestation, and accompanied by a final certification as to the genuineness of the signature and official position (A) of the executing or attesting person, or (B) of any foreign official whose certificate of genuineness of signature and official position relates to the execution or attestation or is in a chain of certificates of genuineness of signature and official position relating to the execution or attestation. A final certification may be made by a secretary of embassy or legation, consul general, consul, vice consul, or consular agent of the United States, or a diplomatic or consular official of the foreign country assigned or accredited to the United States. If reasonable opportunity has been given to all parties to investigate the authenticity and accuracy of official documents, the court may, for good cause shown, order that they be treated as presumptively authentic without final certification or permit them to be evidenced by an attested summary with or without final certification.

(4) Certified copies of public records. A copy of an official record or report or entry therein, or of a document authorized by law to be recorded or filed and actually recorded or filed in a public office, including data compilations in any form, certified as correct by the custodian or other person authorized to make the certification, by certificate complying with paragraph (1), (2), or (3) of this rule or complying with any law of the United States or this state.

3)(5) Official publications. Books, pamphlets, or other publications issued by public authority.

4)(6) Newspapers and periodicals. Printed materials purporting to be newspapers or periodicals.

5)(7) Trade inscriptions and the like. Inscriptions, signs, tags, or labels purporting to have been affixed in the course of business and indicating ownership, control, or origin.

6)(8) Acknowledged documents. Original documents accompanied by a certificate of acknowledgement executed in the manner provided by law by a notary public or other officer authorized by law to take acknowledgments.

7)(9) Commercial paper and related documents. Commercial paper, signatures thereon, and documents relating thereto to the extent provided by general commercial law.

8)(10) Presumptions created by law. Any signature, document, or other matter declared by any law of the United States or of this state, to be presumptively or prima facie genuine or authentic.

9)(11) Certified ~~domestic~~ records of regularly conducted activity. ~~Unless the source of information or the circumstances of preparation indicate lack of trustworthiness.~~ The original or a duplicate of a ~~domestic~~ record of regularly conducted activity within the scope of Rule 803(6), which the custodian thereof or another qualified

person certifies ~~under oath~~ (i) was made at or near the time of the occurrence of the matters set forth, by or from information transmitted by, a person with knowledge of those matters; (ii) is kept in the course of the regularly conducted activity, and (iii) was made by the regularly conducted activity as a regular practice <u>unless the source of information or the method or circumstances of preparation indicate lack of trustworthiness;</u> but a record so certified is not self-authenticating under this subsection unless the proponent makes his or her intention to offer it known to the adverse party and makes it available for inspection sufficiently in advance of its offer in evidence to provide the adverse party with a fair opportunity to challenge it. <u>The word "certifies" as used in this subsection means, with respect to a domestic record, a written declaration under oath subject to the penalty of perjury and, with respect to a foreign record, a written declaration signed in a foreign country which, if falsely made, would subject the maker to criminal penalty under the laws of that country. The certificate relating to a foreign record must be accompanied by a final certification as to the genuineness of the signature and official position (i) of the person executing the certificate or (ii) of any foreign official who certifies the genuineness of signature and official position of the executing person or is the last in a chain of certificates that collectively certify the genuineness of signature and official position of the executing person. A final certification must be made by a secretary of embassy or legation, consul general, consul, vice consul, or consular agent of the United States, or a diplomatic or consular official of the foreign country assigned or accredited to the United States.</u>

~~(10) Certified foreign records of regularly conducted activity. Unless the source of information or the circumstances of preparation indicate lack of trustworthiness, the original or a duplicate of a foreign record of regularly conducted activity within the scope of Rule 803(6), which is accompanied by a written declaration by the custodian thereof or another qualified person that the record (i) was made at or near the time of the occurrence of the matters set forth, by or from information transmitted by, a person with knowledge of those matters; (ii) is kept in the course of the regularly conducted activity, and (iii) was made by the regularly conducted activity as a regular practice. The record must be signed in a foreign country in a manner which, if falsely made, would subject the maker to criminal penalty under the laws of that country, and the signature certified by a government official in the manner provided in Trial Rule 44(A)(2). The record is not self-authenticating under this subsection unless the proponent makes his or her intention to offer it known to the adverse party and makes it available for inspection sufficiently in advance of its offer in evidence to provide the adverse party with a fair opportunity to challenge it.~~

The FRE differs slightly from the URE. It is reprinted below, with the differences highlighted:

<u>(4) Certified copies of public records. A copy of an official record or report or entry therein, or of a document authorized by law to be recorded or filed and actually recorded or filed in a public office, including data compilations in any form, certified as correct by the custodian or other person authorized to make the certification, by certificate complying with paragraph (1), (2), or (3) of this rule or complying with</u>

any Act of Congress or rule prescribed by the Supreme Court pursuant to statutory authority.

(5) Official publications. Books, pamphlets, or other publications purporting to be issued by public authority.

*   *   *

(10) Presumptions created by law ~~under Acts of Congress.~~ Any signature, document, or other matter declared by Act of Congress any law of the United States or of this state, to be presumptively or prima facie genuine or authentic.

C. State variations.

Many states adopted the FRE or URE verbatim, but a number of them have modified this rule to reference existing state rules.

D. Committee commentary.

Rather than spell out what constitutes adequate certification, the committee cross-referenced Indiana Trial Rule 44 which adequately covers the subject. Otherwise, an amendment to the Indiana Trial Rules could create an unintentional conflict with the Indiana Rules of Evidence.

E. Consistent existing law.

Ind.Code § 34-1-17-7 provides that copies of records kept in any public office in Indiana shall be admitted as legal evidence if properly certified. There are two methods of certification. If the public office has an official seal then the keeper of the records must attest under seal that the copy is true and complete. If the office has no seal, the keeper of the records must still attest that the copy is true and complete, but the proponent must also obtain the certification of the court clerk (under seal) that the keeper is the proper official. Official records certified by the clerk of court are self-authenticating and admissible without live testimonial sponsorship. *Connell v. State* (1984), Ind., 470 N.E.2d 701.

Indiana Trial Rule 44 provides a method of certifying a copy of a public record from other states or foreign countries. Copies of official records may be certified as true and complete by the public official having custody of the record or his deputy and do not have to be under seal. In *Gross v. State* (1983), Ind., 444 N.E.2d 296, the court suggests that a judge or notary public from the country in which the records are kept must certify that the record keeper who certifies the record is the proper custodian. A properly certified official record is self-authenticating. *Luttrull v. State* (1986), 499 N.E.2d 1139.

Some kinds of official records are covered by statute:

   (a)   Certified records of all courts within the United States. *Ind.Code* §§ 34-1-17-3, 34-1-17-4, 34-1-18-7, 34-4-3-8, 34-4-6-5.

   (b)   Certified copies of court records showing a conviction for a traffic offense. *Ind.Code* § 9-30-6-14.

   (c)   State, territorial and United States printed statute books. *Ind.Code* §§ 34-1-17-1, 34-1-17-2, 34-3-1-1.

   (d)   Certified acts of state or federal legislatures. *Ind.Code* § 34-1-18-4.

(e)   Reports of common law cases from other states and territories. *Ind.Code* § 34-1-18-11.

(f)   Copies of laws of foreign countries. *Ind.Code* § 34-1-18-12.

(g)   Certificates of notaries public. *Ind.Code* § 34-1-17-5.

(h)   Certificate of secretary of state as to the time when an act of the general assembly was deposited. *Ind.Code* § 34-1-17-6.

(i)   Schedules, rates, tariffs, etc., filed with the interstate commerce commission or the public service commission. *Ind.Code* § 34-3-14-1.

(j)   Records of land ownership, grants and deeds. *See Ind.Code* §§ 32-1-2-28, 34-1-17-8, 34-1-17-9, 34-1-18-5, 34-3-8-1, 34-3-12-1, 34-3-12-2.

(k)   Certified copies of official bonds. *Ind.Code* § 5-4-1-14.

(l)   Certified records of insurance commissioner relating to bail bonds. *Ind.Code* § 35-4-5-2.

(m)   Written findings on the official status of missing servicemen. *Ind.Code* §§ 34-3-4-1, 34-3-4-2.

(n)   Certificates issued by school of medicine relating to breathalyzer operators and equipment. *Ind.Code* § 9-30-6-5.

(o)   Certificates of trademark registration. *Ind.Code* § 24-2-1-5.

(p)   Certificates of recordation of livestock brands are admissible when title to livestock must be proved. *Ind.Code* § 15-5-14-6.

(q)   Certified copies of a person's driving record obtained from the department of motor vehicles, *Ind.Code* § 9-30-6-14, but such records are not admissible as evidence in actions arising out of a motor vehicle accident. Ind.Code § 9-14-3-7. Notations in driving records showing that notice of suspension was mailed are admissible. Ind.Code § 9-14-3-7.

In commercial actions, third-party documents are self-authenticating. Ind.Code § 26-1-1-202.

The inclusion of "sounds" in URE 1001 is probably consistent with Indiana law, if a "plain meaning" analysis is used. *See King v. State* (1989), Ind., 540 N.E.2d 1203 (foundation required for admission of audio recording is same as for document). FRE 1001(1) does not include "sounds."

URE 1001(3) is in accord with current Indiana law. *Morris v. State* (1980) Ind., 406 N.E.2d 1187 (carbon copies considered originals); *Brandon v. State* (1979), 272 Ind. 92, 396 N.E.2d 365 (computer print-outs are originals).

URE 1001(4) is identical to FRE 1001(4), which Indiana has adopted. *See Wilson v. State* (1976), 169 Ind.App. 297, 348 N.E.2d 90.

This is the familiar original document or best evidence rule. The purpose of the rule is to secure the most reliable information as to the contents of writings and recordings when those terms are disputed. *Jackson v. State* (1980), 274 Ind. 297, 411 N.E.2d 609. It is recommended that Indiana's best evidence rule be expanded to include photographs as defined in Rule 1001(2).

Adoption of URE 1002 will create consistency in Indiana with respect to application of the original document or best evidence rule to photographs; *See Lilly v. State* (1985), Ind., 482 N.E.2d 457 (best evidence rule not applicable where photograph of gun used to prove existence of the gun); *Pinkerton v. State* (1972), 258 Ind. 610, 283 N.E.2d 376 (best evidence rule not applicable because x-rays contain scientific evidence which must be explained to the jury); *Jackson v. State* (1980), Ind., 411 N.E.2d 609 (rule applied to videotape).

Indiana follows the "pictorial testimony theory" of photographic evidence: the photograph is admitted into evidence solely to illustrate the relevant testimony of the witness who has properly authenticated the photograph as a fair and accurate representation of something the witness personally viewed. *Wilson v. State* (1978), 268 Ind. 112, 374 N.E.2d 45; 3 *John H. Wigmore, Wigmore on Evidence* § 790 (Chadbourn rev. 1979). Under the pictorial testimony theory, the photograph is not admitted as substantive evidence and therefore the best evidence rule would never apply. However, where a photograph is admitted without an authenticating witness, or in the case of x-rays, the item is admitted for substantive purposes, if properly authenticated, pursuant to the silent witness theory. *Bergner v. State* (1979), Ind.App., 397 N.E.2d 1012; *but see Howard v. State* (1976), 264 Ind. 275, 342 N.E.2d 604 (x-rays properly verified treated as scientific, as opposed to photographic, evidence). In these situations, the best evidence rule should apply.

Indiana adopted FRE 1003 in *Wilson v. State* (1976), 169 Ind.App. 297, 348 N.E.2d 90. This rule differs from URE 1003 in deleting the phrase "or continuing effectiveness" at the end of part (1).

Under URE 1004, if the best evidence rule does not apply, there is no other hierarchy of probative value of evidence which is offered in lieu of the original.

URE 1004(1) is consistent with Indiana law. *Freyermuth v. State ex rel. Burns* (1936), 210 Ind. 235, 2 N.E.2d 399.

URE 1004(2) is consistent with Indiana law. *Thom v. Wilson's Executor* (1886), 27 Ind. 370.

Although current Indiana law is consistent with URE 1004(3) to the extent that Indiana Trial Rule 9.2(E) requires production, it is recommended that the URE approach be adopted, which applies the exception to the best evidence rule if a party is put on notice by way of pleadings or otherwise.

Indiana law is consistent with URE 1004(4).

Indiana law is consistent with URE 1005. *See Walker v. State* (1965), 246 Ind. 386, 204 N.E.2d 850, *cert. denied*, 382 U.S. 991 (1966) (copies admitted to prove contents of public records). Parol evidence may be used. *See White v. Allman* (1952), 122 Ind.App. 208, 103 N.E.2d 901.

Although Indiana does not extend the public records exception to attestations on public records offered to prove prior criminal convictions in criminal habitual offender proceedings, *Kelly v. State* (1990), Ind., 561 N.E.2d 771, it is recommended that the Indiana rule on public records not limit the court's discretion on the issue.

This is URE 1006. Indiana law is consistent with URE 1006, inasmuch as the underlying records need not be admitted, but must be admissible in evidence and made available to the opposing party. *See Crawford v. State* (1980), Ind.App., 401 N.E.2d 715. It is recommended that the standard imposed by "convenient examination in court," as provided in URE 1006, rather than "of such a nature as to make it difficult for the trier of fact to understand" as used in earlier Indiana cases. *Chicago, St. L. and Pittsburgh R.R. Co. v. Wolcott* (1894), 141 Ind. 267, 39 N.E. 451. The law of summaries, which is grounded in policies of efficiency and economy, will be better served by adoption of URE 1006.

This is URE 1007. Indiana law is consistent with URE 1007. *Mark v. City of Indianapolis* (1966), 247 Ind. 511, 219 N.E.2d 434 (contents of a writing); *Coca-Cola Bottling Co. v. International Filter Co.* (1916), 62 Ind.App. 421, 113 N.E. 17 (admission of a party).

The reference to URE 104 provides for the distinction between those preliminary questions which are for the court, URE 104(a), and those which pertain to relevancy conditioned upon fact and are for the fact finder (with the court performing its "gate-keeping" function under URE 104(b). Decisions made under Rule 1008 are reviewed for an abuse of discretion. *Marksill Specialties, Inc. v. Barger* (1981), Ind.App., 428 N.E.2d 65.

This rule provides that the Committee on Rules of Practice and Procedure shall serve as the Evidence Rules Review Committee. The committee shall conduct a continuous study of the Indiana Rules of Evidence and shall submit to the Supreme Court recommendations and proposed amendment to the rules. The committee would review current case law, legislative enactment, and proposed amendment or comment from the Bench, Bar, and Public to determine whether changes are appropriate in the rules of evidence.